Also in the Variorum Collected Studies Series:

H.S. OFFLER (Ed. A.J. Piper and A.I. Doyle)
North of the Tees: Studies in Medieval British History

PATRICK SIMS-WILLIAMS
Britain and Early Christian Europe: Studies in Early Medieval History and Culture

HELMUT GNEUSS
Language and History in Early England

HELMUT GNEUSS
Books and Libraries in Early England

RICHARD W. PFAFF
Liturgical Calendars, Saints and Services in Medieval England

ROSAMOND McKITTERICK
The Frankish Kings and Culture in the Early Middle Ages

MARJORIE CHIBNALL
Piety, Power and History in Medieval England and Normandy

MILTON McC. GATCH
Eschatology and Christian Nurture: Themes in Anglo-Saxon and Medieval Religious Life

JOHN H. MUNRO
Textiles, Towns and Trade: Essays in the Economic History of Late-Medieval England and the Low Countries

CHARLES W. JONES (Ed. Wesley M. Stevens)
Bede, the Schools and the Computus

DAVID N. DUMVILLE
Britons and Anglo-Saxons in the Early Middle Ages

E.M.C. VAN HOUTS
History and Family Traditions in England and the Continent, 1000–1200

ROGER E. REYNOLDS
Clerical Orders in the Early Middle Ages: Duties and Ordination

VARIORUM COLLECTED STUDIES SERIES

Church and Crown in the Fourteenth Century

Professor H. S. Offler
(1913–1991)

H.S. Offler

Church and Crown in the Fourteenth Century

Studies in European History and Political Thought

edited by A.I. Doyle

Routledge
Taylor & Francis Group
LONDON AND NEW YORK

First published in the Variorum Collected Studies Series by 2000 by Ashgate Publishing

Reissued 2018 by Routledge
2 Park Square, Milton Park, Abingdon, Oxon OX14 4RN
711 Third Avenue, New York, NY 10017, USA

Routledge is an imprint of the Taylor & Francis Group, an informa business

A Library of Congress record exists under LC control number: 0102913

ISBN 13: 978-1-138-72723-6 (hbk)
ISBN 13: 978-1-138-72721-2 (pbk)
ISBN 13: 978-1-315-19094-5 (ebk)

VARIORUM COLLECTED STUDIES SERIES CS692

CONTENTS

This volume contains xxxviii + 336 pages

INTRODUCTION

The writings published here form the second volume of Professor Offler's collected papers. The first selection, under the title *North of the Tees*, appeared in 1996, and brought together his work on the north-east of England in the Middle Ages. The subject matter of the present volume is quite different: the history of the western Empire, especially in the time of Lewis IV 'the Bavarian' (1314–1347), and of its dealings with other European powers, above all the Avignon papacy; and fourteenth-century political thought, with a particular concentration upon the writings of William of Ockham. While these are the last of Offler's papers to be published in collected form, they include the fruits of his earliest scholarly activity, and touch on matters that concerned him – albeit with some changes in emphasis – from his time as a Cambridge doctoral student in the 1930s until the end of his life.[1]

Offler's work is distinguished by its subject matter, which to a significant degree lies in fields little worked by English-speaking medievalists. A decision to concentrate on 'Lewis IV of Bavaria' had already been taken when Offler commenced graduate studies in 1934. A resumé of his proposed research, dating from that time, makes clear that Lewis was intended to serve as a starting-point for a wide-ranging study of the political character and condition of Germany in the first half of the fourteenth century, which Offler hoped might shed fresh light on 'the current generalizations as to the decay of the Imperial power' in that period.[2] C.W. Previté Orton, his supervisor, doubtless had a hand in shaping the direction of his research. Previté Orton himself had expertise in the history of northern Italy and in north Italian political thought in the central and later Middle Ages, and something of these interests was to mark Offler's work also: he gave close attention to the Italian context of fourteenth-century imperial politics and, like his mentor, later published on the Italian publicist Marsilius of Padua (IX). Offler also began quickly acquiring the means to investigate the German foundations of Lewis' reign, mastering the German language and, from 1931, making a series of visits to German-speaking Europe. In 1937 he undertook a major tour of Continental archives, gathering materials which were to underpin his publications for at least the next two decades. With the award of a research fellowship 1936 his work began to take on a sharper focus, concentrating upon Lewis' dealings with the Avignon popes, viewed in a European context. The thesis which he submitted for a doctorate in 1938 had as its title 'The Emperor Lewis IV and the Curia from 1330 to 1347: Canon Law and International Relationship in the first half of the Fourteenth Century'.

Offler's subject was well chosen, since the inter-war years had seen significant advances in the study of Lewis' reign. There had appeared a number of important monographs and essays, particularly from the pens of German scholars such as Edmund Ernst Stengel, Friedrich Bock and Richard Scholz, as well as some major edited source collections. The respect which Offler's work quickly gained among leading specialists of the time is attested by the acceptance in 1939 of an essay on 'Kaiser Ludwig IV. und die Prokuratorienfrage' for publication in *Deutsches Archiv für Geschichte des Mittelalters*, house journal of the *Monumenta Germaniae Historica*. The editor was Stengel, whose own *Avignon und Rhens*, published in 1930, had made a major contribution in Offler's field.[3] Stengel would have been a keen judge of the young Cambridge researcher's work.

It was doubtless political pressures in Hitler's Germany that frustrated the essay's publication, and Offler's first published article, in the *English Historical Review*, addressed a different aspect of imperial diplomacy under Lewis IV: his court's dealings with Edward III of England (III). Medieval Anglo-German relations were not a wholly improbable topic for an English-speaking scholar to choose, and in the years which fell on either side of the Second World War a number of medievalists on both sides of the Atlantic – among them Geoffrey Barraclough, C.C. Bayley, N. Denholm Young, H.S. Lucas and Austin Lane Poole – also published in this area. Yet, in contrast to some of these, the main burden of Offler's work lay not in the English but the Continental sources, and it was to these that he again applied himself when, after distinguished war service, he returned to academic life in the late 1940s. He did not, it is true, ever again go back to the archives; but his writing leave no doubt that he followed keenly new developments in his field, particularly when they related to the manuscript sources.

For several years Offler continued in his published work to develop elements from his doctoral research, concentrating particularly upon Lewis' negotiations for a settlement with the Curia in the 1330s and early 1340s. His first post-war essay took up again the subject of Lewis' procurations (V). This appeared in 1951 in *Deutsches Archiv*, which had been re-constituted after the war with a new editorial board. It centred upon the relationship between the emperor's procurations and the instructions issued to the envoys who were to negotiate on his behalf at Avignon. A second piece was published in the same journal three years later, this time examining the role of different groups – Lewis' German clerics and nobles and the exiled Michaelist Franciscans – in shaping his court's approach to the Curia (IV). The 'collatio' of Clement VI, which Offler published with an introduction in 1955, is also best placed under the rubric of imperial-papal relations (XI). The final 'political' essay on Lewis' reign is the 1956 paper in the *Transactions of the Royal Historical Society*, which recounts, and places in its several contexts, the emperor's Italian expedition of 1327–1330 (II). This covers slightly earlier ground than the other pieces, and has a somewhat different focus – broader, and more concerned with the unfolding of events. It ranges well beyond the expedition itself and, perhaps reflecting something of Offler's early interest in the state of the fourteenth-century *Reich*, finds space for such problems as the extent of the monarch's material resources and the politics of the German princes. What gives these early essays their unity as a group is not only their subject matter – the reign of Lewis IV in international perspective – but also their characteristic preoccupations: with the relationship between political ideas and the play of events; with the complex interactions of groups and personalities at Lewis' court; and with questions surrounding the authorship and purpose of key contemporary writings.

Judged by his published work, Offler's interests appear to change direction during the 1950s. Henceforth questions of imperial politics and diplomacy have a much smaller place, and the later essays concentrate upon the political ideas and polemics which are such a conspicuous element in Lewis' reign – and particularly upon the political writings of William of Ockham. But the change of emphasis, while real enough, should not be mistaken or exaggerated. Ockham had been an early interest for Offler, who in 1937 was invited to join a group of Cambridge scholars with the aim of publishing all of Ockham's political writings. Already in his Cambridge days Offler put on record a determination to study political ideas as an integral element in Lewis' reign, and one of the objectives of his *Forschungsreise* to the Continent had been to undertake a systematic search for Ockham manuscripts.[4] A concern for the ideological framework of Lewis' actions is evident throughout the early essays, and the 1954 paper has as a secondary objective establishing whether one particular work from Lewis' circle, *Quoniam scriptura*, could be ascribed to Ockham.

Offler's main activity for the greater part of his scholarly career lay, of course, in bringing to fruition the four-volume edition of Ockham's *Opera politica*. This work, the final volume of which appeared posthumously, constitutes his single greatest achievement, and the later essays in this volume have to be viewed in light of the project which inspired them. Most of them engage with problems arising out of the editorial work; but they do so in different ways, and they illuminate different elements of Offler's interests and approach. Indeed, it could not have been otherwise, since the peculiar difficulties of establishing and elucidating the Ockham *corpus* called for a range of skills, and for a knowledge of political thought and actions extending well beyond the master himself. Offler's concern with publishing accurate and usable texts is well illustrated in the pieces printed here, a number of which either include edited documents or propose improvements to texts already published. But they also reveal something of the breadth of Offler's learning in fourteenth-century political ideas and, in particular, his deep familiarity with the writings of Ockham's contemporaries: not only Marsilius (IX) and Bonagratia (VI), but also Lupold of Bebenburg (VII) and Ockham's German adversary Conrad of Megenberg, whom Offler unmasked as the likely author of a 'minor literary fraud' at Ockham's expense (XII). Offler, as these papers make clear, was not much engaged by the abstractions of political philosophy as such. His interest lay, first, in the technicalities of reconstructing, elucidating and editing texts; but also in understanding those texts as elements in a contemporary world whose substance and importance did not consist of thought alone. The paper on Ockham's *Octo quaestiones* (VII) shows well how the challenges of editorial work kept Offler rooted in the problems of events and personalities with which he had begun, as he traced the work's likely impulse back to Baldwin of Luxemburg's circle and to questions surrounding the succession to the Bohemian throne.

Another reminder of the breadth, as well as the depth, of Offler's scholarship comes from a perusal of his book reviewing, which was formidable in both quantity and range. He concentrated throughout his career particularly upon works on German and Swiss history, social and economic as well as political and ecclesiastical, though he also reviewed widely in the general history of medieval Europe. For many volumes, particularly on Germany, Offler was clearly the only reviewer to whom an editor could have turned, and the short pieces that resulted are works of concentrated scholarship in their own right. Indeed, it would be possible for the student with no German to pick up a good deal of late medieval German history just from a thorough perusal of Offler's reviews in the field. Taken together they constitute a further reason for not overstating the extent of his disengagement from the German history of his earlier years.

Something of the fruits of his familiarity with the German literature can be seen in his 1965 introduction to the government of the late medieval

Empire, thematically perhaps the most ambitious of the papers in this volume (I). Even in its own terms Offler's treatment might today be judged as slightly narrow in conception. Like many of the German medievalists whose work he followed, he concentrated mainly upon the imperial monarchy, and on the consequences that flowed from its weakness as a form of government. While this probably has the advantage of making his subject more readily accessible to a reader schooled in the English tradition, it does result in a somewhat unbalanced picture, since – as Offler himself is at pains to make clear – monarchy was scarcely the most important element in the 'government' experienced by most Germans at the end of the Middle Ages. Principalities, towns, and other local and regional bodies are certainly dealt with, but more as elements in the 'particularism' resulting from the Empire's feebleness than as sources of rule in their own right. Nonetheless, as a lucid and detailed yet concise introduction to imperial institutions Offler's paper remains unmatched. Indeed, it is hard to think of another scholar, past or present, writing in English who has gained a comparable mastery of the constitutional and political history of later medieval Germany.

On only one other occasion did Offler attempt a major synthetic treatment of an aspect of medieval German history: in the series of chapters which he contributed to *A Short History of Switzerland*, a collaborative volume aimed at a non-specialist audience, which appeared in 1952.[5] It must be a matter of regret that he never undertook the monograph on fourteenth-century imperial politics and diplomacy that he was so eminently qualified to write. For Ockham, his monument is the *Opera politica*, but there is in addition a last major essay, published in 1990, which considers Ockham's writings as an element in the political thought of the later Middle Ages (X). This forms a fitting conclusion to Offler's work on medieval political ideas. In showing how small was the contemporary audience for Ockham's publicist writings, how limited the early circulation of manuscripts, yet how substantial their later role in the time of the Councils, he traces patterns which resonate with the development of late medieval political writings more broadly. His firm rejection of the possibility of showing any relationship between Ockham's thought as philosopher and as publicist likewise raises questions with a more general application.

Another medievalist has spoken with approval of 'the hard, gritty bricks from which the Great Wall of history is slowly but steadily built'.[6] With this he had in mind the sort of historical writing which is concerned with detailed, technical problems arising out of the sources – 'historians' history', as Offler himself once characterised it. The metaphor seems to fit aptly the greater part of Offler's own work. When the papers published here are read in the light of later scholarship it becomes clear just how solidly fashioned were Offler's own 'bricks', and consequently how remarkably intact remains his own section of the 'Great Wall'. Certainly, not everything he wrote has gone unchallenged. His work on political thought was largely concerned with establishing convincing attributions and reliable texts for difficult and obscure writings. Consensus is scarcely to be looked for in such a field, and Offler's correspondence reveals vigorous debate with other specialists.[7] German scholars, moreover, have on occasion proposed revisions to certain detailed points in his earlier writings.[8] Nor is it surprising to discover that some of Offler's essays on imperial history now stand in the shadow of later and larger studies – though these betray in their apparatus the part that Offler's papers had in their making.[9] Yet the abiding impression is of how well the conclusions of these essays – some of them now half a century old – have on the whole worn. They continue to provide a foundation upon which any serious study of Lewis IV's reign, or of the political writings which it generated, has to be constructed.[10] Not only the interpretations which Offler proposed and the information which he brought to light, but also the avenues of study which he helped to open up, remain live and fruitful. His preference for viewing political writings in relationship to the circles that produced and consumed them – the only possible means of making headway with the intractable publicist literature from Lewis' court – has found affirmation in important later studies, which build upon and develop further Offler's own lines of inquiry.[11] That his writings thus continue to be of use, and to receive the praise of those best qualified to judge them,[12] would surely have pleased him.

LEONARD E. SCALES

University of Durham
February 2000

[1] I am grateful for the help which I received in preparing this essay from Dr Ian Doyle and from my medievalist colleagues in the Department of History at Durham. I owe a particular debt to Professor P.D.A. Harvey, who kindly allowed me access to the materials which he collected while preparing his memoir of Offler, published in *Proceedings of the British Academy*, 80 (1991) and reprinted in *North of the Tees*.

[2] Emmanuel College, Cambridge, tutorial file for Offler. The document, in Offler's handwriting, is headed 'Proposed Course of Research'. I am indebted to Professor Harvey for letting me see photocopies of the Emmanuel material.

[3] E.E. Stengel, *Avignon und Rhens. Forschungen zur Geschichte des Kampfes um das Recht am Reich in der ersten Hälfte des 14. Jahrhunderts* (Quellen und Studien zur

Verfassungsgeschichte des deutschen Reiches im Mittelalter und Neuzeit, VI, 1, Weimar, 1930).

[4] He explains this in his report to the Master of Emmanuel, 10 May 1938, applying for a renewal of his research fellowship and giving an account of progress to date. From Offler's personal file at Emmanuel. I follow here Professor Harvey's transcription.

[5] E. Bonjour, H.S. Offler and G.R. Potter, *A Short History of Switzerland* (Oxford, 1952).

[6] Denys Hay, quoted in John Larner's obituary of him in *Proceedings of the British Academy*, 90 (1995), p. 406.

[7] A fragment of it has been published in G. Knysh, *Ockham Perspectives* (Ukrainian Academy of Arts and Sciences in Canada, Winnipeg, 1994), pp. 16–24. The volume's dedication, 'To the memory of Hilary Seton Offler who led us through the wilderness', reveals something of Offler's standing in the eyes of his peers.

[8] Thus H.O. Schwöbel, *Der diplomatische Kampf zwischen Ludwig dem Bayern und der Römischen Kurie im Rahmen des kanonischen Absolutionsprozesses, 1330–1346* (Weimar, 1968), pp. 291–4, where Offler's view of the role of Italy in Lewis IV's plans, developed in (II) and (III), is challenged; F. Trautz, *Die Könige von England und das Reich, 1272–1377* (Heidelberg, 1961), pp. 274–5, questioning Offler's interpretation of Edward III's imperial vicariate, again in (III).

[9] Examples are the volumes by Schwöbel and Trautz, cited above.

[10] Offler's 1950s pieces in *Deutsches Archiv* and *TRHS* are thus cited in a recent major biography of Lewis IV: H. Thomas, *Ludwig der Bayer (1282–1347). Kaiser und Ketzer* (Graz, Vienna, Cologne, 1993).

[11] For a single example see: J. Miethke, 'Wirkungen politischer Theorie auf die Praxis der Politik im Römischen Reich des 14. Jahrhunderts', in *Political Thought and the Realities of Power in the Middle Ages/Politisches Denken und die Wirklichkeit der Macht im Mittelalter*, ed. J. Canning and O.G. Oexle (Veröffentlichungen des Max-Planck-Instituts für Geschichte, 147, Göttingen, 1998), pp. 173–210.

[12] Thus ibid., p. 194, n. 67, for 'die methodisch vorbildliche literaturkritische Studie', which (VI) in Miethke's view represents.

PUBLISHER'S NOTE

The articles in this volume, as in all others in the Variorum Collected Studies Series, have not been given a new, continuous pagination. In order to avoid confusion, and to facilitate their use where these same studies have been referred to elsewhere, the original pagination has been maintained wherever possible.

Each article has been given a Roman number in order of appearance, as listed in the Contents. This number is repeated on each page and is quoted in the index entries.

Corrections noted in the Addenda and Corrigenda have been marked by an asterisk in the margin corresponding to the relevant text to be amended.

ACKNOWLEDGEMENTS

The thanks of the estate of the late H.S. Offler, the editor and publishers are owing to Dr R.W. Dyson and Dr L.E. Scales for addenda, to Professor D.J.A. Matthew for bringing up to date his list of the author's publications (first compiled and privately issued at the time of his retirement from the chair of Medieval History in the University of Durham), and for permission to reproduce previously published items to: Faber and Faber (I); the Royal Historical Society (II); Oxford University Press (III, VII); Böhlau Verlag (IV, V, VI); the Editor of *Franciscan Studies* (VII); Anton Hiersemann Verlag (IX); VCH Verlag (X); and the Editor of *Revue Bénédictine* (XI, XII). The Frontispiece (also in the first volume of the author's Variorum Collected Studies, *North of the Tees* [1996]), was taken by Dr Peter Rowe, tragically killed in the Yemen in 1998.

A LIST OF THE HISTORICAL WRITINGS OF HILARY SETON OFFLER (1936–97)

Compiled by D.J.A. Matthew

Abbreviations:

D.U.J. Durham University Journal
E.H.R. English Historical Review
J.T.S. Journal of Theological Studies

1936

E.K. Winter: *Rudolph IV von Österreich*, Bd. 1 (1934)
Review: E.H.R., LI, 520–23

1937

E.K. Winter: *Rudolph IV von Österreich*, Bd. 2 (1936)
Review: E.H.R., LII, 322–5

1938

E. Ziehen: *Mittelrhein und Reich im Zeitalter der Reichsreform, 1356–1504*, 2 Bde. (1934, 1937)
Review: E.H.R., LIII, 500–501

1939

'England and Germany at the beginning of the Hundred Years War' E.H.R., LIV, 608–31

H. & G. Mortensen, *Die Besiedlung des nordöstlich Ostpreussens bis zum Beginn des 17-Jahrhunderts*, Teil 1 (1937)
Review: E.H.R., LIV, 747–8

1940

Guillelmi de Ockham Opera politica accuravit J.G. Sikes sociis adscitis B.L. Manning, R.F. Bennett, H.S. Offler, R.H. Snape, vol I (Manchester University Press, pp. viii + 374)

pp. 224–71: An Princeps pro suo succursu, scilicet guerrae possit recipere bona ecclesiarum, etiam invito Papa [with R.H. Snape]
pp. 274–86: Consultatio de causa matrimoniali

H.Quednau: *Livland im politischen Wollen Herzog Albrechts von Preussen* (1939)
Review: E.H.R., LV, 158

1948

F.M. Powicke: *Three lectures given in the Hall of Balliol College Oxford in May 1947* (1947)
Review: (anon) D.U.J., XL, 62–3

C.M.L. Bouch: *Prelates and People of the Lake Counties* (1948)
Review: (anon) D.U.J., XLI, 36–7

1949

'Edward Gibbon and the Making of his "Swiss History"'
D.U.J., XLI, 64–7

1950

'William of St. Calais, first Norman Bishop of Durham', *Transactions of the Architectural and Archaeological Society of Durham and Northumberland*, X, 258–79

F. Güterbock: *Engelbergs Gründung und erste Blüte, 1120–1223* (1948)
Review: E.H.R., LXV, 539–40

G. Partsch: *Die Steuern des Habsburger Urbars, 1303–1308* (1946)
Review: E.H.R., LXV, 544–5

W. Ullmann: *Medieval Papalism: the Political Theories of the Medieval Canonists* (1949)
Review: (anon) D.U.J., XLII, 73–4

Frank Barlow: *Durham Jurisdictional Peculiars* (1950)
Review: (anon) D.U.J., XLII, 123–5

C.C. Bayley: *The Formation of the German College of Electors in the Mid-thirteenth Century* (1950)
Review: (anon) D.U.J., XLIII, 34–6

1951

'Über die Prokuratorien Ludwigs des Bayern für die römische Kurie', *Deutsches Archiv für Erforschung des Mittelalters*, 8. Jahrgang, Heft 2, 461–87

'The tractate De iniusta vexacione Willelmi episcopi primi' [William of St. Calais, bishop of Durham]
E.H.R., LXVI, 321–41

E.Meyer-Marthaler: *Rätien im frühen Mittelalter* (1948)
Review: E.H.R., LXVI, 129–30

William Ockham (1349–1949) *Aufsätze zu seiner Philosophie und Theologie* (*Franziskanische Studien*, 32. Jahrgang, Heft 1/2) (1950)
Review: E.H.R., LXVI, 578–9

Quellenwerk zur Entstehung der Schweizerischen Eidgenossenschaft, Abt. II: Urbare und Rödel bis zum Jahre 1400, Bd. 3 (1951)
Review: E.H.R., LXVI, 614–15

D. Knowles: The Episcopal Colleagues of Archbishop Thomas Becket (1951)
Review: (anon) D.U.J., XLIII, 115–16

1952

E. Bonjour, H.S. Offler and G.R. Potter: A Short History of Switzerland (Oxford, Clarendon Press), pp. 1–106:

Chapter I The Country and its people
II Celts and Romans
III Germanic Switzerland
IV The Origins of the Confederation
V Growth and Consolidation

H. Ammann: *Mittelalterliche Wirtschaft im Alltag*, Teile 1–2 (1942, 1950)
Review: E.H.R., LXVII, 116–17

H. Ammann & K. Schib (edd.): *Historischer Atlas der Schweiz* (1951)
Review: E.H.R., LXVII, 160

1953

E.F. Jacob: *Essays in the Conciliar Epoch* (1953)
Review: D.U.J., XLVI, 39–40

1954

'Meinungsverschiedenheiten am Hof Ludwigs des Bayern im Herbst 1331', *Deutsches Archiv für Erforschung des Mittlelalters*, 11. Jahrgang, Heft 1, 191–206

H. Strahm: *Die Berner Handfeste* (1953)
Review: E.H.R., LXIX, 476–7

1955

'A Political "Collatio" of Pope Clement VI O.S.B.', *Revue Bénédictine*, LXV, 126–44

H. Ammann: *Die Stadt Bern in der mittelalterlichen Wirtschaft* (1951)
Review: E.H.R., LXX, 321

E. Lewis: *Medieval Political Ideas* (1954)
Review: E.H.R., LXX, 633–5

Dante Alighieri: *Monarchy and Three Political Letters*, with an introduction by Donald Nicholl and a note on the chronology of Dante's Political Works by Colin Hardie
Review: D.U.J., XLVII, 130–32

1956

'Empire and Papacy: The Last Struggle', *Transactions of the Royal Historical Society*, 5th series, VI, 21–47

Guillelmi de Ockham Opera politica accuraverunt R.F. Bennett et H.S. Offler: Vol III edidit H.S. Offler (Manchester University Press, pp. ix + 322)

Epistola ad Fratres Minores
Tractatus contra Johannem

Tractatus contra Benedictum

B. Tierney: *Foundations of the Conciliar Theory: The contribution of the medieval canonists from Gratian to the Great Schism* (1955)
Review: E.H.R., LXXI, 642–5

Urkundenbuch zur Geschichte der Babenberger in Österreich
Bd. 2: Die Siegelurkunden der Babenberger und ihrer Nachkommen von 1216 bis 1279, ed. H. Fichtenau & E. Zöllner (1955)
Bd. 3: Die Siegel der Babenberger, ed. Oskar Freiherr von Mitis & F. Gall (1954)
Review: E.H.R., LXXI, 645–7

H. Butterfield: *Man on His Past: The Study of the History of Classical Scholarship* (1955)
Review: D.U.J., XLVIII, 117–19

1957

P. Duparc: *Le Comté de Genève, ixe–xve siecle* (1955)
Review: E.H.R., LXXII, 98–100

Marie José [reine d'Italie]: *La Maison de Savoie* (1956)
Review: E.H.R., LXXII, 356

Felix's Life of St Guthlac: introduction, text, translation and notes by Bertram Colgrave (1956)
Review: D.U.J., XLIX, 84–5

1958

Medieval Historians of Durham: inaugural lecture of the Professor of Medieval History delivered 14 March 1958, University of Durham, 24 pp.

G.V. Scammell: *Hugh du Puiset, Bishop of Durham* (1956)
Review: E.H.R., LXXIII, 95–9

P.N. Riesenberg: *Inalienability of Sovereignty in Medieval Political Thought* (1956)
Review: E.H.R., LXXIII, 144

D. Hay: *Europe: the Emergence of an Idea* (1957)
Review: D.U.J., LI, 41–2

1959

G. Leff: *Bradwardine and the Pelagians* (1957)
Review: E.H.R., LXXIV, 110–12

M. Pacaut: *La Théocratie: L'église et le pouvoir au moyen-âge* (1957)
Review: E.H.R., LXXIV, 146–7

H. Mitteis: *Die Rechtsidee in der Geschichte: Gesammelte Abhandlungen und Vorträge* (1957)
Review: E.H.R., LXXIV, 289–92

P.E. Schramm: *Sphaira, Globus, Reichsapfel, Wanderung und Wandlung eines Herrschaftszeichens* (1958)
Review: E.H.R., LXXIV, 680–81

P.E. Schramm: *Herrschaftszeichen: gestiftet, verschenkt, verkauft, verpfändet* (1957)
Review: E.H.R., LXXIV, 715

H. Helbling: *Saeculum Humanum: Ansätze zu einen Versuchüber spätmittelalterliches Geschichtsdenken* (1958)
Review: E.H.R., LXXIV, 717–18

O. Chadwick: *Creighton on Luther*
Review: D.U.J., LI, 143–4

Götz Freiherr von Pölnitz: *Anton Fugger*, Bd. 1: 1453–1535 (1958)
Review: *Erasmus*, XII, 56–60

1960

E.H. Kantorowicz: *The King's Two Bodies: A Study in Medieval Political Theology* (1957)
Review: E.H.R., LXXV, 295–8

G.S.H.L. Washington: *Early Westmorland MPs, 1258–1327* (1959)
Review: *Transactions of the Cumberland and Westmorland Antiquarian and Archaeological Society*, n.s., LIX, 165–71

1961

H. Segall: *Der 'Defensor Pacis' des Marsilius von Padua: Grundfragen der Interpretation* (1959)

Review: E.H.R., LXXVI, 351–2

Mario delle Piane: *Vecchio e nuovo nelle idee politiche di Pietro Dubois* (1959)
Review: E.H.R., LXXVI, 519–20

M. Seidlmayer: *Currents of Medieval Thought* (1960)
Review: History, XLVI, 124–5

Rosalind K. Brooke: *Early Franciscan Government* (1959)
Review: D.U.J., LIII, 82–3

Joseph Gill: *The Council of Florence* (1959)
Review: D.U.J., LIII, 89–92

1962

'The Early Archdeacons in the Diocese of Durham', *Transactions of the Architectural and Archaeological Society of Durham and Northumberland*, XI, 189–207

'A Note on the last medieval Bishops of Hexham', *Archaeologia Aeliana*, 4th series, XL, 163–9

'The Date of *Durham (Carmen de Situ Dunelmi)*', *Journal of English and Germanic Philology*, LXI, 591–4

John Taylor: *Medieval Historical Writing in Yorkshire* (1961)
Review: E.H.R., LXXVII, 746–7

Philobiblon Ricardi de Bury : Textum editum et anglice redditum ab Ernesto Thomas nunc recensuit Michael Maclagan (1960)
Review: The Library (Transactions of the Bibliographical Society), 5th series, XVIII, 159–61

H.G. Richardson: *The English Jewry under Angevin Kings* (1960)
Review: *Notes and Queries*, CCVII, 78–9

W. Ullmann: *Principles of Government and Politics in the Middle Ages* (1961)
Review: *Cahiers de civilisation médiévale*, V, 485–6

1963

Guillelmi de Ockham Opera politica accuraverunt R.F. Bennett et H.S. Offler: Vol II recognovit J.G.Sikes retractavit H.S. Offler (Manchester University Press, xix + pp. 375–858) Opus Nonaginta Dierum cap. 7–124

H. Obenaus: *Recht und Verfassung der Gesellschaften mit St. Jörgenschild in Schwaben* (1961)
Review: E.H.R., LXXVIII, 564–5

B. Ita: *Antiker Bau and Frühmittelalterliche Kirche* (1961)
Review: E.H.R., LXXVIII, 759

G. Inger: *Das kirchliche Visitationsinstitut im mittelalterlichen Schweden* (1961)
Review: E.H.R., LXXVIII, 767–8

M.D. Knowles: *The Evolution of Medieval Thought* (1962)
Review: History, XLVII, 200

G. Leff: *Gregory of Rimini* (1961)
Review: *Medium Aevum*, XXXII, 71–2

D. Hay: *The Italian Renaissance in its Historical Background* (1961)
Review: D.U.J., LV, 98–9

J.M. Wallace-Hadrill: *Bede's Europe* (1962)
Review: D.U.J., LV, 135

O. Brandt, A.O. Meyer, L.Just: *Handbuch der Deutschen Geschichte*, 4 Bde. (1957)
Review: *Erasmus*, XV, 174–7

1964

W. Schlesinger: *Mitteldeutsche Beiträge zur deutschen Verfassungsgeschichte des Mittelalters* (1961)
Review: E.H.R., LXXIX, 100–101

J.L. Santschy: *Manuel analytique et critique de la bibliographie générale de l'histoire suisse* (1961)
Review: E.H.R., LXXIX, 223

A. Bruckner: *Das Herkommen der Schwyzer und Oberhasler* (1961)
Review: E.H.R., LXXIX, 407

F.J. Pegues: *The Lawyers of the Last Capetians* (1961)
Review: E.H.R., LXXIX, 828–9

A.C. Chibnall: *Richard de Badew and the University of Cambridge, 1315–1340* (1963)
Review: *Notes and Queries*, CCIX, 280

M.J. Wilks: *The Problem of Sovereignty in the Later Middle Ages* (1963)
Review: *History*, XLIX, 216–18

G. Kitson Clark & G.R. Elton: *Guide to Research Facilities in History in the Universities of Great Britain and Ireland*
Review: D.U.J., LVI, 201–2

C.H. Wilson: *History in Special and in General: An Inaugural Lecture* (1964)
Review: D.U.J., LVII, 70–71

Götz Freiherr von Pölnitz: *Anton Fugger*, Bd. 2, Teil 1 1536–48 (1963)
Review: *Erasmus*, XVI, 493–6

1965

'Aspects of Government in the Late Medieval Empire', in J.R. Hale, J.R.L. Highfield and B. Smalley (eds): *Europe in the Late Middle Ages*, Faber and Faber, London, pp. 217–47

'A Note on the Early History of the Priory of Carlisle', *Transactions of the Cumberland and Westmorland Antiquarian and Archaeological Society*, n.s. LXV, 176–181

Deutsche Königspfalzen: Beiträge zu ihrer historischen und archäologischen Erforschung, Bd. 1 (1963)
Review: E.H.R., LXXX, 377–8

H. Wolfram: *Splendor imperiii: Die Epiphanie von Tugend und Heil in Herrschaft und Reich*; Festschrift zur Jahrtausendfeier der Kaiserkrönung Ottos des Grossen, Teil III (1963)
Review: E.H.R., LXXX, 815

1966

F. Oakley: *The Political Thought of Pierre d'Ailly: the Voluntarist Tradition* (1964)
Review: E.H.R., LXXXI, 560–62

G. Post: *Studies in Medieval Legal Thought* (1964)
Review: E.H.R., LXXXI, 581–2

J.C. Holt: *Magna Carta* (1965)
Review: D.U.J., LVIII, 96–7

H. Westpfahl (ed.): *Vita Dorotheae Montoviensis Magistri Johannis Marienwerder* (1964)
Review: *Erasmus*, XVIII, 629–32

1967

'The Origin of Ockham's *Octo Quaestiones*', E.H.R., LXXXII, 323–32

'A Northumberland Charter of King Henry I', *Archaeologia Aeliana*, 4th series, XIV, 181–8

B. Smalley (ed.): *Trends in Medieval Political Thought* (1965)
Review: E.H.R., LXXII, 157

Deutsche Königspfalzen: Beiträge zu ihrer historischen und archäologischen Erforschung, Bd. 2 (1965)
Review: E.H.R., LXXXII, 374–5

La storia del diritto nel quadro delle scienze storiche: Atti del Primo Congresso Internazionale della Società Italiana di Storia del Diritto (1966)
Review: E.H.R., LXXXII, 595–6

S. Kuttner & J.J. Ryan (eds.): *The Proceedings of the Second International Congress of Medieval Canon Law, Boston, 1963*, vol 1 (1965)
Review: E.H.R., LXXXII, 597

J.A. Watt: *The Theory of Papal Monarchy in the Thirteenth Century* (1965)
Review: E.H.R., LXXXII, 598–9

D.J. Geanakoplos: *Byzantine East and Latin West* (1966)
Review: J.T.S., n.s., XVIII, 516–17

1968

Durham Episcopal Charters, 1071–1152, *Publications of the Surtees Society*, CLXXIX, 192

[with J.M. Todd]
'A medieval Chronicle from Scotland', *Scottish Historical Review*, XLVII, 151–9

K. Schnith (ed.): *Festiva Lanx: Studien zum mittelalterlichen Geistesleben* [Festschrift Johannes Sporl] (1966)
Review: E.H.R., LXXXVIII, 822

Margaret Aston: *Thomas Arundel: a Study of Church Life in the Reign of Richard II* (1967)
Review: J.T.S., n.s., XIX, 358–60

H. Angermeier: *Königtum und Landfriede im deutschen Spätmittelalter* (1966)
Review: *Erasmus*, XX, 42–5

U. Dirlmeier: *Mittelalterliche Hoheitsträger im wirtschaftlichen Wettbewerb* (1966)
Review: *Erasmus*, XX, 181–3

E.E. Unger: *Die Fugger in Hall in Tirol* (1967)
Review: *Erasmus*, XX, 246–9

1969

E. Freiherr von Guttenberg and A. Wendehorst: *Germania Sacra*. Alte Folge, 2. Abt. *Die Bistümer der Kirchenprovinz Mainz*. 1. Bd. *Das Bistum Bamberg*, 2. Teil: *Die Pfarreiorganisation* (1966)
Review: E.H.R., LXXXIV, 380–81

G. Leff: *Heresy in the Later Middle Ages* (1967)
Review: E.H.R., LXXXIV, 572–6

Carlo Pincin: *Marsilio* (1967)
Review: *Rivista Storica Italiana*, LXXX, 1022–6

A. Patschovsky: *Der Passauer Anonymus: Ein Sammelwerk über Ketzer, Juden. Antichrist aus der Mitte des XIII Jahrhunderts* (1968)
Review: J.T.S., n.s. XX, 338–40

Marsile de Padoue: *Le Défenseur de la Paix*, translated by Jeannine Quillet (1968)
Review: J.T.S., n.s., XX, 340–41

F.D. Logan: *Excommunication and the Secular Arm in Medieval England* (1968)
Review: J.T.S., n.s., XX, 683–5

W. Brandmüller: *Das Konzil von Pavia-Siena, 1423–1424*, Bd. 1 (1968)
Review: J.T.S., n.s., XX, 685–8

Dorothy Whitelock: *The Genuine Asser* (1968)
Review: D.U.J., LXI, 163–4

Götz Freiherr von Pöllnitz: *Anton Fugger*, Bd. 2, Teil II (1967)

Review: *Erasmus*, XXI, 59–63

H. Butte: *Geschichte Dresdens bis zur Reformationszeit* (1967)
Review: *Erasmus*, XXI, 109–11

J. Fleckenstein: *Die Hofkapelle der deutschen Könige*, 2 Teile (1959, 1966)
Review: *Erasmus*, XXI, 245–8

H. Steinbach: *Die Reichsgewalt und Niederdeutschland in nachstaufischer Zeit 1247 bis 1308* (1968)
Review: *Erasmus*, XXI, 439–40

H.O. Schwöbel: *Der diplomatische Kampf zwischen Ludwig dem Bayern und der römischen Kurie im Rahmen des kanonischen Absolutionsprozesses, 1330–46* (1968)
Review: *Erasmus*, XXI, 566–71

Richard Feller & Edgar Bonjour: *Geschichtsschreibung der Schweiz vom Spätmittelalter zur Neuzeit* (1962)
Review: *Erasmus*, XXI, 694–8

1970

H. Bansa: *Studies zur Kanzlei Kaiser Ludwigs des Bayern vom Tage der Wahl bis zur Rückkehr aus Italien, 1314–29* (1968)
Review: E.H.R., LXXXV, 157–8

J. Benzinger: *Invectiva in Romam: Romkritik im Mittelalter vom 9. bis zum 12. Jahrhundert* (1968)
Review: E.H.R., LXXXV, 827–8

E.M. Meijers: *Etudes d'histoire du droit international privé*, translated by P.C. Timbal & J. Metman (1967)
Review: E.H.R., LXXXV, 832

H.Schneider: *Adel-Burgen-Waffen* (1968)
Review: E.H.R., LXXXV, 832–3

R.R. Betts: *Essays in Czech History* (1969)
Review: J.T.S., n.s., XXI, 238–40

Rosalind M.T. Hill: *The Labourer in the Vineyard: the Visitations of Archbishop Melton in the Archdeaconry of Richmond* (1969)
Review: D.U.J., LXII, 182–3

K.Ganzer: *Papsttum und Bistumsbesetzungen in der Zeit von Gregor IX bis*

Bonifaz VIII (1968)
Review: *Erasmus*, XXII, 631–4

W. Kehn: *Der Handel im Oderraum im 13. und 14. Jahrhundert* (1968)
Review: *Erasmus*, XXII, 757–9

1971

'Hexham and the Historia Regum', *Transactions of the Architectural and Archaeological Society of Durham and Northumberland*, n.s., II, 51–62

Ranulf Flambard as Bishop of Durham (1099–1128): The Cathedral Lecture for 1971, given in the Monks' Dormitory of Durham Cathedral, 4th March 1971, published by the Dean and Chapter of Durham 14 pp. and also in D.U.J., LXIV, 14–25

Die Urkunden Konrads III und seines Sohnes Heinrich, ed. F.Hausmann (M.G.H. Diplomata Regum et Imperatorum Germaniae, IX) (1969)
Review: E.H.R., LXXXVI, 118–20

W. Mager: *Zur Entstehung des modernen Staatsbegriffs* (1968)
Review: E.H.R., LXXXVI, 163–4

S. Haider: *Die Wahlversprechungen der römish-deutschen Könige bis zum Ende des zwölften Jahrhunderts* (1968)
Review: E.H.R., LXXXVI, 386–7

A. Largiadèr: *Die Papsturkunden des Schweiz von Innozenz III bis Martin V ohne Zürich*. 1. Teil, *Von Innozenz III bis Benedikt XI, 1198 bis 1304* (1968)
Review: E.H.R., LXXXVI, 387

Hérésies et sociétés dans l'Europe préindustrielle, 11e–18e siècles. Communications et débats du Colloque de Royaumont, présentés par Jacques Le Goff (1968)
Review: E.H.R., LXXXVI, 387–8

D.Knowles: *Christian Monasticism* (1969)
Review: E.H.R., LXXXVI, 600

Jürgen Miethke: *Ockhams Weg zur Sozialphilosophie* (1969)
Review: *Journal of Ecclesiastical History*, XXII, 71–3

Jürg Füchtner: *Die Bündnisse der Bodenseestädte bis zum Jahre 1390* (1970)
Review: *History*, LVI, 88–9

Helmut Roscher: *Papst Innozenz III und die Kreuzzüge* (1970)
Review: J.T.S., n.s., XXII, 261–3

A.J. Black: *Monarchy and Community: Political Ideas in the Later Conciliar Controversy, 1430–1450* (1970)
Review: J.T.S., n.s., XXII, 645–7

Bede's Ecclesiastical History of the English People, ed. B. Colgrave and R.A.B. Mynors (1969)
Review: D.U.J., LXIII, 234–6

F. Häusler: *Das Emmental im Staate Bern bis 1798*, 2 Bde. (1958, 1968)
Review: *Erasmus*, XXIII, 379–81

P.E. Schramm: *Kaiser, Könige und Päpste* 2 Bde. (1968, 1969)
Review: *Erasmus*, XXIII, 889–92

Wolfgang von Stromer: *Oberdeutsche Hochfinanz, 1350–1450*, 3. Teil (1970)
Review: *Erasmus*, XXIII, 953–6

E.Meissner: *Fürstbischof Anton Ignaz Fugger, 1711–87* (1969)
Review: *Erasmus*, XXIII, 1012–14

1972

R.W. Southern: *Medieval Humanism and Other Studies* (1970)
Review: E.H.R., LXXXVII, 576–7

J.R. Strayer: *On the Medieval Origins of the Modern State* (1971)
Review: E.H.R., LXXXVII, 85

P.Eitel: *Die oberschwäbischen Reichsstädte im Zeitalter der Zunftherrschaft* (1970)
Review: *Erasmus*, XXIV, 48–50

O. Nübel: *Mittelalterliche Beginen und Sozialsiedlungen in den Niederlanden* (1970)
Review: *Erasmus*, XXIV, 115–17

Thomas Grütter: *Johannes von Müllers Begegnung mit England* (1967)
Review: *Erasmus*, XXIV, 370–73

1973

P. Herde: *Audientia litterarum contradictarum* (1970)

Review: E.H.R., LXXXVIII, 368–71

Brian Tierney: *Origins of Papal Infallibility, 1150–1350* (1972)
Review: *American Historical Review*, LXXVIII, 664–6

G. Strauss (ed.): *Pre-Reformation Germany* (1972)
Review: History, LVIII, 267–8

A. Haverkamp: *Herrschaftsformen der Frühstaufer in Reichsitalien* (1970–71)
Review: *Erasmus*, XXV, 310–14

A. Lhotsky: *Aufsätze und Vorträge*, Bd. 2. *Das Haus Habsburg* (1971)
Review: *Erasmus*, XXV, 431–4

K. Schib: *Johannes von Müller, 1752–1809* (1967)
Review: *Erasmus*, XXV, 439–42

1974

Guillelmi de Ockham Opera politica accuravit H.S.Offler, Vol.1, editio altera. Recensuit H.S.Offler. (Manchester University Press, pp. 368)

Octo Quaestiones de Potestate Papae
An Princeps
Consultatio de Causa Matrimoniale
Opus Nonaginta Dierum cap.1–6

'An Interpolated "Collatio" of Pope Clement VI O.S.B. ?', *Revue Bénédictine*, LXXXIV, 111–25

Schwabenspiegel Kurzform III (Tambacher Handschrift), ed. K.A. Eckhardt (M.G.H. Fontes Iuris Germanici Antiqui) (1972)
Review: E.H.R., LXXXIX, 161

R.E. Lerner: *The Heresy of the Free Spirit in the later Middle Ages* (1972)
Review: E.H.R., LXXXIX, 165

J.N. Hillgarth: *Ramon Lull and Lullism in Fourteenth-century France* (1971)
Review: E.H.R., LXXXIX, 382–4

K.J. Klinkhammer, S.J.: *Adolf von Essen und seine Werke* (1972)
Review: J.T.S., n.s., XXV, 207–9

Canterbury Professions, ed. M.Richter (Canterbury and York Society LXVII) (1973)
Review: D.U.J., LXVII, 107–9

Bruno Meyer: *Die Bildung der Eidgenossenschaft in 14. Jahrhundert* (1972)
Review: *Erasmus*, XXVI, 180–83

E. Bonjour: *Die Schweiz und Europe* (1973)
Review: *Erasmus*, XXVI, 813–16

1975

Festschrift für Hermann Heimpel, 3 Bde. (1971–3)
Review: E.H.R., XC, 118–21

B. Schimmelpfennig: *Die Zeremonienbücher der römischer Kurie im Mittelalter* (1973)
Review: E.H.R., XC, 164–5

C.Trinkhaus and H.A. Oberman: *The Pursuit of Holiness in late Medieval and Renaissance Religion* (1974)
Review: J.T.S., n.s., XXVI, 204–6

L. Binz: *Vie religieuse et réforme ecclésiastique dans le diocèse de Genève, 1378–1450*, tom. 1 (1973)
Review: *History*, LX, 286

W. Brandmüller: *Das Konzil von Pavia-Siena, 1423–1424*, Bd. II (1974)
Review: J.T.S., n.s., XXVI, 481–3

R.M. Helmholz: *Marriage Litigation in Medieval England* (1974)
Review: D.U.J., LXVIII, 98–100

Elsbet Orth: *Die Fehden der Reichsstadt Frankfurt am Main im Spätmittelalter* (1973)
Review: *Erasmus*, XXVII, 119–22

Emanuel Peter La Roche: *Das Interregnum und die Entstehung der schweizerischen Eidgenossenschaft* (1971)
Review: *Erasmus*, XXVII, 367–70

1976

Germania Sacra, neue Folge 8: *Die Bistümer der Kirchenprovinz Mainz, Das Bistum Hildesheim*, 2. ed. H.Goetting (1974)
Review: E.H.R., XCI, 366–9

W. Ullmann: *Law and Politics in the Middle Ages* (1975)
Review: E.H.R., XCI, 855–7

A.B. Cobban: *The Medieval Universities, their Development and Organisation* (1975)
Review: D.U.J., LXIX, 138–40

K. Schib: *Geschichte der Stadt und Landschaft Schaffhausen* (1972)
Review: Erasmus, XXVIII, 437–9

P.E. Schramm: *Kaiser, Könige und Päpste*, Bd. IV. 1 und 2 Hälfte (1970, 1971)
Review: *Erasmus*, XXVIII, 698–700

A.S. McGrade: *The Political Thought of William of Ockham* (1974)
Review: History, LXI, 101–2

M. Dykmans: *Pour et contre Jean XXII en 1333: deux traités avignonnais sur la vision béatifique* (1975)
Review: J.T.S., n.s., XXVII, 500–501

1977

'The three modes of natural law in Ockham: a revision of the text', *Franciscan Studies*, vol.37, annual XV, 207–18

H. Patze & W. Schlesinger: *Geschichte Thüringens*, Vol. II, pt.1. Hohen und spätes Mittelalter (1974)
Review: E.H.R., XCII, 188–9

Codex diplomaticus et epistolaris regni Bohemiae, Vol. V, fasc. 1, ed. J. Sebánek & S. Dusková (1974)
Review: E.H.R., XCII, 884–5

P. Bloesch: *Das Anniversarbuch der Basler Domstifts, 1334/8–1610* (1975)
Review: E.H.R., XCII, 889–90

A. Patschovsky: *Die Anfänge einer ständigen Inquisition in Böhmen* (1975)
Review: J.T.S., n.s., XXVIII, 219–21

F.H. Russell: *The Just War in the Middle Ages* (1975)
Review: D.U.J., LXIX, 285–7

Christopher Brooke (ed.): *Church and Government in the Middle Ages; Essays presented to C.R.Cheney* (1976)
Review: D.U.J., LXX, 91–2

H. Beumann: *Wissenschaft vom Mittelalter* (1972)
Review: *Erasmus*, XXIX, 42–4

A. Lhotsky: *Aufsätze und Vorträge*, Bd. 1 (1970), Bd. III (1972)
Review: *Erasmus*, XXIX, 435–37

K. Bosl: *Die Grundlagen der modernen Gesellschaft im Mittelalter*, II Teile (1972)
F. Prinz, F.J. Schmale & F. Seibt (edd.): *Geschichte in der Gesellschaft: Festschrift für Karl Bosl* (1974)
Review: *Erasmus*, XXIX, 752–5

O. Pustejovsky: *Schlesiens Übergang an die böhmische Krone* (1975)
Review: *Erasmus*, XXIX, 756–8

W. Setz: *Hochschulschriften zur Geschichte und Kultur der Mittelalters, 1939–1972/4: Deutschland, Österreich, Schweiz* (1975)
Review: *Erasmus*, XXIX, 758–60

1978

Rudolf Pfeiffer: *History of Classical Scholarship, 1300–1850* (1976)
Review: *History*, LXIII, 77–8

Die Burgen in deutschen Sprachraum: ihre rechts- und verfassung-geschichtliche Bedeutung, edited by H. Patze (1976)
Review: E.H.R., XCIII, 607–11

1979

E.E. Stengel: *Nova Alamanniae. Urkunden, Briefe und andere Quellen besonders zur deutschen Geschichte des 14. Jahrhunderts*, 2. Hälfte, II Teil (1976)
Review: E.H.R., XCIV, 444–5

Herrschaft und Stand. Untersuchungen zur Sozialgeschichte im 13. Jahrhundert, edited by J. Fleckenstein (1977)
Review: E.H.R., XCIV, 591–3

A. Wendehorst: *Die Bistümer der Kirchenprovinz Mainz. Das Bistum Würzburg*, Teil 3: *Die Bischofsreihe von 1455 bis 1617* (1978)
Review: E.H.R., XCIV, 918–19

1980

G.H.M.P. Meyjes: *Jean Gerson et l'Assemblée de Vincennes: ses conceptions*

de la juridiction temporelle de l'Église (1978)
Review: J.T.S., n.s., XXXI, 249–51

Die Akten des Kanonisationsprozesses Dorothea von Montau von 1394 bis 1521, edited by R. Stachnik (1978)
Review: *Journal of Ecclesiastical History*, XXXI, 386–7

1981

The Medieval Nobility. Studies on the ruling classes of France and Germany from the sixth to the twelfth century, edited and translated by T. Reuter (1979)
Review: E.H.R., XCVI, 190

A. Borst: *Mönche am Bodensee, 610–1525* (1978)
Review: E.H.R., XCVI, 192–3

L.G. Duggan: *Bishop and Chapter. The Governance of the Bishopric of Speyer to 1552* (1978)
Review: E.H.R., XCVI, 199–200

1982

'Notes on the text of Marsilius of Padua's "Defensor Minor"', *Mittellateinisches Jahrbuch*, Bd. 17, 212–16

1983

B. Resmini: *Das Arelat im Kräftefeld der französischen, englischen und angiovinischen Politik nach 1250 und das Einwirken Rudolfs von Habsburg* (1980)
Review: E.H.R., XCVIII, 404–5

St Thomas Cantilupe, Bishop of Hereford: essays in his honour, edited by Meryl Jancey (1982)
Review: D.U.J., LXXVI, 115–16

1984

'A note on the northern Franciscan chronicle', *Nottingham Medieval Studies*, 28, 45–59

1986

'Zum Verfasser der "*Allegaciones de potestate imperiali*" (1338)'
Deutsches Archiv für Erforschung des Mittelalters, 42. Jahrgang, Heft 2, 555–619

F.R.H. Du Boulay: *Germany in the Later Middle Ages* (1983)
Review: E.H.R., CI, 975–6

M. Dykmans: *Le Pontifical romain revisé au XVe siecle* (1985)
Review: *Journal of Ecclesiastical History*, XXXVII, 162–3

F. Oakley: *The Western Church in the Later Middle Ages* 1985 (first published 1979)
Review: *Journal of Ecclesiastical History*, XXXVII, 493–4

1987

Rudolf von Biberach: *De septem itineribus aeternitatis. Nachdruck der Ausgabe von Peltier 1866, mit einer Einleitung in die lateinische Überlieferung und Corrigenda zum Text*, edited by Margot Schmidt (1985)

Rudolf von Biberach: *Die sieben strassen zu got. Recividierte hochalemannische Übertragung nach der Handschrift Einsiedeln 278 mit hochdeutschen Übersetzung*, edited by Margot Schmidt (1985)
Review: *Journal of Ecclesiastical History*, XXXVIII, 292–3

1988

'Murder on Framwellgate Bridge', *Archaeologia Aeliana*, 5th series, 16, 193–211

J. H. Overfield, *Humanism and Scholasticism in Late Medieval Germany* (1984)
Review: E.H.R., CIII, 189

Das ritterliche Turnier im Mittelalter. Beiträge zu einer vergleichenden Formen- und Verhaltengeschichte des Rittertums, edited by J. Fleckenstein (1985)
Review: E.H.R., CIII, 1028–9

From Ockham to Wyclif, edited by Anne Hudson and M. Wilks (1987)
Review: *Journal of Ecclesiastical History*, XXXIX, 466–9

1989

Die Deutschen Königspfalzen Band I, Hessen. Lieferung 1–3, edited by T. Zotz (1983–86)
Review: E.H.R., CIV, 714–15

A. Meyer: *Zürich und Rom: ordentliche Kollatur und päpstliche Provisionen am Frau- und Grossmünster, 1316–1523* (1986)
Review: E.H.R., CIV, 1018

1990

'The Influence of Ockham's Political Thinking: the first century', in *Die Gegenwart Ockhams* [Papers for a Conference in 1988], edited by W. Vossenkuhl and R. Schönberger, 338–65 Weinheim-Berlin VCH Verlagsgesellschaft (1990)

Das spätmittelalterliche Königtum im europäischen Vergleich, edited by R. Schneider (1987)
Review: E.H.R., CV, 454

1991

S. Wefers: *Das politische System Kaiser Sigmunds* (1989)
E. Mályusz: *Kaiser Sigismund in Ungarn, 1387–1437* (1990)
Review: E.H.R., CVI, 393–4

Überlieferung, Frommigkeit, Bildund als Leitthemen des Geschichtsforschung (Festschrift Otto Meyer), edited by Jürgen Petersohn (1987)
Review: E.H.R., CVI, 693–4

Margaret Bonney: *Lordship and the Urban Community: Durham and its Overlords, 1250–1540* (1990)
Review: D.U.J., LXXXIII, 102–3

1992

W. Hölscher: *Kirchenschutz als Herrschaftsinstrument: Personelle und funktionale Aspekte der Bistumspolitik Karls IV* (1985)
D. Veldtrup: *Zwischen Eherecht und Familienpolitik. Studien zu den dynastischen Heiratsprojekten Karls IV* (1988)
Review: E.H.R., CVII, 451–2

F. Graus, *Pest - Geissler - Judenmorde. Das 14. Jahrhundert als Krisenzeit* (1987, 2nd edn 1988)
Review: E.H.R., CVII, 991–2

1993

Die Urkunden der Deutschen Könige und Kaiser, Band XVIII, Teil I: *Die Urkunden Heinrich Raspes und Wilhelms von Holland 1246–52*, edited by D. Hägermann & J.G. Kruisheer (1989)
Review: E.H.R., CVIII, 435

1994

Nord und Süd in der deutschen Geschichte des Mittelalters. Akten des Kolloquiums veranstaltet zu Ehren von Karl Jordan, 1907–1984, edited by W. Paravicini (1990)
Review: E.H.R., CIX, 153–4

1996

North of the Tees: Studies in Medieval British History. Edited by A.J. Piper and A.I. Doyle. [Reprints with addenda and three previously unpublished pieces; a Foreword by A.J. Piper, a memoir of the author by P.D.A. Harvey, two photographs, a general index and and an index of manuscripts.] Variorum Collected Studies Series [each item with original pagination] xxxii, 287 pp.

Medieval Historians of Durham (1958)
A note on the last medieval bishops of Hexham (1962)
The early archdeacons in the diocese of Durham (1962)
The date of Durham (*Carmen de situ Dunelmi*) (1962)
William of St Calais, first Norman bishop of Durham (1950)
The tractate *De iniusta vexacione Willelmi episcopi primi* (1951)
Ranulf Flambard as bishop of Durham (1099–1128) (1971)
A Northumberland charter of King Henry I (1967)
A note on the early history of the Priory of Carlisle (1965)
Hexham and the Historia Regum (1971)
A medieval chronicle from Scotland (1968)
Re-reading Boldon Book (1996)
Fitz Meldred, Neville and Hansard (1996)
Murder on Framwellgate Bridge (1988)

A note on the northern Franciscan chronicle (1984)
Reason in Politics 1363–4, a *Quaestio* from Scotland (1996)

1997

William Ockham Opera politica, Vol. IV, edited by H.S. Offler (Foreword by D. Luscombe). Auctores Britannici Medii Aevi XIV (Oxford University Press for the British Academy, pp. xviii + 486)

I Compendium errorum Ioannis papae XXII
II Breviloquium de principatu tyrannico
III De imperatorum et pontificum potestate
IV Allegationes de potestate imperiali
V De electione Caroli Quarti

De iniusta vexatione Willelmi episcopi primi per Willelmum regem filium Willelmi magni regis. Edited by H.S. Offler. Revised by A.J. Piper and A.I. Doyle in Chronology, Conquest and Conflict in Medieval England, *Camden Miscellany*, XXXIV, Camden Fifth Series, volume 10 (Cambridge University Press for the Royal Historical Society, pp. 49–104)

I

ASPECTS OF GOVERNMENT IN THE LATE MEDIEVAL EMPIRE[1]

'Every kingdom divided against itself shall be brought to desolation, for its princes have become the companions of thieves.' Reciting these opening words of Charles IV's Golden Bull, the young Goethe caused its learned commentator Johann Daniel von Olenschlager to muse: 'What times those must have been, when an emperor at a great imperial diet had such words thrown in the face of his princes'.[2] The impression persists that the main themes of the history of the late medieval empire were disunity, disorder, corruption. Yet even in respect of government this is not wholly fair. Our grasp of these matters, let it be said at once, remains imperfect. Half a century ago Ludwig Quidde stated that the constitutional history of late medieval Germany was as yet unwritten; this still seemed true

[1] [It may be convenient for the reader to be reminded of the succession of rulers in Germany during the period discussed here:

Rudolf (of Habsburg), king of the Romans 1273–91.
Adolf (of Nassau), king of the Romans 1292–8.
Albert I (of Habsburg), king of the Romans 1298–1308.
Henry VII (of Luxemburg), king of the Romans 1308; emperor 1312–13.
Lewis IV (of Bavaria), king of the Romans 1314; emperor 1328–47.
(Frederick the Fair of Habsburg, anti-king 1314–22; nominally joint king with Lewis 1325–30).
Charles IV (of Luxemburg), king of the Romans 1346; emperor 1355–78.
(Günther of Schwarzburg, anti-king 1349.)
Wenzel (of Luxemburg), king of the Romans 1376–1400 (1419).
Rupert (of the Palatinate), king of the Romans 1400–10.
Sigismund (of Luxemburg), king of the Romans 1410 (1411); emperor 1433–7.
Albert II (of Habsburg), king of the Romans 1438–9.
Frederick III (of Habsburg), king of the Romans 1440; emperor 1452–93.
Maximilian (of Habsburg), king of the Romans 1486; emperor 1508–19.]

[2] *Dichtung und Wahrheit*, i, 4. The bull was combining Luke xi, 17 with Isaiah i, 23.

in 1958 to Quidde's successor in charge of the first series of the *Reichstagsakten*.[1] But much work has been done during the last sixty years or so. Though no new synthesis holds the field, perhaps some indications of the ways in which scholars' ideas and researches have been moving may be useful.

In the fourteenth and fifteenth centuries 'the empire' was a highly equivocal expression. It could be used to denote an area or a community or a mode of government or even the royal insignia, kept from 1424 onwards at Nuremberg.[2] In the background of these meanings was implicit some idea of Germany. By this time the expansive period of medieval German history had ended. The great eastward flow slackened markedly about the middle of the fourteenth century. A strong Slavonic state emerged in Poland-Lithuania, while in Bohemia powerful religious and social emotions nourished Czech particularism. The aggressive ambitions of France and then of Burgundy made themselves felt in the west, where the 'Netherlands' continued to drift outside the political ambit of the Rhineland. But despite these marks of recession the area of Germany remained very large, and men did not commonly have all of it in mind when they talked of the empire. Often they seem to have been thinking of a corridor of territories through which ran the axis Regensburg–Nuremberg–Frankfort–Mainz–Cologne–Aachen, the axis being eccentric until it reached the Rhine and the corridor extending further south and south-west than towards the north. When complaint was heard that this or that king had been absent from the *Reich* for years, it meant that he had not been seen in Franconia, Swabia or the Rhineland. This restricted conception took little notice of parts of Germany immensely important in her national history: the Hanseatic north, for instance, and Prussia. The reason is clear: these areas now had only slight connexion with the government of the empire. A history of the late medieval empire is, then, a good deal less, if also something more, than a history of Germany itself.

Holy since Barbarossa's time, holy and Roman since William of Holland's, after the middle of the fifteenth century the empire

[1] Cf. H. Heimpel, 'Deutsche Reichstagsakten, ältere Reihe', *Die Historische Kommission bei der Bayerischen Akademie der Wissenschaften 1858–1958* (Göttingen, 1958), 92.

[2] 'Insignia, que imperium dicuntur': Mathias von Neuenburg, *Chronica*, ed. A. Hofmeister (M.G.H. *S.S.* n.s. iv), 444.

began to be called 'the Holy Roman Empire of the German Nation'.[1] Possibly national feeling had something to do with the addition, though evidence of a heightened German consciousness can be found much earlier, during the excitements of 1337–9, for instance, or in the writings of Dietrich of Niem and Henry of Langenstein.[2] But the new title should not be misunderstood. It did not claim for the Germans an inalienable right to universal empire: rather it was intended almost as a synonym for Germany itself—for that part of the empire occupied by the German people. This attempt to shake off the incubus of classical and earlier medieval tradition had only limited success. The assumption of the author of the *Reformatio Sigismundi* (1439) that empire and Christendom were still convertible terms was widely shared. The care of Christendom's common interests, whether in restoring unity to a Church rent by schism or in waging war on heretical Hussites and infidel Turks, was thought to lie inescapably on the empire and its ruler. 'Promoted by divine providence to be a head of Christendom' was how Sigismund understood his position.[3] Though the story of his reign did not belie his words, it showed how these continuing universal responsibilities could distract the king from the business of governing Germany. Out-of-date claims which could neither be abandoned nor made good were onerous. The territories listed in Wenzel's grant of the imperial vicariate to Sigismund in March 1396 included Apulia, Calabria and Sicily.[4] It is natural to dismiss this as fantasy. Yet only a few years later the Rhenish electors could use Wenzel's grant of the duchy of Milan to Giangaleazzo Visconti as serious grounds for accusing the king of dilapidating the empire.[5] The reign of Wenzel's supplanter, Rupert of the Palatinate, foundered on the extensive obligations he was forced to undertake before his election: to heal the schism in the Church by the

[1] K. Zeumer, *Heiliges römisches Reich deutscher Nation* (Weimar, 1910), 37.

[2] Cf. A. Diehl, 'Heiliges römisches Reich deutscher Nation', *Hist. Zts.*, clvi (1937), 457 ff.; E. E. Stengel, in *Deutsches Archiv f. Gesch. d. Mittelalters*, ii (1938), 300, n. 1; H. Heimpel, *Dietrich von Niem* (Münster, 1932), 220–2.

[3] 'Von gottlicher schickunge ezu einem haubt der Cristenheit gefodert' (25th October, 1433): *Deutsche Reichstagsakten, ältere Reihe, hrsg. durch die Histor. Kommission bei d. Bayerischen Akademie d. Wissenschaften* [=*R.T.A.*] (Munich, 1867 ff.), xi, no. 87.

[4] *R.T.A.*, ii, no. 247; cf. A. Gerlich, *Habsburg–Luxemburg–Wittelsbach im Kampf um die deutsche Königskrone* (Wiesbaden, 1960), 91–3.

[5] *R.T.A.*, iii, no. 9, art. 2a (Christmas 1397); ibid., no. 204, art. 2 (20th August, 1400).

advice of the ecclesiastical electors and to reunite Milan and Brabant with the empire.[1] Only intermittently was it recognized how the empire as area and community had shrunk since Hohenstaufen times; its ruler was still called, and believed himself to be, *semper augustus, zu allen zeiten merer des reiches.*

As a mode of government the empire was in theory a monarchy. Though there was no king of Germany by that name, the principle that the duly elected king of the Romans had forthwith full power to rule the empire could not be effectively impugned in Germany after the electors' declaration at Rhens in July 1338. Complicated transactions with the Curia about papal recognition of the new ruler took place at the beginning of the reigns of Charles IV, Wenzel and Rupert; but their relevance to the situation north of the Alps was probably small. Already crowned in Germany, the king of the Romans became emperor after coronation at Rome by the pope or his delegates. This step was somewhat a matter of chance. Wenzel, Rupert and Albert II never achieved the imperial title; Charles IV became emperor in 1355, eight years after he had begun to reign; Sigismund had to wait twenty-two years and Frederick III twelve. The monarch's authority as king or emperor was supreme; he promulgated laws for the empire *de imperialis potestatis plenitudine, von Romischer kuniclicher macht, kraft und gewalt.* In official usage, at least, the formula 'Emperor and Empire', *Kaiser und Reich*, remained largely tautological throughout the Middle Ages; the institution was identified with the monarch's person.[2] Thus in August 1338 the Alsatian towns could pledge their support 'to our lord the emperor Lewis, who is the empire'.[3]

Reality did not match the theory. Obviously the late medieval empire was not in fact a system of government in the control of a single ruler. A Heidelberg professor—perhaps it was Conrad of Soest—lifted the veil when he wrote in 1408: 'Every nobleman, however modest his standing, is king in his own territory; every city exercises royal power within its own walls'.[4] Half a century later Aeneas Sylvius denied that monarchy existed in Germany.

[1] *R.T.A.*, iii, no. 200; cf. Gerlich, 346.

[2] R. Smend, 'Zur Geschichte der Formel "Kaiser und Reich" in den letzten Jahrhunderten des alten Reiches', *Historische Aufsätze Karl Zeumer . . . dargebracht* (Weimar, 1910), 442, 447.

[3] 'Unsern herren keiser Ludwigen, der daz rich ist': K. Müller, *Der Kampf Ludwigs d. Baiern mit d. römischen Curie*, ii (Tübingen, 1880), 358, doc. no. 5.

[4] *R.T.A.*, vi, no. 268.

I

GOVERNMENT IN THE LATE MEDIEVAL EMPIRE

The Germans were revelling in a plurality of princes. While they paid lip-service to the emperor as king and master, really he had no power: *nulla eius potentia est.* They obeyed him just as much as they wanted to, and their inclination to obey was minimal. The prelates, the lay princes and the towns were governing their subjects in independence.[1] Aeneas knew what he was talking about, from service in the imperial chancery and close acquaintance with some of the most intelligent Germans of his time. But if not a monarchy, what was the empire?

Corporative ideas did something to help. Admittedly the emperor was head, but there were also members of the empire: the princes, lay and ecclesiastical, led by the electors; the non-princely nobility; the towns, imperial and free; the lesser nobles, often of ministerial origin (the *Ritterschaft*). The attitude of these imperial estates towards the empire was ambivalent. They were proud to belong to it and to stand in direct relation to its head; but all desired for themselves as much freedom as possible within it. While the stronger among them were busily consolidating and extending their territories the small fry sought to escape these voracious pike by insisting that they too were independent members of the imperial body. When in 1426 the Swabian *Ritterschaft* formed their league to protect their common interests and ensure that they should 'continue as members of the empire' they were using language which, though commonplace, was meaningful.[2] With the more powerful estates consciousness of being limbs of the empire led to more positive conclusions. The possibility of distinguishing between the realm itself and the ruler's person had been understood from the early eleventh century, if not before.[3] By the late Middle Ages this distinction had been developed to support the claim that the interests of the empire did not invariably coincide with those of the emperor. Then it might be for the members to take action on behalf of the whole body even against the head. If so, a special responsibility was felt to rest upon the electors as *principaliora membra imperii.* Lupold of Bebenburg's teaching that

[1] Aeneas Silvius, *Germania*, ed. A. Schmidt (Cologne, 1962), 57, 68.

[2] 'Auch dass sie als Glieder beym heiligen Reiche bleiben mügen': quoted by C. F. Stälin, *Wirtembergische Geschichte*, iii (Stuttgart, 1856), 448.

[3] On the well-known phrase in Wipo: 'si rex periit, regnum remansit', *Gesta Chuonradi imperatoris*, ed. H. Bresslau, p. 30, cf. H. Beumann, 'Zur Entwicklung transpersonaler Staatsvorstellungen', in *Das Königtum, seine geistigen u. rechtlichen Grundlagen*, ed. Th. Mayer (Lindau and Constance, 1956), 212 ff.

in choosing the king of the Romans they represented the empire could be extended to other activities on their part.[1] In June 1400 the Rhenish electors threatened Wenzel that if he did not appear to meet them at Lahnstein they would feel themselves released from the oaths they had made to his person, though their obligations to the Holy Roman Empire were to remain binding.[2] Wenzel's deposition a couple of months later on the grounds that he was useless to the empire gave sharp point to the distinction.[3] Nothing less than active copartnership in the empire was claimed for the electors by the terms of the league of Marbach, formed under the leadership of Archbishop John II of Mainz against Rupert in 1405.[4] When the citizens of Cologne complained to Sigismund about the behaviour of their archbishop, Dietrich of Mörs, they got but cold comfort in return, according to Eberhard Windecke: 'he could do nothing for them; the electors were themselves the law'.[5] The facts of power make clear that, whatever theory might suggest, the working constitution of the late medieval empire was dualistic.

But it was not neatly so. Among the different estates capacity for effective political action varied enormously. If the electors had the prestige, superiority in physical resources lay increasingly with other territorial princes. Weaker estates, the non-princely nobles, the towns, the *Ritterschaft*, unable to create significant territories for themselves, had good reason to fear those who could. Mutual rivalries and suspicions made it impossible to harness all the estates for common action against the king. The same factors encouraged individual members among them to seek strength by union with selected allies. Late medieval Germany saw a vast activity of the federative principle, *Einung*.[6] The multitude of leagues defies classification. There were leagues between towns, between knights, between peasant communities, but also leagues in which towns, knights, princes and all sorts of nobles were mingled pell-mell. They did not amount to a federal constitution, or even to a

[1] Lupold of Bebenburg, *De iure regni et imperii*, ch. 5 (Basle, 1566), 353.
[2] *R.T.A.*, iii, nos. 146–7.
[3] *R.T.A.*, iii, no. 204.
[4] *R.T.A.*, v, no. 489.
[5] 'Do sprach der konig . . . die korfursten weren selber das recht': *Eberhard Windeckes Denkwürdigkeiten*, ed. W. Altmann (Berlin, 1893), 101.
[6] Cf. E. Bock, 'Monarchie, Einung u. Territorium im späteren Mittelalter', *Hist. Vierteljahrsschrift* [=*H.V.*], xxiv (1929), 568.

system of confederations: 'public life was dominated by a confusion of confederations subsisting side by side.'[1] As Samuel von Pufendorf realized, there lurked in the empire some indefinable element which made it irreducible to any of the classical categories of political science.[2]

No simple formula can be found to describe the development of this complex structure; the lines of stratification were constantly being fractured. The story of the late medieval empire can no longer be presented in the old terms of the collapse of a formerly strong unitary monarchy, brought to ruin by ambitious and self-seeking territorial princes who had succeeded in usurping the prerogatives of sovereignty. As we recognize more clearly how the intensity with which government can be exercised depends on the relation between what is to be governed and the technical resources available for governing, we are less likely to expect too much of even the ablest medieval rulers. When the level of technical resources was low, the well-governed unit was commonly the small one. The sheer extent of Germany made direct rule by the king impossible once demands on government had become more exacting as the result of population growth and the intensification of settlement. The territorial magnates filled the gap, and it is pointless to abuse them as particularist and disruptive elements for doing what was needed and the king was unable to do.[3] During the last thirty years few books about constitutional developments in late medieval Germany have aroused more discussion than O. Brunner's *Land und Herrschaft*. Perhaps its most valuable lesson is so obvious that it is often overlooked: that medieval constitutional problems have the right to be studied in terms of their own times and circumstances, rather than in those suggested by later experience.[4]

A glance at what fifteenth-century Germans thought about the empire reveals much diversity and also a fundamental agreement. Among the town chroniclers Diebold Schilling of Berne has no doubt that 'Heilig rich' and 'Tutsch nacion' are

[1] L. Quidde, *Histoire de la paix publique en Allemagne au moyen âge* (Recueil des Cours de l'Académie de Droit International, xxviii, Paris, 1930), 551.

[2] [Severinus de Monzambano], *De statu imperii*, vi, 1 and 9, ed. F. Salomon (Weimar, 1910), 116, 127.

[3] Cf. K. S. Bader, 'Volk, Stamm, Territorium', in *Herrschaft u. Staat im Mittelalter*, ed. H. Kämpf (Darmstadt, 1956), 267–8.

[4] O. Brunner, *Land und Herrschaft*, 4th edn. (Vienna and Wiesbaden, 1959), 111 ff.

one. But while he accepts without discussion the universal mission of the empire, it becomes a concrete institution for him only in so far as it provides for the security of his own imperial city and its allies.[1] This attitude, combining the widest conceptions of the empire with the sentiment that in fact it is embodied in the free and imperial towns, is typical.[2] The Augsburg chronicler Burkard Zink complained that the imperial cities were failing to maintain their union among themselves and were seeking alliances with the lords: 'and thus the empire is wholly rent asunder'.[3] For Zink as for Schilling, the towns were the empire; and the quality of individual kings was measured by the extent to which they cherished urban interests.

Schilling was Swiss, of course; but the history of the Swiss cantons in the late Middle Ages was still part of German history. Their emergence represented a successful protest of the old law and its freedoms in face of the newer aggressive efficiencies of the territorial princedoms. By making good the claim to depend directly from the empire they ensured their independence from Habsburg, into whose territory they seemed fated to be absorbed, and also they legitimatized their own exercise of authority. From 1438 onwards, with Habsburgers as kings, the allegiance of the Swiss to the empire was inevitably strained; the gamekeeper, they feared, might turn poacher. Even so, their reluctance to leave the empire is remarkable. Like other German territories, the Confederation was jealous of its freedom of action, and on these grounds refused to accept the decisions of the reforming diet at Worms in 1495. Nevertheless, it has been claimed with some force, even after 1495 the Swiss did not desire separation; though ultimately it came, its story lies wholly outside the Middle Ages.[4] The Swiss chroniclers of the fifteenth century, just as the articulate elements in the south German towns, no doubt viewed the empire in the light of particular interests. But for all of them it seemed a permanent part of the settled and proper order of things.

The same conclusion was implied by many of the theoreticians.

[1] Diebold Schilling, *Berner Chronik*, ed. G. Tobler, i (Berne, 1897), 131.

[2] Cf. H. Schmidt, *Die deutschen Städtechroniken als Spiegel des bürgerlichen Selbsverständnisses im Spätmittelalter* (Göttingen, 1958), 64 ff.

[3] 'Also ist das reich alles zertrent': Burkard Zink, *Augsburger Chronik*, ed. F. Frensdorff (*Chroniken d. deutschen Städte*, v), 231.

[4] Karl Mommsen, *Eidgenossen, Kaiser und Reich* (Basel, 1958), 292.

To the greatest of them, Nicholas of Cues, writing in 1433, it was obvious that the emperor's power had declined markedly since Otto I's time, when imperial edicts were armed *potentia et vigore*. The situation was critical; unless his recommendations were carried out, Nicholas declared, the empire was doomed; in the ensuing confusion the lower orders (*populares*) would devour the princes, just as these were now gobbling up the empire. But Nicholas himself, one feels, was hardly convinced by this alarmist language. He thought that salvation could be found by return to the old trodden ways: regular annual assemblies of the princes; the establishment of a dozen or more standing imperial tribunals; use of ballot in future imperial elections; a permanent imperial army maintained by contributions from throughout the empire.[1] Not everything in these proposals did in fact represent return to the tried ways of the past; much was sketchy and indefinite; some was naïve. Interest attaches less to the proposals than to the fact that Nicholas believed in them. If they could be adopted, in his view a reformed empire was still possible.

Writing from a very different level of experience and ability the unknown author of the *Reformatio Sigismundi* (1439) contributed less directly to the argument. The perspective of his writing is eschatological; though his sense of actuality never dissolves completely, his passionate concern for the right ordering of Christian society is that of a moralist rather than a political thinker. Perhaps his disposition was more conservative than is often assumed—not that he believed that things should remain as they were, but rather that they should again become what they ought to be. But though no precise view of the empire is offered by the *Reformatio*, it remains for the author a fundamental institution coterminous with Christendom; he does not despair of its future.[2] No more did Peter of Andlau in his *Libellus de caesarea monarchia* (1460). The message of this feeble and derivative piece is that the empire will last until the coming of Antichrist. Admittedly, Frederick III is in a weaker position than the first Caesars. Nevertheless he is their legitimate

[1] *De concordantia catholica*, iii, 25–39, ed. G. Kallen, *Opera omnia Nicolai de Cusa*, xiv, 3 (Hamburg, 1959), 420–56.

[2] The manuscript basis of the edition by K. Beer, *Die Reformation Kaiser Sigmunds* (Beiheft to *R.T.A.*, 1933) is incomplete. A new edition by H. Koller for M.G.H. appeared in 1963. What is said above owes much to Lothar Graf zu Dohna, *Reformatio Sigismundi* (Göttingen, 1960), 52 ff.

successor; power lies to his hand, if only he will bestir himself to use it.[1]

Behind all these ideas, with their mingling of present and remote past, of the parochially narrow with the ecumenically wide, lies consciousness that the empire is, and must continue. Some of this consciousness has justly been called negative.[2] The weaker estates were far more likely to show awareness of their imperial status when they felt their independence threatened than when the empire called on them to fulfil their duties. But we may easily underestimate how strongly there persisted a feeling of the potentiality latent in the empire. Just past the middle of the fifteenth century an electoral memorandum emanating from Trier expressed it thus: 'In people, towns, fortresses and all other things which pertain to lordly great affairs our nation is master over all other nations, provided that it is rightly ordered and governed.'[3] It was for the empire to supply this right ordering and governance at the highest level. To maintain peace and justice was its primary concern, as Frederick II had emphasized in 1235.[4] No heavier charge could be found to lay against Wenzel's rule than that war was everywhere and no one knew before whom he should seek justice.[5]

The empire's overriding responsibility for *pax et iustitia* was the business in the first place of its head, but also of its members. At any particular time it was the comparative weights of these elements which swayed the balance in the empire's divided constitution.

A basic fact of kingship in Germany at this period was the way in which its elective nature was stressed and exploited. Only few and obscure voices were raised in the cause of sense against the theory that elective monarchy was superior to other kinds.[6] It is useless to debate whether Albert I, had he escaped being

[1] Peter von Andlau, *Libellus de caesarea monarchia*, ii, 18–20, ed. J. Hürbin, *Zts. d. Savigny-Stiftung f. Rechtsgeschichte, Germanist. Abt.* [=*Z.R.G. G.A.*], xiii (1892), 215–17.

[2] Cf. K. S. Bader, *Der deutsche Südwesten in seiner territorialstaatlichen Entwicklung* (Stuttgart, 1950), 58.

[3] Printed by L. von Ranke, *Deutsche Geschichte im Zeitalter der Reformation*, 6th edn., vi (Leipzig, 1882), 13.

[4] In the preamble to the *Landfriede* of Mainz, M.G.H. *Const.*, ii, no. 196, p. 241, the collocation of *pax* and *iustitia* occurs three times in seven lines.

[5] *R.T.A.*, iii, no. 9 (Christmas 1397).

[6] Cf. A. Werminghoff, 'Zur Lehre von der Erbmonarchie im 14. Jahrhundert'. *H.V.*, xx (1922), 150 ff.

murdered in 1308, might have made the Crown hereditary in the Habsburg family. He did not do so, and for the next 130 years no Habsburger was uncontested king in Germany. The important part played by election in making the king had inescapable consequences. Since he could not rely on the Crown remaining in his dynasty after his death (to contrive this for Wenzel taxed the ability of Charles IV, while it seems doubtful whether Maximilian's election was actively promoted by his father at all),[1] the king was bound to do the best he could for his family while he was alive. An elective kingship was necessarily devoted to the pursuit of dynastic power, *Hausmacht*. Before his death Lewis the Bavarian had established members of his family in possession of Tirol, Brandenburg, Hainault, Holland and Zeeland. The acquisition of Brandenburg for the Luxemburgers, completed in 1373, ranks among the most arduous achievements of Charles IV. Only the tireless attention paid by Frederick III to Habsburg family interests, often under discouraging circumstances, made it possible for his heir to play an active part in European politics.

It is futile to accuse these kings of behaving as step-fathers towards the empire. They could make a show of ruling only by deploying their *Hausmacht*. The empire itself had little to offer the king by way of physical or financial support. By this time he had lost control over the imperial churches and their lands; no territory of consequence, except the imperial towns, came to him as king of the Romans; income from such regalian rights as remained was often anticipated for years in advance and these sources were frequently in hazard as the result of being pledged time and again to Crown creditors. Material from which to write a continuous financial history of the late medieval empire does not survive.[2] From year to year revenue from the chief source, the imperial towns, may have varied between about ten and thirty thousand guldens, an excessively narrow basis for the credit operations which had to be undertaken in any emergency and which in the end were commonly

[1] Cf. E. Bock, 'Die Doppelregierung Friedrichs III. u. Maximilians 1486–1493', in *Aus Reichstagen des 15. u. 16. Jahrhunderts. Festgabe dargebracht der Histor. Kommission . . . von den Herausgebern der deutschen Reichstagsakten* [=*A.R.*], (Göttingen, 1958), 283–5. R. Buchner, *Maximilian I* (Göttingen, 1959), 26, puts forward the view that Frederick wished for Maximilian's election though not for its consequences.

[2] E. B. and M. M. Fryde give a useful conspectus in *The Cambridge Economic History of Europe*, iii (1963), 507–18.

backed by the king's dynastic resources. Though the king was still feudal suzerain of Germany, enfeoffing the princes with their territories, this did not put an adequate armed force at his disposal. In face of the Hussite threat in 1422 the summer diet at Nuremberg demanded specified contingents of troops from named members of the empire, together with a fractional tax on incomes or property from those on whom a quota of service was not imposed, as well as a harsh levy from the Jews.[1] These measures were no more effective than the attempt five years later of the papal legate and the estates to finance an imperial army against the Hussites by elaborate tax proposals on persons and property throughout the empire.[2] Feeling against the foreigner might allow Frederick III to bring together an imperial army to relieve Neuss from Charles of Burgundy in 1475, but he met humiliating discomfiture when he tried to enforce by arms an imperial sentence against his vassal Frederick the Victorious of the Palatinate. As was to be expected, at the centre of the wide proposals for reform in 1495 lay a scheme for a general tax, the Common Penny, to be raised for the purposes of 'maintaining peace and justice in the empire and withstanding the enemies of Christ, the Turks and other enemies of the Holy Empire and the German Nation'.[3] Not least amongst the reasons for the failure of the Common Penny was Maximilian's insistence that the proceeds of it from the Habsburg hereditary lands should come under his control, rather than that of the imperial diet. He can hardly be blamed for not accepting a mediatization of his *Hausmacht* which might have undermined his position in the empire. The king's authority and his power as territorial dynast were inseparably connected.

This limited the possible candidates for the office. Four families—Habsburg, Nassau, Wittelsbach and Luxemburg—monopolized the throne from 1272 to 1486; at times there was talk of widening the circle, but nothing came of it.[4] These families did not serve the empire badly. In their differing ways

[1] *R.T.A.*, viii, nos. 145, 147, 152–4; cf. H. Herre, 'Das Reichskriegssteuergesetz vom Jahre 1422'; *H.V.*, xix (1920), 13 ff.

[2] *R.T.A.*, ix, no. 76.

[3] K. Zeumer, *Quellensammlung zur Geschichte der deutschen Reichsverfassung* [=Zeumer, *Quellen*], 2nd edn. (Leipzig, 1913), no. 176.

[4] Cf. Gerlich, op. cit., 274 for an agreement reached in September 1399 between the electors and a number of princes to accept a future king only from the houses of Bavaria, Meissen, Hesse, Hohenzollern or Württemberg.

nearly all the German kings from Rudolf of Habsburg to Maximilian were able, Rudolf and Charles IV outstandingly so. Perhaps the only exceptions were Adolf and Wenzel; and even for Wenzel something can be said, at least down to 1389.[1] The Crown's problems were institutional rather than personal, and it would be wrong to underrate the technical standards of such government as these kings did offer. Quite recently more light has been thrown on the considerable achievements of Lewis the Bavarian as a legislator;[2] work on the registers of the imperial chancery under Sigismund and Albert II shows that office as an efficient organ of administration under the king's control, and no longer exclusively a clerical preserve. Only in Frederick III's reign did a change for the worse take place.[3]

Procedure for electing the king was codified in the Golden Bull of 1356.[4] The Bull's great merit was that it provided lasting rules for an orderly succession to the throne. At a first reading it is disappointing to find this fundamental law devoting so many of its articles to the small change of ceremony. But they, like the unrealistic demand that the lay electors should be instructed in the Latin, Italian and Slavonic tongues, and the attempt to apply to those who plotted against an elector's life the sanctions of the Roman law of treason, were of the very stuff of the mid-fourteenth century.[5] The Bull was little concerned with new principles; the electors had long enjoyed the constitutional standing and most of the privileges ratified in 1356. Its purpose was to place beyond the doubts which had worked so mischievously in the past the details of what was at once a great ceremony and a vital political transaction: to settle finally who were entitled to elect and how they were to proceed. It did not prove a perfect rule for the future; Wenzel's election during his father's lifetime, though not forbidden by the Bull, neglected some of its prescriptions; only the timely death of Jost of

[1] H. Weigel, 'König Wenzels persönliche Politik', *Deutsches Archiv f. Gesch. d. Mittelalters*, vii (1944), 133–99.

[2] H. Lieberich, 'Kaiser Ludwig der Baier als Gesetzgeber', *Z.R.G. G.A.*, lxxvi (1959), 176–219, 241–5.

[3] Cf. H. Koller, *Das Reichsregister König Albrechts II* (*Mitteilungen d. Österreich. Staatsarchivs*. Erg. Bd. iv, Vienna, 1955), 1–11.

[4] Cf. K. Zeumer, *Die Goldene Bulle Kaiser Karls IV*, 2 vols. (Weimar, 1908); text, ibid., ii, 5–48 and Zeumer, *Quellen*, no. 148.

[5] On the long controversy between Mainz and Cologne as to which archbishop should take the king's right hand, see H. Foerster, 'Kurköln u. Stadt Köln i.d. Goldenen Bulle Kaiser Karls IV', *Rheinische Vierteljahrsblätter*, xix (1954), 59–63.

Moravia offered a clear way out of the complicated situation in 1410.[1] But the real grounds for criticizing the Bull are that it was too successful. In the long run it petrified what it had sought to make stable and regular.

In general the eastern electorates played a secondary part. As long as the Luxemburgers survived the Bohemian vote was under their control; afterwards, despite George Podiebrad's ambitions to shape imperial policy in the early 'sixties, doubts could be felt whether Bohemia stood on quite the same footing as the other electorates.[2] Little effective intervention could be expected from Brandenburg or Saxony until the Hohenzollerns (1415) and Wettiners (1424) had become established. The lead fell to the Rhinelanders, the archbishops of Mainz, Cologne and Trier, and the count palatine. Mainz, with its great historic claims, its archchancellorship of the empire in Germany, and its initiative in the business of royal elections now secured by the Golden Bull, outranked the other two archbishoprics. The count palatine, the only prince before whom the king could be called to answer legal complaint, had too the duty of governing the empire as vicar in the area of Frankish law when there was no king. Mainz and the Palatinate can hardly be said to have dominated the electoral college, but for more than a century after the Golden Bull they were its most consistently influential members.

The special union for joint action, the *Kurverein*, to which the electors on occasion resorted, was always a weighty demonstration. At Rhens in July 1338, between April and September 1399, at Bingen in January 1424, electoral unions originating on the Rhine decided great matters of imperial politics.[3] They rejected papal interference in the making of the king of the Romans, prepared the deposition of Wenzel and election of Rupert, manifested electoral solidarity for policies to be achieved, if need be, in the king's despite. A peak was reached after Sigismund's death, before Albert II had accepted the kingship: the March *Kurverein* of 1438 declared for German neutrality between the conflicting claims of Pope Eugenius IV

[1] R. Lies, 'Die Wahl Wenzels z. Römischen Könige i. ihrem Verhältnis z. Goldenen Bulle', *H.V.*, xxvi (1931), 93–5; J. Leuschner, 'Zur Wahlpolitik im Jahre 1410', *Deutsches Archiv f. Erforschung d. Mittelalters*, xi (1955), 506 ff.

[2] Cf. Zeumer, *Goldene Bulle*, i, 170, 234, 245–55.

[3] Zeumer, *Quellen*, nos. 141a, 141c. *R.T.A.*, iii, nos. 41, 51, 56–8, 204; cf. Gerlich, op. cit., pp. 328, 336. *R.T.A.*, viii, no. 294; cf. H. Angermeier, 'Das Reich u.d. Konziliarismus', *Hist. Zts.*, cxcii (1961), 559–60.

and the Council of Basle.[1] Though the Golden Bull's provision for regular annual meetings between king and electors was disregarded, the electors habitually claimed extensive influence in imperial affairs, even when there was no *Kurverein* for a specific purpose. At times—in 1399–1400, for instance, and from 1405 to the end of Rupert's reign—that influence seemed decisive. Between 1417 and 1430, favoured by Sigismund's long absences, they took over much of the business of government, not always with the king's approval. For much of Sigismund's reign, indeed, they were not just the elective body and highest council of the empire, issuing their individual letters of consent (*Willebriefe*) to royal grants. They arrogated to themselves joint rule with the king, whether he liked it or not.

Such examples should not be pressed too hard; the electors' position was not on the whole as strong as they might suggest. Electoral policy towards pope and council in the *Kurverein* of 1446 did not prevail; Frederick III had other views, and it was he alone who arrived at the concordat of 1448 with Pope Nicholas V.[2] Effective action by the electors depended on unity, and this was not easy to create or maintain. The territories of the four Rhenish electors were not merely contiguous, but confused; the geographical texture of the Palatinate, it has been said, resembled a sponge, in the holes of which lay the most important places, all belonging to Mainz.[3] It was a pattern highly apt to breed controversy. Though as an economic region the middle Rhineland imposed on its rulers some degree of joint action in matters of communications, tolls and currency, from this there grew no steady habit of political co-operation. A particular emergency might bring the Rhenish electors together, to act with impressive effect, but soon local rubs and rivalries would set them at odds again. Within a few years of being made king by the Rhenish bloc Rupert had no more bitter opponent than John II of Mainz; the early 1460s are full of the strife between Frederick the Victorious and Archbishop Adolf II. Above all, the numerical preponderance of the Rhinelanders in the electoral college, the result of old history, perpetuated by the Golden Bull, found no justification in the real balance of forces in late medieval Germany. Even in union

[1] *R.T.A.*, xiii, no. 144; cf. Angermeier, 567.
[2] Angermeier, 575; Zeumer, *Quellen*, no. 168.
[3] The description comes from E. Ziehen, *Mittelrhein u. Reich i. Zeitalter d. Reichsreform*, i (Frankfurt a.M., 1934), 162.

the Rhenish electorates were not big enough nor strong enough nor well enough placed to sustain a dominant role when power had moved elsewhere, to the south and the east.[1] The pretensions of the electors to make decisions for the empire rang hollow when some of the most important political factors in Germany had no electoral voice—the Swiss Confederation, the Wittelsbachers in Bavaria, the Habsburgers in their land of Austria 'which is known to be the shield and heart of the Holy Roman Empire'.

This phrase comes from the *Privilegium maius*, a falsified rehandling in 1358–9 of Barbarossa's privilege for the duchy of Austria.[2] It may well be that in substance the falsification did not go far beyond the genuine privilege of 1156, except in making some high faluting ceremonial claims for the duke and asserting for his territory the judicial immunity of the *privilegium de non evocando*.[3] But it is very likely that Duke Rudolf IV of Habsburg instigated the forgery with the Golden Bull in mind. In 1356, together with the rest of southern Germany, Austria had been excluded from the select circle of electors and so from what Rudolf considered its due influence in the empire; in part the *Maius* was intended to redress the situation. It contained a typical programme of princely 'liberty', reducing to a minimum Austria's obligations to the empire while insisting on the empire's duty to aid the duke. 'In matters favourable to itself it is a member of the empire; not so, when the relation is vexatious.' What Pufendorf said of fourteenth-century Austria had the *Maius* in view.[4] But the comment can be applied further afield. The liberties which Rudolf falsely claimed were granted by Barbarossa he did in fact to a large extent enjoy. So too did many other territorial rulers at this time.

With the princes indeed lay not only the future (as we are often told) but also much of the present. Compared with them the lesser nobility and the towns had little weight in politics. The means chosen by the *Ritterschaft* in its struggle for independence were probably more reputable and intelligent than is

[1] Cf. B. Schmeidler, 'Die Bedeutung d. späteren Mittelalters f. d. deutsche u. europäische Geschichte', *H.V.*, xxix (1935), 100.

[2] Text: M.G.H. *Const.*, i, no. 455, pp. 683–5, and A. Lhotsky, *Privilegium maius. Die Geschichte einer Urkunde* (Munich, 1957), 84.

[3] Lhotsky, 24.

[4] [Severinus de Monzambano], *De statu imperii*, ii, 4, ed. Salomon, p. 53: 'Ergo in favorabilibus est membrum Imperii, in odiosis non item.'

sometimes assumed;[1] in their leagues the lesser nobles could be useful allies. But they were hardly an independent force in the empire. No more were the towns in the fifteenth century. By this time the will for positive political action which had characterized the league of Rhenish towns in 1254 seemed dead.[2] Though numerous, the towns were mostly small: among three thousand or so perhaps only a couple of hundred could boast of more than a thousand inhabitants, with a dozen modest giants exceeding ten thousand.[3] Their resources in money, credit and man-power were far from contemptible; the service quotas of 1422 assessed more than a quarter of the imperial army against the free and imperial towns.[4] But with a few exceptions (Nuremberg, Berne, Zürich, for instance) they failed to create for themselves territories of any importance. Individual citizens, as the history of early capitalism shows, abounded in energy and enterprise, yet the corporate psychology of the towns had become defensive, their consciousness of the empire negative. How shrewd Charles IV had been in preferring to support the princes was shown by the towns' nerveless reaction to encouragement from Sigismund. Probably they never fully recovered from the rough handling given them by the nobles and princes in the 1380s.[5] Even the Hanseatic towns, among whom a far stronger and more aggressive political ethos prevailed than in the south, seemed past their peak by 1400.[6]

There was no lack of dynamism among the princes. By the second half of the fifteenth century they were emerging as personalities: Albert Achilles in Franconia and Brandenburg, Frederick the Victorious in the Palatinate, Eberhard the Bearded in Württemberg, Albert the Wise and George the Rich in Bavaria, and a dozen more. Perhaps there is some danger of forgetting how much was still provisional and incomplete in their territorial constructions and how far short

[1] Cf. H. Obenaus, *Recht u. Verfassung d. Gesellschaften mit St. Jörgenschild in Schwaben* (Göttingen, 1961).

[2] Cf. E. Bielfeldt, *Der Rheinische Bund von 1254. Ein erster Versuch einer Reichsreform* (Berlin, 1937), 33.

[3] H. Bechtel, *Wirtschaftsgeschichte Deutschlands von d. Vorzeit bis zum Ende des Mittelalters*, 2nd edn. (Munich, 1951), pp. 255–6.

[4] Herre, 'Reichskriegssteuergesetz', p. 33.

[5] The situation *c.* 1500 has been described by H. Gollwitzer, '*Capitaneus imperatorio nomine*. Reichshauptleute in Städten u. reichsstädtische Schicksale im Zeitalter Maximilians I.', *A.R.*, 273–8.

[6] Cf. F. Rörig, 'Aussenpolitische u. innerpolitische Wandlungen i.d. Hanse nach d. Stralsunder Frieden (1370)', *Wirtschaftskräfte im Mittelalter* (Cologne, 1959), 161–6.

within them they fell of what the modern world would recognize as sovereignty. The rise of the princes to supremacy within their territories was by no means a story of unbroken success.[1] Bad luck or management in a dynasty could lead to paralysing divisions and dissensions. The chaotic internal conditions in Brandenburg under the Wittelsbachers and Luxemburgers are a commentary on that theme.[2] In Bavaria from 1392 to 1448 the duchy was split between four ruling lines, Munich, Ingolstadt, Landshut and Straubing; not until the first decade of the sixteenth century were its rich potentialities brought together in a single hand and its unity made secure. Such circumstances could gravely hinder the princes in their efforts to master the Church, the nobles and the towns in their territories. They could not afford to be nice about the means they used. There are grounds for supposing that the forged *Privilegium maius* was even more serviceable to the Habsburgers as a means of asserting their supremacy within Austria than of emphasizing their quasi-autonomy in the empire.[3] Even so, it has been argued, not till the sixteenth century was the *Landeshoheit* of Habsburg in Austria complete.[4]

The territorial ruler indeed rarely exercised a solid and uniform authority over a neatly defined geographical area. Rather, he is to be pictured struggling with an untidy bundle of rights and superiorities, very diverse in nature and origin. Over some of them his control was still precarious. Feudal ties, paying little heed to emergent territorial boundaries, added their complications. Not everywhere did the lesser nobles submit to the prince; in Württemberg, the Kraichgau and the Rheingau, for instance, they eventually escaped into the status of imperial knights. Sharp definitions were wanting; in a single

[1] H. Spangenberg, *Vom Lehenstaat zum Ständestaat* (Munich and Berlin, 1912), 120 ff.

[2] Cf. H. Spangenberg, 'Landesherrliche Verwaltung, Feudalismus u. Ständetum i.d. deutschen Territorien d. 13. bis 15. Jahrhunderts', *Hist. Zts.*, ciii (1909), 512 ff.

[3] Lhotsky, *Privilegium maius*, 30.

[4] Cf. O. H. Stowasser, 'Zwei Studien z. oesterreich. Verfassungsgeschichte', *Z.R.G. G.A.*, xliv (1924), 146; id., *Das Land und der Herzog* (Berlin, 1925), 7 ff.; id., 'Die Entwicklung des Landes Oesterreich', *Vierteljahrschrift f. Sozial- u. Wirtschaftsgeschichte*, xix (1927), 429 ff. Of course there are dangers in generalizing from the experience of a particular area. How little, e.g., O. Brunner's conception of *Land* as a community living and working under a unity of law (*Landrecht*), largely based as it is on evidence from south-east Germany (*Land und Herrschaft*, 180–96, 231–9), fits conditions in the mark of Meissen has been pointed out by K. Bosl, *Hist. Zts.*, cxci (1960), 350, with reference to H. Helbig, *Der Wettinische Ständestaat* (Cologne, 1955).

area the rights and claims of various territorial rulers and lords might lie intermingled and overlapping.[1] Only by unremitting effort in administration could the princes consolidate their territories and their own position. This proved their ladder to success. Attempts to turn the prince's council into an instrument of the noble estate giving mandatory advice failed; the council did not become part of the constitutional machinery of the territory but remained an organ of administration.[2] The prince appointed as advisers and administrators those whose abilities could serve him best; as the fifteenth century wore on more and more was heard of the professional bureaucrats, often now trained in Roman law and moving for advancement from one territory to another.[3] Not infrequent complaints about the *doctores* bear involuntary witness to their efficiency.[4] These complaints continued long, and warn us not to antedate establishment or acceptance of the new techniques. In the electorate of Mainz, which we might expect to have been pretty forward in this field, administration was not brought under the control of central departments until the second half of the fifteenth century.[5]

A territory was something more than the expression of a dynasty's will for power. As in the empire itself, so there was a dualism in territorial constitutions. The prince had to reckon with his estates—the churchmen, the nobles, the towns and in a few instances the peasants.[6] Their composition and the extent to which they worked with or against the ruler varied greatly from territory to territory. In ecclesiastical principalities facts of church organization and the canon law might cause departures from the usual pattern. Thus in Mainz relations between the prince-archbishop and his estates were in a sense distorted by the claims of the cathedral chapter. Towards the archbishop the chapter acted as an estate, but to the other estates of Mainz —the nobles, the *Landschaft* of the Rheingau, the towns of the *Oberstift*—it appeared as part of the ruling lordship, the *Herrschaft*, itself.[7] But however they might be organized, the estates

[1] Cf. A. Werminghoff, *Ludwig von Eyb* (Halle, 1919), 58 ff.
[2] Spangenberg, *Vom Lehenstaat zum Ständestaat*, 71–3.
[3] Cf. Henny Grüneisen, 'Herzog Sigmund von Tirol, der Kaiser u. die Ächtung d. Eidgenossen, 1469. Kanzlei u. Räte Herzog Sigmunds', *A.R.*, 157–61, 211–2.
[4] F. L. Carsten, *Princes and Parliaments in Germany* (Oxford, 1959), 11, 355–6.
[5] B. Witte, *Herrschaft und Land im Rheingau* (Meisenheim/Glan, 1959) 141–2.
[6] The nature of the medieval estates is well brought out by Brunner, *Land und Herrschaft*, 394 ff.
[7] Witte, 186.

fulfilled indispensable functions. Without their help it was difficult for the prince to raise taxes; only they were able to protect the community of the territory from the results of dynastic accident or caprice. As guardians of the unity of the territory it was their duty to combat patrimonial conceptions in the ruling house. A chronicler tells us how in 1347, after the death of Count Adolf II, the knights of Mark rejected the demand of his brother Eberhard that the county should forthwith be divided between him and Adolf's son Engelbert. Though it was proper, they conceded, that decent provision should be made for Eberhard, it was essential that the county should be kept as a single unit: and so Engelbert III was brought in as sole ruler.[1] The accent was not always merely on conservation. The action of the estates might also be constructive. Even under the thrusting Dietrich II of Mörs (1414–63), it has been claimed, the development of the territory of Cologne was as much the work of the estates as of the archbishop.[2]

At times the estates met of their own volition. The view that only by converting such meetings into a periodic official occasion, the *Landtag*, did the princes manage to draw the teeth of a threat to their own power, is probably too schematic.[3] The joint meetings of the estates at the summons of the prince, becoming more frequent as the fifteenth century wore on, 'did not come into being as a planned move by one side or the other, but grew up because they fulfilled a useful purpose'.[4] It remains true that they could prove formidable to an unwise or unfortunate ruler, as the dukes in Württemberg experienced; their very existence imposed some limitation on the free play of the princes' ambitions.

There was, then, no single machine of government for the empire. Its politics were shaped by the interplay between head and members, both acting more commonly within the context of this or that league or union than as individuals. Thus authority at a high level in Germany was diffused, at a time

[1] Levold von Northof, *Chronica Comitum de Marka*, ed. F. Zschaeck (M.G.H. *S.S.* n.s. vi), 12.

[2] G. Droege, *Verfassung und Wirtschaft in Kurköln unter Dietrich von Moers, 1414–1463* (Bonn, 1957), 205–7.

[3] Spangenberg, *Vom Lehenstaat zum Ständestaat*, 113, 137–51.

[4] Carsten, *Princes and Parliaments*, 428.

when elsewhere it was becoming more concentrated. We ought not to assume too readily that all the results were bad—that therefore the citizen of Bremen or Augsburg or Leipzig had less chance of realizing his human potentialities than his counterpart in Rouen or Bristol or Barcelona. There is a thought-provoking discrepancy in late medieval Germany between vigorous cultural and economic achievement on the one hand and the complications and incoherencies of governmental structure on the other.[1]

But undoubtedly these structural peculiarities in Germany did pose severe problems. Abundant illustration of this can be found in the sphere of justice. Within their territories the princes now controlled the courts. But what if a territorial court judged perversely or denied justice? What if the subjects of one prince were at odds with those of another, or with some lesser member of the empire whose independence might be jeopardized by submission to the jurisdiction of a neighbouring territory? What remedy could be found for the confusions caused by the simultaneous existence of innumerable sources and varieties of law: popular, feudal, ministerial, manorial, urban, in all their differing provincial and territorial forms? The widespread reception of Roman law (as adapted to current needs by the fourteenth-century legists) helped to supply Germany's want of a single common law, even though we cannot assume that this process was rapid or smooth or universal.[2] But as a supreme imperial tribunal the *Reichshofgericht* proved hopelessly inadequate. The *Hofrichter* exercised no jurisdiction over princes; he had neither professional assistants nor means of ensuring the execution of his judgments; commonly a member of the higher nobility, his impartiality might be suspect to other classes; as he worked at no fixed centre but followed the royal court, access to him was difficult. He and his court could contribute little to the maintenance of justice; after 1451 we hear no more of them.[3] Yet baulked as it was by this defective machinery, the desire for imperial, supraterritorial justice remained strong enough to give fresh life to anomalous survivals from the past.

[1] Cf. H. Heimpel, 'Das deutsche Spätmittelalter. Charakter einer Zeit', *Hist. Zts.*, clviii (1938), 233.

[2] Cf. P. Vinogradoff, *Roman Law in Medieval Europe*, 2nd edn. (Oxford, 1929), 119–45.

[3] A. Schulte, 'Der hohe Adel des deutschen Hofrichters', *Festschrift G. von Hertling . . . dargebracht* (Kempten and Munich, 1913), 539 ff.; H. Mitteis, *Der Staat des hohen Mittelalters*, 3rd edn. (Weimar, 1948), 412.

Only thus can we understand the esteem enjoyed in the later Middle Ages by such a court as the 'Hofgericht' at Rottweil in Swabia. By exploiting the facts that it was held on imperial territory and under royal authority it was able to exercise jurisdiction far beyond its original limited competence. The activities of the Westphalian 'free courts', the *Vemgerichte*, were basically similar, for they too claimed to do justice on authority from the king, at a time when the royal *Bannleihe* had long ceased for the courts in the territories. Favoured by Charles IV and Sigismund, and also by the archbishops of Cologne, who saw in them possibilities of promoting their territorial influence in Westphalia,[1] by the early fifteenth century the *Vemgerichte* had achieved an importance not to be disregarded. Their members, the *Freischöffen*, could be found in many places outside Westphalia, participants in a secret alliance, sworn at their initiation to silence about their knowledge of the courts' workings; on them lay the duty of executing the judgments of the *Vemgerichte*. Undoubtedly at times the actions of this secret society were irresponsible and oppressive; the wish to curb them appears clearly in the so-called *Reformatio Friderici* in 1442.[2] But it is certain that in practice the workings of the 'free courts' were not as considerable nor as dreadful nor as abusive as they appeared to the age of Goethe and Kleist.[3] Their significance lay neither in their efficiency nor in their somewhat spurious mystery. Like the Rottweil court they represented a wholly insufficient attempt to supply from local resources the lack of that supreme imperial tribunal which circumstances continued to demand.

Meanwhile recourse to forcible self-help, vendetta, the *Fehde*, was prevalent. It would be a mistake to infer too hastily from this that might alone was right. At least in theory *Fehde* was not the arbitrary exercise of purposeless and unlimited violence, but a process directed to the recovery of right and the re-establishment of peace. Declaration and conduct of *Fehde* were governed by well-understood conventions with an internal logic of their own. That this was a practice ingrained in the legal conscious-

[1] Cf. E. Bock, 'Der Kampf um die Landfriedenshoheit in Westfalen u. die Freigerichte bis zum Ausgang d. 14. Jahrhunderts', *Z.R.G. G.A.*, xlviii (1928), 379 ff.

[2] *R.T.A.*, xvi, no. 209.

[3] T. Lindner, *Die Feme* (Münster, 1888), xxi. For activity of these 'free courts' outside Westphalia, see C. W. Scherer, *Die westfälischen Femgerichte u. die Eidgenossenschaft* (Aarau, 1941), 21 ff., 52 ff.

ness and habits of German noble society, not just a symptom of the failure of medieval government to meet its obligations, has rightly been stressed by Otto Brunner.[1] *Fehde* found its counterpart in the numberless standing arrangements for settling disputes by arbitration which bulk so large among the documents of this period.[2] In the case of such associations as the St George societies of the Swabian knights arbitral procedures between the members seem quite as important as the protection of their political and class interests against outsiders.[3]

But it would be folly to ignore the disastrous effects on wholly innocent third parties of the plundering and wasting which might accompany *Fehde*. Those who have penetrated most deeply into its nature do not deny that it was an evil.[4] The evidence for a slow but persistent pressure to outlaw *Fehde* is therefore a cogent argument against too pessimistic a view of fifteenth-century Germany. Ineffective proposals in 1431 and 1438 to prohibit *Fehde* were followed in 1442 by the attempt to protect the defenceless against its consequences.[5] In 1467 the sanction of the Roman law of treason was invoked for an imperial decree making recourse to *Fehde* illegal during the next five years;[6] after being renewed in 1471, 1474, 1480 and 1486 (for ten years) the prohibition was made perpetual at the great reforming diet at Worms in 1495.[7] Mere legislation could not, of course, immediately abolish a deep-rooted practice. As many of the less powerful estates of the empire well understood, to declare *Fehde* illegal without providing an acceptable substitute by way of process in the courts was beating the air.[8] Nevertheless, between 1400 and 1500 *Fehde* had become increasingly disreputable. Joint action by the emperor and the estates had played some part in bringing this about.

[1] *Land und Herrschaft*, part i (*Friede und Fehde*), 1–110.

[2] Cf. Ingeborg Most, 'Schiedsgericht, rechtlicheres Rechtgebot, ordentliches Gericht, Kammergericht', *A.R.*, 116 ff.

[3] Cf. Obenaus, *Recht u. Verfassung d. Gesellschaften mit St. Jörgenschild*, 39 ff., 93.

[4] Brunner, *Land und Herrschaft*, 80–95, 106.

[5] *R.T.A.*, xvi, no. 209.

[6] Cf. Ingeborg Most, 'Der Reichslandfriede vom 20 August 1467. Zur Geschichte des Crimen laesae maiestatis u. der Reichsreform unter Kaiser Friedrich III', *Syntagma Friburgense. Historische Studien Hermann Aubin dargebracht* (Lindau and Constance, 1956), 191 ff. See too the remarks of H. Conrad in *Z.R.G. G.A.*, lxxv (1958), 394.

[7] Zeumer, *Quellen*, no. 171 (1486), no. 173 (1495); cf. Quidde, *Paix publique*, 547–9; E. Molitor, *Die Reichsreformbestrebungen d. 15. Jahrhunderts bis zum Tod Kaiser Friedrichs III* (Breslau, 1921), pp. 166–7.

[8] Cf. Obenaus, 227.

I

The theatre for co-operation or controversy between head and members was the diet, the *Reichstag*, in which Ranke recognized the fundamental institution of the late medieval empire.[1] Experience has falsified his estimate that the sources for the history of the diets down to 1519 could all be printed in a couple of quarto volumes after a few years' work.[2] Fourteen volumes of *Reichstagsakten* have been needed to cover the years 1376–1439; another nine will bring the story only as far as 1477.[3] Not until this enterprise is complete will a satisfactory account of the diet as an institution be possible. During the fifteenth century much about the *Reichstag* was still fluid and uncertain; only towards the end of the century were its composition and procedure made more regular and formal by the influence of Berthold of Henneberg, archbishop of Mainz. Clearly by this period the old supreme feudal court of the German ruler, the *Reichshoftag*, had been superseded in idea and practice; the fifteenth-century diet was not a feudal court but an assembly of the estates of the empire.[4] Any conceivable subject might be brought before it. Concern with external affairs bulked large: relations with pope or council, defence against Hussites, Turks or Burgundy. Of internal matters perhaps two were the object of most lively and persistent interest: care for the general public peace in Germany (the *Landfriede*) and reform of the imperial constitution. More must be said of these, at the risk of doing some violence to the facts by separating problems which rarely arose in isolation. For frequently the emperor, calling a *Reichstag* to raise help against the Hussites or the Turks, would be faced by the estates wishing to talk of the *Landfriede* or imperial reform.

The last great act of Hohenstaufen legislation in Germany had been the *Landfriede* promulgated by Frederick II at Mainz in 1235.[5] Many of its principles passed as generally desirable

[1] *Deutsche Geschichte im Zeitalter der Reformation*, 6th edn., i (Leipzig, 1881), Vorrede, v.

[2] Cf. Heimpel, 'Deutsche Reichstagsakten, ältere Reihe', 86.

[3] On present editorial problems see W. Kaemmerer, 'Zum gegenwärtigen Standort der Reichstagsakten', *A.R.*, 11 ff.

[4] H. Spangenberg, 'Die Entstehung des Reichskammergerichts u. die Anfänge der Reichsverwaltung', *Z.R.G. G.A.*, xlvi (1926), 245, n. 2.

[5] Text of Latin version: M.G.H. *Const.*, ii, no. 196, 241–7; German version: Zeumer, *Quellen*, no. 58. On the priority of the Latin version see H. Mitteis, 'Zum Mainzer Reichslandfrieden von 1235', *Z.R.G. G.A.*, lxii (1942), 13 ff. [=*Die Rechtsidee in der Geschichte* (Weimar, 1957), 387 ff.]; E. Klingelhöfer. *Die Reichsgesetze von 1220, 1231/2 u. 1235* (Weimar, 1955), 97 ff.

into the legal consciousness of Germany. But the collapse of Hohenstaufen rule frustrated Frederick's intention that responsibility for maintaining the public peace throughout Germany should rest with the emperor and his *Hofrichter*. However usefully the principles of the *pax publica* might serve as the basis for penal legislation against crimes of violence, its effectiveness as an institution was increasingly restricted by the princes' claim to exclusive rights of justice over their own subjects. Moreover the executive machinery tended to slip out of the king's hands. For much of the fourteenth century, so far as the device of the *Landfriede* was maintained at all, it was by the efforts of particular leagues and unions in various parts of Germany. Initiative in forming them might come from the king; more often it was taken by the territorial rulers in ways best suited to serve their ambitions. The *pax publica*, nation-wide in its original conception, seemed fated to become an adjunct of territorial or regional policy.[1]

The last third of the fourteenth century saw a determined attempt by the Crown to recover control over the *Landfriede*. Charles IV showed the way.[2] But it was under Wenzel that appeared an approach towards a new pattern of local organizations which would maintain the public peace under the authority and in the name of the Crown and be strong enough to escape being dominated by the territories. The towns greeted a first scheme to divide Germany into circles with distrust, for it would have involved them in co-operation with the princes and nobles whom they hated and feared.[3] But after their defeats in 1388 Wenzel was able to promulgate a general *Landfriede* on these lines at Eger in May 1389. Within each of five circles—the Rhineland, Franconia, Bavaria, Swabia and Thuringia—care of the *pax publica* was to be entrusted to an executive committee of nine: a captain appointed by the king, four members chosen by the towns and four by the other estates.[4] Little came of the plan. But at least it had indicated how, by a process of devolution which left wide scope for political manœuvre, the king might hope to fulfil effectively, if

[1] Cf. Quidde, *Paix publique*, 511–31; E. Bock, 'Kampf um die Landfriedenshoheit in Westfalen', cited above, p. 238, n. 1.

[2] Molitor, 22.

[3] Quidde, 534 ff.

[4] *R.T.A.*, ii, no. 72, arts. 2, 39, 40; 35, 37, 38; 44.

indirectly, his duty of maintaining peace throughout Germany.[1]

The lesson was not wholly lost on Sigismund. Possibly he had it in mind to seek as head of a national *Landfriede* the power which otherwise kingship had ceased to offer.[2] But he was unable to give the problem the consistent attention it deserved and his support of the towns and the *Ritterschaft* could do little to redress a balance now swinging decisively in favour of the princes. In face of the Hussite menace in 1431, it is true, private war was proscribed throughout the empire for the first time since the Diet of Roncaglia in 1158, even though this held good only for the duration of the campaign which ended so disastrously at Tauss. Whether Sigismund exercised any real control over affairs in Germany during the last few years of his reign is disputable. What is certain is that at this time reform of the imperial constitution became a lively issue. How far demand for reform is to be explained as resulting from ill-success in the Hussite wars and the contemporary debate at Basle about reform of the Church, how far by reference to the internal situation in Germany and the newly-found strength of the electors, are matters of opinion.[3] The demand itself continued to echo for the rest of the century.

Perhaps historians have been too ready to blame the fifteenth-century reformers for failing to achieve aims which they did not pursue nor could reasonably have pursued, like the establishment of a strong unitary monarchy.[4] They wanted the government of the empire to be made capable of discharging its duties. In theory imperial prerogatives were already adequate to protect the integrity of Germany from foreign attack, preserve the public peace and make justice readily available. The trouble was that these prerogatives were not being fully exercised. The call, then, was less for revolutionary changes than for such rehabilitation and modification of the constitution as would enable the empire to do what was expected of it. At this point, however, confusion was engendered by conflicting views about what the empire was. The emperor was bound to see the matter in personal terms. Much history

[1] For a less favourable view of the Eger *Landfriede* see H. Angermeier, 'Städtebünde und Landfriede im 14. Jahrhundert', *Hist. Jahrbuch*, lxxvi (1956), 44–6.

[2] Molitor, 26.

[3] Cf. H. Angermeier, 'Das Reich u.d. Konziliarismus', 553–67.

[4] Cf. H. Angermeier, 'Begriff u. Inhalt d. Reichsreform', *Z.R.G. G.A.*, lxxv (1958), 197–205.

suggested that he was the empire; proposals for reform which would enable him to be so more effectively (by providing him with funds or troops, for instance) were welcome; all others were to be rejected as diminishing not only his own dignity but also that of the empire which he incorporated. On the other hand there was the claim of the estates to be considered necessary elements of the empire's authority. By reform they hoped to convert a significant part of the emperor's personal powers into impersonal institutions, capable indeed of working efficiently, but ultimately controlled by themselves and so not likely seriously to impair their independence. Their policy was to bring the respective positions of emperor and estates into line with the current facts of power. They could claim, not wholly paradoxically, to be envisaging reform in a conservative fashion: organs they controlled were to exercise in the name of the empire capacities already to be found there, though detained for the time being by an emperor not strong enough to put them to good use.

The short reign of Albert II marked a first climax in the movement for reform. The electors' proposals for a general *Landfriede* at the Nuremberg diet in July 1438 would have abolished recourse to private war. The whole empire save Austria and Bohemia was to be divided into four circles. Over each a prince was to be appointed captain by the king, to do justice in his name in cases of appeal from the ordinary courts.[1] The danger that this scheme would deliver the circles into the hands of the greater princes was countered by amendments which Albert's counsellors suggested. There should be six circles rather than four; in each the captain should be elected by the estates of the circle and aided by ten counsellors chosen from the lords, lesser nobility and the towns.[2] By this plan a far-reaching delegation of authority would have endowed the circles with a considerable degree of self-government. Perhaps by this date in Germany there was no longer a real possibility of movement in the direction of provincial autonomy under control of the local estates rather than towards territorial consolidation under the supremacy of the princes.[3] But though these interchanges in 1438 produced no practical results, they illustrate what very

[1] *R.T.A.*, xiii, no. 223.
[2] *R.T.A.*, xiii, no. 224.
[3] Cf. Molitor, 97 ff.

different ideas about reform were held by the king and the princes. The former wished to use it to strengthen his own hand in Germany; the circles organized as his counsellors proposed would undoubtedly have offered opportunities for political manipulation by the Crown. To the princes, on the other hand, reform seemed a means of subordinating to themselves the less powerful estates of the empire.

Possibly even at the time of Albert's death in 1439 'there was still hope that the empire could be governed and the constitution be reformed'.[1] As yet the lines along which the constitutional relationship between the king and the particularist powers would develop had not become completely rigid. In this respect, it would seem, the reign of Frederick III was decisive. Perhaps we need to know more about the activities centring on the archbishop of Trier, James of Sierck, in the early 'fifties.[2] But for decades, it seems safe to say, imperial reform ceased to be a serious programme and became a party cry in the rivalries of the territorial princes. Thus the real issue between Wittelsbach and Hohenzollern in their long struggle was lands and power in southern Germany; their talk of *Reichsreform* was camouflage.[3] Despite his extraordinarily high conception of imperial majesty Frederick III made little attempt to rule Germany. Interest in the constitutional problem, still real under Sigismund and Albert, flagged until 1486. Characteristic of the change is the contrast offered to the schemes of 1438 by Frederick's so-called *Reformatio* of 1442. For the most part the *Reformatio* repeated existing and unchallenged law. No reform of the judicial system was envisaged, nor any devolution of responsibility to regional authorities; *Fehde* was tolerated, as long as it was kept within the rules. No provision was made for executing the *Reformatio*, which was indeed sadly destitute of any leading idea, either progressive or conservative.[4] And after 1444 Frederick was seen no more in the empire for twenty-seven years.

Discussion of this period cannot go deep until the *Reichstagsakten* for it have been published. It was not wholly barren for the constitutional problem; slowly some things stirred. From 1467

[1] Heimpel, 'Deutsche Reichstagsakten', 106.

[2] Cf. V. von Kraus, *Deutsche Geschichte im Ausgange des Mittelalters*, i (Stuttgart and Berlin, 1905), 310–20; H. Weigel, 'Kaiser, Kurfürst u. Jurist', *A.R.*, 80–115.

[3] Molitor, 116.

[4] *R.T.A.*, xvi, no. 209; cf. Molitor, 109; Quidde, *Paix publique*, 543.

onwards, as we have seen, the pressure against *Fehde* increased. But if self-help were to be prohibited effectively a supreme imperial court was needed, to do what the now defunct *Reichshofgericht* had never succeeded in doing. In his *Kammergericht* the king already had a partly professional court; shortly after the Grosse Christentag in 1471 Frederick, it seems, gave this court a new establishment and farmed it to Archbishop Adolf II of Mainz, who brought it to a state of some efficiency during the next few years.[1] Though Adolf's death in 1475 checked this development, the interest of the archsee of Mainz had been awakened, and in June 1494 we find Archbishop Berthold of Henneberg taking charge of the *Kammergericht* as of right. For years Berthold and his fellow reformers had been urging the need for a permanent imperial court independent of the emperor. Frederick's tenacity had foiled their attempt at Frankfort in 1486 to impose on him a tribunal divorced from his entourage, passing judgment in its own name as well as his, and with a composition on which his influence would have been markedly less than that of the estates.[2] But the reformers were not permanently to be denied. The setting up of the *Reichskammergericht* as supreme court for the empire at the diet of Worms in August 1495 met many of their wishes; for all its limitations, this proved perhaps the most central and lasting achievement of the whole reform movement.[3]

Berthold's leadership was vastly important for the emergence at this time of a comprehensive policy of reform.[4] Though much of the legislation at Worms bore the marks of compromise, its range was impressive: *Fehde* abolished, at least in principle, for all time by the *Ewige Landfriede*; a supreme court organized by the *Reichskammergerichtsordnung*; proposals for a general system of taxation, the Common Penny, as the basis for an imperial army; the diet itself to become an assembly meeting regularly to

[1] Cf. Spangenberg, 'Entstehung d. Kammergerichts', 286–8; J. Lechner, 'Reichshofgericht u. königliches Kammergericht i. 15. Jahrhundert', *Mitteilungen d. Instituts f. österreich. Geschichtsforschung*, Erg. Bd. vii (1907), 109 ff. While only 2 sessions of the court are known in 1466, 11 in 1467 and 1 in 1468, in 1471 the number had increased to 36 and in the next year to 85.

[2] Molitor, 182,

[3] Zeumer, *Quellen*, no. 174; cf. R. Smend, *Das Reichskammergericht* (Weimar, 1911), 1–23.

[4] Cf. F. Hartung, 'Die Reichsreform von 1485–1495. Ihr Verlauf u. ihr Wesen', *H.V.*, xvi (1913), 24 ff., 181 ff.; K. S. Bader, 'Kaiserliche u. ständische Reformgedanken i.d. Reichsreform d. endenden 15. Jahrhunderts', *Hist. Jahrbuch*, lxxiii (1954), 74–94.

exercise extensive powers in accordance with defined procedures. A campaign which produced results on such a scale as this was clearly not negligible. But the press and complexity of political events during these years, which nearly coincide with the period (1486–93) when Frederick and Maximilian were reigning in double harness,[1] make it difficult to isolate reform and bring it into focus. In 1488, for instance, the Swabian League was born, perhaps the strongest, best articulated and most interesting example of confederative practice in late medieval Germany. Originally it had nothing to do with reform, for it was rooted in the political circumstances of the south-west, where fear of the Wittelsbachers and the Swiss caused the princes, the towns and the lesser nobility to band together for mutual protection. Only gradually, as it gained strength and Maximilian became concerned with the fate of the Habsburg *Vorlande*, did the Swabian League come to be intimately involved in the politics of the empire and the reforming movement.[2]

Then too there is much to puzzle us in the attitudes of the chief actors in this drama. Almost any talk of reform offended Frederick's sense of majesty; he would listen at all only if by so doing he could hope to get help for Habsburg policy. On the other hand Maximilian's approach to this problem, it can be argued, was a good deal more positive. He seemed willing to accept some diminution of the Crown's theoretic rights in return for an increased efficiency in imperial government to be reflected in financial and military support for his own schemes.[3] Seventeenth-century scholars gave all the credit for the reforming legislation of 1495 to Maximilian, none to Berthold of Henneberg.[4] Though we know better, Berthold's personality has remained elusive.[5] There is no doubt, however, that this

[1] E. Bock, 'Die Doppelregierung Friedrichs III u. Maximilians 1486–1493', *A.R.*, 283 ff.

[2] E. Bock, *Der Schwäbische Bund u. seine Verfassungen 1488–1534* (Breslau, 1927), 9; F. Ernst, 'Reichs- und Landespolitik i. Süden Deutschlands am Ende d. Mittelalters', *H.V.*, xxx (1935), 726.

[3] Cf. Bock, 'Doppelregierung', 324–7.

[4] F. H. Schubert, 'Die Reichstage Kaiser Maximilians I. i. Urteil d. 17. Jahrhunderts', *A.R.*, 242.

[5] I have not seen K. S. Bader's essay *Ein Staatsmann vom Mittelrhein: Gestalt u. Werk d. Mainzer Kurfürsten u. Erzbischofs Berthold v. Henneberg* (Mainz, n.d.). That E. Ziehen's learned but disorderly *Mittelrhein u. Reich i. Zeitalter d. Reichsreform*, 2 vols. (Frankfurt a.M., 1934–7) writes Maximilian down excessively in favour of Berthold has been made clear by H. Baron, 'Imperial Reform and the Habsburgs, 1486–1504', *American Hist. Review*, xliv (1939), 293 ff.

great prelate from the heart of Germany, whose house had rendered notable services to the Crown during the fourteenth century, did combine with his passionate loyalty to the empire clear ideas of what needed to be done if it were to play a worthy role in Germany and western Europe.[1] For him the empire was far greater than its monarch, and there was urgent need to strengthen it against the particularist elements in Germany, which were represented just as much by the territorial interests of the king as by the strivings of the princes towards irresponsible independence.[2] Only by turning its administrative institutions into bureaucratic departments of state and so freeing them from the king's personal whims could they be made strong enough to serve their proper purposes. In their technical aspects Berthold's ideas deserved and enjoyed some success. But from the point of view of politics, most would agree, they came too late. Admirable as was his sense of responsibility, Berthold looked too much to the past with its intimations that the electors in union might lead the empire's estates in controlling a system of government directly effective throughout Germany.[3] He failed to get honest support from Maximilian or many of the princes for a permanent collegiate executive for the empire: a *Reichsregiment* in which electoral influence would predominate. After all, Maximilian had good grounds for claiming that it was his business to rule the empire; and the princes had passed the point of being ready to tolerate the amount of imperial government which Berthold's schemes envisaged. The pertinacity with which he fought them through to partial acceptance at Worms in 1495 forbids us to discount him as a mere doctrinaire. Some of his reforms continued to work usefully until the end of the Holy Roman Empire in 1806. But though he has no real competitor for the title of the last statesman of the medieval empire, his understanding of its structural changes had fallen behind the times. By 1500 the shell of that superior authority under shelter of which the territories had grown seemed very thin. How tough it still remained the story of the next three centuries was to show.

[1] Berthold was the seventh son of Count George I of Henneberg-Römhild (in the basin of the upper Werra, south of Meiningen in Thuringia). In Count Berthold VII of Henneberg-Schleusingen the family had produced one of the most important figures in imperial politics between 1310 and 1340; cf. Ziehen, i, 167–9.

[2] Cf. F. Hartung, 'Berthold von Henneberg, Kurfürst von Mainz', *Hist. Zts.*, ciii (1909), 539.

[3] Cf. Bader, 'Reformgedanken', 89.

II

EMPIRE AND PAPACY: THE LAST STRUGGLE

IN the early months of 1327 the communities of the Angevin kingdom of Sicily were ordered to send representatives to Naples, there to discuss means of opposing 'the lord Lewis, duke of Bavaria: *qui in Italiam transire disposuit et regnum Sicilie invadere, servans antiquum odium belli et interitus Corradini.*'[1] The reference to the last Hohenstaufen in this contemporary comment on Lewis' Italian enterprise is at first sight surprising. During the half-century following Conradin's execution the prestige of the empire in German hands had fallen steeply in the estimation of western Europe; all the activity of Dante's emperor could not disguise that fact. From time to time the Angevins at Naples urged the abolition of the institution, as something of which the usefulness was now outworn.[2] Other solutions were being talked of, such as the setting up of a separate hereditary kingdom in Lombardy[3] or the transference by election or papal provision

[1] Quoted from Carlo De Lellis' extracts from the Angevin archives by T. E. Mommsen, *Italienische Analekten zur Reichsgeschichte des 14. Jahrhunderts* (*Schriften der M*[*onumenta*] *G*[*ermaniae*] *H*[*istorica*], xi. Stuttgart, 1952), nr. 160, p. 75.

[2] Cf. the instruction given to the Angevin envoys to the Curia after the death of the Emperor Henry VII in August 1313, *MGH Const*[*itutiones*], iv, nr. 1253, p. 1369, and a similar memorandum from 1334 printed by C. Müller, *Der Kampf Ludwigs des Baiern mit der römischen Curie*, i (Tübingen, 1879), p. 393. The so-called 'bull' *Ne praetereat*, which is either an exercise in style or a hasty Angevin draft in the same sense, has provoked an enormous literature, out of proportion to its importance. The most recent discussion is by G. Tabacco, 'Un presunto disegno per l'unificazione dell'Italia', *Rivista storica italiana*, lxi (1949), 509.

[3] This scheme was adumbrated by Bernard Gui in his *Extractiones* from the *Opusculum tripartitum* of Humbert de Romanis: Martène et Durand, *Collectio Amplissima*, vii. 198. It was suggested again in the report which Bernard and Bertrand de la Tour sent to the Curia from Lombardy in 1317, S. Riezler, *V*[*atikanische*] *A*[*kten zur deutschen Geschichte in der Zeit Kaiser Ludwigs des Bayern*] (Innsbruck, 1891), nr. 50, p. 37. It came into the realm

of the imperial title to the ruling house of France. Perhaps too much importance has been attributed to some of these schemes, though there is no reason to doubt the seriousness of French ambitions to acquire as much as possible of the western possessions of the empire.[1] But their frequent recurrence, together with the known weakness of the German kingship, does indicate a climate uncongenial to a repetition of the themes of Hohenstaufen imperialism by a German ruler in the third decade of the fourteenth century. Consequently Lewis' conflict with the papacy has an anachronistic air. Long ago Gregorovius cast a stereotype destined to wear well, when he wrote that 'this afterpiece' was saved from being 'an utterly unbearable caricature of a great past' only by the 'progress of human thought' with which it was associated.[2]

'The progress of human thought' is scarcely a subject to be dealt with in the span of an hour, and the aim of this paper is much less ambitious. It is to discuss the conflict at the level of political action. What significance had 'this afterpiece' outside the realm of theory? Admittedly, the question can be posed thus only at the cost of an artificial distinction, but that may perhaps be justified by the sheer weight of the material which calls for consideration.

Much spadework on the sources was done in the second third of the nineteenth century by J. F. Boehmer and Julius Ficker, and somewhat later the opening of the Vatican Archives promoted a busy and fruitful, if rather disorderly, activity in publication. In

of practical politics in 1330–1, when there was a serious proposal to create a kingdom in Lombardy for Philip VI of France. Cf. H. Otto, 'Zur italienischen Politik Johanns XXII', *Quellen und Forschungen aus italienischen Archiven und Bibliotheken*, xiv (1911), 189; F. Bock, 'Kaisertum, Kurie und Nationalstaat im Beginn des 14 Jahrhunderts', *Römische Quartalschrift f. christliche Altertumskunde*, xliv (1936), 204.

[1] See G. Zeller, 'Les rois de France candidats à l'empire', *Revue historique*, clxxiv (1934), 273 sqq., and for a sceptical view R. Fawtier, *Les Capétiens et la France* (Paris, 1942), p. 87. Philip VI's concern to secure and to project his eastern frontier at the expense of the empire is illustrated by the terms of his treaties with John of Bohemia at Fontainebleau in January 1332 and with Henry XIV of Lower Bavaria at Frankfort in December 1333: J. Emler, *Regesta diplomatica necnon epistolaria Bohemiae et Moraviae*, iii (Prague, 1890), nr. 1867, p. 727; J. F. Boehmer, *Acta Imperii Selecta* (Innsbruck, 1870), nr. 1033, p. 724.

[2] F. Gregorovius, *Rome in the Middle Ages*, xi. 3, trans. by A. Hamilton, vi (i) (London, 1906), p. 114.

this century Finke's edition of the *Acta Aragonensia* has offered us, through the eyes of the Aragonese agents at the Curia and elsewhere, an intimate view of some of the workings of the higher diplomacy, to say nothing of a good deal of gossip which requires careful sifting. Professor Stengel's elaborate publication of the manuscript collections of Rudolf Losse has proved a rich mine, though the ore has sometimes been excessively refined. A generation has passed since the *Monumenta* edition of the *Constitutiones* for Lewis' reign was brought down to 1330; more than half the reign has still to be covered and what has already been published needs some revision. In the 'thirties, useful gleanings for these purposes were being made by collaborators in the *Monumenta*, particularly at the Vatican and in the Italian archives and among the English records.[1] More recently some interesting things have come to light at Trier and Rome and Marseilles, and no doubt further discoveries await the making.[2] Perhaps the time for a new large-scale narrative of Lewis' relations with the papacy has not yet come, but the materials to hand are sufficient for an interim attempt at interpretation.[3]

No better clue to the nature of the conflict can be found than the first papal process issued against Lewis on 8 October 1323. Lewis was threatened with excommunication for offences under three heads: (i) though his election as king of the Romans had

[1] Cf. C. Erdmann, 'Vatikanische Analekten zur Geschichte Ludwigs des Baiern', *Archivalische Zeitschrift*, xli (1932); T. E. Mommsen, *Italienische Analekten* (above, note 1), which publishes the result of researches carried out in 1933–5; and the numerous papers by Dr. Friedrich Bock cited in his book (note 3 below).

[2] Cf. F. Pelster, 'Die zweite Rede Markwarts von Randeck für die Aussöhnung des Papstes mit Ludwig dem Bayern', *Historisches Jahrbuch*, lx (1940), 88 sqq.; A. Mercati, 'Dall'Archivio Vaticano. Proposte di Giovanni, il francofilo re di Boemia, a Giovanni XXII', *Mélanges d'archéologie et d'histoire*, lxi (1949), 195 sqq.; H. S. Offler, 'Über die Prokuratorien Ludwigs des Bayern für die römische Kurie', *Deutsches Archiv für die Erforschung des Mittelalters*, viii (1951), 476 sqq.

[3] Carl Müller's valuable book (p. 21, n. 2 above) was published before the material in the Vatican Archives was readily available. Friedrich Bock's *Reichsidee und Nationalstaaten vom Untergang des alten Reiches bis zur Kündigung des deutsch-englischen Bündnisses im Jahre 1341* (Munich, 1943) is based on an unrivalled knowledge of the sources, but not all its judgements have found or are likely to find acceptance. There is a balanced account of Lewis' reign by Herbert Grundmann in the new edition of B. Gebhardt, *Handbuch der deutschen Geschichte*, i (Stuttgart, 1954), pp. 427–58.

been made *in discordia*, he had dared to assume the royal title without papal approval; (ii) he had performed acts of administration in the realm and the empire, although the empire was vacant and its administration consequently pertained to the pope; (iii) he had shown favour to the Visconti of Milan, who had been condemned for heresy, and to various other rebels against the Church.[1] The third item need not detain us. Though the *fautoria* of heretics was indeed an offence automatically involving canonical penalties, he who had incurred them normally had little to fear, unless his relations with the ecclesiastical authorities were otherwise bad; in any case, there was a strongly political flavour about the condemnation of the Visconti.[2] But the first two charges had graver implications, which touched sensitive areas in the public law of the German kingdom and the empire. That the choice of the German electors must be submitted for papal approval and that it was the pope's right to administer the empire as long as no emperor had been crowned were claims which, though not novel, could hardly expect undisputed acceptance. About them much has been written,[3] and for the next quarter of a century the struggle largely turned around their application. Pressed to an extreme conclusion they might seem to imply that the successful candidate in a German royal election would be powerless even within Germany until his person had been approved by the pope. They sharply affronted Lewis' respectably founded contention that the king of the Romans as the result of his election immediately gained the right to administer not only in Germany, but in Italy as well: as in fact Lewis had been doing through his lieutenants in Lombardy since March 1323.[4] In this opposition of legal standpoints neither Lewis nor the pope could give way without seeming to prejudice the rights of the institution which he represented. And this was not merely a theoretical dispute about formalities. Seen in the context of the

[1] *MGH Const.*, v, nr. 792, p. 617; for the force of the phrase *in discordia* see H. Mitteis, *Die deutsche Königswahl* (Baden bei Wien, 1938), pp. 168, 185.

[2] Bock, 'Studien zum politischen Inquisitionsprozess Johanns XXII', *Quellen u. Forsch. aus italien. Archiven u. Bibliotheken*, xxvi (1936), 21 sqq.

[3] See, e.g., F. Baethgen, 'Der Anspruch des Papsttums auf das Reichsvikariat', *Zts. d. Savigny-Stiftung f. Rechtsgeschichte*, xli, *Kan. Abt.*, x (1920), 168 sqq.; H. E. Feine, 'Die Approbation der Luxemburgischen Kaiser in ihren Rechtsformen an der Kurie', *ibid.*, xxvii (1938), 364.

[4] *MGH Const.*, v, nr. 729, p. 568.

process of October 1323, issued at a date when Lewis, having defeated his competitor for the German throne, was beginning for the first time to intervene effectively in Lombardy, the papal claims reveal John XXII's preoccupation with Italy and his determination that no German ruler should exercise influence there except on terms acceptable to the papacy. At the root of Lewis' controversy with the papacy lay this clash of interests in Italy. To it, the religious issues arising from Lewis' choice of methods and allies were only consequential.

There is nothing new in this diagnosis. Herwart von Hohenburg expressed it pointedly against Abraham Bzovius in 1618: *Lis fuit de terris non de religione, Bzoui.*[1] But it is worth repeating because, although the tendency of much recent work has been to confirm it, sometimes it is still overlooked. The events of 1328 were so sensational that we are tempted to treat them as if they were the whole story. The flouting of the established church order; Lewis' coronation at Rome at the hands of the representatives of the Roman people; the creation of the anti-pope Peter of Corbara; Marsilio of Padua acting as vicar in spirituals in Rome and John of Jandun appointed bishop of Ferrara; the dissident Franciscans with their leader Michael of Cesena fleeing by night from Avignon to find refuge with Lewis at Pisa: these are indeed exciting happenings, but they need to be kept in perspective. The character of this long struggle is not to be resumed in the events of a single year. In the course of a *collatio* delivered in April 1343 Pope Clement VI declared that Lewis had been 'abandoned unto Satan' for twenty-six years. That takes us back to 1317; and it is significant that the first item in the Curia's register of the processes against Lewis is not the process of October 1323 but the constitution *Si fratrum* of March 1317, which assumed that the empire was vacant and declared penalties against any who might meddle with it in defiance of the papal claim to administer during the vacancy.[2] Within a few months of his election John XXII had thus turned his eyes to Italy, and it

[1] J. G. Herwart von Hohenburg, *Ludovicus Quartus Imperator defensus; Bzovius injuriarum postulatus* (Munich, 1618), p. 173.

[2] An edition of a copy of the *Liber processuum* is given in Martène et Durand, *Thesaurus Novus Anecdotorum*, ii. 641 sqq. Clement's *collatio* is to be found in Paris, Bibliothèque Ste Geneviève, cod. 240, and the phrase cited at fo. 64.

would seem that Clement, by construction, regarded Lewis as having fallen under the penalties for contravening *Si fratrum* almost from the date when the constitution was promulgated. It would not in fact be easy to show that Lewis was taking any great interest in Italian affairs in 1317; at this early period of his reign he was pretty fully occupied by the struggle for survival in Germany. On the other hand, the end of his Roman expedition certainly did not mark the end of his concern with Italy. Among the reasons which led him to discard his alliance with England in 1341 his wish to conduct an active Italian policy may well have played a part; probably he was encouraged by the same motive to interfere in the marriage between John Henry of Luxemburg and Margaret Maultasch of Tirol, the action which in 1342 caused his 'sweet reputation to begin to stink in the nostrils of the princes'.[1] Even in the summer of 1346, while an anti-king was being raised against him in Germany, he lingered in Tirol, planning another descent to the south.[2] At no time during the negotiations for his reconciliation with the Church which dragged their long course from 1330 to 1345 was Lewis willing to accept terms which might impair his freedom to act in imperial Italy.[3]

That freedom the papacy was led to deny in the interests of its own Italian policy. The broad outlines of its aims are not in doubt. The restoration of order and papal authority in the States of the Church was necessary for the health of the Camera; it was also a condition for the return of the Curia to Italy, a consideration never long out of mind.[4] But the Italian problem was not

[1] Johann von Viktring, *Lib. certarum historiarum*, ed. F. Schneider, ii (*MGH SS. in usum scholarum*, 1910), p. 228; cf. Offler, 'England and Germany at the beginning of the Hundred Years' War', *English Historical Review*, liv (1939), 619–22.

[2] E. Werunsky, *Geschichte Kaiser Karls IV und seiner Zeit*, i (Innsbruck, 1880), p. 435.

[3] Lewis' attitude is plainly expressed in his instruction for his envoys to the Curia dated 28 October 1343: 'Item der artikel dar inn wir uns verbinden solten daz wir gen Ytali nicht chomen solten e wir von dem stuol approbiert wuerden, der wirt auch abgant', in Munich, Geheimes Haus-Archiv, 1/5 259 fo. 15 = S. Reizler, *Die literarischen Widersacher der Päpste zur Zeit Ludwig des Baiers* (Leipzig, 1874), p. 333.

[4] E. Kraack, *Rom oder Avignon? Die römische Frage unter den Päpsten Clemens V und Johann XXII* (Marburg, 1929), pp. 57–8. I cannot share the negative judgement of E. Duprè-Theseider, *I papi di Avignone e la questione romana* (Florence, 1939), pp. 49, 73–5.

patient of a piecemeal solution. A Lombardy given over to the *signori* would be a focus of unrest against the ecclesiastical interest throughout the peninsula. So a general pacification of Italy was necessary, directed—and here is the divergence from Dante's ideal—by the pope. How this design might be accomplished was a question which provoked varying answers. John XXII was inexhaustible in energy and expedients, the cost of which is reflected in the leaping expenditure of the Camera at this time.[1] Early in his pontificate he decided that the Ghibelline lords of Lombardy, Matteo Visconti in Milan, Can Grande della Scala in Verona, Passerino Bonnacolsi in Mantua, might and must be broken. For this purpose he tried to use the secular allies of the Church: Robert of Naples, whom he confirmed in the appointment of vicar-general over all imperial territory in Italy except Genoa; Philip count of Maine, later Philip VI of France; even, for a short period, the Habsburg contestants for the German throne.[2] None of them answered expectations. More promising was direct action by the Church in Lombardy under the leadership of the cardinal legate Bertrand du Poujet. It is not easy to decide whether Bertrand's long mission from 1320 to 1334 had more than the negative aim of reducing the Lombard *signori*. Was there also the ambition to create a papal state in Lombardy, or a Lombard kingdom under papal control? In the complicated negotiations which accompanied John of Bohemia's intervention in north Italy in 1331–3 there are glimpses of a scheme whereby he was to hold his Lombard lordships from Philip of France, who in turn was to recognize papal suzerainty.[3] But a united Italian opposition drove John of Bohemia from Lombardy and

[1] Between the financial years 1320–1 and 1325–6 it increased from 112,490 to 528,857 florins: K. H. Schäfer, *Die Ausgaben der apostolischen Kammer unter Johann XXII* (*Vatikanische Quellen zur Geschichte der päpstlichen Hof- und Finanzverwaltung 1316–1378*, ii, Paderborn, 1911), p. 13*. A rough calculation from Schäfer's sources, *ibid.*, pp. 470–6, shows that about 336,000 florins of the total for 1325–6 were assigned to the war in Lombardy.

[2] *MGH Const.* v, nr. 443, p. 367, reviving the intention of Clement V, *ibid.*, iv, nr. 1164, p. 1205. On the problems concerning the date and text of Robert's appointment, see most recently G. Tabacco, *La Casa di Francia nell' azione politica di papa Giovanni XXII* (Rome, 1953), pp. 161, n.3, 164. John's negotiations with Philip of Maine are to be found in *MGH Const.*, v, nr. 577, pp. 462–3; with Habsburg *ibid.*, nrs. 655–7, pp. 520–2.

[3] Carla Dumontel, *L'impresa italiana di Giovànni di Lussemburgo, re di Boemia* (Turin, 1952), pp. 114–15.

brought the long labours of Bertrand du Poujet to nothing. John XXII's successor conformed to the facts. The destruction of the *signori* had proved impossible; Benedict XII's alternative was to attach them to him by the grant of local vicariates *vacante imperio*. It was a system which, though it did not establish peace in north Italy, at least gave some semblance of regularity to the situation and meant income rather than expense to the Camera. But however the methods might change, the design persisted. And the pacification of Italy under papal direction could hardly be hoped for if the German king were free to intervene as he pleased and as, on his own theory of his rights, he was entitled to. It is at this point that the force of the papal claims to approve the choice of the German electors and to administer *vacante imperio* really becomes appreciable. When granting the vicariate over Verona, Parma and Vicenza to Alberto and Mastino della Scala in September 1339, Benedict expressed matters very clearly. The grant was to last for ten years or for as long as the empire was vacant: 'and we understand and we wish it to be understood by others, that this vacancy lasts until some one shall have been elected as emperor or king of the Romans *concorditer et canonice*, and shall have been approved by the Apostolic See.' [1]

Lewis' preoccupation with Italy can be explained in large part by reference to the known facts of the position of the kingship in fourteenth-century Germany. There the character of his reign was shaped by the circumstances of his accession. He had been brought to the throne in the double election of 1314 as the Luxemburg candidate against Habsburg. The Luxemburg promoters, Peter Aspelt, archbishop of Mainz, and Baldwin, archbishop of Trier, had esteemed his chances to be better than those of Baldwin's nephew, the young John of Bohemia; it was not expected that this surrogate would achieve much independence of his makers.[2] His hereditary endowment in land was scanty. For much of his reign he controlled directly only a fraction of the divided duchy of Bavaria; both Lower Bavaria and the Palatinate were in the hands of other Wittelsbachers, with whom he did not enjoy

[1] Raynaldus, *Annales ecclesiastici*, 1339, § 65.

[2] See H. Schrohe, *Der Kampf der Gegenkönige Ludwig und Friedrich um das Reich bis zur Entscheidungsschlacht bei Mühldorf* (*Hist. Studien*, xxix. Berlin, 1902), pp. 45 *sqq.*; H. S. Lucas, 'The Low Countries and the disputed imperial election of 1314', *Speculum*, xxi (1946), 72–114.

that steady habit of dynastic unity which was generally such a strength to Habsburg at this period.[1] And if possession of the kingship seemed to offer opportunities to remedy this deficiency, the steps which Lewis took as king to strengthen his territorial resources seriously affected his relations with the Luxemburg family. Shortly after the victory over the Habsburgs at Mühldorf in 1322 Lewis granted to his eldest son the Mark of Brandenburg, which since the failure of the Ascanian line in 1319–20 had remained exposed to the covetousness of the neighbouring princes.[2] The prospects of a window to the north-east and mastery of an additional electoral vote were tempting. But to establish the Wittelsbachers in the Mark was not to be a quick or easy matter, and this momentous action set in motion some of the most important currents in German politics during the next quarter of a century. Here, perhaps more than at any other juncture in the reign, it would be interesting to know what part in forming Lewis' decision was played by the counsel of Berthold VII of Henneberg-Schleusingen, that shadowy figure whose great importance in the affairs of the realm under three successive kings we can sense rather than measure.[3] Combined, as it had to be, with action to secure the alliance of the young margrave of Thuringia,[4] Lewis' enfeoffment of his son with Brandenburg represented an interference in a sphere of influence which John of Bohemia had marked out as his own, and so led to a loosening of the Luxemburg-Wittelsbach connexion which had brought Lewis to the throne and to victory over Frederick the Fair of Austria.[5]

The break was long retarded, first by Baldwin of Trier's

[1] Undoubtedly there were passing disagreements between Frederick the Fair and his brothers; cf. *MGH Const.*, vi, nr. 402, p. 303. But they never threatened to compromise the substantial unity of the family against the outside world.

[2] G. Salchow, *Der Übergang der Mark Brandenburg an das Wittelsbachse Hause* (Halle, 1893), pp. 42–4.

[3] A comprehensive study of Berthold would be valuable. W. Füsslein's *Berthold VII, Graf von Henneberg* (Hamburg, 1905) is more concerned with Berthold's local activities as a dynast than with the part he played in national politics and covers only the earlier part of his career.

[4] W. Lippert, *Wettiner und Wittelsbacher sowie die Niederlausitz im XIV Jahrhundert* (Dresden, 1894), p. 5.

[5] So Bock, 'Politischen Inquisitionsprozess', p. 58; cf. Franz Meltzer, *Die Ostraumpolitik König Johanns von Böhmen* (Jena, 1940), p. 28.

obstinate attempt to maintain himself in the administratorship of the archbishopric of Mainz, which from 1328 to 1337 set him at odds with the papacy and so inclined him to cautious communication with Lewis; then by the prospects of profit which the English alliance offered to Lewis' supporters in the next few years. Perhaps even as late as 1344 Baldwin, the senior and the wisest of the Luxemburg family, was still unwilling to go all the way with John of Bohemia and Charles of Moravia in opposition to Lewis.[1] But by the middle 'twenties the initial harmony was gone and Lewis found it necessary to seek compensation elsewhere. The peace of Hagenau in August 1330 and the agreement at Augsburg in November signalized a revolution in the complex system of dynastic rivalries in Germany. After sixteen years of intermittent strife Lewis came to an understanding with Habsburg which lasted for the rest of his reign.[2] The offered price, the enfeoffment of the Habsburgers with the duchy of Carinthia after the death of Henry of Tirol, was paid in 1335, and in the next year Lewis appeared as the ally in arms of Habsburg against John of Bohemia.[3] In effect Lewis' kingship for the most part depended on his ability to maintain a precarious balance between the two major dynasties of Germany. Merely to survive as king made calls on his energy which did not leave much wherewith to rule.

That impression is reinforced when the nature of the records of Lewis' reign is considered. Measured by the standard of efficiency in business, kingship in Germany was at a level of effectiveness markedly lower than the average in the west. A royal chancery had to be improvised when Lewis came to the throne, for it was one of the curses of the elective system that a change in the royal dynasty meant that the new king reaped little or no benefit from the administrative staff and experience gathered by his predecessor. That Lewis' chancery attracted some able men to serve in it and learned to produce documents creditable in form and in number is witnessed by such a collection as the *Kaiser Ludwig Selekt* of the Hauptstaatsarchiv in Munich. But there are only

[1] Perhaps it was Baldwin's political perplexities at this time which caused him to think of resigning his archbishopric; cf. Riezler, *VA*, nrs. 2199, 2211, pp. 795, 799.

[2] *MGH Const.*, vi, nrs. 834, 882–6, pp. 701, 734 sqq.

[3] Johann von Viktring, *Lib. certarum historiarum*, *ed. cit.*, ii. 165–7.

fragmentary traces of registration;[1] nothing survives to suggest that in the systematic keeping of records the methods of Lewis' chancery were nearly as advanced as those being used in Avignon and Naples, Aragon and England at this time. The historian of Lewis has to hunt for individual *Acta*, as if he were writing of Henry II Plantagenet—and he has no Pipe Rolls to help him. This weakness in documentation indicates that royal government in Germany was not intensive. Nor, in a land of sovereign princes, did it stretch very far. Lewis' itinerary shows how limited was the area of his influence. The imperial towns in Swabia, Franconia and the Wetterau saw him pretty often; he could expect to find at least some partisan support in Alsace; exceptionally he might descend the Rhine as far as Coblenz, though he never visited the lower Rhineland after the occasion of his coronation.[2] A phrase in a document which he issued in 1331 reveals that parts of Germany were as a foreign land to him: Otto of Habsburg was granted the office of vicar of the empire, to come into effect when Lewis passed over the Alps to Lombardy *oder uber den Duringer Walt*. Never in fact did he enter northern Germany.[3]

Impecunious kings were not rare in fourteenth-century Europe. But Lewis' lack of money was chronic and desperate to a degree which sets him apart from most of his contemporaries. No corpus of financial records for his reign seems to have survived; it may be doubted whether there was ever reason for such records to exist on any elaborate scale, since the financial resources at his disposal were ludicrously inadequate to sustain a kingly activity. The yearly tax of the imperial towns was probably the most important single source of regular income; it may have amounted

[1] Harry Bresslau, *Urkundenlehre*, i (2nd ed., Leipzig, 1912), pp. 133–6; W. Erben, 'Berthold von Tuttlingen, Registrator und Notar in der Kanzlei Kaiser Ludwigs des Baiern', *Denkschriften d. Akademie d. Wissenschaften in Wien, phil.-hist. Kl.*, lxvi (1923), 49 sqq.

[2] The early appearance of J. F. Boehmer's *Regesta Imperii inde ab anno 1314 usque ad annum 1347* (Frankfort, 1839; supplements 1–3, 1841–63) means that a good deal of revision of the details of Lewis' itinerary still needs to be done. But it seems unlikely that such a revision would invalidate the generalization in the text.

[3] 4 May 1331, printed by A. F. Oefele, *Rerum Boicarum Scriptores*, i (Augsburg, 1763), p. 758; cf. E. von Freeden, *Die Reichsgewalt in Norddeutschland von der Mitte des 13. bis zur Mitte des 14. Jahrhunderts* (Göttingen, 1931), pp. 90–3.

to 25,000 florins.[1] By now the Rhine tolls had in large part escaped the king's control; the ecclesiastical tenths which periodically refreshed royal finances elsewhere were denied to Lewis. His hereditary lands, though on occasion he taxed them hard enough to cause complaint, could not do much to remedy these deficiencies;[2] what credit he could command was often on ruinous terms: the pledging to his creditors of sovereign rights for capital sums which he had not received and could scarcely hope to repay.[3] The rumour reported by the Fürstenfeld chronicler, that there were barely eleven pounds in Lewis' chamber when he set out for the Mühldorf campaign, at least conveys a valid impression.[4] After Mühldorf as before, Lewis' attempts on quite minor occasions to impose his will in Germany were liable to end in fiasco because of insufficient means.[5]

Thus the temptation for Lewis to exploit his claims in Italy was strong. We know that his Italian enterprise failed, but we are not entitled to conclude that therefore it was hopeless or irrational, though the terms on which it offered possibilities need definition. In the twenty years following the death of the emperor Henry VII northern and central Italy had failed to find a political coherence to match their high economic development. Though some of the *signori* had long histories behind them by now, their grip had not yet hardened; it was still an unstable world, where the interposition of a moderate force might be expected to produce

[1] This is the figure suggested by Werunsky, *Geschichte Karls IV*, ii. 31. J. Knöpfler's reckoning of the taxes from the imperial towns in Swabia, Alsace and the upper Rhineland indicates a total of about 12,500 florins a year from this area: 'Die Reichsstädesteuer in Schwaben, Elsass und am Oberrhein zur Zeit Kaiser Ludwigs des Baiers', *Württembergische Vierteljahrshefte für Landesgeschichte, Neue Folge*, xi (1902). I have not seen the Erlangen dissertation by H. Gradenwitz, *Beiträge z. Finanzgeschichte d. deutschen Reichs unter Ludwig. d. B.* (1908).

[2] See the complaint of Heinrich Taube von Selbach in his *Chronica*, ed. H. Bresslau (*MGH Scriptores, nova series*, i, 1922), p. 58.

[3] On the ruinous device of the 'unabniezendes Pfand' see A. Werminghoff, *Die Verpfändungen der mittel- und niederrheinischen Reichsstädte während des 13. und 14. Jahrhunderts* (Breslau, 1893), pp. 30 sqq.

[4] *Chronica de Gestis Principum*, ed. G. Leidinger, in *Chronicae Bavaricae Saeculi XIV* (*MGH Scriptores in usum scholarum*, 1918), p. 94.

[5] As, for example, his vain attempt to capture Burgau in 1324–5, *Chronica de Gestis Principum*, pp. 100–3, and his futile intervention on behalf of Albrecht von Hohenberg in the struggle for the see of Constance in 1334, on which see Bock, *Reichsidee und Nationalstaaten*, pp. 353–5.

far-reaching results.[1] That view was not peculiar to Lewis, for it was shared by Pope John XXII and by John of Bohemia; perhaps it was not until the failure of their schemes in 1333–4 that it became clear that the opportunity had passed and that Italy was not to be reshaped by foreign hands. Ten years before, the prospects for intervention were much more promising; it seemed possible for a determined leader with 5,000 men-at-arms to play an imposing role in Italy. That was the sort of figure which contemporary Italians thought of;[2] their insistence that the men-at-arms should originally have come from beyond the Alps reminds us that German mercenaries formed a large proportion of the effective troops already in Italy. Their first interest was their pay, but it was suspected, not wholly without reason, that they might not prove deaf to a call from their national ruler.[3]

How high did Lewis pitch his Italian expectations? Did he envisage conquest, the imposition of direct administration on the Hohenstaufen model, the destruction of the Angevin kingdom of Naples with the aid of Frederick of Sicily? The sources hardly allow definite answers. There is a world of difference between some of the claims which Lewis made during the exaltation of his Italian expedition and his willingness in 1330 to agree that he would not intervene in the territories of the Visconti provided that they paid him something every year.[4] Probably it would be unwise to underestimate the range of Lewis' ambition. But at the lowest, could he but appear in imperial Italy he had a valuable commodity to sell. The power of the *signori* was a matter of fact; in a world curious and persistent in its enquiries about the origin of authority they lacked convincing titles to legitimacy. That

[1] P. S. Leicht, 'Staatsformen in der italienischen Renaissance', *Quellen u. Forsch. aus italien. Archiven u. Bibliotheken*, xxxi (1940), 207–22; Luigi Simeoni, *Le signorie*, i (Milan, 1950), pp. 52, 87.

[2] As, for instance, Florence, when she was trying to organize a combined Guelf force to oppose Lewis in January 1329, *MGH Const.*, vi, nr. 539, p. 449.

[3] K. H. Schäfer, *Deutsche Ritter und Edelknechte in Italien während des 14. Jahrhunderts*, i (*Quellen und Forschungen aus dem Gebiet der Geschichte*, xv (i). Paderborn, 1911), pp. 75–9. For the fear that German mercenaries in Guelf service might fall away to Lewis there is evidence in a letter dated 22 April 1342 from Florence to Robert of Naples, summarized by Mommsen, *Italienischen Analekten*, nr. 267, p. 112.

[4] It would seem that this offer was made to Azzo Visconti by John of Bohemia on Lewis' behalf: Riezler, *VA*, nr. 1386a, p. 482.

lack Lewis could supply by the grant of imperial vicariates. How profitable such a transaction might be to both parties is well illustrated by the story of Lewis' relations with Castruccio Castracani of Lucca; we know that the papacy soon learned to imitate the device.[1]

If he would limit his purposes, the Lombard *signori* were willing to have Lewis in Italy. Provided that he left their position and their territories intact he was welcome to come to help them against their enemies and to do what he pleased against the Tuscan Guelfs and Robert of Naples. But there was little or no question of a gratuitous Ghibelline sentiment at this time. The Italian Ghibellines could still write a pro-imperial brief; probably they played no inconsiderable part in providing the store of arguments and ideas on which Lewis drew in his polemics with the papacy.[2] But their actions were dictated solely by their own interests, and if those were threatened by a German ruler, then Guelf allies were becoming entirely acceptable to them. The way was pointed in 1332–3 by the alliance of Florence with the Lombard *signori* against John of Bohemia and the papal legate;[3] in June 1341 the Visconti, the Gonzaga and the Estensi were allied to Florence, Bologna and Robert of Naples 'against the Bavarian and his accomplices and any other person tyrannically entering or hostilely invading Italy.'[4] In the early 'twenties, however, the *signori* were being so hard pressed by John XXII that they were willing to look for help from beyond the Alps. A few days after Mühldorf Lewis sent news of his victory to Italy, where previously, except for a short burst of activity at the beginning of his reign, he had shown far less interest than had his defeated rival.[5] By January

[1] T. E. Mommsen, 'Castruccio e l'impero', *Atti della R. Accademia Lucchese, nuova serie*, iii (1934), 33 sqq.; P. J. Jones, 'The Vicariate of the Malatesta of Rimini', *English Historical Review*, lxvii (1952), 321–51.

[2] See the memorandum of Ugolino of Celle dated April 1323, printed by E. E. Stengel, *N[ova] A[lamanniae]*, i (Berlin, 1921), nr. 123, p. 73, or the memorandum composed some ten years earlier and printed *MGH Const.*, iv, nr. 1248, pp. 1308–17; Bock, *Reichsidee*, pp. 210–11.

[3] Giovanni Villani, *Cronaca*, lib. x, c. 203; cf. Dumontel, *op. cit.*, pp. 99–101.

[4] N. Rodolico, *Dal Comune alla Signoria* (Bologna, 1898), doc. 73, p. 273; other documents concerning this league are printed by Mommsen, *Italienische Analekten*, nrs. 252–62, pp. 107–10.

[5] *MGH Const.*, v, nr. 676, p. 539. On Frederick the Fair's Italian interests see T. E. Mommsen, 'Das Habsburgisch-Angiovinische Ehe-Bündnis von

1323 envoys from Milan were at Lewis' court soliciting the intervention by Lewis' lieutenants which later in the year helped the Lombard Ghibellines to resist a dangerous attack by the papal legate.[1] The pope's first counter-measure was the process of October 1323 against Lewis.

This brusque gesture left Lewis no real choice, for he knew what his rights were. To have yielded to the papal threat would have been to diminish himself disastrously in his own eyes and in those of his contemporaries. In his appeals against the papal processes he began to develop an aggressive reply, which culminated in the Italian expedition in 1327–9.[2] Though he claimed authority in the empire from the fact of his election as king of the Romans, fully to convince the Italians of the validity of the wares he had to offer he needed to add the imperial title. Coronation as emperor by a hostile pope was not to be hoped for, and so we find Lewis putting into practice a programme sketched by Manfred sixty years before. He had recourse to the 'Roman theory of the empire', which maintained that an emperor could legitimately be created by the act of the Roman people, without the participation of the Roman Church.[3] Long abandonment by the papal court had soured relations between the inhabitants of Rome and their bishop, and they were willing to play their part. Lewis' strange coronation at Rome in January 1328 has no deep ideological significance. It was an act of necessity; a practical expedient to meet immediate difficulties.[4]

The motives of Lewis' Italian expedition are comprehensible

1316', *Neues Archiv d. Gesellschaft f. ältere deutsche Geschichtskunde*, l. (1935), 600–15; G. Tabacco, 'La politica italiana di Federico il Bello, re dei Romani', *Archivio storico italiano*, cviii (1950), 3–77.

[1] *MGH Const.*, v, nr. 723, p. 564.

[2] The most recent discussion of Lewis' appeals is by F. Bock, 'Die Appellationschriften König Ludwigs IV', *Deutsches Archiv f. Gesch. d. Mittelalters*, iv (1941), 179 sqq. The problem of the interpolation in the Sachsenhausen appeal of 22 May 1324 (*MGH Const.*, v, nr. 909, p. 722) of the extreme Franciscan *Tractatus de paupertate Christi* remains obscure.

[3] Manfred's manifesto of 25 May 1265, *MGH Const.*, ii, nr. 424, p. 559, is discussed by R. Folz, *L'Idée d'Empire en Occident du Ve au XIVe siècle* (Paris, 1953), pp. 138–42. A clear indication of the nature of Lewis' coronation is given in the encyclical issued by Castruccio Castracani on 17 January 1328, *MGH Const.*, vi, nr. 383, p. 286.

[4] See E. Duprè-Theseider, *Roma dal Comune di Popolo alla Signoria Pontificia (1252–1377)* (Bologna, 1952), p. 467.

enough. But that it was an ill-managed affair can scarcely be doubted. When he set out for Trent at the beginning of 1327 he apparently intended to do no more than hold preliminary discussions with the envoys of the Italian Ghibellines.[1] In fact he went on to Italy, persuaded by the promises—perhaps also by the threats—of some of the Italians.[2] We know the form of expedition which they envisaged. They wanted Lewis at the head of some 1,500–2,000 men-at-arms, for whom they would supply the pay together with reinforcements up to twice that number from their own German mercenaries.[3] It was a plan devised to keep Lewis strictly under their control; it ruled out an imperial progress in the old manner, with the emperor-elect sustained by the feudal service of the German kingdom. To it Lewis had to conform.[4] He had had no time to organize support in Germany before he entered Italy and his attempts later to remind the German estates of their traditional obligations met with little response.[5] The witness lists of the documents which he issued soon after the imperial coronation disclose an unimpressive entourage lacking German names of independent standing. There was a single electoral prince, Lewis' nephew, the young Rudolf II of the Palatinate; of the two dukes, Lewis of Teck's title was an historical curiosity without territorial significance, while Henry II of Braunschweig-Grubenhagen was little more than an adventurer errant. A more solid element was provided by the landgrave of Alsace and the Hohenzollern burgrave of Nürnberg.

[1] This is Lewis' own account, *MGH Const.*, vi, nr. 241, p. 158.

[2] *Ibid.*, nr. 266, p. 174. Simeoni, *Le Signorie*, i. 105 emphasizes that not all the *signori* welcomed Lewis' coming. It may well have been made clear to Lewis at Trent that if he delayed his Italian expedition there was the danger that the *signori* would come to terms with the papacy.

[3] So the Aragonese proctor at the Curia had reported to his master, 26 September 1325, *Acta Aragonensia*, ed. H. Finke, i (Berlin, 1908), nr. 274, p. 416.

[4] That Lewis himself recognized that this must be so appears from his reply to the envoys of the Estensi on 19 October 1324, *MGH Const.*, v, nr. 1006, p. 835. For the way in which the obligation of the German estates to help the crown 'uber daz gebirge gegen Lamparten' was being whittled away by royal privileges, see *ibid.*, nr. 25, § 3, p. 24; nr. 191, § 8, p. 177.

[5] See *MGH Const.*, vi, nrs. 266, 289–91, 326–9, pp. 173, 205, 238. By the end of August 1327 Lewis' father-in-law, William of Holland, had bound himself by oath to the pope not to aid Lewis, *ibid.*, nrs. 335–6, pp. 245–7.

For the rest, Lewis' German following consisted of faithful servants and fighting men from the smaller nobility.[1]

In effect Lewis was the leader of a mercenary force, much of which he picked up in Italy. The absence of financial records makes it difficult to be precise about the number of his German men-at-arms. There are indications that he crossed the Alps with a few hundred; by September 1327 they had increased to about 3,000, at Rome four months later they had reached a maximum of about 4,000 and they were still more than 2,000 strong in November 1329.[2] At its largest, this was a small army with which to brave the three concentrations of Lewis' enemies in Italy: the papal forces under Bertrand du Poujet, based on Bologna; Florence and the Tuscan Guelfs; Robert of Anjou and the forces of the kingdom of Naples. But it represented a monthly bill for wages which cannot have fallen far short of 50,000 florins.[3] Levies from the towns which he occupied did not enable Lewis to meet his troops' demands for regular pay, though of course they helped to make his enterprise unpopular; in time his Lombard allies grew disinclined to share a financial burden on behalf of a ruler who was showing altogether more appetite for power than they had bargained for. The break with the Visconti came early. Perhaps from the outset Galeazzo Visconti's relations with Lewis had been equivocal; on 20 July 1327, less than a fortnight after his appointment as imperial vicar of Milan, Galeazzo together with his son and his brothers Luchino and Giovanni was imprisoned, seemingly on the charge of covert communication with the pope.[4] The reconciliation which was patched up when Lewis

[1] *Ibid.*, vi, nrs. 390, 395, 401, pp. 293, 297, 300.

[2] These figures are those of Villani, *Cronaca*, lib. x, cc. 17, 31, 47, 53, 54, 146. Collateral evidence suggests that they were not much exaggerated. While Villani, x. 47, says that the advance guard on Lewis' march to Rome in December 1327 consisted of 700 horse and 2,000 foot, Robert of Naples writing to the Justiciar of the Terra di Bari on 22 December puts the numbers at 400 horse and 2,000 foot, Mommsen, *Italienischen Analekten*, nr. 158, p. 74.

[3] In 1337 Edward III was offering 15 florins a month for a mounted man-at-arms, Rymer, *Foedera*, ii (ii), 984. Schäfer, *Deutsche Ritter und Edelknechte*, i. 45 sqq. gives Italian rates from the 'twenties to the 'fifties which are considerably lower: 10, 8, 7, 6, even 5 florins a month for a simple man-at-arms; a troop leader might get three times this. *MGH Const.*, vi, nr. 513, p. 423, suggests that Lewis could get men at 6 florins a month.

[4] Simeoni, *op. cit.*, i. 106–7.

returned to Lombardy in 1329 was certainly not sincere and before the end of the year the Visconti and the Estensi had come to terms with the Church.[1]

The two allies who did show some zeal for Lewis' cause were Castruccio Castracani and the Aragonese king of Sicily, Frederick. Could their actions have been combined, so that Castruccio held Guelf Tuscany in check while Lewis and the Sicilians attacked the kingdom of Naples, then Lewis might possibly have gained the sort of victory which would have made him a power in Italy. But the rebellion of Pistoia at the end of January 1328 called Castruccio from Lewis' side, and by early autumn he was dead. The Sicilians were slow to start, and when they did move it was too late, for Lewis had begun his journey northwards from Rome.[2] Already he was having difficulties with his troops, and at Pisa in the autumn he was faced by a mass desertion of nearly a thousand of his mercenaries whose pay was in arrears.[3] Nevertheless, Lewis was still capable of cutting a considerable figure in north Italy and his withdrawal to Germany at the end of 1329 was in no sense a debacle. Its timing seems to have been as fortuitous as that of the start of his expedition. Towards the end of December he made his way to Trent, intending to meet Frederick of Austria there.[4] Instead, he received the news of Frederick's death which made his presence in Germany urgently necessary. There are good reasons to believe that he intended to return to Italy. But in fact he never did return: the Guelfs had beaten him. Harsh things were said at the time, and are still being said, about the generalship of the Guelf forces which allowed Lewis to complete his perilous march to Rome without meeting serious opposition.[5] But the Guelf leaders knew their business. Time, poverty and the incompatibility between his ultimate aims and those of most of his

[1] C. Erdmann, 'Vatikanische Analekten', pp. 14, 22; Mommsen, *Italienischen Analekten*, nr. 190, p. 84.

[2] *MGH Const.*, vi, nr. 486, p. 399, gives the report sent to Frederick III of Sicily by an anonymous observer with the Sicilian fleet during the last week of August.

[3] *Ibid.*, vi, nrs. 512–13, pp. 421–3; cf. R. Davidsohn, *Geschichte von Florenz*, iii (Berlin, 1912), pp. 851 sqq.

[4] John XXII had heard this rumour of Lewis' intentions before 28 October 1329, *MGH Const.*, vi, nr. 658, p. 556.

[5] By Villani, for instance, *Cronaca*, lib. x, cc. 31, 47, and by Bock, *Reichsidee*, p. 284.

allies could and did defeat Lewis in Italy; it was sufficient to have denied him the opportunity of securing that victory in a large-scale engagement which might have made him really formidable.

In Italy Lewis had incurred heavy liabilities as the result of his deposition of Pope John XXII and his promotion of a grotesquely ineffective schism. How these actions at Rome are to be explained is not clear. Lewis' temperamental proclivity to a radical gesture may have counted for something. It is often supposed that here, for once, the advice of Marsilio of Padua played a large part and if this be so, he was perhaps the most damaging gift that the Lombard Ghibellines ever slipped into Lewis' pocket.[1] For what had been done at Rome in 1328 greatly complicated the question of Lewis' reconciliation with the Church during the next decade and a half. The documents faithfully reflect the double nature of the problem.[2] On the one hand, there were the religious aspects: the offences which Lewis had perpetrated by his attacks on John XXII, his schism, his harbouring of heretics. But there were also political considerations. Some arose from Lewis' acts of government, in Germany as well as in Italy, in defiance of the papal approbation theory, and from his Roman coronation; others from the fact that the papacy would not and could not envisage a settlement with Lewis which did not respect the interests of its friends. The business of Lewis' reconciliation was cast into the legal form of a process for absolution. But both sides knew that behind the canonical formalities, inevitably affecting their pace and their issue, lay the great political questions of the time: the future of Italy, the search for alliances by the states of the west as they prepared for the outbreak of the Hundred Years' War, the acute though irregular sensitivity to these western

[1] On the use of Marsilio by Matteo Visconti in the spring of 1319, see C. W. Previté-Orton, 'Marsilius of Padua and the Visconti', *English Historical Review*, xliv (1929), 278–9. Marsilio seems to have been known in Milan. The two witnesses who testified before the papal inquisitor at Bologna in December 1329 as having recognized Marsilio riding with Lewis in Parma on 28 November were both Milanese, Bock, 'Politischen Inquisitionsprozess', p. 68.

[2] They are discussed by F. Bock, 'Die Prokuratorien Kaiser Ludwigs IV an Papst Benedict XII', *Quellen u. Forsch. aus italienischen Archiven u. Bibliotheken*, xxv (1933), 251 sqq.; Offler, 'Die Prokuratorien Ludwigs des Bayern' (above, p. 23, n. 2).

motions of a more eastern Europe in Bohemia and Poland and Hungary.[1]

Lewis' attitude was more consistent and less pliant than the older historians believed. Two precious items in the Geheimes Haus-Archiv in Munich, which contain the instructions given to his autumn embassies to the Curia in 1331, 1336 and 1343, seem conclusive on this point.[2] Lewis refused to admit that he had been justly excommunicated for acting as king without papal approval or that he had in any way jeopardized his personal orthodoxy. The imperial coronation, the deposition of John XXII and the election of Peter of Corbara were improprieties into which he had been forced in defence of imperial rights and he was prepared to make amends for them. He had never, he declared, accepted the theological opinions of Marsilio and the rebel Minorites; he had kept them at his court as learned men, who might help to protect his rights and those of the monarchy; if they proved obdurate and would not be reconciled to the Church when he was, his protection would be withdrawn from them. As to the papal claim to approve the elected king of the Romans, Lewis declined to concede anything more than his predecessors had conceded. In effect he was willing to ask for and accept papal approval of his person, provided the concession in no way affected the validity of the acts which he had already performed as king; but he would enter into no engagement which limited his freedom of action in imperial Italy. Slight changes of emphasis there were during these fifteen years. Lewis had not by 1331 yet made up his mind to the unconditional surrender of his imperial title; in 1344 he may have been willing to accept for a moment the full papal approbation theory, though only with safeguards which made the concession nugatory in practice.[3] But there was never

[1] A good example of this is offered by the tentative negotiations for an alliance between Hungary and England in 1345–6. See F. Trautz, 'Die Reise eines englischen Gesandten nach Ungarn im Jahr 1346', *Mitteilungen des Instituts für Österreichische Geschichtsforschung*, lx (1952), 359 sqq.

[2] Munich, Geheimes Haus-Archiv 1/5 256 has the instruction for October 1331, imperfectly printed in Ch. Gewold, *Defensio Ludovici imperatoris ratione electionis contra Abr. Bzovium* (Ingolstadt, 1618), pp. 118–20. At fo. 12 of 1/5 259 is the instruction for October 1336, and at fos. 14–15 that for October 1343. Both are printed in Riezler, *Literarischen Widersacher*, pp. 328, 332.

[3] Clement VI's demands in 1344 survive in a contemporary German translation presumably made in Lewis' chancery, Munich, Geheimes Haus-

a real change of ground. Seemingly unconscious of the burden of his enormities Lewis continued to bargain as if from strength.

The springs of papal policy were more complicated. There was the duty of reconciling the penitent—if such he sincerely was—to the Church. But there were other responsibilities also. The papacy had its general concern for the political order of the west, its own particular stake in Italy, its allies and special friends, some of whom were much interested in the future of the empire and the German kingdom. Could the terms of Lewis' reconciliation be so contrived as to satisfy at one and the same time the papal demands, both canonical and political, Lewis' reserves and the interests of the papacy's allies? We can expect no single answer of the three very different popes who had to deal with this question, though some preoccupations were constant: the need to control any future activity of Lewis in Italy, for instance, and the demand that as a prerequisite of his reconciliation Lewis should reach agreement about outstanding controversies with France and Naples and Luxemburg.[1] Probably to John XXII the problem seemed insoluble on terms which would have allowed Lewis to keep the German crown. In his person John had borne the brunt of Lewis' outrages against papal dignity and he was not to be convinced of the sincerity of Lewis' repentance. From the late autumn of 1327 until the spring of 1330 his agent Peter of Ungula was busy in Germany in the vain attempt to raise an anti-king against Lewis.[2] When in 1333–4 the kings of France

Archiv, 1/5 260; cf. Offler, 'Die Prokuratorien Ludwigs des Bayern', pp. 480–3. The 20th article of Clement's political demands was that Lewis' proctors should be empowered to swear on his behalf that he would perform no actions under the imperial or royal title without the special permission of the pope (fo. 9v.). In the margin is the note (which presumably represents the decision of Lewis and his counsellors): 'Das urlop sol der bapst geben das er under den kuenklichen titel sinen gwalt ueben und gefuern mueg des tags und der wil so des keisers procurator vor den Bapst in dem consistori fuerlegent und tuend als begriffen ist in den artikeln der procuratorien und sol auch sinen brief geben mit der bulle was der keiser daran tuet daz dem stuol und dem rich keinen schaden bringen mueg.'

[1] This is clear from the terms of Lewis' instructions to his envoys in 1331 and 1336 (above, p. 40, n. 2). See also Riezler, *VA*, nrs. 1748a, 1842, pp. 592, 651, and the documents preserved in the register of Jean de Revets, Marseilles, Archives départmentales des Bouches du Rhône, B. 176, fos. 113–14, referred to in my paper 'Die Prokuratorien Ludwigs d.B.', pp. 476–7.

[2] E. E. Stengel, *Avignon und Rhens* (Weimar, 1930), pp. 40–59.

and Bohemia were supporting a scheme whereby Lewis was to abdicate in favour of his cousin Henry XIV of Lower Bavaria, John engaged himself to an extent which strained his relations with Robert of Naples.[1]

During the early years of the next pontificate the prospects for Lewis' reconciliation seemed much more hopeful. Lewis treated Benedict XII with deference;[2] he was willing to go some way to meet the demands of Robert of Naples, and by the end of 1336 his envoys had reached agreement on his behalf with Philip VI of France.[3] All seemed favourable for the success of Lewis' proctors at the Curia in February and March 1337. But in April negotiations broke down. Opinion in Germany imputed the blame to the French king and the documents do seem to indicate that in this instance Benedict, despite his later protestations to the contrary, yielded to French pressure.[4] At this time Benedict was hoping to bring about a slackening of political tension in the west by papal mediation between France and England; in this design Lewis' reconciliation had a part to play. Philip VI was less sanguine. He was rightly nervous lest Lewis, notwithstanding the recent pact, should ally with England against him.[5] With his canonical disabilities still about him Lewis would be a less useful ally to Edward III and a less formidable opponent to France. Philip's view prevailed at the Curia and an opportunity passed. There was little energy in the negotiations between Lewis and the papacy which continued intermittently for the rest of

[1] E. E. Stengel, *Avignon und Rhens* pp. 60 sqq.; Bock, *Reichsidee*, pp. 348 sqq., and in *Historische Zeitschrift*, cxlvii (1933), 398. The tension between John and Robert of Naples is discussed by E. G. Léonard, *Les Angevins de Naples* (Paris, 1954), pp. 267–9.

[2] See his care to avoid using the royal and imperial titles in his letter to Benedict dated 2 August 1335, Riezler, *VA*, nr. 1748, p. 592.

[3] On 23 December 1336 Miles of Noyers swore on behalf of Philip that he would make no hindrance to Lewis' reconciliation, Riezler, *VA*, nr. 1876, p. 668. Lewis ratified the agreement in February 1337 and denounced it on 7 July, Bock, *Reichsidee*, pp. 375, 386.

[4] I have not been convinced by the learned attempt of F. Pelster, *art. cit.* (above, p. 23, n. 2), pp. 102–9, to minimize the effect of French pressure and place the main responsibility for the break on Benedict's rigour for what he considered to be papal rights in the matter of Lewis' approbation. The decisive document seems to be Benedict's letter to Philip of 4 April 1337, Riezler, *VA*, nr. 1876, p. 668.

[5] Stengel, *NA*, i, nr. 408.

Benedict's lifetime. For some years the English alliance stood in the way; when in January 1341 Lewis changed over to friendship with Philip of Valois this did him no good in Benedict's eyes: in anticipation of pressure to come Philip was told that Lewis could be treated by the Curia only *secundum formam iuris*.[1]

Clement VI was at once more experienced and more deeply involved in politics than his predecessor. It is not easy to determine how soon he became convinced that further negotiations with Lewis would serve no purpose. During his first eighteen months as pope he showed great skill in bringing Lewis to reveal how far in concession he was willing to go.[2] When the papal demands were formulated in the spring of 1344 they were such as neither Lewis nor the German electors could accept; it may be that they were not intended to be found acceptable.[3] Lewis' last independent embassy left the Curia in mid-May 1345. On 22 April 1346 Charles of Luxemburg made to the papacy the promises which Clement claimed as the price of his support and on 11 July he was elected king at Rhens in opposition to Lewis.

But Lewis still held the German crown at his death in October 1347. Although the Wittelsbachers failed to find a rival candidate for the monarchy capable of holding out against Charles, to Lewis' heirs were left a united Upper and Lower Bavaria, the Mark of Brandenburg, the county of Tirol and a footing in the Low Countries. In that achievement (though some if it was not lasting) lies the answer to those who ask why men competed for the German kingship in the fourteenth century. It leads also to a final problem. How was it that Lewis managed to survive for so long? Partly, it may be supposed, because after his withdrawal from Italy and the submission of his anti-pope to John XXII in the summer of 1330, the papacy ceased to be much frightened of him: he declined from a menace into an embarrassment not calling

[1] *Benoît XII (1334–1342). Lettres closes, patentes et curiales se rapportant à la France*, ed. G. Daumet (Paris, 1920), nr. 832.

[2] As I have tried to show in my paper, 'A political *collatio* of Pope Clement VI', *Revue Bénedictine*, lxv (1955), 127–9.

[3] For Clement's demands, see p. 40, n. 3 above. An electoral commentary on them is printed by Stengel, *NA*, ii, nr. 773, p. 495. Another opinion of them (presumably that of some representative of the imperial towns) was published by F. von Weech, *Kaiser Ludwig der Bayer und König Johann von Böhmen* (Munich, 1860), pp. 126–30.

for urgent action.[1] We badly need a new comprehensive account of the effects of the struggle on the Church in Germany at large.[2] But without prejudging the findings of that enquiry it seems fair to record a general impression. Throughout the period when the lands of Lewis and his supporters lay under interdict, ecclesiastical conditions remained more nearly normal than might have been expected. Germany was a large country and the area effectively controlled by Lewis was comparatively small. Consequently the interdict was supposed to be in force precisely in those places where Lewis was best able to prevent it from operating. German princes who for years had communicated with Lewis and had thus in theory brought the interdict upon their territories found at the Curia pretty ready acceptance of the plea that they had acted from that just fear which can fall even upon a constant man.[3] That the papal sentences were from time to time the source of disorders and violence is undoubted; for instance, they could offer the communal movement in an episcopal town a convenient excuse for disobedience to an unpopular *Stadtherr* when he tried to carry out the pope's orders. Individuals and religious communities were sometimes faced by anxious problems of conscience and division of allegiance. But on the whole the situation, though often difficult, never became intolerable; the condition of the Church in Germany, however deplorable, did not deteriorate so far as to make it imperative for the papacy to aim a final blow at Lewis.

There was also a more positive consideration. The complications of international politics, which had wrecked Lewis' chance of reconciliation in 1336–7, worked in the next few years to group most of the German princes around him. Lewis' alliance with Edward III in the summer of 1337 was based on a misapprehension about Edward's ability to fulfil the financial obligations which he then undertook. Nevertheless, the prospect of English subsidies and an excited atmosphere in which some

[1] Early in 1340 Benedict XII seems to have been unmoved by the fears of Florence that Lewis was planning a new descent on Italy: G. Gorrini, 'Lettere inedite degli ambasciatori fiorentini alla corte dei papi in Avignone anno 1340', *Archivio storico italiano*, iv[a] serie, xiv (1884), 166.

[2] The account by A. Hauck, *Kirchengeschichte Deutschlands*, v (i) (Leipzig, 1911), pp. 492–7, 557, is still valuable.

[3] See, for instance, the form of absolution of Baldwin of Trier, 24 November 1342, Reizler, *VA*, nr. 2134, p. 768.

genuine stir of anti-French feeling was discernible helped to bring the electoral princes—the Rhenish archbishops in the forefront—nearer to the crown than ever before.[1] They were willing to acknowledge that the papal approbation theory, if pressed to its logical conclusion, led to an absurdity which it was their duty as well as their interest to resist. Perhaps there was nothing very original in the terms of the declarations made at Rhens in July 1338.[2] What mattered was the circumstances in which the declarations were made and the political cooperation (however occasional and involuntary) with Lewis which they implied. It may well be that the part taken by Baldwin of Trier in these transactions has been exaggerated; that his initiative at Rhens and his altruistic enthusiasm for the rights of the German crown were less than has sometimes been supposed.[3] But this great nobleman and churchman, brother of one emperor and great-uncle of another, cannot be denied a proper sense of what was due to his dignity as an elector. His adhesion to the declarations, however cautious and reserved it may have been, marks his understanding that papal policy towards Lewis held dangers for the public law of Germany. The German constitutional assemblies of 1338–9, themselves in a sense the offspring of the Anglo-imperial alliance, gave a sort of galvanic shock to Lewis' kingship, and the effect lasted for some years. As late as 1344 German princes who had no reason to wish Lewis well had not resolved the puzzle how to be rid of

[1] Offler, 'England and Germany at the beginning of the Hundred Years' War', p. 616.

[2] In declaring that it was old and approved law that he whom the electors or a majority of them had chosen might take the royal title and administer the Empire 'nulla approbatione vel licencia dicte sedis apostolice super hoc habita et obtenta' (M. Krammer, *Quellen zur Geschichte der deutschen Königswahl und des Kurfürstenkollegs*, ii (Leipzig, 1912), p. 91) the electors in their *Weisthum* at Rhens were not going substantially beyond the position of Lewis in his Sachsenhausen appeal in 1324, *MGH Const.*, v, nr. 909, § 12, p. 726.

[3] The highly favourable view of Baldwin taken by E. E. Stengel in *Avignon und Rhens* and his *Baldewin von Luxemburg. Ein grenzdeutscher Staatsmann des 14. Jahrhunderts* (Weimar, 1937) is sharply criticized by implication by Bock, *Reichsidee*, pp. 396–405. The document printed by Stengel, *NA*, i, nr. 547, p. 365, seems to show Baldwin as something less than a whole-hearted supporter of the Rhens declarations. Stengel's attempts to explain it away, *Avignon und Rhens*, pp. 142 sqq., are not wholly convincing.

him without at the same time prejudicing their own rights as electors.[1]

Lastly, this long survival tells us something of Lewis himself. What influence his counsellors exerted on him at various periods is a question needing further investigation, though it is certain that he was not always well or faithfully served.[2] But like any medieval ruler Lewis must carry the responsibility for his own decisions. His character is not easily read and those scholars who would claim for him a consistent realism in politics hardly do justice to his variety. There was, for instance, his strange foundation at Ettal for twenty Benedictine monks together with thirteen knights and their wives. It has been explained with much critical skill in political terms: as a device designed to abolish old imperial rights in the Ammergau for the benefit of the duchy of Bavaria and to secure an area of strategic importance in the approaches to the Alps.[3] But can such an explanation wholly satisfy? This illiterate man, with his sincere conventional piety,[4] was capable of headstrong decisions; then liable in a fit of depression to talk of renouncing the throne. There was rumour of his wish to abdicate in 1319; in January 1326 he promised to give up the kingdom to his defeated rival, if Frederick could get the pope's approval; in 1333–4 half Europe was kept interested or alarmed by a scheme that he should make way for his cousin, Henry of Lower Bavaria.[5] Nothing came of these proposals and much in-

[1] See *NA*, ii, nr. 773, p. 495, and Stengel's comments, *Avignon u. Rhens*, p. 202, n. 1.

[2] Offler, 'Meinungsverschiedenheiten am Hof Ludwigs des Bayern im Herbst 1331', *Deutsches Archiv f. Erforschung des Mittelalters*, xi (1954), 191–206. The rediscovered *Oeconomica* of Conrad of Megenberg even brings a charge of disloyalty against Lewis' experienced protonotary and diplomatic agent Ulrich Hofmaier of Augsburg: Th. Käppeli, 'L'Oeconomica de Conrad de Megenberg retrouvée', *Revue d'histoire ecclésiastique*, xlv (1950), p. 618, n. 8.

[3] F. Bock, 'Die Gründung des Klosters Ettal', *Oberbayerisches Archiv*, lxvi (1929), pp. 78, 84.

[4] Offler, 'England and Germany', p. 619, n. 3. When under the papal sentences Lewis remained an extremely generous *Landesherr* to the regular clergy in Bavaria: O. Bornhak, *Staatskirchliche Anschauungen und Handlungen am Hofe Kaiser Ludwigs des Bayern* (Weimar, 1930), pp. 102–3.

[5] *Chronica de Gestis Principum*, *ed. cit.*, p. 89; *MGH Const.*, vi, nrs. 140–1, pp. 96–7 (cf. *Regesta Habsburgica*, iii, ed. L. Gross, nr. 1636, p. 202); p. 42, n. 1 above.

genuity has been spent in maintaining that Lewis was never in earnest with them, but was always playing some deep game for the confusion of his opponents. Perhaps there is something to be said for a less subtle explanation: circumstances improved, the depression of the moment passed and Lewis changed his mind. The trait contemporaries fastened on was his duplicity.[1] In a sense that was the obvious resource of a ruler who had so often and so long to contend against the odds, but with Lewis one may feel that it was sometimes less the consequence of calculation than of a certain instability of temperament. Against it must be weighed his tenacious defence of what he considered to be the rights of the German kingship. Certainly Lewis was not a simple nor a negligible man. Hauck went so far as to declare that it was on him that the claims of the papacy to world dominion broke down.[2] Those are excessively dramatic terms. At the level of political action Lewis' struggle with the papacy represented a conflict over claims in an Italy much of which was rapidly developing out of the reach of either of the contestants. Surely that was why it was the last?

[1] See the passages collected by Stengel, *Avignon und Rhens*, pp. 78–80.
[2] *Op. cit.*, p. 582.

III

England and Germany at the Beginning of the Hundred Years' War

THE preliminary alliances and agreements by which both France and England prepared for the Hundred Years' War have been the subject of a number of recent studies,[1] and perhaps little more remains to be said about them, except that the story of English diplomatic activity in this period could be enriched in detail by a more exhaustive examination of the evidence of the exchequer and wardrobe accounts than has yet been undertaken. The facts of the situation are well enough established. When Edward III landed on the continent in July 1338 he was allied to a number of territorial rulers in the Low Countries, to the excommunicate emperor, Lewis the Bavarian, to the dukes of Austria, and to the towns of Flanders. Against him the French king could rely on the support of the two Luxemburgers, John of Bohemia and his son Charles of Moravia, the counts of Flanders and Savoy, and the bishop of Liège. Edward had been led to make his engagements by elementary strategic considerations and perhaps also by reminiscence of his grandfather's action in planning an attack on France from the east as well as from Gascony ; Philip of Valois had countered in the way which was to be expected. Thus Germany was to be implicated very thoroughly in the Anglo-French national war. Two incidents in Edward III's relations with the nominal sovereign power in Germany, the Holy Roman Empire, merit perhaps more attention than they have yet been given.[2] No attempt is intended here to give a detailed account of the exchanges between Edward and Lewis the Bavarian ;[3] the object of this paper is to put forward

[1] H. Weiss, *Frankreichs Politik in den Rheinlanden am Vorabend des Hundertjährigen Krieges* (1927) ; H. S. Lucas, *The Low Countries and the Hundred Years' War* (1929) ; J. de Sturler, *Les relations politiques et les échanges commerciaux entre le duché de Brabant et l'Angleterre au moyen âge* (1936).

[2] The accounts of W. Longman, *Life and Times of Edward III*, i. 142, 293 ; J. H. Ramsay, *The Genesis of Lancaster*, i. 261, 357 ; and T. F. Tout, *The History of England from the Accession of Henry III to the Death of Edward III*, 335, are very insufficient.

* [3] The materials for this have been collected by Dr. F. Bock for the forthcoming completion of the *Constitutiones* of Lewis' reign in the *Monumenta Germaniae Historica.* Dr. Bock announced a work on Anglo-German relations in the fourteenth century in *ante* xlv. 353.

Reprinted from the *English Historical Review* 54 (1939), pp. 608–63, by permission of Oxford University Press.

some suggestions about the imperial vicariate granted to Edward in 1338 and his refusal of the imperial crown in 1348.

It is necessary at this point to notice a complication which at once arises in any discussion of Edward's relations with the empire at this time. For it was possible to argue, and it was in fact argued, that the empire was without an emperor. Lewis the Bavarian's election as king of the Romans in 1314 had been impugned by a counter-claimant, Frederick the Fair of Austria, and even Lewis' military success near Mühldorf in 1322 had not given him an undisputed title. For since the time of Innocent III the papacy had been elaborating a theory of the necessity of papal approval of the elected king of the Romans before he could perform legitimate acts of administration,[1] and under Clement V this theory had received sharp definition in the bulls *Romani Principes* and *Pastoralis Cura*. Primarily, it was a claim whereby the pope could hope to control the actions of the future emperor in Italy, and point was added to it by the preoccupations of the papacy with the interests of France and Naples in the peninsula.[2] Lewis had flatly disregarded this papal theory ; he had not asked for papal approval of his election and he had performed acts of administration in Italy and Germany as if his election alone had given him full and sufficient title. On these political grounds had arisen the last great struggle between the empire and the papacy. Once the issue was joined Lewis proceeded to even more radical measures against the papacy ; he welcomed to his court Marsilio of Padua and John of Jandun ; after receiving the imperial crown at Rome in democratic form he deposed Pope John XXII and created an anti-pope ; he gave shelter to the rebellious Franciscans who, under Michael of Cesena, had fallen foul of John XXII over the question of evangelical poverty. Had the pope wished to depose Lewis he could have found pretext enough in these excesses, but from the papal standpoint there was little need for such action. According to the papal theory Lewis had never been king of the Romans, nor even effective ruler of Germany [3] because his election had not been approved by the pope. Since the death of Henry VII the empire had been vacant, and *vacante imperio* the pope had the right to administer. This claim was quite generally accepted in Europe ; it was in the interest of France and Naples to deal with a friendly

[1] Cf. H. E. Feine, 'Die Approbation der Luxemburgischen Kaiser in ihren Rechtsformen an der Kurie' (*Zeitschrift der Savigny-Stiftung für Rechtsgeschichte*, lviii (1938)), *Kanon. Abt.* xxvii. 364–5.

[2] See most recently on this subject F. Bock, 'Kaisertum Kurie und Nationalstaat im Beginn des 14 Jahrhunderts' (*Römische Quartalschrift f. christl. Altertumsk.* xliv (1936)).

[3] Cf. G. Frotscher, *Die Anschauungen von Papst Johann XXII über Kirche und Staat*, 99–107, where the rich and confusing literature on this point is discussed.

III

pope rather than with a German ruler capable of resisting French aggression on the western frontiers of the empire and the advance of Neapolitan power in Italy; John of Bohemia subscribed to it, as a weapon against one of his greatest rivals for dynastic influence in Germany; and in the privacy of the English records Lewis was not infrequently denied the imperial title which it was an essential part of English policy to grant him in public.[1]

There was thus from the beginning an element of risk in Edward's relations with Lewis. At best the political position of the German partner was beset with doubts; at worst he might bring upon his ally the canonical penalties for *fautoria* of heretics.

I

Edward opened his negotiations with Lewis in August 1335.[2] Despite the opposition of the curia and some vacillation on the part of Lewis, by the summer of 1337 the English envoys had concluded a treaty with the emperor. Edward's ratification of the treaty on 26 August announced that it had been struck for the recovery, defence, and conservation of the rights and possessions of Lewis and the empire from French usurpation. A scheme was adumbrated whereby Lewis and Edward were to appear in person at the curia, there to coerce the pope into reconciling Lewis. Moreover, Lewis was to join Edward in his expedition against France, meeting him on 30 November with two thousand men-at-arms. For this service he was to receive 400,000 florins, to be paid at Dordrecht in two instalments, 300,000 florins on 29 September and the remainder on 2 February 1338.[3]

Edward did not appear on the continent until the summer of 1338. In early September he met Lewis at the *Reichstag* of Coblence, and a little later began to use the title of Vicar of the Holy Roman Empire. The grant of this title had obviously been a stipulation of the earlier negotiations, during which even higher honours for Edward had been considered.[4] In July 1337

[1] In the English records Lewis was frequently referred to as '*dux Bavarr*' or '*dominus Bavarr*'. Cf., e.g., the account of John Thrandeston for his embassy to Germany in May 1340 in the Wardrobe counter-roll of William Cusance (Public Record Office, E. 101, 389/8); and the account of the expenses of Brother Geoffrey de Maldon, on his continental mission from 1336 to 1338, preserved in the Pipe Roll of 19 Edward III (P.R.O., E. 372, 190, m. 40).

* [2] John of Shoreditch and William Fitzwarin were then sent to Lewis at Nürnberg (*ibid.* 180, m. 44; 187, m. 48d).

[3] Rymer, *Foedera*, II, ii. 991.

[4] On 20 July 1337 Edward's envoys declared that he would make no use of the title or powers of vicar which he might have been granted unless Lewis failed to join him within six weeks of the payment of 300,000 florins at Dordrecht. As soon as Lewis and his army joined Edward the vicariate was to expire (I. A. Nijhoff, *Gedenkwaardigheden uit de Geschiedenis van Gelderland*, i. 317). Here the grant is referred to as a possibility, not as an existent fact, and the limited scope envisaged at this date is of interest.

Edward himself seems to have thought it possible that he might become king of Germany,[1] while in November rumours had reached the curia that Lewis intended to cede the imperial title to Edward, remaining ruler of Germany himself, or alternatively that Edward was to become both emperor and German king.[2]

The grant of the vicariate to Edward has generally been brought into connexion with the meeting of Lewis and Edward at Coblence, but, as Dr. Bock's researches have shown, it was from Frankfort on 15 September 1338 that Lewis issued Edward's letter of appointment, together with an announcement of his action to the empire.[3] The latter, proclaiming to all subjects of the empire that Edward had been created imperial vicar *per totam Alemanniam et Germaniam*, contained a general exhortation to obey him ; the terms of Lewis' letter to Edward are far more interesting. Herein Lewis declared that in view of Edward's proved zeal for the interests of the empire he had made him imperial vicar-general *per Alemanniam et Galliam et universas earum provincias sive partes*, with as much power as any former imperial vicar had had. If Edward resigned the office, Lewis would consult him about his successor, and the grant was not to be recalled before Edward had secured possession of the realm of France or the greater part of it, though otherwise Lewis reserved the right of disposing about the vicariate at his pleasure.

Despite the restriction implied in this last phrase, the grant was very extensive. In allowing Edward as much power as any former vicar had exercised, Lewis was in fact giving him sovereign rights in Germany. When Lewis' predecessor in the empire, Henry VII of Luxemburg, had left Germany on his Italian expedition he had made his son John of Bohemia his vicar, and there is record that in this capacity John pledged imperial possessions, exercised supreme jurisdictionary rights, confirmed imperial grants, and enfeoffed ecclesiastical princes with their regalities.[4] By the terms of his appointment Edward was to

[1] In an agreement with William, count of Holland, on 12 July Edward used the phrase : 'en cas . . . ke nous fussiens Roys d'Allemaigne ou vicaires del Empereur . . .' (*Foedera*, II, ii. 984).

[2] Benedict XII to Philip of France, 6 November (G. Daumet, *Benoît XII Lettres closes, patentes, et curiales se rapportant à la France*, 374). I cannot agree with J. de Sturler's conclusion in his article, 'Une démarche politique inconnue de Jean III, duc de Brabant' (*Revue Belge de Philologie et d'Histoire*, xiv. 1319–27), that Edward's letter of 20 August 1337 (*Foedera*, II, ii. 989) proves that at this date John had done homage to Edward as future emperor.

[3] Cf. Bock's articles in *ante*, xlv. 353 ff., and *Neues Archiv*, xlviii. 435–40, * announcing the discovery of these letters in Brit. Mus. Add. MS. 24062, fo. 151v, and John Rylands Library, Latin MS. 404, fos. 35v–36r.

[4] Cf. the Acta Vicariatus Generalis per Alemanniam, in *M.G.H. Constitutiones*, * IV, ii. appendix ii, especially 1104, 1117–20, 1132–3. Charles IV created some vicars with equally extensive powers, and others with far more restricted. Cf. L. Hüttebraüker, 'Die Vikare Karls IV in Deutschland' (*Festschrift Albert Brackmann*, 546–68).

have similar powers, even though the continued presence of Lewis in Germany would leave him a narrower field of action; and this fact was emphasized at the *Reichstag* of Coblence, when Archbishop Baldwin of Trier declared in the name of the electoral princes that a vicar of the empire possessed all the powers of the emperor himself.[1]

It thus becomes clear that in September 1338 Edward III, already the holder of one kingdom and claimant to another, was solemnly granted sovereign rights in a third. No very adequate reason has as yet been brought forward to explain why Edward was at pains to obtain this third title, and his imperial vicariate has commonly been dismissed as a rather fantastic episode. Such treatment, it may be suggested, does not do justice to Edward's intentions; the imperial vicariate was to him a piece of political calculation rather than a mere satisfaction of his illusions of greatness. But even if Edward's action in accepting the vicariate can be shown to be reasonable enough, there remains the question of Lewis' motives in granting it. What did he hope to gain from this delegation of his authority?

Some hint of the underlying rationality of the transaction may perhaps be discovered by a closer examination of the terms of the grant to Edward. While John of Bohemia had been 'vicar-general of the Holy Empire on this side of the mountains', 'vicar of the Roman Empire over Germany', 'common warden of the Roman Empire in Germany on this side of the mountains', Edward was to be vicar *per Alemanniam et Galliam et universas earum provincias sive partes*. The inclusion of *Gallia* in Edward's title is significant. The middle ages, depending on Caesar rather than the administrative terminology of the Roman Empire, considered all land west of the Rhine as *Gallia*, and French expansionist theory in the thirteenth century had made useful play of the equation of *Gallia* with France.[2] As the power of the empire declined, France steadily pushed her frontier eastwards at the expense of that part of the Empire which fell within Caesar's *Gallia*. The grant to Edward of a vicar's powers in precisely that part of the empire which suffered from French aggression is thus a valuable indication of the connexion of his title with a German policy of revendication of imperial rights in the west. What community of political interest existed between England and Germany in the fourteenth century lay in their opposition to the French monarchy; the technique which the French kings were using to expel the English from Aquitaine was also being used to bring under French control territory which for centuries had lain inside the imperial frontiers. The empire

[1] Kervyn de Lettenhove, *Oeuvres de Froissart*, ii. 548.

[2] F. Kern, *Die Anfänge der französischen Ausdehnungspolitik*, 19.

could hope to profit by Edward's attack on the Valois, and Edward found it convenient to operate from a base on the lower Rhine and with the help of German mercenaries. This interdependence of interests was reflected in the form of Edward's title.

Lewis, indeed, was willing to interpret *Gallia* very widely for Edward's benefit. On 13 March 1339 he wrote to the town of Ypres, addressing its inhabitants as *fideles* of the empire. Announcing his intention of proceeding against Philip of Valois, he warned the town to prepare for his coming, and to obey the commands of his vicar 'on the faith by which you are bound to us and to the Holy Roman Empire '.[1] But Lewis had no obvious right to send orders to Ypres, for the 'natural lords' of the town were the count of Flanders immediately and the king of France supremely, as Pope Benedict XII correctly pointed out a little later.[2] Only by an extension of imperial claims in *Gallia* as gross as any made by France could Lewis justify his commands to a town which lay well to the west of the Scheldt frontier. A double reason may be suggested for his action. In the first place it may well seem that Lewis in granting the vicariate and Edward in receiving it were attempting to establish a basis of right for the latter's dealings with the Flemish towns, analogous to that which he created when he obtained recognition as king of France: Edward could claim a legitimate footing in Flanders and give the Flemish towns a pretext of rebellion against their count either because as rightful king of France he was overlord of Flanders, or because Flanders, as part of *Gallia*, could be assumed to be subject to the empire of which he was vicar.[3] In the second place, Lewis' emphasis on imperial rights on the left bank of the Rhine, and even on rights which were not his on the left bank of the Scheldt, was evidence of an intention to place a bar to the eastward expansion of France even if he had to combat usurpation with the dubious weapons of counter-usurpation.

In the first half of the fourteenth century the French crown did not relax the ambitions which had guided it in the thirteenth century. The ideal of its policy was the Holy Roman Empire in French hands. In 1308 Philip the Fair of France strove to secure the election as king of the Romans of his brother, Charles of Valois, and after the death of the Emperor Henry VII there

[1] J. F. Boehmer, *Acta Imperii Selecta*, 788.

[2] Daumet, 677. There were, of course, still current at this time vague ideas of the universal supremacy of the emperor.

[3] At the very time when Lewis was writing to Ypres in the above terms Edward was appealing to the towns of Flanders to obey him as rightful king of France. Cf. the 'Sommacien an den grave omme syn leen 't ontfanghene van den keyserike, ende ooc van den croone van Vranckerike', printed by Kervyn de Lettenhove, 'Du vicariat impérial conféré à Edouard III' (*Annales de la Société d'Émulation pour l'étude de l'histoire et des antiquités de la Flandre*, ix. 2e serie, 338–53).

III

was another project for a French candidature. The idea was alive in 1324, and perhaps also in 1328.[1] Meanwhile Philip VI of Valois was willing to work for gains less complete than the absorption of the whole empire. More moderate, though still important aims appeared in the agreement (undoubtedly of French composition) made between Philip and Henry XIV, duke of Lower Bavaria, in 1333, when a scheme was on foot to secure Lewis the Bavarian's abdication of the empire and Henry's succession to it.[2] In return for Philip's help Henry engaged to respect the existing boundaries of France: a concession which amounted to a ratification of past usurpations. Moreover, he promised to hand over certain territories to Philip, and though this transaction was disguised by the fiction of pawn it would have amounted in fact to a transfer of sovereignty. The territories which were thus to pass to France included the counties of Provence and Forcalquier, the ecclesiastical temporalities of Arles, Avignon, Orange, St. Paul-Trois-Châteaux, Valence, Embrun, Vienne, Geneva, Besançon, Sion, and Lausanne, with the cities of the same name, the Dauphiny, Faucigny, Savoy, and Bresse, the Free County of Burgundy, the city of Die, the temporalities of the bishopric of Cambrai together with the city and county of Cambrai, and anything of the temporalities of Lyons and Viviers which might lie within the empire. These were territories where the empire had ceased to exercise effective control, but legally and historically they belonged to the empire, for which they would again be claimed by Charles IV,[3] and it was far more tolerable from the German point of view that they should continue to lead an independent existence under nominal German suzerainty than that they should be incorporated into the aggressive French state, which would thereby be brought within striking distance of the Rhine and Italy.

This particular scheme came to nothing, but it gives a clear indication of the aims which French policy was engaged in realizing piecemeal during Lewis the Bavarian's reign. In 1343 the dauphin of Vienne was persuaded to sell his lands to France, a show of legitimacy being given the business by its ratification by Pope Clement VI, administrator of the empire, as he claimed, *vacante imperio*.[4] The Dauphin Humbert had long been subject

[1] Cf. K. Wenck, 'Französische Werbungen um die deutsche Königskrone' (*Historische Zeitschrift*, lxxxvi. 252 ff.); *M.G.H. Constitutiones*, v. 952; E. E. Stengel, *Avignon und Rhens*, 36 ff.

[2] Boehmer, 1033; cf. G. Sievers, *Die politischen Beziehungen Kaiser Ludwigs des Baiern zu Frankreich*, 191.

[3] Cf. B. Mendl and F. Quicke, 'Les relations franco-impériales de 1355 à 1356' (*Revue Belge de Philologie et d'Histoire*, viii).

[4] C. U. J. Chevalier, *Regeste dauphinois*, vi. 31952. Clement's confirmation, 'tam apostolica quam imperiali auctoritate', is printed by E. Déprez, *Clément VI, Lettres closes, patentes, et curiales se rapportant à la France*, 1013.

to French influence ; he was a feudatory of the French crown as well as of the empire. The count of Savoy found himself in the same position, and as a French vassal took part in the autumn campaign of 1339 against Lewis' vicar.[1] In the Argonne the process of penetration which had taken the French frontier under Philip the Fair up to the Meuse [2] was continued under his successors, whose goal was now Verdun. French 'safeguard' was imposed on this imperial city in 1315, 1318, and 1327, and though there was some pretence of respecting imperial rights the value of this formality can be gauged from the French claim inserted in all three treaties : *quod ipsa civitas est infra regni nostri limites situata.*[3] Elsewhere in this region French influence was being strengthened by the usual devices of 'safeguard' and *pariage.*[4] Further north, in the district of Ostrevant, which was a dependency of Hainault and had been considered imperial territory from the twelfth century onwards, France attempted to establish her claims, first raised under Philip the Fair, by performing acts of administration and encouraging appeals to Paris.[5] There is no reason to doubt the complaint of William, count of Holland and Hainault, when in 1340 he accused the French king of committing usurpations at various places 'in Ostrevant, at St. Amand en Peble, and on the borders of my castleries of Ath and Lens '.[6]

Equally tempting to France was the ambiguity of the position of Cambrai, a French-speaking city of the empire, which had as its lord the bishop, who was at once a prince of the empire and a suffragan of the province of Rheims. In August 1335 Lewis the Bavarian found it necessary to order Bishop Guido of Auvergne to prevent the acquisition of fortified places in his territory by certain French nobles.[7] Lewis' grounds were plainly expressed as those of public policy : such a transfer would do no small damage to the rights of the empire. His fears were amply justified when the importance of these fortifications and the person of the purchaser were revealed. In February 1337 Engergier, lord of Amboise, and Marie de Flandres his wife ceded to Philip VI of France their titles to the fortresses of Crèvecoeur,

[1] Cf. J. Cordey, *Les comtes de Savoie et les rois de France pendant la Guerre de Cent Ans*, ch. ii.

[2] Cf. Kern, *Ausdehnungspolitik*, 212 ; Ch. Aimond, *Les relations de la France et du Verdunois*, 80.

[3] Aimond, *Pièces justificatives*, ix, x, xiii.

[4] J. Havet, 'La frontière de l'Empire dans l'Argonne' (*Bibliothèque de l'École de Chartes*, xlii. 392). *

[5] Cf. E. Delcambre, 'L'Ostrevant du IXe au XIIIe siècle' (*Le Moyen Age*, 2e série, xxviii) ; J. Viard, 'L'Ostrevant—Enquête au sujet de la frontière française sous Philippe de Valois' (*Bibliothèque de l'École de Chartes*, lxxxii. 325–6).

[6] Kervyn de Lettenhove, *Oeuvres de Froissart*, xviii. 136.

[7] *Neues Archiv*, l. 627; cf. H. Dubrulle, *Cambrai à la fin du moyen-âge*, 280 ; Lucas, *op. cit.* 196. *

Arleux, St. Soupplet, Rumilly, and the castlery of Cambrai.[1] In the form of a private purchase the French king thus obtained a number of important posts to the east of the Scheldt and well within the imperial border.

The German reaction was immediate and strong; Lewis quickly concluded the alliance for which the English envoys had been angling, and he appointed Reinald, count of Gelders, and William, margrave of Jülich, as imperial vicars throughout the diocese and city of Cambrai.[2] The warmth of national feeling aroused seems to have disconcerted Philip, who thought it necessary to send circular letters to the Rhineland denying that he had usurped any imperial rights.[3] But his soft speeches deceived no one; the tendencies of French policy had been too continuous to be misunderstood.[4] Not even the most international circle in Germany, the *curia* of Baldwin, archbishop of Trier, was impervious to the nationalist excitement.[5] And it was to French usurpations, as much as to the papal claim to approve the elected king of the Romans, that the electoral princes were referring when they declared in the *Kurverein* at Lahnstein on 15 July 1338: *das selbe Romische riche an seinem eren, rechten und guden . . . angegriffen, gecrenket und beswert sin.*

Under these circumstances there seem very strong reasons for not dismissing as mere rhetoric the expressed intention of the treaty of alliance between Edward and Lewis in 1337: *pro adquisitione recuperatione et conservatione cunctorum . . . iurium honorum hereditatum possessionum rerum et querelarum imperii.* The empire had considerable wrongs to avenge, and a favourable opportunity would be offered by the outbreak of the Anglo-French war. It seems certain that the grant of the vicariate or its equivalent was among the conditions of the alliance. What was the advantage which was expected to accrue to the English for their help in recovering lost imperial rights: the advantage

[1] It was not until May 1340 that the bishop of Cambrai, from whom these possessions depended, enfeoffed Philip's eldest son, John of Normandy, with them, on the condition that they should never be held directly by the king of France (Kervyn de Lettenhove, *Oeuvres de Froissart*, xviii. 144: Dubrulle, 281).

[2] Nijhoff, *Gedenkwaardigheden*, i. 315.

[3] One copy of the circular, addressed to the *Raugraf* Georg is printed by E. E. Stengel, *Nova Alamanniae*, 477. Another was brought to Cologne by two French envoys and read before the city council on 23 October (*Chronique de Richard Lescot*, ed. by J. Lemoine, app. iv).

[4] The inevitable course of relations between France and the Empire was exactly hit off by Robert of Anjou, in his plea to the curia after the death of Henry VII to confirm no one as king of the Romans: 'Ecce quidem statim quod eligitur rex Alamanie . . . statim habet oculum livoris et punicionis contra regem Francie, eo pretextu quod dicitur dictum regem Francie occupasse multa iura et terras imperiales et specialiter a flumine Saone citra versus Franciam' (*M.G.H. Constitutiones*, IV, ii. 1253).

[5] Cf. the memorandum written by Baldwin's councillor, Rudolf Losse, between September and December 1338, printed by Stengel, *Nova Alamanniae*, 581.

which could be secured only by making Edward III vicar of the empire ?

A clue to the answer to this question is to be found in a piece of imperial legislation carried through at the *Reichstag* of Coblence on 5 September 1338. Here, in a solemn assembly of the electoral princes and in the presence of Edward, the emperor decreed that all subjects of the empire were bound to stand by him or his vicar to maintain and defend the honours, customs, and rights of the empire. He then demanded of the electors present their *Weisthum* as to how those who broke this ruling offended against him and the empire, and what remedy was to be had against them. The electors declared that such a crime was treason, and Lewis thereupon pronounced their opinion to be imperial law.[1] Consequently, when Edward became vicar, he gained the right to enforce service against France from the subjects of the Empire under penalties of treason. Thereby he was armed not only with a ready excuse for attacking those imperial vassals who were allied to France, such as the bishop of Liège, John of Bohemia, and the count of Flanders, but also (and this was probably the more important consideration) with a means of coercion by which his German mercenaries might be held to their engagements. By the end of September 1338 a great number of the territorial rulers in the Rhineland had covenanted to help Edward against France in return for payment, and if he might neglect as being far from disinterested papal warnings about the untrustworthiness of the Germans,[2] he could not forget the experience of his grandfather. Edward I's carefully constructed system of alliances with Adolf of Nassau and the German princes had not withstood the bribes of the French king,[3] and so Edward III had good cause to reflect on the weakness of a simple mercenary bond between himself and his allies. By obtaining the public authority of the empire he could hope to strengthen his private treaties with the dynasts and princes of Germany. So much weight did he lay on this point that he was willing to affront the papal contention that the empire was vacant and its administration rested with the papacy. While Edward used his vicariate to prepare his inroad into France through Cambrai, and his

[1] Stengel, *op. cit.* 556.

[2] Cf. Benedict XII's letter to Edward, 5 March 1340 (Daumet, 699), in which he warns him that he will find the Flemings and Germans loyal as long as he has any money left, and no longer.

[3] Cf. Kern, 'Die Bestechung K. Adolfs von Nassau' (*Mitteilungen des österreichischen Instituts für Geschichtsforschung*, xxx. 423 ff.); Bock, 'Englands Beziehungen zum Reich unter Adolf von Nassau' (*ibid.* Erg. Bd. xii. 244). V. Samanek's latest attempt to defend Adolf's honesty, in his article, 'Der angebliche Verrat Adolfs von Nassau' (*Historische Vierteljahrschrift*, xxix. 326–35), does not shake the damning evidence of the memorandum of Musciatto Franzesi (*M.G.H. Constitutiones*, iii. 645). *

campaign in 1339 was based, as Benedict XII complained, 'on the pretext of a certain process which he, wrongfully calling himself vicar of the empire, is said to have made against the church and county of Cambrai,' [1] it seems probable that the vicariate was intended less for use against the few imperial feudatories who were openly hostile than as a potential means of making Edward's avowed allies stand by their obligations.

Support for this theory is found in two of Edward's few recorded acts [2] as vicar. On 18 September 1338 he called a meeting of the great lords of the lower Rhine at Herck for 12 October, for the publication of the orders and intentions of the emperor. In the summons the legislation of Coblence was specifically mentioned, and the penalty of deprivation of their imperial fees was threatened against absentees.[3] On 20 November Edward called upon John, duke of Brabant, William, count of Holland and Hainault, Reinald of Gelders, William of Jülich, Adolph, count of Marck, and others to appear in arms between Mons and Binche on 18 December, thence to proceed to recover the imperial rights and possessions long usurped in the counties of Flanders, Cambrai, and Burgundy by Philip of Valois.[4] Again there was reference to the enactments of Coblence, invoked against imperial feudatories who were all in Edward's pay. The vicar's intention to use imperial authority to enforce his private contracts clearly appears. So also does the limitation of the use he could make of that authority. Edward could not hope to make the German vassals attack France at their own expense, as on a strict interpretation of feudal law they were bound to do. They were to proceed, said Edward, *nostris expensis :* the private treaty peeps through the public summons.

II

It is well known that the agreement between Edward III and Lewis failed completely ; that Edward obtained no substantial assistance from Germany for his autumn campaign of 1339 ; and that Lewis, having made a treaty with Philip of Valois in January 1341, recalled Edward's vicariate three months later. This

[1] Daumet, 648.

[2] The roll of Edward's acts as vicar (P.R.O., Chancery Misc. 32/1) remains only in fragments, containing at present seven documents.

* [3] H. Laurent, *Actes et documents intéressant la Belgique conservés aux Archives de l'État à Vienne*, 83, prints from the original the summons sent to John of Brabant. For the enrolment of the summons in Chancery Misc. 32/1 and its registration in John Rylands Library, Latin MS. 404, cf. Bock, *ante*, xlv. 366. On 12 October from Diest Edward sent out the summons again, for a meeting at Malines on 26 October (Nijhoff, *Gedenkwaardigheden*, i. 336).

[4] Laurent, 84 ; enrolment and registration as above. Laurent and Lucas (*op. cit.* 298) have confused Adolph, count of Marck, with Adolph, bishop of Liège.

diplomatic revolution has commonly been explained by reference to Lewis' qualms of conscience and his intense desire to gain reconciliation with the church. His appreciation of French influence at the curia led him, it is supposed, to trust in the mediation of Philip of Valois, and thus to commit the gross political error of exchanging the English alliance, by which the pope might have been forced into granting reconciliation, for a mere promise of French support at Avignon : a promise which the whole trend of French policy at the time shows never to have been honestly intended.[1]

Serious objections may, however, be raised against this construction. In the first place it is based on the assumption that Lewis' repeated efforts to make peace with the church were the result of overwhelming spiritual anxieties.[2] But there seems evidence enough to show, on the contrary, that these efforts proceeded very largely from Lewis' desire to escape from the unhappy political consequences of excommunication. The personal, spiritual dangers of his condition as an outlaw from the church were counteracted by the simple theory that an unjust excommunication had no binding force, and in fact while under the church's ban Lewis continued his conventional religious exercises and had no difficulty in finding clergy willing to conduct his services for him.[3] His eagerness to accept reconciliation was constantly tempered by a stubborn refusal to agree to the Papacy's demand that he should admit the validity of its theory of approbation ; and in 1338 and the years following this attitude was fortified by national support expressed in a succession of great assemblies of the German estates.[4] The supposition, therefore, that it was fears for the safety of his soul which drove Lewis into an alliance with France as the surest means of obtaining reconciliation with the church is unwarranted. And secondly, it may be doubted whether the hope of French mediation at the curia played any part at all in deciding Lewis for the French alliance.

As an alternative, it may be suggested that the Anglo-German agreement broke down for two reasons : Edward's inability to fulfil his promised payments to the emperor, and Lewis' continued obsession with Italy, which prevented him from supporting whole-heartedly any scheme for a concerted attack on France.

Edward's difficulties in carrying out the financial side of his

[1] Cf., e.g., W. T. Waugh, *Cambridge Med. Hist.* vii. 133.

[2] Cf. the phrase of the late Edward Armstrong : 'the alternations between violence and remorse of a rough superstitious soldier' (*Italian Studies,* 45).

[3] In 1336 Lewis declared that he had 'gotz dienst all zeit geheort und och gotes lichnam dick enphangen' (S. Riezler, *Die literarischen Widersacher der Päpste zur Zeit Ludwig des Baiers,* 328).

[4] Cf. R. Moeller, *Ludwig der Bayer und die Kurie im Kampf um das Reich ;* E. E. Stengel, *Avignon und Rhens,* ch. 4.

engagements to Lewis appeared at the very beginning of his vicariate. When he met Lewis at Coblence in September 1338 he admitted that he had paid only 80,000 of the 400,000 florins stipulated in the agreement of 1337, and engaged to clear off the debt by 21 March 1339, under pain of losing the active support of the emperor.[1] Before this date, on 12 March, Edward made a new arrangement through William of Jülich and Reinald of Gelders : his debt for the 2000 men whom Lewis was to lead against France was fixed at 300,000 Florentine florins, and Lewis was not bound to move against France until two-thirds of this sum had been paid to him at Frankfurt and the remainder placed to his credit at Cologne.[2] From the wardrobe account of William Northwell it is possible to gauge how far short Edward fell of satisfying these obligations. Between 11 July 1338 and 23 January 1339 Lewis received from Edward's agent, John Montgomery, 32,464 florins *de scuto* and 1 florin *de florentia*, in two instalments ; on 16 April 1339, 100 more florins were paid, and
* on 21 April, 4000 florins.[3] With this Edward's payments to Lewis seem to have come to an end, leaving a huge discrepancy between promise and fulfilment which sapped the foundations of the Anglo-German alliance. In August 1339 it was thought necessary to make a declaration that the pacts between the two rulers were still in existence and would be kept as long as they lived,[4] but Edward's failure to carry out his part in the agreement of March completely excused Lewis' passivity during the autumn campaign of 1339. Edward's impecuniosity, together with his ill success in the field, gravely shook his standing in Germany. When in the following year the domestic crisis called him back to England, the truce which he made at Esplechin in September with the French without consulting Lewis provided the latter with a pretext to break the Anglo-German agreement.

It may be doubted, however, whether Lewis would have put much energy into the attack on France even if Edward had been able to pay him the promised subsidies. His attention was still concentrated on Italy, for despite the failure of his *Römerzug* he did not relinquish the hope of making the resources of Italy available for the empire. And at the very time that the alliance with England was being made, conditions in Italy became propitious for imperial intervention. Mastino and Alberto, heirs of Cangrande della Scala, had formed a mighty dominion in north Italy, comprising Verona, Padua, Vicenza, Treviso, Brescia, Feltre, Belluno, Parma, and Lucca. This had aroused fears and jealousies throughout north Italy ; Venice went to war with the Scaligeri in May 1336, being joined a month later by Florence,

[1] *Neues Archiv*, xxiii, 350.
[2] *Ibid.* 352.
[3] P.R.O., E. 36, 203, p. 328.
[4] *Neues Archiv*, xxiii. 358.

and in March 1337 by the Visconti, Obizzo d'Este and Alois Gonzaga. In July 1337 Charles of Moravia, the son of Lewis' great rival, the Luxemburger, John of Bohemia, allied himself to these confederates. Against these enemies Mastino and Alberto were incompetent and unsuccessful, and their only hope lay in help from Lewis, which they were begging desperately in January 1337.[1] Throughout 1336 and 1337 Lewis was in touch with the Scaligeri through his most experienced Italian agent, John of Chiaramonte,[2] and he did his best to help them by diplomatic means. At the beginning of 1338, for instance, he attempted to detach Alois Gonzaga from the league against Verona ; in January Alois was promised an imperial vicariate over Reggio, Asola, and various territories of Cremona, and it was hardly a coincidence that on 10 February a treaty of peace and perpetual friendship was made between the Scaligeri and Alois, in which mutual aid was pledged against all *excepto Romano imperio*.[3]

Lewis did not intend to limit his assistance to mere diplomatic action of this kind ; he planned a new expedition over the Alps. Rumours of this had reached the curia at the end of December 1337, when the patriarch of Aquileia was praised for the steps he had taken to oppose Lewis' passage, and was granted a crusading indulgence to aid him further.[4] In his renewal to the Habsburgers of their imperial vicariate over Treviso and Padua on 4 January 1338 Lewis hinted that he would soon be in Lombardy, and a few weeks later, when ordering Venice to disband the army which it was maintaining on imperial soil, he announced that he was collecting forces wherewith to crush those who had rebelled against the imperial authority in Italy.[5]

At the time these plans came to nothing. Throughout 1338

[1] *Historia Cortusiorum*, ed. Muratori, 875.

[2] John of Chiaramonte, count of Modica and lord of Ragusa, fled from Sicily finally in 1332, as a result of the long feud between the families of Chiaramonte and Ventimiglia (cf. Haberkern, *Der Kampf um Sizilien in den Jahren 1302–37*, 141–7). From 1325 onwards he appears as Lewis' expert adviser on Italian affairs, acting as rector for Peter of Corbara in the Mark of Ancona, and falling under the papal ban in January 1330 (*M.G.H. Constitutiones*, vi. 686). In 1335 he entered the service of Robert of Naples, commanding the Neapolitan fleet against Sicily, but soon returned to his old master, Lewis. Then he entered the service of Mastino della Scala (G. Villani, *Cronaca*, lib. xi, c. 29). He was at Verona in February 1336, and was fighting for the Scaligeri in July, and also in the next year. In February 1338 he went as envoy from Lewis to Alois Gonzaga (*Historia Cortusiorum*, 869, 871 ; *Vita Karoli*, ed. Boehmer, 255 ; J. F. Boehmer, *Acta Imperii Selecta*, 781).

[3] *Ibid.* 777, 781 ; C. Cipolla, 'Documenti per la storia delle relazioni diplomatiche fra Verona e Mantova nel secolo xiv' (*Miscellanea di Storia Veneta*, 2ª serie, xii, parte 1, 316).

[4] J. M. Vidal, *Benoît XII Lettres closes et patentes intéressant les pays autres que la France*, 1608, 9.

[5] G-B. Verci, *Storia della Marca Trivigiana e Veronese*, xi, doc. mcccxxv ; Boehmer, *Acta Imperii Selecta*, 780.

Lewis was too occupied with the business of constitutional definition and in waiting for the often postponed appearance of Edward III on the continent to intervene actively in Italy. Left to their own resources the Scaligeri fared badly and were forced to accept an unfavourable peace in January 1339, their bitterness at Lewis' failure to help them being such that they immediately sought agreement with the papacy. Yet despite the sorry issue of his projects there can be no doubt that the years 1337–8 brought a revival of Lewis' Italian ambitions, and so introduced an awkward dualism into his policy.[1] An active Italian policy was incompatible with the fulfilment of the terms of his alliance with Edward; if such a policy was to be carried into effect it demanded peace on the western frontier of the empire.

Philip of Valois was not unaware of Lewis' distracted interests, and even in 1338 attempted to seduce him from the English alliance. From June to September 1338 the French intermediary, the duke of Lorraine, was trying to arrange a meeting between Philip and Lewis, or at least a conference between their representatives. Though these efforts gave the pope some cause for alarm, they were hardly regarded seriously on the imperial side, and it seems safe to suppose that Lewis' good faith to Edward was still unimpaired, and that he tolerated the French advances only in order to engage Philip's attention until Edward could cross the channel.[2] The critical period for the Anglo-German alliance did not come until the spring of 1340. Although in February and March rumours had reached the curia that Lewis and Edward were planning a joint attack on France through Besançon,[3] the failure of Edward's campaign in the Cambrésis and his return to England had strained Lewis' loyalty too far. Edward found it quite impossible to make the payments he had promised to his allies and seems himself to have considered that the game was up with his system of German alliances; at the beginning of 1340 he withdrew from the Austrian court his little daughter Johanna, whose proposed marriage to a Habsburg prince had been intended to corroborate one of the most important details of this system.[4]

Rapprochement between Lewis and France soon followed. On 13 June Philip informed the pope that he had accepted Lewis'

[1] This dualism is well illustrated in Lewis' quittance to the imperial town of Wetzlar in May 1338 for ' eine gewonliche stuir ze hilf und ze dienst zu unsere vart gen Frankrich und gen Lampparten ' (*Urkundenbuch d. Stadt Wetzlar*, i. 1323).

[2] Cf. J. Reichert, *Die politischen Beziehungen Kaiser Ludwigs des Bayern zu England und Frankreich im Jahre 1337–47* (Diss. Heidelberg, 1931), 11 ff.

[3] G. Gorrini, ' Lettere inedite degli ambasciatori fiorentini alla Corte dei Papi in Avignone, anno 1340 ' (*Archivio Storico Italiano*, 4ª serie, xiv, lett. 2, 4, and 5).

[4] Edward's agent, John Montgomery, drew wages between 16 December 1339 and 15 April 1340 for his journey to Austria to fetch Johanna (P.R.O., E. 36, 203, p. 184).

offer to mediate in the quarrel between England and France, but on condition that the pope also should be allowed to make efforts in this direction. Philip's statement that this proposal had been made by his niece Margaret, Lewis' wife, was probably disingenuous ; it seems likely that the initiative had lain with Philip.[1]

Benedict XII would have nothing to do with this scheme ; he could not regard an open enemy of the church as a fit person to mediate. But contact had been established between Lewis and Philip, and with the failure of Edward's new campaign before Tournai and his retreat to England at the end of October, the way lay open for an alliance of the Empire with France.

On 24 January 1341 Lewis swore lifelong friendship to France, and four days later he promised to leave Philip in peaceful possession of all the territories, jurisdictions, and so forth, which he held *de facto* at that moment.[2] Lewis completed the abandonment of his policy of revindication of lost imperial rights in the West by promising to recall Edward's imperial vicariate as soon as he had received Philip's ratification of the treaty.[3] Philip issued the necessary documents on 15 March, and a month later Lewis formally revoked Edward's vicariate, at the same time announcing that Philip had entrusted him with the task of making peace between France and England.[4] It may be suspected that this stipulation was as empty as its counterpart, the power given to Philip to negotiate a settlement of Lewis' quarrel with the church ; such respect for the decencies could not hide the fact

[1] It seems permissible to deduce French initiative from the grant made in June 1340 by Philip to Geoffroi de Nancy of the *corvées* in Rigny-la-Salle, Thusey, and Chalaines, ' pour considération des bons et agréables services qu'il nous a faiz et fait de jour en jour, en exposant sa personne a plusieurs et divers perilz et esperons que il nous face encore ou temps avenir ' (J. Viard, *Bulletin de la Société historique et archéologique de Langres*, iii. 430 ff.). As clerk in the service of the duke of Lorraine, Geoffroi had been engaged in the pourparlers between Lewis and France in 1338 (cf. E. Winkelmann, *Acta Imperii Inedita*, ii. 602, 604), and in that year appears in receipt of a pension from the French king (*Journaux du Trésor de Philippe VI de Valois*, ed. by J. Viard, 5381). When Lewis made his oath of friendship to France at Vilshofen in Bavaria on 24 January 1341 ' Jofridus de Nanceyo ' was among the witnesses (Kervyn de Lettenhove, *Oeuvres de Froissart*, xviii, doc. xlviii) ; it was presumably for his part in bringing about this alliance that Geoffroi in March 1341 was granted an additional 100 livres a year on his fees from the French crown (Bibliothèque Nationale, nouv. acq. lat. 2314, pièce 10). It is almost certain that the account of Mathias von Neuenburg (*Chronica*, ed. by A. Hofmeister, i. 155) of the *rapprochement* between Lewis and Philip in 1340, ' Tunc misit Francus nuncium et litteras imperatrici filie sororis sue, quam dominam Alamanniae scripsit, ut inter ipsum et principem concordiam ordinaret et sibi nuncium de quo princeps confiderat, destinaret ', should be applied to Geoffroi. The German envoy sent in return was Ulrich von Augsburg (cf. Daumet, 727 ; J. F. Boehmer, *Regesta Imperii . . . ab anno 1314 usque ad annum 1347*, 2122).

[2] Kervyn de Lettenhove, *loc. cit.* ; Winkelmann, 626.

[3] *Ibid.* 627.

[4] Stengel, *Nova Alamanniae*, 669 ; Winkelmann, 629.

that the new arrangement implied desertion of Edward by Lewis and of the pope by Philip.[1]

It was suggested above that Lewis' motive for making an alliance with France lay in a wish to satisfy his Italian ambitions. This suggestion is supported by evidence of his continued interest in Italian affairs after 1338. From 1339 to 1342 Italy was full of rumours of an impending invasion from Germany,[2] and in the latter year imperial troops under the duke of Teck and the burgrave of Nürnberg entered Italy at the request of Florence to help her in her war for Lucca.[3] Action of this kind was certain to aggravate the discord between Lewis and the pope, who demanded as an invariable pre-requisite of Lewis' reconciliation that he should abstain from Italian politics. Yet it was precisely freedom for such action which Lewis had bought by making the French alliance. It is therefore impossible to consider the diplomatic revolution of 1340–1 as the result of Lewis' painful anxiety for peace with the church. It was for Italy, not to quieten qualms of conscience, that Lewis gave up the western policy symbolized in Edward's vicariate.

III

Edward was left both anxious and resentful by this breakdown. He had risked canonical censure by communicating with a condemned heretic, and after the avowed French partisan Clement VI had succeeded Benedict XII in May 1342 there was a genuine fear in England that the pope might help the French cause by proceeding against Edward for his past relations with Lewis. Evidence of this fear is to be found in the draft of an appeal by Edward to a general council, which may be dated between Easter 1343 and the end of 1345.[4] In this Edward

[1] Both Benedict XII and Edward III took the desertion ill. In a letter to Philip dated 23 April 1341, Benedict expressed dismay at the break in the tradition of common action by France and the Curia in the matter of Lewis' reconciliation (Daumet, 832). On 14 July Edward sent a very cool reply to Lewis' letter of 25 June, in which had been announced the recall of Edward's vicariate and Lewis' offer to mediate (*Foedera*, II, ii. 1166, 1167–8).

[2] In August 1339 it was expected in Italy that Lewis would come to Lombardy before the end of September (Winkelmann, 1147); in November 1340 Benedict XII informed Robert of Naples that he had heard from the patriarch of Aquileia that Lewis was seeking to pass into Italy (S. Riezler, *Vatikanische Akten zur deutschen Geschichte in der Zeit Kaiser Ludwigs des Bayern*, 2087); in May 1341 Alois Gonzaga informed Robert of Naples that Lewis was attempting to persuade John Henry of Tirol to allow him passage through his county to Italy (Winkelmann, 1152).

[3] G. Villani, *Cronaca*, lib. xi, c. 138. The importance of this incident has probably been exaggerated, and the work of a small clique in Florence has been magnified into an official act of the Commune. Cf. R. Caggese, *Roberto d'Angio e i suoi tempi*, ii. 277–9, against A. Sapori, *La crisi delle compagnie mercantili dei Bardi e dei Peruzzi*, 144.

* [4] This appeal is to be found in the *Opus collectum et compilatum per venerabilem patrem Thomam Bekyntone Bath. et Wellens. episcopum*, a collection of materials made

makes a variety of excuses for his alliance with Lewis : extreme necessity, advice of the learned, hope of persuading Lewis to abjure his excesses against the church, and ignorance of the papal processes against Lewis, which were not then published in Germany. He now annuls all the dealings which he has had with Lewis, so far as they offend the church, and offers to submit himself to the church's correction. Since Clement VI is a suspect judge, however, because of his sympathies with Philip of Valois, Edward appeals to the judgement of a general council. This appeal remained in the form of a draft and was never published. But the fact of its composition is evidence of Edward's fears, and his wish to dissociate himself from the German connexion.[1]

In this wish was reflected a change in the strategic elements of the Anglo-French war. Though it was obvious that the truce made at Esplechin in 1340 would not be renewed after its expiry at midsummer 1342, the occasion and the theatre of renewed hostilities were now to be found in Brittany. Duke John III of Brittany died in April 1341, in September the parlement of Paris adjudged the duchy to Philip's nephew, Charles de Blois, and between August and October Edward III had allied himself to the other claimant, Jean de Montfort. The first English contingent under Walter Manny landed in December 1341, the second under Robert of Artois in August 1342 ; Edward was to appear in person in October. This change in the English point of attack made the support of the Low Countries (where in any case Edward's influence was rapidly declining) [2] and of Germany far less important to Edward than it had been in 1337–8. When Frederick of Austria wrote in October 1343, asking that the arrangement for his marriage to Edward's daughter Johanna, which had formed part of the English system of alliances in Germany from 1336 onwards, should now be carried out, Edward found no difficulty in giving an oblique refusal and expressed his disgust at the conduct of his former allies : *speratum et promissum auxilium per amicos et parentes vestros nobis factum nec pactiones inter nos et ipsos unitae statutis fuerunt temporibus observatae.*[3] Johanna was intended to play a part in a more promising scheme,

between 1443 and 1465 to support the English claim to the crown of France : Brit. Mus. Cottonian MS. Tiberius B. xii. fos. 6v–8v ; Brit. Mus. Harleian MS. 4763, fos. 3r–5r ; Brit. Mus. Harleian MS. 861, fos. 3r–5r.

[1] It may be noticed that among the papers taken by the English embassy to Avignon in September 1344 was a legal opinion about the excuses which might be made for Edward's alliance with Lewis : ' Si rex ductus huiusmodi necessitate aliquotiens excesserit prohibitionem papalem in communicando cum persona vetita, dum tamen non in prohibitionis causa sed aliunde pro bono iuris recuperandi communicaverit, excusabilis reputabitur ' (Brit. Mus. Cottonian MS. Cleopatra E. ii. fos. 44r–v).

[2] Cf. Lucas, *op. cit.* ch. xii.

[3] Frederick's letter to Edward, dated 28 October, P.R.O., SC. 1, 37/182 ; Edward's answer, 1 March 1344, *Foedera*, III, i. 7.

a dynastic union with Castile. Such a union offered great strategic advantages, for it would protect Edward's rear in Guyenne and deprive Philip of Valois of a possible source of sea power,[1] and in September 1344 Edward was angling for a marriage between Johanna and Pedro, eldest son of Alfonso XI of Castile.[2] In this transaction is typified the difference between the first and second phases of the Hundred Years' War.

Under these circumstances the connexion between Edward and Lewis lapsed almost completely for some years after 1341.[3] Its renewal was the result of the progressive deterioration of the relations of both these princes with the papacy. The war in Brittany was interrupted in January 1343 by the truce of Malestroit, but all attempts by Clement VI to turn this truce, which his agents had contrived, into a definite peace failed, and at the same time Edward's administrative action against papal provisions to English benefices embittered Clement against him.[4] In May 1345 Lewis' last independent effort to gain reconciliation with the church broke down, in June Edward denounced the truce with France, and in the same month he replied favourably to a suggestion of Lewis' eldest son, the margrave of Brandenburg, that the Anglo-Imperial treaty should be revived.[5] But though envoys to discuss this matter in Germany were accredited in June and July, not until December do any active steps seem to have been taken.[6]

By this time, however, the prospects of a new alliance between Edward and Lewis had been destroyed by a new controversy. In September 1345 Count William IV of Holland-Hainault died, leaving no male heirs. The nearest of kin were his sisters, Margaret, Philippa, and Johanna, the wives of Lewis the Bavarian,

[1] Cf. G. Daumet, *Étude sur l'alliance de la France et de la Castille au XIV et XV siècles*, 2.

[2] *Foedera*, III, i. 21.

* [3] Between 1 February and 29 April 1341 John Thrandeston and John Burton were sent by Edward 'versus partes Alemannie ad imperatorem et ad omnes magnates et dominos de electione imperatoris' (P.R.O., E. 372, 187, m. 48). But we lack further information of the purpose of this embassy.

[4] Cf. E. Déprez, 'La conférence d'Avignon, 1344' (*Essays in Medieval History Presented to T. F. Tout*). M. Déprez confines himself to a discussion of the papal attempts to arbitrate in the Anglo-French struggle. The material for the question of provisions, which became very acute from 1343 onwards, has not yet been fully explored. The papers of the English embassy at the Curia in September 1344 (Brit. Mus. Cottonian MS. Cleopatra E. ii. fos. 36r–58v) show how vivid was the fear that Clement might be provoked to extreme action by the English measures against provisions.

* [5] Cf. *Foedera*, III, i. 43, Edward to Lewis of Brandenburg, 6 June.

[6] *Ibid. loc. cit.* (6 June); C.P.R. 1374–7, 508 (21 July); *Ibid.* III, i. 65, 66 (27 December). None of the envoys here accredited seems to have gone to Germany before Yves de Clinton, who travelled to High Germany to Lewis the Bavarian and William of Jülich between 29 December 1345 and 21 March 1346 (P.R.O., E. 101, 312/19).

Edward III, and William, margrave of Jülich, respectively. The question arose whether they were to succeed (female succession was a settled matter in Hainault) or whether William's territories were to be treated as fees of the Empire which had fallen in. Lewis settled the question to the advantage of his house in January 1346 by granting the whole patrimony of Avesnes to his wife, investing Margaret *de prescriptis comitatibus . . . iuribus et pertinentiis a nobis et Sacro Romano Imperio in feodum descendentibus tanquam veriorem proximiorem et antiquiorem heredem.*[1] Edward was greatly offended at this slighting of Philippa's claims, which he had taken immediate steps to assert, and on the satisfaction of which he seems to have made the conclusion of any new agreement with Lewis depend.[2] An alliance was now out of the question; indeed, in December 1345 and October 1346 the Wittelsbachers feared that the English would attempt to seize Zeeland. Both the pope and the French king did their best to widen this rift,[3] and though at a meeting between Philippa and Margaret at Ypres in October 1346 a personal agreement was approached, it was not until November that negotiations for the alliance could be resumed.[4] As the result of this dispute Edward fought and won the campaign of Crécy without official German support.

IV

Among Edward's opponents at Crécy was Charles of Moravia, whom, at the orders of the pope, five of the electors had chosen as king of the Romans at Rhens on 11 July 1346. As anti-king Charles had no great success during the lifetime of Lewis the Bavarian. The tough old victor of Gammelsdorf and Mühldorf, who fought battles reluctantly but almost always successfully, was more than a match for his young rival. But Lewis' sudden death on 11 October 1347 changed the aspect of German politics. The Wittelsbach party had to continue to oppose Charles, for

[1] Lewis' grant of 15 January 1346 is printed by F. van Mieris, *Groot Charterboek der Graaven van Holland, van Zeeland en Heeren van Vriesland*, ii. 702.

[2] On 20 October 1345 Edward appointed commissioners to defend Philippa's rights in Zeeland (*Foedera*, III, i. 61). A further commission appointed on 27 December for the same purpose was almost identical with that created on the same day to treat with Lewis about an alliance (*ibid.* 65).

[3] Margaret was allowed by Philip of Valois to reach her new possessions in the winter of 1345 through Lorraine and France. Mathias von Neuenburg comments, 'promovit autem rex Francie imperatricem neptem suam, non forsan amore principis set quia terras per Anglum timuit occupari' (*Chronica*, ed. Hofmeister, i. 201). In September 1346 Clement agreed to Philip's suggestion that he should not pass sentence on the county of Hainault for receiving as its ruler the wife of the excommunicate emperor (Riezler, *Vatikanische Akten*, 2304).

[4] Cf. *Foedera*, III, i. 92; Mathias von Neuenburg, *Chronica*, i. 219. The question of the Holland-Hainault inheritance is treated at length, but with some inaccuracies of detail, by Lucas, *op. cit.* 535–43, 556–9. *

general recognition of him would imply a victory of papal policy in Germany, and according to the theory of the curia all Lewis' grants to his relatives and allies were illegitimate. If Charles could establish himself as king of the Romans the Margrave Lewis would have to fear for his province of Brandenburg, with which his father had enfeoffed him in 1323; Henry of Virneburg, archbishop of Mainz, who had already been deposed by the pope for his support of Lewis, could hope to maintain himself in his see only by successful opposition to the Luxemburger. The obvious course for the Wittelsbachers was to impugn the validity of Charles' election and elect a king of their own.

This they could do with some plausibility. The *Weisthum* of Rhens in 1338 had declared him to be king of the Romans who had secured the majority of the electoral votes, and Charles had been elected by Baldwin, archbishop of Trier, Walram, archbishop of Cologne, John of Bohemia, Gerlach of Nassau, archbishop of Mainz, and Rudolf, duke of Saxony (-Wittenberg)—thus by five voices, apparently a clear majority in a college of seven. But the legality of two of these votes could be questioned. Gerlach had been provided to Mainz by Clement VI in April 1346, in place of the deposed adherent of Lewis, Henry of Virneburg. Henry, however, with strong support from his chapter, continued in effectual possession of his see, and Gerlach was little recognized. And since the ducal house of Saxony had divided into two branches, Lauenburg and Wittenberg, in 1295, there had been disputes as to which branch had the vote in imperial elections. In the election of 1308 Wittenberg had voted, under protest from Lauenburg; in the double election of 1314 the Lauenburger had voted for Lewis and the Wittenberger for Frederick the Fair of Austria. In 1347 the Lauenburgers were still attached to the Wittelsbach interest, and were willing to contend that Rudolf's vote in 1346 was invalid.[1] The Bavarian party could thus argue that Charles had received only three valid votes, those of Trier, Cologne, and Bohemia, against which they could oppose four, those of Lewis, margrave of Brandenburg, of the Count Palatine Rudolf II, Lewis the Bavarian's nephew, of Henry of Virneburg as archbishop of Mainz, and of the Lauenburg branch of the Saxon house. Moreover, there were formal difficulties about Charles' claim. He had been elected and crowned at Rhens and Bonn, instead of at Frankfort and Aachen, as custom demanded.

After Lewis' death the Wittelsbachers lost little time in picking on the English king as their candidate against Charles. By the beginning of December Edward had received envoys from Lewis of Brandenburg, Henry of Virneburg, and the powerful

[1] Cf. F. Lammert, 'Der Streit um die Kurwürde zwischen Sachsen-Lauenburg und Sachsen-Wittenberg' (*Historische Vierteljahrschrift*, xxx. 305–15).

provost of Mainz, Conrad of Kirkel. On 3 and 4 December he informed his correspondents that he was sending back their envoys with his answer to their requests ; his own envoys would soon appear in Germany.[1] On 10 January 1348 his representative, Ives de Clinton,[2] met the confidential advisers of Lewis of Brandenburg, the Count Palatine, Henry of Mainz, and Eric, duke of Saxony (-Lauenburg) at Oberlahnstein in the Rhineland, and was there informed that these four electors had decided to elect Edward king of the Romans.[3] This was not a full *electio* but merely a *conversio intuitus* of the electors towards Edward, an expression of present intention, not a completed act.[4] This intention was communicated to the towns of the empire in a circular letter, which also set out the grounds for opposing Charles : he had been chosen by some of the electors at the pope's behest while Lewis was still alive, he had not gained effective control of the empire, and his election had not been celebrated at the customary place. The four electors of the Wittelsbach party claimed, moreover, to form a majority of the college.[5]

Mathias von Neuenburg states that at the meeting of Oberlahnstein it was publicly announced that Edward wished to go forward with the plan for his election.[6] But it is unlikely that he had committed himself so far. On 10 May he wrote to the confederates that Ives de Clinton and Hugh Nevill would meet them or their representatives at Cologne to reply to their proposal for his election, and to hear their further wishes.[7] Clinton and Nevill went to Cologne, but by this time the scheme was dead.[8] Nothing more is heard of Edward's candidature, and a little later the Wittelsbachers transferred their hopes to Frederick, margrave of Meissen.

[1] *M.G.H. Constitutiones*, viii. 380, 1, 2.

[2] Cf. the account of Ives's expenses in the Rhineland from 7 December 1347 to 31 January 1348 (P.R.O., E. 101, 312/28).

[3] Mathias von Neuenburg, *Chronica*, i. 248.

[4] So R. Salomon, 'Zur Geschichte des englischen Politik Karls IV' (*Historische Aufsätze Karl Zeumer . . . dargebracht*, 402, n. 4). Salomon's contention is fully borne out by the wording of the confederates' letter of 16 January. *

[5] A copy of this letter, sent to Hagenau on 16 January by Lewis of Brandenburg and the Counts Palatine, Rudolf II and Rupert I, from Ingolstadt, is printed by T. E. Mommsen, 'Beiträge zur Reichsgeschichte von 1313–49' (*Neues Archiv*, l. 421). On 7 March the Lauenburgers pledged themselves to vote for whomever Lewis of Brandenburg chose as king of the Romans (*M.G.H. Constitutiones*, viii. 545).

[6] Mathias, *loc. cit.*

[7] *M.G.H. Constitutiones*, viii. 575. The duke of Saxony to whom Edward wrote was Eric, not, as H. Otto erroneously supposes, Rudolf (*Regesten der Erzbischöfe von Mainz*, I, ii. 5661). Edward's letter was in reply to an embassy of the confederates which met him at a council after Easter (20 April), according to Geoffrey le Baker, *Chronicon*, ed. Giles, 187. Ramsay, *op. cit.* 357, errs in saying that on 10 May Edward finally declined the imperial throne.

[8] Ives de Clinton and Hugh Nevill were absent, 'ad partes Brabantie et ad civitatem Colonie', from 12 May to 20 June (P.R.O., E. 101, 312/30, 31).

III

Edward had in fact been disingenuous in pretending in May that he might still be ready to go on with the Wittelsbach scheme. For on 23 April he had made an agreement with Charles of Moravia in which he promised to do nothing *quominus idem rex . . . imperio et eius possessione gaudere libere valeat et habere.*[1] The architect of this alliance was William of Jülich, who received his commission from Charles on 19 January.[2] Charles was obviously anxious about the plans of his opponents,[3] and Edward was thus able to make favourable terms. Charles indeed declined to co-operate in an offensive against Philip of Valois, unless a quarrel should arise *pro iuribus imperii*, but he promised not to aid Philip against Edward, and thus renounced the long tradition of faithful assistance by Luxemburg to France. And Edward gained also the right of freely recruiting men in the empire, a concession probably of far more weight than would have been the promise of an offensive alliance such as he had experienced in 1337–40.[4]

The English chroniclers explain Edward's refusal of the German crown on the grounds that he declined to be distracted from the pursuit of his claims to the kingdom of France.[5] This is only half the truth ; Edward was tempted away from the Wittelsbach offer by the more solid advantages of the agreement with Charles. This agreement offered prospects not only of imperial neutrality and an open recruiting ground in Germany, but also of a settlement of the question of the Avesnes inheritance, on which the Wittelsbachers were not likely to make concessions. On 16 January 1348 Charles declared that the inheritance, on the death of William IV of Holland-Hainault, had fallen into four parts, one of which was the right of each of William's three sisters, and the fourth, of the empire. At the same time Charles enfeoffed William of Jülich with the quarter which was due to his wife, together with the quarter which had fallen to the Empire.[6] Three days after this William was empowered by Charles to negotiate with Edward for an alliance, and there can be no doubt that William on his mission to England was able to hold out the expectation that Philippa would receive her share of the inheritance of Holland and Hainault. At the end of July it was being rumoured in Germany that Charles had bought Edward's

[1] Edward does not seem to have had any relations with Charles before this date. Lucas, *op. cit.* 538, bases his statement that Edward and Charles exchanged letters in October 1346 on *Regesta Imperii*, viii. 525, which misplaces in 1346 a document which belongs to 1355. Cf. Salomon, *op. cit.* 397–402.

* [2] Cf. Bock, *ante*, xlv. 366.

[3] On 9 February he sent his *diffidatio* to Rupert I, Count Palatine, because of the latter's complicity in the confederates' letter to the imperial cities on 16 January (*M.G.H. Constitutiones*, viii. 524).

[4] Edward's letter of 23 April, *ibid.* 569 ; Charles' reversals of 24 June, *ibid.* 613.

[5] Cf. Geoffrey le Baker, *loc. cit.* ; Knighton, *Chronicon*, ed. Lumby, ii. 56.

[6] *M.G.H. Constitutiones*, viii. 490.

friendship by granting Holland and Zeeland to the children of Edward III and William of Jülich.[1] The rumour was incorrect, and Philippa never received her due, but Charles' apparent willingness to be accommodating on this subject probably eased the way to the Anglo-Luxemburg agreement.

It is tempting to contrast Edward's 'realist' attitude in refusing the Wittelsbach offer in 1348 with the romanticism of the period of the vicariate. Such an antithesis is unreal, however. On both occasions he followed the course he thought best fitted to promote the war with France; the course in 1348 differed from that of 1337–40, not because Edward had in the meantime gained more political wisdom, but rather because the whole strategic scheme of the Hundred Years' War had changed, and no longer was it to be fought from a base in Low Germany. In the fourteenth century England and Germany had common interests against France, and it was perfectly sensible for Edward at the very outbreak of the war against Philip of Valois to seek German aid. That the attempt failed in the form in which it was first made is not sufficient grounds for condemning the form as fantastic. The grant of the vicariate, it has been suggested above, was based on reasonable motives; it broke down not because it was inherently ridiculous, but on certain external factors, such as Edward's lack of money and Lewis' preoccupation with Italy.

[1] Mathias von Neuenburg, *Chronica*, i. 259.

IV

Meinungsverschiedenheiten am Hof Ludwigs des Bayern im Herbst 1331

Seit 1874 Riezlers Literarische Widersacher der Päpste zur Zeit Ludwigs des Baiern erschienen, ist unser Wissen von den Schriften der ausgezeichneten Gruppe von emigrierten Intellektuellen, welche in München Zuflucht gefunden hatte, bedeutend gewachsen. Die Untersuchungen und Editionen von Richard Scholz hatten hier richtungweisend gewirkt. Und obgleich die Aufgabe der Texteditionen noch nicht vollendet ist, so sind wir doch in viel günstigerer Lage als Riezler, Inhalt, Quellen und Zusammenhänge der Schriften des Marsilius von Padua und jener oppositionellen Minoriten zu erörtern, welche wegen ihrer Stellung gegen die Avignonpäpste Michael von Cesena an den Hof Ludwigs gefolgt waren [1]).

Doch obwohl der Wert jener ungeheueren Literaturmasse für die Ideengeschichte nun besser abgeschätzt werden kann, hat die Diskussion einer verwandten Frage noch keine vergleichbaren Fortschritte gemacht: welches war der wirkliche Einfluß, den diese Intellektuellen auf Ludwigs politisches Handeln ausübten? Oder, mit anderen Worten, inwieweit gestalteten sie kaiserliche Politik während des langen Zeitraums,

---

[1]) Nur einige der bemerkenswerteren Titel der sehr ausgedehnten Literatur zu diesem Thema müssen erwähnt werden: R. Scholz, Unbekannte kirchenpolitische Streitschriften aus der Zeit Ludwigs des Bayern 1327—1354, 1—2 (1911—14); die Ausgaben von Marsilius, Defensor pacis durch C. W. Previté-Orton (1928) und durch Scholz, MG. Fontes iuris Germ. ant. 7 (1932); O. Bornhak, Staatskirchliche Anschauungen und Handlungen am Hofe Ludwigs des Bayern (Quellen und Studien zur Verfassungsgeschichte des deutschen Reiches 7, 1933); G. de Lagarde, La naissance de l'esprit laïque au déclin du moyen âge 1—6 (1934—46); Guillelmi de Ockham Opera Politica ed. J. G. Sikes et al. 1 (1940); R. Scholz, Wilhelm von Ockham als politischer Denker und sein Breviloquium de principatu tyrannico (Schriften des Reichsinstituts für ältere deutsche Geschichtskunde 8, 1944); L. Baudry, Guillaume d'Occam: sa vie, ses œuvres, ses idées sociales et politiques 1 (1950); A. Gewirth, Marsilius of Padua: The Defender of Peace 1 (1951).

in dem sie in Ludwigs Umgebung wirkten? Jeder Versuch, diese Frage zu beantworten, ist natürlich mit dem schwierigen Problem von Ludwigs Persönlichkeit und Charakter verknüpft. War er imstande, eine eigene, folgerichtige Politik zu entwickeln und zu behaupten? Riezler hatte wenig Zweifel; ihm erschien Ludwig als Schwächling, verführt zu extremen und unzeitgemäßen Maßnahmen durch Doktrinäre, deren Theorien umgekehrt zur Fruchtlosigkeit verurteilt waren, weil sie einem so unfähigen Herrn dienten [2]). Neuerdings hat Friedrich Bock gegen die Auffassung protestiert, daß der Schlüssel zu den Unternehmungen Ludwigs stets in fremden Ideen zu finden sei, deren Grundlage fremde Interessen waren. Bock meint, die wichtigsten theoretischen Einflüsse hätte Ludwig von der Reichstradition der italienischen Ghibellinen empfangen. Marsilius war in gewissem Sinn ein Exponent dieser Tradition. Michael von Cesena und seine Anhänger, welche nicht vor September 1328 in direkte Verbindung mit dem Kaiser kamen, wurden von Ludwig nur für seine Zwecke ausgenützt, weil sie wirkungsvolle antipäpstliche Propagandisten waren [3]).

Es gibt nur einen Weg, der uns hoffen läßt, angesichts solcher Meinungsverschiedenheiten weiterzukommen: man muß diese Urteile, wo immer es die Quellen ermöglichen, durch ins Einzelne gehende Untersuchungen über die Tätigkeit der Emigrantengruppe an Ludwigs Hof zu verschiedenen Zeiten prüfen. E. E. Stengel hat bereits wertvolle Hinweise darauf gegeben, wie unbeständig die Einflußnahme der Minoriten während der großen verfassungsrechtlichen Beratungen von 1338 gewesen ist [4]). Es ist die Absicht der folgenden Ausführungen, ausdrücklich darauf hinzuweisen, daß eine erneute Beurteilung der Quellen für 1331 (deren meiste seit langem gedruckt vorliegen) einiges Licht auf das gleiche Problem werfen kann.

*

Nachdem Ludwig anfangs des Jahres 1330 von Italien zurückgekehrt war, verschwindet Marsilius aus unserem Blickfeld, bis 1341 seine Meinung über die Tiroler Heiratsaffäre angefordert (aber nicht befolgt)

---

[2]) Riezler S. 49, 52, 296. Aber vgl. S. 336.

[3]) F. Bock, Reichsidee und Nationalstaaten vom Untergang des alten Reiches bis zur Kündigung des deutsch-englischen Bündnisses im Jahre 1341 (1943) S. 210, 240, 271.

[4]) E. E. Stengel, Avignon und Rhens (Quellen und Studien zur Verfassungsgeschichte des deutschen Reiches 6, 1930) S. 104 ff. u. 178.

wurde [5]). Zwar lassen sich von Zeit zu Zeit [6]) Spuren seiner Gedankengänge nachweisen, aber für sein persönliches Eingreifen in Staatsgeschäfte gibt es keine direkten Anhaltspunkte. Andererseits steht die Tätigkeit Michaels und der Minoriten außer jedem Zweifel: Es gibt einen Bericht über eine Unterredung Michaels mit dem Kaiser im April 1330 [7]); am 12. Juni befahl Ludwig den städtischen Behörden von Aachen in einem Brief, welcher minoritischen Einfluß in der kaiserlichen Kanzlei am Werke zu zeigen scheint, an Michael alle Franziskaner auszuliefern, die ihm den Gehorsam verweigerten [8]); diesem Jahr dürften mutmaßlich Michaels „Litterae deprecatoriae“ zuzuweisen sein, die an Ludwig *ceterisque principibus, baronibus et nobilibus secum in parlamento existentibus* gerichtet sind und sie auffordern, die Irrtümer Johanns XXII. der christlichen Welt anzuzeigen [9]); und dies war bloß ein Stück eines un-

---

[5]) Bornhak S. 116 ff. Es ist wahrscheinlich, daß Marsilius' Radikalismus durch das klägliche Scheitern der Unternehmungen in Rom vom Januar bis Mai 1328 diskreditiert wurde. Redewendungen wie die, daß die emigrierten Intellektuellen eine „Münchner Akademie“ bildeten (Bock S. 268, 321) können irreführen, wenn sie den weiten Abstand in Temperament und Ansichten zwischen Marsilius und den Minoriten übersehen: vgl. G. de Lagarde, Marsile de Padoue et Guillaume d'Ockham, Revue des sciences religieuses 17 (1937) 168 ff.

[6]) Für eine solche Spur im Jahr 1331 vgl. unten S. 197 Anm. 24.

[7]) MG. Const. 6 Nr. 743.

[8]) Ebda. Nr. 788. Zu dem Versuch von E. Knotte, Untersuchungen zur Chronologie von Schriften der Minoriten am Hofe Ludwig des Bayern (phil. Diss. Bonn 1903) S. 54 ff., zu zeigen, daß Ockham diesen Brief entweder schrieb oder an seiner Abfassung beteiligt war, vgl. Baudry S. 146 Anm. 1.

[9]) M. Goldast, Monarchia Romani Imperii 2 (1614) 1344—60. W. Preger, Beiträge und Erörterungen zur Geschichte des deutschen Reiches in den Jahren 1330—34 (Abh. Münch. III. Kl. 15, 2, 1880) S. 38 f., Anm., nahm an, daß die Versammlung, an welche die „Litterae deprecatoriae“ gerichtet waren, während Ludwigs Anwesenheit zwischen 20. Mai und 22. Juni 1330 in Speyer zusammentrat. Man sollte die Annahme vorziehen, daß Michael seine Streitschrift entweder in Vorbereitung für die zum 8. Juli nach Eisenach (MG. Const. 6 Nr. 753: 17. Mai 1330) oder für die zum 27. Januar 1331 nach Frankfurt einberufene Versammlung verfaßte (ebda. Nr. 865: 5. September 1330). 1330 erweist sich als Jahr der Abfassung durch Michaels Bezugnahme auf eine Predigt mit sabellianischen Tendenzen über die Schriftstelle *Gaudete in Domino semper;* sie sei von Johann XXII. *hoc anno* gehalten worden; denn das Datum dieser Predigt war der 17. Dezember 1329: Paris, Bibl. Nat., Cod. lat. 5154, fol. 253 v; Rom, Cod. vat. lat. 4009, fol. 183 r. Der Einwand Baudrys, S. 139 u. Anm. 7, die „Litterae deprecatoriae“ könnten nicht vor 1332 geschrieben sein, beruht auf einer Verwechslung der Predigt *Gaudete* von 1329 mit einer über die gleiche Schriftstelle, aber mit anderem Thema *

unterbrochenen Propagandafeldzuges gegen die Legitimität von Johanns Pontifikat, welcher vom März 1330 bis April 1331 geführt wurde [10]). Aber dann folgt eine Pause. Geraldus Oddonis, jetzt Generalminister der päpstlichen Observanz der Franziskaner, hat vermutlich sein „Quid niteris" gegen Michael bald nach dem Generalkapitel zu Perpignan zu Pfingsten 1331 verfaßt; Michaels Gegenschrift „Teste Salomone" trägt das Datum des Dezember 1332. Die rebellierenden Minoriten ließen Angriffe normalerweise nicht so lange unerwidert! [11])

Die Erklärung für diese Verzögerung kann in dem offiziellen Verbot gesucht werden, welches Ludwig für einige Zeit während des Sommers oder Frühherbstes des Jahres 1331 über die propagandistische Tätigkeit der Minoriten verhängt hatte. Von der Existenz dieses Verbotes sind wir durch einen Minoritentraktat mit dem Incipit „Quoniam scriptura testante divina" unterrichtet, der während des Oktobers 1331 oder kurz zuvor geschrieben ist. Darin finden wir die bezeichnende Klage: *Nunc autem facta est in derisum iusticia, quia sapientes, quibus est cognita, ipsam declarare minime permittuntur* [12]). Der Inhalt dieses Traktats, Warnungen vor den Gefahren, in welche Ludwig sich stürze, wenn er mit Johann XXII. Frieden schlösse, kennzeichnet den Zweck des Verbots. Ludwig erwog ernsthaft den Versuch, eine Übereinkunft mit dem Papst zu erreichen, und eine für Verhandlungen günstige Atmosphäre konnte nicht erreicht werden, ohne Michael und seine Anhänger für diese Zeit zum Schweigen zu bringen. Für die Minoriten war es eine erschreckende Aussicht, daß ihr Beschützer zu einer Einigung mit dem Papst kommen könnte, den sie als einen Ketzer ansahen und dem sie die Anerkennung verweigerten. Ihre Sorge fand nicht nur in „Quoniam scriptura", sondern auch in einem längeren Traktat mit dem Incipit „Ut

---

(Visio beatifica), welche Johann am 15. Dezember 1331 hielt: Cambridge, Univ. Bibl., Cod. lat. Jj, 3. 10 fol. 4—10.

[10]) Michaels Appellation vom 26. März 1330 gegen die Bulle *Quia vir reprobus,* C. Eubel, Bullarium francisc. 5 (1898) 426 f. Anm.; seine Briefe an den Franziskanerorden vom 24. Januar und 25. April 1331 ebda., S. 427—38 Anm.; S. 497—500 Anm.

[11]) A. Heysse, Duo documenta de polemica inter Gerardum Oddonem et Michaelem de Caesena, Arch. francisc. hist. 9 (1916) 140 ff.; 153 ff.

[12]) Herausgegeben von Preger S. 76—82 aus clm. 17 833 fol. 178 v ff. Die zitierte Stelle: S. 82. Knotte, S. 1—12, setzt die Entstehungszeit des Traktats zwischen Juni und Oktober 1331 fest. Über die Autorschaft vgl. unten S. 203—206.

in composicione“ Ausdruck, der offenbar in denselben historischen Zusammenhang gehört [13]).

Ludwig hatte im Sommer 1331 direkte Verhandlungen mit dem Papst über seine Versöhnung mit der Kirche eröffnet. Im vorhergehenden Jahr hatten Vermittlungsbemühungen von dritter Seite keine Erfolge bei der Kurie verzeichnen können [14]). Aber die internationale Situation von 1331, kompliziert wie sie durch Johanns von Böhmen italienisches Abenteuer war, eröffnete vielleicht eine günstigere Gelegenheit. Im Juni und Juli wurden Geleitsbriefe für die Gesandten Ludwigs nach Avignon ausgestellt [15]); um Mitte Oktober brachten diese die Bedingungen nach Deutschland zurück, von welchen Johann XXII. weitere Fortschritte in den Verhandlungen über eine Aussöhnung mit Ludwig abhängig machte.

Diese Bedingungen sind im Original nicht erhalten, aber eine deutsche Fassung, gekürzt auf zehn Forderungen des Papstes an den Kaiser, ist in München im Geheimen Hausarchiv 1/5 259 fol. 13 zu finden (fortan als C bezeichnet). Sie sind in diesem Dokument von zehn vorgeschlagenen Erwiderungen begleitet, gefolgt von einer Aufstellung von zehn Gravamina oder Forderungen des Kaisers an den Papst. Der Text, von Riezler als Stück C im dritten Appendix seiner Literarischen Widersacher [16]) herausgegeben, trägt kein Datum, aber 1914 brachte ihn R. Moeller [17]) folgerichtig in Verbindung mit den Verhandlungen von 1331. Er konnte gleichwohl nicht glauben, daß das letzte Drittel des Textes, die zehn Gravamina, den offiziellen Charakter des übrigen teilte; vielmehr, meinte er, sei dies nichts anderes als ein Entwurf eines Theoretikers und in das Jahr 1331 zu setzen [18]). Doch 1933 gelangten Bornhak und Bock unabhängig voneinander zu dem Schluß, daß

---

[13]) Herausgegeben von Hans Foerster, Ein unbekannter Traktat aus dem Streit Ludwigs des Bayern mit Johann XXII., Miscell. francesc. 37 (1937) 592—614 aus Cod. 23 J. 60 fol. 153 ff. des Franziskanerkonventes zu Freiburg i. Ü.

[14]) Zu den Unternehmungen des Grafen Wilhelm III. von Holland-Hennegau im Frühjahr 1330 vgl. Wilhelm von Egmond, Chronicon, in A. Matthaeus, Veteris Aevi Analecta 2 (1738) 704; zu den habsburg-luxemburgischen Versuchen im Sommer MG. Const. 6 Nr. 761—763, 811—819; H. Finke, Acta Aragonensia 1 (1908) Nr. 299.

[15]) S. Riezler, Vat. Akten z. dt. Gesch. i. d. Zeit Kaiser Ludwigs d. Bayern (1891) Nr. 1465—6.

[16]) Riezler S. 329—32.

[17]) R. Moeller, Ludwig der Bayer und die Kurie im Kampf um das Reich (Hist. Studien 116, 1914) 62 ff.

[18]) Moeller S. 67.

alle dreißig Artikel ein geschlossenes Ganzes bildeten. Dessen Eigenart werde durch eine Formulierung erläutert, welche die kaiserliche Antwort auf die päpstlichen Forderungen eröffnete: *Ze dem ersten antwrt der kaiser vnd all sein weiser rat, pfaffen vnd layen, daz* ... etc. Das ganze Schriftstück stellt danach den amtlichen Bericht über eine Sitzung von Ludwigs Beratern dar, welche die Antwort auf die päpstlichen Bedingungen für die Versöhnung mit Ludwig erwägen sollten. Die Bedingungen sind zusammengestellt, eine Erwiderung ist für jede von ihnen vorgesehen, und um die päpstlichen Forderungen auszugleichen und die Position des Kaisers als gleichberechtigter Verhandlungspartner zu wahren, sind zehn kaiserliche Forderungen hinzugefügt [19]).

Nehmen wir die Hypothese als gegeben, in C das Protokoll einer Sitzung von Ludwigs Rat vor uns zu haben, dann müssen wir ebenso einräumen, daß dieser Rat sehr stark von den Ideen der Minoriten beeinflußt war. Die dreißig Artikel wurden von Bock zusammengefaßt [20]) und müssen daher nicht noch einmal in extenso behandelt werden. Einige Beispiele werden genügen, um die Tendenz dieser Ratsbeschlüsse darzulegen. Zur ersten päpstlichen Forderung, Ludwig solle nötigenfalls Marsilius und die Minoriten zum Gehorsam gegen den Papst zwingen, wird erwidert, daß Marsilius, die Minoriten und alle anderen Helfer Ludwigs gleichermaßen wie Ludwig selbst zu behandeln, d. h. in die Versöhnung einzubeziehen seien [21]). Wenn dies geschehen sei, müßten die Kardinäle eine öffentliche Diskussion über die Behauptungen des Marsilius und der Minoriten herbeiführen, und nur, wenn diese tadelnswert befunden würden und ihre Verfasser den Widerruf verweigerten, werde Ludwig auf kirchliches Geheiß unternehmen, was die Gerechtigkeit erfordere. Es dürfte schwerlich zu leugnen sein, daß diese Antwort ihren gewichtigen Platz und ihre vorsichtige Formulierung unmittelbarer Inspiration durch die Emigranten verdankt, vornehmlich da wir darin eine der hartnäckigen Forderungen der Minoriten nach öffentlicher Debatte ihres Streites mit Johann XXII. wiederholt sehen [22]). Dasselbe

---

[19]) Bornhak S. 41 Anm. 2; F. Bock, Die Prokuratorien Kaiser Ludwigs IV. an Papst Benedikt XII., QFIAB. 25 (1933) 256.

[20]) Bock, Reichsidee S. 323 f.

[21]) Dies halte ich für die volle Bedeutung der Redewendung: *mit dem kaiser besamt sullen sein,* a. a. O. S. 330. Ludwigs Wiederaufnahme soll von der seiner Helfer begleitet sein.

[22]) Vgl. die Aufforderung der Minoriten an Benedikt XII. 1338: *quod predicti magistri et iuris periti erant parati in publico consistorio predicta sustinere ... offerentes se portare debitam penam, si deficerent in predictis,* J. F. Boehmer, Fontes rer. germ. 4 (1868) 608.

scheint bei dem Entwurf der Antwort auf die neunte Forderung des Papstes vorzuliegen, daß die deutschen Fürsten den Papst schriftlich um Ludwigs Krönung bitten sollten. Hier wird die Erwiderung zur Zurückweisung. Der Papst mag geziemend gebeten werden, die Krönung Ludwigs (nämlich die Krönung in Rom 1328) anzuerkennen, gutzuheißen und ihr seinen Segen zu geben. Aber nichts mehr! Die Möglichkeit einer erneuten Krönung ist ausgeschlossen, denn die Krönung ist ein unwiderrufliches Sakrament: *wan di kroenung ist ein sacrament, daz man nicht aendern muoz* [23]).

Der minoritische Beigeschmack wird noch stärker, wenn wir uns der Aufstellung von kaiserlichen Beschwerden zuwenden. Daß die ersten sechs von ihnen enge Beziehungen zu dem Minoritentraktat „Quoniam scriptura" besitzen, hat Bornhak bereits herausgestellt [24]); ein Beispiel ist vielleicht des Verweilens wert: der vierte Klagepunkt der Kaiserlichen lautet, der Papst habe sich angemaßt, Grenzen zwischen dem Reich und Frankreich zu des Reiches Schaden zu ziehen und löse die Lombardei aus dem Reichsverband. Für diese Handlungen könne er sich weder auf eine Vollmacht von Gott, noch von St. Peter oder St. Paul berufen [25]). Ob wir hier eine Anspielung auf die sog. Bulle „Ne praetereat" vor uns haben, oder, wie Bock behauptet [26]), auf den päpstlichen Plan von 1331, für Philipp von Valois ein Königreich Lombardei zu errichten, es sind fast stets Minoritenschriften, in denen man in den nächsten Jahren die Wiederholungen dieser Anklage finden kann. Sie taucht auf in den Traktaten „Quoniam scriptura" und „Ut in composicione" [27]); in dem Konzept für eine Appellation Baldwins von Trier an ein allgemeines Konzil gegen Johann XXII., das von den Minoriten zwischen zwischen dem 14. Juli und dem 12. August 1333

---

[23]) A. a. O. S. 331. Bock, Reichsidee S. 323, scheint den Sinn dieser Erwiderung mißzuverstehen, wenn er sie zusammenfassend wiedergibt mit: „Um die päpstliche Krönung will der Kaiser gern bitten." Alles, worum Johann XXII. gebeten werden sollte, war nur, die Krönung zu bestätigen, welche bereits stattgefunden hatte.

[24]) Bornhak S. 41 Anm. 2. Es soll ausdrücklich bemerkt werden, daß es sich dabei in der zweiten kaiserlichen Beschwerde um einen Gedankengang des Marsilius handelt: *wan ... werltlich gerichte von dem keysertuom ist vnd geistlich gerichte von dem stuol, doch von gab der kaiser*, a. a. O. S. 331; vgl. Defensor pacis II, 5 § 10 ed. Scholz S. 197.

[25]) A. a. O. S. 331.

[26]) F. Bock, Kaisertum, Kurie und Nationalstaat im Beginn des 14. Jahrhunderts, Röm. Quartalschr. 44 (1936) 204.

[27]) Preger S. 78; Foerster S. 609.

entworfen wurde [28]); in dem kaiserlichen Manifest „Fidem catholicam" von 1338 [29]); und in einem anderen Traktat desselben Jahres „Inferius describuntur articuli", welchen wahrscheinlich die Minoriten für den Erzbischof von Mainz, Heinrich von Virneburg, verfaßt hatten [30]). Die einzige mir bekannte zeitgenössische Beziehung zu dieser Anklage von anderer als minoritischer Seite ist in der Tat ihre Aufnahme in das Dictionarium iuris des Bergamasker Juristen Alberich von Rosciate [31]). Folglich scheint eine fast überwältigend starke Stütze für die Annahme gegeben, der vierte kaiserliche Klagepunkt sei aus minoritischen Quellen geschöpft.

In einer Sitzung des kaiserlichen Rates, der äußerst aufnahmefähig für minoritische Ideen war, wurde also beraten, welche Antwort auf die päpstlichen Forderungen zu geben sei. Doch als die Instruktionen für die Gesandten aufgesetzt wurden, welche Ludwigs Antworten zur Kurie zu bringen hatten, basierten diese Instruktionen da noch auf den Entscheidungen, von welchen C der Niederschlag ist? Bocks überzeugte Behauptung, daß dem so sei, kann nicht ohne weiteres übernommen werden [32]). Instruktion und Beglaubigungen für Arnold Minnepeck und Ulrich von Augsburg sind unter 1/256 im Geheimen Hausarchiv in München erhalten (fortan als I bezeichnet) [33]), und ein Ver-

---

[28]) Rom, Cod. Vat. lat. 4009 fol. 185v.

[29]) Anal. Francisc. 2 (1887) 171; zum minoritischen Ursprung von „Fidem catholicam" vgl. Stengel, Avignon und Rhens S. 109.

[30]) E. E. Stengel, Nova Alamanniae 2 (1930) Nr. 583. Wiewohl Stengel, Avignon und Rhens S. 131, für die Entstehung dieses Traktates in Mainz argumentiert, räumt er doch ebda. S. 178 ein, daß er einen Teil der von Nikolaus Minorita an die Kurie gesandten Sammlung bilde.

[31]) Unter *papa*. Das Dictionarium wurde 1498 in Pavia gedruckt. Zu Alberich vgl. F. C. von Savigny, Geschichte des römischen Rechts 6², 126 ff.

[32]) Bock, Prokuratorien S. 257. Bornhak bemerkte S. 19, daß die Instruktionen für Arnold und Ulrich nicht auf C basierten, aber zog aus diesem Umstand keine weiteren Schlüsse.

[33]) Hg. v. Ch. Gewold, Defensio Ludovici IV. imperatoris ratione electionis contra Abr. Bzovium (1618) S. 118—24. Riezler, Widersacher S. 311, beschreibt das Schriftstück als Originalurkunde; Bock a. a. O. als unbenütztes Konzept. Gegen das letztere läßt sich die Tatsache einwenden, daß, obwohl das Schriftstück keine Siegel trägt, es doch am unteren Rand Einschnitte zeigt, welche zum Siegeln gedient haben dürften. Gewold bemerkt nicht, daß spätere Zusätze zu I gemacht worden sind, welche anzeigen, daß es in der Folgezeit als Vorbild für das Beglaubigungsschreiben des Grafen Ludwig von Öttingen bei einer Mission an die Kurie diente (vermutlich Ende 1332: vgl. Vat. Akten Nr. 1598; Heinrich Taube von Selbach, Chronica [MG. SS. NS. 1] S. 45).

gleich zwischen den Anerbieten, zu welchen Ludwigs Gesandte in I ermächtigt waren, und den Entschließungen, deren Formulierung wir in C vor uns zu haben glauben, wirkt äußerst hinderlich für den Schluß, daß C zur unmittelbaren Grundlage für I gedient habe.

So findet der Vorschlag der ersten Erwiderung in C zur Erörterung der Meinungen des Marsilius und der Minoriten keinen Platz in I. C hatte eine ganz unnachgiebige Haltung gegenüber der zweiten und dritten päpstlichen Forderung gezeigt, Ludwig solle für alle seine Unternehmungen gegen den Heiligen Stuhl Vergebung erstreben, für seine Verfehlungen, wie es einem Christen zieme, Buße leisten, und die Aufhebung des Kirchenbannes, der über ihn verhängt war, erbitten. Gemäß C wollten Ludwig und seine Ratgeber um Absolution bitten, aber nur *ad cautelam*, und wollten keine Zugeständnisse machen, welche ihren gegenwärtigen oder zukünftigen Rechten schaden könnten; Ludwig wollte nichts tun, das seiner persönlichen Ehre oder kaiserlichen Würde abträglich sein könnte; seine früheren Handlungen als König und Kaiser hatten rechtskräftig zu bleiben. In I sind diese Vorbehalte fortgefallen; während Ludwigs Gesandte nicht zulassen dürfen, daß seine persönliche Rechtgläubigkeit bestritten werde, dürfen sie seine Bereitwilligkeit zur Buße für seine Verfehlungen gegen die Kirche erklären. Die sechste und die neunte päpstliche Forderung, Ludwig solle für eine zeitlang Königs- und Kaisertitel ablegen und die deutschen Fürsten sollten den Papst schriftlich um die Krönung Ludwigs bitten, erfährt wiederum eine auffällig unterschiedliche Behandlung in C und I. Der erste Punkt ist in C umgangen [34]), und die Antwort zum zweiten kommt, wie wir gesehen haben [35]), dort einer Zurückweisung gleich. Während I andererseits nichts unmittelbar zur neunten Forderung aussagt, sucht es wenigstens einen Weg, sich mit der sechsten auseinanderzusetzen. Ludwigs Gesandte dürfen zustimmen, daß er, falls der Papst seine Vertreter sendet um die Krönung zu vollziehen, für kurze Zeit des kaiserlichen Titels entsagt, um ihn als unmittelbare Folge der vom Papst angeordneten Weihe und Krönung gleich wieder anzunehmen. Die Notwendigkeit einer erneuten Kaiserkrönung für Ludwig, welche C geleugnet hatte, ist in I dadurch eingeräumt. Ebenfalls zugestanden wurde die achte päpstliche Forderung, daß Ludwig bei Vergabungen an den römischen Stuhl sich als ebenso großzügig erweisen solle wie alle seine

---

[34]) *der kaiser tet nicht, daz an seines leibes oder seines onmechtes ere gat.* A. a. O. S. 330.

[35]) Siehe oben S. 196 f. und Anm. 23.

Vorgänger — eine Klausel, welche C verächtlich zur Seite geschoben hatte.

Ebenso scheint es auch nicht möglich, in den Formulierungen von I irgend eine Spur des Einflusses der kaiserlichen Gravamina zu entdecken, welche C enthielt. Selbst wenn man das damit erklärte, daß die Verfasser der kaiserlichen Forderungen nicht wirklich an die Erfüllung ihrer Ansprüche glaubten, sondern sie als rein formale Erwiderungen für den Gebrauch der deutschen Gesandten bei der Kurie abgefaßt hatten [36]), bleibt es dennoch erstaunlich, einen Artikel von I in glattem Widerspruch zu einem der Gravamina zu finden. In C gilt gleich die erste der vorgeschlagenen kaiserlichen Forderungen an den Papst der Rückkehr des Königreiches Sizilien, über welches die Päpste nach dem Tode Friedrichs II. widerrechtlich verfügt hätten, zum Reiche. Mit dieser Forderung ist es völlig unvereinbar, daß die Gesandten in I angewiesen werden, Ludwigs Bereitwilligkeit zu einer Übereinkunft nicht nur mit Philipp von Valois, sondern auch mit Robert von Neapel auszudrücken, und als Garantie dafür sein Einverständnis zu erklären, daß eines seiner Kinder für eine Heiratsverbindung nach päpstlichem Wunsch vorgesehen werde.

Offensichtlich weichen demnach die Erwiderungen, welche Arnold Minnepeck und Ulrich von Augsburg gemäß ihrer Instruktion vom 14. Oktober auf die päpstlichen Forderungen zu geben hatten, in recht entscheidender Weise von den in C vorgeschlagenen Antworten ab. Doch eben diese Antworten stellten nach dem Zeugnis von C selbst eine Entscheidung des Kaisers in seinem Rate dar: *antwrt der kaiser vnd all sein weiser rat, pfaffen vnd layen.* Notwendigerweise ist deshalb zu folgern, daß zwischen dieser Entscheidung und der Zusammenstellung der Instruktionen vom 14. Oktober der Kaiser und sein Rat ihre Stellungnahme änderten, was dazu führte, daß sie ihre ursprüngliche Haltung zum großen Teil aufgaben.

Wenn die kaiserlichen Antworten und Beschwerden in C Auffassungen der Minoriten wiedergeben (wie es ihr Inhalt und ihr Bezug zu zeitgenössischen Streitschriften deutlich zeigen), dann müssen wir annehmen, Ludwig habe die päpstlichen Forderungen zuerst mit einem Rate behandelt, in dem die Meinung der Minoriten die Oberhand hatte. Daß das Gutachten der Minoriten in der Tat von Amts wegen abgegeben

---

[36]) So Bock, Prokuratorien S. 255 Anm. 1 u. S. 256. Ich kann diese Meinung nicht teilen. Es erschiene zwecklos, eine Liste von Beschwerden aufzustellen, für welche keine Abhilfe erwartet wurde.

wurde und nicht nur ein vertraulich erörterter Entwurf war, darf man daraus schließen, daß es in C, einem amtlichen Bericht, aufgezeichnet wurde. Hätte man an diesem Gutachten ständig festgehalten, so bleibt kaum ein Zweifel, daß es die Aussichten auf einen Friedensschluß zwischen Papst und Kaiser von Anbeginn zerstört haben würde. Es bot keine erwägenswerte Verhandlungsbasis und war möglicherweise auch gar nicht darauf angelegt. Denn die Aussicht auf einen erreichten Ausgleich zwischen Ludwig und dem Papst war höchst unwillkommen für Michael und seine Anhänger im Hinblick auf ihren theologischen Streit mit Johann. Sie für ihren Teil wünschten eine Erörterung ihrer Sache gegen den Papst vor einem allgemeinen Konzil [37]). Aber man hielt sich nicht durchwegs an ihr Gutachten. Die Antworten, welche Arnold und Ulrich der Kurie überbringen sollten, bewegten sich in viel mäßigeren Grenzen, denen die Unversöhnlichkeit der Minoriten in C fern liegt. Demnach, so muß geschlossen werden, hatten die Minoriten vor dem 14. Oktober ihren vorwaltenden Einfluß unter Ludwigs Ratgebern an eine Partei verloren, welche ernsthaft bereit war, die Möglichkeiten einer Versöhnung mit Johann XXII. zu erwägen.

Eine deutliche Anspielung auf diese Partei erscheint in dem Traktat „Quoniam scriptura", der eine feindselige Anspielung auf jene macht, *qui vel infideliter consulunt, vel causam imperatoris minus bene cognoscunt, scripturam sacram et rationem naturalem ac historias fide dignas, in quibus imperii iura fundantur, ignorantes* [38]). Vielleicht schimmert in diesen Worten der Groll von geringschätzig behandelten Intellektuellen gegen die praktischeren Politiker durch, deren Einfluß den ihren verdrängt hatte. Wir können nur vermuten, wer diese Männer waren, aber es liegt nahe, sie unter den heimischen Ratgebern Ludwigs zu suchen, von denen im allgemeinen eine enge Verbindung zum Kaiser bekannt ist; es waren in dieser Zeit vertraute, seit langem bewährte Diener, wie etwa Berthold von Henneberg, der Kanzler Hermann von Lichtenberg, Ludwig und Friedrich von Oettingen und Heinrich von Zipplingen, Landkomtur des Deutschen Ritterordens in Franken [39]). Die

---

[37]) „Ut in composicione" a. a. O. S. 605.

[38]) A. a. O. S. 76 f.

[39]) Alle diese Namen erscheinen in einer vom 24. April 1332 datierten Liste von Ludwigs Räten, welche bestimmt waren, die Ausführung eines Übereinkommens zwischen Ludwig und Johann von Böhmen zu garantieren: Preger Nr. 29 S. 75 f.; W. Fuesslein, Berthold VII. Graf von Henneberg (1905) ist unvollständig. Zu Hermann von Lichtenberg vgl. Bruno Schilling, Kaiser Ludwig der Baier in seinen Beziehungen zum Elsaß (Veröff. d. Hist.

Ansichten solcher Männer, so darf man vermuten, eroberten schließlich im Herbst 1331 Ludwigs Gunst; und ihre erfolgreich vertretene Politik der Verhandlungen mit der Kurie erregte die Zweifel und Befürchtungen, welche die Traktate der Minoriten ausdrücken und machte das amtliche Verbot der propagandistischen Betätigung der Minoriten notwendig, über welches „Quoniam scriptura" Klage führt.

Ihre Verhandlungsbereitschaft brandmarkt diese Männer nicht als die Männer der Kapitulation; sie waren unnachgiebig in der Verteidigung des nach ihrer Auffassung Wesentlichen innerhalb Ludwigs verfassungsrechtlicher Stellung [40]), und sie haben anscheinend gehofft, unter den Kardinälen einige Sympathie für den deutschen Standpunkt zu finden [41]). Obgleich die Angebote, welche Ludwig auf ihr Anraten machen ließ, den päpstlichen Forderungen viel näher kamen, als die vordem unter Einfluß der Minoriten gefaßten Beschlüsse, so genügten sie doch nicht, Johann XXII. zufriedenzustellen. Der Aufenthalt der Gesandten Ludwigs in Avignon war kurz; am 20. November erhielten Arnold und Ulrich Geleitsbriefe für ihre Rückkehr nach Deutschland [42]). Die Verhandlungen brachen nicht vollständig ab; sie wurden tatsächlich bis zum letzten Jahr von Johanns Pontifikat von Zeit zu Zeit wieder aufgenommen [43]). Aber lange ehe sie endlich im Sande verliefen, war es un-

---

Seminars d. Univ. Graz 11, 1932) S. 81 f. Eine nähere Untersuchung dieser Gruppe von Männern wäre sicher recht lohnend.

[40]) Ein späterer Zusatz zu I (vgl. oben S. 198 Anm. 33) formuliert treffend, was man für das Ziel dieser Partei halten kann: *Daz unser vorgen. herre Chaiser Lud. und daz Romisch Reich bei iren rehten und eren beleiben sullen.*

[41]) Arnold und Ulrich wurden instruiert, ihre Verhandlungen mit den Kardinälen zu beginnen, nicht mit dem Papst: B o c k , Reichsidee S. 325.

[42]) Vat. Akten Nr. 1497.

[43]) Über die Mission Ludwigs von Öttingen nach Avignon Ende 1332 vgl. die oben S. 198 Anm. 33 zitierten Verfasser. Er wurde zusammen mit dem Grafen von Hals durch Albert von Habsburg abgesandt, der kraft Vollmacht Ludwigs handelte. Eine französische Intervention wegen Ludwig ist ausdrücklich in einem Brief Johanns XXII. vom 18. Dezember 1332 erwähnt, Vat. Akten Nr. 1592; Johanns Klage, daß die Angebote der deutschen Gesandten ungenügend seien, ebda. Nr. 1598. Geleitsbriefe für die Reise nach Avignon wurden bei der Kurie ausgestellt für Arnold Minnebeck, Ulrich von Augsburg, von Öttingen und von Hals am 12. März 1333; weiter für von Öttingen am 29. April und 19. August, C. E r d m a n n , Vat. Analekten z. Gesch. Ludwigs d. Bayern, Archiv. Zs. 41 (1932) 32—34. Vor dem 22. Oktober 1333 waren von Öttingen und der Kartäuserprior Gottfried von Mauerbach mit Bitten Alberts von Habsburg zugunsten Ludwigs zur Kurie gekommen. Johann sandte sie *imperfecto negotio* unter dem üblichen Vorwand ungenügender Vollmachten zurück, P r e g e r Nr. 20, S. 72; vgl. ebda. Nr. 22, S. 73.

verkennbar, daß, was Ludwig anzubieten bereit war, nicht einmal die Mindestforderungen Johanns erreichte, welche diesen zu mehr als Präliminarverhandlungen veranlaßt hätten. Und als die Aussichten auf Verständigung dürftiger wurden, war nicht mehr länger Grund dafür, die minoritische Polemik gegen den Papst zurückzuhalten, welcher durch seine Predigten über die Visio beatifica im November und Dezember 1331 selbst seine Gegner mit weiterem Agitationsmaterial versorgte. Als am 10. April 1332 Bonagratia von Bergamo im Franziskanerkonvent zu München im Namen der oppositionellen Minoriten eine Appellation gegen die jüngsten Irrlehren Johanns XXII. veröffentlichte, wurde der Akt durch Zeugenunterschriften einer Anzahl von Klerikern aus der engsten Umgebung der königlichen Familie einschließlich Ludwigs benediktinischem Beichtvater bekräftigt [44]). Die Minoriten waren auf gutem Wege, ihren Einfluß bei Hofe wieder zu erobern, welchen sie — es liegt auf der Hand — im Herbst 1331 zeitweilig verloren hatten.

*

Über die Autorschaft der anonymen Traktate „Quoniam scriptura" und „Ut in composicione" mögen noch einige Worte gesagt sein. Bemühungen, einen oder beide Marsilius zuzuweisen, vermögen nicht zu überzeugen; Inhalt und Wortlaut lassen keinen Zweifel über ihren minoritischen Ursprung [45]). Aber können wir es präziser fassen? Knottes Behauptung, Ockham sei der Autor von „Quoniam scriptura", wurde von Hauck als möglich, und von einem so überragenden Kenner von Ockhams politischen Schriften wie Richard Scholz als sicher angenommen [46]). Gewiß finden manche Gedankengänge des Traktats Parallelen in Abhandlungen, deren Autor ganz ohne Frage Ockham ist: Zum Beispiel, daß das Reich gegenwärtig genau so frei sei als jemals

---

[44]) *presentibus testibus ... frederico abbate de richienbach ordinis sancti benedicti confessore domini imperatoris ... dominis Johanne ac bernardo capellanis domine marchionisse Brandenburgen. ... bertoldo notario domine imperatricis,* Cod. vat. lat. 4009 fol. 213 (der Entwurf der Appellation); vgl. L. Oliger, Fr. Bonagratia de Bergamo et eius tractatus de Christi et apostolorum paupertate, Arch. francisc. hist. 22 (1929) 310.

[45]) Riezler denkt daran, „Quoniam scriptura" könne Marsilius' Werk sein, HZ. 45 (1880) 508. Bock, Reichsidee S. 321, hält Marsilius für den Autor beider Traktate; aber er gibt S. 322 eine Mitarbeit der Minoriten an „Ut in composicione" zu, wiewohl er sie für „Quoniam scriptura" verneint.

[46]) Knotte S. 12 ff.; Hauck S. 534 Anm. 3; Scholz, Wilhelm von Ockham S. 5.

vorher [47]); daß der Kaiser von wem er wolle gekrönt werden kann [48]); daß ein Kaiser nicht seine Nachfolger eidlich binden könne, *cum non habeat imperium par in parem* [49]); daß der Kanon 3 C. XV qu. 6, der die Absetzung Childerichs enthält, im Zusammenhang mit seinen Glossen verstanden werden müsse [50]); daß Kleriker verpflichtet seien, dem Kaiser für ihren weltlichen Besitz Abgaben zu leisten, außer er habe ihnen Exemptionsrechte gewährt [51]); daß weder Laien noch Kleriker innerhalb des Reiches weltliche Gerichtsbarkeit *iure divino*, sondern nur kraft kaiserlicher Verleihung übten [52]). Überdies entwickelt „Quoniam scriptura" einen Doppelschluß, den wir bei Ockham an mehr als einer Stelle wiederholt finden, um zu zeigen, daß Johann XXII., ob er ein Ketzer sei oder nicht, kein rechtmäßiger Papst sein könne, nämlich: da die von ihm hartnäckig gelehrten Doktrinen denen seiner Vorgänger entgegengesetzt seien, sei er entweder ein Ketzer (und daher kein rechtmäßiger Papst) oder, wenn nicht, seien seine Vorgänger Ketzer gewesen. Doch wenn diese Ketzer waren, seien sie weder rechtmäßige Päpste noch die von ihnen kreierten Kardinäle rechtmäßige Kardinäle gewesen. Aber diesen Kardinälen verdankte Johann seine Wahl und sei deshalb nicht rechtmäßiger Papst [53]). Schließlich findet man die Betonung der Notwendigkeit für Ludwig, seine Unschuld und die Gerechtigkeit seiner Sache öffentlich zu bekunden, worauf „Quoniam scriptura" mit großem Nachdruck hinweist, auch bei Ockham in seinem Traktat „Contra Benedictum" von 1337—38 wieder [54]).

---

[47]) „Quoniam scriptura" a. a. O. S. 77; vgl. Ockham, Octo Quaestiones II, 6, 12 ed. Sikes S. 80 u. 93. Angesichts Ockhams endloser Wiederholungen seiner Argumente sind die Hinweise in dieser Anmerkung und in den folgenden nur eine kleine Auswahl von Parallelen in seinen Werken, die herangezogen werden könnten.

[48]) S. 77; vgl. Octo Quaest. I, 13 S. 57.

[49]) S. 77; vgl. Octo Quaest. I, 15 S. 58; ebda. II, 12 S. 93; Decretales Gregorii IX, I, 6, 20.

[50]) S. 77; vgl. Octo Quaest. II, 9 S. 87; Breviloquium VI, 2 ed. Scholz S. 198.

[51]) S. 79; vgl. Octo Quaest. II, 12 S. 92 f.; „An princeps" c. 7 ed. Snape und Offler S. 256.

[52]) S. 79; vgl. Octo Quaest. II, 8 S. 85.

[53]) S. 80; vgl. Ockhams Abhandlung „Contra Joannem" c. 29, Paris, Bibliothèque Nationale, fonds lat. 3387 fol. 202r—v; und seine Abhandlung „Contra Benedictum" I, 6, ebda. fol. 220r—v; V, 7, ebda. fol. 248v—249.

[54]) S. 82; vgl. Contra Benedictum VI, 19 fol. 256.

Diese Parallelen sind schlagend, doch sie bringen noch nicht den Beweis, daß Ockham „Quoniam scriptura" schrieb, denn ähnliche Übereinstimmungen in Gedanken und Argumenten können leicht zwischen „Quoniam scriptura" und den Schriften anderer oppositioneller Minoriten wie Michael von Cesena und Bonagratia gefunden werden. So ist zum Beispiel der oben angeführte Doppelschluß von Michael bereits im April 1328 benützt [55]). Die Ähnlichkeiten zwischen „Quoniam scriptura" und Teilen von Ockhams Werken stellen nichts anderes dar, als eine Bekräftigung der unverkennbaren Wahrheit, daß Ockham, als er sich dem politischen Schrifttum zuwandte, heftig nach Argumenten und Erklärungen unter dem bereits von seinen Gesinnungsfreunden im Franziskanerkonvent zu München Verfaßten suchte. Es zeigt sich nichts (außer der Hypothese, er sei der Autor von „Quoniam scriptura") zur Unterstützung der Annahme, daß Ockham sich mit dieser Art des Schrifttums schon 1331 befaßt habe; das erste glaubwürdige Zeugnis für seine Anteilnahme an zeitgenössischen verfassungsrechtlichen Problemen des Reiches, an der päpstlichen Forderung nach dem Anerkennungsrecht der Wahl der deutschen Kurfürsten usw., ist in Buch VI und VII seiner Abhandlung „Contra Benedictum" zu finden, die 1337—38 geschrieben ist [56]); und diese Bücher machen den Eindruck eines ersten versuchenden Tastens in einem dem Autor neuen Problemkreis [57]). Knottes gewichtigste Argumente für die Zuteilung von „Quoniam scriptura" an Ockham sind von Baudry in einer schlüssig erscheinenden Weise kritisiert worden [58]); die Anonymität der Schrift bleibt noch bestehen [59]).

---

[55]) Appellatio Avinionensis (Baluze-Mansi, Miscellanea 3, 1762) S. 238 f.

[56]) Scholz, Streitschriften 1, 153.

[57]) Diesen Eindruck empfand ich sehr stark, während ich eine vollständige Ausgabe von Contra Benedictum für Guillelmi de Ockham Opera Politica Band 3 vorbereitete. Das unterstützt durchaus die Meinung von Scholz, Wilhelm von Ockham S. 10, daß das Jahr 1337 einen Einschnitt in der Entwicklung der politischen Ideen Ockhams bezeichne. Damit soll natürlich nicht geleugnet sein, daß Ockham in früheren Werken die Beziehungen zwischen Kirche und Staat in allgemeinen Wendungen berührt hat: zum Beispiel in c. 93 des Opus Nonaginta Dierum, etwa 1332 geschrieben. Aber niemals bis zu Contra Benedictum gilt die allgemeine Erörterung aktuellen politischen Ereignissen.

[58]) Baudry S. 133—135.

[59]) Eine weitere Überlegung, soweit sie wichtig ist, mag gegen Ockhams Autorschaft sprechen. „Quoniam scriptura" a. a. O. S. 76 nennt Johann XXII. Jacobus de Carecto (es sollte heißen de Caturco): Jakob von Cahors. Diese heruntersetzende Bezeichnung war recht verbreitet, sowohl in Urkunden der

Ebenso wenig kann man zu Gunsten der Annahme sagen, daß „Ut in composicione" Ockhams Werk sei, wie das der Herausgeber auf Grund ihrer „Quoniam scriptura" ähnlichen Tendenz (F o e r s t e r hatte, K n o t t e folgend, „Quoniam scriptura" für Ockham in Anspruch genommen) und infolge einer Parallele zu den „Allegationes de potestate imperiali" von 1338 getan hat [60]). Es scheint sicher, daß der Autor von „Ut in composicione" Minorit war [61]), doch es wäre schwierig, darin irgendwelche spezifisch ockhamistischen Züge zu erkennen. Im Gegenteil, die Untersuchung von mindestens einem wichtigen Punkt kann positiv zeigen, daß Ockham nicht der Autor war. Denn die Schrift stellt in derart scharfer und absoluter Weise eine Trennung zwischen göttlicher und weltlicher Gewalt auf, daß kein Raum mehr bleibt für Ockhams typischen Vorbehalt, eine jede Macht habe im Notfall die Pflicht, in die Sphäre der anderen einzugreifen [62]).

Folglich kann weder „Quoniam scriptura" noch „Ut in composicione" überzeugend den Anspruch auf einen Platz in der Liste der politischen Schriften Ockhams erheben. Ihre wirkliche Bedeutung liegt in dem zufälligen Schlaglicht, das sie auf die zeitweilige Einbuße von Gunst und Einfluß an Ludwigs Hof werfen, die Michael von Cesena und seine Anhänger in der zweiten Hälfte des Jahres 1331 erlitten.

---

kaiserlichen Kanzlei als auch unter den Minoriten: vgl. Bonagratias Appellationen von 1332 und 1334, Cod. vat. lat. 4009 fol. 207 u. 164. Aber ich fand sie niemals gebracht in irgendeiner Schrift, welche fraglos Ockham zugeschrieben werden kann.

[60]) F o e r s t e r S. 595. Ockhams Autorschaft der Allegationes ist noch nicht gegen jeden Zweifel gesichert: vgl. B a u d r y S. 202.

[61]) Nicht nur wegen des Inhaltes, sondern auch wegen der handschriftlichen Überlieferung: vgl. F o e r s t e r S. 593.

[62]) Ebda. S. 602.

V

Über die Prokuratorien Ludwigs des Bayern für die römische Kurie

Es ist seit langem anerkannt, daß die wichtigste Quelle für die Geschichte der Versuche Ludwigs des Bayern nach seiner Rückkehr vom Römerzug, Frieden mit dem Papsttum zu schließen, in den Prokuratorien zu suchen ist, in denen Ludwig seine Beauftragten ermächtigte, der Kurie in seinem Namen gewisse Zugeständnisse und Garantien zu gewähren, die seine Rekonziliation mit der Kirche sichern sollten. Solche Urkunden werden bereits im Jahre 1335 gebraucht worden sein, das im Prozeß der Rekonziliation einen Fortschritt von der einfachen Verhandlung der früheren Jahre zu einer strengeren kanonischen Prozedur bringt[1]). Aber die einzigen noch erhaltenen Prokuratorien sind die der Gesandtschaften vom März u. Oktober 1336 und vom September 1343, auf Grund deren man zu weitreichenden Schlüssen auf Ludwigs Haltung zu den päpstlichen Bedingungen der Rekonziliation gekommen ist. Wie schwach die Grundlage mancher dieser Verallgemeinerungen ist, hat kürzlich F. Bock gezeigt, dessen sorgfältige archivalische Forschungen im Vatikanischen Archiv und anderswo viel dazu beigetragen haben, das Problem aufzuhellen, was für Prokuratorien tatsächlich den Prokuratoren im Jahre 1336 von Ludwig ausgehändigt worden sind[2]). Bock hat überdies die an-

[1]) J. Schwalm hat im NA. 26 (1901) 713 gezeigt, welchen neuen kanonischen Aspekt die Verhandlungen durch den Gebrauch von formalen Prokuratorien gewinnen. Die Instrumente der Gesandtschaft, welche Ludwig im August 1335 an die Kurie schickte, wurden *procuratoria* genannt, doch sind diese nun verloren, und es ist unmöglich, zu entscheiden, ob die verlorenen Urkunden schon in der technischen Form abgefaßt waren, welche die Instrumente vom März und Oktober 1336 und vom September 1343 auszeichnet.

[2]) F. Bock, Die Prokuratorien Kaiser Ludwigs IV. an Papst Benedikt XII., QFIAB. 25 (1933) 251 ff. Die ausgedehnte frühere Literatur ist kurz erwähnt S. 251 Anm. 1.

regende und wertvolle Vermutung ausgesprochen, daß der Schlüssel zur richtigen Interpretation der Prokuratorien in der bisher versäumten gründlicheren Prüfung des kanonischen Verfahrens, insbesondere der politischen Verwendung des inquisitorischen Verfahrens durch die Kurie zu finden ist[1]).

Während Bock sich hauptsächlich mit den Prokuratorien von 1336 beschäftigt, haben mich meine eigenen Studien über das kanonische Verfahren zu einer Untersuchung der Urkunden von 1343 geführt. Der Hauptzweck dieses Aufsatzes ist daher, die herrschende Auffassung der Prokuratorien von 1343 auf Grund von bisher noch unveröffentlichten Urkunden zu revidieren. Die Ergebnisse, zu denen ich gekommen bin, haben mich veranlaßt, gegen einige der Behauptungen Bocks über die Prokuratorien von 1336 Bedenken zu äußern. Doch schien es mir wünschenswert, einleitend einige Bemerkungen über die rechtliche Bedeutung der Prokuratorien überhaupt vorauszuschicken.

I.

Der Gebrauch von Prokuratoren als Prozeßbevollmächtigten ging vom zivilen in das kanonische Recht über, und das 13. Jh., welches die auswärtige Politik fast allgemein als Beanspruchung oder Verteidigung von legalen Rechten auffaßte, dehnte die Verwendung von Prokuratoren auch auf das Gebiet der internationalen Beziehungen aus[2]). Im 14. Jh. wurde der diplomatische Brauch üblich, einem Verhandlungsbevollmächtigten ein in ganz allgemeinen Ausdrücken gehaltenes Prokuratorium für den Zweck seiner Sendung mitzugeben. Eine solche Urkunde umschrieb formell den Umfang der Vollmacht des Prokurators. Wenn seine Aufgabe war, Frieden oder einen Waffenstillstand oder eine Heirat oder ein Bündnis zu schließen, so ver-

---

[1]) Über die päpstliche Anwendung der inquisitorischen Prozedur zu politischen Zwecken vgl. ferner Bock, Studien zum politischen Inquisitionsprozeß Johanns XXII., QFIAB. 26 (1936) 21ff. und Derselbe, Der Este-Prozeß von 1321, Archivum Fratrum Praedicatorum 7 (1937) 41.

[2]) Ein interessanter Unterschied zwischen einem Prokurator und einem gewöhnlichen Gesandten wird zum Ausdruck gebracht von Gondissalvus de Villadiego, Tractatus de legato, pars III quaestio I, 19 (Hrabar, De legatis et legationibus tractatus varii, 1905): *Colliguntur aliquae differentiae inter nuncium et procuratorem. Et inter caeteras est illa, quod in actu gerendo procurator concipit verba in personam suam, nominando dominum, non sic autem in nuncio, qui concipit verba in personam domini et est ut picca et organum, loquitur enim per se et non a se.*

sicherte das Prokuratorium die Partei, an die der Gesandte geschickt werden sollte, daß er von seinem Auftraggeber bevollmächtigt worden sei, Frieden usw. zu schließen. Aber das Prokuratorium stellte nur fest, was der Prokurator im Namen seines Herrn tun könnte, nicht was er tun sollte. Die Einzelheiten seines Verhaltens wurden durch weniger formelle mündliche oder schriftliche Angaben bestimmt, auf Grund deren er die Verhandlungen innerhalb des allgemeinen Rahmens seines Prokuratoriums zu führen hatte. Diese Angaben waren die Instruktionen des Prokurators, das formelle Prokuratorium war sein Mandat: „Mandat und Instruktion ergänzen sich mithin inhaltlich; jenes enthält die bedingte Vollmacht, diese die Bedingung[1].“ So ist vieles von unserer Kenntnis der internationalen Politik des Mittelalters lückenhaft, weil nur die formalen Urkunden einer Verhandlung erhalten sind. Instruktionen waren ihrer Art nach formlos, sie waren häufig dazu bestimmt, geheimgehalten zu werden und mögen zuweilen wohl bloß dem Gedächtnis des Prokurators bei einer Besprechung mit dem Auftraggeber anvertraut worden sein.

Keine Verlegenheit dieser Art erhebt sich in bezug auf Ludwigs Verhandlungen mit der Kurie im März und Oktober 1336 und im September 1343, denn die Instruktionen für die beiden letzten Gesandtschaften sind vorhanden und es ist möglich, sie für die erstere mit ziemlicher Sicherheit zu rekonstruieren[2]. Die Schwierigkeit liegt vielmehr in der Entscheidung der Frage, in welchem Verhältnis hier Prokuratorien und Instruktionen zueinander stehen. Denn während Ludwig in den Prokuratorien seine Gesandten bevollmächtigte, sogar in noch ausgedehnterem Maße als ausdrücklich gesagt wird[3]), dem Papst gewisse einzelne Zugeständnisse zu machen,

---

[1]) V. Menzel, Deutsches Gesandtschaftswesen im Mittelalter (1892) S. 108.

[2]) Bock, Prokuratorien S. 270.

[3]) In den allgemeinen und speziellen Prokuratorien vom März 1336, den beiden speziellen Prokuratorien vom Oktober 1336, und den speziellen politischen und kirchlichen Prokuratorien vom September 1343 bevollmächtigte Ludwig seine Prokuratoren: *Suprascriptis articulis omnibus singulis et unicuique ipsorum addendi, supplendi et adiungendi ac ipsos et quemlibet eorum mutandi, corrigendi et emendandi.* — In den speziellen politischen Prokuratorien vom März und Oktober 1336 und vom September 1343 sagt Ludwig: *Damus dictis procuratoribus nostris plenam potestatem . . . ad consentiendum et promittendum quod, si in premissis articulis vel aliquo eorundem aliquid esset ambiguum, dubium et incertum, declarationi, interpretationi, correctioni et suppletioni ac ordinationi sanctitatis vestre et domini summi pontificis, qui pro tempore fuerit, stabimus cum effectu.*

V

Eide zu leisten und Forderungen zu erfüllen, und während er schwor, alles das gutzuheißen, was die Prokuratoren in seinem Namen tun würden, enthalten die Instruktionen Bedingungen, die mit der wörtlichen Erfüllung der Prokuratorien unverträglich sind[1]). Das würde leicht verständlich sein, wenn es sich einfach um ein politisches Geschäft gehandelt hätte. Es würde bei einem Herrscher in keiner Weise befremden, wenn er, um aus bestimmten Gründen Zeit zu gewinnen, zu einem andern einen Prokurator senden würde mit Vollmacht, Frieden zu schließen, jedoch mit der geheimen Instruktion, die Verhandlungen zu sabotieren. Aber Ludwigs Gesandtschaften waren nicht mit politischen Verhandlungen beauftragt. Sie spielten ihre Rolle in einem kanonischen Absolutionsprozeß; der Inhalt ihrer Vollmacht war vom Papste, nicht von ihrem Auftraggeber Ludwig vorgeschrieben worden[2]). Und es scheint so, als hätte Ludwig bei Aus-

---

[1]) Dies wird deutlich, wenn wir die Instruktionen der Gesandten vom Oktober 1336, bei S. Riezler, Die literarischen Widersacher der Päpste zur Zeit Ludwigs des Bayern (1874) S. 328, mit zwei detaillierten Prokuratorien in den Vatikanischen Akten zur Deutschen Geschichte aus der Zeit Kaiser Ludwigs des Bayern (1891) Nr. 1842 vom selben Datum vergleichen. In den Prokuratorien scheint Ludwig zuzugeben, daß er die Exkommunikation verdient habe, weil er das Kaisertum angetreten habe, ohne sich der päpstlichen Approbation seiner Wahl zu versichern. Die Instruktion verbot seinen Prokuratoren, einer solchen Zumutung zu willfahren. Während in VA. Nr. 1842 Ludwig seine Prokuratoren bevollmächtigte, die Auferlegung von automatisch wirkenden Sanktionen zuzugestehen für den Fall, daß er oder seine Beamten die Integrität der territorialen Besitzungen der Kirche antasten würden, und er ihnen die Vollmacht gab, dem Papste das Recht zuzugestehen, die Artikel des Prokuratoriums zu interpretieren und zuzustimmen, daß Robert von Neapel zum lebenslänglichen Vikar von Toskana ernannt werden solle, belehrte die Instruktion die Prokuratoren, daß sie sich keinesfalls auf solche Zugeständnisse einlassen dürften. Wenn Ludwig auch in dem Prokuratorium willig schien, die Notwendigkeit der päpstlichen Approbation seiner Wahl zuzugeben, so vernichtete er den praktischen Wert dieses Zugeständnisses dadurch, daß er den Prokuratoren in ihrer Instruktion verbot, ihn zu verpflichten, von Italien fern zu bleiben, bis er vom Papst approbiert sei. Vgl. R. Möller, Ludwig d. B. und die Kurie im Kampf um das Reich (Hist. Stud. 116, 1914) S. 89, wo Möller übrigens durch ein Mißverständnis die Instruktion vom Oktober 1336 in das Jahr 1335 verlegt.

[2]) E. E. Stengel, Avignon und Rhens (Quellen und Studien zur Verfassungsgeschichte des Deutschen Reichs 6, 1930) S. 193 Anm. 1 geht so weit, anzunehmen, daß die Kurie „fertige Entwürfe sandte, die, um Schlußformeln und einzelne Namen ergänzt, unverändert mundiert wurden“. Ich kann dem nicht ganz zustimmen; es erscheint fast sicher, daß die päpstlichen Bedingungen zuweilen in ihrem Wortlaut in Deutschland revidiert wurden. Das spezielle kirchliche Prokuratorium vom Jahre 1343 hat z.B. den Satz *quia credidimus et adhuc credimus nos*

stellung der Prokuratorien die päpstlichen Vorschriften angenommen. Wie läßt sich diese anscheinende Unterwerfung mit der Tatsache vereinigen, daß die Instruktionen der Prokuratoren in manchen Punkten den päpstlichen Forderungen widersprachen?

Die Schwierigkeit scheint noch größer zu werden, wenn wir die übliche kirchliche Prozedur der Rekonziliation untersuchen. Die Strafe der Exkommunikation wurde nicht als Rache, sondern als Heilmittel betrachtet: *Disciplina enim est excommunicatio et non eradicatio* war ein Grundsatz, der in das Corpus Iuris Canonici Eingang gefunden hatte[1]). Demgemäß war es die Pflicht der Kirche, die Verhängung der Exkommunikation aufzuheben, wenn sie ihren Zweck erfüllt und der von ihr Betroffene seine Haltung geändert hatte[2]). Den Beweis für eine solche Änderung konnte der Pönitent nur dadurch erbringen, daß er die von der Kirche vorgeschriebene Form der Rekonziliation gehorsam annahm. Diese Form umfaßte so, wie sie vom Hostiensis in seiner *Summa aurea* beschrieben, von Antoninus von Florenz im 15. Jh. gebilligt, und als *Ordo excommunicandi et absolvendi* in das Pontificale Romanum einverleibt worden war, vier Elemente[3]). Erstens, der Pönitent mußte schwören, den Befehlen der Kirche in bezug auf die Angelegenheit, derentwegen er exkommuniziert worden war, zu gehorchen. Zweitens, wenn das Urteil gefällt worden war *ab homine* wegen offenbarer Verstöße, mußte dem Gekränkten genügende Genugtuung gewährt werden; war es aber gefällt *a canone*, so mußte unter Umständen (wie im Falle

---

iniuste fuisse privatos; eine solche Meinung würde der Papst Ludwig nicht in den Mund gelegt haben. Auch ist es nicht wahrscheinlich, daß in Ludwigs Prokuratorium vom September 1343 die Kurie die Stelle formuliert hat, welche den Papst ermächtigte, ein Abkommen zwischen ihm und den Luxemburgern zu treffen, wobei Ludwig sich beklagt über jene Familie, *cum revera et ipsi potius nos multis offenderint et honori nostro et statui repugnent.* Es ist höchst wahrscheinlich, daß in dem kurzen allgemeinen Prokuratorium, das Ludwig im September 1343 aufsetzte, die päpstlichen Bedingungen von Ludwig verstümmelt worden waren, vgl. unten S. 478 Anm. 1.

1) c. 37. C. XXIV q. 3.

2) D. B. Schilling, Der Kirchenbann nach canonischem Rechte (1859) S. 1; N. München, Das kanonische Gerichtsverfahren und Strafrecht 2 (1866) 255.

3) Hostiensis, *Summa aurea* lib. V. *De sententia excommunicationis* (ed. Colonia 1612, cc. 1706ff.); Antonini Archiep. Flor. Summa, pars III. tit. 24 c. 77 (ed. Venedig 1582, 459); *Pontificale Romanum (Clementis VIII. pont. max. iussu restitutum atque editum* ed. Antwerpen 1627). München S. 259 betrachtet die Garantie, die Verletzung nicht zu wiederholen *(Cautela de futuris)*, als eine wesentliche Vorbedingung der Absolution.

V

der Häresie) eine beschworene Garantie dafür gegeben werden, daß der Verstoß sich nicht wiederholen werde. Drittens kam hinzu der formale Akt der Rekonziliation mit der symbolischen Züchtigung des Pönitenten, der Rezitation der Bußpsalmen usw. Endlich hatte der Pönitent die gerechten und vernünftigen Vorschriften der Kirche hinzunehmen. Die Theorie war also, daß ein Exkommunizierter, der die Rekonziliation wünschte, sich der Kirche voll unterwerfen und solche Forderungen erfüllen müsse, welche die Kirche zu stellen beliebte. Nur diese völlige Unterwerfung konnte den Zweifel an der Aufrichtigkeit des Pönitenten ausschließen.

Man kann beobachten, wie dieser kirchliche Grundsatz in die Praxis umgesetzt wurde, und zwar in einigen Fällen, in denen die Pönitenten Absolution suchten von den Kirchenstrafen, die sie durch ihre Anhängerschaft an Ludwig erlitten hatten. Am 9. Februar 1330 erschien Henricus Roberti im Konsistorium zu Avignon, um als Prokurator der Kommune von Viterbo die Rekonziliation mit der Kirche zu erbitten[1]). Sein Prokuratorium gab ihm Vollmacht zu sehr ausgedehnten Zugeständnissen und Garantien an den Papst und schloß die Klausel ein, daß dieselben nach dem Wunsch des Papstes geändert werden könnten[2]). Aus einem notariellen Protokoll des Konsistoriums erfahren wir, daß Henricus am 9. Februar alle Akte vollzog, zu denen er in seinem Prokuratorium ermächtigt worden war, indem er sich im Namen der Kommune erbot, *stare ac parere mandatis ecclesie* in allen Punkten, in denen sie die Kirche beleidigt hatte[3]). Aber die Entscheidung wurde verschoben, bis Henricus nochmals am 15. Februar im Konsistorium erschien und mehrere Artikel beschwor, die ihm nun vorgelesen wurden. Diese Artikel decken sich nur teilweise mit den Zugeständnissen, die Henricus früher im Rahmen seines Prokuratoriums gemacht hatte, und fügen gewisse Einzelheiten hinzu, die völlig neu sind[4]). Erst als Henricus diese neuen Bedingungen formell

---

[1]) Das Prokuratorium für Henricus Roberti vom 11. Dezember 1329 ist abgedruckt von F. Bussi, Istoria della Città di Viterbo (1742) S. 423.

[2]) *quod huiusmodi instrumentum possit corrigi et emendari, et in eo addi et minui ac etiam de novo fieri secundum quod visum fuerit dicto sanctissimo patri.*

[3]) Das Protokoll des Konsistoriums ist erhalten in dem Register des Kammerklerikers Guilelmus de Petrilla, abgedruckt bei Erdmann, Vatikanische Analekten zur Geschichte Ludwigs des Bayern, Archiv. Zs. 41 (1932) 23.

[4]) Die endgültigen Bestimmungen sind enthalten in Johanns XXII. Brief an Viterbo vom 15. Februar 1330 (Bussi S. 420). Viterbo mußte den Befehlen der Kirche gehorsamen in allen Punkten, in denen es geirrt

angenommen hatte, gewährte Johann XXII. Viterbo die Absolution unter der Bedingung, daß die Stadt die Akte ihres Prokurators binnen 15 Tagen ratifiziere.

Hier kommt die Haltung der Kurie gegenüber einem Pönitenten gut zum Ausdruck. Viterbo hatte seinem Prokurator weitgehende Vollmachten für die Unterwerfung gegeben. Es ist nicht unwahrscheinlich, daß die Bedingungen des Prokuratoriums von der Kurie diktiert waren. Aber diese Bedingungen waren vom Papst beliebig ausgedehnt und der kanonische Grundsatz nachdrücklich betont worden, daß die vollständige Unterwerfung unter die Diktate der Kirche in den fraglichen Punkten die Vorbedingung der Absolution sei.

Dies Ergebnis wird bestätigt durch das Beweismaterial, das der Prozeß um die Rekonziliation der Visconti im Jahre 1329 liefert. Am 20. Mai bestellten fünf Glieder dieser Mailänder Familie zwei Prokuratoren mit der Vollmacht, Johann XXII. als rechten Papst anzuerkennen und zu bekennen, daß sie gesündigt hätten durch Unterstützung Ludwigs des Bayern, durch Annahme von Ämtern von ihm und seinem Gegenpapst, durch Rebellion gegen die päpstlichen Legaten und Mißachtung der päpstlichen Prozesse. Überdies waren die Prokuratoren bevollmächtigt, zu Händen des Papstes auf die Herrschaft von Mailand zu verzichten, die Azzo Visconti von Ludwig verliehen war, und auf den Titel des Kardinallegaten, den Johann Visconti von der kaiserlichen Partei empfangen hatte. Sie durften sich im Namen der Visconti allen Befehlen, Sprüchen und Strafen unterwerfen, die der Papst ihnen aufzuerlegen für gut finde, durften bei dem Seelenheil ihrer Auftraggeber schwören, daß sie den Befehlen der Kirche gehorchen wollten und durften sie unter Garantie aller ihrer Besitzungen dazu verpflichten, alle in ihrem Namen gemachten Versprechungen zu erfüllen[1]). Die Prokuratoren der Visconti erschienen vor dem Papst in einem am 15. September gehaltenen Konsistorium und bekannten, nachdem sie ihr Prokuratorium hatten verlesen lassen, daß alles, was es enthalte, wahr sei. Knieend erbaten sie Absolution für ihre Auftraggeber und erboten sich, alle Urteilsprüche und Strafen anzunehmen, die der Papst ihnen etwa aufzuerlegen wünsche und alle Eide zu schwören, die man nur von

hatte, *in procuratorio predicto contentis implicite vel explicite confessatis et non confessatis*. Außer den in den Prokuratorien gemachten Zusagen mußte Viterbo sich verpflichten, niemals einen als Kaiser aufzunehmen, der nicht vom Heiligen Stuhl approbiert wäre, und insbesondere keinerlei Bündnis einzugehen mit Ludwig dem Bayern oder seinem Gegenpapst.

[1]) Erdmann S. 14.

ihnen verlangen werde. Dann beschworen sie einige Artikel, die ein Kardinal ihnen vorlas. Manche von diesen waren denen ähnlich, die im Falle von Viterbo gebraucht waren und in den vielen Rekonziliationen, die nach der Abreise Ludwigs aus Italien erfolgten, offenbar schematisch wiederkehren[1]). Andere bezogen sich speziell auf Mailand. Die Prokuratoren schwuren, sie wollten die Stadt vom Papst zu Lehen nehmen, genügend Truppen zu ihrer Verteidigung gegen Ludwig halten usw. Als diese Eide geleistet worden waren, absolvierte Johann XXII. die Visconti, indem er sich das Recht vorbehielt, Bußen aufzuerlegen und bestimmte, daß bei Strafe des Widerrufs alle Akte der Prokuratoren bis zum Tage Aller Heiligen von ihren Auftraggebern ratifiziert werden müßten[2]). In der Tat ratifizierten die Visconti die Akte ihrer Prokuratoren am 26. November *prout in procuratorio ... in consistorio et in capitulorum per ipsos iuratorum rotulo plenius continetur*[3]).

Ein drittes Beispiel der Art, wie das Papsttum einem die Absolution begehrenden Pönitenten Bedingungen diktierte, kann in den Akten der Rekonziliation des Erzbischofs Baldewin von Trier gefunden werden. Im März 1341 hatte Baldewin nach einer langen Periode vorsichtiger Verbindung mit Ludwig dem Bayern wieder Beziehungen mit der Kurie aufgenommen. Bald nach dem Regierungsantritt Clemens' VI. versuchte er die Rekonziliation zu erlangen. Schon vor dem Oktober 1342 erhielt er von Avignon einen Entwurf der Vollmachten, die er seinen Prokuratoren geben sollte, um Lossprechung von dem Urteil zu erlangen, das ihn wegen seiner Parteinahme für Ludwig getroffen hatte[4]). Aber seine Gesandten ermangelten formeller Urkunden, und der Papst weigerte sich zu handeln[5]). Im November 1342 kamen sie aufs neue nach Avignon mit einem regelrechten Prokuratorium, in dem ihnen Vollmacht gegeben war, zu schwören, daß Baldewin Clemens und seinen Nachfolgern gehorsam sein wolle,

---

[1]) Die ersten sieben von den Prokuratoren der Visconti beschworenen Artikel können in Parallele gestellt werden mit den von Henricus Roberti für Viterbo geleisteten Eiden.

[2]) Das Register des Guillelmus de Petrilla enthält das Protokoll dieses Konsistoriums, Erdmann S. 14ff.

[3]) Erdmann S. 22.

[4]) H. V. Sauerland, Urk. und Reg. zur Gesch. der Rheinlande aus dem Vatikanischen Archiv 3 (1905) Nr. 70a. Das Konzept wird dadurch gesichert, daß es den päpstlichen Registern für das sechste Jahr Benedikts XII. angeheftet ist.

[5]) Clemens VI. an Baldewin, den 16. November 1342 (nur Konzept), Erdmann 41.

daß er dafür halte, der Glaube, den die Kirche lehre, sei der rechte Glaube, daß er nicht glaube, der Kaiser habe irgendein Recht, den Papst abzusetzen oder zu erwählen, daß er nicht mit Willen die Partei Ludwigs des Bayern ergreifen oder ihm gegen die römische Kirche beistehen wolle, daß er glaube, Ludwig habe die kaiserliche Krone ungesetzlich empfangen und deshalb seien seine Entscheidungen kraftlos, daß er keinem als Kaiser gehorchen wolle, der nicht auf gehörige Weise die kaiserlichen Insignien empfangen habe, daß er die Prozesse Johanns XXII. gegen Ludwig in seiner Stadt und Diözese veröffentlichen wolle und daß er Ludwig auf gewissen Reichstagen nur begegnet sei aus Furcht vor den Folgen seiner Abwesenheit. Wenn Baldewin wegen der Verletzung irgendeines dieser Punkte in der Vergangenheit exkommuniziert worden sei, so sollten seine Prokuratoren um Absolution für ihn bitten und schwören, daß er den Befehlen des Papstes in Bezug auf seine Verfehlungen gegen die Kirche nachkommen werde[1]).

Im allgemeinen entsprach dies Prokuratorium vom Oktober 1342 dem Entwurf, den Baldewin von Avignon erhalten hatte. Aber politische Gründe veranlaßten ihn, die Bedingungen des Entwurfs in der Weise zu ändern, daß in dem Prokuratorium nicht deutlich ausgesprochen wurde, daß Ludwig ein Häretiker sei, und daß nicht bestimmt die Theorie der vollen päpstlichen Approbation anerkannt wurde, wonach der erwählte König der Römer so lange keine Macht habe, bis er vom Papste bestätigt sei[2]). Es könnte hiernach scheinen, daß wir hier einen Fall haben, in dem nicht der Papst, sondern vielmehr der Supplikant die Bedingungen der Absolution festsetzte. Dieser Eindruck wird indessen abgeschwächt durch den Vorgang der Rekonziliation selber. Am 16. November wurde den Prokuratoren im Konsistorium eine päpstliche Urkunde vorgelesen, und sie be-

[1]) Sauerland Nr. 70b.

[2]) Stengel, Avignon und Rhens S. 188—192, betont die Wichtigkeit dieser Veränderungen für die Beurteilung von Baldewins damaliger politischer Haltung. Aber er unterschätzte wohl die Fähigkeit des Papstes, die Ausflüchte Baldewins zu bemerken und zu durchkreuzen. Der geistige Kampf zwischen Baldewin und Clemens endete unentschieden; denn wenn Baldewin auch sicherlich in manchen Punkten eine Modifikation der päpstlichen Bedingungen erlangte, in einem (den übrigens auch Stengel S. 194 Anm. 1 bemerkt hat) erlitt er deutlich eine Niederlage. Daß Baldewin überhaupt Erfolg hatte, verdankt er der Stärke seiner Position. Das deutet auch hin auf die unten ausführlicher behandelte Tatsache, daß es im Falle eines starken und unabhängigen Supplikanten um Absolution für das Papsttum nicht möglich war, das Element der Verhandlung über die Bedingungen völlig auszuschließen.

V

schworen dann die darin enthaltenen Erklärungen und Forderungen im Namen ihres Auftraggebers[1]). Sie enthielt nicht allein die Wiederholung von Baldewins Prokuratorium und Clemens' Absolutionsdekret, sondern auch die Verpflichtung Baldewins, gemäß dem Gehorsamseid, den er dem Papst bei seiner Promotion zum Erzbischof von Trier geleistet hatte, und dem generellen Eid seiner Prokuratoren, daß er den Geboten des Papstes gehorchen wolle, zu erklären, daß es häretisch sei zu lehren, daß der Papst vom Kaiser abgesetzt werden könne. So war eine von den Stipulationen des Entwurfs, die Baldewin in seinem Prokuratorium ausgelassen hatte, wieder eingefügt worden[2]), und ihre Annahme durch Baldewin wurde zu einer Bedingung seiner Absolution gemacht, die ja davon abhing, daß er nicht nur ratifizierte *omnes supradictos articulos in dicto tuo procuratorio expressos et tuo nomine per eosdem procuratores tuos et nuncios confessatos*, sondern auch *ea que per nos* (Clemens) *sunt tibi ut prefertur, iniuncta*[3]). Der Versuch des deutschen Prälaten, die Bedingungen der Rekonziliation zu mildern, war wenigstens teilweise mißlungen.

Auf den ersten Blick scheinen diese drei Fälle lediglich die kanonische Theorie der Absolution zu bestätigen und kein neues Licht auf die Frage zu werfen, wie Ludwig hoffen konnte, die päpstlichen Forderungen, denen er doch anscheinend durch die Aufsetzung der Prokuratorien schon zugestimmt hatte, dadurch modifizieren zu können, daß er seinen Prokuratoren Instruktionen erteilte, die von dieser Vollmacht abweichen. In der Angelegenheit der Rekonziliation von Viterbo, der Visconti und, vielleicht weniger streng genommen, in der des Baldewin von Trier, hat offenbar das Papsttum sein Recht ausgeübt, den Bittstellern um Absolution beliebige Bedingungen der Unterwerfung aufzuerlegen. In jedem Fall machte das Papsttum die Absolution davon abhängig, daß der Supplikant mehr erfüllte, als in den Einzelheiten der Vollmachten seiner Prokuratoren aufgezählt war: Das Recht hierzu ist in den Prokuratorien von Viterbo

---

1) Das Protokoll des Konsistoriums ist aus dem Register des Michael Ricomanni abgedruckt bei Erdmann S. 42.

2) Vgl. schon Stengel S. 194 Anm. 1.

3) Sauerland Nr. 87. Bischof Daniel von Verden wurde vom Papst beauftragt, Baldewin erst dann die Buße abzunehmen und das Interdikt über seine Diözese aufzuheben, wenn er die Akte seiner Prokuratoren ratifiziert und die päpstlichen Vorschriften erfüllt hätte. E. E. Stengel, Nova Alamanniae, Urkunden, Briefe und andere Quellen, besonders zur deutschen Gesch. des 14. Jh.s 2 (1930) 723.

und der Visconti deutlich anerkannt[1]). Ebenso ist in den Prokuratorien von 1336 und 1343 das päpstliche Recht, Ludwigs Unterwerfung auch auf Angelegenheiten auszudehnen, die in den Instrumenten nicht besonders erwähnt waren, ausdrücklich vorbehalten[2]). Wie kann die Tatsache, daß Ludwig seinen Prokuratoren Instruktionen gab, welche die in den Prokuratorien bereits gemachten Zugeständnisse herabminderten, sich mit der päpstlichen Praxis vertragen?

Die Erklärung dürfte zum Teil abhängen von dem richtigen Verständnis des Wesens der Prokuratorien, und hier ist das in den drei oben behandelten Fällen vorliegende Beweismaterial für die Art der Prozedur aufschlußreich. In jedem Fall kamen die Prokuratoren in das Konsistorium und vollzogen dort die Akte, zu denen sie durch ihre Prokuratorien bevollmächtigt waren, bekannten die Verfehlungen ihrer Auftraggeber, unterwarfen sie der Gnade der Kirche, baten um ihre Absolution usw. Wenn diese Akte vollzogen waren, waren die Auftraggeber gebunden durch die Bedingungen ihrer Prokuratorien, aber erst dann, nicht früher. Bei dem Akt des Vollzugs und der Veröffentlichung eines Prokuratoriums tat der Auftraggeber weiter nichts, als sich zu verpflichten, alles das gutzuheißen, was seine Prokuratoren im Rahmen ihres Instruments tun würden; er garantierte damit aber nicht, daß sie alles tun würden, was in dem Prokuratorium aufgezählt war. Wenn und sobald sie es nach seiner Instruktion taten, war er durch ihre Akte gebunden[3]). Es ist also ersichtlich, daß in den oben behandelten drei Fällen der Rekonziliation die Auftraggeber an die Bedingungen ihrer Prokuratorien erst von dem Augenblick an gebunden waren, wenn ihre Prokuratoren im Konsistorium bekannt, geschworen, gebeten hatten usw., wie ihre Vollmacht lautete. Im Augenblick ihres Erlasses legten die Prokuratorien dem Auftraggeber

---

[1]) Henricus Roberti wurde in dem Prokuratorium von Viterbo ermächtigt, die Eide über die aufgezählten Einzelheiten abzulegen und jeden andern Eid zu leisten, der notwendig sein würde, um die Absolution zu erlangen (Bussi S. 423). Die Prokuratoren der Visconti wurden ermächtigt, alle Bekenntnisse abzulegen, die in dem Prokuratorium einzeln aufgeführt waren, *et quascumque alias confessiones* (Erdmann S. 14).

[2]) Vgl. oben S. 463 Anm. 3.

[3]) Die Situation kommt gut zum Ausdruck bei R. Möller S. 86. Durch die Prokuratorien bekamen die Gesandten des Kaisers „wohl die Vollmacht, aber nicht den Befehl, auf die Bedingungen abzuschließen. Sie konnten die Ratifizierung vollziehen, und der Kaiser schwur, das, was sie auf Grund der Prokuratorien zum Abschluß bringen würden, zu erfüllen. Die Unterhändler aber handelten nicht nach eigenem Ermessen, sondern nach den Direktiven, die sie mitbekamen; sie waren an ihre Instruktionen gebunden.“

V

lediglich hypothetische und potentielle Verpflichtungen auf. Real und wirksam wurden diese Verpflichtungen erst infolge der Vollziehung des Aktes durch die Prokuratoren.

Auf dieses erste Stadium, als seine Prokuratorien noch bloß potentiell bindende Kraft hatten, müssen Ludwigs Instruktionen von 1336 und 1343 bezogen werden. Die Folgerung ist unmißverständlich die, daß Ludwig, während das Papsttum darauf bestanden hatte, daß seinen Prokuratoren gewisse Vollmachten gegeben würden als Vorbedingung für eine Erwägung der Rekonziliation überhaupt, nicht gewillt war, die päpstlichen Forderungen so anzunehmen, wie sie sich in den Prokuratorien spiegelten. Doch wünschte er seinen Friedensversuch mit der Kirche nicht völlig abzubrechen. So schickte er seine Gesandten zur Kurie mit der Vollmacht, die päpstlichen Forderungen anzunehmen, und mit festen Instruktionen, es nicht zu tun. Auf diese Weise lag keine Gefahr in der Ausstellung der Vollmacht für die Prokuratoren, wenn sie nur wußten, daß sie sich hüten müßten, ohne weiteres die Akte zu vollziehen, welche allein die Prokuratorien für Ludwig bindend machen konnten. Man mochte hoffen, daß die Prokuratoren nach ihrer Ankunft bei der Kurie den Papst überreden könnten, seine Forderungen so zu mildern, daß sie sich mit den Bedingungen ihrer Instruktionen vereinigen ließen. Aber wie läßt sich Ludwigs Hoffnung, daß der Papst zur Milderung seiner Forderungen überredet werden könne, mit der kirchlichen Theorie vereinen, daß der Pönitent seine vollständige Unterwerfung vollziehen müsse, um die Absolution zu erlangen? War nicht Verhandlung und Kompromiß im Falle der Rekonziliation durch die kanonische Theorie völlig ausgeschlossen?

Die Antwort auf diese Fragen liegt in der Tatsache, daß es gewisse Grenzen gab, welche die Kirche bei ihrem Anspruch auf völlige Unterwerfung als Vorbedingung der Rekonziliation nicht überschreiten durfte. Ihre Forderungen mußten vernünftig[1]) sein, und sie durften nicht für den Pönitenten so untragbar sein, daß er die Rekonziliation unter diesen Bedingungen verweigern würde. Die Gefahr, in der Exkommunikation in *foro externo* verharren zu müssen, verringerte sich je nach der weltlichen Machtstellung des Betroffenen. Ein Großer, der die unangenehmen Seiten der Rekonziliation abwog gegen die Folgen der Verstocktheit, war vielleicht nicht geneigt, die ersteren vorzuziehen. Es war also Raum für Verhandlungen zwischen

[1]) Vgl. die Bemerkung des Antoninus von Florenz a. a. O.: *absolvens faciat illi mandata iusta et rationabilia; alias appellare possit.*

einem mächtigen Exkommunizierten und der Kirche. Denn wenn auch der Anspruch der Kirche auf Unterwerfung formell absolut war, so war er doch in der Praxis durch die Möglichkeit begrenzt, daß der Exkommunizierte die ersten Schritte zur Erlangung der Absolution nicht unternehmen werde, wenn er sich nicht vorher vergewissert hätte, daß ihm nicht zu drückende Bedingungen auferlegt würden.

Die Rolle, welche hier die Verhandlung spielt, tritt deutlich genug hervor in jenem Prozeß um die Rekonziliation Friedrichs II. von Hohenstaufen, der unter dem Namen des „Vertrags“ oder „Friedens“ von San Germano bekannt ist. Am 10. November 1229 bevollmächtigte Papst Gregor IX. Thomas von Capua, den exkommunizierten Kaiser loszusprechen gemäß einem ihm anvertrauten Formular, welches die üblichen kanonischen Bedingungen der Unterwerfung unter die Kirche enthielt (vgl. den Eid *stare praecise mandatis ecclesie et sine aliqua conditione secundum formam ecclesie . . . super omnibus pro quibus est excommunicatus*): die Verpflichtung, abzubitten für offenbare Beleidigungen, und das Gelübde, etwaigen Mandaten des Papstes zu gehorchen, erscheinen hier als die Vorbedingungen der Absolution[1]). Später wurden einige weitere Bürgschaftsbedingungen dieser ursprünglichen Form hinzugefügt, die sich besonders auf das Schicksal von Gaeta und S. Agata bezogen. Am 4. Februar 1230 hatte Friedrich die ursprünglichen Bedingungen angenommen; aber die weitere *cautio* betr. Gaeta und S. Agata wollte er nicht zulassen. Erst nach langen politischen Verhandlungen kam über diese Frage eine beiden Teilen genehme Formulierung zustande. Und erst als dies geschehen war, leistete Friedrich am 23. Juli dem Papst den Unterwerfungseid, auf Grund dessen am 28. August seine Absolution in Ceperano stattfand[2]). An diesem Beispiel wird klar, welche Rolle in einem Pro-

[1]) K. Hampe, Die Aktenstücke zum Frieden von S. Germano 1230 (MG. Epp. sel. 4) S. 24, 27, 32.

[2]) Papst Gregor IX. schlug als zusätzliche Garantie vor, daß die Kirche Gaeta und S. Agata besetzen solle, bis eine befriedigende Abmachung darüber getroffen sei und bis Friedrich die Garantie der Fürsten, Grafen und Herren von Deutschland und der Kommunen der Lombardei, Tusciens, der Mark und Romagnola beigebracht habe, daß sie die Kirche gegen ihn unterstützen würden, falls er ihren Befehlen nicht gehorche und den Frieden breche (Hampe S. 31). Ende März, als Friedrichs Verweigerung dieses Vorschlags klar wurde, wurde ein Alternativvorschlag angeregt, aber ebenfalls verworfen (Hampe S. 39 Nr. 2). Erst am 12. Juli legte die päpstliche Partei einen Garantievorschlag vor, den Friedrich annahm. Wenn nach Ablauf eines Jahres eine befriedigende Entscheidung

zeß um die Rekonziliation eines mächtigen weltlichen Herrschers die vorherige Beilegung der politischen Differenzen zwischen Papst und Pönitent spielen konnte, ehe der letztere den Unterwerfungseid schwur, und wie — als Ergebnis dieser Vorverhandlungen — der Eid nicht mehr bedeutete, als daß der Pönitent die Bedingungen erfüllen wolle, über die er sich bei der Verhandlung mit dem Papst geeinigt hatte.

Ludwigs des Bayern Versuche vom März und Oktober 1336 sowie vom September 1343, die Rekonziliation zu erlangen, unterschieden sich vom Falle Friedrichs insofern, als sie nicht persönlich in Gegenwart päpstlicher Legaten, sondern bei der Kurie in Vertretung durch Prokuratoren unternommen wurden. Aber gerade die Schwierigkeiten, welche die Verwendung von Prokuratorien für das Verständnis von Ludwigs Beziehungen zum Papsttum bedeutet, haben wir oben teilweise lösen und zeigen können, daß Ludwig bei Ausstellung der Prokuratorien sich nicht ohne weiteres den darin enthaltenen Forderungen unterwarf und daß er sich nicht meineidig machte, wenn er später die Ausführung ablehnte. Die Möglichkeit von Verhandlungen, die wir bei der Rekonziliation Friedrichs nachweisen konnten, liegt auch bei den Versuchen Ludwigs von 1336 und 1343 vor; sie folgt aus den Instruktionen an seine Prokuratoren. Als Ludwigs Wunsch, die Rekonziliation mit der Kirche zu erlangen, bekannt wurde, teilte ihm der Papst die Bedingungen mit, zu deren Erfüllung die Prokuratoren bevollmächtigt sein müßten, wenn sie bei der Kurie empfangen werden wollten. Ludwig stellte zwar die Prokuratorien mehr oder weniger nach dem päpstlichen Muster aus[1]), instruierte aber seine Prokuratoren, ihn nicht zur Erfüllung ihres Inhalts zu verpflichten; vielmehr sollten sie durch Verhandlung eine Herabminderung der päpstlichen Forderungen versuchen. So angesehen, darf man nicht, wie Preger, in dem Dualismus zwischen den Prokuratorien und den Instruktionen einen diplomatischen Kniff argwöhnen[2]). Ludwig wollte damit nur das tun, was jeder um Absolution Bittende, der sich in

---

über Gaeta nicht gefunden wäre, so sollten von jeder Seite zwei Schiedsrichter ernannt werden mit Vollmacht, einen fünften zu kooptieren, um dann mit Stimmenmehrheit zu einer Entscheidung zu gelangen. Die Garantie, der Kirche zu helfen, wenn Friedrich die Friedensbedingungen verletze, wurde nun bloß von den deutschen Fürsten verlangt, die mit Friedrich in S. Germano waren (Hampe S. 48—49). Friedrichs Eid, *stare precise mandatis ecclesie* (Hampe S. 57).

[1]) Vgl. oben S. 464 Anm. 2.

[2]) W. Preger, Der kirchenpolitische Kampf unter Ludwig dem Bayern (Abh. Münch. III. Kl. 14, 1879) S. 27.

seiner geistlichen und weltlichen Position sicher fühlen konnte[1]), versuchen durfte, nämlich über die etwaige Form der Unterwerfung verhandeln, ehe er sich der Gnade der Kirche anvertraute.

Wir kommen so zu einer einfachen Schlußfolgerung über den Wert von Ludwigs Prokuratorien und Instruktionen für die Erkenntnis der Beziehungen zwischen Papst und Kaiser. Die Prokuratorien enthalten die päpstlichen Forderungen[2]), die Instruktionen den Kommentar des Kaisers, der seine Zweifel und Bedenken erledigt haben wollte, ehe er sich der Kirche unterwarf.

II.

Die Beurteilung der Forderungen, welche das Papsttum an Ludwig 1343 und 1344 als Preis für seine Rekonziliation stellte, ist infolge des unvollständigen Urkundenmaterials und der irrtümlichen Verwertung desselben lange verworren geblieben. Es ist bekannt, daß im Spätsommer 1343 Marquard von Randeck mit einem von der Kurie aufgesetzten Formular der Prokuratorien[3]) aus Avignon zu Ludwig zurückkehrte und daß Ludwig am 18. September seine Gesandten mit den entsprechenden Prokuratorien bevollmächtigte. Als diese Gesandten im Mai 1344 wiederum von der Kurie heimkamen, brachten sie Prokuratorien mit, welche die Bedingungen enthielten, unter welchen die Rekonziliation Ludwigs stattfinden könne, und diese Bedingungen unterbreitete Ludwig den Kurfürsten, deren Stellungnahme in einem Memorandum erhalten ist, das ich SNA[4]) nennen will. So muß es einerseits möglich sein, aus den Prokuratorien des 18. September 1343 zu entnehmen, welches die 1343 von Marquard mitgebrachten päpstlichen Forderungen waren; andererseits wird

---

[1]) Es scheint sehr wenig Grund für die weitverbreitete Annahme zu bestehen, daß Ludwig sich durch Gewissensbisse gedrängt fühlte, die Rekonziliation zu suchen. Er betrachtete die gegen ihn gefällten Urteile als ungerecht und daher nichtig, und setzte die üblichen frommen Übungen fort; vgl. die Feststellung in der Instruktion vom Oktober 1336, er habe *gotz dienst all zeit gehoert vnd och gotes lichnam dick enpfangen*, Riezler, Widersacher S. 328.

[2]) Man muß die Einschränkung machen, daß hier die Möglichkeit besteht, daß die päpstlichen Bedingungen zuweilen stillschweigend abgeändert wurden, ehe Ludwig sie in der Form von Prokuratorien ausgehen ließ; vgl. oben S. 464 Anm. 2.

[3]) Dies ist im wesentlichen der Bericht des Mathias von Neuenburg, Chronica (MG. SS. NS. 4/1) S. 189, wenn auch Mathias einige Einzelheiten des nächsten Jahres in das Jahr 1343 vorverlegt haben mag.

[4]) Stengel, Nova Alamanniae Nr. 773.

man die Revision dieser Forderungen in den Urkunden zu finden haben, welche den Kurfürsten vorgelegt wurden. Aber bis jetzt ist die Identität der Prokuratorien von 1343 noch nicht sicher festgestellt worden, und das hat zu verwirrten Vorstellungen von den Bedingungen von 1344 geführt.

In der jüngsten Diskussion hierüber hat Stengel[1]) angenommen, daß die ausführlichen Prokuratorien vom September 1343 in zwei Urkunden zu finden seien, die Gewold[2]) in seiner Übersetzung des deutschen Kodizills 1/5 260 des Geheimen Haus-Archivs in München[3]) gedruckt hat, und daß die päpstlichen Forderungen von 1344 nicht mehr erhalten seien, sondern durch einen Vergleich von MGHA mit SNA rekonstruiert werden müßten.

Die Theorie, daß MGHA eine Fassung der ausführlichen Prokuratorien vom September 1343 darstelle, wird indessen völlig ausgeschlossen durch die Tatsache, daß in Marseille Abschriften von sechs Prokuratorien erhalten sind, die Ludwig am 18. September für seine Verhandlungen mit Papst Clemens VI. ausstellte. Sie stehen in einem Register von Urkunden, die zusammengestellt sind auf Befehl von Jean de Revest, *magister rationalis* der Provence, der in den Frühjahren der Regierung Johannas von Neapel bei der Kurie die neapolitanischen Interessen vertrat[4]). In seinem Register hat Revest Abschriften von solchen vom Papst kommenden oder an ihn gerichteten Briefen und Dokumenten genommen, welche für die Leiter der neapolitanischen Politik von Interesse sein könnten; und Urkunden, welche sich auf die Frage der Rekonziliation Ludwigs bezogen, mußten sie schon interessieren; wünschte doch Neapel mehr als jeder andere Staat in Europa die kaiserliche Macht gelähmt, wenn nicht völlig zerstört zu sehen[5]).

---

[1]) Avignon und Rhens, S. 192—194; G. Dahrmann, Ludwigs des Bayern Kampf mit der Kurie von 1338 bis zu seinem Tode (Diss. Rostock, ungedruckt, 1920), habe ich nicht gesehen.

[2]) Ch. Gewold, Defensio Ludovici IV imperatoris ratione electionis contra Alb. Bzovium (1618) S. 181—208.

[3]) Beschrieben von C. Müller, Der Kampf Ludwigs d. B. mit d. römischen Kurie 2 (1880) 306.

[4]) Archives départementales des Bouches du Rhône, 176. Das Register ist beschrieben von E. G. Léonard, Histoire de Jeanne 1re Reine de Naples 1 (1932) XXXVII—IX.

[5]) Über die neapolitanische Haltung dem Kaiser gegenüber vgl. F. Bock, Kaisertum, Kurie und Nationalstaat im Beginn des 14. Jahrhunderts, Römische Quartalschrift 44 (1936) 169ff.

Es handelt sich um folgende Dokumente[1]), die wir mit unterscheidenden Siglen bezeichnen:

ff. 108^r—111^v. Ein Spezialprokuratorium, welches die Submissionen behandelt, die Ludwig in Bezug auf politische Angelegenheiten machen sollte (SP);

ff. 112^r—113^r. Ein kurzes allgemeines Prokuratorium, welches die Einzelheiten der andern Prokuratorien zusammenfaßt. Es ist bereits zweimal nach anderen Kopien gedruckt[2]) (SA);

ff. 113^{r-v}. Ein Prokuratorium, in dem Ludwig alle mit Frankreich streitigen Sachen der päpstlichen Entscheidung unterwirft (SF);

ff. 113^v. Ein Prokuratorium, welches Ludwig bei seinen Streitigkeiten mit den Luxemburgern der päpstlichen Entscheidung unterwirft (SL);

ff. 113^v. Ein Prokuratorium, in dem Ludwig den Papst ermächtigt, seine Streitigkeiten mit allen Königen und Fürsten usw. beizulegen (SG);

ff. 113^v—114^r. Ein Prokuratorium, durch welches Ludwigs Prokuratoren den Papst bitten sollen, Ludwigs Wahl zum König der Römer zu billigen (SW).

Ein weiteres Prokuratorium vom selben Datum, das seit dem 18. Jh. gedruckt[3]), aber von vielen Gelehrten seltsamerweise übersehen worden ist, beschäftigt sich fast ausschließlich und sehr ausführlich mit Ludwigs Irrlehren (SC).

Auf Grund dieser Reihe von sieben Prokuratorien erscheint es möglich, mit Sicherheit eine vollständige Übersicht über die Forderungen Clemens' VI. im Jahre 1343 zu geben. Die Meinung, sie seien viel schroffer als die seines Vorgängers[4]), ist nicht richtig, denn

---

[1]) Ich danke M. Raoul Busquet, Archiviste en chef des Archives départementales des Bouches du Rhône, für die Erlaubnis, Photographien dieser Urkunden zu erwerben.

[2]) VA. Nr. 2167 nach einer Kopie im Vatikan; und Gewold, Defensio Ludovici 173—180, nach einer jetzt im Geheimen Haus-Archiv München befindlichen Kopie 1/5, 253, datiert vom Jahre 1355 (vgl. Schwalm, NA. 23 [1898] 25).

[3]) J. P. de Bourchenu, Marquis de Valbonnays, Histoire de Dauphiné 2 (1722) 473 ff.

[4]) Vgl. C. Müller 2, 176—177: „Man kann ohne weiteres behaupten, daß diese Bedingungen nur aufgestellt worden sind, um eine Vereinbarung mit Ludwig auf ihrer Grundlage unmöglich zu machen. Man wollte jetzt keine Aussöhnung mehr mit ihm; zu bestimmt hatte Clemens sein Ziel schon ins Auge gefaßt.“ Aber über die Natur der päpstlichen Bedingungen war Müller falsch unterrichtet.

die Ludwig zur Ausführung übersandten Prokuratorien beruhen auf denen von 1336, und die Unterschiede betreffen mehr Einzelheiten als Hauptsachen.

Die Artikel des langen politischen Prokuratoriums vom Oktober 1336 (OP) werden fast wörtlich von SP wiederholt. Nur läßt das letztere die Klauseln von OP aus, die sich auf eine Allianz mit Robert von Sizilien beziehen, denn dieser war nun tot. Es mag auch nicht ganz bedeutungslos sein, daß zweimal der Ausdruck *post approbationem persone nostre* von OP[1]) ersetzt wird durch den weniger zuversichtlichen *si approbationem persone nostre obtinuerimus*. Überdies mildert SP, in Übereinstimmung mit SC und SA, das absolute Verbot der Prokuratorien von 1336, die Prokuratoren *pendente negotio* abzuberufen. Ludwig darf sie, durch versiegelte Briefe an den Papst, jetzt abberufen; aber in diesem Falle ist alles, was sie bisher verrichtet haben, für ihren Auftraggeber bindend.

SC enthält vielleicht noch mehr Spuren kaiserlicher Redaktion[2]) als das Ludwigs Verstöße gegen die Lehre und das Gesetz der Kirche behandelnde lange spezialisierte Prokuratorium vom Oktober 1336 (OC), auf dem es übrigens weithin beruht. Wenn der Artikel von OC, in dem Ludwigs Prokuratoren bevollmächtigt wurden, die päpstliche Billigung der Wahl Ludwigs zum König der Römer zu erbitten, in SC fehlt, so doch nur deshalb, weil 1343 ein besonderes Prokuratorium für diesen Zweck aufgesetzt worden ist (SW). Zwei Neuerungen finden sich indessen in SC: es enthält einen Artikel, nach dem Ludwigs Prokuratoren ihn verpflichten können, die Fürsten und Herren Deutschlands zu überreden, daß sie um seine Absolution und um die Erlaubnis der Annahme des Titels eines Königs der Römer bitten, während Ludwigs Verzicht auf seine kaiserliche Krone nun in ursächlichen Zusammenhang mit seinen Verfehlungen gegen das Gesetz und die Lehre der Kirche gebracht werden soll[3]).

---

[1]) Man kann auch feststellen, daß in SP der Artikel, welcher von der Revokation der Urteile über Heinrich VII. handelt, nicht mehr, wie in OP, eingeschränkt ist durch den Satz *postquam assumpti fuerimus a sanctitate vestra in regem Romanorum.*

[2]) Vgl. oben S. 464 Anm. 2.

[3]) OC. *Dictis nostris procuratoribus* . . . *damus* . . . *potestatem ad renunciandum et dimittendum et totaliter deponendum vice et nomine nostro et pro nobis titulum imperialem Rome per nos receptum et quo utimur et hactenus usi sumus* . . . *SC: quod in emendam et satisfactionem et nomine emende et satisfactionis excessuum predictorum per nos commissorum coram sanctitate vestra* . . . *titulum imperialem per nos Rome assumptum et quo hactenus usi fuerimus* . . . *tanquam male et iniuste et perverse receptum deponant et dimittant* . . .

Das kurze allgemeine Prokuratorium von 1343 (SA) summiert, aber keineswegs vollständig, die Einzelheiten der sechs übrigen Prokuratorien vom selben Datum. Es ist möglich, daß die Unvollständigkeit von einer radikalen Redigierung des päpstlichen Konzepts kaiserlicherseits herrührt. Im Gegensatz zum kurzen allgemeinen Prokuratorium vom März 1336 (MA), dem es am meisten ähnelt, wird in SA nicht erwähnt: daß die Prokuratoren bevollmächtigt waren, die päpstliche Genehmigung zur Wahl Ludwigs zu erbitten, Bündnisse mit Robert von Neapel zu schließen, dem Papst zu gestatten, die von Heinrich VII. in Italien gefällten Entscheidungen umzustoßen, Ludwig zu verpflichten, vor der Billigung seiner Wahl durch den Papst nicht nach Italien zu kommen und Rom vor dem für seine Krönung bestimmten Tage nicht zu betreten, dem Papst die Schlichtung aller Meinungsverschiedenheiten, die sich über den Sinn der Artikel des Prokuratoriums ergeben könnten, zu erlauben, Absolution zu erbitten für die bisherigen Anhänger Ludwigs, sowie Milderung des Interdikts in den Städten, die ihn aufgenommen hatten. Aber das Verschwinden dieser Punkte in SA läßt nicht auf irgendwelche Abschwächung der päpstlichen Forderungen im Jahre 1343 schließen; denn mit Ausnahme der Klauseln über Robert von Neapel kommen sie alle in den anderen Prokuratorien vom September 1343 wieder vor. Das Zusammentreffen von manchen dieser Auslassungen mit der Tendenz von Ludwigs Instruktion für seine Prokuratoren im Oktober 1343 läßt indessen vermuten, daß die ursprüngliche Form von SA, die Ludwig als päpstliches Konzept vorlag, von ihm im Sinne der kaiserlichen Vorbehalte abgeändert wurde, bevor er sie siegelte und ausgehen ließ[1]). In einer Hinsicht ging SA über MA

[1]) Ludwigs Instruktion, datiert vom 28. Oktober 1343, ist bei Riezler, Widersacher S. 332—333, aus MGHA 1/5, 259 abgedruckt. Der Schlüssel zu SA liegt in dem rechten Verständnis von der Bedeutung der kurzen allgemeinen Form des Prokuratoriums. Es war die für die aktive Verhandlung bestimmte Vollmacht der Prokuratoren. Als Ludwigs Prokuratoren am 16. Januar 1344 im Konsistorium vor dem Papst erschienen, wurde diese Form allein verlesen; nach ihren Bedingungen handelten Ludwigs Prokuratoren, indem sie die darin enthaltenen Submissionen, Konzessionen, Eide usw. leisteten (vgl. die erste Fassung des offiziellen Konsistorialprotokolls in dem Manual des Richard Ricomanni, Protokollführers der päpstlichen Camera, bei H. Schröder, Die Protokollbücher der päpstlichen Kammerkleriker, Archiv f. Kulturgesch. 27 [1937] 263—271). Wir dürfen daraus schließen, daß die allgemeine Form des Prokuratoriums als ein vollständiges Resumé der speziellen Vollmachten dienen sollte, welche in den speziellen besonderen Prokuratorien gegeben waren, und daß die Fassung von SA, die von der Kurie an Ludwig geschickt war, solch ein vollständiges Resumé war. Ludwig

hinaus: die Prokuratoren wurden nun bevollmächtigt, Ludwig der Entscheidung des Papstes in allen Streitigkeiten mit dem König von Frankreich und den Luxemburgern zu unterstellen, Zugeständnisse, für die auch noch besondere Prokuratorien (SF und SL oben) ausgestellt wurden.

Zusammenfassend können wir sagen, die Prokuratorien von 1343 beweisen schlüssig, daß die Forderungen des Papsttums seit der Zeit, als die Bedingungen für Ludwigs Absolution zuerst festgelegt wurden, sich nicht geändert hatten. Die politischen Interessen des Papsttums und seiner Verbündeten waren noch immer ausschlaggebend. Hinter der Forderung, daß Ludwig seine Wahl der päpstlichen Genehmigung unterbreiten solle, stand der Wunsch, Garantien für die päpstlichen Territorien und für den päpstlichen Einfluß in Italien zu erlangen. Die Luxemburger waren für das päpstliche Interesse auf den durch den Tod Roberts von Neapel freigewordenen Platz gerückt, und Ludwig wurde ersucht, ihre Wünsche ebensowohl zu erfüllen wie die des Königs von Frankreich. Wenn die päpstlichen Forderungen nicht merklich strenger waren als 1336, so waren sie auch sicherlich nicht leichter.

Was hat es nun auf sich mit dem Kodizill, das bisher als eine deutsche Übersetzung von zwei langen spezialisierten Prokuratorien von 1343 angesehen wurde (MGHA)? Dieses Kodizill[1]) umfaßt zwei undatierte Urkunden, jede gefolgt von einer Inhaltsangabe der Eide, die zu leisten waren, wenn die Urkunden tatsächlich erlassen und verwendet werden sollten. Auf fol. 1^r—6^r steht die deutsche Übersetzung eines Konzepts für ein notarielles Protokoll über ein von Ludwig auszustellendes Prokuratorium, welches hauptsächlich von Ludwigs Verfehlungen gegen die Lehre und das Gesetz der Kirche

---

änderte diese päpstliche Fassung von SA in der Weise, daß sie in Übereinstimmung gebracht wurde mit seiner beständigen Haltung gegenüber den päpstlichen Forderungen, die am besten ihren Ausdruck findet in den Instruktionen vom Oktober 1336 und Oktober 1343. Die Prokuratoren konnten also unbedenklich in dem Konsistorium vom 16. Januar 1344 die Unterwerfung nach den Bedingungen von SA vollziehen, obgleich sie nach dem gegenteiligen Auftrag ihrer Instruktion die Unterwerfung nach den detaillierten Prokuratorien vom September 1343 nicht hätten vollziehen dürfen; in diesen waren die päpstlichen Bedingungen im wesentlichen unverändert geblieben, wenn sie auch Spuren einer kaiserlichen Redaktion an sich tragen (vgl. oben S. 464 Anm. 2).

[1]) Ich habe dem Generaldirektor der staatlichen Archive Bayerns für die Erlaubnis zu danken, daß ich diese und andere Urkunden im Geheimen Haus-Archiv benutzen konnte.

handeln sollte (BC)[1]. fol. 7ʳ—11ᵛ enthalten das Konzept für ein Protokoll über ein Prokuratorium, welches politische Zugeständnisse enthält (BP). BC ist erkennbar verschieden von den entsprechenden Prokuratorien vom September 1343 (SC); BP ist völlig verschieden von SP[2]).

---

[1]) Diese Auffassung von der Natur von BC und BP kann durch folgende Erwägungen gerechtfertigt werden. Die Urkunden sprechen von Ludwig in der dritten Person (vgl. BC art. 1: *Zem ersten gibt er sein procuraturen vollen woren und frein gewalt*... MGHA 1/5, 260, fol. 1ʳ); vom Papst in der zweiten (vgl. BC art. 12: *vor ewer hailkeit und wa es ewer hailchait guot duncht*... fol. 4ʳ); und von den Notaren in der ersten Person (BC art. 27: *und satz darumb allin siniu guot, diu er ietzo hat oder noch gewint, uns Notarien und schribern* ... fol. 5ᵛ). Überdies sind beide Urkunden durchweg im Präsens abgefaßt. Sie scheinen also ein für den Papst aufgesetztes Protokoll von gewissen Akten zu sein, die damals von Ludwig vollzogen wurden. Aber dieser Anschein ist trügerisch. Sowohl BC als BP ist angehängt ein Verzeichnis der in diesen Urkunden geforderten Eide, und Ludwigs Eid, alles, was seine Prokuratoren tun würden, zu erfüllen — ein Eid, der ein wesentlicher Teil des Aktes der Prokuratie war —, ist so abgefaßt, daß er offenbar noch nicht abgelegt war (vgl. fol. 12ʳ: *Ir wert auch hie uz selb swern vor den notarien, was ewer procuratur tuond in den vorgeschriben sachen, als si begriffen sint in den artikeln, daz ir das stuet habt begriffen ist in dem iungsten artikel*). Es dürfte daher zur Genüge klar sein, daß zu der Zeit, wo die Summarien der nach BC und BP zu leistenden Eide aufgezeichnet wurden, Ludwig den Akt des Prokuratoriums noch nicht vollzogen hatte, und daß die Summarien selbst später als BC und BP sein müssen. BC und BP sind also bloß Entwürfe für ein Protokoll von Akten, die Ludwig noch nicht vollzogen hatte und tatsächlich niemals vollzog.

[2]) Nach den Bedingungen von BP sollten alle im Namen des Königs der Römer erfolgten Akte Ludwigs sowie seine Akte als Kaiser annulliert werden, wenn ihm auch Aussicht gemacht wurde, daß er nach seiner Absolution vielleicht durch einen Gnadenakt des Papstes einige oder alle Verleihungen, die er als König vorgenommen hatte, erneuern dürfe (Artikel 2 und 6). Heinrichs VII. Garantie der päpstlichen Länder, die am 11. Oktober 1310 in Lausanne gegeben war, wurde nicht mehr, wie in OP und SP vollständig, aber immerhin, in Artikel 9—15, doch zu einem beträchtlichen Teil in den Text aufgenommen. Neue Artikel bestimmten nun, daß Ludwig nichts im Namen des Kaisers oder Königs ohne päpstliche Erlaubnis tun dürfe und daß er um Aufhebung aller Urteile bitten müsse, die Clemens VI. und seine Vorgänger gegen ihn ausgesprochen hätten. Er sollte auch den Antrag stellen, daß er wieder eingesetzt werde in den Stand vor dem gegen ihn gerichteten Prozesse, und daß er nach seiner Absolution wieder regieren dürfe (Artikel 20, 31, 32, 21). Gewisse Artikel von SP kamen in BP überhaupt nicht mehr vor. Sie sind alle von der gleichen Tendenz und beziehen sich auf Ludwigs Annullierung der Prozesse Heinrichs VII. gegen Robert von Sizilien, auf die Gewährung der Erlaubnis an den Papst, allen in Italien die in den letzten fünfzig Jahren gegen das Reich begangenen Injurien, Rebellionen und Verletzungen zu verzeihen, auf den Eid Ludwigs, vor dem festgesetzten Tag seiner Krönung nicht nach Rom zu kommen, auf die Verpflichtung, die er seinen Beamten

BC und BP können somit nicht zu den Prokuratorien vom September 1343 gehören. Wenn man sie aber vergleicht mit der Denkschrift der Kurfürsten vom August 1344 (SNA), wird es klar, daß die letztere Urkunde in enger Beziehung zu ihnen steht. In SNA ist kein einziger Artikel, der nicht in BP sein Gegenstück fände, und die leichte Abweichung in der Zählung der Artikel in den beiden Urkunden kann leicht erklärt werden: SNA behandelt die Artikel 4 und 5 von BP als einen, und in ähnlicher Weise Artikel 14 und 15 von BP. Von den vier Artikeln in SNA, welche kanonische Fragen behandeln, können drei auf Artikel in BC bezogen werden[1]). Die Schlußfolgerung erscheint klar, daß BC und BP die Artikel enthalten, zu denen SNA den Kommentar der Kurfürsten gibt, das will sagen, daß die Prokuratorien, die BC und BP zugrunde liegen, die *forma procuratoriorum* darstellen, welche von Ludwigs Gesandten im Mai 1344[2]) von der Kurie

---

in Italien auferlegen sollte, dort die päpstlichen Rechte zu wahren und zu schwören, daß sie keinerlei Autorität in Rom oder dem päpstlichen Territorium ausüben wollten, und endlich auf seinen Eid, alles dies binnen drei Tagen nach seiner Approbation und noch einmal binnen acht Tagen nach seiner Krönung als Kaiser wiederholen zu wollen. Der Grund, weshalb Clemens in BP nicht länger Garantien für Ludwigs Verhalten in Italien und als Kaiser erzwang, war, daß er nicht mehr mit der Möglichkeit rechnete, daß Ludwig Kaiser wurde oder in Italien handle. Diese Behauptung wird gestützt durch gewisse Unterschiede im Wortlaut der BP und SP gemeinsamen Artikel. Artikel 22 von BP lautet, daß Ludwig nicht nach Italien kommen oder sich mit den dortigen Händeln befassen solle „*ann besunder urlop des stuls ze Rome*"; SP hatte gelautet: *donec approbationem persone nostre fuerimus assecuti*. Wenn Ludwig die territoriale Integrität des Papsttums antastet, kann er nach SP beraubt werden *imperiali, regia et qualibet alia dignitate*; in BP heißt es *ain ieglich wirdicheit und herrschaft* (Artikel 16). In diesen beiden Fällen vermeidet BP sorgfältig, die Möglichkeit einzuschließen, daß Ludwig König der Römer und nachher Kaiser werden würde.

[1]) Daß BC keinen Artikel enthält, auf den die 62. Entgegnung von SNA sich bezieht, kann angesichts der überwältigenden Übereinstimmung von BC und BP mit SNA nicht dazu benutzt werden, die obige Beweisführung zu entkräften, wenn es auch die Vermutung nahe legt, daß die päpstlichen Forderungen den Kurfürsten in einer von der in MGHA erhaltenen sehr abweichenden Form unterbreitet wurden.

[2]) Freies Geleit für die Rückkehr nach Deutschland wurde Ludwigs Prokuratoren am 2. Mai 1344 zugesichert (VA. Nr. 2183); sie brachten mit eine *forma procuratoriorum ad hoc sufficienter cum deliberatione magni et maturi consilii ordinata* (Clemens VI. an Herzog Albert von Österreich am 27. Juni 1344, VA. Nr. 2186). Mathias von Neuenburg S. 191 sagt, daß die von Ludwig zu erfüllenden Artikel *non tangebant personam eius sed statum imperii*, eine Angabe, die sich sehr gut verträgt mit BC und BP; denn BC, das kirchliche Prokuratorium, welches die persönlichen

mitgebracht wurden und die revidierten päpstlichen Forderungen von 1344 enthielten[1]).

Diese Behauptung findet eine gewisse Stütze in der eigentümlichen Form von BC und BP. Diese Urkunden sind unvollzogene Konzepte für Notariatsinstrumente über den Akt der Prokuratorien[2]). Die notarielle Prozedur kommt in Verbindung mit den Prokuratorien von 1336 und 1343 nicht vor. Diese Prokuratorien wurden in Gegenwart von Notaren aufgesetzt und von ihnen beglaubigt, aber von Ludwigs Akt selbst scheint ein notarielles Protokoll nicht gemacht worden zu sein. Dagegen ist bekannt, daß der Papst im Mai 1344 zwei päpstliche Notare nach Deutschland sandte[3]). Er wußte, daß Vorsicht am Platze war, wollte man sicher gehen, daß Ludwig sich nicht der Erfüllung von Zugeständnissen entziehen könne, die seine Prokuratoren etwa machen würden; und die Vermutung scheint berechtigt, daß der Auftrag der päpstlichen Notare, die nach Deutschland geschickt wurden, der gewesen ist, gerade solch ein Protokoll von dem Akt des Prokuratoriums zu machen, wie wir es im Konzept in BC und BP vor uns haben. Sie konnten ein solches Konzept im voraus bereithalten, da sie wußten, daß der Akt des Prokuratoriums sich nur in der Form vollziehen konnte, die vom Papst schriftlich niedergelegt war, und die ihnen zweifellos bekannt war.

III.

In dem oben[4]) berührten Aufsatz hat Bock sich eingehend mit den Urkunden beschäftigt, die Ludwig bei seinen beiden Versuchen des Jahres 1336, die Rekonziliation mit der Kirche zu erlangen, ausgehen ließ. Seine Ergebnisse können, soweit sie diese Prokuratorien angehen, folgendermaßen zusammengefaßt werden:

Irrungen Ludwigs betrifft, ist im wesentlichen gegen SC nicht geändert, während BP, das politische Prokuratorium, das sich unter anderem auch mit der Frage des Imperiums befaßt, im Vergleich zu SP manche Neuerungen enthält.

[1]) F. von Weech, Kaiser Ludwig d. Bayer und König Johann von Böhmen (1860) S. 89 kommt zu diesem Ergebnis, obgleich er nur Gewolds lateinische Übersetzung der Prokuratorien zur Unterlage hat.

[2]) Daß die Entwürfe nicht ausgeführt wurden, ist klar; vgl. oben S. 481 Anm. 1.

[3]) Am 2. Mai 1344 wurden Freigeleitscheine für die Reise von Avignon nach Deutschland ausgestellt zugunsten zweier päpstlicher Notare; ihnen wurden 200 Florin ausgezahlt (VA. Nr. 2183 n. 2; Erdmann S. 42).

[4]) S. 461 Anm. 2.

März 1336. Ein allgemeines Prokuratorium, welches sich auf politische und kirchliche Angelegenheiten, namentlich aber auf letztere bezieht (MA).

Ein spezielles Prokuratorium, welches sich hauptsächlich auf politische Angelegenheiten bezieht (MP).

Oktober 1336. Ein spezielles Prokuratorium, das sich mit den mehr kirchlichen Seiten der Rekonziliation Ludwigs befaßt und das allgemeine Prokuratorium vom März ersetzt (OC).

Ein spezielles Prokuratorium, das sich hauptsächlich mit politischen Angelegenheiten befaßt (OP).

Drei von diesen Prokuratorien sind im Original erhalten, das vierte (MP) in einer gleichzeitigen Kopie[1]). Bock behauptet, daß wir in diesen vier Stücken die formellen Prokuratorien von Ludwigs Gesandtschaften an die Kurie im März und Oktober 1336 vollständig besitzen; keines sei vermißt oder verloren. Er meint auch, dieses Ergebnis vertrage sich mit dem Befund des Inventars der päpstlichen Archive, das 1366 von Arnold von Auch aufgestellt wurde[2]).

Bock hat seine Ergebnisse auf gründliche urkundliche Forschungen aufgebaut; aber sie sind doch auch von gewissen vorgefaßten Meinungen über das gegenseitige Verhältnis der Prokuratorien abhängig. Er sieht MA und MP als im wesentlichen identisch an — es „unterscheiden sich beide Stücke nur in der Ausführlichkeit" (S. 266) — und meint, daß als Ergebnis der Verhandlungen von Ludwigs Gesandten im Frühjahr 1336 die Form MA im Oktober durch die detailliertere Form OC (S. 273) ersetzt wurde. Es wären also nach Bock nur zwei Prokuratorien im März und zwei weitere im Oktober 1336 von Ludwig ausgestellt worden. Von diesen vier seien MP und OP praktisch identisch; aber OC, das sich mehr mit der kirchlichen Seite von Ludwigs Submissionen in vielen Einzelheiten befaßt, wäre eine neue, erstmals im Oktober eingeführte Form des Prokuratoriums.

Uns scheinen von vornherein sehr starke Gründe dagegen zu sprechen, daß irgendeine solche Änderung in der Verhandlungsgrundlage eingetreten wäre, die ihren Niederschlag in der Einführung einer neuen Form des Prokuratoriums gefunden hätte, wie Bock mit der

---

[1]) MA ist NA. 26 (1901) 713ff. nach dem Original gedruckt; OP in VA. Nr. 1842 nach dem Original; OC in VA. Nr. 1841 nach dem Original; MP in Bzovius, Annalium ecclesiasticorum . . . tom. 14 (1618) 1336 c. 2, nach einer Kopie.

[2]) L. A. Muratori, Antiquitates Italicae 6 (1742) 75ff.

Begründung vorschlägt, daß im Oktober OC MA ersetzt habe. Denn es dürfte sehr wahrscheinlich sein, daß die von Ludwig im Oktober 1336 an die Kurie geschickte Gesandtschaft lediglich eine Fortsetzung der März-Gesandtschaft war und daß die Ausstellung besonderer Prokuratorien im Oktober nicht in einer Änderung der Vollmacht der Gesandtschaft, sondern in einer Änderung ihres persönlichen Bestandes begründet war. Im März waren Ludwigs Prokuratoren der ältere und jüngere Graf von Öttingen, Eberhard von Tumnau, Heinrich von Zipplingen, Marquard von Randeck und Ulrich von Augsburg gewesen. Im Oktober schieden die beiden Grafen von Öttingen und Eberhard von Tumnau aus und wurden durch Graf Wilhelm von Jülich und Ruprecht von der Pfalz[1]) ersetzt. Diese beiden neuen Mitglieder bedurften einer Verhandlungsvollmacht, und diese wurde ihnen in OC und OP gegeben. Aber da keine neuen Vollmachten für Heinrich, Marquard und Ulrich ausgestellt wurden, müssen wir schließen, daß ihre alten Vollmachten ausreichten. Sie hatten ein detailliertes Prokuratorium für politische Angelegenheiten (MP), fast wörtlich übereinstimmend mit dem für Wilhelm und Ruprecht ausgestellten politischen Prokuratorium (OP)[2]); die Annahme scheint notwendig, daß sie auch eine detaillierte kirchliche Prokuratie im Sinne von OC hatten. Sonst würden ja Wilhelm und Ruprecht im Oktober ihren Gefährten gegenüber eine Ausnahmestellung gehabt haben. Dieses detaillierte kirchliche Prokuratorium der März-Gesandtschaft wollen wir MC nennen.

Diese Theorie, wonach schon die März-Gesandtschaft ein ausführliches kirchliches Prokuratorium besaß, das nun verloren ist, wird gestützt durch das neue Material der Vollmachten von 1343. Die Tatsache, daß wir 1343 sowohl ein kurzes allgemeines Prokuratorium (SA) als auch zwei spezielle Prokuratorien haben, von denen das eine hauptsächlich politische, das andere vorwiegend kirchliche Angelegenheiten behandelt, erschüttern Bocks Behauptung, daß

---

[1]) Ludwig an Benedikt XII. am 3. November 1336 mit der Ankündigung der Rückkehr von Heinrich, Marquard und Ulrich nach Avignon, VA. Nr. 1843.

[2]) Die einzigen Unterschiede zwischen MP und OP sind folgende: OP fügt eine dahingehende Erklärung hinzu, daß frühere Prokuratorien durch die neuen nicht berührt werden. Ferner soll in MP dem Papst für zwei Jahre Gewalt gegeben werden, alle in Italien gegen das Reich in den letzten fünfzig Jahren begangenen Missetaten zu vergeben, während OP vorsah, daß Ludwig, falls er selbst innerhalb dieser beiden Jahre nach Italien käme, die Vergebung in den Fällen, wo er es wünsche, ohne Beeinträchtigung der päpstlichen Rechte selbst vollziehen dürfe.

die kurze allgemeine Form vom März 1336 (MA) im Oktober verschwinde, weil sie zu dem speziellen kirchlichen Prokuratorium OC erweitert worden sei, und daß man also für die März-Gesandtschaft eine nun verlorene spezielle kirchliche Form nicht anzunehmen brauche. Denn 1343 existiert die allgemeine Form SA noch immer zusammen mit den speziellen Formen SC und SP, und es scheint daher, daß wir der kurzen allgemeinen Form des Prokuratoriums eine selbständige Bedeutung zuschreiben müssen. Wenn man SA auf seine Beziehungen zu den anderen Prokuratorien von 1343 prüft, wird es klar, daß seine Aufgabe war, eine große Menge der Einzelheiten der andern sechs Prokuratorien vom selben Datum in einem Dokument zusammenzufassen. Es war die für die aktiven Verhandlungen bestimmte Fassung der Vollmachten der Prokuratoren, und als dieselben vor Clemens VI. im Konsistorium des 16. Januar 1344 erschienen, war es diese Fassung, die sie verlasen und auf Grund deren sie als Prokuratoren verhandelten. SA hat im wesentlichen dieselbe Fassung wie MA, nur daß es aus gewissen Gründen seine anliegenden detaillierten Prokuratorien viel weniger vollständig wiedergibt[1]); gerade so wie MA die Substanz von MP enthält, wiederholt SA einen großen Teil von SP. Aber SA gibt auch den Inhalt von SC und einer Anzahl anderer Prokuratorien wieder; und es kann so vermutet werden, daß die Artikel von MA, die nicht aus MP abstrahiert sind, von einem verlorenen speziellen kirchlichen Prokuratorium vom März 1336 (MC) stammen, das wir mutatis mutandis mit OC und SC gleichsetzen können.

Bock nimmt keinen Bezug auf ein wichtiges Beweisstück für die Existenz von MC. Schon Stengel[2]) hat bemerkt, daß das Msc. jur. fol. 25 der Hessischen Landesbibliothek in Kassel eine Form von OP (Nr. 569 bei Stengel) bringt, die nicht vom Original, sondern einer früheren Fassung, vielleicht dem Konzept abgeleitet ist. Sie hat zahlreiche kleine Abweichungen von dem Original von OP gemeinsam mit MP. Überdies findet sich in demselben Manuskript eine Fassung von OC, welche verschiedene Lesarten enthält, die sich nicht im Original finden und die teilweise den Differenzen zwischen Nr. 569 und dem Original von OP entsprechen. Stengel schließt daraus, daß OC eine Urkunde zugrunde liegt, die zu ihm in demselben Verhältnis steht wie MP zu OP, d.h. er vermutet die Existenz von MC. Diese glänzende kritische Konstruktion findet ihre Bestätigung durch die

---

1) Vgl. oben S. 479 Anm. 1. 2) Nova Alamanniae S. 259.

Entdeckung, daß im Jahre 1343 MA, MP und MC sämtlich ihre Äquivalente haben, nämlich SA, SP und SC.

Auch Karl Rümler kommt zu dem Schluß, daß es drei Prokuratorien für die März-Gesandtschaft von 1336 gab, aber auf einem ziemlich anderen Wege, nämlich auf Grund von Beweismaterial, das Arnold von Auchs Inventar der päpstlichen Archive bietet[1]). Bock hat auf Grund der Aufschrift auf der Rückseite des Originals bündig gezeigt, daß ein Eintrag im Inventar sich auf MA beziehen muß. Ein anderer Eintrag im Inventar bezieht sich auf das verlorene Original von MP; aber es ist noch ein dritter Eintrag übrig, der ein Dokument vom selben Datum wie MA und MP verzeichnet, für das sich kein Original finden läßt. Bock versucht diesen dritten Eintrag durch die Annahme zu erklären, daß er sich auf MA beziehe, das infolge eines Irrtums des Abschreibers zweimal registriert worden sei. Rümlers Schluß indessen, so scheint es, ist dieser ziemlich gezwungenen Erklärung vorzuziehen: der dritte Eintrag des Inventars bezieht sich auf ein drittes, jetzt verlorenes Prokuratorium vom März 1336, mit anderen Worten auf MC.

Durch eine dreifache Kette von Beweisen sind wir also genötigt, die Existenz eines speziellen kirchlichen Prokuratoriums in der Art von OC und SC als eines der Instrumente der Gesandtschaft vom März 1336 anzunehmen. Wenn diese Annahme richtig ist, wird man die Annahme verwerfen müssen, daß jene Gesandtschaft während ihres Aufenthalts an der Kurie neue Bedingungen für Ludwigs Rekonziliation mit der Kirche — als Ergebnis detaillierter Verhandlungen auf der Grundlage von Ludwigs Instruktionen — erhalten habe[2]).

---

[1]) K. Rümler, Die Akten der Gesandtschaften Ludwigs des B. an Benedikt XII. und Klemens VI. (Quellenstudien aus d. histor. Seminar d. Univ. Innsbruck 2, 1910) 126—131.

[2]) Vgl. Bock, Prokuratorien S. 274.

VI

Zum Verfasser der ‚Allegaciones de potestate imperiali' (1338)*

Inhalt: 1. Handschriften S. 563. – 2. Der Aufbau S. 569. – 3. Das Verfasserproblem im Lichte der Inhaltsanalyse S. 575; a) Artikel I S. 576; b) Artikel II S. 581; c) Artikel III S. 587; d) Artikel IV S. 601; e) Artikel V S. 604; f) Artikel VI S. 613; g) Artikel VII S. 615. 4. Schlußbetrachtung S. 616.

Das Manifest ‚Fidem catholicam' – im Namen Ludwigs des Bayern in Frankfurt am Main am 6. August 1338 verkündet – ist von seinem jüngsten Herausgeber als kaiserliches Mandat bezeichnet worden[1]. Es sollte die Nichtigkeit der päpstlichen Prozesse gegen Ludwig erklären und denjenigen Strafe androhen, die ihnen Folge leisteten. Auf seine Formulierung haben in bestimmender Weise die franziskanischen ‚Dissidenten' um den abgesetzten Generalminister des Ordens, Michael von Cesena, Einfluß genommen; diese hatten sich unter dem bisweilen prekären Schutz des Kaisers in Deutschland halten können, seit es mit Johannes XXII. über der Armutsfrage 1328 zum Bruch gekommen war. Mehr oder weniger gleichzeitig mit ‚Fidem catholicam' entfalteten die Anhänger Michaels eine lebhafte publizistische Tätigkeit zugunsten Ludwigs und seines Manifests. Unter den Erzeugnissen dieser Kampagne nun befindet sich ein Traktat, bekannt als ‚Allegaciones de potestate imperiali'. Obwohl von Karl Müller vor einem Jahrhundert als „sachlich ganz interesselos" zur Seite geschoben[2], haben diese ‚Allegaciones' doch ein nicht unbeträchtliches Interesse

*) Es ist dem Vf. ein Vergnügen, Prof. Jürgen Miethke (Heidelberg) Dank zu sagen für alle Ermutigung und Hilfe bei der Abfassung dieses Aufsatzes, desgleichen Dr. Sibylle Patschovsky (München) für die Mühen bei der Übersetzung des nicht ganz einfachen Textes ins Deutsche.

[1]) H.-J. Becker, Das Mandat „Fidem catholicam" Ludwigs des Bayern von 1338, DA 26 (1970) S. 468-470. Es lag am 18. Mai im Entwurf vor, wurde aber erst am 6. August verkündet; ebd. S. 461, 463. Zu der ersten Fassung siehe Nova Alamanniae 1, hg. von E. E. Stengel (1921) S. 343f. Nr. 522.

[2]) K. Müller, Einige Aktenstücke und Schriften zur Geschichte der Streitigkeiten unter den Minoriten in der ersten Hälfte des 14. Jahrhunderts, ZKG 6 (1884) S. 77.

gefunden, zumal seit sie Richard Scholz 1911 näher untersuchte und 1914 umfangreiche Textauszüge daraus veröffentlichte[3]. Doch während es nie einem Zweifel unterlag, daß der Traktat im Umkreis der Anhänger Michaels entstand, ist doch einer genaueren Klärung der Verfasserschaft wenig Aufmerksamkeit zugewandt worden. Dieser Frage soll hier nachgegangen werden, und zwar auf der Grundlage des vollständigen Textes, von dem Scholz unter Heranziehung nur einer der erhaltenen Handschriften lediglich ein knappes Drittel abgedruckt hat.

Den Titel ‚Allegaciones de potestate imperiali' hat Scholz erfunden[4]. Zu ihm scheint er gelangt zu sein, indem er die Eingangsworte des Prologs – *Inferius describuntur allegaciones* – mit einer Überschrift verband, die er in der Handschrift Pal. lat. 679 der Biblioteca Apostolica Vaticana fand: *Tractatus Oquam de potestate imperiali;* sie ist dort von der Texthand am oberen Rand des ersten Folio eingetragen, mit dem der Traktat einsetzt, und zwar noch vor dem Kolophon des vorausgehenden Textstücks[5]. Diese Konstruktion ist ein wenig irreführend, da sich die ‚Allegaciones' in erster Linie mit der päpstlichen und nicht so sehr mit der kaiserlichen Gewalt befassen; zudem liefern die anderen beiden Handschriften, die eine Überschrift enthalten, keine wirkliche Bestätigung für Scholz' Titelwahl. Die Überschrift der Hs. Kassel, Murhardsche und Landesbibliothek, 2° iurid. 25, fol. 95^v lautet: *Tractatus Occam pro iuribus imperii,* und stammt von einer nur wenig, wenn überhaupt späteren Hand als der Texthand[6]; und in der Hs. Wien, Österreichische Nationalbibliothek, 4613 fol. 242^r hat eine spätere Hand dem Beginn des Traktats hinzugefügt: *Determinacio Okam de dominio Christi satis incongrua, quia contra determinacionem sancte matris ecclesie.* Diese drei Überschriften sind offensichtlich spätere inhaltliche Charakterisierungen der ‚Allegaciones' und nicht deren originaler Titel (den das Werk vermutlich nie besessen hat). Ihnen allen ist gemeinsam, daß sie Ockham als Verfasser nennen; es sind vornehmlich diese Überschriften, auf die sich äußeren Merkmalen nach eine Zuschreibung der ‚Allegaciones' an Ockham

---

3) R. Scholz, Unbekannte kirchenpolitische Streitschriften aus der Zeit Ludwigs des Bayern (1327–1354) 1 (1911) S. 161-167; 2 (1914) S. 417-431.

4) Scholz, ebd. 2, 417. In gewisser Hinsicht sind die ‚Allegationes religiosorum virorum' vergleichbar, 1329 von Anhängern Michaels von Cesena verfaßt; aber dort sind die Verfasser namentlich genannt: Baluze - Mansi, Miscellanea 3 (Lucca 1762) S. 315-323; Bullarium Franciscanum 5, hg. von Conrad Eubel (1898) S. 388-396.

5) Fol. 117^v. Das war die einzige Scholz bekannte Handschrift; er beschreibt sie in: Unbekannte Streitschriften 1, 162.

6) Hand 8 nach Stengel, Nova Alamanniae 1, 390 Nr. 582*; siehe auch Nova Alamanniae 2, 2, hg. von E. E. Stengel und Klaus Schäfer (1976) S. LXXVII f. und Tafel 5.

stützen läßt; zudem endet aber auch in der Hs. Wien 4613 der Traktat fol. 263^r – und zwar von der Texthand – mit dem Kolophon: *Explicit quedam determinacio de dominio Christi etc. falsa,* gefolgt von dem Zusatz (nicht ganz sicher, ob ebenfalls von der Texthand): *Wilhelmi Ockham*[7].

Autorenzuschreibungen in mittelalterlichen Handschriften sind oftmals irreführend[8]. Scholz selbst hat das einmal eingeräumt, und Léon Baudry betonte dies in einer Studie, die gegenwärtig als die eindringendste Untersuchung der Frage gelten darf, wieweit man Ockham für die ‚Allegaciones' als Verfasser in Anspruch nehmen kann[9]. An polemischen Werken, die von späteren Schreiben irrig mit Ockhams Namen versehen wurden, konnte Baudry das ‚Defensorium', die ‚Determinatio compendiosa' des Tolomeus von Lucca, die ‚Disputatio inter clericum et militem' der Zeit Bonifaz' VIII. und den ‚Defensor pacis' des Marsilius von Padua anführen[10]. Die Liste falscher Zuschreibungen ließe sich verlängern: z. B. behaupten zwei Pariser Handschriften mit dem Traktat ‚De potestate regia et papali' des Johannes Quidort von Paris die Autorschaft Ockhams[11]. In Bezug auf die ‚Allegaciones' ist nicht einmal diese Art der Beweisgrundlage widerspruchsfrei: Es gibt eine anderslautende Zuschreibung – zwar nicht für das Gesamtwerk, aber doch für eine ziemlich vollständige Zusammenfassung und Paraphrase – in einer Handschrift des 15. Jahrhunderts mit der Überschrift: *Ex dictis fratris Bonagracie sive vera sint sive falsa*[12]. Diese Verbindung von Bonagra-

[7]) Verglichen mit der Überschrift und dem Kolophon der Hs. Wien 4613 kommt den sechs Ranglossen eines späteren Bearbeiters, in denen Ockham als Verfasser behandelt wurde, nur geringes Gewicht zu: fol. 243^r; 244^v; 249^v; 250^v (zweimal); 252^r. Auf das Kolophon auf fol. 263^r ließ die Hand, die fol. 242^r die Überschrift anbrachte, folgen: *Nolo quod a quoquam dogmatizetur Okam. Nota preceptum: Argumenta bona, sed doctrina mala etc.* Dann eine andere Hand: *Quare? Quia non placet pape.*

[8]) Es ist freilich anzumerken, daß die Überschrift in der Kasseler Hs., von der man annimmt, daß sie zwischen 1338 und 1344 geschrieben wurde (oben Anm. 6), nicht viel jünger sein kann als der Text. Indessen hat Rudolf Losse, der Auftraggeber der Hs., bei der Anlage des Inhaltsverzeichnisses für diesen Band Ockham nicht als den Autor der ‚Allegaciones' bezeichnet; siehe Nova Alamanniae 1, 390 Nr. 582*; 2, 2 1009 Nr. 1828.

[9]) Scholz, Unbekannte Streitschriften 1, 163; L. Baudry, Guillaume d'Occam, Bd. 1: L'homme et les oeuvres (1950) S. 199-204.

[10]) So konnte Thomas Gascoigne seine Abschrift des ‚Defensor pacis' überschreiben: *Incipit* (folgt getilgt *inceptoris*) *doctoris Okkam fratris minoris in suo defensorio;* London, British Library, Royal ms. 10 A. XV, fol. 3^r. Ein ähnliches Durcheinander ist etwa zur selben Zeit bei Laurentius von Arezzo zu beobachten; vgl. das Prooemium zu Buch II seines Traktats ‚De ecclesiastica potestate', am besten hg. von A.-H. Chroust und J. A. Corbett, The fifteenth-century *Review of Politics* of Laurentius of Arezzo, Mediaeval Studies 11 (1949) S. 64f., 73.

[11]) Paris, BN cod. lat. 4364, fol. 40^r; cod. lat. 14619, fol. 121^v.

[12]) Biblioteca Apostolica Vaticana, cod. Pal. lat. 606, fol. 94^v.

tias Namen mit den ‚Allegaciones' dürfte nicht zufällig sein, wie noch zu zeigen sein wird. Sie sollte so wenig wie die Nennung Ockhams in anderen Überschriften voreilig verworfen werden. Doch muß man sich dessen bewußt sein, daß all solch Zuschreibungen nur begrenzten Wert für die Klärung der Verfasserschaft eines Werkes besitzen.

Allein die Überschrift in der Kasseler Handschrift (künftig: K) läßt sich der Lebenszeit Ockhams zuweisen; bislang ist keine weitere zeitgenössische Zuschreibung der ‚Allegaciones' an Ockham bekannt geworden. Die nächstjüngere Zuschreibung wenigstens von Teilen des Traktats an ihn begegnet in der ‚Chronica de ducibus Bavariae', verfaßt höchstwahrscheinlich von einem Benediktiner in Oberaltaich, ca. 1371/2[13]. Der Chronist zitiert wörtlich einige Zeilen der ‚Allegaciones'[14]; für ihn sind die Verfasser dieses Werkes und von ‚Fidem catholicam' *quidam fratres de ordine Minorum, videlicet Franciscus ⟨de Esculo et⟩ Wilhelmus Okka*[15]. Es ist durchaus anzunehmen, daß Ockham bei der Abfassung von ‚Fidem catholicam' mitwirkte, wenn auch sein Anteil daran mit Sicherheit weitaus geringer war als Bonagratias[16]. Aber Schwierigkeiten ergeben sich sofort, nimmt man die Angabe des Chronisten ernst, daß sowohl ‚Fidem catholicam' wie die ‚Allegaciones' das Ergebnis gemeinsamer Bemühungen von Ockham und Franz von Ascoli waren. Denn irgendwann zwischen dem Frühjahr 1337 und dem Sommer 1338 scheint Franz auf seinem langen Weg zurück zu einer Versöhnung mit dem Papsttum die Dissidentengruppe um Michael in München verlassen zu haben[17]. Denn wenn er auch zusammen mit anderen prominenten Anhängern Michaels in einem päpstlichen Dokument noch des Zeitraums Dezember 1338/Januar 1339 zu finden ist, wird hier doch auf längst zurückliegende Ereignisse Bezug genommen; er fehlt auf der Liste der Unterzeichner der Appellation, die Michael am 23. August 1338 von

---

[13]) Hg. von G. Leidinger, Bayerische Chroniken des XIV. Jahrhunderts, MGH SS rer. Germ. (1918) S. 141. Leidinger weist Weilands Versuch zurück, die Chronik auf Konrad von Megenberg zurückzuführen; ebd. S. 149f.

[14]) S. 164 Z. 9 bis 165 Z. 5 von Leidingers Ausgabe; siehe E. E. Stengel, Avignon und Rhens (1930) S. 109 Anm. 4; Becker (wie Anm. 1) S. 484 Anm. 150.

[15]) Ebd. S. 164 Z. 1–2. Leidinger übernahm den Zusatz *de Esculo* von Veit Arnpecks ‚Chronica Baioariorum' und Nikolaus Glassbergers Chronik. Nikolaus könnte den Zusatz in einem verbesserten Text der ‚Chronica pontificum et imperatorum' des Andreas von Regensburg gefunden haben; Veit Arnpeck eventuell auch, aber vielleicht hatte er Zugang zu einer besseren Überlieferung der ‚Chronica de ducibus Bavariae', als wir sie heute besitzen.

[16]) Siehe Becker (wie Anm. 1) S. 482.

[17]) Clément Schmitt, Un Pape réformateur et un défenseur de l'unité de l'Église: Benoit XII et l'Ordre des Frères Mineurs (1334–1342) (1959) S. 243f.

München aus an Benedikt XII. richtete[18]. Obwohl ‚Fidem catholicam' Mitte Mai 1338 vorlag[19] und möglicherweise auch die ‚Allegaciones' etwa zur selben Zeit zur Verfügung standen, ist es doch zweifelhaft, ob Franz damals in München anwesend war, um bei der Abfassung beider Schriftstücke eine aktive Rolle gespielt zu haben. Wenn aber die mehr als dreißig Jahre später abgefaßte ‚Chronica de ducibus Bavariae' hinsichtlich der Beteiligung des Franz von Ascoli irrte, könnte dies ebensogut bei Ockham der Fall sein. Das Schweigen Konrads von Megenberg in seinem Werk ‚De translacione Romani imperii' hat da mehr Gewicht. Als Konrad sich 1354 mit Argumenten auseinandersetzte, die er wörtlich den ‚Allegaciones' entnommen hatte, machte er keinen Versuch, Ockham oder Franz dafür verantwortlich zu machen[20]. Er nahm vielmehr die Aussage des Prooemiums der ersten Fassung der ‚Allegaciones' wörtlich: *Inferius describuntur allegaciones per plures magistros in sacra pagina approbate;* d. h. er ging von einer Mehrzahl von Verfassern aus, von anonymen Theologen, die eine theologische Debatte führten[21]. Konrad rieb sich bekanntlich mit Vorliebe an Ockham[22]. Hätte er geahnt, daß die ihm anstößigen Auffassungen der ‚Allegaciones' mit Ockhams Namen hätten gebrandmarkt werden können, wäre es befremdlich, wenn er die Gelegenheit dazu ungenutzt hätte vorübergehen lassen. Ein argumentum e silentio ist zwar nie ohne Risiko; aber daß Konrad keinen Zusammenhang zwischen den ‚Allegaciones' und Ockham oder Franz herstellte, scheint mindestens ebenso beweiskräftig wie die dezidierte gegenteilige Aussage des bayerischen Chronisten.

Die ziemlich fragwürdigen Nennungen Ockhams als Autor der ‚Allegaciones'; die Behauptung der ‚Chronica de ducibus Bavariae', Franz von Ascoli habe gemeinsam mit Ockham das Werk verfaßt; die durch den Prolog der ‚Allegaciones' nahegelegte Deutung, sie seien ein weiteres Gemeinschaftsprodukt von Michaels gelehrten Parteigängern[23] – das alles hat in er-

---

[18]) Nova Alamanniae 1, 408f. Nr. 597; wo auch der 1328 verstorbene Johannes von Jandun erwähnt wird; siehe L. Schmugge, Johannes von Jandun, 1285/89 – 1328 (1966) S. 121f. Zu Michaels Appellation vgl. Paris, BN cod. lat. 5154, fol. 330^r.

[19]) Siehe oben Anm. 1.

[20]) Kap. 23–25 von ‚De translacione', hg. von Scholz, Unbekannte Streitschriften 2, 322–345.

[21]) Kassel, 2° ms. iurid. 25, fol. 95v. Konrad S. 324: *aliqui theologorum;* S. 328: *adversarios;* S. 328: *alii;* S. 332: *adversarii;* S. 341: *raciones theologicas.*

[22]) Siehe H. S. Offler, An interpolated *collatio* of Pope Clement VI, O.S.B.?, Revue bénédictine 84 (1974) S. 120f.

[23]) In der ersten Fassung der ‚Allegaciones' war lediglich davon die Rede gewesen, daß Magister der Theologie sie gebilligt hätten: *Inferius describuntur allegaciones per plures magistros in sacra pagina approbate;* Kassel, 2° ms. iurid. 25, fol. 95^v. Aber

heblichem Maße bezüglich des Verfassers der ‚Allegaciones' zu Unsicherheiten geführt, die sich in unterschiedlichen Auffassungen der Forschung niederschlugen. Zum Teil liegt die Schuld an dieser schwankenden Beurteilung, wie man sich eingestehen muß, an Richard Scholz, der wie kein zweiter dazu beitrug, den Traktat bekanntzumachen, und dessen Anteil an der Erforschung der polemischen lateinischen Literatur in Europa des 14. Jahrhunderts von niemandem übertroffen wird[24]. Während A. G. Little 1892 und J. Sullivan 1896 die ‚Allegaciones' in gutem Glauben Ockham zugeschrieben hatten, gestützt auf die Überschriften in Pal. lat. 679[25], kam Scholz 1911 zu einem eher widersprüchlichen Urteil. Ihm erschienen die ‚Allegaciones' als ein Werk, das „wir wenigstens teilweise für Occam in Anspruch nehmen dürfen"[26]; und obwohl er den Wert der Zuschreibung in Pal. lat. 679 nicht sonderlich hoch veranschlagte, meinte er doch, daß sich zumindest nichts dagegen einwenden ließe[27]. Da er den Traktat seinem Stil nach eher für das Werk eines Theologen als eines Juristen hielt, glaubte er sich mit hoher Wahrscheinlichkeit dafür aussprechen zu können, daß Ockham daran beteiligt war, vielleicht in Zusammenarbeit mit Bonagratia und Michael von Cesena[28]. An anderer Stelle desselben Buches hielt es Scholz für angebracht zu erwägen, es sei gut möglich, in Ockham zumindest den Herausgeber der ‚Allegaciones' zu sehen. Genauso wie franziskanische Dissidenten – offensichtlich vor allem Bonagratia und Ockham – an der Promulgierung von ‚Fidem catholicam' beteiligt waren, so waren sie vielleicht auch die Verfasser der gleichsam offiziellen Verteidigungsschrift für dieses Dokument: „vielleicht beide Male dieselben Autoren"[29]. Trotz der vorsich-

---

in der Einführung zu seiner Fassung behauptet ‚Nikolaus Minorita', sie seien gemeinschaftlich verfaßt worden: *Propter quod nonnulli in sacra pagina magistri et alii in utroque iure periti, super hiis a prefato domino Ludovico et nonnullis aliis cum instancia requisiti, ad supradictorum clariorem evidenciam cunctis fidelibus intimandam composuerunt et fecerunt allegaciones et raciones efficaces et veritate plenas in divino et humano iure fundatas, ostendentes aperte, quod nec iure divino nec humano summus pontifex habet talem plenitudinem potestatis;* Paris, BN cod. lat. 5154, fol. 344r, gedruckt von K. Müller (wie Anm. 2) S. 102f.

24) Scholz starb 1946. Der ‚Nachruf' auf ihn aus der Feder von Hermann Heimpel, in: DA 8 (1951) S. 264–266, läßt den Verdiensten dieses ebenso bescheidenen wie bedeutenden Gelehrten Gerechtigkeit widerfahren.

25) A. G. Little, The Grey Friars in Oxford (1892) S. 232f.; J. Sullivan, Marsiglio of Padua and William of Ockham, American Historical Review 2 (1896) S. 414. Mir ist nicht klar, weshalb Sullivan den Traktat auf ‚nach 1339' datiert.

26) Scholz, Unbekannte Streitschriften 1, 161f.

27) Ebd. 1, 163.

28) Ebd. 1, 164f.

29) Ebd. 1, 119.

tigen Ausdrucksweise von Scholz scheint es doch nicht unbillig, ihm den Wunsch zu unterstellen, die ‚Allegaciones' unter die Schriften Ockhams einzureihen, obgleich er sich sehr wohl der Tatsache bewußt war, daß die Beweise dafür nicht gerade erdrückend waren. Schon 1911 ging er so weit, die ‚Allegaciones' als „den Occamschen Traktat" zu apostrophieren, eine Meinung, die sich zwanzig Jahre später bei E. E. Stengel wiederfindet[30]. Im Jahre 1944 hat Scholz dann alle Vorbehalte beiseite gelassen, jedoch nicht, wie es scheint, auf Grund neuer Belege. Unter den Werken, die Ockham 1338 verfaßt habe, führt er nun auch an: „die sogen. Allegationes de potestate imperiali, einer der wenigen offiziösen Traktate, dessen Abfassung durch Ockham ausdrücklich bezeugt ist"; er zitiert sie als unzweifelhaftes Werk Ockhams[31].

Scholz' Urteil, das im gleichen Maße Autorität besitzt wie es nicht ganz überzeugt, hat in jüngster Zeit so manchen Gelehrten im Hinblick auf den Verfasser der ‚Allegaciones' zu widersprüchlichen Feststellungen veranlaßt. Georges de Lagarde etwa, der einerseits die Ansicht übernahm, die ‚Allegaciones' seien ein Gemeinschaftsunternehmen, stellte sie andererseits 1962 zu den unbestreitbar Ockham zuzuschreibenden Werken, die unmittelbaren Einblick in sein Denken gewährten; an wenigstens zehn Stellen zitiert er die ‚Allegaciones' als Beleg für Ockhams eigene Ansichten[32]. Im nächstfolgenden Jahr behandelte er die ‚Allegaciones' weiterhin als Ockhams Werk, obwohl er hatte einräumen müssen, daß darin eine in Ockhams Schriften unübliche Ausdrucksweise anzutreffen ist[33]. Gleichfalls 1963 führte M. J. Wilks in seiner Bibliographie die ‚Allegaciones' ohne nähere Erläuterung unter Ockhams Werken an und nahm sie für Ockhams Auffassungen in Anspruch[34]. Diese vorschnelle Annahme von Ockhams Verfasserschaft ist um so überraschender, als Léon Baudry schon 1950 zur Vor-

---

30) Ebd. 1, 120; S t e n g e l, Avignon und Rhens S. 178.

31) R. S c h o l z, Wilhelm von Ockham als politischer Denker und sein Breviloquium de principatu tyrannico (Schriften der MGH 8, 1944) S. 13 und 26 Anm. 1.

32) Georges de L a g a r d e, La naissance de l'esprit laïque au déclin du moyen-âge, Bd. 4: Guillaume d'Ockham: Défense de l'Empire (1962) S. 32, 61, 108, 115, 122, 135, 147, 159 mit Anm. 98, 164, 167, 173 mit Anm. 91, 200. Ich verstehe nicht, was der Vf. mit den Worten meint: „Les *Allegationes*, qui font décidément l'office de filtre de la pensée d'Ockham" (S. 169).

33) Ebd. Bd. 5: Guillaume d'Ockham: Critique des structures ecclésiales (1963) S. 33 mit Anm. 19, 253.

34) M. J. W i l k s, The Problem of Sovereignty in the later Middle Ages (1963) S. 566; siehe ebd. S. 191 Anm. 3, 196 Anm. 3, 243 mit Anm. 2, 281 mit Anm. 3, 315 Anm. 1, 502 Anm. 3.

sicht geraten hatte: Die ‚Allegaciones' wurden nach seinem wohlbegründeten Urteil von den um Michael gescharten Theologen und Juristen an Ludwigs des Bayern Hof verfaßt; ohne Zweifel habe Ockham bei ihrer Abfassung eine Rolle gespielt, aber die Annahme, er habe die Hauptverantwortung dabei getragen, sei zwar vielleicht einleuchtend, aber keinesfalls sicher[35]. Noch stärkere Vorbehalte wurden 1962 von Wilhelm Kölmel und 1969 von Jürgen Miethke vorgebracht; geleitet von der Überlegung, daß Ockhams Anteil an den ‚Allegaciones' sich nicht näher bestimmen lasse, neigten beide dazu, ihren Wert als Quelle für Ockhams Gedankenwelt gering einzuschätzen[36]. Doch 1970 konnte Hans-Jürgen Becker Ockham immer noch als die führende Gestalt unter den Autoren der ‚Allegaciones' bezeichnen, obwohl er zu einem früheren Zeitpunkt einen längeren Abschnitt darin als Werk Bonagratias nachgewiesen hatte und die Ansicht vertrat, daß Bonagratia an den ‚Allegaciones' „in modo determinante" mitgearbeitet habe[37]. A. S. McGrade vermied es 1974 klugerweise, den Traktat für die Untersuchung von Ockhams politischem Denken heranzuziehen. Doch während Marino Damiata 1979 die ‚Allegaciones' unter der Überschrift „Ockham collaboratore, non autore" in seine Arbeit einführte, wobei er sich Baudrys Auffassung ausdrücklich zu eigen machte, kreist seine Gedankenführung in beträchtlichem Maße um den Aufweis von Übereinstimmungen zwischen den in den ‚Allegaciones' und in authentischen Werken Ockhams zum Ausdruck gebrachten Ansichten[38]. Auf der anderen Seite hat die subtile Interpretation, die P. Marc Dykmans dem ursprünglichen Prolog der ‚Allegaciones' hat angedeihen lassen, einer etwas

---

35) L. Baudry, Guillaume d'Occam S. 202.

36) Wilhelm Kölmel, Wilhelm Ockham und seine kirchenpolitischen Schriften (1962) S. 163: „Da sie nur teilweise sichere Spuren der Arbeit Ockhams verrät, besitzt sie keinen primären Zeugniswert." Jürgen Miethke, Ockhams Weg zur Sozialphilosophie (1969) S. 104: „Es ist daher wohl wahrscheinlich, daß Ockham an der Ausarbeitung beteiligt war, allerdings darf auch eine ‚federführende' Rolle nicht angesetzt werden." Helmar Junghans, Ockham im Lichte der neueren Forschung (1968) S. 98, führt die ‚Allegaciones' unter Ockhams Werken auf, obwohl er meint, sie seien wahrscheinlich eine Gemeinschaftsarbeit; in der Datierung folgt er Baudry.

37) Becker (wie Anm. 1) S. 484; ders., Kanonistische Schriften Bonagratias von Bergamo, QFIAB 46 (1966) S. 251 Anm. 1; ders., Bonagrazia di Bergamo, in: Dizionario biografico degli Italiani 11 (1969) S. 508.

38) A. S. McGrade, The Political Thought of William of Ockham (1974). Marino Damiata, Guglielmo d'Ockham: Povertà e Potere 2 (1979) S. 138–146. Späterhin geht Damiata stillschweigend dazu über, die ‚Allegaciones' als Zeugnis für Ockhams Ansichten heranzuziehen: ebd. S. 426 Anm. 191 u. 199, S. 453f.

tiefergehenden Lösung der Verfasserfrage die Richtung gewiesen, und zwar nicht gerade zugunsten Ockhams[39].

Aus diesem Meinungsdurcheinander schälen sich zwei Hauptrichtungen heraus: Einerseits zögert man, eine größere oder geringere Beteiligung Ockhams an den ‚Allegaciones' in Abrede zu stellen, auf der anderen Seite ist man sich bewußt, daß der eine oder andere Gefolgsmann Michaels dabei wahrscheinlich seine Hände mit im Spiel gehabt haben dürfte. Ein ziemlich unbequemer und prekärer Balanceakt! Nur indem man die ‚Allegaciones' genauer befragt als bisher, kann man hoffen, über diesen Stand hinauszukommen. Muß man die ‚Allegaciones' eher zwei oder mehr Verfassern zuschreiben als Ockham allein? Wenn ja: was läßt sich davon guten Gewissens Ockham zuweisen, was Franz von Ascoli oder Bonagratia oder einem anderen ihrer namhaft zu machenden Mitstreiter im Lichte von deren bekannten Schriften? Falls der Traktat sich tatsächlich als Gemeinschaftswerk erweist: wurden dann die verschiedenen Beiträge zum Schluß der einheitsstiftenden Redaktion eines Einzelnen unterworfen? Wenn ja: wessen? Das sind ohne Zweifel schwierige Fragen, und es wäre leichtfertig anzunehmen, daß sich für alle restlos befriedigende Antworten finden lassen. Aber ein entschlossener Versuch in dieser Richtung ist eine unausweichliche Vorbedingung, um den Platz der ‚Allegaciones' im vierten Band der Edition von Ockhams ‚Opera politica' zu bestimmen: Sind sie unter seine unzweifelhaft echten Schriften einzuordnen?

Der Versuch muß einsetzen mit einer Untersuchung der Handschriften, des Aufbaus und des Inhalts des Traktats in seiner vollen Länge.

1. Die Handschriften

Soweit bekannt, haben sich die ‚Allegaciones' in den folgenden Handschriften erhalten:

---

[39]) M. Dykmans, De Jean XXII au Concile de Florence, RHE 48 (1973) S. 54: „...car le titre même de l'opuscule indique une révision faite par des docteurs en théologie pour un auteur qui ne devait pas l'être ... Cet auteur, qu'on peut appeler Occam sous cette réserve ..." Aber obwohl der Venerabilis Inceptor nie förmlich Doktor der Theologie geworden ist, galt er im Umkreis Michaels als solcher; vgl. z.B. die Liste derjenigen, die Michaels Appellation vom 23. August 1338 unterstützten, wo Ockham genau wie Heinrich von Talheim als *in sacra theologia magister* angeführt wird: Paris, BN cod. lat. 5154, fol. 330^r. Dykmans Argumentation scheint darauf hinauszulaufen, daß es sich bei dem Verfasser der ‚Allegaciones' um jemanden gehandelt habe, der seinem Titel nach überhaupt kein Theologe war.

Kassel, Murhardsche Bibliothek und Landesbibliothek, Cod. 2° iurid. 25 (14. Jh.), fol. 95^{v}–107^{r} (= K)[40].
Città del Vaticano, Biblioteca Apostolica Vaticana, Cod. Pal. lat. 679 (15. Jh.), fol. 117^{v}–156^{r} (= A)[41].
Wien, Österreichische Nationalbibliothek, Cod. 4613 (früher Univ. 687; 15. Jh.), fol. 242^{r}–263^{r} (= Vi)[42].
München, Bayerische Staatsbibliothek, Clm 17833 (15. Jh.), fol. 152^{v}–174^{v} (= M)[43].
Paris, Bibliothèque nationale, Cod. lat. 5154 (14. Jh.), fol. 344^{r}–370^{r} (= P)[44].
Città del Vaticano, Biblioteca Apostolica Vaticana, Cod. Vat. lat. 4008 (14. Jh.), fol. 200^{r}–211^{v} (= N)[45].
Außerdem gibt es noch eine ziemlich vollständige paraphrasierende Zusammenfassung der in den Hss. KAViM überlieferten Fassung: Città del Vaticano, Biblioteca Apostolica Vaticana, Cod. Pal. lat. 606 (15. Jh.), fol. 94^{v}–104^{r} (= C)[46].

Die Handschriften zeigen, daß die ‚Allegaciones' in zwei deutlich unterschiedenen Fassungen auf uns gekommen sind. Die jüngere (künftig Z) wird weiter unten zu besprechen sein. Die ältere, repräsentiert durch KAViM(C), möchte ich G nennen; Verweise darauf beziehen sich auf die Fundstellen in K[47]. Die Anspielung im Prolog von G auf *processus factus et sentencia lata in Franckfort per dominum Ludewicum dei gracia Romanorum imperatorem* (K, fol. 95^{v}) bezieht sich eindeutig auf ‚Fidem catholicam'.

---

[40]) Ausführlich beschrieben von E. E. Stengel und K. Schäfer, Nova Alamanniae 2, 2 S. XVI–XXXVII. Der Anfang der ‚Allegaciones' auf fol. 95^{v} ist durch eine rote Initiale gekennzeichnet. Die weit ausgreifende Materialsammlung dieses Bandes ist 1344 abgeschlossen worden.

[41]) Beschrieben von Scholz, Unbekannte Streitschriften 1, 162.

[42]) Siehe Tabulae codicum manu scriptorum praeter Graecos et Orientales in Bibliotheca Palatina Vindobonensi asservatorum 3 (1869) S. 329f.

[43]) Siehe Catalogus codicum manu scriptorum Bibliothecae Regiae Monacensis IV, 3 (1878) S. 124 Nr. 1007. Die Hs. ist auf ca. 1467–1478 datiert von H. Grundmann und H. Heimpel, Die Schriften des Alexander von Roes (MGH Staatsschriften 1, 1, 1958) S. 78.

[44]) Siehe K. Müller (wie Anm. 2) S. 63–77.

[45]) Siehe H. Kämpf, Die Codices Latini 4008–4010 der Vatikanischen Bibliothek, QFIAB 26 (1935–1936) S. 143–171.

[46]) Siehe H. Stevenson, jr., und I. B. De Rossi, Codices Palatini Latini Bibliothecae Vaticanae 1 (1886) S. 210f.

[47]) Bd. 4 der Opera politica Ockhams wird einen detaillierten Apparatus criticus erhalten müssen.

Obwohl dieses Schriftstück rechtzeitig vor Ludwigs Zusammenkunft mit den deutschen Fürsten in Frankfurt in der dritten Mai-Woche des Jahres 1338 im Entwurf vorlag und sich eine auf den 18. Mai datierte Fassung erhalten hat, scheint die formelle Publikation bis zum 6. August auf dem Reichstag zu Frankfurt hinausgeschoben worden zu sein[48]. Fassung G, die die Aufgabe hatte, ‚Fidem catholicam' näher zu begründen, wird nicht lange nach dem 6. August fertiggestellt worden sein; verfaßt von derselben Gruppe um Michael, die tätigen Anteil an der Konzipierung von ‚Fidem catholicam' gehabt hat, mag G recht gut schon im Mai oder noch früher in Arbeit gewesen sein. Daher ist Scholz' Datierung „zwischen Mai und Herbst 1338" dem Versuch Baudrys vorzuziehen, die Abfassung von G auf den Zeitraum zwischen den Reichstagen von Frankfurt im August und in Koblenz Anfang September 1338 einzugrenzen[49].

Die bei weitem älteste und beste der bekannten Handschriften der Fassung G der ‚Allegaciones' ist K. Der Kodex, der sie überliefert, ist Teil der Kollektaneen Rudolf Losses aus Eisenach. Nach einem Studium des kanonischen Rechts in Montpellier war Losse um 1332 in die Dienste des bedeutenden Luxemburgers Erzbischof Balduin von Trier getreten und dessen Offizial geworden; er starb 1364 als Dekan des Mainzer Domkapitels. Losse zeigte reges Interesse am Streit Ludwigs des Bayern mit dem Papsttum und besaß infolge seiner Beziehung zu Balduin von Trier einflußreiche Verbindungen. Es scheint, als habe er sich kurz nach Abfassung von G bereits mit einer Abschrift versehen können, denn K stammt von einem Schreiber, von dem man weiß, daß er zwischen 1338 und 1340 für Losse tätig war[50]. Die Textüberlieferung von K mit ihren von wenigstens zwei Händen ausgeführten sorgsamen Korrekturen bietet fraglos die Grundlage für die Textkonstitution der Fassung G. Dennoch: K ist nicht ganz frei von Fehlern; es finden sich eine Reihe kleinerer Schreiberversehen und es gibt auch einige Auslassungen. Eine davon auf fol. 105^{v} – hervorgerufen durch Homoioteleuton – ist von besonderer Bedeutung. Denn A – eine weitaus jüngere Handschrift als K und im allgemeinen sehr viel weniger sorgfältig angelegt – enthält gerade diesen Fehler nicht und erweist sich damit als eine von K unabhängige Überlieferung, obwohl beide Handschriften mehr als dreißig Trennfehler gemeinsam haben. Vermutlich gehen K wie A unabhängig

---

48) Siehe oben Anm. 1.

49) S c h o l z, Wilhelm von Ockham als politischer Denker S. 13; B a u d r y, Guillaume d'Occam S. 203.

50) Hand 7 nach der Zählung Stengels; siehe Nova Alamanniae 2, 2 S. LXXVII und Tafel 4. Zur Überschrift von Hand 8 siehe oben Anm. 6.

voneinander auf eine gemeinsame Vorlage zurück, die jünger sein müßte als die Urschrift von G. Die späte und sorglos geschriebene Hs. M hat wenig Bedeutung für die Texterstellung; am nächsten steht sie der ebenso sorglos und noch eigenwilliger geschriebenen Hs. Vi, mit der sie mehr als hundert Lesarten gemein hat. Aber von einiger Bedeutung ist die Tatsache, daß M und Vi einzeln wie zusammen eine ganze Reihe von Varianten mit P und N, den Hss. der Fassung Z, gemeinsam haben. Eine mögliche Erklärung dafür wäre, daß, wenn sich schon keine direkte Abhängigkeit zwischen M und Vi nachweisen läßt, beide Hss. letztlich doch gemeinsam auf eine Vorlage zurückgehen, die ihrerseits von einer Überlieferung abhängt, die PN näher steht als KA. K bleibt der bei weitem verläßlichste Textzeuge für G, eine Handschrift, die, wie wir sahen, zeitlich nah an die Urschrift der ‚Allegaciones' heranreicht. Dennoch kann man sich darauf nicht wie auf die Urschrift selbst stützen[51].

Obwohl das Material für die Aufstellung eines bis ins letzte überzeugenden Stemmas nicht ganz hinreicht, läßt sich das ungefähre Verhältnis der Handschriften auf folgende Weise graphisch verdeutlichen:

[51]) Zwei mögliche Differenzen zwischen K und dem Original der Fassung G scheinen der Anzeige wert: 1. Bei dem Verweis auf den Kanon ‚Monomachiam' (C. 2 q. 5 c. 22) – in K fol. 106^{v} – haben KA *Monachiam*, MPN *Monarchiam*, und in V fehlt das Wort; nur die Kurzfassung C, fol. 104^{r}, schreibt korrekt *Monomachiam*. Das braucht nicht mehr zu sein als die Emendation eines im kanonischen Recht bewanderten Schreibers; indessen ist es möglich, daß C eine bessere Vorlage vor sich hatte als die heute erhaltenen Handschriften der ‚Allegaciones'. – 2. Vielleicht besaß Konrad von Megenberg, als er 1354 an ‚De translacione imperii' arbeitete, Zugang zu einem etwas vollständigeren Text, als ihn K überliefert. Denn in c. 23 nachdem er aus den ‚Allegaciones' den Beweis gegen die päpstliche Vollgewalt in wesentlichen Dingen, beruhend auf dem Kanon ‚Si habes', zitiert hatte (K, fol. 95^{v}), fügt Konrad noch ein weiteres Argument hinzu, wie wenn es aus derselben Quelle stammte: *Item oracione qua legitur et cantatur ... tradidisti* (S c h o l z, Unbekannte Streitschriften 2, 324f.); in c. 25 nun greift er die Behauptung, daß dies die päpstliche Gewalt auf geistliche Dinge einschränke, in demselben Kontext an, in dem er die gleichgerichteten Argumente der ‚Allegaciones' zurückgewiesen hatte. Man ist daher versucht anzunehmen, daß Konrad dieses zusätzliche Argument von einer etwas längeren Fassung der ‚Allegaciones' übernahm, als sie heute bekannt ist. Auch ist festzuhalten, daß Konrad in c. 24 – wo er überwiegend wortwörtlich der Argumentationslinie der ‚Allegaciones' bezüglich der Zwei Schwerter-Lehre folgt, insbesondere bei den Ambrosius- und Lukas-Zitaten – seinen Gegnern Meinungen in den Mund legt, die den Stoff in einer besser geordneten Abfolge als die uns erhaltenen Handschriften der ‚Allegaciones' bieten (S c h o l z, Unbekannte Streitschriften 2, 332; vgl. K, fol. 100^{v}–101^{r}).

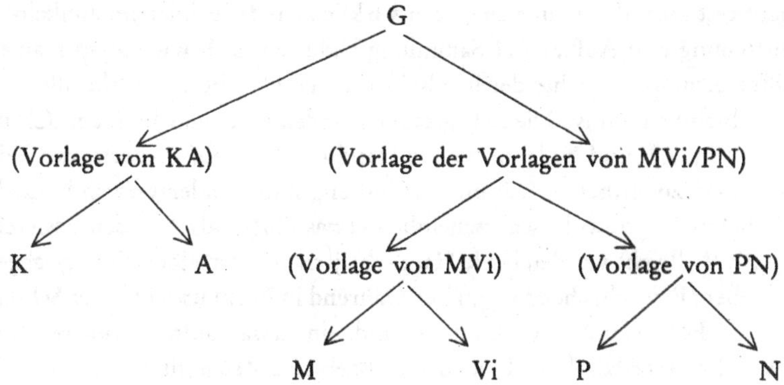

Die jüngere Fassung Z der ‚Allegaciones' wird von P und N überliefert. Sie ordnet den Stoff nach Gutdünken neu, um ihn der sog. ‚Chronik des Nikolaus Minorita' leichter einfügen zu können. Diese Chronik ist nichts anderes als eine Sammlung von pièces justificatives, entstanden in der Umgebung Michaels von Cesena mit dem Zweck, die Rebellion Michaels und seines Anhangs gegen die avignonesischen Päpste Johannes XXII. und Benedikt XII. zu rechtfertigen. Dazu wurden päpstliche und kaiserliche Verfügungen zusammen mit polemischen Traktaten aus der Umgebung Michaels, Briefe und Appellationen von 1322 an in chronologischer Folge aneinandergereiht, zusammengehalten von einem für Michael und seine Gruppe Partei ergreifenden Kommentar. Die ‚Chronik' hat seit den 1840er Jahren als Fundgrube für Materialien zur deutschen Geschichte gedient[52], und ihren Inhalt hat Karl Müller 1883 auf der Grundlage von P erschöpfend bekannt gemacht[53]. Doch seit Konrad Eubels 1897 erschienenen Studien sind die Fragen, die dieses Sammelwerk aufwirft, als Gegenstand eigener Untersuchung einer Lösung nicht nennenswert nähergebracht worden.[54] Zwar ist der Name des angeblichen Verfassers, ‚Nikolaus', auf Ver-

---

[52]) Siehe Alfons Huber, Vorrede zu J. F. Böhmer, Fontes rerum Germanicarum 4 (1886) S. LXIV.

[53]) K. Müller (wie Anm. 2) S. 68–77.

[54]) Konrad Eubel, Zu Nicolaus Minorita, HJb 18 (1897) S. 375–386; ders., Nachträgliches zu Nicolaus Minorita, HJb 20 (1899) S. 767–769. Die Sammlung mag von einer ähnlichen Bemühung aus früherer Zeit angeregt worden sein, entstanden 1317–1318 und befaßt mit der *magna disceptatio* zwischen den Franziskaner-Konventualen und -Spiritualen; siehe Franz Ehrle, Zur Vorgeschichte des Concils von Vienne, 2: Des Ordensprocurators Raymund von Fronsac Actensammlung zur Geschichte der Spiritualen, Archiv für Litteratur- und Kirchengeschichte des Mittelalters 3 (1887) S. 1–32. Obwohl Ehrle dazu neigte, Raymund von Fronsac die Verfasserschaft an der Sammlung zuzusprechen, hielt er es doch für gut möglich, daß Bonagratia von Bergamo dabei seine Hand mit im Spiele hatte; ebd. S. 3–6.

dacht gestoßen, doch um wen es sich wirklich handelte, blieb im dunkeln[55]. Entstehung und Aufbau der Sammlung bedürfen nach wie vor sorgsamer Untersuchung im Lichte der handschriftlichen Überlieferung, die alles andere als einheitlich ist. Die ‚Allegaciones' finden sich am Schluß der ‚Chronik' allein in P und N; keine andere Handschrift scheint Material der Zeit nach 1335 zu enthalten[56]. P und N sind eng miteinander verwandt, doch überliefert P – obwohl wahrscheinlich etwas jünger als N – den besseren Text[57]. Vielleicht wurden beide Handschriften von derselben Vorlage abgeschrieben, P durchgehend sorgfältig, während in N ein unachtsamer Schreiber die Folien 200^r–210^v kopierte und ein etwas aufmerksamerer fol. 211^{r-v}. Im Regelfall kann P als der maßgebende Zeuge für die Fassung Z der ‚Allegaciones' angesehen werden.

---

[55]) Siehe H. S. Offler, in: Guillelmi de Ockham Opera politica 2 (1963) S. XVIIIf.

[56]) In der Hs. Florenz, Biblioteca Medicea Laurenziana, S. Crucis, Plut. XX sin. cod. 12 (geschrieben um 1350) endet die ‚Chronik' auf fol. 161^v mit dem Brief ‚Teste Salomone' Michaels von Cesena vom Dezember 1332 (Nr. 35 von Müllers Inhaltsübersicht für den ‚Nikolaus': Einige Aktenstücke [wie Anm. 2] S. 76); auf fol. 161^v – 168^v befindet sich Bonagratias Münchener Appellation von 1334, während eine Hand des 15. Jh. auf fol. 169^r – 171^r eine unvollständige Fassung des Traktates ‚Quoniam ut ait Leo papa' hinzugefügt hat (Müller S. 76 Nr. 37); siehe A. M. Bandini, Catalogus codicum Latinorum Bibliothecae Mediceae Laurentianae 4 (Florenz 1777) Sp. 152; Marc Dykmans, Les sermons de Jean XXII sur la vision béatifique, Miscellanea Historiae Pontificiae 34 (1973) S. 196, 213. Die Fassung des ‚Nikolaus' in: Biblioteca Apostolica Vaticana, cod. Vat. lat. 7316 – geschrieben für Kardinal Domenico Capranica und 1798 vom Collegio Capranica in die Vatikanische Bibliothek überführt – bricht mit dem auf den 24. Januar 1331 datierten Brief ‚Christianae fidei fundamentum' Michaels von Cesena ab (Müller S. 75 Nr. 29). Von dieser Handschrift des 15. Jh. stammt die bei Baluze – Mansi, Miscellanea 3 (Lucca 1762) S. 206 – 358 gedruckte Fassung der ‚Chronik'. Die Hs. Vat. lat. 4128 ist eine sorgfältig angefertigte unmittelbare Abschrift des Vat lat. 7316, mit einem ähnlichen Schluß; sie wurde für Piero da Monte geschrieben, dem späteren Bischof von Brescia. Beide vatikanischen Handschriften sind beschrieben von Scholz, Unbekannte Streitschriften 2, 565f.; zu ihrem Abhängigkeitsverhältnis vgl. J. Miethke, Die handschriftliche Überlieferung der Schriften des Juan González, Bischof von Cadiz, QFIAB 60 (1980) S. 286 Anm. 35; siehe auch ebd. S. 284 Anm. 29, 289 Anm. 40. Die Hs. Venedig, Biblioteca Nazionale Marciana, cod. Zan. lat. I. 196 scheint inhaltlich mit cod. Vat. lat. 7316 übereinzustimmen, aber leider läßt sich das mit Hilfe der Beschreibung bei J. Valentinelli, Bibl. manuscripta ad S. Marci Venetiarum. Codices mss. Latini 2 (Venedig 1869) S. 354f., nicht klären. Kämpf (wie Anm. 45) S. 164f., hat gezeigt, daß cod. Vat. lat. 4010 zwar vielleicht eine Quelle für ‚Nikolaus' war, aber nicht die ‚Chronik' selbst überliefert; die Hs. endet mit ‚Quoniam ut ait Leo papa'.

[57]) A. Heysse, Duo documenta de polemica inter Gerardum Oddonem et Michaelem de Caesena, Archivum Franciscanum Historicum 9 (1916) S. 139; Dykmans, Les sermons de Jean XXII S. 213.

Es war in keiner Weise ungewöhnlich, wenn der Kompilator oder die Kompilatoren des ‚Nikolaus Minorita' ursprünglich selbständig zirkulierende Traktate aus der Umgebung Michaels in die ‚Chronik' aufnahmen und für deren Zwecke umarbeiteten. So erging es z. B. einem 1338 entstandenen Textstück, das sich unter Rudolf Losses Kollektaneen mit dem Incipit *Inferius describuntur articuli* erhalten hat; es taucht mit textlichen Veränderungen erneut im ‚Nikolaus Minorita' auf unter dem Titel *Subsequenter ponuntur articuli*[58]. So wurde auch die im Umkreis Michaels verfaßte Schrift ‚Quoniam ut ait Leo papa' – entstanden 1335 – umgearbeitet, bevor sie in den ‚Nikolaus' aufgenommen wurde[59], während Bonagratias Denkschrift von 1338 über die Ungültigkeit von Eiden, die Ludwig dem Bayern zum Nachteil ausschlügen, in einer im Vergleich zur Erstfassung merklich veränderten Form in den ‚Nikolaus' gelangte[60]. Es ist daher nicht überraschend, die ‚Allegaciones' im ‚Nikolaus' in einer Gestalt vorzufinden, die sich von der ursprünglichen Fassung deutlich unterscheidet. Die Einzelheiten der Umformung in Z gegenüber G lassen sich nur namhaft machen, wenn wir den Aufbau des gesamten Traktats einer eingehenden Betrachtung unterziehen.

2. Der Aufbau

Auf den ersten Blick scheint der Text der ‚Allegaciones' – mehr als 20 000 Worte – in den Handschriften nicht weiter in Kapitel oder Abschnitte untergliedert worden zu sein. Eine nähere Untersuchung zeigt jedoch, daß das Werk in eine Reihe selbständiger Abschnitte zerfällt, oder – um die werkeigene Terminologie zu gebrauchen – in *articuli*[61]: den sechs in G ist ein siebenter in Z hinzugefügt worden. Spuren dieser ursprünglichen Einteilung in ‚Artikel' lassen sich – freilich nur ganz schwach – auch in den Handschriften ausmachen.

Artikel I führt aus, daß *iure divino* die Vollgewalt des Papstes auf geistliche Angelegenheiten begrenzt sei; seine Gewalt könne nicht die Gewalt

---

[58]) Inferius in K, fol. 119r–122r, ed. Stengel, Nova Alamanniae 1, 391–401 Nr. 583; Subsequenter in P, fol. 335r–340v, ed. Böhmer, Fontes rerum Germanicarum 4, 592–605.

[59]) Dykmans, Les sermons S. 196, 213.

[60]) Siehe H.-J. Becker, Kanonistische Schriften (wie Anm. 37) S. 263–271; vgl. unten Anm. 192.

[61]) K, fol. 104v: *Sed non habet de iure divino, ut superius in primo articulo probatum est plene.*

Christi *inquantum homo viator* übersteigen, da Christus nach dem Zeugnis der Schrift weltliche Herrschaft zurückgewiesen habe.

Artikel II kommt auf einem anderen Weg zum selben Ergebnis. Die Gewalt Christi in seiner göttlichen Vollkommenheit, sein *dominium increatum*, wird unterschieden von seiner Gewalt als vollkommener Mensch, dem *dominium creatum;* das letztere wird noch einmal differenziert in *dominium creatum* vor der Passion und nach der Auferstehung. Nur Christi *dominium creatum* vor der Passion sei Petrus und seinen Nachfolgern übertragen worden. Und das sei eine rein geistliche Gewalt gewesen; anzunehmen daß sie sich auf Weltliches erstreckt habe, würde Christi Armut, Demut, Liebe und Rechtschaffenheit in Abrede stellen. Belege aus den Apostel- und den Väterschriften, aus dem römischen und dem kanonischen Recht werden angeführt, um die These zu untermauern, daß die päpstliche Gewalt *iure divino* auf den geistlichen Bereich beschränkt sei. Artikel I und II gelangen also zum selben Ergebnis, doch unterscheiden sie sich (wie noch zu zeigen sein wird) augenfällig in Substanz und Form der Argumentation. Die Schreiber von K (fol. 96^{v}) und A (fol. 121^{r}) versuchen eine Zäsur zwischen den beiden *articuli* zu markieren, A in Gestalt einer weitausholenden Initiale für den Anfangsbuchstaben von Artikel II. In M wird nichts dergleichen versucht, doch ist dort auf fol. 154^{r} dem Schluß von Artikel I ein weiteres Belegstück zugefügt worden. In Vi, P und N läuft der Text von Artikel I zu Artikel II kontinuierlich weiter ohne sichtbares Zeichen einer Unterbrechung.

Artikel III erwidert auf Einwände, die sich gegen die in Artikel I und II aufgestellten Thesen erheben ließen. Dabei werden fünfzehn der gängigsten hierokratischen Argumente, daß sich die päpstliche Gewalt auch auf den weltlichen Bereich erstrecke, widerlegt. Die Schreiber markieren den Übergang von Artikel II zu Artikel III klar und deutlich, und zwar sowohl in K (fol. 100^{r}) wie in A (fol. 132^{r}) und in M (vol. 159va); dabei werden als Mittel der Unterscheidung zu Beginn der detaillierten Ausführungen von Artikel III erneut Initialbuchstaben verwendet (fol. 100^{r} bzw. 132^{v} und 159vb).

Artikel IV argumentiert auf der Grundlage von elf Textstellen aus dem kanonischen und fünfen aus dem römischen Recht, daß der Papst von Rechts wegen *iure humano* nicht universale Herrschaft über Temporalien beanspruchen könne. Von einer ganz leichten Andeutung in K vielleicht abgesehen (fol. 103^{v}), enthalten die Handschriften nichts, um Artikel III und IV optisch voneinander abzugrenzen.

Artikel V weist Argumente zugunsten einer universalen weltlichen Herrschaft des Papstes zurück, die sich auf die Translatio imperii, die Absetzung

Childerichs und die Konstantinische Schenkung stützten. Die Trennlinie zwischen den Artikeln IV und V ist in A (fol. 147^{v}) verhältnismäßig klar markiert, weniger deutlich in K (fol. 104^{v}); sie ist auch in P (fol. 368^{v}) und N (fol. 200^{r}) gut erkennbar.

Artikel VI ist der Schlußabschnitt in G. Er gelangt zu dem Schluß, päpstliche und kaiserliche Gewalt leiteten sich unabhängig voneinander unmittelbar von Gott her; sie hätten klar getrennte Wirkungsbereiche, die Domäne der ersteren sei die geistliche, die der letzteren die weltliche Sphäre. Schwache Spuren einer Abgrenzung zwischen den Artikeln V und VI lassen sich bei gutem Willen in K (fol. 106^{v}) wahrnehmen, aber nichts dergleichen in den anderen Handschriften.

Ohne diesen Rahmen in den Grundzügen zu verlassen und ohne die Textgestalt wirklich schwerwiegend zu verändern, präsentiert die für die ‚Chronik des Nikolaus Minorita' angefertigte Fassung Z dennoch eine umfassende, durchgreifende und zweckvoll ausgerichtete Umarbeitung von G. Der Kompilator der ‚Chronik' steuerte eine einführende Vorbemerkung bei: Als Johannes' XXII. Anspruch auf Vollgewalt sowohl im geistlichen wie im weltlichen Bereich die Frage aufwarf, auf welches Recht, göttliches oder menschliches, gestützt er diese unerhörte *plenitudo potestatis* an sich riß, da habe auf des Kaisers Geheiß eine Anzahl in der Theologie wie in den Rechten bewanderter Männer ‚Allegaciones' zusammengestellt, um zu zeigen, daß weder nach göttlichem noch nach menschlichem Recht der Papst diese unbegrenzte Macht innehabe[62]. Darauf folgt der Prolog der ‚Allegaciones' in der für Z eigentümlichen Gestalt. Die Abweichungen gegenüber G lassen gerade hier die für die spätere Redaktion insgesamt bezeichnende Tendenz hervortreten. Während Fassung G der ‚Allegaciones' ganz einfach darauf ausgerichtet ist, den ersten Artikel von ‚Fidem catholicam' zu rechtfertigen – päpstliche Vollgewalt ist eingegrenzt auf geistliche Angelegenheiten[63] –, verkündet Z ein weitaus ehrgeizigeres Programm. Die Verfasser der ‚Allegaciones' seien – nach Z – um schriftliche Abgabe ihres Votums bezüglich päpstlicher Gewalt *tam in spiritualibus quam in temporalibus* gebeten worden; sie gelangten zu dem Urteil, daß der *summus pontifex nec iure divino nec iure humano habet plenitudinem universalis iurisdictionis in temporalibus e t s p i r i t u a l i b u s*[64]. Das dehnt die ursprüngliche Zielrichtung des Traktats, wie sie G zum Ausdruck brachte, ganz entschieden

62) Siehe oben Anm. 23.

63) K, fol. 95^{v}.

64) P, fol. 344^{r}; N, fol. 200va; M ü l l e r (wie Anm. 2) S. 103.

aus; über die Leugnung päpstlicher Vollgewalt in weltlichen Dingen hinaus möchte Z auch die geistliche Prärogative ins Visier nehmen.

Ein Zusatz in Z zu Beginn des Artikels II macht den Wandel augenfällig[65]. Während G sofort mit der Argumentation einsetzt, daß päpstliche Vollgewalt sich ausschließlich auf Geistliches erstrecke, fügt Z Augustins Ausspruch ein, aller Besitz beruhe auf göttlichem oder menschlichem Recht[66]. Wenn der Papst die volle, freie und universale Jurisdiktion sowohl im weltlichen wie im geistlichen Bereich habe, dann müßte sie entweder unmittelbar nach göttlichem oder menschlichem Recht an ihn gelangt sein. So hat man zu prüfen: (a) ob der Papst die volle Jurisdiktion in weltlichen Dingen *de iure divino* besitze, und (b) ob er sie *de iure humano* innehabe. Sodann (c) seien – in der stillschweigenden Annahme, daß das Resultat der Überprüfung negativ ausfallen würde – Einwände dagegen zu entkräften. Schließlich (d) sei zu fragen, ob der Papst Vollgewalt *in spiritualibus* besitze[67]. G entspricht diesem Schema im Hinblick auf (a) in Artikel II und III; bezüglich (b) in Artikel IV; hinsichtlich (c) in Artikel V. Aber (d) wird dort selbstverständlich überhaupt nicht behandelt. Entsprechend hält es Z für angebracht, einen eigenen Abschnitt speziell dieser Frage zu widmen: Artikel VII, der keinerlei Gegenstück in G besitzt. Dieses ist der einzige Abschnitt der ‚Allegaciones', dessen Verfasser zweifelsfrei feststeht, denn er ist wörtlich jenem Traktat entnommen, den Ockham 1337/38 gegen Papst Benedikt XII. gerichtet hat[68].

Z's Absicht, die päpstliche Autorität in geistlichen Dingen einer Überprüfung zu unterziehen und dabei deutlich zwischen zwei Formen der Vollgewalt – im weltlichen sowie im geistlichen Bereich – zu unterscheiden, hat offenkundig die Art der Umformung von G's Text bestimmt[69]; so

---

[65]) K, fol. 96v; P, fol. 346v.

[66]) Augustin, Ep. 93.12.50, ed. A. Goldbacher, CSEL 34, 2 (1898) S. 493; = Decretum Gratiani C. 23 q. 7 c. 1.

[67]) P, fol. 346v; N, fol. 201rb-va: *Quamvis res quecunque terrena non recte a quocumque possideri possit nisi iure divino, quo cuncta sunt iustorum, vel iure humano, quod est in potestate regum terre, ut ait Augustinus ad Vincencium rogatistam, ideo si papa habet universalem et plenam ac liberam in temporalibus et spiritualibus iurisdictionem, vel habet eam immediate de iure divino vel de iure humano. Propter quod primo videndum est, utrum papa habeat plenitudinem iurisdictionis in temporalibus de iure divino, secundo utrum habeat de iure humano, tercio obiecta in contrarium excludentur, ultimo utrum habeat in spiritualibus plenitudinem potestatis.*

[68]) ‚Contra Benedictum' VI 3–4, in: Guillelmi de Ockham Opera politica 3, ed. H. S. Offler (1956) S. 274f.

[69]) Man vergleiche etwa K, fol. 102v, mit P, fol. 360v: Auslassung von *sed solum in spiritualibus;* K, fol. 104v, mit P, fol. 364r: Zusatz von *potestatis in temporalibus;* K, fol..

ist beim Anfang von Artikel IV der Text von G neu formuliert worden, um ganz unmißverständlich deutlich zu machen, daß es hier speziell um die päpstliche *plenitudo potestatis* im weltlichen Bereich geht[70]. Aber nicht alle Veränderungen, die Z an G vornahm, sind auf diese Tendenz zurückzuführen. Manches sind bloße redaktionelle Eingriffe, die auf größere sprachliche Eleganz oder knappere Form des Ausdrucks zielen; gelegentlich mildert Z harte Formulierungen in G, bringt leichte sachliche Korrekturen an, kürzt ein Zitat oder ergänzt einen Verfassernamen[71]. Abweichend von seiner sonstigen Übung ergänzt Z bei Artikel II an vier Stellen die von G angeführten Autoritäten, und zwar um je zwei Hilarius- und Augustin-Zitate[72]. Als bedeutsam wird man festhalten müssen, daß Z in Artikel V den Vorwurf an die Griechen wegläßt, sie behaupteten, dem römischen Bischof keinen Gehorsam zu schulden; daß G's Auslegung der ‚Glossa ordinaria' zu X 1. 6. 34 einen möglicherweise tendenziösen Zusatz enthält; schließlich daß ein Satz ausgelassen wird, der die verfassungsrechtliche Wirkung des Wahlakts auf die Titulatur des deutschen Herrschers zum Inhalt hat[73]. Die lange Passage, die Z der Erörterung G's zur Zwei-Schwerter-Lehre in Artikel III hinzufügte, wird weiter unten noch näher zu betrachten sein[74].

Z hat sich als eine sorgfältige und durchdachte Überarbeitung von G erwiesen. G war höchstwahrscheinlich im Herbst 1338 bereits vorhanden. Wie bald danach ist Z hergestellt worden? Dafür läßt sich ein ziemlich genauer terminus a quo anführen: Das ist in P und N das letzte Textstück der

---

104^{v}, mit P, fol. 364^{v}: Auslassung von *et spiritualibus;* K, fol. 106^{v}, mit P, fol. 368^{r}: Zusatz von *plenitudinem potestatis et.*

70) K, fol. 103^{v}: *Tamen adhuc restat plenius ostendere, quod papa eciam a iure humano non habet talem potestatem et quod omnibus obiectionibus, que fiunt in oppositum quantum ad hunc articulum, plenarie respondeatur. Quod autem papa non habeat a iure humano talem potestatem ...* P, fol. 362^{v}: *Nunc restat plenius ostendere, quod papa eciam a iure canonico et civili non habet universale dominium rerum temporalium nec plenitudinem potestatis et iurisdictionis super regnum et imperium temporale. Et obiectiones, que per nonnullos fiunt ad oppositum, inferius dissolventur. Quod autem papa non habeat temporale dominium omnium regnorum et imperiorum terrenorum de iure humano ...*

71) K, fol. 106^{r}, P, fol. 367^{r-v}; K, fol. 98^{v}, P, fol. 351^{r}; K, fol. 98^{v}, P, fol. 351^{v}; K, fol. 99^{v}, P, fol. 353^{r}.

72) K, fol. 97^{r}, P, fol. 347^{v}; K, fol. 97^{v}, P, fol. 348^{v}; K, fol. 97^{v}, P, fol. 349^{r}; K, fol. 98^{r}, P, fol. 350^{v}. Zitiert werden Hilarius von Poitiers, ‚In Ps.' 2, 26 u. 69, 5; Augustin, ‚Enarr. in Ps.' 1, 1 u. ‚De catechizand. rud.' 40.

73) K, fol. 105^{v}, P, fol. 366^{r}; K, fol. 105^{r}, P, fol. 365^{r}; K, fol. 105^{v}: *Et hoc patet, quia statim postquam electus est appellatur et vocatur rex Romanorum,* fehlt P, fol. 366^{v} und N, fol. 210ra.

74) K, fol. 101^{r}, P, fol. 356^{v}–357^{r} und N, fol. 205^{va-vb}.

‚Chronik des Nikolaus Minorita'[75]. Das vorletzte Textstück ist Bonagratias Traktat ‚Ad predictam questionem' in der ihm 1338 gegebenen Fassung[76]; ihm sind vorangestellt die auf München, den 23. August 1338 datierte Appellation Michaels von Cesena sowie sieben weitere Dokumente, die alle mit der Diskussion um die Reichsrechte in Zusammenhang stehen, wie sie in jenem Jahre in Deutschland geführt wurde[77]. Nach Abschrift von ‚Ad predictam questionem' merkt ‚Nikolaus' an, daß der gesamte Inhalt der Sammlung bis zu dieser Stelle von Kaiser und Kurfürsten nach Avignon geschickt worden sei. Zur selben Zeit hätten die *periti* um Michael von Cesena Benedikt XII. und die Kardinäle aufgefordert, sich der Diskussion mit ihnen zu stellen. Sie hätten angeboten, in öffentlichem Konsistorium ihre Ansichten zu verteidigen, und um sicheres Geleit an die Kurie gebeten. Avignon habe die Herausforderung nicht angenommen, sagt ‚Nikolaus', weil Papst und Kardinäle keine Diskussion über die Sache Michaels und seines Anhangs wollten[78]. Erst auf diesen Hinweis lassen P und N die Vorbemerkung des ‚Nikolaus Minorita' zu den ‚Allegaciones' folgen, und im Anschluß daran Z.

Des Kaisers Gesandtschaft hatte die Kurie im Dezember 1338 erreicht[79]. Benedikts Weigerung, den Gefolgsleuten Michaels freies Geleit zu gewähren, ist in einem auf den 23. Januar 1339 datierten Brief enthalten[80]. ‚Nikolaus' kann daher seine Bemerkung am Schluß von ‚Ad predictam questionem' nicht geschrieben haben, bevor dieser Brief nach Deutschland gelangt war, d. h. frühestens im Februar 1339. Da er seiner Bemerkung in der

---

75) In N kommt noch ein sehr detailliertes Inhaltsverzeichnis der gesamten ‚Chronik' hinzu. Der letzte Eintrag (fol. 220v) betrifft die ‚Allegaciones', bei der eine Dreiteilung vorgenommen wird:
Item allegaciones nonnullorum magistrorum et aliorum peritorum in iure, quod papa non habeat plenitudinem potestatis in temporalibus. Incipit: Quoniam a nonnullis etc.
Item responsiones ad allegata, quod papa non habeat postetatis plenitudinem in temporalibus. Incipit: Nunc autem restat respondere etc. (d.i. Artikel III).
Item allegaciones, quod papa non habeat potestatis plenitudinem in spiritualibus. Incipit: Viso et multipliciter ostenso etc. (d.i.Artikel VII).

76) Zu den verschiedenen Fassungen dieses Werkes vgl. unten Anm. 192.

77) Müller (wie Anm. 2) S. 77 Nr. 40–46.

78) P, fol. 344r; N, fol. 200rb.

79) Siehe Stengel, Avignon und Rhens S. 170 Anm. 1, 179 Anm. 3; Becker (wie Anm. 1) S. 466. Zum Hintergrund: H. O. Schwöbel, Der diplomatische Kampf zwischen Ludwig dem Bayern und der römischen Kurie im Rahmen des kanonischen Absolutionsprozesses, 1330 – 1346 (1968) S. 278–291.

80) G. Daumet, Benoît XII (1334 – 1342). Lettres closes, patentes et curiales se rapportant à la France (Bibliothèque des Écoles françaises d'Athènes et de Rome, 3e série 2, 1899–1920) Sp. 346 Nr. 560.

‚Chronik' Z folgen läßt, dürfte die Annahme begründet sein, Z habe noch nicht existiert, als die Gesandtschaft im Spätherbst 1338 Deutschland in Richtung Avignon verließ; Z wird vielmehr im oder nach dem Februar 1339 verfertigt worden sein. Ein terminus ante quem kann nicht mit hinreichender Sicherheit angegeben werden, bevor man nicht etwas mehr über die Identität jenes ‚Nikolaus' und die Art des Zustandekommens seiner ‚Chronik' weiß als jetzt. Aber man wird in diesem Zusammenhang nicht aus dem Auge verlieren dürfen, daß Bonagratia von Bergamo am 19. Juni 1340 starb und Ockham wohl am 9. oder 10. April 1348 oder 1349[81].

3. Das Verfasserproblem im Lichte der Inhaltsanalyse

Wenn wir die ausdrückliche Feststellung im Prolog von Z ernst nehmen, die ‚Allegaciones' seien ein Gemeinschaftswerk, dann müssen wir einräumen, daß die Gruppe jener *nonulli in sacra pagina magistri et alii in utroque iure periti* unter den Anhängern Michaels von Cesena – die nie sehr zahlreich gewesen waren – im Jahre 1338 nur noch schemenhaften Charakter besaß[82]. Unter den Zeugen für Michaels Appellation im August jenes Jahres lassen sich als Theologen Michael selbst, Ockham und Heinrich von Talheim identifizieren; der einzige Jurist war Bonagratia[83]. Ob der andere bekannte Theologe unter den Flüchtlingen, Franz von Ascoli, sich um diese Zeit noch bei ihnen befand, ist schon oben in Zweifel gezogen worden[84]. Allerhöchstens vier oder fünf Koautoren können an der Entstehung der ‚Allegaciones' beteiligt gewesen sein. Und natürlich wirft jede Annahme der Beteiligung mehrerer Autoren die Frage nach der praktischen Seite des Vorgangs auf: Wie kam das Werk konkret zustande? War ein Einzelner federführend, indem er Anregungen, Argumente und Beweisstellen der anderen – oder einiger von ihnen – entgegennahm und in das Werk einarbeitete? Oder hat jeder einzelne aus der Gruppe einen oder mehrere Abschnitte

[81]) Zum Tode Bonagratias siehe S c h m i t t (wie Anm. 17) S. 245f.; zu Ockhams: J. M i e t h k e, Zu Wilhelm Ockhams Tod, Archivum Franciscanum Historicum 61 (1968) S. 98.

[82]) Das Zitat nach ‚Nikolaus'. Es wird von Z bestätigt; siehe M ü l l e r (wie Anm. 2) S. 103. G ist zurückhaltender und behauptet nur, die ‚Allegaciones' seien *per plures magistros in sacra pagina approbate;* K, fol. 95^{v}. Siehe oben Anm. 39.

[83]) Paris, BN cod. lat. 5154, fol. 330^{r}. Der Guardian des Münchener Franziskaner-Konvents, *fr. Fredericus de Vilperg,* tritt als Zeuge auf ohne akademischen Titel, wie auch sein Vorgänger, *fr. Henricus Brunone.*

[84]) Siehe oben Anm. 17.

fertiggestellt und hat einer von ihnen das alles dann zu einem einheitlichen Ganzen zusammengefaßt? Es steht fest, daß Merkmale, die auf das Werk eines einzigen Autors oder eines hauptverantwortlichen Redaktors schließen lassen, schon in G anzutreffen sind; darauf weisen rund vierzehn Querverweise zwischen den sechs *articuli* hin sowie die durchgehend gleiche Form, in der Autoritäten angeführt werden[85]. Unsere einzige Hoffnung, den Schleier der Anonymität zu lüften, der über Zustandekommen und Publikation der ‚Allegaciones' liegt, besteht in der systematischen Untersuchung dieser Merkmale, Abschnitt für Abschnitt.

Die Hypothese, daß einige oder alle Abschnitte der ‚Allegaciones' ursprünglich selbständige Einheiten aus der Feder unterschiedlicher Verfasser gewesen sind, läßt sich bei Betrachtung der Beziehungen zwischen Artikel I und II erhärten. Beide haben dieselbe Zielrichtung: Sie sollen zeigen, daß die päpstliche Vollgewalt und Jurisdiktion auf den geistlichen Bereich beschränkt ist. Blickt man auf die Gesamtanlage des Werkes, macht das Nebeneinander dieser beiden *articuli* einen denkbar schlechten Eindruck: einer von beiden ist faktisch überflüssig. Artikel II behandelt den Gegenstand in sehr viel umfassenderer und besser ausgearbeiteter Form, und Z macht von ihm in einer Weise Gebrauch, als sei er der eigentliche Beginn des Traktats[86]. Aber so wenig wie G verzichtet Z auf Artikel I. Diese offenkundige Unausgeglichenheit der ‚Allegaciones', in zwei überaus unterschiedlichen Abhandlungen dasselbe eingangs gestellte Thema bearbeiten zu lassen, läßt sich am einfachsten mit der Annahme erklären, daß Artikel I und II unabhängig voneinander entstanden.

a) Artikel I

Artikel I ist ziemlich einfach aufgebaut: Er stellt zwei Thesen nebeneinander. In der ersten wird behauptet, daß die Schlüssel, die Christus an Petrus und dessen Nachfolger übergab, für das Himmelreich bestimmt waren, nicht für ein Reich auf Erden; die Gewalt zu binden und zu lösen habe nur geistliche Übertretungen betroffen. Diese Deutung von Matth. 16, 19 wird gestützt durch Verweise auf Joh. 20, 22–23, auf den hl. Bernhard und den hl. Augustinus[87]. Die zweite These ist in einen Syllogismus gekleidet: Des

---

[85]) Auf Artikel I wird immerhin je einmal von Artikel II, IV und V verwiesen; K, fol. 98^{v}, 104^{v}. Vier Rückverweise gibt es von Artikel III auf Artikel II; K, fol. 100^{r}. Vier auf Artikel II von Artikel IV und einen von Artikel V; K, fol. 103^{v}, 104^{r}, 104^{v}, 105^{v}. Zwei von Artikel V auf Artikel IV; K, fol. 106^{v}.

[86]) Siehe oben Anm. 67.

[87]) K, fol. 95^{v}.

Papstes Macht als Vikar Christi kann nicht größer sein als Christi selbst; aber als *homo viator* hat Christus allumfassende Gewalt und Jurisdiktion in weltlichen Dingen weder besessen noch danach gestrebt; ergo usw. Um den ‚minor' zu beweisen, werden zehn Belegstellen angeführt, die etwa drei Viertel des *articulus* ausmachen; alle beruhen auf der Heiligen Schrift. In der Tat verrät Artikel I seiner ganzen Machart nach sehr viel eher die Hand eines Theologen als die eines Juristen[88]. Einer der Theologen um Michael, der recht gut der Verfasser hätte sein können, muß leider sofort aus dem Kreis der Kandidaten ausscheiden: wir haben kein Vergleichsmaterial, das als Grundlage dienen könnte, um die Ansichten Heinrichs von Talheim zu erörtern[89]. Aber die anderen drei – Michael selbst, Ockham und Franz von Ascoli – hatten in ihren Kampfschriften gegen Johannes' XXII. Konstitution ‚Quia vir reprobus' des langen und breiten die Frage von Christi weltlicher Herrschaft behandelt. Eine Betrachtung, wie sie sich über diesen Gegenstand ausließen, kann vielleicht Licht auf den Verfasser von Artikel I werfen.

Zuerst zu Ockham, der sich 1332 in cap. 93 seines ‚Opus Nonaginta Dierum' mit wenigstens fünf Schriftstellen befaßt hatte, die in den ‚Allegaciones' angeführt wurden, um den ‚minor' des Syllogismus in Artikel I zu beweisen. In diesem Werk ging es Ockham sicherlich um dasselbe wie in Artikel I: die Vorstellung als gänzlich abwegig zu erweisen, daß Christus als weltlicher Herrscher aufgetreten sei. Aber nirgends lassen wörtliche oder stilistische Übereinstimmungen zwischen dem ‚Opus Nonanginta Dierum' und Artikel I auch nur von ferne daran denken, daß Ockham der Verfasser des letzteren gewesen sein könnte[90].

Bei Franz von Ascoli ist die Sache komplizierter. Es gibt schlagende Parallelen zwischen Artikel I und der ‚Improbacio ... contra libellum domini Iohannis qui incipit „Quia vir reprobus"', die Franz 1330 verfaßt hat. Ins-

---

[88]) Artikel I erhält nur drei Verweise auf das kanonische Recht, alle auf Gratians Dekret; K, fol. 95^{v}, 96^{v}.

[89]) Zu dem wenigen, das wir von Heinrichs Lebenslauf wissen, nachdem er seine Tätigkeit in Ludwigs des Bayern Kanzlei eingestellt hatte, vgl. S c h m i t t (wie Anm. 17) S. 245.

[90]) ‚Opus Nonaginta Dierum', in: Guillelmi de Ockham Opera politica 2, hg. von J. G. S i k e s und H. S. O f f l e r (1963). Vgl. ‚Allegaciones', erster Beweis nach Luc. 12, 13–14 (K, fol. 95^{v}) mit ‚Opus Non. Dierum' c. 93 Z. 490–493; zweiter Beweis, nach Joh. 6, 15 (K, fol. 96^{r}) mit ‚Opus Non. Dierum' c. 93 Z. 513–517; dritter Beweis, nach Joh. 18, 36 (K, fol. 96^{r}) mit ‚Opus Non. Dierum' c. 93 Z. 210–425; sechster Beweis, nach Luc. 1, 32–33 (K, fol. 96^{r}) mit ‚Opus Non. Dierum' c. 93 Z. 426–482, 1222–1228; achter Beweis, nach Matth. 22, 21 usw. (K, fol. 96^{r-v}) mit ‚Opus Non. Dierum' c. 93 Z. 533–558.

besondere fallen die Übereinstimmungen zwischen der ‚Improbacio‘ und dem zehnten Beweis des ‚minor‘ in der zweiten Hauptthese von Artikel I ins Auge[91]. Man ist versucht, auf Grund der Textübereinstimmungen anzunehmen, daß Franz zumindest für diesen Teil von Artikel I direkt verantwortlich ist. Es wäre voreilig, das zu tun! Denn es läßt sich eine Quelle ausfindig machen, die noch enger mit jener Passage in Artikel I übereinstimmt: die im Namen Michaels ergangene Appellation gegen ‚Quia vir reprobus‘, datiert auf München, den 26. März 1330[92]. Stellt man die einschlägigen Stellen der drei Werke nebeneinander, wird es ganz klar, daß der Wortlaut von Artikel I der Appellation Michaels sehr viel näher steht als der ‚Improbacio‘.

(Im folgenden sind die Textteile, die in den ‚Allegaciones‘ sowohl mit der Appellation wie mit der ‚Improbacio‘ übereinstimmen, in allen drei Vergleichsstücken kursiv gesetzt worden; Sperrung wurde dort verwendet, wo die ‚Allegaciones‘ nur mit der ‚Improbacio‘ textgleich sind.)

Franz, ‚Improbacio‘ fol. 71rb:	*‚Allegaciones‘ Artikel I, K, fol. 96^{v}:*	Appellation vom 26. März 1330, fol. 185^{v}:
Item *tale fuit regnum Christi pro hac vita* passibili *quale commisit seu recommendavit suis principibus primis,* scilicet *apostolis.* Unde *Luce XXII.* l e g i t u r : *„Et ego dispono vobis regnum sicut disposuit michi*	*Decimo ex eo, quod tale fuerit regnum Christi pro hac vita mortali quale commisit seu recommendavit suis apostolis primis principibus ecclesie, sicut patet Luce XXII°, ubi* l e g i t u r *Christum apostolis dixisse: „Et ego dispono vobis regnum si-*	Item *tale fuit Christi regnum pro hac vita mortali quale commisit seu recommendavit suis apostolis primis principibus ecclesie, sicut patet Luce XXII.* c., *ubi Christus apostolis dixit: „Et ego dispono vobis regnum sicut disposuit michi pater* meus, ut edatis et bibatis super mensam meam in regno meo et sedeatis super thronos iudicantes XII tribus Israel.“ *In quibus verbis Christus* secundum quod homo viator *manifeste demonstrat,*

[91]) ‚Allegaciones‘ Artikel I, K, fol. 96^{v}; Franz von Ascoli, ‚Improbacio‘, in: Florenz, Biblioteca Medicea Laurenziana, S. Crucis, Plut. XXXI sin. cod. 3, fol. 71rb. Zu anderen Handschriften der ‚Improbacio‘ vgl. Anneliese M a i e r, Eine unbeachtete Quaestio aus dem Visio-Streit unter Johann XXII., Archivum Franciscanum Historicum 63 (1970) S. 287 Anm. 3 (= d i e s., Ausgehendes Mittelalter 3 [1977] S. 512 Anm. 22).

[92]) Überliefert in der Hs. Paris, BN cod. lat. 5154, fol. 185^{v}.

Franz, ‚Improbacio‘ fol. 71rb:	*‚Allegaciones‘ Artikel I, K, fol. 96^{v}:*	Appellation vom 26. März 1330, fol. 185^{v}:
pater, ut edatis et bibatis super mensam meam in regno meo.“ Et hoc fuit racionabile, quia sui principes debuerunt esse consortes et comparticipes sui regni sicut fuerunt consortes et participes evangelii et persecucionis mundi. Sed Christus *recommendavit* suis *apostolis regnum* ecclesie *spirituale* et *non temporale,* quia *regnum temporale* admonuit et *docuit eos relinquere et contempnere.* Unde *et Petrus in persona omnium apostolorum* dixit: „Domine, *ecce nos reliqui-*	*cut disposuit michi pater*“ etc. *In quibus verbis Christus manifeste demonstrat, quod* ipse *tale regnum recommendabat apostolis quale pater* suus *sibi commiserat,* et hoc *non fuit temporale sed spirituale,* ut dictum est. Ergo Christus *non* commisit sive *commendavit regnum* et dominium rerum *temporalium apostolis, immo regnum* et dominium rerum *temporalium docuit eos relinquere et contempnere, quia* ut dicitur *Matthei XIX. et Luce XVIII.:* „Vade et *vende omnia que habes et da pauperibus* et sequere me!“ *Et Petrus in persona omnium apostolorum ostendens se* et apostolos hoc	*quod tale regnum recommendavit apostolis quale* sibi *commiserat pater.* Sed *apostolis non recommendavit regnum temporale sed spirituale, ymo regnum temporale docuit eos contempnere et relinquere, quia* „Si vis,“ inquit, „perfectus esse, *vende omnia que habes et da pauperibus!*“ *Et Petrus in persona omnium apostolorum ostendens se* predictum *Christi consilium adimplesse respondit: „Ecce nos reliquimus omnia*“ etc. Que autem apostoli semel ex perfectione apostolica reliquerunt, stante perfectione apostolica illa amplius non resumpserunt, quia stante causa stat effectus[93]. Et Luce IX. dicitur: „Nemo mittens manum ad aratrum et aspiciens retro dignus est regno dei.“ Sed apostoli ex perfectione virtutis, ut dictum est, omnia temporalia reliquerunt, ergo stante apostolica perfectione amplius illa non resumpserunt et a Christo regnum temporale non receperunt. *Ergo regnum Christi* inquantum homo viator *non fuit temporale sed spirituale,* quia, ut premissum est, tale fuit eius regnum quale suis *apostolis*

---

93) Variation der bekannten Parömie: *Cessante causa cessat effectus* (zuerst X 2.24.26, Innocenz III.); vgl. H. Krause, in: ZRG Kan. 46 (1960) S. 85.

Franz, ‚Improbacio' fol. 71rb:	‚Allegaciones' Artikel I, K, fol. 96^{v}:	Appellation vom 26. März 1330, fol. 185^{v}:
mus omnia et secuti sumus te:" *Ergo regnum Christi non fuit temporale, sed spirituale* et celeste.	*Christi consilium adimplesse respondit: „Ecce nos reliquimus omnia* et secuti sumus te!" *Ergo regnum Christi* et Petri eius vicarii *non fuit temporale sed spirituale.*	*commendavit.* Item quod *regnum Christi* inquantum homo viator *non fuerit temporale sed spirituale* et celeste, apparet per hoc, quod tale fuit regnum Christi quale venit predicare et annunciare, et non tale quale venit contempnere et despicere, cum magister perfectionis non aliud verbo aliud facto predicare debuerit, ne eius predicacio contemptui haberetur. Sed Christus venit predicare et annunciare regnum celorum, *quia „Vende,"* inquit, *„omnia que habes et da pauperibus* et habebis thesaurum in celo", *Mat. XIX* et Marci X. *et Luce XVIII. Ergo Christi regnum non fuit temporale* et terrenum, *sed spirituale* et celeste.

Es kommt hinzu, daß die Appellation, nicht die ‚Improbacio' für einen Großteil des achten und neunten Beweises für den ‚minor' der zweiten Hauptthese von Artikel I bis in den Wortlaut hinein die Vorlage abgab[94].

Diese Entlehnungen beweisen natürlich nicht, daß Michael von Cesena selbst den Artikel I verfaßt hat. Im Jahre 1338 hätte jeder der *periti* aus der Umgebung Michaels die Appellation von 1330 ausbeuten können – wie das etwa Ockham tat, als er 1332 sein ‚Opus Nonaginta Dierum' schrieb[95]. Zudem darf man nicht zu selbstverständlich davon ausgehen, daß Michael die Appellation von 1330 persönlich abgefaßt hat, sowenig wie die zahllosen anderen Manifeste und Appellationen, die nach seiner Rebellion gegen Johannes XXII. unter seinem Namen und gedeckt von seiner vorgeblichen

---

[94]) ‚Allegaciones' Artikel I, K, fol. 96^{r-v}; Appellation fol. 183^{v} – 184^{r}.

[95]) Siehe Guillelmi de Ockham Opera politica 2, S. XVIIf.

Autorität als Generalminister in die Welt gingen. Es ist viel eher wahrscheinlich, daß es sich um das Ergebnis vereinter Bemühungen der um Michael gescharten Gelehrtengruppe handelte, wobei im Hinblick auf Rechtskenntnis Bonagratia eine besondere Bedeutung zukam[96]. Ohne Zweifel billigte Michael diese Dokumente; er war von seinem Rang her der verantwortliche Mann, und sie drückten seine Ansichten aus. Aber gerade weil er der Rangobere war, könnte sein eigener Anteil an ihrer Abfassung gering gewesen sein. Dennoch, läßt man Heinrich von Talheim beiseite, über den wir so gar nichts wissen, dann wird man Michael auf der Liste der potentiellen Verfasser von Artikel I der „Allegaciones' einen Spitzenplatz zuweisen müssen. Wahrscheinlich ist er noch vor Franz von Ascoli einzustufen. Denn selbst wenn die oben erwähnte Argumentationskette, die in so gleichartigen Wendungen in der ‚Improbacio', in der Appellation von 1330 und in den ‚Allegaciones' anzutreffen ist, letztlich auf Franz zurückginge, erschiene es zweifelhaft, ob er einen direkten Anteil an der Abfassung von Artikel I gehabt haben kann. Denn seine Anwesenheit im Kreise der Anhänger Michaels kann zu diesem Zeitpunkt nicht mehr als gesichert gelten; und stammte Artikel I von seiner Hand: hätte er es dann nicht vorgezogen, seiner eigenen ‚Improbacio' die Textanleihen zu entnehmen statt Michaels Appellation, zu der er nur als einer von mehreren beigetragen haben kann? Wie immer das gewesen sein mag: man wird ohne Zögern sagen können, daß nichts unverwechselbar nach Ockham klingt in Artikel I, weder nach Stil, Temperament noch Kraft der Gedankenführung.

b) Artikel II

Artikel II der ‚Allegaciones' sucht sehr viel eindringender als Artikel I Christi *dominium potestatis* zu ergründen. Dieses *dominium*, so wird argumentiert, war und ist ein zweifaches: eine ungeschaffene, ewige Herrschaft gemäß Christi Göttlichkeit, und ein *dominium creatum* gemäß seiner Menschlichkeit. Die ungeschaffene Herrschaft ist eine absolute, allumfassende Gewalt, die Christus keinem menschlichen Wesen übertragen hat.

---

[96]) Die ungeprüfte Annahme, Michael habe seine offiziellen Erklärungen selbst geschrieben, mindert ein wenig den Wert einiger tiefdringender Erörterungen seiner Ansichten: z.B. Brian Tierney, The Origins of Papal Infallibility 1150–1350 (1972) S. 196–201, sowie Carlo Dolcini, Il pensiero politico di Michele da Cesena 1328–1338 (1977) passim. Wenn Becker Recht hat mit der Annahme, daß Bonagratia das Material für die drei Appellationen Michaels von 1328 zusammenstellte, könnte er recht gut auch an der Abfassung der Appellation von 1330 beteiligt gewesen sein; siehe Becker, Bonagrazia (wie Anm. 37) S. 508.

Hinsichtlich Christi geschaffener Herrschaft wiederum muß man unterscheiden zwischen der, die er vor der Passion besaß, und jener, die er nach der Auferstehung innehatte. Gemäß der letzteren war und ist Christus der Herr aller körperlichen und geistlichen Dinge, aller Menschen und aller Engel. Diese Gewalt hat er niemandem übertragen, weder an Petrus noch an irgendjemanden sonst. Die geschaffene Herrschaft, die Christus seinem Stellvertreter Petrus zusagte und dessen Nachfolgern, war seine Herrschaft vor der Passion: eine ausschließlich geistliche Gewalthabe, da weltliche Herrschaft ein Widerspruch gewesen wäre zu Armut, Demut, Liebe und Rechtschaffenheit *(equitati et honestati)* Christi und der Apostel. Daß deren Lebensform unvereinbar war mit weltlicher Herrschaft, wird anhand biblischer und patristischer Autoritäten aufgezeigt.

Artikel II gelangt zu dem unausweichlichen Schluß: Der Papst ist nach göttlichem Recht nicht mit universaler Herrschaft ausgestattet oder mit Gewalt über den weltlichen Bereich. Daraus ergeben sich eine negative und eine positive Folgerung, beide gestützt zum einen auf die Kirchenväter (Augustin, Ambrosius und Johannes Chrysostomus, dazu Papst Leo I. und der hl. Bernhard), zum anderen auf Gratians ‚Dekret' und dessen Glossen, zum Schluß auf das römische Recht. Negativ: Da Christus und die Apostel Herrschaft in dieser Welt weder innehatten noch ersehnten, besitzt der Papst – ihr Nachfolger – keine Vollgewalt in weltlichen Dingen. Positiv: Gemäß päpstlichen Verfügungen und auch nach Gesetzen des römischen Rechts, die die Kirche approbiert hat, erfreut sich allein der Kaiser voller weltlicher Gewalt; kaiserliche Gewalt hat ihren Ursprung unmittelbar von Gott, nicht vom Papst, denn dessen Wirkungsbereich ist eingeschränkt auf geistliche Angelegenheiten.

Der Art nach, wie die positive Folgerung aus dem kanonischen und dem römischen Recht begründet wird, ist Artikel II offensichtlich unselbständig. Der Text lehnt sich über weite Strecken kontinuierlich und wörtlich an ‚Fidem catholicam' an[97] und verläßt diese Vorlage lediglich, um eine Reihe von Allegationen aus dem römischen Recht (mit einer Appendix aus dem kanonischen Recht) einzufügen, die wortgleich in einer Allegationskette des aus Franziskanerkreisen stammenden Traktats ‚Inferius describuntur articuli' begegnet[98]. Wie Becker nachwies, stimmt die gesamte Beweisführung weitgehend mit einem älteren, 1331 entstandenen Werk aus demselben Milieu überein: mit ‚Ut in composicione[99]. Es gibt keinen trifti-

[97]) K, fol. 99^v: vgl. ‚Fidem catholicam', ed. B e c k e r (wie Anm. 1) S. 497ff.

[98]) K, fol. 99^v; vgl. ‚Inferius', in: Nova Alamanniae 1, 391 Nr. 583.

[99]) B e c k e r (wie Anm. 1) S. 484. K, fol. 99^v; vgl. ‚Ut in composicione', ed. H. F o e r s t e r, Miscellanea Francescana 37 (1937) S. 599–601.

gen Grund zu zweifeln, daß ‚Inferius describuntur articuli' aus dem Umkreis der Anhänger Michaels hervorgegangen ist[100]; und einen gewichtigen, wenn nicht dominierenden Anteil sowohl an ‚Fidem catholicam' wie an ‚Ut in composicione' wird man mit guten Gründen dem einzigen ausgebildeten Juristen in ihrer Mitte zuzuschreiben haben: Bonagratia von Bergamo[101]. Er scheint am ehesten als Autor zumindest für diesen Teil von Artikel II in Frage zu kommen.

Direkte wörtliche Entlehnungen aus Michaels Appellation vom 26. März 1330 (künftig Appellation IV), die in Artikel I der ‚Allegaciones' eine so bedeutende Rolle spielten, haben sich in Artikel II nicht aufweisen lassen. Aber der oder die Verfasser kannten die Appellation offenkundig gut und bezogen sich sogar direkt darauf[102]. Die Unterscheidung in Artikel II zwischen Christi *dominium creatum* vor der Passion und nach der Auferstehung begegnet bereits in Appellation IV[103]. Indem nun aus dem Herrenwort: „Gebt dem Kaiser, was des Kaisers ist," abgeleitet wird, daß des Kaisers Gewalt nicht ihren Ursprung im Papst habe, noch des Papstes im Kaiser, weil Christus *iura imperialia et iura pontificalia ... ex opposito adinvicem distinxit et divisit*, kommt Artikel II schon sehr nahe an das heran, was die Appellation IV acht Jahre zuvor ausgeführt hatte[104]. Christi Ausspruch: *Regnum meum non est de hoc mundo*, schließt nach Ansicht von Artikel II jeglichen Anspruch auf weltliche Herrschaft aus; wäre Christi Reich von dieser Welt gewesen, dann hätte das der Herrschaft anderer Könige und Fürsten Eintrag getan, *quia in eodem regno sive imperio temporali plures reges et domini simul et in solidum esse non possunt.* Artikel I hatte dasselbe ausgeführt, aber unter direktem Rückgriff auf Appellation IV[105].

Es ist natürlich in keiner Weise überraschend, daß Artikel II und Appellation IV häufig die selbe Textpassage aus der gleichen patristischen Quelle

---

100) Entgegen den Ausführungen S t e n g e l s, Avignon und Rhens S. 131. Indessen ist in keiner Weise die von Becker vertretene Annahme gesichert, daß ‚Inferius' von den ‚Allegaciones' abhängt: B e c k e r (wie Anm. 1) S. 486 Anm. 1. Für die Überarbeitung von ‚Inferius' in ‚Nikolaus Minorita' siehe oben Anm. 58.

101) B e c k e r, ebd. S. 482; *ders.*, Bonagrazia S. 505–508.

102) K, fol. 98r: *Ponere et dogmatizare Christi regnum fuisse temporale et terrenum ... sapit carnalem errorem Herodis et Iudeorum et incidit in heresim dampnatam, sicut plene ostenditur et probatur in appellacione contra dictum errorem facta;* vgl. Appellation IV, Paris, BN cod. lat. 5154, fol. 192r–v.

103) K, fol. 96v; Appellation IV, fol. 188v, 189r, 189v.

104) K, fol. 98v; Appellation IV, fol. 183v. Es ist unwahrscheinlich, daß Ockham diese Begriffe benutzt haben würde; vgl. seine nuancierte Behandlung des Problems in qu. 1 der ‚Octo Quaestiones', in: Opera politica ²1, ed. H. S. O f f l e r (1974) S. 16–68.

105) ‚Allegaciones' Artikel I, K, fol. 96v; Appellation IV, fol. 183v.

zitieren, hält man sich die ähnliche Thematik der beiden Werke sowie die Tatsache vor Augen, daß deren Verfasser auf einen gemeinsamen zusammengetragenen Grundstock an Materialien zurückgreifen konnten. An manchen Stellen, wo die Zitate in Artikel II umfangreicher sind als in Appellation IV, ist es klar, daß zwischen beiden Texten keine direkte Abhängigkeit besteht[106]. Anderswo ist das weniger deutlich: Das Leo-Zitat ist vielleicht aus Appellation IV übernommen, obwohl es der Kreis um Michael auch andernorts verwendet hat[107]; möglicherweise gilt das auch für eine längere Passage aus dem Apokalypsenkommentar Haymos, bei der als Quelle Remigius von Auxerre angegeben wurde[108]. Aber an zumindest einem Beispiel läßt sich der Nachweis führen, daß Artikel II auf Appellation IV beruht (oder auf einer von Appellation IV benutzten Materialsammlung): Die Auffassung, daß weltliche Herrschaft nicht in Einklang zu bringen sei mit Christi Demut, sucht Artikel II mit Hilfe einer Zitatenkette zu untermauern, entnommen aus Hieronymus, In Matth. 1, 9, der Glosse des Johannes Chrysostomus zu Matth. 8, 20 und Anselm, De sacrament. divers. III. Einzeln sind all diese Belegstellen wiederholt von franziskanischen Autoren benutzt worden: die Glosse des Johannes Chrysostomus beispielsweise von Bonagratia und Ockham[109], desgleichen Anselm von Bonaventura[110]. Aber die Allegationskette in Artikel II führt diese Passagen in genau der gleichen Ordnung und in exakt demselben Umfang an, wie sie in Appellation IV erscheinen[111]. Die Übereinstimmung kann kaum zufällig sein.

Es gibt folglich Anzeichen, daß Artikel II mit Werken zusammenhängt, an denen Bonagratia so gut wie sicher beteiligt war[112], sowie mit der unter

---

106) K, fol. 97^r, 97^v (bis), 98^v; vgl. Appellation IV, fol. 195^r, 190^v, 190^r, 191^r.

107) K, fol. 99^r; vgl. Appellation IV, fol. 190^v. Das Zitat findet sich auch bei Franz von Ascoli, ‚Improbacio' (wie Anm. 91), fol. 70rb. Ockham hat es in derselben Form Form im ‚Opus Non. Dierum', in: Opera politica 2, c. 93 Z. 470–473, und gekürzt im ‚Breviloquium' IV 8, ed. S c h o l z, Wilhelm von Ockham (wie Anm. 31) S. 155f.

108) K, fol. 96^v; Appellation IV, fol. 186^r; ebenso bei Franz von Ascoli, ‚Improbacio', fol. 71vb.

109) Bonagratia, ‚De paupertate Christi', ed. L. O l i g e r, Archivum Franciscanum Historicum 22 (1929) S. 499; Ockham, ‚Opus Non. Dierum', in: Opera politica 2, c. 93 Z. 920–922.

110) Bonaventura, ‚Apologia pauperum' VII, in: Opera omnia 8 (1898) S. 274; Bonagratia, ‚De paupertate' S. 496; Ockham, ‚Opus Non. Dierum', in: Opera politica 2, c. 93 Z. 932–937.

111) K, fol. 97^{r-v}; Appellation IV, fol. 183^v.

112) Es sollte allerdings angemerkt werden, daß es wenig Gemeinsames gibt zwischen Artikel II und Bonagratias Erörterung von Christi Herrschertum in zwei unzweifelhaft aus seiner Feder stammenden Werken: in der auf den 10. April 1332 datierten Appellation, überliefert in Vat. lat. 4009, fol. 212^r, und in dem Entwurf einer Art Appellation für Balduin von Trier aus dem Jahre 1334, ebd. fol. 184^v–185^v.

Michaels Namen laufenden Appellation IV, wer immer deren Autoren gewesen sein mögen. Möglicherweise waren Franz von Ascoli und Ockham darunter. Andererseits ließen sich keine zwingenden Übereinstimmungen zwischen Franz' ‚Improbacio' und Artikel II aufdecken. Dort ist auch nichts enthalten, was unmißverständlich auf Ockham hindeutete. Er erwähnt zwar durchaus des öfteren den Unterschied zwischen *increatum et creatum dominium Christi*, aber nie in Form engerer wörtlicher Anklänge an Artikel II[113]. Ein anderes Beispiel führt zu einem ähnlich fruchtlosen Vergleich: Weil Petrus und die anderen Apostel die heidnischen Herrscher ihrer Zeit als die gesetzliche Regierung ansahen, so argumentiert Artikel II, können sie nicht selbst weltliche Macht ausgeübt haben, da nicht gut zwei Herrscher zu derselben Zeit in demselben Reich vollkommen unabhängig voneinander regieren können. Ockham entwickelt den gleichen Gedankengang in seinem ‚Breviloquium de principatu tyrannico', in der Absicht, die Legitimität weltlicher Herrschaft selbst unter Heiden aufzuzeigen: *potestas concessa et ordinata, non solummodo permissa*[114]. Es ist unvermeidlich, daß beide Werke die eine oder andere Schriftautorität in gleicher Weise anführen. Aber ein Vergleich der einschlägigen Textstellen hinterläßt nicht den Eindruck, beide Werke stammten von demselben Verfasser. Ebensowenig führt in diesem Zusammenhang ein Vergleich zwischen Artikel II und einer ganz ähnlich aufgebauten Erörterung in Ockhams ‚Octo Quaestiones' zu einem anderen Resultat[115].

Der Augenschein legt vielmehr nahe, daß Ockham den Artikel II der ‚Allegaciones' ausgebeutet, aber nicht, daß er ihn verfaßt hat: Im ‚Breviloquium' IV 8 argumentiert er, das römische Reich sei von Gott gestiftet worden auf dem Wege freiwilliger Unterwerfung der Menschen unter den Kaiser, dem sie ein für allemal Gewalt und Jurisdiktion über sich übertragen hätten; als sterblicher Mensch war Christus folglich kein weltlicher Herrscher. Die von Ockham zum Beweis angeführten Autoritäten gleichen denen, die in Artikel II den Widerspruch weltlicher Herrschaft zur Demut Christi und der Apostel belegen sollen. Die Art der Übereinstimmung läßt freilich in aller Deutlichkeit erkennen, daß Ockham hier der Schuldner, nicht der Gläubiger war. Die erste Autorität in Artikel II: Gregor d. Gr., ‚Regula pastoralis' I 3, erscheint verkürzt im Breviloquium; dasselbe bei der zweiten:

---

113) K, fol. 96v; vgl. Ockham, ‚An princeps', in: Opera politica $^{2}1$, c. 4 Z. 9–13; d e r s., ‚Breviloquium' II 9, ed. S c h o l z S. 69f.; d e r s., ‚Octo Quaestiones', in: Opera politica $^{2}1$, q. 1 c. 13 Z. 5–9.

114) K, fol. 97r–v; vgl. ‚Breviloquium' III 3, ed. S c h o l z S. 117f.

115) ‚Octo Quaestiones', in: Opera politica $^{2}1$, q. 1 c. 10 Z. 97–129.

Augustin, Ep. 132[116]. Artikel II zitiert danach aus Johannes Chrysostomus, In Matth. homil. 86, und das ‚Breviloquium' führt exakt dieselbe Textpassage an[117]; dann folgt in beiden Werken dasselbe Zitat aus dem Markus-Kommentar von Pseudo-Hieronymus[118]. Artikel II setzt fort mit dem Beweisgang für die These, weltliche Herrschaft sei unvereinbar mit Christi Liebe, und nennt in diesem Zusammenhang als erste Autorität Augustin, Super Ioann. tr. 115; dieser Text erscheint, wenn auch stark verkürzt, auch im ‚Breviloquium' IV 8[119]. Und so geht es weiter: Die nächsten sieben patristischen Autoritäten in Artikel II begegnen allesamt, wenn auch bisweilen verkürzt, im selben Kapitel des ‚Breviloquium'[120]. Es grenzt ans Unmögliche, den Schluß zu vermeiden, Ockham fuße hier direkt auf Artikel II[121]; das könnte an anderen Stellen seines ‚Breviloquium' ebenso der Fall sein[122].

So gibt es keine überzeugenden Beweise für Ockham oder Franz von Ascoli als Verfasser von Artikel II; vielmehr läßt sich eher das Gegenteil behaupten[123]. Belegbar ist der Einfluß Bonagratias auf Artikel II – ganz deut-

---

116) K, fol. 97^{v}; vgl. ‚Breviloquium' IV 8, ed. S c h o l z S. 154f. Die Textstelle aus Gregor d. Gr. wird zitiert von Bonaventura, ‚Apologia pauperum' IX, in: Opera omnia 8, 297 und in gekürzter Form von Michael von Cesena, Appellation IV, fol. 191^{r}, sowie von Ockham, ‚Opus Non. Dierum', in: Opera politica 2, c. 95 Z. 67–75; Augustin ist in gekürzter Fassung anzutreffen in Appellation IV, fol. 190^{v} und im ‚Opus Non. Dierum', in: Opera politica 2, c. 95 Z. 64–67.

117) K, fol. 97^{v}; ‚Breviloquium', ebd. S. 154.

118) K, fol. 97^{v}; ‚Breviloquium', ebd., wo Scholz den Schreibfehler *super Matth.* im Text beibehält.

119) K, fol. 97^{v}; ‚Breviloquium', ebd. Ausführlicher als im ‚Breviloquium' zitiert von Michael, Appellation IV, fol. 190^{r}; Franz von Ascoli, ‚Improbacio', fol. 69vb: Ockham, ‚Opus Non. Dierum', in: Opera politica 2, c. 93 Z. 378–399.

120) K, fol. 98^{r-v}; ‚Breviloquium' IV 8, ed. S c h o l z S. 155ff.

121) Die mögliche andere Erklärung, daß Artikel II und das ‚Breviloquium' unabhängig voneinander auf eine schon vorhandene Autoritäten-Sammlung zurückgehen, erscheint zu weit hergeholt. In ‚Breviloquium' IV 8 steht Ockham Artikel II erheblich näher als in der ähnlichen Allegationsreihe von der er zu ganz demselben Zweck im ‚Opus Non. Dierum', in: Opera politica 2, c. 95 Z. 48–107 Gebrauch gemacht hatte.

122) In K, fol. 98^{v}–99^{r}, zitiert Artikel II Ambrosius, ‚Super Luc.' IV; das Zitat begegnet im ‚Breviloquium' II 16, ed. S c h o l z S. 88. Ambrosius, ‚Super Luc.' IX findet sich Artikel II in K, fol. 99^{r}; dasselbe Zitat steht im ‚Breviloquium' II 11, ed. S c h o l z S. 74, und Ockham benutzt es auch in ‚An princeps', in: Opera politica ^{2}1, c. 3 Z. 12–20.

123) Markant ist die unterschiedliche Zitierweise von Johannes Chrysostomus in den ‚Allegaciones' und bei Ockham: In den ‚Allegaciones' haben die Verweise auf die echten Matthäus-Homilien die Form: *Ioannes Chrysostomus in homeliario super Mattheum homelia* ... (z.B. K, fol. 97^{v}, 98^{r}), während bei Verweisen auf das ‚Opus imperfectum' des Pseudo-Chrysostomus die Bezeichnungen ‚commentarium' und ‚commentum' gebraucht werden (z.B. K, fol. 98^{r}: *In commentario super Mattheum commento III° idem Io-*

lich im hinteren Teil – sowie des oder der Verfasser der Appellation IV, unter denen Bonagratia recht gut federführend gewesen sein kann, obgleich sich die Mitarbeit anderer bei der Abfassung der Appellation – inclusive Michael und natürlich auch Franz von Ascoli und Ockham – nicht ausschließen läßt. Woher das die Einzelelemente zusammenhaltende Grundschema in Artikel II stammt: die vierfach begründete Zurückweisung weltlicher Herrschaft Christi und seiner Jünger auf Grund ihrer Armut, Demut, Liebe und Rechtschaffenheit, hat sich nicht feststellen lassen. Ich habe es nicht in Werken nachweisen können, deren Zurückweisung an Ockham unstrittig ist.

c) Artikel III

Artikel III ist der umfangreichste Abschnitt der ‚Allegaciones' und deren eigentlicher Kern. Er setzt sich mit fünfzehn Argumenten zugunsten der päpstlichen Vollgewalt in weltlichen Dingen auseinander. Diese Argumente waren längst Gemeinplätze in der Diskussion um das Verhältnis zwischen Staat und Kirche geworden; ob sie in den ‚Allegaciones' auf eine einzige Quelle zurückgehen, war nicht möglich herauszufinden. Ganz offensichtlich jedoch hat Ockham Artikel III vor sich gehabt, als er Buch V und VI des ‚Breviloquium' schrieb.

Der schlüssige Beleg ist die wörtliche Übernahme von rund einem halben Dutzend Zeilen von Artikel III in das ‚Breviloquium' VI 1; weil er das bei seiner Edition des ‚Breviloquium' übersah, ließ sich Scholz die Möglichkeit entgehen, die verdorbene Überlieferung seiner einzigen Handschrift zu verbessern[124]. Aber es lassen sich unschwer weitere Belege für Ockhams Benutzung von Artikel III im ‚Breviloquium' ausfindig machen. In Buch V

annes Chrysostomus ...; K, fol. 99r: *sanctus Ioannes Chrysostomus super Mattheum commento III°*; vgl. auch in Artikel III und IV K, fol. 101v, 102r, 104r). Im Gegensatz dazu bezieht sich Ockham gewöhnlich mit *super Mattheum* oder ähnlich ohne jede Unterscheidung auf beide Werke, wenn er auch gelegentlich eine Nummer für eine der echten Homilien angibt; vgl. ‚Opus Non. Dierum', in: Opera politica 2, c. 76 Z. 140–141 und c. 115 Z. 75; ‚An princeps', in: Opera politica ²1, c. 3 Z. 41; ‚Breviloquium' IV 8, ed. Scholz S. 155.

[124]) ‚Breviloquium' VI 1, ed. Scholz S. 196, im Kontext der Auseinandersetzung mit dem Kanon ‚Omnes': *Dicunt autem quidam, quod Nicholaus non accipit ius terreni[a] imperii pro iure divino[b] temporalium et spiritualium rerum, sed pro spirituali potestate solvendi et ligandi universa peccata, de qua potestate dixit Christus Petro: „Tibi dabo claves regni celorum... erit solutum et in celo."* Die gesperrten Worte stammen aus Artikel III, K, fol. 102r–v, der die besseren Lesarten *terreni et celestis* (a) und *iure et dominio* (b) aufweist.

war es Ockhams Absicht, der Heiligen Schrift entnommene Argumente zugunsten der These abzuweisen, daß sich das römische Reich vom Papste herleite[125]; Buch VI sollte darüber hinaus prüfen, ob sich die These dem Rechte nach (vor allem dem kanonischen Rechte nach) oder auf Grund politischer oder theologischer *rationes* rechtfertigen ließ[126]. In diesen zwei Büchern befaßte sich Ockham mit neun der fünfzehn pro-päpstlichen Argumente, die in Artikel III aufs Korn genommen wurden; ohne Zweifel hat ihm Artikel III das gesamte Material für seine Angriffe geliefert. Es wird unumgänglich sein, in der Folge besondere Aufmerksamkeit den in Artikel III widerlegten Argumenten 3 und 4 zuzuwenden, die sich auf die Zwei-Schwerter-Lehre bzw. auf 1. Cor. 6, 2–6 beziehen[127]; mit ihnen beschäftigen sich ‚Breviloquium' V 3–5 und V 9. Das sechste in Artikel III attackierte Argument, das sich auf Christi Austreibung der Geldwechsler aus dem Tempel stützte, wird in ‚Breviloquium' V 8 zurückgewiesen; desgleichen im selben Kapitel die siebente, achte und neunte der in Artikel III behandelten pro-päpstlichen *rationes*[128]: d. h. die Argumente, die sich auf Christi Erlaubnis an die Apostel stützen, Schwerter zu tragen; sodann seine Weisung an die Jünger, ihm eine Eselin und deren Füllen zu bringen; schließlich die Gaben der drei Weisen bei Christi Geburt (besonders in diesem Punkt kommt die Abhängigkeit des ‚Breviloquium' vom Text des Artikel III sehr deutlich zum Ausdruck)[129]. Das zehnte Argument von Artikel III, das sich auf die *Duo luminaria magna* bezieht (Gen. 1, 16), wird in ‚Breviloquium' V 6 widerlegt; in ‚Breviloquium' V 7 geschieht dasselbe hinsichtlich des dreizehnten, wo es um die Unterordnung des weltlichen Herrschers unter den, der ihn salbt und weiht, geht. Die Behandlung des elften pro-päpstlichen Arguments in Artikel III, das sich auf den Kanon ‚Omnes' gründet (D. 22 c. 1), hat ihr Gegenstück in ‚Breviloquium' VI 1, ein Abschnitt, der, wie wir bereits feststellten[130], an dieser Stelle Artikel III entlehnt ist.

---

125) ‚Breviloquium' V 1, ed. Scholz S. 168.

126) ‚Breviloquium' VI 1, ebd. S. 194

127) K, fol. 100v–101r.

128) K, fol. 101v–102r.

129) Artikel III, fol. 102r, zitiert zuerst in der ihm eigentümlichen Form das ‚Opus imperfectum' des Pseudo-Chrysostomus: *In commento super Mattheum III° commento;* dann die echte Homilie 8 ‚super Matthaeum' des Johannes Chrysostomus. Im ‚Breviloquium' V 8, ed. Scholz S. 186, zitiert Ockham lediglich die letztere Stelle, und auch dies nur in Kurzform. Aber er führt diesen verstümmelten Auszug der Homilie mit den Worten ein: *Iohannes Crisostomus ... dicens in commento super Matth.* Offensichtlich hat er Artikel III nachlässig gelesen und verkürzt und dabei übersehen, daß dort zwei verschiedene Werke angeführt werden.

130) Siehe oben Anm. 124.

Obwohl Buch V und VI des ‚Breviloquium‘ auf die übrigen sechs in Artikel III angegriffenen pro-päpstlichen Argumente nicht eingehen[131], ist der enge Zusammenhang zwischen beiden Werken doch unverkennbar. Ockham nun war mit Sicherheit der Verfasser des ‚Breviloquium‘. Aber war er auch verantwortlich für Artikel III, von dem das ‚Breviloquium‘ so deutlich abhängt[132]? Es ist niemals leicht, auf eine derartige Frage eine negative Antwort schlüssig zu begründen. Dennoch legt ein systematischer Vergleich zwischen der in Artikel III vorgenommenen Behandlung der hierokratischen Topoi mit Ockhams gesicherten Ansichten die Unwahrscheinlichkeit nahe, daß er bei der Abfassung von Artikel III eine nennenswerte Rolle gespielt hat. Damit er von Nutzen ist, muß ein solcher Vergleich ins Detail gehen; dabei läßt sich kaum erhoffen, Langeweile ganz zu vermeiden oder zu absolut sicheren Erkenntnissen vorzustoßen. Aber es gibt keinen anderen Weg, um über vage Eindrücke hinauszukommen.

Ein geeigneter Ausgangspunkt ist das vierte Argument, mit dem sich Artikel III auseinandersetzt[133]. Gestützt auf 1. Cor. 6, 3 argumentierten die Anhänger einer hierokratischen Ordnung, daß, wenn die Apostel in der künftigen Welt die in die Dinge dieser Welt verstrickten Menschen und die gefallenen Engel zu richten hätten, sie a fortiori in der jetzt bestehenden Welt die Gewalt besäßen, in weltlichen Angelegenheiten richtend einzugreifen. In Artikel III wird darauf erwidert, daß sich Paulus hier auf die weltlichen Belange der armen Mitglieder der Kirche bezöge, deren Interessenvertretung die Apostel wahrnähmen: nicht aber auf weltliche Angelegenheiten von Bedeutung, betrieben von Menschen, für die die Geschäfte dieser Welt der Lebensinhalt sind. Was das letztere angeht, so habe Paulus in der Tat sogleich hinzugefügt: *Saecularia igitur iudicia si habueritis, contemptibiles qui sunt in ecclesia, illos constituite ad iudicandum*, eine Anweisung, die er kaum erteilt hätte, würde er universale Jurisdiktion in weltlichen Angelegenheiten für sich als Apostel beansprucht haben. Zudem, so wird in Artikel III argumentiert, würde es, folgte man der papalistischen Deutung der Paulus-Worte, zu der offenkundig falschen Schlußfolgerung führen, daß jeder heiliggesprochene Christ, der künftig Engel zu richten hätte, die volle Gewalt besäße, alle Vergehen im säkularen Bereich hier und jetzt zu ahnden. Dementsprechend, so wird in Artikel III weiter ausgeführt, sei der Paulus-Text auf die Gerichtsgewalt der Kirche als ganzer zu bezie-

---

131) Einwände Nr. 1, 2, 5, 12, 14, 15; in K fol. 100^r, 100^{r-v}, 101^{r-v}, 102^v, 103^r, 103^{r-v}.

132) Siehe oben Anm. 124 und 129.

133) Die Quelle ist möglicherweise (Innocentius papa IV), ‚Eger cui lenia‘ (1245–1246), ed. P. Herde, DA 23 (1967) S. 518.

hen; Paulus habe nichts für sich persönlich oder für seine Apostel-Gefährten gefordert[134].

Ockhams Behandlung desselben Textes im ‚Breviloquium' weicht von dieser Deutung entschieden ab, und zwar nicht nur in der ganzen Anlage der Argumentation, sondern großenteils auch in der Sache[135], und dies, obwohl er wie Artikel III davon ausgeht, daß Paulus nicht für sich selbst, sondern für die Kirche als ganze gesprochen habe[136]. Auch benutzt er genau wie Artikel III an dieser Stelle 2. Tim. 2, 4 als Beweis, um Männer der Kirche von der Regelung weltlicher Dinge auszuschließen. Aber er tut das mit dem charakteristischen Vorbehalt: *extra articulum urgentis necessitatis et evidentis utilitatis*[137]. Vor allem räumt er den legitimen Gerichtsrechten der weltlichen Herrscher (selbst wenn sie Heiden wären) eine Bedeutung ein, die sie in Artikel III nicht besitzen. Das ist ein Gedanke, den er auch andernorts vertritt, wenn er auf diese Stelle des Korinther-Briefs zu sprechen kommt: in ‚An princeps', den ‚Octo Quaestiones', der ‚Consultatio de causa matrimoniali' (hier ganz besonders!), und im zweiten Traktat von Teil III des ‚Dialogus'[138]. In ihrer Behandlung von 1. Cor. 6, 3 stimmen all diese Werke in den Grundzügen mit dem ‚Breviloquium' überein, aber nicht mit Artikel III. Demzufolge ist es wenig wahrscheinlich, daß Ockham die Widerlegung des vierten pro-päpstlichen Arguments in Artikel III verfaßt hat.

Einem Versuch derselben Art läßt sich auch Franz von Ascoli unterwerfen, der 1. Cor. 6, 3 an zwei Stellen seiner ‚Improbacio' erörtert hat. Franz lehnt es ab anzuerkennen, der Text würde einer unmittelbaren Gerichtsgewalt der Apostel das Wort reden. Ihrem Rang und persönlichen Verdienst nach hätten sie zwar die Fähigkeit zur Ausübung des Richteramtes besessen, aber es sei ihrem Amte nicht angemessen gewesen, sich mit derlei Dingen zu beschäftigen. Und daher habe Paulus im Hinblick auf weltliche Streitigkeiten gelehrt: *contemptibiles qui sunt in ecclesia, illos constituite ad iudicandum;* der einzig mögliche Bereich, der den Aposteln zum Richten verblieben sei, habe die Rechtsfälle der Armen, der Witwen und der Waisen

---

[134]) K, fol. 101^r.

[135]) ‚Breviloquium' V 9, ed. Scholz S. 186–190.

[136]) ‚Breviloquium', ebd. S. 190: *Apostolus non est ibi locutus in persona pape illius, sed in persona totius congregationis fidelium ;* vgl. Artikel III, K, fol. 101^r: *loquitur ibi Apostolus in persona corporis ecclesie.*

[137]) ‚Breviloquium', ebd. S. 190; K, fol. 101^r.

[138]) ‚An princeps', in: Opera politica ^{2}1, c. 6 Z. 104–147; ‚Octo Quaestiones' q. 1 c. 11 Z. 1–70; ‚Consultatio de causa matrimoniali, in: Opera politica ^{2}1, Z. 278–300; ‚Dialogus' 3.2.2.18.

betroffen[139]. Andernorts zitierte Franz zustimmend Gregors d. Gr. Bemerkungen, ‚Moralia' XIX 25, zur selben Stelle; *viri spirituales*, deren Sinn auf Höheres gerichtet sei, sollten sich nicht in die Niederungen weltlicher Geschäfte begeben. Franz unterlegt Paulus wie Gregor die Ansicht, daß *iudices rerum temporalium debent esse infimi in ecclesia; suppremi vero non debent terrenis negociis implicari*[140]. All dem läßt sich nicht der geringste Hinweis darauf entnehmen, Franz könnte eher noch als Ockham für die Erwiderung auf das mit 1. Cor. 6, 3 begründete hierokratische Argument in Artikel III verantwortlich gewesen sein.

Zu einem ähnlichen Resultat gelangt man bei dem Vergleich zwischen Ockhams gesicherten Ansichten und der breit ausgearbeiteten Antwort in Artikel III auf das zehnte pro-päpstliche Argument. Auf der Grundlage von Innocenz' III. Dekretale ‚Solitae' (X 1.33.6) wird dort der Versuch unternommen, die Überlegenheit der päpstlichen über die weltliche Gewalt mit dem Hinweis auf den Unterschied zwischen Sonne (Sinnbild der ersteren) und Mond (Sinnbild der letzteren) zu beweisen. Artikel III mißt diesem Argument größere Bedeutung bei als Ockham. Es wird erwidert, Sonne und Mond seien beide unmittelbare Schöpfungen Gottes. Der Mond habe seine eigene Quelle für den Antrieb und für sein Licht, wie sich bei Eklipsen beobachten lasse; in gleicher Weise habe die königliche Gewalt ihre eigenen Gesetze und Zwangsmittel, unabhängig von priesterlichen Einrichtungen, außer in Sachen, die den Weg zum Heil betreffen. Ein wenig inkonsequent fährt Artikel III dann fort mit der Anführung von vier Gleichnissen, die für die Überlegenheit der geistlichen über die laikale Gewalt sprechen, ohne daß der Versuch gemacht wird, den Widerspruch aufzulösen[141]. Bei der Erwähnung des auf ‚Solitae' gegründeten Arguments verschwendet Ockham darauf in den ‚Octo Quaestiones' kein einziges Wort[142]. Wenn er sich im ‚Breviloquium' und im ‚Dialogus' 3.2.1 dann doch etwas näher darüber ausläßt, so ist seine Zurückweisung des Arguments sehr viel schärfer

---

139) Franz von Ascoli, ‚Improbacio' (wie Anm. 91), fol. 72va: *Patet quod illud, quod dicit Apostolus prima ad Corinth. VI. capitulo: „An nescitis, quoniam angelos iudicabimus? Quanto magis negocia secularia!"*, ⟨*quod*⟩ *est intelligendum quantum ad apostolos attinet de potestate iudicandi rerum secularium mediata et non immediata, et de auctoritate iudicandi quantum ad condignitatem honoris et meriti et non quantum ad oportunitatem laboris et officii. Ideo subdit ibi Apostolus: „Secularia igitur iudicia si habueritis, contemptibiles qui sunt in ecclesia, illos constituite ad iudicandum," nisi fortassis in causa pia pauperum et pupillorum ac viduarum.*

140) ‚Improbacio', fol. 83va.

141) K, fol. 102^{r}; Gold und Blei (Ambrosius); Herz und Haupt (Chrysostomus); zwei kleine Fische (Augustin); Kalb und Bock von Lev. 4,3 u. 4,22-3.

142) ‚Octo Quaestiones', in: Opera politica ^{2}1, q. 2 c. 1 Z. 44–48; q. 2 c. 14 Z. 1–3.

und knapper gefaßt als in Artikel III. Das Argument kann, so führt er aus, keine Beweiskraft haben, da es vollkommen auf einer allegorischen Auslegung der Schrift beruht. Selbst wenn man die Gleichsetzung der Sonne mit der *potestas pontificalis* und des Mondes mit der *potestas regalis* akzeptierte, wäre daraus das Gegenteil der papalistischen Absichten zu folgern. Denn der Mond hat sein Sein von Gott, nicht von der Sonne, und übt eine Macht – *scilicet super aquas et humores* – originärer Art aus, nicht abgeleitet von der Sonne; daher würde das Gleichnis einräumen, daß das *imperium* eine Macht besäße, die ihm nicht von seiten des *sacerdotium* zugeflossen sei. In der Tat könne – nach Ockham – das Gleichnis allenfalls zeigen, daß, so wie der Mond kleiner ist als die Sonne und etwas Licht von ihr empfängt, das *imperium* an Würde dem *sacerdotium* nachstehe und der Kaiser der geistlichen Leitung durch Papst und Prälaten bedürfe[143]. Auch hier läßt die unterschiedliche Behandlung derselben Frage bei Ockham und in Artikel III die Autorschaft Ockhams als zweifelhaft erscheinen.

Der Unterschied ist sogar noch schärfer ausgeprägt im Falle des elften pro-päpstlichen Arguments, das den Kanon ‚Omnes' (D. 22. c. 1) heranzog, um zu begründen, daß Petrus universale Jurisdiktion im weltlichen wie geistlichen Bereich übertragen erhielt, als Christus die Rechtsgewalt im Himmel wie auf Erden in seine Hände legte[144]. Artikel III behalf sich bei der Erwiderung mit der Deutung, das *ius terreni et caelestis imperii* des Kanons meine, Christus habe Petrus die geistliche Gewalt zugesprochen, alle Sünder im Himmel und auf Erden zu binden und zu lösen (Matth. 16, 19); es meine aber nicht die weltliche Jurisdiktion, wie sich aus dem Kanon ‚Si habes' ersehen lasse in Verbindung mit zwei Passagen aus ‚De sacerdotio' des Johannes Chrysostomus[145]. Christus gab Petrus Jurisdiktion nur im geistlichen Bereich; in weltlichen Angelegenheiten sei der Kaiser dem Papste übergeordnet, während es in geistlichen Dingen umgekehrt sei, wie sich aus Gratians Dictum zu dem Kanon ‚Nos si incompetenter' ergebe[146].

Wie wir bereits sahen, hat Ockham in dem hier in Frage stehenden Zusammenhang den Text von Artikel III im ‚Breviloquium' VI 1 wörtlich zi-

---

143) ‚Breviloquium' V 6, ed. S c h o l z S. 179f. ‚Dialogus' 3.2.1.24 fügt dem Text des ‚Breviloquium', das hier die wörtliche Vorlage zu bilden scheint, nichts hinzu.

144) D. 22 c. 1, Papst Nikolaus II. (1058–1061) zugeschrieben, aber in Wirklichkeit von Petrus Damiani, Opusc. V (‚ad Hildebrandum'), Migne PL 145, 91. K auf fol. 102^{r-v}.

145) C. 24 q. 3 c. 1; Ioannes Chrysostomus, ‚De sacerdocio' III 5 und VI 1, Migne PG 48, 643, 678f.

146) C. 2 q. 7 Dictum post c. 41. K, fol. 102^{v}; dort wird Gratian in einer Form zitiert, als sei die Textstelle dem Kanon selbst entnommen, der auf einen Brief Papst Leos IV. (847–855) an Kaiser Ludwig II. (850–875) zurückgeht.

tiert[147]. Um so bemerkenswerter ist daher die Tatsache, daß er in vier verschiedenen Werken das auf ‚Omnes‘ gestützte papalistische Argument angriff, ohne sich im geringsten auf die Autoritäten des Artikels III zu beziehen. Als er im ‚Opus Nonaginta Dierum‘ auf die Stelle erstmals einging, referierte er lediglich die Ansicht, Papst Nikolaus II., der vermeintliche Autor von ‚Omnes‘, habe mit *imperium caeleste* die Guten in der ‚kämpfenden Kirche‘ gemeint, mit *imperium terrenum* hingegen die Bösen. So war gar kein Anlaß gegeben, die Möglichkeit zu erwägen, Petrus könne die weltliche Jurisdiktion über den Kaiser zugesprochen worden sein[148]. Doch im ‚Breviloquium‘, in den ‚Octo Quaestiones‘ und im ‚Dialogus‘ 3.2 ist Ockhams Zurückweisung des auf ‚Omnes‘ gestützten Arguments dann weitaus sorgfältiger begründet. Sich mit den Papalisten auf den Kanon zu berufen, wie er prima facie zu verstehen sei, führe zu häretischen Absurditäten: beispielsweise, daß das Himmelreich Petrus gehöre, so daß jeder, der dahingelangt, verpflichtet wäre, als Vasall die Lehnshoheit Petri und des Papstes anzuerkennen; oder, daß alle Reiche dieser Welt vom Papst zu Lehen gingen, und folglich der König von Frankreich, weil er hartnäckig leugnet, daß er einen *superior in temporalibus* habe, ein Ketzer wäre und die Päpste, die seine Häresie weder korrigierten noch zurückwiesen, sich ihrer Begünstigung schuldig machten[149]. Um derart abwegige Folgerungen zu vermeiden, müsse daher für Nikolaus' Worte eine andere Deutung gefunden werden.

Im ‚Breviloquium‘ schlägt Ockham vier mögliche Deutungen vor, wobei er behauptet, sie würden einander nicht wechselweise aufheben[150]. Zuerst zitiert er wörtlich die in Artikel III wiedergegebene Ansicht: das *ius terreni et caelestis imperii* sei die geistliche Gewalt, Sünder zu binden und zu lösen. Sein zweiter Vorschlag ist, ‚caeleste imperium‘ als die ‚triumphierende Kirche‘ aufzufassen, ‚terrenum imperium‘ hingegen als die ‚kämpfende Kirche‘, nicht aber als das weltliche Reich. Christus habe Petrus keine unumschränkte Herrschaft über diese zwei Kirchen übertragen, sondern nur bestimmte Rechte: das Recht, z. B., die ‚kämpfende Kirche‘ zu hegen und zu pflegen; Ungläubige mittels Taufe zum Eintritt zu veranlassen; ihre Glieder von Sünden loszusprechen und sie gute Werke zu lehren, und dergestalt ihre Aufnahme in die ‚triumphierende Kirche‘ zu befördern. Der dritte Deutungsvorschlag ist der des ‚Opus Nonaginta Dierum‘: unter himmli-

147) Siehe oben Anm. 124.

148) ‚Opus Non. Dierum‘, in: Opera politica 2, c. 93 Z. 696–701, 712–723.

149) ‚Breviloquium‘ VI 1, ed. Scholz S. 194f.; ‚Octo Quaestiones‘, in: Opera politica ²1, q. 2 c. 1 Z. 15–19 und q. 2 c. 7 Z. 7–61; ‚Dialogus‘ 3.2.1.19.

150) ‚Breviloquium‘, ebd. S. 196f.

schem und irdischem Reich seien die Guten und die Bösen in der ‚kämpfenden Kirche' zu verstehen. Letzter Vorschlag schließlich: Die Worte könnten meinen, Christus habe Petrus die Wahrnehmung bestimmter Rechte über das weltliche Reich zugesprochen, jedoch nicht unter dem Begriff von Eigentum oder Herrschaft, sondern in bezug auf die Unterrichtung der Kaiser im rechten Glauben. Sollten sie diese Belehrung annehmen, würde Petrus über sie geistliche Gewalt besitzen und er hätte auch das Recht, materielle Unterstützung für sich und sein Amt entgegenzunehmen. Während die ‚Octo Quaestiones' – mit manchen Verfeinerungen – in der Substanz die Gesamtheit der Deutungsvorschläge des ‚Breviloquium' wiederholt, beschränkt sich der ‚Dialogus' 3.2 auf die letzten zwei. Aber bei allen Unterschieden befassen sich diese Werke Ockhams mit ‚Omnes' in einer Weise, die deutlich anders ist als in Artikel III.

Das dritte pro-päpstliche Argument, das in Artikel III zurückgewiesen wurde, stützte sich auf das Bild der zwei Schwerter bei Luc. 22, 36–38. Hier läßt sich nicht umgehen, Probleme der Textüberlieferung in die Betrachtung einzubeziehen; denn möglicherweise ist G an dieser Stelle nicht ganz vollständig[151], während Z einen umfangreichen Zusatz aufweist, mit dem wir uns später noch beschäftigen werden. Aber bei der Behandlung dieses wohlbekannten Topos[152] hält sich Artikel III im allgemeinen an eine Argumentationslinie, die seit etwa 1300 sehr verbreitet gewesen ist. Das hierokratische Argument beruhte auf der allegorischen Interpretation der zwei Schwerter, die die Apostel führten: das waren das weltliche und das geistliche Schwert, sprich: die kaiserliche und die päpstliche Gewalt, beides in der Hand der Apostel. Diese Auslegung, so wird in Artikel III entgegengehalten, läßt sich aus keinem Schriftwort schlüssig belegen; sie muß daher gemäß Augustins Lehre über die Verbindlichkeit allegorischer Interpretationen zurückgewiesen werden. In Artikel III werden dann eingehend andere patristische Erklärungen des Textes untersucht: Drei Passagen aus Ambrosius' Lukas-Kommentar legen nahe, das Bild entweder auf das Schwert des Gotteswortes und auf das Schwert des Martyriums zu beziehen, oder auf die Lehren des Neuen und des Alten Testaments. Nach der in Artikel III vertretenen Ansicht hat Ambrosius, ungeachtet seiner Einschätzung des Textes als dunkel und zweideutig, doch in gar keinem Fall eine Gleichsetzung der beiden Schwerter mit der geistlichen und der weltlichen Gewalt

---

151) K, fol. 100^{v}–101^{r}. Siehe oben Anm. 51.

152) „Überreif" hat ihn Wilhelm L e v i s o n zu Recht genannt, in: Die mittelalterliche Lehre von den beiden Schwertern, DA 9 (1951) S. 39.

vorzunehmen gewagt[153]. Bei Johannes Chrysostomus kommt die Untersuchung zum selben Ergebnis. Wir dürfen die Schwerter zwar nicht als bloße materielle Gegenstände ansehen; aber selbst wenn man annähme, daß sie die geistliche und die kaiserliche Jurisdiktion verkörperten, wird doch nirgends berichtet, daß Petrus oder ein anderer Apostel beide Schwerter führte. *Ecce duo gladii hic* deute nur an, daß es innerhalb der Gemeinschaft der ‚kämpfenden Kirche' zwei Arten von Jurisdiktion gebe: geistliche Jurisdiktion als Sache der Priester, weltliche als Sache der Laienherrscher.

Ockhams Erörterung des Zwei-Schwerter-Gleichnisses im ‚Breviloquium' spiegelt Teile der abschließenden Argumentation in Artikel III wider[154]. Zudem beruft er sich wie Artikel III auf Augustin, Ep. 93, um zu bestreiten, daß die allegorische Deutung einer Schriftstelle beweiskräftig sei, ohne daß sie durch ein anderes Bibelwort gestützt werde oder – wie er hinzufügt – auf einer *ratio evidens* beruhe. Indessen geht er auf die Frage sehr viel gründlicher ein als Artikel III, reserviert ihr ein ganzes Kapitel im ‚Breviloquium' und beantwortet in einem weiteren mögliche Einwände auf die von ihm vorgetragenen Ansichten[155]. Bei der Interpretation von Luc. 22, 36–38 begnügt er sich nicht wie Artikel III damit, lediglich die Meinung der Kirchenväter wiederzugeben, die Stelle sei zweideutig; er führt das vielmehr selbst vor Augen: Während *gladius* manchmal dasselbe wie *potestas* hieße, seien ebensogut andere Bedeutungen möglich, z. B. *verbum Dei,* wie in Ephes. 6, 17, was darauf hinausliefe, akzeptierte man diese Interpretation, daß die beiden Schwerter auf die *predicatio novi testamenti et veteris* hindeuteten – und hier bezieht er sich auf die zweite im Artikel III zitierte Stelle aus Ambrosius' Lukas-Kommentar.

Aber das Hauptgewicht von Ockhams Argumentation liegt woanders:

---

[153]) Demgegenüber nahm Konrad von Megenberg (wie Anm. 51) an, daß Ambrosius bei der dritten Textstelle zu verstehen gab, Luc. 22, 36–38 beziehe sich auf das weltliche und das geistliche Schwert. Christus hatte seine Jünger beauftragt, ein ‚materielles' Schwert zu kaufen, dessen Benutzung er indessen Petrus untersagte; es war nur zur Verteidigung gedacht, und selbst da nicht zur Verteidigung Christi, weil an diesem Tag niemandem der Versuch gestattet war, Christi Tod aufzuhalten. Dennoch beweist, auch Konrad zufolge, Ambrosius' dritte Textstelle: *sacerdotium habere gladium auctoritative, sed non exercitative, nisi casu necessitatis imminente.* Ambrosius rückt auf diese Weise als Zeuge in die Nachbarschaft des hl. Bernhard: S c h o l z, Unbekannte Streitschriften 2, 332.

[154]) ‚Breviloquium' V 5, ed. S c h o l z S. 178: *Aliter dicitur, quod quamvis due potestates predicte intelligerentur per duos gladios, tamen ex hoc concludi non posset, quod papa regulariter haberet utrumque, vel quod imperium esset a papa, quia non dicitur, quod Petrus habebat duos gladios, nec quod aliquis unus habebat duos gladios; nec est verisimile, quod aliquis unus portaverit ambos, sed duo.*

[155]) ‚Breviloquium' V 3–4, ebd. S. 171–176.

Auch wenn die zwei Schwerter zwei Gewalten bedeuteten, so würde daraus noch nicht folgen, daß die eine geistlich und die andere weltlich sei; die eine sei nicht weniger geistlich als die andere, diese wiederum nicht weniger weltlich sei als jene. Vielmehr könnten recht gut beide Gewalten geistlich sein: die eine könnte die Gewalt sein zu predigen, und die andere die Macht, Wunder zu vollbringen; die eine könnte rechtschaffenes Leben, die andere unanstößige Lehre bedeuten. Andererseits könnten beide Gewalten auch weltlich sein, wie im Falle des *imperium merum et mixtum*, das weltliche Herrscher gegenüber Ketzern ausübten. Nähme man an, die beiden Schwerter bedeuteten tatsächlich sowohl geistliche wie weltliche Gewalt, dann ließe sich daraus noch nicht ableiten, daß der Papst von Rechts wegen beide besäße, da uns jede Nachricht fehlt, daß Petrus oder ein anderer Apostel zwei Schwerter geführt hätte. Einzig zulässig sei, so erklärt Ockham mit einiger Ungeduld, bei Luc. 22, 36–38 die am Wortsinn orientierte Deutung: jede allegorische Interpretation kann die zwei Schwerter ganz nach Belieben in irgendwelche zwei Gewalten verwandeln: beide weltlich, beide geistlich, eine weltlich und die andere geistlich, eine gerecht und die andere tyrannisch, legitime päpstliche Gewalt hier und angemaßte päpstliche Gewalt dort usw.

Nirgendwo sonst erörtert Ockham *Ecce duo gladii* in solcher Ausführlichkeit; als er in den ‚Octo Quaestiones' auf die Stelle zu sprechen kam, lieferte er nicht viel mehr als eine knappe Ablehnung der Gültigkeit allegorischer Schriftauslegung[156]. Seine Ausführungen dazu im ‚Breviloquium' mögen die Wahrscheinlichkeit nahelegen, daß er die Darlegung des Problems in Artikel III in der von G überlieferten ursprünglichen Fassung gekannt hat; aber nichts scheint den Verdacht zu begründen, er sei der Verfasser dieser Darlegung gewesen.

Die Fassung Z der ‚Allegaciones' bietet indessen in diesem Punkt ein anderes Bild: Mit Hilfe einer beträchtlichen Texterweiterung gegenüber G vermag sie das dort erarbeitete dualistische Konzept entschieden zu verändern[157]. In diesem Textzusatz wird zwar eingeräumt, daß nach göttlichem Recht keines von beiden Schwertern von dem anderen abhängt; jedoch in Fragen des Glaubens und der guten Sitten, so wird argumentiert, hat sich das weltliche Schwert der Leitung des geistlichen Schwertes anzuvertrauen und sich ihm zu unterwerfen. In solchen Fragen habe sich die weltliche Ge-

---

[156]) ‚Octo Quaestiones', in: Opera politica ^{2}1, q. 2 c. 13 Z. 1–11.

[157]) K, fol. 101^{r}: *Sed spiritualis* (sc. *gladius) directe et immediate spectat ad pontifices et sacerdotes; temporalis vero directe et immediate de iure divino spectat ad reges et seculi principes.*

walt demütig der geistlichen unterzuordnen; sie kann in Übereinstimmung mit 2. Cor. 10, 4–6 durchaus auch zum Gehorsam gezwungen werden. Daher, so wird in dem Textzusatz gefolgert, gehören die beiden Schwerter in gewisser Beziehung *(quodammodo)* in der Tat dem Papst, wenn auch in ungleichartiger Weise: Von Rechts wegen und unmittelbar hat er die Kontrolle über das geistliche Schwert, soweit die Schlüsselgewalt betroffen ist. Hingegen ist ihm das weltliche Schwert nur mittelbar unterworfen, indem er sich zu dessen Gebrauch anderer Personen als seiner Werkzeuge bedient, und auch das nur für die Zwecke des Glaubens: *casualiter et mediate quoad fidei religionem et morum disciplinam directionemque salutis eterne.* Der passende Beleg findet sich in einem Ausspruch des hl. Bernhard mit der berühmten Klimax: das ‚materielle Schwert' sei zu führen *militis manu, sed sane ad nutum sacerdotis et iussum imperatoris*[158].

---

[158]) Unmittelbar auf das Ende der Widerlegung des dritten pro-päpstlichen Arguments: *que sunt dei deo* (K, fol. 101r), läßt Z folgen (P, fol. 356v; N, fol. 205va): *Sed quamvis neuter gladius de iure divino sit ab alio gladio effective, tamen in hiis que sunt fidei et bonorum morum gladius temporalis debet dirigi et subici gladio spirituali, sicut terra, quamvis non sit facta nec creata a celo, tamen terra subditur celo et recipit influenciam ab eo. Caro eciam, licet non sit creata ab anima sed a deo, tamen caro debet subdi et regi ab anima et non e converso. Sensus eciam corporeus (corporis* N*), licet non sit factus ab hominis racione vel intellectu, tamen debet regi et disciplinari per racionem et intellectum. Luna eciam, licet non sit creata a sole sed a deo, tamen luna illustratur et perficitur a sole. Sic potestas terrena et carnalis atque temporalis, quamvis de iure divino non sit a potestate spirituali et pontificali, tamen debet pro fidei et morum ecclesieque catholice defensione et gubernacione subdi et humiliter subici spirituali et celesti pontificalique dignitati quia, licet hec potestas non sit ab illa, debet tamen humiliter esse sub illa. Quod si subesse in hiis que ad fidem pertinent finaliter renuerit, virtute clavium poterit salubriter coherceri secundum illud Apostoli II. ad Cor. X (V* PN*) c.: „Arma nostre milicie non sunt carnalia, sed potencia deo ad de-* / (P, fol. 357r) *structionem municionum, consilia destruentes, et omnem altitudinem se extollentem adversus scienciam dei, et in captivitatem redigentes (redigentem* PN*) omnem intellectum in obsequium Christi, in promptu eciam habentes ulcisci omnem inobedienciam, cum impleta fuerit obediencia vestra." Hec Apostolus. Et ita uterque gladius quodammodo subest potestati summi pontificis, sed differenter. Quia unus, scilicet spiritualis, subest ei per se regulariter et immediate quoad clavium potestatem. Alius vero, scilicet temporalis, subest ei solummodo per alium casualiter et mediate (immediate* N*) quoad fidei religionem et morum disciplinam directionemque salutis eterne. Et hoc est quod beatus Bernardus valde pulcre dicit IIII° libro de consideracione ad Eugenium papam scribens sic: „Quid tu denuo usurpare gladium temptes, quem semel iussus es reponere in vaginam? Quem tamen, si tuum negas, non satis michi videtur actendere verbum domini dicentis: ‚Convertere gladium tuum in vaginam'. Tuus ergo et ipse, tuo forsitan nutu etsi non tua manu evaginandus. Alioquin, si nullo modo ad te pertineret et is, dicentibus apostolis: ‚Ecce duo gladii hic,' non respondisset dominus: ‚Satis est,' sed: ‚Nimis.' Uterque ergo ecclesie, et spiritualis scilicet gladius et materialis. Sed is quidem pro ecclesia, ille vero et ab ecclesia exercendus; ille sacerdotis, is militis manu, sed sane ad nutum sacerdotis et iussum imperatoris." Hec Bernardus* (De consid. IV 7, in: Opera omnia 3, ed. J. Leclercq und H. M. Rochais, 1963, S. 454).

Hier endlich findet sich ein unmißverständlicher Anklang an Ockham. In seinem Traktat ,An princeps' hatte er die These erwogen, daß absolute Machtfülle genieße, wer zugleich beide Schwerter besitze. Obwohl er dem Papst solch undifferenzierte *plenitudo potestatis* verweigerte, war er nichtsdestoweniger bereit zuzugestehen, *quod uterque gladius aliquo modo spectat ad papam,* indem er zustimmend Bernhards Ansicht aufnahm, das ,materielle Schwert' sei vom Laien zu führen *ad nutum sacerdotis et ad iussum imperatoris*[159]. Die Argumentation in Z's Zusatz zu Artikel III gleicht zwar nicht vollständig jener in ,An princeps', da dort eine Unterscheidung zwischen des Papstes regulärem und dem fallweisen Gebrauch des weltlichen Schwertes getroffen wird, die in dem Zusatz keine direkte Entsprechung hat[160]. Aber eine Einwirkung ockhamscher Gedanken auf Z läßt sich schwerlich in Abrede bringen. Wie sie zustande kam, ist ein Problem, das eng verbunden ist mit der weiterreichenden Frage, wann, wie und von wem die sog. ,Chronik des Nikolaus Minorita' zusammengestellt worden ist[161].

Im übrigen gibt es allem Anschein nach jedoch nur wenige Spuren in Artikel III, die auf Ockham als Verfasser hindeuten: Da die Kirche ein einziger Körper sei, könne sie auch nur ein einziges Haupt haben, und das sei der Papst; dies ist das zwölfte von Artikel III zurückgewiesene papalistische Argument. Darauf nimmt Ockham in den ,Octo Quaestiones' und im ,Dialogus' 3.2 Bezug, aber in beiden Fällen läßt das, was er sagt, keine nähere Übereinstimmung mit Artikel III erkennen[162]. Und obgleich die Erwiderung in Artikel III auf das sechste pro-päpstliche Argument, das sich auf Christi Vertreibung der Geldwechsler aus dem Tempel stützt, in den Grundzügen eine gewisse Ähnlichkeit mit der Art und Weise erkennen läßt, in der Ockham die Problematik im ,Opus Nonaginta Dierum', im ersten Teil des ,Dialogus' und im ,Breviloquium' behandelt, klingt die Argumentation in einem bestimmten Punkte anders: Die Rolle, die Artikel III

---

159) ,An princeps', in: Opera politica ^{2}1, c. 6 Z. 1–72.

160) ,An princeps', ebd. Z. 29f.: *Gladius autem materialis isto modo ad regularem potestatem papae quodammodo spectat.* In ,Octo Quaestiones', Opera politica ^{2}1, q. 8 c. 6 Z. 63–71, scheint Ockham diese Unterscheidung aufzugeben.

161) An den wichtigsten anderen Stellen, an denen Ockham auf die Zwei-Schwerter-Lehre Bezug nimmt – ,Octo Quaestiones', ebd., q. 1 c. 13 Z. 33–43 und q. 1 c. 19 Z. 19–24 sowie ,Dialogus' 3.2.1.22 – geht er nicht auf den Text *Ecce duo gladii hic* ein. In ,Contra Benedictum' VI 5, ebd. 3, 280 zitierte er die Glosse zu X 2.1.13 ad v. ,iurisdictionem nostram' zugunsten der Ansicht, daß weder die Kirche noch der Papst beide Schwerter besäßen.

162) K, fol. 102^{v}; vgl. dazu ,Octo Quaestiones' q. 8 c. 6 Z. 42–62; ,Dialogus' 3.2.1.24.

dem *pontifex* zuweist, wird von Ockham in allen drei Werken einem *hostiarius* zugesprochen[163]. Mit diesem Beispiel kann die Aneinanderreihung negativer Funde beendet werden. Der Schluß scheint angebracht, daß Ockham kein nennenswertes Maß an Verantwortung für die Abfassung von Artikel III zugeschrieben werden kann, obwohl er den Text ganz sicherlich kannte und benutzte, als er das ‚Breviloquium' schrieb.

Viel spärlicher bietet sich der Stoff für eine Untersuchung dieser Art über Franz von Ascoli, der, wie schon erwähnt, gleichfalls 1. Cor. 6, 3 behandelt hat. Doch was man hier greifen kann, vermittelt nicht den Eindruck, daß Franz mit diesem Abschnitt der ‚Allegaciones' viel zu tun hatte. Wie viele andere beschäftigte er sich sodann ausführlich mit Luc. 22, 38. Aber die Art, wie er auf das Thema einging, zeigt nur geringe oder gar keine Übereinstimmung mit der in Artikel III anzutreffenden Behandlung der Zwei-Schwerter-Lehre. An keiner Stelle verwirft er ausdrücklich eine allegorische Deutung des Textes. Ihm scheinen die beiden Schwerter die zwei Wirkweisen von Petri geistlicher Gewalt zu versinnbildlichen: die Gewalt geistlich zu töten oder zu beleben, das heißt zu binden und zu lösen. Alternativ dazu ließen sich die beiden Schwerter auch verstehen als des geistlichen Pontifex Gewalt, für Sünde eine zweifache Buße zu verhängen: eine geistliche und eine weltliche. Franz sprach sich nicht zugunsten der Ansicht aus, daß die beiden Schwerter zwei voneinander verschiedene Gewalten bezeichneten, die päpstliche und die königliche bzw. die geistliche und die weltliche, obwohl diese Deutung, wie ihm durchaus bewußt war, seine Generalthese unterstützt hätte, daß Christus keine weltliche Herrschaft ausgeübt habe. Denn obwohl Petrus sagte: „Herr, siehe, hier sind zwei Schwerter," gebrauchte er doch nur eines. Nähme man an, die zwei Schwerter bedeuteten die beiden Gewalten, so würde das zu dem Schluß führen, daß nur das die geistliche Gewalt symbolisierende Schwert direkt im Besitze Petri und seiner Nachfolger wäre; über das andere, das weltliche Schwert, bzw. die weltliche oder kaiserliche Gewalt, verfügten sie hingegen nur mittelbar, namens der Christengemeinde, die in ihre Obhut gegeben ist. Schließlich berührt Franz noch zwei mögliche Bedeutungen des Textes: Nach Ambrosius' Annahme könnten die beiden Schwerter auch Sinnbilder für die Autorität der beiden Testamente sein. Oder sie könnten für des Papstes Schwert der geistlichen Wahrheit stehen, womit er durch Predigt und Unterweisung Sünden zerstört, sowie für sein Schwert als Instrument rea-

---

163) K, fol. 101v; vgl. dazu ‚Opus Non. Dierum', in: Opera politica 2, c. 96 Z. 213–238; ‚Dialogus' 1.6.3; ‚Breviloquium' V 8, ed. Scholz S. 184f.

ler Macht, mit dem er Sünden korrigiert und bestraft[164]. Zögernd und ohne über ein Ausbreiten miteinander unvereinbarer Lösungsvorschläge hinauszukommen, erörtert Franz *Ecce duo gladii hic* in einer Weise, die der Behandlung in Artikel III überwiegend fernsteht.

Nicht viel anders verhält es sich mit seinen Ausführungen zu Luc. 22, 36. Das siebente von Artikel III referierte und widerlegte pro-päpstliche Argument gab vor, diese Textstelle zeige Christus, wie er als weltlicher Herrscher auftrat, indem er seinen Jüngern gestattete, Waffen zu besitzen und zu tragen. Franz' Verständnis bezüglich der aus der Weisung *Et emat gladium* zu ziehenden Folgerungen blieben im traditionellen Rahmen franziskanischer Denkweise: Die Schwerter gehörten den Jüngern nicht *quoad domi-*

---

[164]) Franz, ‚Improbacio' (wie Anm. 91), fol. 72rb: *Nec movere debet, quod Luce XXII. c. Petrus dixit Christo: „Domine, ecce duo gladii hic!" Cui Christus ait: „Satis est." Quoniam per duos gladios significari videtur duplex potestas spiritualis Petri, scilicet potestas spiritualiter occidendi et potestas spiritualiter vivificandi, quo modo secundo libro Regum VIII. c. legitur, quod David „mensus est duos funiculos, unum funiculum ad occidendum" et alium funiculum „ad vivificandum", et significabant duplicem potestatem pontificis, scilicet potestatem ligandi et solvendi. Et ita eadem potestas, quamquam aliter, significatur per duplicem funiculum, duplicem gladium et duplicem clavem, scilicet potestas spiritualiter occidendi et potestas spiritualiter vivificandi seu potestas spiritualiter ligandi et solvendi, que est eadem potestas in re, licet differat racione.*

Vel eciam per duos gladios potest intelligi potestas pontificalis spiritualis infligendi pro delicto duplicem penam, spiritualem et temporalem, quia ecclesie pontifex potest racione delicti atque peccati infligere reo duplicem penam, spiritualem vel temporalem. Non quod per duos gladios significetur potestas pontificalis et potestas regalis sive potestas spiritualis et potestas temporalis, ut aliqui autumant, quamquam, etsi illa significarentur per duos gladios, non esset contra sed pro nobis. Quamvis Petrus dixerit: „Domine, ecce gladii duo hic!", tamen Petrus non legitur habuisse nec portasse nisi tantum unum illorum gladiorum duorum, sed alium gladium non legitur Petrum portasse nec usum fuisse. Ex quo datur intelligi, quod unus illorum, scilicet potestas spiritualis, pertinebat directe et immediate ad Petrum et eius successores, reliquus vero gladius, scilicet potestas temporalis seu imperialis, pertinebat ad Petrum et eius successores tantum mediate racione communitatis ecclesie sibi commisse, que in collegio apostolorum et discipulorum representabatur. Ideo Petrus dixit: „Ecce duos gladios hic!", scilicet in ecclesia militante, et non dixit: „Habeo vel habemus duos gladios," sed dixit: „Hic," dans intelligere, quod „hic", scilicet in ecclesia militante, est duplex potestas per duplicem gladium significata, scilicet potestas spiritualis seu pontificalis et potestas / (fol. 72va) *temporalis seu imperialis. Set una illarum potestatum spectabat ad Petrum directe et immediate, alia vero potestas spectabat ad eum indirecte et mediate racione communitatis ecclesie sibi commisse. Ideo unum illorum gladiorum legitur Petrus portasse et habuisse immediate ac ipso usum fuisse, alium vero gladium non legitur Petrus portasse nec eciam immediate habuisse et multo minus usum fuisse.*

Quamvis eciam per duos gladios utriusque testamenti auctoritas congrue posset intelligi secundum Ambrosium; vel eciam per duos gladios posset intelligi gladius spiritualis sciencie et veritatis et gladius potencie seu potestatis que pertinet ad pontificem, quia pastor ecclesie secat ac necat vicia et peccata et gladio veritatis per predicacionem et informacionem et gladio potestatis per correccionem et debitam punicionem ...

nium, sed solum dispensative quoad usum – eine sehr viel andere Auffassung, als sie in Artikel III zum Ausdruck gebracht wird[165]. In dieser Frage kommt Ockhams Gedankenführung im ‚Breviloquium' sehr viel näher an Artikel III heran als Franz, obwohl dem Wortlaut nach auch hier keine Übereinstimmung besteht[166].

Aufs Ganze gesehen ist also in Artikel III kein ockhamscher Einfluß im ursprünglichen Text auszumachen, sondern nur in einem von Z überlieferten späteren Zusatz zur Argumentation bezüglich der Zwei-Schwerter-Lehre. Des weiteren hat sich in keiner der beiden Fassungen, weder in G noch in Z, in Artikel III irgendein zwingender Hinweis auf Franz von Ascoli ergeben. Damit sind mehr als zwei Drittel der ‚Allegaciones' Stück für Stück überprüft worden. Es läßt sich nicht leugnen, daß die Belege für eine aktive Beteiligung der beiden traditionell mit dem Werk in Beziehung gebrachten Franziskaner bislang überaus dürftig geblieben sind.

d) Artikel IV

Artikel IV versucht auf der Grundlage des auf menschlicher Satzung beruhenden Rechtes – d. h. des kanonischen und des römischen – zu zeigen, daß der Papst keine Vollgewalt und keine universale Jurisdiktion besitzt, weder im geistlichen noch im weltlichen Bereich. Das Ergebnis ist eine klar umrissene dualistische Konzeption konventioneller Prägung: Geistliche und weltliche Gewalt sind verschieden in ihrer Zwecksetzung[167]; beide sind unabhängig voneinander von Gott abgeleitet, der Papst hat Gewalt im

165) K, fol. 101v: *Tamen in casu, in quo divina et humana iura publice violarentur et disciparentur, licencia portandi gladios pertineret ex causa racionabili non solum ad reges et principes sed eciam ad alios dei ministros. Constat autem, quod in passione domini publice et manifeste divina simul et humana iura fuerunt profanata et exsecrata, quare Christus de iure divino et naturali potuit tunc concedere vel permittere apostolis licenciam portandi gladios, non sicut rex et dominus in temporalibus sed sicut pius pastor et pater in spiritualibus.* Vgl. damit Franz, ‚Improbacio', fol. 78rb: *Christus dispensative relaxavit ad tempus prioris precepti rigorem. Et si nunquam alias dixisset, hoc patet evidenter ex eo, quod dixit: „Et qui non habet, vendat tunicam suam et emat gladium." Certum est autem nec alicui intelligenti debet verti in dubium, quod apostolis non licuit antea nec post portare arma ad offendendum nec ad defendendum ... Ergo Christus tempore passionis propter imminentem timorem dispensative concessit apostolis, quod possent portare gladios. Unde nec ante nec post nunquam leguntur gladios portasse nec habuisse. Et eadem racione dispensative concessit eis tunc sacculum et peram, quia sub eadem lege concessit eis omnia prefata. Ergo sicut cum apostolis fuit tunc misericorditer dispensatum, quod possent portare gladios, quos alias eis portare non licebat, ita tunc fuit cum eis benigne dispensatum, quod possent habere sacculum et peram pro se ipsis.*

166) ‚Breviloquium' V 8, ed. Scholz S. 185.

167) K, fol. 104r: *Iudicare in spiritualibus pertinet ad papam, et iudicare in temporalibus pertinet ad imperatorem.*

geistlichen und nicht im weltlichen Bereich, der Kaiser im weltlichen, nicht im geistlichen. Auf diese Verschiedenheit wird wiederholt Bezug genommen[168]. Es läßt sich keine Spur finden von Ockhams gewohnter Neigung, den Unterschied näher zu bestimmen oder jeder der beiden Gewalten Raum zu geben für stellvertretendes Eingreifen in die Sphäre der anderen.

Die aus dem kanonischen Recht angeführten Belegstellen sind die Dekretalen ‚Si duobus' (X 2.28.7), ‚Per venerabilem' (X 4.17.13), ‚Solitae' (X 1.33.6), ‚Novit' (X 2.1.13) und ‚Causam, quae' (X 4.17.7) sowie die Kanones ‚Cum ad verum' (D. 96 c. 6), ‚Duo sunt' (D. 96 c. 10), ‚Si imperator' (D. 96 c. 11), ‚Ecclesiae meae' (D 97 c. 1), 'Quoniam idem' (D. 10 c. 8) und ‚Non liceat' (C. 12 q. 2 c. 48), zusammen mit den zugehörigen Glossen. Dieses Material war in der Kanonistik und in der Streitschriftenliteratur generationenlang unablässig bearbeitet worden[169]; der Gebrauch, den Artikel IV davon machte, weist weder Originalität noch besondere Merkmale auf. Ockhams authentische Schriften bieten selbstverständlich ebenfalls zahlreiche Beispiele für den Rekurs auf diese Stellen (mit Ausnahme vielleicht von ‚Ecclesiae meae', wofür ich keinen Nachweis habe finden können); z. B. beruft er sich bei einem guten Dutzend Gelegenheiten auf ‚Per venerabilem'[170]. Er zitiert acht der elf Autoritäten des kanonischen Rechts innerhalb weniger Zeilen in ‚An princeps', und fünf im Kontext nur eines einzigen Kapitels im ‚Breviloquium'[171]. Doch zieht Artikel IV diese Autoritäten – mit einer einzigen gewichtigen Ausnahme – stets in einer Weise heran, für die es keine überzeugenden Parallelen in unbestritten authentischen Werken Ockhams gibt.

Die Ausnahme ist der Kanon ‚Non liceat', dessen relativ umfangreiche Erörterung in Artikel IV großenteils wörtlich in Ockhams ‚Contra Benedictum' wiederzufinden ist, verfaßt Ende 1337 oder Anfang 1338[172]. Wahrscheinlich hat Artikel IV Ockham hier ausgeschrieben. Aber selbst wenn das so wäre – und die Möglichkeit, daß ‚Contra Benedictum' und Artikel

---

168) K, fol. 104r–v: *Ostenditur evidenter, quod utraque potestas, scilicet pontificalis et imperialis, est immediate a deo. Et quod pontificalis est in spiritualibus et non in temporalibus, et imperialis est in temporalibus et non in spiritualibus.*

169) Siehe z. B. J. A. W a t t, The Theory of Papal Monarchy in the Thirteenth Century (1965) passim.

170) ‚Per venerabilem' etwa, in: ‚An princeps', Opera politica [2]1, c. 2 Z. 169 und c. 5 Z. 127; ‚Breviloquium' II 10 und 15, IV 4, VI 1; ‚Octo Quaestiones', Opera politica [2]1, q. 1 c. 7 Z. 143; q. 1 c. 9 Z. 6; q. 1 c. 12 Z. 234; q. 2 c. 7 Z. 60; De imperatorum et pontificum potestate' c. 19; ‚Dialogus' 1.6.6; 3.1.1.9 und 3.1.1.15; 3.2.1.18/19/23, 3.2.2.15.

171) ‚An princeps' c. 2 Z. 166–171; ‚Breviloquium' II 10, ed. S c h o l z S. 71ff.

172) K, fol. 104r–v; vgl. dazu ‚Contra Benedictum' VI 4, in: Opera politica 3, 275f.; zur Datierung ebd. s. 161f.

IV hier auf eine gemeinsame, bislang nicht identifizierte Quelle zurückgehen, kann nicht ganz ausgeschlossen werden –, so zwingt doch nichts zu dem Schluß, Ockham selbst habe die Übernahme vorgenommen. Fast unmittelbar auf die Passage aus ‚Non liceat' läßt Artikel IV eine uneingestandene Entlehnung aus der Appellation Michaels von Cesena vom 18. September 1328 in deren längerer Fassung folgen; was daran anschließt, beruht offensichtlich auf der Kurzfassung derselben Appellantion[173]. Es wäre leichtfertig, in einem solchen Sammelsurium einen bestimmten Verfasser namhaft machen zu wollen.

Bei der Argumentation gemäß römischen wie kanonischem Recht ist in Artikel IV bewußt auf Artikel II zurückgegriffen worden, dessen Erörterungen, wie gezeigt, überwiegend wörtlich auf ‚Fidem catholicam' beruhen[174]. Alle Verweise auf das römische Recht sowie auf zwei im selben Zusammenhang angeführte Kanones – ‚Quo iure' (D. 8 c. 1) und ‚Convenior' (C. 23 q. 8 c. 21) – finden sich in Artikel II wieder; dessen Quelle ist teils ‚Fidem catholicam', teils, wie es scheint, ‚Inferius describuntur articuli'[175]. Dieselbe Mischung begegnet in einer Allegationskette der aus Michaels Umkreis stammenden Kompilation ‚Ut in composicione', und offensichtlich spiegelt sich darin der Einfluß kanonistischer Glossen wider[176]. In diesem Abschnitt des Artikels IV findet sich nichts an charakteristischen Eigentümlichkeiten Ockhams. Obwohl Ockham wiederholt den ersten Beleg dieser Art in Artikel IV zitiert – Nov. 6 pr.[177] –, beruft er sich, sehe ich recht, doch nirgendwo auf die anderen Gesetzesstellen der Allegationsreihe, nicht einmal dort, wo man das am ehesten erwarten würde: im ‚Dialogus' 3.2.2. Denn obgleich er sich mit einiger Gewandtheit im kanonischen Recht zu bewegen vermochte, gelang ihm das beim römischen Recht nicht im gleichen Maße.

Artikel IV legt daher weder seiner Gesamtanlage nach noch im Detail (abgesehen vielleicht von der Passage über ‚Non liceat') Ockhams Verfas-

---

173) K, fol. 104v; Michaels Appellation in der Langfassung: B a l u z e – M a n s i, Miscellanea 3, 279f.; in der Kurzfassung Bullarium Franciscanum 5 (wie Anm. 4) S. 417.

174) K, fol. 103v: *Licet autem eciam superius per iura canonica et civilia sit aliqualiter ostensum, quod papa eciam a iure humano, scilicet canonico et civili, non habeat hanc potestatem ...;* vgl. dazu Artikel II, K, fol. 99v, und oben Anm. 97.

175) K, fol. 99v, 104v; dazu vgl. ‚Fidem catholicam', ed. B e c k e r (wie Anm. 1) S. 499; ‚Inferius describuntur articuli', ed. S t e n g e l, Nova Alamanniae 1, 391 Nr. 583.

176) ‚Ut in composicione', ed. F o e r s t e r (wie Anm. 99) S. 600f. Die Verweise der Allegationsreihe auf Cod. 7.37.3.1, Dig. 14.2.9 und auf ‚Quo iure' und ‚Convenior' sind alle in der Glosse zur Dekretale ‚Venerabilem' (X 1.6.34) zu finden, ad v. ‚in Germanos'.

177) ‚Breviloquium' IV 2, ed. S c h o l z S. 147; ‚Octo Quaestiones' q. 1 c. 6 Z. 103–107.

serschaft nahe. Von Franz von Ascoli hat sich nichts erhalten, was sich für einen ähnlichen Vergleich heranziehen ließe. Soweit sich aus seiner ‚Improbacio' ersehen läßt, hatte er mit dem ‚ius humanum' als solchem nicht viel im Sinn.

e) Artikel V

Artikel V enthält sorgfältig ausgefeilte Angriffe auf drei sattsam bekannte Hauptargumente, die seit eh und je zugunsten der Überordnung des Papstes über den Kaiser in weltlichen Angelegenheiten ins Feld geführt wurden.

Beim ersten, das sich auf die Translatio imperii berief, wie sie in der Dekretale ‚Venerabilem' (X 1.6.34) ihren Ausdruck gefunden hatte, wendet sich Artikel V ohne Umschweife der Glossa ordinaria zu[178]. In Verfolg ihrer Darlegung, die hier auf Tancreds berühmter Glosse ‚Ut in chronicis' fußt[179], nimmt es Artikel V als gegeben hin, daß die römische Kirche, als sie der Langobardenkönig Aistulf bedrückte, Hilfe bei den Kaisern in Konstantinopel gesucht habe, bei Konstantin (V., 741–775) und Leo (IV., 775–780); da diese sich nicht dazu bereitfanden, die Kirche zu schützen, habe Papst Stephan II. (752–757!) das Kaisertum auf den Franken Karl, Pippins Sohn, übertragen[180]. Aber nach Artikel V hat Stephan das nicht als oberster Herr in weltlichen Dingen getan; vielmehr sei das als ein Akt geistlicher Jurisdiktion zu betrachten, der wegen der Verbrechen der Griechen an der römischen Kirche gerechtfertigt gewesen sei. Denn dieselben Chroniken, denen die Glosse ihre Darstellung entnahm, wissen zu berichten, daß die beiden griechischen Kaiser Ungläubige, Schismatiker und Verfolger der Gläubigen waren. Auch Otto von Freising sagt über die Translatio nicht mehr, als daß 801 das *regnum Romanorum,* das seinen Mittelpunkt seit den Zeiten Konstantins d. Gr. in Konstantinopel hatte, *ad Francos derivatum* sei; er nennt niemanden, der das veranlaßt hätte[181]. Papst Stephans Erwähnung in der Glosse bedeute lediglich, daß er einer schon stattgehabten Translatio seine Zustimmung gab. Folglich bleibe ‚Venerabilem' den Beweis schuldig, daß der Papst in weltlichen Angelegenheiten Vollgewalt über weltliche Herrscher ausübt: *quia illa translacio facta fuit racione criminis et delicti spiritualis.*

---

[178]) K, fol. 104ᵛ–106ʳ.

[179]) Zitiert in der Glossa ordinaria zu X 1.6.34 ad v. ‚transtulit'.

[180]) Zu diesem chronologischen Unstimmigkeiten, die von Tancreds Abhängigkeit von Marianus Scotus herrühren, vgl. W. G o e z, Translatio imperii (1958) S. 195–198.

[181]) Siehe Otto von Freising, Chron. V. 31, ed. H o f m e i s t e r, MGH SS rer. Germ. (1912) S. 256.

Um diese Folgerung weiter abzustützen, verbreitet sich Artikel V dann über Augustins Unterscheidung (Ep. 173 = C. 23 q. 4 c. 38) zwischen der Verfassung der Urkirche und dem Zustand, in dem sich die Kirche befand, nachdem Gott sie unter den christlichen Kaisern erhöht hatte. In der älteren Phase ihrer Geschichte hätten Christus und die Apostel die heidnischen weltlichen Herrscher als legitim angesehen; soweit sie nicht göttlichem Recht widersprachen, habe man ihren Geboten Folge leisten müssen. Daher hätten die christlichen Soldaten des Kaisers Julian Apostata jenen Befehlen gehorcht, die sich auf die Verteidigung des Reiches bezogen, aber sie hätten sich geweigert, die Waffen gegen Mitchristen zu richten. Aber in der jüngeren Phase ihrer Geschichte errang die Kirche ein Mehr an geistlicher Macht; sie war willens und fähig, Ketzer zu verdammen und zu unterwerfen, mögen sie noch so groß und mächtig gewesen sein. Da nun die Griechen und ihre Kaiser die Einheit der Kirche verlassen hätten und in mancherlei Häresien fielen – sie werden nach Thomas, ‚Contra errores Graecorum', aufgezählt, zusammen mit weiteren ‚Irrtümern', die die Verzögerung der ‚glückseligen Schau' und den Beginn der Bestrafung der Verdammten betrafen –, hätten sie ihren Anspruch auf das Reich verwirkt. Es sei daher auf die Deutschen übertragen worden; auf Grund seiner Wahl werde der deutsche König wahrer und rechtmäßiger Kaiser und oberster weltlicher Herr. Der Papst habe, so betont Artikel V, das Reich von den Griechen auf die Deutschen nicht auf Grund eines Rechtstitels übertragen, der ihm nach göttlichem oder menschlichem Recht auf weltliche Superiorität zugekommen sei, sondern *racione criminis et delicti heresis et scismatis Grecorum.* Er habe gehandelt auf Grund der Gewalt und der Vollmacht, die ihm in geistlichen Dingen gewährt worden seien[182].

Ockhams zahlreiche und eingehende Ausführungen über die Translatio imperii zeigen, daß er ihr erhebliche Bedeutung zuerkannte. Aber sie weichen beträchtlich von der Behandlung des Themas in Artikel V ab. Seine Ansichten bedürfen einer ins einzelne gehenden Untersuchung, denn ihnen kommt ausschlaggebende Bedeutung zu für unseren Vergleich zwischen den ‚Allegaciones' und den Ockham sicher zuzuweisenden Schriften.

Im ‚Opus Nonaginta Dierum', im ersten Teil des ‚Dialogus' und in ‚Contra Benedictum' leugnete er, daß die Autorität zur Übertragung des Reiches wesensmäßig zum päpstlichen Amt gehörte. Sie rührte von den Römern her, die *ex causa rationabili* dem Papst Gewalt gegeben hätten, so zu handeln. Diese Übertragung habe ihre Ursache nicht, wie Artikel V behauptete, in den Häresien der Griechen gehabt, sondern in der verdammenswer-

---

[182]) K, fol. 105^{v}–106^{r}.

ten Nachlässigkeit der griechischen Kaiser, die es versäumt hätten, die Römer zu schützen. Sollte jemand nach einem Beleg fragen, daß der Papst nur auf Grund der Vollmacht der Römer tätig geworden sei, so lautet die Antwort in ‚Contra Benedictum': *ex gestis Romanorum colligitur, quod hoc factum fuit assensu et auctoritate Romanorum* – eine Angabe, die Ockham mit einem Hinweis auf bestimmte Quellen nicht zu präzisieren vermag[183].

Was Ockham im ‚Breviloquium' über des Papstes Macht zur Translatio imperii auszuführen für nötig findet, bleibt im Rahmen von den alttestamentlichen Präzedenzfällen, er vermeidet Anspielungen auf die Translation von den Griechen auf die Deutschen, auf ‚Venerabilem' und auf die damit verbundenen Fragen[184]. Damit beschäftigt er sich indessen an zwei Stellen der ‚Octo Quaestiones', vielleicht um der Auseinandersetzung mit Lupold von Bebenburg Genüge zu tun. In der zweiten Quaestio, die auf den Anspruch eingeht, der Papst genieße in solchem Maße Vollgewalt, daß, wenn der gemeine Nutzen es erfordere, er – ohne irgendjemanden um Rat fragen zu müssen – das Reich von einem Volke auf das andere übertragen könne, füllt Ockham ein ganzes Kapitel mit ausgefeilten Distinktionen[185]: Die Notwendigkeit für eine Übertragung könne sich entweder aus einem Verbrechen im geistlichen Bereich von seiten der weltlichen Herrscher ergeben, oder auf Grund ihres Versagens in weltlichen Dingen. Im ersteren Fall sagten einige, daß der Papst das Reich *iure divino* übertragen könne. Andere wiederum würden ihm nur zugestehen zu handeln, wenn das Laienvolk sich als schuldhaft nachlässig im Verfolg der Angelegenheit erwiese; denn es sei primär ihre Pflicht, Maßnahmen zu ergreifen, wenn sie der Papst alarmiert, es sei denn sie wünschten ihre Macht dem Papst zu delegieren. Nur wenn das Laienvolk nicht handeln will oder kann, fällt die Macht zur Translation an den Papst. Im zweiten Fall, wenn es nur um rein weltliche Versäumnisse von des Reiches Herrschern geht, kann der Papst auf Grund eigener Vollmacht überhaupt nichts tun, es sei denn, die Römer und andere Laien erwiesen sich als verdammenswert nachlässig in ihrem Bemühen, die Situation zu meistern. Was tatsächlich vorgefallen sei, als das Reich von den Griechen auf die Lateiner übertragen wurde, das könnte nur jemand beurteilen, der mit der gesamten historischen Überlieferung vertraut sei – ein

---

183) ‚Contra Benedictum' VI 13, Opera politica 3, 295f. Im ‚Opus Non. Dierum', ebd. 2, c. 93 Z. 740–742, drückt sich Ockham noch einfacher aus: *Dicunt nonnulli, quod papa transfert Romanum imperium non inquantum successor beati Petri sed auctoritate Romanorum, qui sibi potestatem huiusmodi concesserunt;* vgl. auch ‚Dialogus' 1.6.9.

184) ‚Breviloquium' V 10, ed. Scholz S. 191ff.

185) ‚Octo Quaestiones', Opera politica ^{2}1, q. 2 c. 2 Z. 37–41.

Wissen, von dem Ockham nicht behauptete, daß es ihm zur Verfügung stünde. Einige, denen dieses besondere Wissen fehle (und zu denen sich Ockham vermutlich zählte), sagen, daß, wenn der Papst das Reich ohne gerechten Grund übertrüge, oder wenn er das auf Grund eigener Vollmacht täte, ohne dazu von den Römern ein Mandat erhalten zu haben, dies als eine tadelnswerte Amtsanmaßung von seiner Seite her zu bewerten sei. Hingegen hätte er korrekt gehandelt, wäre er namens oder mit Zustimmung der Römer vorgegangen, oder wenn sie schuldhaft nachlässig darin gewesen wären, selbst etwas zu unternehmen. Der Papst könne in solchen Angelegenheiten Gewalt ausüben *solummodo casualiter, et non regulariter*[186].

Diese Linie der Beweisführung verfolgte Ockham im wesentlichen auch in der vierten der ‚Octo Quaestiones‘[187]. Dort referiert er zwei Ansichten, wer das Reich von den Griechen auf die Deutschen übertragen habe: Einige sagen – unter Berufung auf ‚Venerabilem‘ –, der Papst, doch gehen die Ansichten darüber auseinander, welcher Papst. Rationale Erwägungen legen eine andere Sicht der Dinge nahe: Die Übertragung wurde vom römischen Volk vorgenommen (eingeschlossen Papst und Klerus), wie sich aus einer Passage der ‚Annales regni Francorum‘ über Karls d. Gr. Krönung als Kaiser ableiten läßt[188]. Es war das römische Volk, das das römische Reich begründet hatte; es war seine Sache, es auf andere zu übertragen. Translation ist ein weltliches Geschäft, und der Papst sollte sich in weltliche Belange *regulariter* nicht einmischen. Nur wenn die Römer nicht bereit sind, die nötigen Schritte zu unternehmen, darf er *casualiter* tätig werden; nach dem gewöhnlichen Lauf der Dinge kann er das nicht auf Grund eigener Autorität tun, ausgenommen er handelt als einzelner Römer unter vielen. Daher fordert ‚Venerabilem‘ eine vorsichtige Ausdeutung. Mögliche Ansichten sind, daß der Papst namens der Römer Karl zum Kaiser krönte, oder daß die Römer den Papst als ihren vornehmsten Bürger bevollmächtigten, das Reich zu übertragen, oder daß Papst und Klerus in ihrer Qualität als Römer das Reich in Verbindung mit ihren römischen Mitbürgern übertrugen, oder daß der Papst ganz einfach den Römern den Rat gab, die Übertragung vorzunehmen. In jedem Fall betont Ockham die Verantwortlichkeit der Römer, und das tut er auch in einem späteren Kapitel derselben Quaestio[189].

---

186) Ebd. q. 2 c. 10 Z. 53f.
187) Ebd. q. 4 c. 6 Z. 67–106.
188) Annales regni Francorum, ed. F. Kurze, MGH SS rer. Germ. (1895) S. 112.
189) ‚Octo Quaestiones‘ q. 4 c. 9 Z. 117f.

Nicht viel anders sieht es zunächst im ,Dialogus' 3.2 aus: Der Papst übertrug das Reich *auctoritate Romanorum;* als Alternative wird erwogen, er habe nicht mehr getan, als einer Aktion der Römer seine Zustimmung zu gewähren[190]. Erst später durchbricht Ockham in demselben Werk den von ,Venerabilem' gesteckten Rahmen und erkennt die Notwendigkeit an, drei Translationes imperii zu erklären: von den Römern an die Griechen, von den Griechen an die Franken, und von den Franken an die Deutschen. Die Macht zu übertragen liegt nun *principalissime apud universitatem mortalium* des römischen Erdkreises. Ockham faßt ins Auge, daß die Römer ihr Recht auf diese Translation delegieren oder auch darauf verzichten können, ganz oder teilweise. Aber welche Gewalt über das Reich sie tatsächlich dem Papst zugestanden haben, könne nur wissen, wer Zugang zu den authentischen Akten habe[191].

Bei all diesen Ausführungen kommt Ockham an keiner Stelle in die Nähe der Behandlung des Translationsthemas in Artikel V. Was Artikel V in diesem Zusammenhang erkennen läßt, ist eine enge und bisweilen wörtliche Übereinstimmung mit einem Werk, das uns in dem Autograph Bonagratias von Bergamo erhalten ist. Das ist ein Addendum mit dem Titel ,Responsio ad oppositionem fratris Gisalberti de Pergamo olim ministri provincie Mediolanensis', das Bonagratia vielleicht im Jahre 1333 einer ,quaestio' anfügte, die sich mit der bindenden Kraft von Eiden befaßte, die einem Ketzer geleistet worden seien[192]. Als H.-J. Becker 1966 ,quaestio' und ,responsio' publizierte, erkannte er, daß die letztere in den ,Allegaciones' her-

---

[190]) ,Dialogus' 3.2.1.20.

[191]) ,Dialogus' 3.2.1.29–30.

[192]) Gedruckt von Becker, Kanonistische Schriften (wie Anm. 37) S. 263–276, von cod. Vat. lat. 4009, fol. 203^r–204^v; die ,responsio' ist von Bonagratias Hand. Zur Datierung siehe Anneliese Maier, Zwei unbekannte Streitschriften gegen Johann XXII. aus dem Kreis der Münchener Minoriten, Archivum Historiae Pontificiae 5 (1967) S. 53 (= dies., Ausgehendes Mittelalter 3, 1977, S. 386). Sie betrachtete die ,responsio' als einen Nachtrag zur ,quaestio', nicht, wie Becker, als Antwort auf einen von Ghisalbert erhobenen formalen Einwand. Integriert in eine Denkschrift über die Gültigkeit von Eiden zum Nachteil Ludwigs des Bayern und mit ausdrücklicher Zuweisung an Bonagratia, fand eine gekürzte und überarbeitete Fassung der ,quaestio' Aufnahme in die ,Chronik' des ,Nikolaus Minorita': P, fol. 343^{r-v}; N, fol. 199^v–200^r; danach gedruckt bei Böhmer, Fontes rerum Germanicarum 4, 606–608. Zu einem früheren Zeitpunkt hatte die ,quaestio' Teil eines aus dem Umkreis Michaels herrührenden Traktats mit dem Incipit ,Quia sepe iuris ignari' gebildet, datiert auf 1328/29, den A. Maier in cod. Ottob. lat. 2520, fol. 115^v–116^r der Biblioteca Apostolica Vaticana entdeckte: Zwei unbekannte Streitschriften, S. 49–52 (=Ausgehendes Mittelalter 3, 382–385). Ich bin nicht überzeugt von ihrer Annahme, Ockham könne der Verfasser von ,Quia sepe' gewesen sein: S. 55–57 (=Ausgehendes Mittelalter 3, 389f.).

angezogen worden war; obwohl er zu der Annahme neigte, in Ockham den Verfasser der ‚Allegaciones' zu sehen, fühlte er sich doch gedrängt, Raum für eine Zusammenarbeit mit Bonagratia zu lassen[193]. Ein Vergleich der Texte läßt keinen Zweifel, daß die Beweisführung des Artikels V hinsichtlich einer gewandelten Einstellung der Kirche gegenüber weltlichen Herrschern nach Konstantins Bekehrung von Bonagratias ‚responsio' übernommen wurde[194]. Es ist wahrscheinlich, wenn auch nicht nachweisbar, daß Bonagratia selbst diese Passage dem Artikel V einfügte. Vollkommen klar ist es indessen, daß die ganze Art und Weise, in der in Artikel V ‚Venerabilem' und das Translationsthema behandelt wurden, keine spezifisch ockhamschen Merkmale aufweist.

Zu dem gleichen negativen Ergebnis gelangt man bei Betrachtung der Schlußfolgerungen, die in Artikel V auf der Ebene der Reichsverfassung aus dem Ergebnis der Diskussion um die Dekretale ‚Venerabilem' gezogen werden[195]. Deren oft zitierte Wendung: *in imperatorem postmodum promovendum,* könne die wesensmäßig kaiserlichen Rechten des frisch gewählten deutschen Königs nicht in Frage stellen; denn der, den die Kurfürsten wählten, wird im gleichen Moment wirklicher Kaiser *ex sola electione* und kann als solcher handeln, noch ehe er gekrönt, gesalbt und geweiht worden ist. Diese Lehre findet zwar in der Tat einen Widerhall in der im Umkreis Michaels von Cesena entstandenen Streitschrift ‚Subscripta', aber es ließ sich kein überzeugendes Argument für eine Zuweisung der Schrift an Ockham beibringen[196]. Die Sprache, deren sich Artikel V zur Behandlung des Themas bediente, ist spürbar weniger verklausuliert als Ockhams Ausdrucksweise in seinem etwas früher entstandenen ‚Contra Benedictum'. In der Substanz bildet die in Artikel V vertretene Ansicht natürlich den Endpunkt einer weit zurückreichenden Entwicklung, die sich von den deutschen verfassungrechtlichen Erklärungen von Juli und August 1338 über die italieniche Tradition, wie sie etwa Ugolino von Celle 1323 repräsentiert, bis hin zu dem Weistum der deutschen Fürsten aus dem Jahre 1252 zurückverfolgen läßt, von dem uns Hostiensis berichtet[197].

---

193) Becker, ebd. S. 248, 251 Anm. 114.

194) K, fol. 105^{r-v}; siehe die ‚responsio', a.a.O. S. 271–273.

195) K, fol. 105^{v}–106^{r}: *Unde statim postquam electus est in imperatorem ex sola electione est verus imperator et statim potest legitimare et iura et leges condere et tollere, eciam antequam coronetur, inungatur vel consecretur a papa, quoniam coronacio, unctio et consecracio nichil omnino ad verum esse imperatoris operantur.*

196) Nach einer ins einzelne gehenden Prüfung des Verfasserproblems zog es Baudry, Guillaume d'Occam, App. II, S. 254ff., klugerweise vor, die Sache unentschieden zu lassen; siehe Guillaumi de Ockham Opera politica ^{2}1, 10f.

197) ‚Contra Bendictum' VI 6, Opera politica 3, 280: *Electus in regem Romanorum, an-*

Sehr viel kürzer faßt sich Artikel V bei der Behandlung des zweiten Hauptarguments zugunsten der päpstlichen Vollgewalt in weltlichen Angelegenheiten: das ist die Rolle, die Papst Zacharias nach dem Kanon ‚Alius' bei der Ablösung Childerichs als König der Franken durch Pippin d. J. spielte[198]. Artikel V repliziert mit einem Hinweis auf die Darstellung dieses Vorgangs in der Glossa ordinaria: *dicitur (Zacharias) deposuisse, quia deponentibus consensit.* Zusätzlich gestützt durch eine Textstelle bei Martin von Troppau, wird in Artikel V argumentiert, die Initiative bei Childerichs Absetzung habe beim fränkischen Adel gelegen; der Papst habe lediglich dessen Aktion *ex post facto* gebilligt. Als Alternative wird erwogen, daß, wenn Zacharias tatsächlich allein Childerich absetzte, dies auf Grund von geistlichen Vergehen des letzteren geschehen sein müsse; eine Absetzung aber aus geistlichen Gründen rechtfertige in keiner Weise den Schluß, daß der Papst in weltlichen Belangen Superiorität über alle Reiche und Herrscher besitze[199]. Berufung auf diese Glosse war seit langem üblich, um der hierokratischen Ausdeutung von ‚Alius' zu begegnen[200]. Ockham greift ebenfalls darauf zurück, aber mit Nuancierungen, die man in Artikel V vermißt und die darauf angelegt waren zu betonen, daß die Absetzung in erster Linie ein Akt des fränkischen Volkes war. Im Endeffekt glossiert er die Glosse – ganz ausdrücklich im ‚Dialogus' 3.2: ‚*Quia deponentibus consensit*', *recipiendo scilicet ab eis potestatem deponendi. Ideo quasi una cum eis deposuit*[201]. Wenn Zacharias tatsächlich Childerich absetzte, müsse er dafür die Vollmacht von den Franken bekommen haben. Aber Ockham zieht auch andere Möglichkeiten in Erwägung: daß Zacharias entweder die Absetzung überhaupt nicht vornahm, oder daß er sich dieses Amt einfach anmaßte[202].

---

tequam persona vel electio a pontifice sit approbata et admissa, potest sibi nomen et titulum regium assumere, ut sit verus rex et valeat se administrationi regni et imperii immiscere. Zu Ugolino vgl. Nova Alamanniae 1, 71–79 Nr. 123; zu Hostiensis siehe ‚Octo Quaestiones' q. 4 c. 2 Z. 2.

198) C. 15 q. 6 c. 3, von Gregors VII. Brief vom 15. März 1081 an Hermann von Metz, Reg. VIII 21, ed. E. Caspar, MGH Epp. sel. 2, 554.

199) K, fol. 106r. In der Tat behauptete der Kanon nicht mehr, als daß Childerich *inutilis* gewesen sei, wozu die Glosssa ordinaria anmerkte: *dissolutus et effeminatus.*

200) Vgl. beispielsweise Johannes von Paris, ‚De potestate regia et papali' c. 14, ed. J. Leclercq (1942) S. 218f.

201) ‚Dialogus' 3.2.1.18. Siehe auch ‚Opus Non. Dierum', Opera politica 2, c. 93 Z. 735: ‚*Quia deponentibus consensit*', *hoc est, auctoritate populi reputantis regem deponendum eundem regem deposuit.* Im gleichen Sinn argumentiert Ockham im ‚Dialogus' 1.6.9, und erneut in ‚Octo Quaestiones', Opera politica ²1, q. 2 c. 9 Z. 21–23: ‚*Quia deponentibus consensit*': *laudando eorum propositum et consulendo, ut non timerent in hoc potestatem suam contra regem pro communi utilitate omnium exercere.*

202) ‚Octo Quaestiones' q. 8 c. 7 Z. 26–31; ‚Dialogus' 3.2.1.18.

Der Unterschied zwischen Artikel V und Ockham in der Art, wie sie auf ‚Alius‘ eingehen, kommt ganz deutlich im ‚Breviloquium‘ zum Ausdruck. Weit davon entfernt, sich wie Artikel V hinsichtlich der geschichtlichen Umstände der Absetzung auf Martins Chronik zu berufen, lehnt es Ockham ab, eine Festlegung vorzunehmen, wie Pippin an die Stelle Childerichs getreten sei, weil ihm die einschlägigen Quellen nicht erreichbar waren[203]. Er begnügt sich mit zwei Hypothesen, wie der Wechsel vernünftigerweise vonstatten gegangen sein könne: Entweder delegierten die Franken ihre Gewalt an den Papst – *et tunc papa vere deposuisset;* oder sie nahmen die Dinge selbst in die Hand, mit des Papstes Rat und Zustimmung. In diesem Fall gibt die Glosse korrekt wieder, in welchem Sinne man sagen könne, der Papst habe Childerich abgesetzt: *deponentibus consensit.* In bezug auf Gründlichkeit wie Vorsicht hält Artikel V bei der Behandlung von ‚Alius‘ den Vergleich nicht aus mit dem, was unserer Kenntnis nach Ockham darüber geschrieben hat.

Das dritte und letzte von Artikel V attackierte Argument zugunsten von des Papstes universaler Oberhoheit in weltlichen Dingen gründete sich auf die sog. ‚konstantinische Schenkung‘, wie sie Gratians Dekret D. 96 c. 14 überliefert. Trotz der Erwähnung, daß der Kanon ‚Constantinus‘ als Palea bezeichnet wird, wirft Artikel V keine Zweifel an seiner Echtheit auf, sondern wendet sich umgehend der Frage zu, wie er zu verstehen sei[204]. Das pro-päpstliche Argument bezog seine Durchschlagskraft vornehmlich aus der angeblichen Erklärung Konstantins, daß er, seine Satrapen und Notabeln, der Senat und das ganze römische Volk Macht, Ruhm, Würde und kaiserliches Recht auf Papst Silvester übertragen hätten. Artikel V repliziert mit einem Hinweis auf eine später folgende Textstelle, die den Umfang der Übertragung einzuschränken scheint auf *ea, que ad cultum Dei vel fidei Christianorum stabilitatem procuranda fuerint*[205]. In der Tat hätte Silvester das Angebot auf die kaiserliche Krone abgeschlagen[206], weil er sich dessen wohlbewußt war, daß die Verstrickung in weltliche Angelegenheiten der Würde des ‚supremus pontifex‘ abträglich wäre, denn seine Macht liegt

---

203) ‚Breviloquium‘ VI 2, ed. S c h o l z S. 172: *Quia gesta illius regni non habeo.*

204) K, fol. 106^{r-v}. Der zur gleichen Zeit lebende englische Kanonist Wilhelm von Paull *(de Pagula)* hatte für die Frage: *Que sunt illa privilegia, que imperator Constantinus concessit ecclesie Romane ⟨X⟩ C ⟨VI⟩ d. ‚Constantinus imperator‘?*, nur zwei Worte übrig: *Palea est!;* ‚Summa summarum‘ 1.10.1, London, British Library, Royal ms. 10 D. X, fol. 25ra.

205) ‚Constitutum Constantini‘, ed. Horst F u h r m a n n, MGH Fontes iuris 10 (1968) Z. 158–160, 169–170, 174–177.

206) ‚Constitutum Constantini‘ Z. 249–255.

im geistlichen Bereich, wie mit Zitaten aus Gregor d. Gr. und Pseudo-Chrysostomus belegt wird[207]. Doch selbst wenn Konstantin mit den Worten seines Erlasses wirklich weltliche Gewalt über die Stadt Rom und bestimmte Gebiete des Reiches an Silvester übertrug[208], dann war der Umfang dieser Übertragung doch nicht allumfassend. Konstantin baute im Ostreich seine eigene souveräne Herrschaft auf, während in bezug auf den Westen – wie die Glosse zu ‚Per venerabilem' bezeuge[209] – Papst Innocenz III. einräumte, daß des Papstes Recht, in weltlichen Dingen etwas zu legitimieren, nicht über das Patrimonium Petri hinausreiche. Was auch immer Silvester und seine Nachfolger aus der ‚Schenkung' an Gewinn gezogen haben mögen, so haben sie doch keine Herrschaft darüber ausgeübt; wie in Artikel IV gezeigt[210], ist der Papst nicht Herr, sondern Verwalter des Kirchenbesitzes.

Leider geht Ockham im ‚Breviloquium' auf die Konstantinische Schenkung erst sehr spät ausführlicher ein, und der Text bricht in der einzigen Handschrift unvollendet ab[211]. Unleugbar bringt er Zweifel am Zeugniswert des Kapitels ‚Constantinus' in einer Weise zum Ausdruck, die kein Äquivalent in Artikel V besitzt: Einige sagen, seine Worte seien *apocripha et nullius auctoritatis*, weit unterlegen dem Zeugnis von Ratio, Geschichtswerken und anderer glaubwürdiger Quellen. Es ist nicht sicher, daß sie von der Kirche gebilligt worden sind; vielen scheinen sie *non ... tante auctoritatis, ut rationi debeant prevalere*[212]. Dennoch gibt Ockham zu, daß sich dem Kapitel ‚Constantinus' ein guter Sinn abgewinnen lasse. Denn ehe unser Text des ‚Breviloquium' abbricht, gibt er noch einen Fingerzeig auf die Richtung, in die sich Ockhams Interpretation wahrscheinlich bewegte. Danach wäre der Erlaß im Lichte jener Textpassage zu verstehen, die auch Artikel V hervorgehoben hatte: Er übertrug Gewalt an Silvester in bezug auf jene Dinge, die die Verehrung Gottes und die Ungestörtheit des christlichen Glaubens gewährleisteten[213]. Es scheint, daß in Ockhams Sicht die

---

[207]) Gregor d. Gr., Hom. in Evang. X 1, Migne PL 76, 1110, teilweise auch zitiert von Franz von Ascoli, ‚Improbacio', fol. 71rb; Pseudo-Chrysostomus, Opus imperfectum in Matth., hom. VII, Migne PG 56, 675, schon zitiert in Artikel IV der ‚Allegaciones', K, fol. 104^{r}.

[208]) ‚Constitutum Constantini' Z. 261–276.

[209]) Glossa ordinaria zu X 4.17.13 ad v. ‚libere'.

[210]) K, fol. 104^{r}.

[211]) ‚Breviloquium' VI 3–5, ed. Scholz S. 201–209.

[212]) ‚Breviloquium' VI 4, ebd. S. 205f.: *apocripha* hat wohl eher den Sinn von ‚unkanonisch' als von ‚unecht'.

[213]) ‚Constitutum Constantini' Z. 171–177.

Wirkung der ‚Schenkung' auf das Papsttum allein darin bestand, dessen Einfluß im geistlichen Bereich zu verstärken.

In dieser Hinsicht läßt sich eine gewisse Ähnlichkeit zwischen ‚Breviloquium' und Artikel V erkennen, die aber nicht sehr weit reicht. Andere Stellen, an denen sich Ockham mit der Donatio beschäftigt, zeigen nicht einmal dieses Maß an Übereinstimmung. In der ersten der ‚Octo Quaestiones' war Ockham damit befaßt, das päpstliche Argument zu widerlegen, daß Konstantin mit seiner Schenkung lediglich dem Papst jene Gewalt zurückgab, in deren Besitz er zuvor als Kaiser unrechtmäßig gewesen war[214]. Im Gegenteil, führt Ockham aus: Konstantin gewährte Silvester *de novo* Vorteile im weltlichen Bereich, wie sie im Kanon ‚Constantinus' aufgezählt würden; daraus läßt sich ableiten, daß er sich als des Papstes Oberherr in weltlichen Belangen fühlte. Nur in der geistlichen Sphäre werde des Papstes Überlegenheit anerkannt, wenn die ‚Schenkung' erlaubt: *Et eius* (d. h. des Papstes) *iudicio, quae ad cultum Dei et ⟨fidei⟩ Christianorum stabilitatem procuranda fuerint, disponantur*[215]. Hinsichtlich des weltlichen Bereichs, so führt Ockham an anderer Stelle in den ‚Octo Quaestiones' aus, hat Konstantin an Silvester nicht gleichviel Gewalt über die westliche Reichshälfte verleihen können und auch nicht verliehen, wie er sie zuvor über das ungeteilte Reich ausgeübt hat[216].

Die Vergleiche zwischen der Art und Weise, wie diese drei klassischen hierokratischen Topoi in Artikel V und in Ockhams zweifelsfrei echten Schriften abgehandelt wurden, haben wenig ans Tageslicht gefördert, was die Annahme rechtfertigen würde, daß Ockham der Verfasser oder der spiritus rector dieses Abschnitts der ‚Allegaciones' gewesen sei. Die erste Widerlegung läßt an Bonagratia denken; nur die dritte hat überhaupt etwas gemein mit Ockhams gesicherten Ansichten. Es fand sich keine andere Schrift aus dem Umkreis Michaels, die sich in gleicher Weise hätte überprüfen lassen.

f) Artikel VI

Mit dem sechsten und letzten Abschnitt in G schicken sich die ‚Allegaciones' in ihrer ursprünglichen Gestalt an, die Konsequenzen aus ihrer Beweisführung zu ziehen. Diese haben einen stark dualistischen Einschlag,

---

214) ‚Octo Quaestiones' q. 1 c. 12 Z. 134–174; vgl. dazu (Innocentius papa IV), ‚Eger cui lenia', ed. Herde (wie Anm. 133) S. 521; ‚Octo Quaestiones' q. 3 c. 13 Z. 20–25.

215) ‚Octo Quaestiones' q. 1 c. 12 Z. 170f.

216) ‚Octo Quaestiones' q. 8 c. 7 Z. 5–25, in Erwiderung auf ebd. q. 8 c. 2 Z. 5–12. Die Erörterung in ‚Dialogus' 3.2.1.27 bringt keine neuen Elemente.

wie dem bayerischen Mönch auffiel, als er in den 1370er Jahren seine Auszüge anfertigte[217]: Jede der beiden Gewalten leite sich unmittelbar und unabhängig von der anderen von Gott her und habe ihren eigenen autonomen Wirkungsbereich – päpstliche Gewalt ist beschränkt auf geistliche Dinge, kaiserliche auf weltliche; es fehlt jeder Hinweis auf ein ersatzweises Eintreten der einen für die andere. Das Kaisertum habe weder seinen Ursprung im Papst noch gehe es von ihm zu Lehen; mit deutlichem Bezug auf ‚Fidem catholicam' verkündet Artikel VI, daß einzig durch den Akt der Wahl der, der zum Kaiser erwählt sei, römischer König werde[218]. Johannes' XXII. Vorgehen gegen Kaiser Ludwig sei daher als unwirksame Amtsanmaßung zu bewerten; Ludwigs Gegenangriff auf Johannes aber sei vernünftig und gerecht.

Es gebe zahlreiche Belege, behauptet Artikel VI, daß die Maßnahmen Johannes' XXII. und seines Nachfolgers Benedikt XII. gegen Ludwig keine bindende Kraft besäßen, aber da der Nachweis darüber schon in anderen Appellationen und Allegationen geführt worden sei, brauche das nicht nochmals wiederholt zu werden. Das hindert nicht daran, das besondere Augenmerk auf Johannes' XXII. ‚häretische' Erklärung, in ‚Quia vir reprobus' zu richten, daß vom Augenblick seiner Empfängnis als Mensch an Christus universale weltliche Herrschaft als wahrer Herr und König innegehabt habe. Auf diese ‚Häresie' hätten Johannes und Benedikt ihren Anspruch gegründet, daß der Papst als Christi Stellvertreter die Oberhoheit über alle weltlichen Dinge besitze; daß er über alle Königreiche und Fürstentümer dieser Welt frei verfügen könne, sie austeilen an wen er wolle, sie verkleinern oder vergrößern oder ihre Grenzen nach Belieben festsetzen. Das war in der Tat eine alte Klage Michaels und seines Anhangs über das avignonesische Papsttum. Zum Großteil in dieselben Worte gekleidet, erscheint die Klage in Michaels Appellation von 1330, in den franziskanischen Traktaten ‚Quoniam scriptura testante divina' und ‚Ut in composicione' von 1331, und 1338 im zweiten Teil von ‚Inferius describuntur articuli', wo die Argumentenfolge in diesem Punkt nahe an die ‚Allegaciones' herankommt[219]. Aber die unmittelbare Quelle von Artikel VI scheint hier

217) K, fol. 106v; siehe oben Anm. 14.

218) ‚Fidem catholicam', ed. B e c k e r (wie Anm. 1) s. 499.

219) Michael, Appellation IV vom 26. März 1330 (wie oben Anm. 92), fol. 193v; ‚Quoniam scriptura testante divina', gedruckt bei Carlo D o l c i n i, Marsilio e Ockham (1981) S. 127 (Dolcinis These, S. 65–89, daß es sich hier um ein zusammengesetztes Textstück handelt, bei dem sich Spuren einer Tätigkeit nicht nur von Ockham und Bonagratia, sondern vielleicht auch von Marsilius von Padua auffinden ließen, hat mich nicht überzeugen können); ‚Ut in composicione', ed. F o e r s t e r (wie Anm. 99) S. 609;

Wort für Wort der Entwurf jener Appellation zu sein, den Bonagratia von Bergamo Juli/August 1333 für Erzbischof Balduin von Trier angefertigt hatte[220]. Der genannten ‚häretischen‘ Erklärung wegen und auf Grund anderer ‚Häresien‘ hätten Johannes XXII. und Benedikt XII. jedes Vorrecht verwirkt, das ihnen aus Konstantins Schenkung zugekommen sein mag; *ipso iure et facto* seien sie aller päpstlichen Gewalt, Jurisdiktion und Autorität entkleidet. So endet Artikel VI und damit Fassung G der ‚Allegaciones‘.

Nichts an dieser abschließenden Folgerung deutet auf Ockham als den Autor hin. Artikel VI weist mehr Verwandtschaft auf mit jener umfangreichen Literatur aus dem Umkreis Michaels in Gestalt von Appellationen und Denkschriften, auf deren Zusammenstellung niemand so beständig und in seinem Anteil so mühelos identifizierbar Einfluß genommen hat wie Bonagratia von Bergamo.

g) Artikel VII

An den Schluß nun von G fügt ‚Nikolaus Minorita‘ seiner Fassung der ‚Allegaciones‘ einen weiteren kurzen Abschnitt an. Dieser Artikel VII macht Ernst mit der in Fassung Z sich deutlich angekündigenden Absicht, die Zielrichtung des ganzen Traktats radikal auszuweiten. Jetzt, wo es zutage liege, daß der Papst keine *plenitudo potestatis* in weltlichen Dingen besitze, gelte es noch nachzuweisen, daß es ihm auch an Vollgewalt im geistlichen Bereich mangele. Der in Z eingeschlagene Weg, dieses Ziel zu erreichen, besteht darin, als Artikel VII aus Ockhams ‚Contra Benedictum‘ wortwörtlich Kapitel 3 und 4 des VI. Buches auszuschreiben. Insgesamt hielt sich der Schreiber dabei getreu an seine Vorlage. Aber an zwei Stellen unterläßt er es mitzuteilen, daß Ockham in diesen beiden Kapiteln seines ‚Contra Benedictum‘ keineswegs beabsichtigte, dem Papst rundweg jede Vollgewalt in geistlichen Dingen zu bestreiten, sondern nur eine *plenitudo*, die er folgendermaßen definiert: *Ut de potentia absoluta omnia possit, quae non sunt contra legem divinam vel legem naturae, ita ut in omnibus talibus omnes Christiani ei de necessitate salutis obedire firmiter teneantur*[221]. Im weiteren Verlauf der Diskussion folgt Fassung Z ihrer Quelle an drei Stellen ganz akkurat bei der Niederschrift der Worte *talem plenitudinem potestatis;*

‚Contra vero predicta‘ (das ist der zweite Abschnitt von ‚Inferius describuntur articuli‘), art. 3, ed. Stengel, Nova Alamanniae 1, 396f. Nr. 583. Vgl. dazu ‚Fidem catholicam‘, ed. Becker S. 500.

220) K, fol. 107r; vgl. dazu Bonagratias Entwurf in cod. Vat. lat. 4009, fol. 184v, 185v. Beide Texte kommen Michaels Appellation IV, fol. 193v sehr nahe.

221) ‚Contra Benedictum‘ VI 2–4, Opera politica 3, 273–277.

an zwei anderen Stellen läßt sie jedoch *talem* weg[222]. Die Auslassungen könnten anzeigen, daß dem Abschreiber eine wichtige präzisierende Zuspitzung in Ockhams Denken entgangen ist.

4. Schlußbetrachtung

Wenn die zuletzt getroffene Beobachtung richtig ist, so wäre das ein Grund, der gegen die vorschnelle Aufstellung einer Hypothese spräche, die in mancher Hinsicht nicht ohne Reiz ist: daß nämlich Ockham selbst die ursprüngliche Gestalt der ‚Allegaciones' zur Fassung Z umarbeitete, wie sie in der ‚Chronik des Nikolaus Minorita' anzutreffen ist. Zugunsten dieser Theorie ließe sich nicht nur der aus ‚Contra Benedictum' übernommene Schlußabschnitt in Z anführen sowie die vorbereitenden Stufen für dessen Einfügung, die sich besonders deutlich an der Überarbeitung des ursprünglichen Prologs zu den ‚Allegaciones' und am Textanfang von Artikel II ablesen lassen[223]; sondern man könnte auch auf die gehaltvolle Weiterentwicklung des Zwei-Schwerter-Arguments im ockhamschen Sinne hinweisen, die Z dem Artikel III hat angedeihen lassen[224]. Aber nur eine tiefer eindringende Untersuchung, als sie bisher vorliegt, über die Art und Weise, wie ‚Nikolaus' seine ‚Chronik' zusammengestellt hat, könnte vielleicht zu einer angemessenen Prüfung dieser Hypothese führen. Doch bestenfalls würde auch dann das Ergebnis sein, Ockhams Anteil an den ‚Allegaciones' als den eines Herausgebers und Redaktors zu sichern, mit Spuren seiner Tätigkeit nur in der zweiten, der jüngeren Fassung. Hinsichtlich der ursprünglichen Fassung G hat es sich als außerordentlich schwierig herausgestellt, Ockham einen klar umrissenen Anteil zuzuweisen, denn es ließ sich lediglich feststellen, daß er von Artikel III der Fassung G Kenntnis hatte und im ‚Breviloquium' davon Gebrauch machte, und daß Artikel IV eine Textstelle mit seinem ‚Contra Benedictum' gemein hat[225]. Der Vergleich zwischen der Behandlung einzelner Fragen in G und in Ockhams unstrittigen Werken hat eher Unterschiede als Gemeinsamkeiten zutage gefördert. Es gibt hier deutlich sichtbare Grenzen für die Tragfähigkeit eines Beweisgangs, der darauf beruht, von einer bekannten Größe auf eine unbekannte zu schließen: Autoren können ihren Sinn ändern und sie können unter-

---

222) P, fol. 369^{v}–370^{r}; N, fol. 211^{rb-va}.

223) Siehe oben Anm. 62–70.

224) Siehe oben Anm. 158.

225) Siehe oben Anm. 124–131, 172.

schiedliche Dinge bei unterschiedlichen Gelegenheiten von sich geben. Indessen sind Häufigkeit und Ausmaß der von uns festgestellten Abweichungen doch bezeichnend. Sie lassen jede Behauptung als nicht plausibel erscheinen, daß Ockham einen beherrschenden Einfluß auf Substanz und Struktur der Fassung G ausgeübt hat.

Das Material, von dem her sich beurteilen ließe, ob Franz von Ascoli an den ‚Allegaciones‘ beteiligt war, ist weniger reich. Was davon erhalten ist, weist in dieselbe Richtung. Selbst wenn man außer acht läßt, auf wie schwachen Füßen die Annahme steht, Franz habe zur Zeit der Abfassung der ‚Allegaciones‘ kontinuierlich mit dem Münchener Kreis um Michael in Verbindung gestanden[226], sind konkrete Spuren einer möglichen Beteiligung an den ‚Allegaciones‘ kaum über Artikel I hinaus zu verfolgen. Auch wenn die ungeschickte Form, in der Artikel I und II zusammengefügt worden sind, nahelegt, daß wenigstens zwei Verfasser bei der Herstellung von G am Werke waren, kann man sie doch nicht sicher identifizieren. Denn daß Franz und Ockham eine Generation später von der ‚Chronica de ducibus Bavariae‘ dafür namhaft gemacht werden, hat keinen endgültigen Beweiswert. Ihre Ideen werden bei der Abfassung der ‚Allegaciones‘ eine gewisse stimulierende Rolle gespielt haben, aber der Nachweis, daß sie bei der Herstellung von G auch ihre Federn in Bewegung setzten, läßt sich nicht führen. In Band IV von Ockhams ‚Opera politica‘ werden die ‚Allegaciones‘ unter den ‚dubia et spuria‘ ihren Platz finden müssen.

Sucht man nach einer Zuschreibung, die einen höheren Grad an Wahrscheinlichkeit beanspruchen könnte, so stößt man immer wieder auf den Namen Bonagratias von Bergamo. Bei einer Reihe von Textstellen innerhalb der ‚Allegaciones‘ ließ sich sein Einfluß mit Händen greifen. Was immer das konkret besagen mag: die Überschrift der Exzerpte in cod. Pal. lat. 606 (C) gibt vor, Bonagratia sei der Verfasser[227]. Der Prolog zu G vermag vielleicht ein überzeugenderes Argument beizubringen: Wie P. Marc Dykmans zu Recht bemerkte, stellt der Prolog trotz seiner Mitteilung, die ‚Allegaciones‘ seien von einer Anzahl Magister der Theologie gebilligt worden, nicht die Behauptung auf, diese hätten die Schrift auch verfaßt[228]. Ließe sich nicht daraus folgern, daß die ‚Allegaciones‘ das Werk des einzigen prominenten Vertreters aus Michaels Umkreis waren, der nicht den Titel eines Magisters der Theologie führte – d. h. des Juristen Bonagratia? Es ist

---

226) Siehe oben Anm. 17–18.

227) Biblioteca Apostolica Vaticana, cod. Pal. lat. 606, fol. 94v; siehe oben Anm. 12.

228) K, fol. 95v: *Allegaciones per plures magistros in sacris litteris approbate;* siehe oben Anm. 39.

hinreichend wahrscheinlich, daß Bonagratia in der Tat einen beträchtlichen Anteil an der Abfassung der ‚Allegaciones' hatte. Aber es wäre unklug, ihn allein dafür verantwortlich zu machen.

Denn es wäre ein Gebot wissenschaftlicher Redlichkeit, ähnlich wie zuvor bei Ockham und Franz die Verfasserschaft Bonagratias auf Herz und Nieren zu prüfen. Wenn man das tut, wird klar, daß die Darlegungen der Artikel II und III über Christi Erdenherrschaft trotz mancher Übereinstimmungen in ihrer allgemeinen Tendenz Bonagratias schriftlichen Äußerungen über diesen Gegenstand, die er nur wenige Jahre vor 1338 zu Papier brachte, nicht ganz entsprechen[229]. Als Beispiel mag die Widerlegung des aus Matth. 21, 2–3 abgeleiteten hierokratischen Arguments in Artikel III dienen: Christi Befehl an die Jünger, ihm eine Eselin und ihr Füllen zu bringen mit der Begründung, *quia Dominus hiis opus habet.* Artikel III beginnt seine etwas weitschweifigen und verwickelten Ausführungen mit der Behauptung, daß Christus hier nicht als weltlicher Herr handelte, sondern *pontificali auctoritate.* Mit der Bemerkung, *Dominus hiis opus habet,* könne Christus *secundum divinitatem* gesprochen haben, oder auch in seiner Eigenschaft als Mensch im Namen Gottes als *sacerdos et pontifex Dei;* aber auch eine dritte Möglichkeit sei nicht ganz auszuschließen, daß nämlich Christi Befehl eine jener außergewöhnlichen Handlungen darstellte, *significantia secreta Dei misteria,* aus denen sich überhaupt keine allgemeinen Schlüsse ziehen ließen[230]. Im Gegensatz dazu ist Bonagratias Exegese von Matth. 21, 3 eindeutig und entschieden: *Et vere non obstat, quia dominus ibi reffertur ad Christi divinitatem et non ad humanitatem,* wie es die Glosse ausdrückt[231]. Dieselbe Sicht der Dinge ist in Michaels Appellation von 1330 und in Franz' ‚Improbacio' anzutreffen, wobei beide noch einen Hinweis auf die Glosse zu Luc. 19, 31 anbringen[232]. Nur Ockham war bereit, noch eine andere Möglichkeit ins Auge zu fassen: Während Christus *secundum divinitatem* gesprochen haben könnte, tat er das vielleicht doch *secundum humanitatem;* doch ist Ockham hier sorgsam darum bemüht, seine Begriffe zu klären, die wiederum in keiner Weise mit den in Artikel III verwendeten

---

229) Siehe oben Anm. 112.

230) K, fol. 101ᵛ.

231) Cod. Vat. lat. 4009, fol. 185ᵛ.

232) Michael, Appellation IV, fol. 187ᵛ: *Quia illud intelligitur de dominio Christi secundum divinitatem;* Franz, ‚Improbacio', fol. 72ʳᵃ: *Talia et similia sunt intelligenda de Christo secundum divinitatem, que omnia continet.* Die Gedankenführung ist bei der Argumentation in diesen beiden Werken so ähnlich, daß es schwer vorstellbar erscheint, sie hätten verschiedene Verfasser.

übereinstimmen[233]. In diesem Fall drückten die ‚Allegaciones‘ also Ansichten aus, von denen sich nicht zeigen läßt, daß Bonagratia oder Franz oder Michael (falls er diesen Teil der Appellation abfaßte) sie vertreten hätten[234]; und nur in einem sehr ungefähren Sinne lassen sie sich mit Ockham in Verbindung bringen. Eher läßt sich sagen, daß sie die Merkmale eines nicht ganz zum Ausgleich gelangten Kompromisses aufweisen, wie es bei einem echten Gemeinschaftswerk nur natürlich wäre.

Die Suche nach einem einzigen Verfasser der ‚Allegaciones‘ erscheint illusorisch. Notgedrungen müssen wir uns mit der Aussage gemeinschaftlicher Verantwortung des um Michael gescharten Personenkreises begnügen, wie es ‚Niklolaus Minorita‘ ausdrücklich angibt und womit sich Konrad von Megenberg abgefunden hat[235]. Indessen erscheint es nicht zu kühn, auf die eingangs gestellten Fragen die folgenden Antworten zu wagen: War an den ‚Allegaciones‘ in ihrer ursprünglichen Gestalt mehr als ein Verfasser beteiligt? Ja! Gab es nur einen einzigen Redaktor von G? Das ist sehr wahrscheinlich, obwohl es sich nicht mit gleicher Sicherheit nachweisen läßt wie die Überarbeitung des Werkes in der Fassung Z, für die sich der weite Begriff ‚ockhamistischer‘ Einfluß in Anspruch nehmen läßt. Enthält G Anteile, die eindeutig Franz von Ascoli oder Ockham zum Autor haben, in so nennenswertem Umfang, daß sie eine Zuweisung an beide rechtfertigen, wie in der ‚Chronica de ducibus Bavariae‘, oder an Ockham allein, wie von einigen Handschriften behauptet? Nein! Wer aus dem Umkreis Michaels erweckt den Anschein, er habe am meisten Einfluß auf Tendenz und Inhalt der Fassung G ausgeübt? Bonagratia von Bergamo.

---

233) ‚Opus Non. Dierum“, Opera politica 2, c. 93 Z. 1391ff.: *Potest etiam dici dominus secundum humanitatem propter praerogativam gratiarum.* ‚Breviloquium V 8, ed. Scholz S. 185: *Quod autem dixit: „Dominus hiis opus habet,“ potest intelligi, quod vocavit se dominum vel ratione divinitatis vel ratione spiritualis potestatis, quasi in spiritualibus erat prelatus.* Möglicherweise spiegelt sich in diesen Worten Ockhams die Lehre Ubertins von Casale vom doppelten Status Christi und seiner Jünger wider: als Bettler, aber auch als Prälaten der Kirche; vgl. Ubertinus de Casale, ‚Responsio ad inquisitum papae Johannis XXII‘, in: Baluze – Mansi, Miscellanea 2 (Lucca 1761) S. 279f.

234) Siehe oben Anm. 96.

235) Siehe oben Anm. 23.

VII

The Origin of Ockham's Octo Quaestiones

OCKHAM'S treatment of the *Octo Quaestiones* justly ranks high among his polemical writings. Less burdened than many of the others by his obsession that the contemporary Avignon popes were heretics,[1] this lengthy work has a certain quality of academic detachment which heightens its effect. Its concern is to examine (though it does not explicitly determine) eight questions about the relations between the spiritual and secular powers put before Ockham, he tells us, by 'vir quidam venerabilis', who, without disclosing why he wished them to be discussed, had deigned humbly to beg Ockham to solve them.[2] Probably Ockham had finished this work during the lifetime of Pope Benedict XII, or at any rate before news of Benedict's death on 25 April 1342 had reached Germany.[3] As they pay much attention to views expressed by Lupold of Bebenburg in his *Tractatus de iuribus regni et imperii*, of which the earliest form was completed on 3 February 1340,[4] the *Octo Quaestiones* must have been composed after this date. It may be possible to narrow these limits somewhat. Considerations to be put forward below suggest that the *Octo Quaestiones* had probably been finished by the autumn of 1341. Ockham could be a very quick worker, and he mentions haste as a possible cause of the imperfections of this treatise.[5] The most likely period for its composition would thus seem to lie between the summer of 1340 and the late summer of 1341.[6]

1. Though see *Octo Quaest.* viii. 7. ed. J. G. Sikes, *Guillelmi de Ockham Opera Politica* i (Manchester, 1940), 209–19. 2. i, 1, p. 14; viii, 9, p. 221.

3. In his *Opus Nonaginta Dierum*, written during the pontificate of John XXII, Ockham had reported the allegation that since Sylvester I about 27 popes had been involved in notorious crimes: c. 124, lines 339–45, *Opera Politica*, ed. J. G. Sikes and H. S. Offler, ii (1963), 854. In a very similar passage in OQ viii, 7, p. 218, the number of errant popes has increased to about 28. It seems pretty safe to assume that had Ockham been writing the *Octo Quaestiones* after Clement VI had succeeded Benedict XII he would have given the number as 29.

4. A note that the treatise was completed at Würzburg on the day after the feast of the Purification of the Blessed Virgin Mary 1340 appears at the end of the version in Leipzig, Universitätsbibliothek, cod. lat. 543, fo. 62v; see H. Meyer, *Lupold von Bebenburg* (Freiburg im B., 1909), pp. 69–70. There is the same note in Besançon, Bibliothèque municipale, cod. 1166, fo. 90; see *Cat. gén. des manuscrits des bibliothèques publiques de France* xxxii (1897), 818. According to the *stilus Moguntinensis* this would be 3 Feb. 1340, the date accepted by Meyer, Sikes, *ed. cit.* p. 4, and R. Most, 'Der Reichsgedanke des Lupold von Bebenburg', *Deutsches Archiv für Geschichte des Mittelalters* iv (1941), 444.

5. viii, 9, p. 221.

6. L. Baudry, *Guillaume d'Occam* i (Paris, 1950), 220–1, is less definite; Sikes, *ed. cit.* p. 5, suggests August 1342 as the *terminus ante quem.*

Reprinted from the *English Historical Review* 82 (1967), pp. 323–332, by permission of Oxford University Press.

There has been much debate about the identity of the propounder of the questions, 'vir quidam venerabilis' or, as he is called elsewhere,[1] 'dominus michi quamplurimum venerandus'. J. G. Sikes was in a respectable tradition in supposing that he was Ockham's protector, the Emperor Lewis the Bavarian.[2] But, as Hauck pointed out long ago, there are substantial difficulties in the way of accepting the emperor as inspirer or transmitter, not to say author, of these questions, formulated as they were in scholastic terms which could hardly have been intelligible or interesting to the unlearned Lewis.[3] It seems unlikely that Lewis would have humbly begged Ockham to discuss the questions, or felt it necessary to induce his protégé to write 'suis precibus'.[4] Had Ockham been composing his work in response to a request by the emperor, it is not easy to believe that in the course of it he would have referred to Lewis as 'dominum Ludovicum de Bavaria, quem aliqui Bavarum, aliqui imperatorem appellant'.[5] Neither 'vir venerabilis' nor 'dominus venerandus' was an adequate title of respect for an emperor, however controverted his claim and shaky his position. 'Venerandus dominus' was how the archbishop of Mainz addressed his suffragan of Spires in 1344; 'vir venerabilis' was commonly used at this time as a title for cathedral dignitaries.[6] Proper as it may have been in 1340 or 1341 to call a dean or provost or archdeacon 'vir venerabilis', this was no way in which to refer to the ruler of Germany. In the light of contemporary usage the man who propounded the eight questions to Ockham was probably a churchman of decent, though scarcely of eminent standing. To such a man the expert scholastic formulation of the questions would present no difficulties. And though for the time being we may have to regard him as 'unknown',[7] perhaps something more can usefully be said about where the questions originated.

But first it may seem advisable to establish that he did exist. At times the suspicion had crossed my mind that the whole story of the eight questions and their anonymous transmitter was no more than a deliberate mystification on the part of Ockham, who was really himself responsible for inventing as well as discussing them. This suspicion was dispelled by looking again at a piece of evidence which has hitherto been misunderstood. Cod. lat. b. 35 in the Stadtbibliothek at Bremen is a quite well-known manuscript. It was written, not

1. viii, 9, p. 221.

2. *ed. cit.* p. 2.

3. A. Hauck, *Kirchengeschichte Deutschlands*, v, i (Leipzig, 1911), 562, n. 3; *cf.* R. Scholz, *Wilhelm von Ockham als politischer Denker* (*Schriften des Reichsinstituts für ältere deutsche Geschichtskunde* 8, 1944/52), p. 12, n. 2. Baudry's objection, *op. cit.* p. 220, n. 2, is unconvincing. It seems justifiable to call Lewis unlearned, though it would hardly do to call him illiterate; see F. Bock, 'Bemerkungen zur Beurteilung Kaiser Ludwigs IV in der neueren Literatur', *Zeitschrift für bayerische Landesgeschichte*, xxiii (1960), 125–6.

4. See p. 323, note 2.

5. viii, 2, p. 183.

6. *Nova Alamanniae*, ed. E. E. Stengel (Berlin, 1921-30), no. 770; *ibid.* nos. 733, 852, 875, 876, 906.

7. W. Kölmel, *Wilhelm Ockham und seine kirchenpolitischen Schriften* (Essen, 1962), p. 125.

before *c.* 1360,[1] by a single somewhat careless scribe, who had at his disposal an important collection of writings by and adaptations from Lupold of Bebenburg, Marsilius of Padua, Ockham and others, first brought together, it seems likely, in the early 1340s.[2] On fos. 152v–155v, immediately following Ptolemy of Lucca's *Determinatio compendiosa*, it has a short treatise with the title 'Questiones circa eandem materiam. De iurisdictione inperii'. This piece has repeatedly been described as excerpts from or an abstract of Ockham's *Octo Quaestiones*.[3] A re-examination of the text of the Bremen treatise [henceforward B] has convinced me that this is not so: B is in fact an independent treatment of the eight questions. Like Ockham, the author of B discusses the questions without solving them, though the balance of the arguments is such that it is not difficult to surmise which point of view he favoured. His sentiments seem German, patriotic and evangelical. Though he made some use of the canon law, his background would seem to have been philosophy and theology; nothing suggests that he was a lawyer by training or profession. Something of this can be seen in his discussion of the third question:

[fo. 153v] Utrum papa et ecclesia romana ex institucione Christi habeat conmittere inperatori et aliis principibus secularibus iurisdictiones temporales et ipsi alias eas non habeant exercere. Videtur quod non. Quidquid enim repugnat vite et doctrine Christi hoc non potest papa facere ex institucione Christi. Sed talis comissio est huiusmodi. Maior videtur nota. Minor probatur, quia ex tali commissione papa usurparet sibi plus quam inperialem et regiam potestatem, cum plus esset inperatorem facere quam regem esse. Sed Christus exemplo docuit contrarium, quia cum vellent eum regem facere ipse fugit, ut patet Johannis vi [15], item Luce xxii [25–26], 'Reges gentium dominantur eorum, vos autem non sic', etc. Et illud optime videtur deducere Augustinus in libro de vera religione c. 29, ubi sic dicit, 'Non enim ullum peccatum committi

1. The last item, on fos. 176v–186v, the *Vademecum in tribulacione* of Johannes de Rupescissa O.F.M., was not composed until 1356; see J. Bignami-Odier, *Études sur Jean de Roquetaillade* (Paris, 1952), p. 158. In the Bremen MS. (not noticed by Bignami-Odier) the *Vademecum* is preceded by John's letters, as in the edition by Edward Brown, *Appendix ad fasciculum rerum expetendarum et fugiendarum . . . ab Orthwino Gratio* (London, 1690), pp. 494 ff.

2. The manuscript is described by Meyer, *op. cit.* pp. 24–25, and by Offler, in *Opera Politica*, i. 275–6, where by error it was said to be of paper, instead of parchment. It is the unique source of Ockham's *Consultatio de causa matrimoniali* and of the so-called *Tractatus de matrimonio* of Marsilius, most recently discussed by M. Grignaschi, 'Il matrimonio di Margarete Maultasch e il "Tractatus de matrimonio" di Marsilio da Padova', *Rivista di storia del diretto italiano*, xxv (1952), 195–204. The view of the relation of the *Tractatus* to the *Defensor minor* taken by Grignaschi, p. 200, following C. K. Brampton in his edition of the *Defensor minor* (Birmingham, 1922), pp. vi ff., seems to me disputable.

3. H. Theobald, *Beiträge zur Geschichte Ludwigs des Bayern. Beilage zum Jahresberichte des Grossherzogl. Gymnasiums Mannheim für das Schuljahr 1896/7*, p. 5; Meyer, *op. cit.* p. 24; R. Scholz, *Marsilii de Padua Defensor Pacis* (Hannover, 1932), p. xliv; Sikes, *ed. cit.* p. 10; Offler, *Opera Politica*, i. 276.

potest nisi dum appetuntur ea que Christus contempsit aut fugiuntur que ille sustinuit. Tota namque vita eius in terris per hominem quem suscipere dignatus est disciplina morum fuit.' Et quod est ad propositum premisit dicens, 'Satellites voluptatum divitias appetebant, pauper esse voluit. Honoribus et inperiis inhyabant, rex fieri noluit.'[1] In contrarium est illud Jeremie [i. 10], 'Ecce constitui te super gentes et super regna.' Per quod videtur pape et spirituali potestati commisisse institucionem etiam principum, ut probatur extra de maior. et obedientia, solite [c. 6 *X* I, 33].

Again, when discussing the fourth question (whether election by the princes entitles the new king of the Romans to full rights of administration), B's author is found arguing for the affirmative thus:

[fo. 154] Et illud videtur rationabile. Cum enim deus fecerit homines liberi arbitrii et ipse dimiserit quemlibet 'in manu consilii sui', ut patet Ecclesiastici [xv. 14], iustum videtur quod sola libertas electorum, in quorum personis totus populus regni tam virtualiter continetur, possit et ipsum populum et iura regni sibi tradere in plenariam potestatem. Cum enim esset contra rationem liberi arbitrii quod etiam cogeretur a deo, nunquam deus in veteri testamento alicui quantumcunque per ipsum electo vel a prophetis inuncto populi et iurium regni tradidit plenariam potestatem et amministrandi liberam facultatem donec populus libere se subiecit, ut patet in exemplis Saule, David et Iheu regibus [*sic*] Israel... [fo. 154v] Non obstat si aliud statutum est in electione prelatorum ecclesiasticorum. Hoc variare non debet iura inperii prout a divina institucione et naturali origine iuris gentium et libero arbitrio processit, quia contra rationem libere electionis esset quod populus temporalis christianorum et principes in temporalibus sibi dominum constituere non possent nisi secundum alterius voluntatem vel nisi regimen et defensio populi ab alio dependeret. Immo videretur contra ius naturale. Cum enim liber homo etiam christianus et quilibet de populo possit sibi dominum christianum iuste constituere quem vult et quem sibi iudicat expedire, et ille statim super sua servitute habet liberam executionem eo quod electio talis domini immediate dependet a deo et libero arbitrio quod deus cogere non vult, ymmo non potest secundum multos, quod totus populus et principes essent minoris libertatis quam quilibet de populo hoc esset contra rationem penitus et absurdum.

These are perhaps as favourable examples of the author's skill as B can show. Clearly he works at a very different level of subtlety and thoroughness from Ockham: only questions 1 and 4 are treated at any length; the others are dismissed in twenty lines or so apiece. All that he finds to say about question 3 is reproduced above; Ockham's treatment of the same question demands 28 octavo pages of print. The interesting thing is that B reveals no acquaintance with Ockham's work and no borrowing from his arguments. On occasion, indeed, a sentiment is expressed which seems diametrically opposed

1. Augustine, *de vera relig.* 31–32, ed. Daur (*Corpus Christ.* xxii, 1962), pp. 206–7.

to Ockham's way of thinking. Thus, when the author is discussing whether election by the princes is as effective for the king of the Romans as is legitimate succession in an hereditary monarchy, he argues:

[fo. 155] Et videtur quod sic. Primo quia ipsa electio principum fuit data loco et vice hereditarie successionis per Ottonem tercium vel secundum alios per Gregorium quintum qui fuit de genere dicti Ottonis, quia ante tempora illa fuit in inperatoribus successio hereditaria.

This comes close to the view of Lupold of Bebenburg, though Lupold makes no mention of Pope Gregory V. But it cannot be reconciled with Ockham's position that the empire had always been an elective dignity and that hereditary succession to it in any true sense had never existed.[1] It is probable that the author of B had read Lupold's *Tractatus de iuribus regni et imperii.* Though he words it differently, he echoes Lupold's idea that the electoral princes in choosing the new ruler represent all the people of the empire.[2] When he vouches to witness 'cronica Eusebii' and 'historia Francorum' for Charlemagne's administration before 800, he is citing Frutolf of Michelsberg and the *Annalista Saxo* in the way which was habitual to Lupold.[3] On the other hand nowhere does his thought or language impel us to believe that he had studied Ockham's *Octo Quaestiones* or was relying on them.

It seems clear, then, that B was not an abstract or abbreviation of Ockham's work. But may not the author have used this as his source for the questions themselves, while going on to discuss them quite independently of what Ockham had written? Slight but pervasive differences in the wording of the questions as they appear in the two works, and a significant variation in the order in which they are presented, seem to rule out this possibility. A few examples will illustrate the differences:

Octo Quaestiones, qu. i: Utrum potestas spiritualis suprema et laicalis suprema ex natura rei in tantum ex opposito distinguantur, quod non possint formaliter et simul cadere in eundem hominem.
B fo. 152^{v}: Utrum potestas spiritualis in supremo gradu sue perfectionis et potestas suprema laycalis ex opposito distingwantur quod non possint cadere formaliter in unum subiectum simul vel suppositum.

1. Lupold, *Tractatus de iuribus regni et imperii*, c. 2, ed. S. Schard (Basle, 1566), p. 339; OQ iv, 9, p. 151; viii, 4, p. 195.

2. B fo. 154: Electio autem principum virtualiter habet potentiam totius populi regni et inperii ... libertas electorum, in quorum personis totus populus regni tam virtualiter continetur. Lupold, c. 5, pp. 352–3: mortuo rege uel Imperatore ... principes Electores ratione iam dictae institutionis, habent eligere regem seu Imperatorem, repraesentantes in hoc omnes principes et populum Germaniae, Italiae et aliarum provinciarum et terrarum regni et Imperii, quasi uice omnium eligendo.

3. Meyer, pp. 222–3.

OQ qu. ii: Utrum suprema potestas laicalis proprietatem sibi proprie propriam habeat immediate a Deo.
B fo. 153: Utrum potestas inperialis iurisdictionem sibi proprie propriam habeat immediate a deo.

OQ qu. vi: Utrum rex hereditarie succedens suo coronatori in aliquo sit subiectus.
B fo. 155: Utrum rex hereditarie succedens ex ipsa coronatione et consecratione consecratori in aliquibus temporalibus sit subiectus.

From the cumulation of such verbal discrepancies[1] it seems necessary to infer that the author of B did not rely on Ockham for his wording of the eight questions. Possibly the version he preserves is closer to the original than is Ockham's. This view gains some support from a comparison of the order of the questions in the two works. Questions 1 to 4 are the same in both; then B takes as its fifth question the one which Ockham treats last, so that in B the equivalents of Ockham's fifth, sixth and seventh questions come sixth, seventh and eighth. B's order appears the more logical of the two. For its fifth question (Ockham's eighth and last) – whether the king of the Romans is created as effectively as the result of canonical election by the electors as is an hereditary king by legitimate succession – provides as it were a bridge between discussion of the problems of the empire in the first four questions and those concerning hereditary monarchy in the last three. Ockham's arrangement, on the other hand, suggests that he had adapted the original order of the questions to suit his own purposes.

It has not proved possible to identify the rather naïve evangelical responsible for B, nor the precise date at which he composed it, which may lie anywhere between 1340 and the time when the Bremen manuscript was written. In itself his work is of only moderate interest. Its extrinsic significance, however, is more considerable. Its survival allows us to infer that the list of eight questions once had an independent existence in Germany, and to surmise that Ockham, when he came to discuss them, may have treated their original wording and arrangement with some freedom. We can now say with confidence that 'vir quidam venerabilis', 'dominus michi quamplurimum venerandus' was no mere fiction of Ockham's.

Who he was is still unknown. But it is not quite hopeless to ask where he found the questions he put to Ockham. For this enquiry the fact that nearly half the questions were concerned with problems of

1. Probably the most significant occurs in the formulation of question 4. OQ iv, 1, p. 126: utrum electio alicuius in regem Romanorum vel imperatorem sibi det plenam administrationem ex eo quod sua potestas est immediate a Deo. B fo. 153ᵛ, though otherwise verbally the same, omits 'vel imperatorem'. This omission may imply that the author of B did not accept the proposition that election by the princes immediately made the object of their choice full emperor in name and fact. If so, his view was closer to that expressed in the electoral *Weisthum* of Rhens (16 July 1338) than to that of the imperial constitution *Licet iuris* (6 Aug. 1338); *cf.* M. Krammer, *Quellen zur Geschichte der deutschen Königswahl* (Leipzig-Berlin, 1912), pp. 91–92, 97.

hereditary monarchy has an importance which Ockham's concentration on the imperial aspects has tended to obscure. Compared with his exhaustive treatment of questions 1–4, which have to do with the supreme secular power, the attention Ockham pays to questions 5–7 concerning hereditary monarchy seems almost perfunctory. His position in Germany as a Michaelist emigré depending on the emperor's patronage makes this natural enough. But that so many of the questions seemed of minor interest to an imperial pamphleteer suggests doubts about supposing that they originated in imperialist circles. It has indeed been argued that question 7 – whether, if a king by hereditary succession were crowned by an archbishop other than the customary one, or crowned himself, he would thereby forfeit his royal power and title – was related to the circumstance that Lewis the Bavarian had been crowned king of the Romans in 1314 by the archbishop of Mainz, not by the archbishop of Cologne who claimed a customary right to this office.[1] It seems fair to object to this not only that the events of 1314 were very old history by 1340/1, but also that question 7, like the two questions which preceded it, was concerned with the relations to the archbishop who crowns and consecrates him of a ruler by hereditary succession. Quite clearly the king of the Romans was not such a ruler. Within the empire there was only one king who could be regarded in this light. He was the king of Bohemia.

Early in 1340 John of Bohemia went blind. In his will dated 9 September 1340 he treated his kingdom as bequeathable to his eldest son, Charles of Moravia.[2] On 11 June 1341 John announced to the estates at Prague that he had appointed Charles and his male heirs as successors to the Bohemian crown after his own death. Without making difficulties the estates recognized Charles as John's successor, and so in effect the hereditary right of the Luxemburgers to the Bohemian crown.[3] John's blindness suggested that it would be advisable to have Charles crowned in his father's lifetime. But here an awkward complication arose. The customary consecrator of Bohemian kings was the metropolitan, the archbishop of Mainz, who at this time was Henry of Virneburg. He had become archbishop in 1328 as a papal partisan and provisee, but in the summer of 1337 he had made his peace with Lewis the Bavarian and had done fealty to him. For participating with the heretical and schismatical emperor he had fallen under the Church's ban, so that he was canonically disabled from crowning the successor to Bohemia.[4] This posed a

1. Sikes, *ed. cit.* p. 4.

2. J. Emler, *Regesta diplomatica necnon epistolaria Bohemiae et Moraviae*, iv (Prague, 1892), no. 819.

3. E. Werunsky, *Geschichte Karls IV*, i (Innsbruck, 1880), 278: 'Von diesem Tage an war Böhmen ein luxemburgisches Erbland.'

4. H. Otto, *Regesten der Erzbischöfe von Mainz*, 1, ii (Darmstadt, 1934), nos. 3802, 4043, 4130.

problem for the Luxemburgers. If Henry crowned Charles, the ceremony would be illegal in the eyes of the pope; if some other churchman performed the ceremony, it would almost certainly be alleged that this was an unlawful derogation from the rights of Mainz. To postpone the crowning might leave doubts whether Charles was properly king. It was the pope who cut the knot. On 15 October 1341 Pope Benedict XII granted permission to Bishop John of Prague to consecrate and crown Charles as king of Bohemia, since the archbishop of Mainz was under the Church's ban and his suffragan had previously been forbidden to obey him.[1] The coronation of Charles did not in fact take place at this time, perhaps because, when it came to the point, John of Bohemia was unwilling to relinquish all his power.[2] But the importance of this situation for the present enquiry is clear. In the absence of any plausible alternative explanation it is natural to suppose that the 5th, 6th and 7th of the eight questions, concerned as they were with the relations between a king by hereditary succession and the churchman who consecrates and crowns him, had reference to the Luxemburgers' difficulties in 1341 about the coronation of Charles of Moravia.

Of the three leading Luxemburgers at this time it was the eldest, John's uncle Baldwin, archbishop of Trier, who was most interested in the problems of the empire and imperial election which the rest of the eight questions treated.[3] The nature and extent of the influence Baldwin exerted in 1338, the great year of German constitutional definition, are still disputed.[4] But his deep involvement in the debate about the rights of the German electors to create a king independently of papal approval cannot be doubted. It seems a reasonable hypothesis, then, that the author of the eight questions stood pretty close to Baldwin, whether or not the author himself was the 'vir venerabilis' who transmitted them to Ockham. Little weight need be accorded to Hauck's objection that Ockham cannot have received his impulse from this quarter because his *Octo Quaestiones* combat Lupold of Bebenburg, who had dedicated his *Tractatus de iuribus* to Baldwin.[5] The recipient of a dedication is not necessarily committed to the views of its author. Ockham does indeed criticize very thoroughly one of Lupold's most important positions – the distinction drawn in the *Tractatus* between the power of the elected king

1. Otto, nos. 4701, 4733.

2. Werunsky, p. 279. John handed over the regency of Bohemia to Charles in February 1342, *ibid.* p. 297.

3. *Cf.* E. E. Stengel, *Avignon und Rhens* (Weimar, 1930), pp. 85 ff., and the same author's *Baldewin von Luxemburg. Ein grenzdeutscher Staatsmann des 14. Jahrhunderts* (Weimar, 1937).

4. *Cf.* F. Bock, *Reichsidee und Nationalstaaten vom Untergang des alten Reiches bis zur Kündigung des deutsch-englischen Bündnisses im Jahre 1341* (Munich, 1943), pp. 398 ff.

5. *Kirchengeschichte Deutschlands*, v, i, 562, n. 3. Hauck mentions, but does not support, Henry of Mainz as a possible alternative to Baldwin. In my opinion the tendency of questions 5, 6 and 7 makes it very unlikely that the eight questions originated at Mainz.

of the Romans to administer immediately those areas held by Charlemagne before his coronation in 800, and his need to be crowned emperor by the pope before he could administer the rest of the empire.[1] But he shows no inclination to attack the five articles in which Lupold set out his conclusions, and could himself, I believe, granted some freedom of interpretation, have subscribed to any or all of them.[2] His references to Lupold personally are notably courteous.[3] Nor had Lupold reasonable cause to complain of criticism of the kind he was given in the *Octo Quaestiones*. For at the end of his treatise he had asked Baldwin to submit it for amendment to abler and more acute scholars than he esteemed himself to be.[4] It looks very much as if he was taken at his word. The publication of his treatise, together with the complications foreseen as likely to arise about securing the coronation of Charles of Moravia as king of Bohemia, may well have led to the eight questions being drawn up by someone in the entourage of Baldwin of Trier. This argument, of course, falls considerably short of a demonstration. But, as far as I can see, nowhere does it conflict with the available evidence, and it seems to have a fair degree of probability on its side.

If it be accepted that the questions were formulated at Trier, how did they come to Ockham's attention? Here it is useful to bear in mind that the Luxemburgers were on exceptionally good terms with the emperor from 1339 until late in 1341, when relations were embittered by Lewis's scheme to make his eldest son, Lewis of Brandenburg, husband of Margaret Maultasch of Tirol in place of John Henry of Luxemburg.[5] We do scant justice to the variety and fluidity of German politics between 1337 and 1341 if we assume them to have been dominated by a rigid opposition between Baldwin of Trier with his theorist Lupold on the one side, and Lewis with his Michaelist pamphleteers on the other: lining up, as it were, 'eine kurfürstliche Reichspartei' against 'eine minoristische kaiserliche Partei'.[6] In 1340 or early 1341 it would have been easy and natural enough for Baldwin to seek through this or that middleman an opinion about the eight questions from Trier from the emperor's outstanding expert in this field. It seems to me likely that it was in some such fashion as this that Ockham was made aware of the questions. If there is substance in this suggestion, then we must conclude that the impulse for Ockham to compose one of his most

1. OQ iv. *passim*; viii. 3–4.

2. *Cf.* Lupold, *Tractatus*, c. 5, p. 351; c. 6, pp. 356–7; c. 7, p. 358; c. 8, p. 363; c. 9, p. 368.

3. OQ iv, 3, p. 128: "a quodam venerabili doctore'; viii, 3, p. 184: 'doctor quidam venerabilis'; viii, 8, p. 219: 'homo non mediocris scientiae'.

4. *Tractatus*, c. 19, p. 409; Peto igitur pater magnifice ut ad resecandum superflua, et ad supplendum defectuosa, necnon ad corrigendum falsa in eo contenta, peritiores et perspicaciores, uestra procurante et ordinante solicitudine, diligentius elaborent.

5. Stengel, *Avignon und Rhens*, pp. 186, 240–1.

6. Most, 'Reichsgedanke des Lupold von Bebenburg', p. 465.

important polemical works originated not from his overt patron, Lewis the Bavarian, but from the Luxemburgers who were ultimately to prove Lewis's successful rivals. As a corollary we would have to suppose that the *Octo Quaestiones* had been completed before the rapid deterioration of Wittelsbach-Luxemburg relations in the autumn of 1341.

VIII

THE THREE MODES OF NATURAL LAW IN OCKHAM: A REVISION OF THE TEXT

The significance of the concept of natural law in Ockham's thinking can hardly be decided on *a priori* grounds.[1] Only close attention to what he wrote can help towards an estimate. During the last forty years or so a central place in the lively if inconclusive debate about his views on this subject has been occupied by chapter six of book three of the second treatise of part three of his *Dialogus*. To it Max. A. Shepard drew attention in 1932 and Georges de Lagarde devoted almost a whole chapter of discussion in 1946[2]. Father W. Kölmel's attempt in 1953 to rebut Lagarde's conclusions, though rightly insisting that IIusIIIae *Dial.* iii. 6 does not reveal the whole story, nevertheless concentrated most of its attention upon this text.[3] When in the sixties Lagarde rehandled his Ockham volumes IIusIIIae *Dial.* iii. 6 still had a considerable part to play in his defence of his earlier views against Kölmel's criticisms.[4] In his recent study of Ockham's political thought Professor McGrade engages in a lengthy tussle with this same passage; if only in passing, Professor

---

[1] That seems to be the tendency, for example, of A. P. d'Entrèves, *Natural Law* (London, 1951), pp. 68–69, when he remarks on the Nominalist theory of ethics as an "insidious menace to the doctrine of natural law" and on Ockham as drawing out fully all the implications of "voluntarist ethics."

[2] Max A. Shepard, "William of Occam and the Higher Law," *American Political Science Review*, 26 (1932), 1011–12; 27 (1933), 24, 32. Georges de Lagarde, *La Naissance de l'Esprit Laïque au Déclin du Moyen-Age*. Tom. VI. *Ockham: La Morale et le droit* (Paris, 1946), chapter 6, pp. 140–63.

[3] W. Kölmel, 'Das Naturrecht bei Wilhelm Ockham,' *Franziskanische Studien*, 35 (1953), 39–85. For the reservations, cf. pp. 56, 76; for the discussion, pp. 55–76.

[4] Cf. especially *La Naissance de l'Esprit Laïque*. Tom. V. *Guillaume d'Ockham: Critique des structures ecclésiales* (Paris/Louvain, 1963), pp. 112–19, 271, 286.

Gordon Leff has not failed to notice it.[5] Of course, none of these scholars confined his attention to IIusIIIae *Dial.* iii. 6 or built his argument upon it exclusively: the early chapters of book i of the same treatise contain an important alternative definition of natural law, as Lagarde perceived, and the value of Ockham's *Opus Nonaginta Dierum* for the investigation of this problem has been indicated by Dr. J. B. Morrall and Professor Miethke, recently followed by Leff.[6] Yet IIusIIIae *Dial.* iii. 6 remains, as Professor Francis Oakley has said, Ockham's "best known text on natural law."[7] Modern scholarship has in fact endorsed the high opinion of this passage expressed by medieval annotators: "pulchra definitio iuris naturalis," or, as Pierre d'Ailly characterized it, "novam distinctionem de iure naturali valde bonam."[8]

In view of the strategic importance so generally attributed to this text we are left asking why modern interpretations of it have been so notably diverse. At least part of the answer lies in the deficiencies of the version which the commentators have used. Ultimately only one version is at issue. Shepard, Lagarde, Kölmel and Oakley rely on Goldast's edition of the *Dialogus* in vol. ii of his *Monarchia Sancti Romani Imperii* (1614; in vol. iii of later editions of the same work); McGrade and Leff have gone back to the Lyons edition of 1494 (reproduced in 1962). But Goldast offered no more than a reprint of the Lyons edition, which has thus provided all these scholars with the basis for their varied conclusions. Though both Lagarde and McGrade have also consulted manuscripts, neither seems to have pursued this line systematically or very far; Lagarde indeed, possibly not without irony, appears at one point to make rather light of textual problems.[9] The result has been that the difficulties of inter-

[5] A. S. McGrade, *The Political Thought of William of Ockham* (Cambridge, 1974), pp. 177–85; Gordon Leff, *William of Ockham: The Metamorphosis of Scholastic Discourse* (Manchester, 1975), pp. 622–23.

[6] Georges de Lagarde, *La Naissance de l'Esprit Laïque.* Tom. IV. *Guillaume d'Ockham: Défense de l'empire* (Paris/Louvain, 1962), pp. 118–20. J. B. Morrall, "Some Notes on a Recent Interpretation of William of Ockham's Political Philosophy," *Franciscan Studies,* 9 (1949), 335–69; Jürgen Miethke, *Ockhams Weg zur Sozialphilosophie* (Berlin, 1969), pp. 480–502; Leff, pp. 620–22.

[7] F. Oakley, "Medieval Theories of Natural Law: William of Ockham and the Significance of the Voluntarist Tradition," *Natural Law Forum,* 6 (1961), 66.

[8] Paris, BN cod. lat. 14619, fol. 143r, cited by Lagarde, *La Morale et le droit,* p. 143, n. 7; BN cod. lat. 14579, fol. 101r, cited by McGrade, p. 175, n. 4.

[9] Lagarde, *La Morale et le droit,* p. 150, n. 25; McGrade, p. 178, n. 17. Cf.

preting what is in any case an intricate piece of reasoning on Ockham's part have been compounded by reliance on the corrupt text published by Johannes Trechsel at Lyons in 1494.

How desperate an obstacle this version presents to an accurate understanding of Ockham can be illustrated by Oakley's valiant attempt in 1963 to render the whole of IIusIIIae *Dial.* iii. 6 into English from Goldast's text.[10] We may take the crucial definition of the second mode of natural law, which according to Ockham 'ought to be observed by those who rely solely on natural equity without any recourse to custom and human regulation.' Goldast (p. 932) proceeds: "quod ideo est naturale, quia est contra statum naturae institutae, et si omnes homines viverent secundum rationem naturalem aut legem divinam, non esset faciendum nec seruandum." Oakley appreciates the difficulty of making coherent sense of this, and amends Goldast by moving *non* from before *esset* to after *quia*, translating thus (p. 500; cf. p. 506, n. 9): "and which is natural because it is [not] contrary to the state of nature as it was established and would have to be followed or observed if all men lived in accordance with natural reason or the divine law." Recourse to the manuscripts, however, suggests that what Ockham wrote was nearer this: "quod ideo dicitur naturale quia contrarium est contra statum nature institute et, si homines viverent secundum rationem naturalem aut legem divinam, non esset servandum nec faciendum."[11] This can be rendered in a way which, compared with Oakley's translation, gives a markedly different and, I think, better sense: "which is called natural because its contrary is opposed to the state of nature before the Fall and, if

Lagarde, *Défense*, p. 59: "Ce ne sont pas les hésitations sur telle ou telle variante des manuscrits qui constituent la principale des difficultés qu'ait à vaincre le commentateur d'Ockham."

[10] In R. Lerner and M. Mahdi (editors), *Medieval Political Philosophy: A Sourcebook* (New York, 1963), pp. 499–505.

[11] See below, note 4 to text. In the light of the reading offered by a number of the mss. Lagarde, *La Morale et le droit*, p. 150, n. 25, suggested that *statutum* should here be preferred to *statum* (though the omission by Goldast of *contrarium* escaped his notice). But *statum*, given by Mazarine, cod. 3522, fol. 282rb, seems to me to make much better sense. On the tendency of medieval scribes to confuse *statum* and *statutum* and the need to refer to the context rather than to abide blindly by the wording of the mss., see Gaines, Post, "Copyists' Errors and the Problems of Papal Dispensations *Contra Statutum Generale Ecclesiae* or *Contra Statum Generalem Ecclesiae* according to the Decretists and Decretalists ca. 1150–1234," *Studia Gratiana*, 9 (1966), 358–405.

men lived according to natural reason or divine law, [this contrary] would not need to be observed or enacted."

Or again one may cite the passage in which Ockham discusses Isidore's definition of natural law, given below on page 215, lines 2–7. In translation it reads: "When Isidore says: *Natural law is common to all nations*, it means that natural law in the first mode is so common to all nations that all nations are bound indispensably by it; and accordingly it *occurs by instinct of nature*, that is, of natural reason, which never fails." Basing himself on Goldast's defective text Oakley translates (p. 502): "...of all nations, because all nations are indispensably bound by it, and, therefore, that in the state of nature it is the law of reason that in no case fails, then the law of which he is speaking is natural law in the second sense." Here, as with the definition of the second mode of natural law, it seems clear that Oakley has failed to render Ockham's intention. To criticize him for this would be unfair. He has done his best with a poor text, ultimately that of the Lyons edition of 1494; it has misled him.[12]

It is not likely that a modern critical edition of Ockham's *Dialogus* can appear for some years. Because of the admitted significance of IIusIIIae *Dial.* iii. 6 for the understanding of Ockham's ideas about natural law, and to obviate some of the pitfalls which await those who approach this chapter through the older versions available in print, it has seemed useful to produce an interim edition of it backed by respectable manuscript tradition. At this stage of research it cannot be claimed with any certainty that cod. Vat. lat. 4115 is the best surviving manuscript of IIusIIIae *Dial.* But, though comparatively late in date (c. 1411), it undoubtedly represents a good tradition and has been taken as the basis for the edition which follows.[13] It is not impeccable and shows some omissions by homeoteleuton; I have supplemented it by reference to the better of the

[12] The problems of the real *editio princeps* of the *Dialogus*, printed in Paris and dated 5 July 1476, are not immediately relevant here. Professor Astrik L. Gabriel has made clear that the printers were not Petrus Caesarius Wagner and Johannes Stoll, as has often been supposed, but the printers working at the sign of the *Soufflet vert* in the Rue St Jacques, who were perhaps break-away apprentices of Wagner and Stoll: "*Via Antiqua* and *Via Moderna* and the Migration of Paris Students and Masters to the German Universities in the Fifteenth Century," *Antiqui und Moderni* (*Miscellanea Mediaevalia. Veröffentlichungen des Thomas-Instituts der Universität zu Köln*, 9, Berlin, 1974), pp. 452–453.

[13] Cf. Guillelmi de Ockham, *Opera Politica* I, editio altera, ed. H. S. Offler (Manchester, 1974), pp. 223–24.

two versions of IIusIIIae *Dial.* contained in Paris, Mazarine, cod. 3522, from the end of the fourteenth century.[14] In the apparatus V signifies the first hand in cod. Vat. lat. 4115, fols. 101v–104v, and V^2, V^3 the second and third hands; M indicates readings from Mazarine, cod. 3522, fols. 282rb–283vb. Annotation has been confined to verifying Ockham's references to the canon law. Considered as a whole, these references suggest that the discussion of natural law in IIus IIIae *Dial.* iii. 6 was to some extent conditioned, even if not motivated, by the well-known difficulties raised by Gratian's treatment of this subject in the *Tractatus de Legibus* in the *Decretum.*[15]

The issue debated between master and pupil in IIusIIIae *Dial.* iii. 6 had been raised in chapter 5. There the master had argued thus: the right to elect the pope does not derive from the pope; accordingly the Romans' right to elect him comes not from the pope, but from the fact that they are Christians and Catholics. To this the pupil had raised three objections, of which the third reads:

> Amplius, si Romani non habent ius eligendi a papa, quero quo iure habent ius eligendi summum pontificem, aut divino aut humano? Non divino: quia non legitur in scripturis divinis quod Deus eis dederit tale ius. Nec humano: quia ius humanum aut est civile aut canonicum; iura civilia sunt iura imperatoris et regum, iura canonica sunt iura summorum pontificum; ergo Romani haberent ius eligendi ab imperatoribus vel regibus vel a summis pontificibus. Sed non habent ius eligendi ab imperatoribus. Ergo a solis summis pontificibus habent huiusmodi ius eligendi; et ita ius eligendi est a solo papa.[16]

It is this objection which provides the substance for the discussion in chapter 6, which is prefaced by a general consideration of the modes or levels of natural law and the relation of natural to divine law (pages 212–16 of the text below).

---

[14] Ockham, *Opera Politica* I, ed. alt., p. 5. Even with this help I cannot claim to have resolved satisfactorily every difficulty in the text. Only after much hesitation has the *poterunt* of the mss. been retained at n. 51, p. 217. Though the sense of the first sentence in the last paragraph, p. 218, seems clear enough, there appears to be a syntactical confusion, which may, of course, go back to Ockham.

[15] See, for example, Brian Tierney, *Medieval Poor Law* (Berkeley and Los Angeles, 1959), pp. 28–31; Stanley Chodorow, *Christian Political Society and Church Politics in the Mid-Twelfth Century* (Berkeley and Los Angeles, 1972) pp. 98, 105–111.

[16] Text from cod. Vat. lat. 4115, fol. 100v; cf. ed. Lyons, 1494, fol. cclxiiva; Goldast, II, 931.

VIII

IIus IIIae *DIALOGUS*, iii, 6

(Cod. Vat. Lat 4115, fols. 101v–104v, with some readings from Paris, Mazarine, 3522, fols. 282rb–283vb)

DISCIPULUS. Dic qualiter respondetur ad hoc, quod excepi,[1] quod Romani nec iure divino nec iure humano habent ius eligendi summum pontificem.

MAGISTER. Ad hoc respondetur quod extendendo ius divinum ad omne ius[2] naturale Romani ex iure divino habent ius eligendi summum pontificem.

DISCIPULUS. Ista responsio obscura michi videtur; ideo ipsam secundum istam opinionem cupio declarari. Primo autem declara secundum eam quare dicitur "extendendo ius divinum ad omne ius naturale"; secundo quare omne ius naturale potest vocari ius divinum.

MAGISTER. Primum distinguitur propter tres modos iuris naturalis.

Uno enim modo dicitur ius naturale illud, quod est conforme rationi naturali, que in nullo[3] casu fallit, sicut est 'non mechaberis,' 'non mentieris' et huiusmodi.

Aliter dicitur ius naturale, quod servandum est ab illis, qui sola equitate naturali absque omni consuetudine et constitutione humana utuntur. Quod ideo dicitur naturale quia contrarium est contra statum[4] nature institute et, si homines viverent secundum rationem naturalem aut legem divinam, non esset servandum nec faciendum.

Isto modo et non primo modo ex iure naturali omnia sunt communia, quia in statu[5] nature institute omnia fuissent communia, et si post lapsum omnes homines secundum rationem viverent, omnia deberent esse communia et nichil proprium; proprietas enim propter iniquitatem est inducta, xii, q.i, c. *Dilectissimis*.[6] Isto modo loquitur Ysidorus libro v⟨i⟩ Ethimologiarum, et ponitur in decretis di.i, c. *Ius naturale*,[7] cum dicit quod secundum ius naturale est *communis omnium possessio et omnium una libertas*.[8] Non enim communis omnium possessio et omnium

---

[1] excepi: accepi M

[2] ius *om.* V; *in marg.* V^2

[3] nullo M; illo V

[4] statum M; statutum V, Paris, Mazarine cod. 3522, fol. 190, Frankfurt a.M., Stadtbibliothek cod. lat. quart. 4, fol. 380vb (Paris, BN lat. 3657, 14619, 15881: cf. Lagarde, *La Morale et le droit*, p. 150, n. 25); alias instintum V^2

[5] in statu: alias instictu V^2

[6] C. 12 q. 1 c. 2

[7] *Dist.* 1 c. 7 = Isidorus, *Etymol.* v. 4

[8] libertas una *trs.* V

una libertas est de iure naturali primo modo. Tunc enim nullus posset sibi licite aliquid appropriare, nec aliquo iure gentium vel civili posset aliquis fieri servus, quia ius naturale primo modo est immutabile et invariabile ac indispensabile, di. v, § *Nunc autem*[9] et di. vi, § *Hiis itaque respondetur.*[10] Constat autem quod aliqui iure gentium licite fiunt servi, teste beato Gregorio, qui, ut legitur xii, q. ii, c. *Cum Redemptor,*[11] ait: *Salubriter agitur, si homines, quos ab initio natura liberos protulit, et ius gentium iugo substituit*[12] *servitutis, in ea* natura, *qua*[13] *nati fuerant, manumittentis beneficio* liberati[14] *reddantur.* Ex quibus verbis colligitur quod iure naturali omnes homines sunt liberi et tamen aliqui iure gentium fiunt servi; ex quo concluditur quod ius naturale uno[15] modo accepto vocabulo non est immutabile, immo licet contrarium statuere, ut iure fiat contrarium.

Tertio modo dicitur ius naturale illud, quod ex iure gentium vel alio aut ex aliquo facto divino vel humano evidenti ratione colligitur, nisi de consensu illorum, quorum interest, contrarium statuatur. Quod poterit vocari ius naturale ex suppositione, sicut secundum Ysidorum[16] ubi prius: *Ius naturale est deposite rei vel commodate pecunie restitutio, violentie per vim repulsio.* Ista enim non sunt iura naturalia primo modo.[17] Nec etiam secundo modo; quia nec fuissent in statu nature institute nec essent inter illos, qui secundum rationem viventes sola equitate naturali absque omni consuetudine et constitutione humana essent contenti; quia inter illos nulla res esset deposita vel commodata nec aliquis alteri vim inferret. Sunt ergo iura naturalia ex suppositione. Quia, supposito quod res et pecunie sint appropriate iure gentium vel aliquo iure humano, evidenti ratione colligitur quod res deposita et pecunia commodata debent restitui, nisi ex causa per illum vel illos, cuius vel quorum interest, contrarium ordinetur. Similiter, supposito quod aliquis violentiam de facto iniuriose inferat alteri — quod non est de iure naturali, sed contra ius naturale —, evidenti ratione colligitur quod licet per vim violentiam talem repellere.

Propter istos itaque tres modos iuris naturalis dicunt[18] quod Romani ex iure divino habent ius eligendi summum pontificem, extendendo

[9] *Dist.* 5 *ante* c. 1

[10] *Dist.* 6 *post* c. 3

[11] C. 12 q. 2 c. 68 = Gregorius Magnus, *Reg.* v. 12

[12] subistit V

[13] natura qua: in qua *canon*

[14] libertati *canon*

[15] uno: alias secundo V[2]

[16] *Dist.* 1 c. 7

[17] *post* modo: quia uariationem et mutabilitatem recipere possunt *add.* V[3]

[18] dicunt isti *add.* M

ius divinum ad omne ius naturale. Quia si extenderetur solummodo ad ius naturale primo modo dictum, qualiter accipitur ius naturale di. v, § i[19] et di. vi, § *Hiis itaque respondetur*[20] et di. viii, § *Dignitate vero*[21] et di. ix, § i[22] et in multis aliis locis,[23] Romani non haberent ex solo iure divino ius eligendi summum pontificem.

DISCIPULUS. Quia istam distinctionem iuris naturalis alias non audivi, volo obicere contra eam, ut ex solutione obiectionum secundum opinionem istam magis intelligam an contineat aliquid veritatis.

Videtur itaque ista distinctio verbis Ysidori in preallegato capitulo *Ius naturale* apertissime obviare. Tum quia dicit Ysidorus:[24] *Ius naturale est commune omnium nationum, eo quod ubique instinctu nature, non constitutione aliqua habetur.* Ista non possunt competere secundo membro predicte distinctionis; quia illa, quorum contraria possunt esse licita secundum ius gentium, [non sunt communia omnium nationum nec ubique habentur instinctu[25] nature, quia non habentur ibi, ubi contraria secundum ius gentium][26] observantur. Tum quia ibidem dicit Ysidorus:[27] *Hoc, aut*[28] *si quid huic simile est, nunquam iniustum, sed naturale equumque habetur.* Hoc nec de secundo membro nec de tertio potest veritatem habere. Nam illud, quod dicitur ius naturale secundo modo, potest esse iniustum, ex quo contrarium potest esse de iure gentium; quod enim contrariatur iuri gentium est censendum iniustum. Illud etiam, quod dicitur ius naturale tertio modo, potest esse iniustum, ex quo contrarium est de iure nature secundo modo. Cum de iure nature illo secundo modo sit, quod nulla pecunia commodetur et nulla res deponatur, quia secundum ius nature sic accepto vocabulo omnia sunt communia; et ita secundum illud ius nulla pecunia potest commodari nec aliqua res deponi. Ista sunt, que movent me contra distinctionem premissam. Tu vero dic qualiter respondetur ad ipsa.

MAGISTER. Ad ista dupliciter respondetur.

Uno modo quod quedam verba in predicto capitulo *Ius naturale* debent intelligi solummodo de iure naturali primo modo dicto,[29] et sic contra predicta non videntur concludere.

---

[19] *Dist.* 5 *ante* c. 1

[20] *Dist.* 6 *post* c. 3

[21] *Dist.* 8 *post* c. 1

[22] *Dist.* 9 *ante* c. 1

[23] di.viii, § Dignitate vero *scripsi;* di.vii § significate vero V; et di.viii... aliis locis *om.* M

[24] *Dist.* 1 c. 7

[25] instinctu *scripsi;* in statu M

[26] non sunt... gentium M; *om.* V

[27] *Dist.* 1 c. 7

[28] aut *sec. canonem;* autem VM

[29] *post* dicto: et quedam de aliis et ideo verba que accipis obiciendo de iure naturali primo modo dicto tantummodo debent intelligi *add.* M

Aliter dicitur quod illa verba, que obiciendo accipis, de omni iure naturali dicuntur, sed sane debent intelligi. Cum ergo dicit Ysidorus:[30] *Ius naturale est commune omnium nationum* etc., intelligitur quod ius naturale primo modo dictum sic[31] est[32] commune omnium nationum quod[33] omnes nationes indispensabiliter obligantur ad ipsum; et ideo *instinctu nature,* hoc[34] est naturalis rationis, que nunquam fallit, *habetur.* Ius autem naturale secundo modo dictum sic est commune omnium nationum quod omnes nationes, nisi ex causa rationali ordinent contrarium, tenentur ad ipsum; et ideo est ex instinctu nature, hoc est rationis naturalis, antequam contrarium statuatur per ordinationem humanam. Ratio enim dictat quod omnia sunt communia antequam de consensu hominum approprientur. Ius vero naturale tertio modo est commune omnium nationum ex suppositione, si scilicet omnes nationes statuerint vel fecerint illud, ex quo ius illo modo dictum evidenti ratione colligitur; et ideo *instinctu nature,* hoc est rationis [naturalis],[35] *habetur,* illo supposito, ex quo tali modo colligitur.

Consimiliter dicitur de illis verbis,[36] que secundo allegas: *Hoc, aut*[37] *si quid huic simile* etc., quod possunt de secundo membro intelligi, quia tale ius naturale *nunquam iniustum* est,[38] *sed naturale equumque habetur,* nisi contrarium aliquo iure humano ex causa rationabili statuatur. Ius etiam naturale tertio modo dictum aliquo modo *nunquam iniustum, sed* semper *naturale equumque habetur,* quia illo supposito, ex quo evidenti ratione colligitur, *nunquam iniustum,*[39] *sed* semper *naturale equumque habetur,* nisi per illum vel illos, cuius vel quorum interest, contrarium ordinetur.

DISCIPULUS. Videtur quod ista sint inconvenienter dicta, quia secundum ista idem verbum semel positum in verbis premissis Ysidori acciperetur equivoce.

MAGISTER. Hoc non reputatur inconveniens, quia hoc notat Glosa, di. lxiii, c. *Nosse* dicens: *Nota verbum semel hic positum equivoce ponitur; sic xxviii di., 'Presbyterum.'*[40]

DISCIPULUS. Declarasti secundum opinionem prescriptam quare dixit Romanos habere ius eligendi summum pontificem ex iure divino, exten-

[30] *Dist.* 1 c. 7
[31] sic M; nec V
[32] est: alias deest hoc verbum est V²
[33] et quod *add.* V²
[34] hoc M: homo V
[35] naturalis M; *om.* V
[36] *Dist.* 1 c. 7
[37] aut *sec. canonem;* autem VM
[38] est *om.* M *canon*
[39] iniustum V²M; iustum V
[40] *Gl. ord. ad Dist.* 63 c. 12 *s.v.* 'clero et populo'; cf. *Dist.* 28 c. 16

dendo ius divinum ad omne ius naturale. Nunc dic secundum eandem opinionem,, quare dicit omne ius naturale posse vocari ius divinum.

MAGISTER. Hoc ideo dicunt, tum quia omne ius, quod est a Deo, qui est conditor nature, potest vocari ius divinum; omne autem ius naturale est a Deo, qui est conditor nature; ideo, etc.: tum quia omne ius, quod explicite vel implicite continetur in scripturis divinis, potest vocari ius divinum. Quia *ius divinum in scripturis divinis habe*tur, di. viii, *Quo iure;*[41] omne autem ius naturale in scripturis divinis explicite vel implicite continetur, quia in scripturis divinis sunt quedam regule generales, ex quibus vel solis vel cum aliis colligi potest omne ius naturale et primo et secundo et tertio modo dictum, licet in eis non inveniatur explicite.

DISCIPULUS. Declarasti secundum opinionem prescriptam duo, que michi videbantur obscura. Nunc dic qualiter secundum eandem[42] Romani ex iure divino habent ius eligendi summum pontificem.

MAGISTER. [Ad][43] hoc dicitur quod Romani ex iure naturali tertio modo dicto habent ius eligendi summum pontificem.

Supposito enim quod aliquibus sit aliquis prelatus vel princeps aut rector preficiendus, evidenti ratione colligitur quod nisi per illum vel illos, cuius vel quorum interest, [contrarium][44] ordinetur, illi, quibus est preficiendus, habent ius eligendi preficiendum eis, unde nullus debeat dari ipsis invitis. Hoc innumeris rationibus et exemplis videtur posse probari, sed adducam pauca.

Exemplum est ad hoc quod universitati mortalium nullus prefici debet, nisi per electionem et consensum ipsorum.

Amplius, quod omnes tangit, ab omnibus tractari debet; aliquem prefici omnibus omnes tangit; ergo per omnes tractari debet.

Rursus, quorum interest sibi facere iura, illorum est, si voluerint, caput eligere; sed populus quisque et civitas potest sibi proprium ius facere, quod civile vocatur, di. i, *Ius civile;*[45] ergo et populus et civitas potest sibi[46] caput eligere. Et ita semper spectat ad illos, quibus est aliquis preficiendus, preficiendum eligere, nisi per illum vel illos, cuius vel quorum interest, contrarium ordinetur.

Quod ideo dicitur, quia illi possunt saltem in multis casibus cedere iuri suo[47] et transferre ius suum in alium vel alios; per quem modum,

---

[41] *Dist.* 8 c. 1

[42] eandem opinionem *add.* V[3]

[43] Ad *om.* V

[44] contrarium *supplevi; om.* VM

[45] cf. *Dist.* 1 c. 8

[46] sibi proprium ius facere et caput *add.* M

[47] eidem iuri suo renuntiare V[3]

licet populus ex iure naturali tertio dicto vel secundo modo habuerit ius condendi leges, illam tamen potestatem transtulit in imperatorem, et ita fuit in potestate eius transferre in aliquem vel aliquos ius eligendi imperatorem. Similiter, si illi, quibus est aliquis preficiendus, sunt in huiusmodi subiecti alicui superiori, ille superior potest ordinare quod illi non habeant ius eligendi, licet haberent ius eligendi ex iure nature secundo[48] modo dicto, si scilicet nec per ipsos nec per superiorem esset contrarium ordinatum. Et ita videtur istis quod propositio preaccepta est evidens reputanda.

Sed summus pontifex est specialiter quodammodo preficiendus Romanis, quia non habent episcopum alium. Ergo ipsi ex iure naturali tertio[49] modo dicto, scilicet ex iure naturali ex suppositione, ex hoc scilicet supposito quod debent habere episcopum, habent ius eligendi ipsum, nisi per ipsos Romanos vel alium superiorem Romanis, qui habeat[50] in huiusmodi potestatem, contrarium statuatur vel ordinetur. Ipsi enim Romani poterunt[51] cedere iuri suo vel transferre ius eligendi summum pontificem in alium;[52] poterant etiam transferre in alium ius instituendi electores[53] summi pontificis. Superior etiam Romanis, qui [in][54] huiusmodi habuerit potestatem, poterat concedere ius eligendi aliis quam Romanis. Sed ille superior fuit Christus, et non papa, et ideo Christus, et non papa, poterat privare Romanos iure eligendi summum pontificem. Sed Christus non privavit Romanos iure eligendi episcopum suum. Quando enim Christus prefecit beatum P[etrum][55] omnibus Christianis, dans sibi potestatem ut ubi vellet sedem eligeret ita ut ibi esset quodammodo proprius illorum episcopus, non privavit illos iure illo, quod omnibus competit, quibus est aliqua preficienda potestas sive secularis sive ecclesiastica, [nisi per illos, quibus est preficienda potestas secularis sive ecclesiastica,][56] vel[57] per superiorem contrarium ordinetur. Ergo, cum beatus Petrus elegerit sedem Rome, sequitur quod Romani habent ius eligendi successorem beati Petri, qui eis scilicet preficiendus est in spiritualibus. Et ita Romani ex iure divino, extendendo ius divinum ad quodcunque ius naturale, habent ius eligendi summum pontificem.

DISCIPULUS. Videtur quod secundum istam opinionem melius diceretur quod ex iure gentium Romani habent ius eligendi episcopum suum.

---

[48] secundo M; illo V
[49] tertio *scripsi;* illo V; primo M
[50] habeat M; habeant V
[51] poterunt: *sic* VM
[52] alium vel alios M
[53] electores M; electionis V
[54] in M; *om.* V (*lacuna*)
[55] Petrum: P. *cod.* V
[56] nisi... ecclesiastica M; *om.* V
[57] vel VM: alias donech V[2]

218

Quia hoc est de iure gentium quod omnes, quibus est aliquis preficiendus, habeant ius eligendi preficiendum, nisi cedant iuri suo vel superior eis ordinet contrarium.

MAGISTER. Quamvis multa, que spectant ad ius gentium, sint iura naturalia tertio modo sumpto iure naturali, tamen secundum istam opinionem magis proprie dicitur quod Romani habent ius eligendi episcopum suum ex iure divino sive ex iure naturali tertio modo dicto quam ex iure gentium, pro eo quod ad ius gentium non spectat habere episcopum catholicum, sed hoc spectat ad ius divinum. Preficiendum etiam eligi ab illis, quibus est preficiendus, licet spectet ad ius gentium, spectat nichilominus ad ius divinum, pro eo quod concludi potest ex illis, que in scripturis sacris habentur, una cum aliis. Et ita illa duo supposita, ex quibus colligitur quod Romani habent ius eligendi episcopum suum, specta[n]t[58] ad ius divinum, quamvis diversimode; unum autem solum spectat ad ius gentium. Et propter hoc magis proprie dicitur quod Romani habent ius eligendi episcopum suum ex iure divino sive ex iure naturali tertio modo dicto quam ex iure gentium.

Isti tamen, quia de verbis non curant contendere, dicunt quod sufficit eis quod Romani habent ius eligendi episcopum suum ex hoc ipso quod debent habere episcopum et quod illi, quibus est aliquis preficiendus, ab illis eligi debet, nisi cedant iuri suo vel per[59] superiorem contrarium ordinetur. Utrum autem debeat proprie loquendo dici quod Romani habent ius eligendi ex iure divino vel ex iure naturali tertio modo dicto vel ex iure gentium vel simul ex iure divino et iure gentium, magnam vim non faciunt. Apparet tamen nonnullis quod proprie dicitur quod habent ius eligendi simul ex iure divino et iure gentium. Et ideo, cum queris an habeant ius eligendi ex iure divino vel ex iure humano, dicunt quod nec ex solo iure divino nec ex solo iure humano, sed ex utroque simul, et hoc extendendo ius humanum ad ius gentium et non solum ad ius civile et canonicum.

---

[58] spectat VM

[59] per *om.* V; *add.* V[2]

IX

Notes on the text of Marsilius of Padua's 'Defensor minor'

The modern editors of Marsilio's 'Defensor pacis' ['DP'] could resort to nearly thirty manuscripts, of which at least one was written in Marsilio's lifetime and stands close to the author's autograph. In contrast, the tradition of 'Defensor minor' ['DM'] is weak. The work survives complete in only a single manuscript, Oxford, Bodleian Library, Canonici misc. 188 [= O], dating from the very end of the fifteenth century. Its first editor, C. K. Brampton in 1922, published what was essentially a transcript of O. This was, I believe, Brampton's first piece of editing. Though he read and copied a difficult manuscript with care and had the benefit of advice from R. Lane Poole and C. W. Previté-Orton, he lacked the aid of the modern editions of 'DP' (Previté-Orton, 1928; R. Scholz, 1932–3). By retaining the punctuation exhibited by O – which there is no guarantee was Marsilio's and certainly is not that of modern times – he made difficulties for his readers, not always resolved by his notes. Above all, he failed to realise how corrupt was his only witness, to which he continued to adhere in his text when considerations of sense or syntax or Marsilio's known modes of expression might have suggested that something had gone wrong. In comparison with the depravity of some fifteenth-century manuscripts, O is by no means a hopeless specimen. But during the century and a half between 'DM''s composition c. 1341 and the writing of O a considerable amount of textual corruption had occurred. Of this some examples were provided by Carlo Pincin in 1967[1].

Unfortunately much the same criticisms apply to the elaborate new edition (1979) of 'DM' offered by Colette Jeudy and Jeannine Quillet, who supplies a French translation 'en face'[2]. O has been read again with meticulous care, and it has been bound possible to correct a few of Brampton's readings; some of Pincin's suggested amendments have been adopted[3]. But in general the text presented shows the same excessive reliance as Bramp-

---

[1] Marsilio (Pubblicazioni dell'Istituto di Scienze Politiche dell'Università di Torino XVII), Turin 1967, 201, n. 1.

[2] C. Jeudy and J. Quillet, Marsile de Padoue. Oeuvres mineures (Éditions du Centre National de la Recherche Scientifique), Paris 1979. The volume also contains Marsilio's 'De translatione imperii' and some related texts. The introduction to 'DM' is at pp. 141–168; text and translation, pp. 170–311.

[3] There is no point in lingering over a few misprints of the kind apt to befall any edition on its way through the press: I 6.5 for *summi* read *sumi*; III 5.11 for *plurimi* read *plurimis*; IV 3.31 for *de aliquid* read *de ea aliquid*; V 11.7 for *salutatem* read *salutem*; XV 5.24 for *hac* read *haec*; XV 8.21–2

ton's on the letter and punctuation of a fallible and defective witness. No doubt, when transcribing a manuscript the old rule *verbatim, litteratim et punctuatim* remains valid. An editor's business does not stop there.

Besides O, we have for about a third of the text of 'DM' a collateral source of evidence. About 1360 a collection of material bearing on Lewis the Bavarian's behaviour concerning the Tirolese marriage imbroglio in 1341–2 was copied into the manuscript now Bremen, Staatliche Bibliothek, cod. lat. b. 35 [= B][4]. Two pieces in this collection, a 'Tractatus super divorcio matrimonii' attributed to Marsilio and what purports to be the formula for an imperial dispensation from the impediment of affinity to the marriage between Lewis of Brandenburg and Margaret Maultasch, show very close relationship to the text of the last four chapters of 'DM'[5]. These pieces, it is now agreed, are posterior to 'DM' from which they must derive[6]. The circumstances under which they were confected remain in some ways obscure, and of course we cannot tell precisely how far they remained verbally faithful to that part of 'DM''s text which they reproduced; though the correspondence seems consistently close, the possibility of an element of conscious rehandling cannot be wholly ruled out. Nevertheless, the copies of these pieces in B had probably been made within twenty years of 'DM' being composed; in time they are thus some 130 years less remote from its original text than O. From its nature, B cannot be accorded the full authority of a direct witness to 'DM'. But for the text of most of chapters XIII–XVI of that work B has considerable value as a control of O. Brampton, who knew the 'Tractatus super divorcio' and 'Forma dispensacionis' only from the seventeenth-century edition in Goldast and mistakenly thought they were anterior to 'DM', made little use of them for textual purposes. Though Jeudy and Quillet have consulted B, and have indeed used it to repair long omissions from O at XIII 9.33–5 and XVI 2.13–16, they could with profit have given greater weight to many of B's variant readings.

Unless hitherto unknown manuscript material comes to light – and that, in view of Jeudy's thorough researches, seems unlikely – we shall never have a really satisfactory text of 'DM'. The conscientious edition of Jeudy and Quillet does not, in my opinion, make the best use of the imperfect material available. Nothing is gained for our understanding of what Marsilio intended to convey in 'DM' by supposing that its text is better based than it is. We must be ready to depart from O's readings more often than the editors of 1922 and 1979 have brought themselves to do. In that conviction the following emendations are offered. More could reasonably have been proposed; not all those put forward will find general acceptance. But perhaps this limited list of suggestions will provoke other scholars into more skilful efforts to better the text of 'DM'[7].

---

omit the repetition of *quae sibi conformiter fieri vel omitti*; XV 10.17 for *tammodo* read *tantummodo*.

[4] Most recently described by JEUDY in her excellent Catalogue des manuscrits, in: Oeuvres mineures, pp. 80–3. But is should be noted that B it not the only ms. to contain 'Informatio de nullitate processuum', as she claims, p. 81, n. 2. It can be found also in cod. lat. Trevirensis 844, whence it was printed by W. FELTEN in 1898. I have given a short account of the Tirolese marriage affair in: Guillelmi de Ockham Opera politica, I, ed. altera (Manchester 1974) 270–272.

[5] Perhaps even to the extent of a common error at DM XIV 2.14; see below.

[6] PINCIN (note 1) showed this conclusively, pp. 202–7; QUILLET agrees, pp. 150–154. PINCIN gave a new edition of the 'Tractatus' at pp. 268–283 and of the 'Forma dispensacionis' at pp. 264–8.

[7] Besides the works mentioned above I have referred to the Italian translation of 'DM' from BRAMPTON's text by C. VASOLI, Marsilio da Padova. Il Difensore Minore, Naples 1975, and two papers by

I 1.5 *quidem*: O's reading, followed by edd. But VASOLI's translation «alcuni» [= *quidam*] is probably right.

I 1.8 *imperatoris*: despite the preference of PINCIN, VASOLI and DOLCINI for *imperatori*, O's reading can stand: «whether in any fashion imperial [i. e. coercive] jurisdiction is due to bishops and priests».

I 4.3-4 *obtinendis*: *omittendis* is to be expected and makes far better sense, as BRAMPTON and VASOLI saw.

I 6.7 punctuate: *status, praeeminentiae vel conditionis.*

I 7.11-12 *ad Romanum principem ... pertinere*: the apparent confusion of *princeps* and *legislator* is untypical and awkward. PREVITÉ-ORTON smelled corruption, and suggested amending: *in quantum legislatoris humani per auctoritatem.* I prefer: *ad Romanum principem, inquantum* [*per*] *humanum legislatorem* [*hab*]*et auctoritatem, solummodo pertinere.*

II 5.4 read: *saeculo,* [*quod*] *praesertim importabile est cuilibet politiae et dudum hactenus fuit, et erit causa.*

II 5.14 *mores*: *moris* seems more likely; *mali moris* is repeatedly used as an adjectival phrase below, XVI 3.

II 6.1-3 read: *ad sacerdotis officium hec (haec) simpliciter non pertineat et regulariter potestas, tamen in casu hec (haec) ipsorum officio conveniret.*

III 4.2-4 O has omitted a word here, and, followed by edd., makes a sad hash of the punctuation, thus obscuring the structure of the argument. Read: *de hoc transibimus, aliquid* [*dicturi*] *ubi de interdicto et excommunicatione dicetur.* [New section] *Tertia conclusio, quae per necessitatem sequitur, est quod ...*; cf. I 6.2; I 7.1; IV 1.1; X 2.1–6.6.

III 7.5 [*quantum*] *ad tributum et censum, concessionem ...* would help the sense.

IV 2.2 BRAMPTON's alternative suggestion of *sacerdotes* seems better than *sacerdot⟨al⟩ibus.*

IV 3.5 add 6, 7 *et* 9 [*secundae*], as BRAMPTON suggests and VASOLI, p. 102, translates.

V 2.1 *quidem*: QUILLET translates as if *quidam* stood in the text; this is probably preferable.

V 2.4 read *tenetur* for the *tamen* in O. VASOLI's translation, p. 105, shows that he has seen this.

V 4.6 if *unumquemque fidelem* in the previous line is correct, one would expect *teneatur* rather than *teneantur.*

V 12.6 *peccatores* rather than *peccatoris,* with the impersonal *poenitet.*

V 13.16 A new sentence should begin with *Consequentia*; cf. *Antecedens* in line 9.

V 13.45-6 *spiritualiter:* should be *specialiter,* in contrast to *indifferenter* in line 39. A common scribal confusion.

V 13.51-3 *et contra*, not *lucretis* marks the end of the gloss, against which Marsilio himself argues: *Nam si peccaverit contra te frater, sive contra proximum te sciente, ipsum corripere debes.* A reference by edd. to Nicolaus de Lira to Matth. 18, 15 would have been relevant.

Carlo DOLCINI, Osservazioni sul Defensor Minor di Marsilio da Padova, in: Atti della Accademia delle Scienze dell'Istituto di Bologna, Rendiconti LXIV (1975–1976) 87–102; and Marsilio contro Ockham. Intorno a una recente edizione del Defensor minor, in: Quaderno della Rubiconia Accademia dei Filopatridi 12 (1980) 1–18. – I am very grateful to J. MIETHKE for allowing me to read in typescript his paper 'Die kleinen politischen Schriften des Marsilius von Padua in neuer Präsentation', see this volume of Mlat. Jb., and for encouraging me to publish my own remarks.
Only after completing these notes could I consult CARLO PINCIN, Storia e Critica di Testi di Marsilio, in: Riv. stor. ital. 93 (1981) 775–94. All the emendations which PINCIN, pp. 792–4, there suggests to the JEUDY/QUILLET text of 'DM' are worth consideration; most of them are convincing. In particular, his suggestion of *sub* for *super* at VIII.3.4 and VIII.4.3 seems clearly right.

V 16.9-10 read: *nisi primum a Deo et aliis, ad quos pertinet, Dei ministris ad hoc auctoritate sacerdotali sibi concessa.*

VIII 3.13 *quando videlicet* would make better sense than *quia videlicet.* Marsilio envisages the possibility of human laws being contrary to divine; see lines 16–17 below.

IX 2.19 *per efficaciam*: JEUDY/QUILLET follow BRAMPTON's rendering of the *efichciam* in O, and VASOLI, p. 130 translates accordingly. But surely this is a corruption of *epieikeiam*, perhaps spelt by Marsilio *epykeiam* or in some similar fashion? In line 38 below there is a reference to '*benigna interpretatio*'. For Marsilio's understanding of the concept *per epieikeiam,* see DP I, XIV. 7 and II, XII. 6.

IX 2.36 *addentes causam*: *addentes tamen* seems more likely; the abbreviations for *tamen* and *causam* were a frequent source of scribal error.

X 2.11 *Et rarius*: this interjection into a straightforward quotation of I Tim. 1,20 is quite meaningless, though both VASOLI, p. 134 and QUILLET have managed to translate it. It is to be rejected as the intrusion of a corrupted gloss. Somewhere along the line of tradition to O the name *Alexander* in the scriptural quotation caught a scribe's eye; facetiously he added *et Darius*; after that, downhill all the way.

X 2.68 *dicitur*: *dicere* or *dictum* would make better sense.

X 5.15-21 PREVITÉ-ORTON, Proc. Brit. Acad. 21 (1935) 177 n. 61, thought the text here «slightly corrupt». But the editors offer no help. Read: *Et dico quo[a]d haereticos aut aliter infideles a consortio fidelium separare, praesertim quantum ad convictum domesticum aut consortium seu contubernium et collocutionem de his, quae pertinent ad ritum fidei conservandum, [quod haeretici] praesertim post.*

XI 3.34 *in modum ad alios divulgata: in mundum* seems simpler and preferable.

XI 3.81-84 by adhering to the punctuation in O the editors have misled the translators, VASOLI, pp. 149–50 and QUILLET. Marsilio regards Christ as the first bishop of Jerusalem, followed in the care of the Church there by a consortium of Peter, James and John, before Peter became bishop at Rome; cf. Gal. 2,9; DP II, XVI. 10. Read: *quoniam princeps pastorum, videlicet Christus, ibidem sedit tamquam episcopus, et apostolorum famosior, cum reliquis duobus famosioribus apostolis, prius quam Romae ibidem rexit.*

XI 3.88 read: *expedienta semper et pro quolibet tempore*: *expedientia similiter* yields no apparent sense.

XII 1.11 *ipsorum*: edd. follow O. But the reference is to *provinciae,* so *ipsarum* seems preferable.

XII 3.6 *unum imperium*: read *verum imperium.* Though QUILLET follows my emendation (Riv. stor. ital. 80 [1968] 1026) in her translation, the JEUDY/QUILLET text continues to follow O. The point at issue was not the unicity of the pagan empire, but its legitimacy.

XII 5.5-6 *Nec obstat paralogismus, quod positiones et divisiones, quo quidam inferunt inducendo*: O calls for amendment. For *quod positiones* read *per compositiones* (palaeographically not improbable, and cf. line 9 below); and *quem*, rather than *quas* with BRAMPTON, for *quo.*

XII 5.8-10 *quoniam licet ... falsa*: O has lost the way in this knotty passage; edd. have not found it. Despite the translators, the subject of the whole sentence is *illatio.* Substituting *certa* for O's *orta* and following edd. with *compositis* for *composita*, read: *quoniam licet in sensu divisio[nis] sit certa in singulis, tamen [de] compositis pronuntiata est falsa.*

XIII 1.5-6 *impediri* would seem to govern *combinari:* «whether or not such persons can be prevented from being joined in marriage for certain causes and by someone's authority?» If so, the translations of QUILLET and VASOLI, p. 157 are inexact.

XIII 2.6-7 *instantia naturarum*: D'ALVERNY is clearly right with the alternative reading: *in scientia naturarum.* Marsilio had used precisely the same phrase DP I, IV.3.

XIII 2.19 *divisione secunda*: probably Marsilio wrote *dictione secunda*, as PINCIN notes, p. 201, n. 1.

XIII 4.3 *spiritualia sunt*: B adds *essentialiter*, and this seems likely.

XIII 4.21 *quos exercent, veluti imperata*: an awkward phrase. B's alternative: *quibus inexistunt veluti paramenta, spiritualia dicta sunt* is not wholly unattractive.

XIII 5.6 *notant*: B's *convenit* seems preferable.

XIII 7.19 *Christus videlicet*: has something of the flavour of a later gloss; B omits.

XIII 9.19 *aperte*: B's *a fratre* is surely superior; cf. Luc. 12,13.

XIII 10.11 *necessitatem*: BRAMPTON hankered after, but did not adopt B's *veritatem*, which he knew from GOLDAST; it seems much the better reading. QUILLET's translation misses Marsilio's point that a double doubt calls for a double enquiry. So does VASOLI's, p. 168.

XIV 2.14 *ad fugiendum vel*: both O and B show this. But *adfligendam ad* makes better sense.

XIV 3.5 read with B: *per quemquam sint tales actus aut opera facta sive omissa*; cf. XIV 1.5–6 above.

XV 2.10 *contrectet*: B's *coartet* is possibly to be preferred.

XV 3.4 *iudicium*: read *iudicem* with B.

XV 3.9 *cum spiritualis non sit essentialiter* with O and edd. would have to refer to *legislator humanus*; *cum spirituales non sint essentialiter* in B relates, more probably, to *actus humani*.

XV 3.33 *docentia:* B's *decentia* is more convincing.

XV 4.1 read *proprie* with B, rather than *propterea* with O and edd.

XV 4.8 *circa spiritualia [seu de ipsis nec circa ipsa temporalia] vel de ipsis* seems the correct reading. Though QUILLET's translation recognises the need to call on B here, the edd. do not.

XV 4.19 *sive temporalia*: Marsilio's gloss; no part of the text of I Cor. 9,11.

XV 5.13-15 The editors do not notice the corruption here. Amend: *Materialis autem causa praeceptorum dictorum una, videlicet homines. [Divinae legis praeceptorum] propinqua materia sunt homines inquantum susceptibiles.*

XV 5.18 *potestatem:* a copyist has erred in extending the abbreviation for the correct reading: *pacem.*

XV 5.21 read: *quemadmodum motus caeli circularis [et] rotae molaris.*

XV 10.5 *secundo* is more difficult than appears from the translations; possibly an abbreviated *vero* has been wrongly extended. The first sentence ends with *signum* in line 4, after which a full stop is necessary. Then read: *Priori vero modo et famoso sumendo sacramentum, pro quibusdam.*

XVI 2.8 *praesertim inter sorores et fratres*: for *inter* B offers a less sensational and perhaps more plausible reading: *infra.*

XVI 2.19-21 The text seems clear, and gave VASOLI, p. 186 no difficulty. But the translation proposed by QUILLET completely misrepresents Marsilio's intention. True to his principles, he says: «It is also proper for the Roman bishop, called pope ... to grant and acknowledge, as truth demands, the same thing» [i.e. that prohibition of marriage between blood relations must be by authority of *legislator humanus* or *principans supremus*].

XVI 4.22-23 *divisione*: as above, XIII 2.19, the correct reading is probably *dictione.*

X

The 'Influence' of Ockham's Political Thinking: The First Century

The belief that intensive study of medieval thinkers can produce results of great interest calls for no defence in a conference such as this. But the enthusiasm necessary to sustain the labour of discovering, deciphering and comparing medieval texts carries with it some dangers. Possibly a student today, if suitably equipped, can sometimes grapple with the thought of this or that fourteenth-century scholar more closely than many of the scholar's contemporaries could have done. Yet he is exposed to a danger: the temptation to be prejudiced towards the significance of the author on whom his efforts have been spent. From the philosopher's point of view, of course, he may turn out to be right in his evaluation. Historians however are bound to see the matter somewhat differently. For them the medieval author's contribution in the context of his own times is one problem; he poses different ones in the context, say, of the Enlightenment or of the twentieth century. What justifies repeating this banal distinction is that in practice the lines so often do get blurred. In 1949, for example, Bertrand Russell could utter about Ockham perhaps the most unhistorical remarks to be made about him since Diderot's *Encyclopédie* in 1765.[1] The immediacy and force of the impact made by pieces of fourteenth-century political or publistic writing need careful weighing in terms of their own and proximate times: for historians this issue is not to be prejudged by modern conclusions, however philosophically justifiable, about the pieces' intrinsic merits as expressions of thought. That is to say, historians wish to know how political treatises were disseminated and published in the later middle ages, and by whom they were read. Only then can it be estimated how influential they were in shaping thinking about politics, in comparison, for instance, with the everyday books from which lawyers and theologians learned their trades, or with calculated manifestos in pictorial or plastic art which could be guaranteed a wider, if not always comprehending audience. Much progress in investigating these problems has been made during the last decade; if I single out for mention Jürgen Miethke's many notable papers, it is because I owe much to them.[2] Thus the general direction of the present communication is not particularly novel. It aims to throw into an already current discussion some considerations focussed on Ockham's political writings viewed historically during the century following his death. How 'influential' were they in that period, within what limits did they come to be so at all?

About those writings and their author discussion continues tirelessly. Scholars are still – and perhaps always will be – far from general agreement about what characterized Ockham as a political thinker. Quite recently Francis E. Kelley, echoing an old phrase of Ernest Jacob's, referred to Ockham's 'stand as a constitutional liberal'.[3] On the other hand, in 1979 another transatlantic scholar esteemed Ockham in his political and social thinking as a 'backward-looking, bookish traditionalist'.[4] Neither of these statements is inept; possibly they could be reconciled more readily than appears at first sight. But I have no wish to attempt that now. The suggestion which this paper will seek to canvass is that the route by which Ockham came to his reputation and influence as a thinker about society and politics was to a considerable extent adventitious. Primarily, both in time and intention, he was a philosopher with a marked bent towards logic, and a theologian. Judgement of how original or profound Ockham was as a logician must be left to experts in this subject. What seems accepted is that in his *Summa logicae* he produced 'the first attempt to present the whole of logic, including medieval novelties, in one systematic exposition'.[5] The number of surviving manuscripts attests the popularity of this textbook; by 1974 sixty-five had been identified, seven of them written during the author's lifetime.[6] That is a far stronger tradition than can be shown for the logical works, however meritorious, of such contemporaries as Richard Campsall.[7] As late as 1675 that strange character Obadiah Walker brought out a new edition of the *Summa logicae* at Oxford; perhaps it was only the appearance sixteen years later of Aldrich's *Artis logicae compendium* which prevented Ockham's *Summa* becoming synonymous with the teaching of logic in Oxford down to the nineteenth century, as Aldrich's book did.[8] It does not seem extravagant to suggest that Ockham was chiefly known both to contemporaries and to succeeding generations in the universities as the author of the clearest and most convenient introduction to the indispensable tool which logic provided for their activities. Compared with his *Summa logicae* even his *Commentary on the Sentences* was less widely diffused; a bare score of manuscripts of his *Ordinatio* of the commentary's first book survive.[9]

That Ockham's reputation should mainly have rested on this sort of basis is by no means unfair. For he leaves little impression of having been interested by temperament in any wide range of political or social enquiry. He did indeed become tolerably acquainted with Aristotle's *Politics* and *Ethics*, and at times leaned heavily on them – for example in book ii of the first treatise of *Dialogus* part III.[10] But lecturing on moral philosophy seems to have begun comparatively late in the mendicant *studia*; not till after 1315 was Galvano Fiamma, O.P., put in charge of a course for the Dominicans at Milan, in which he commented on the *Ethics, Politics* and *Rhetoric* of Aristotle, as well as the pseudo-Aristotelian

Economica and John Holywood's *Sphaera.*[11] Perhaps Ockham was of rather too early a generation to have heard or to have been called upon to give formal instruction in this field within Franciscan *studia*. Nothing of his about such matters has survived at all comparable with works by contemporary seculars such as Walter Burley's *Commentary on the Politics* or Conrad of Megenberg's planned triple disquisition on ethics, economics and politics.[12] It rather looks as if Ockham resorted seriously to the Aristotelian *Politics* and *Ethics* only pretty late in his career as polemicist: somewhere about 1339 or 1340, after such works as I *Dialogus, Contra Benedictum* and *An princeps* had been written. At most, it might be argued that earlier on the weight he laid in *Opus Nonaginta Dierum* upon the distinction between *ius poli* and *ius fori* indicated a willingness, at any rate for polemical purposes, to differentiate between morality and positive law, between ethics and politics.

Of course, when they wanted to, scholastics often did contrive to introduce discussion about politics and the ordering of society into works of which the avowed purpose was very different. We know, for instance, that in the late twelfth century theological discourse provided to Peter the Chanter and his circle ample opportunity to air their social and economic views.[13] One of the most valuable quarries for John of Jandun's ideas about politics – if we are not prepared to take as seriously as perhaps we should his right to be recognised as co-author of *Defensor pacis* – is offered by his *Questions on the Metaphysics.*[14] Part of the substance of Durand of Saint-Pourçain's 'political' treatise *De origine iurisdictionum* had already appeared in his *Commentary on the Sentences.*[15] From late in the fourteenth century comes the example of Henry of Langenstein, who worked pieces of his lengthy commentary on Genesis into his enquiry into the problem of perpetual rent-charges, to form the second part of that *Tractatus bipartitus de contractibus* which has been praised as one of the most lively and informative contributions to economics and moral theology produced by a medieval scholar.[16] Equally well-known is the way in which three generations before Langenstein such secular masters at Paris as Godfrey of Fontaines and Henry of Ghent had used the academic exercise of the *Quodlibeta* to bring under survey a wide range of socio-political questions.[17]

With Ockham there is little or no sign of such self-indulgence. His seven *Quodlibeta* betray no interest at all in problems other than those of philosophic theology;[18] his other philosophical and theological writings are for the most part barren of even incidental social or political comment. It seems certain that he had watched sheep attentively;[19] on the other hand, his sympathies with humankind are well concealed. He claimed that he arrived at Avignon in 1324 as a political innocent, and though he admitted having learned much about human nature during the next four years before he fled with Michael of Cesena to join the excommunicate emperor Lewis, it is hard to believe that by 1328, or indeed at any time, he achieved much understanding of his fellow-men.[20] Evidence of warmth and empathy for the human condition is hard to come by. If he accepts that the unlearned, those without Latin, may sometimes excel in intellectual power, he does not envisage their dispensing with expert aid.[21] His real opinion comes out, one feels, when he quotes with approval the canon *Docendus*: 'the people are there to be taught, not followed'.[22] Though he was willing to argue that the faith of the Universal Church could if necessary be saved in children below the age of reason, that was an essentially theological, not a political position. But did he not state that the secular ruler derived his temporal power from the community *(populus)* acting as God's intermediary? Indeed he did, frequently.[23] Here however he was dealing with a problem which the commentators of Roman civil law, needing to cope with that legal construction which the *lex regia* represented, could not escape confronting; the solution he adopted did not differ basically from theirs, nor from that propounded a generation earlier by John of Paris.[24] Following in the best scholastic tradition, he was far from unmindful of the common good; he recognised that those private property rights he valued so highly must at times be limited by the exigencies of the public interest.[25] But he was certainly no 'democrat' and would have no truck whatever with the view that majority decisions were necessarily right or binding.[26] There is no reason to disbelieve what he wrote at the end of his life in the prologue to *De imperatorum et pontificum potestate*: 'I shall feel no shame at all to be vanquished by truth, but not by mass opinion ... since the crowd *(multitudo)* most commonly gets things wrong.'[27] Ockham was in fact a highly professional scholar, a willing prisoner of his own élitism. He stood apart from that movement toward popularized scholasticism which has attracted attention in recent decades: the tendency, discernible from about the middle of the fourteenth century, to substitute the catechetical and practical for the dogmatic and speculative, and the vernacular for school Latin.[28] Nothing indicates that he ever undertook anything comparable to Conrad of Megenberg's renderings from Thomas of Cantimpré and Bartholomew the Englishman in his *Buch der Natur*, or to Conrad's version in his *Deutsche Sphaera* of John Holywood's Latin treatise on the globe. Not for Ockham the bandwaggon of popular science nor of philosophy made available for those without Latin.

Less than might be expected changed during the twenty years after 1328 when Ockham in exile concentrated so much of his energy on polemics against the Avignon popes. What gave force to that formidable spate of more than a million words was not expansive breadth in choice of subject or in incidental reference. It was much more an obsessive thoroughness in attack on a short series of narrow fronts. Ockham's polemical writings are thin in social comment; it would be difficult to quarrel with Georges de Lagarde's harsh verdict: 'This defender of empirical knowledge shows a total failure to understand the reality of an evolving social life.'[29] In part that failure may have been rooted in Ockham's attitude towards the past, in which yearning was combined with what we would call ignorance. On occasion he can be found undertaking what might be called a minor piece of genuine historical research: in *Octo Quaestiones*, for instance, where to demonstrate his point that emperors can create their successors he appears to have ransacked the universal histories for examples between the first and seventh centuries A.D.[30] But he can hardly be credited with anything recognisable in modern terms as a sense of history. Like many of his contemporaries he displayed as a matter of conviction, not just as a response to the needs of dialectic, the archaic belief that the empire over which Lewis the Bavarian presided so uneasily was the direct and effective inheritor of Augustan Rome. That was the principle on which rested his advisory memorandum at the end of 1341 defending Lewis's right to dispense from the impediment of consanguinity the proposed marriage between Lewis of Brandenburg and Margaret Maultasch of Tirol. Brian Tierney's reminder how little the claims of historical reality affected mendicant polemical writing during Ockham's lifetime is not unjustified.[31]

'Un uomo senza fervore, tutta testa, niente cuore':[32] impossible as it is to agree wholly with the novelist, probably he comes nearer the mark than do the liberation theologians. The mean folly of denigrating the sincerity of Ockham's personal religion because of disagreement with his theological opinions is now, it is to be hoped, a thing of the past. Yet it must be granted that he hardly placed the sacraments at the heart of religious life;[33] he showed only hostile incomprehension for the most significant religious current in the Germany of his time: the teachings of Master Eckhart in their relation to mysticism in the Rhineland.[34] In common with other scholastics Ockham found difficulty in allowing particular experience of his mundane environment to break through that 'high wall of intellectual abstraction and aloofness' which has been claimed as so characteristic a feature in medieval philosophers.[35] In his case that breakthrough of experience remained imperfect. When he came to touch on actualities of his times – for example, on the disordered condition of Italy, or the claims of the king over church property in England – it was not in an especially novel or enlightening fashion.[36] Apart from his warfare with Avignon popes, current circumstances engaged his interest only exceptionally. When they did, the result is sometimes discouraging. In chapter 3 of *Opus Nonaginta Dierum* he is to be found attaching to the *palea Eiciens* in Gratian's *Decretum* a lengthy excursus about usury.[37] Wordy, repetitive and dull, it does not go beyond insisting on the distinction between *mutuum* and *locatio* which had long been a common opinion among the canonists and had been well known to the masters at Paris *c.* 1200.[38] In terms of the economic realities of the 1330s it was out of date. It was out of date too in the light of thinking within Ockham's own order. Alexander of Alexandria, O.F.M., who died as Minister General in 1314 not long after completing his treatise on usury, had helped to make exchange transactions respectable and legitimate by classing *cambium* as *permutatio* rather than as *mutuum*, so breaching an awkward barrier to the development of banking.[39] Why, having so little relevant or new to contribute to this well-worn topic, did Ockham choose to dilate on it? Perhaps for a personal, practical reason. As a licensed confessor, he will have needed to clear his own mind about the sin of usury;[40] the excursus in *Opus Nonaginta Dierum* may reflect his ponderings on the subject a dozen years earlier. Despite the agitated times in which he lived notably little originality or enterprise marks Ockham's approach to many of the tired *topoi* of the papo-imperial debate – the Two Swords, the Translation of the Empire, the Kingship of Christ, and so forth – though possibly a scrap of specifically English experience may show when he argues that Christ never concerned himself with the business of a secular king 'because He did not hold parliaments and courts ...'.[41] In Ockham's political thinking what is explosive is the compound rather than the elements. For him the ordinary functions of the lay ruler were essentially negative, restrictive, punitive; we are not far away from the tradition of Isidore of Seville.[42]

Of course, the ecclesiological themes predominated: the nature of the Church, the structure of the Church, the government of the Church, and above all the problem of the pope's power in the Church. No longer is it respectable to say that Ockham rejected papal *plenitudo potestatis*. He was in fact not at all concerned to reject the concept, but rather to show what he thought it ought to mean. This has proved a stumbling-block for those who have imagined that fullness of power meant absolutely unlimited power, so that when the phrase was used about the pope it implied that he could do whatsoever he pleased. For they have been puzzled by the spectacle of Ockham, undeniably an eminent logician, committed for a dozen years to the apparently illogical enterprise of trying to define how short of full fullness ought to be. It did not seem an illogical enterprise to Ockham, any more than it did to contemporary opponents whose views are classed as highly pro-papal. To a greater or less extent they shared in the same endeavour.[43] Where he differed from them was in the intensity of his aversion from anything like wholly unfettered power in fallible human hands. The concept of papal fullness of power had to be accepted, as a matter of Revelation; Ockham's task, as he saw it, was the delicate one of defining that concept in terms which would permit its necessary truth to be useful while precluding possibilities of harmful excess. Judgements about how far he was successful will always differ. To those who wish to appreciate the subtlety of the position he reached a careful reading of *Octo Quaestiones* i.7 is commended. There, as the result of an elaborately qualified definition of papal *plenitudo potestatis*, he perhaps came nearest to delimiting the functions within a Christian society which should ordinarily be exercised by the pope and those remaining for ordinary exercise by the lay ruler. If Ockham's political writings – in contrast, it would seem, to Wyclif's – can still claim to have something to offer to modern theorists, it is chiefly because they investigate so unremittingly questions about the distribution and limitation of governmental power.[44]

Why was Ockham so obsessed by this problem of the pope's power? Was it, as he himself would have us believe, because as a faithful Franciscan he was shattered by what he regarded as John XXII's heretical constitutions prejudicial to his order's and his own convictions about Evangelical Poverty?[45] Alternatively, did the obsession spring from lower levels: from the injured arrogance of a self-righteous, self-confident Oxonian, appalled at the prospect of finding some of his own theological conclusions being censured at the Curia, with the result that he might be forced to shuffle or recant? Outright choice of either alternative would probably hinder rather than help understanding. Ockham certainly shared with some of his fellow Franciscans firm belief in the abiding validity of Nicholas III's constitution *Exiit qui seminat* in determining the relations between Evangelical Poverty and the Franciscan Order. So inflexibly did he hold this belief that in defending it he got himself into a position in which, it has been plausibly contended, he might by inference be considered a proponent of papal infallibility. But Tierney's adroit argumentation does not, in my opinion, reach the essential Ockham; never was there a man less likely to admit the infallibility of any human being.[46] Decision whether principle or pride or some combination of both gave the impulse to Ockham's polemical treatises would be possible only if we knew far more about his psychological temperament than we can hope to learn. Hints from the substance and the tone of his writings may help a little, but hard evidence is difficult to find, for all that in his *Commentary on the Sentences* he undertook serious philosophical discussion of psychological themes such as love, pleasure and volition.[47] He seems to have lacked the ordinary antidotes to self-regard: there is no humour in his writing, only very occasionally a piece of heavy-footed jocosity.[48] He had no literary grace: *Defuit ei rhetorica*, as Luther justly remarked.[49]

However it is to be explained, Ockham's obsession glares out at us from the polemical works. Personal insecurity and fear may have had a part in making it inveterate. It ought not to be forgotten that he composed all these works between 1330 and 1347 as an alien refugee in Germany, under the pressures inherent in that predicament, and well aware that his protector, the emperor Lewis, was engaged almost continuously from 1331 to 1345 in negotiations for his own reconciliation with Ockham's enemies at Avignon.[50] That may help to explain the shrill importunity to be sensed underlying those wearisome, repetitious lists of 'errors' which proved to Ockham's satisfaction that John XXII and his successors were heretics. The lists are nearly always there, clogging up the discourse by their length; vital though they may be to the author's assumptions, they do become an intolerable bore. They are there in the *Epistola ad fratres*, in *Contra Ioannem*, in *Contra Benedictum*, in *Compendium errorum*, in *Octo Quaestiones*; they still appear in what must surely have been Ockham's last work, *De imperatorum et pontificum potestate*.[51] If *An princeps* and *Breviloquium* survive only as incomplete texts, one is almost tempted to suppose that this is not because Ockham left them so, but because originally they continued with similar lists, which later scribes shirked copying. No wonder that the manuscript tradition of all these treatises, except *Octo Quaestiones*, is so woefully exiguous.

There seem, then, good grounds for claiming that Ockham's activity as a polemicist should be considered secondary to his vocation as philosopher and theologian: almost a deviation from his natural course, though one which preoccupied most (probably not quite all) of his intellectual energy during the last twenty years of his life.[52] What, other than a ready-made reputation, did the polemicist owe to the philosopher and theologian? Rather sadly one has to admit that valiant efforts to show that Ockham's political and social ideas were determined by his philosophical positions seem to have run into a dead end. For what is *a priori* an attractive view only narrow and unsubstantial evidence has been produced. It amounts to little more than Ockham's obdurate rejection of a short passage in John XXII's *Quia quorundam* arguing that the Franciscans enjoyed *usus iuris* in their goods because their order was not a true but an imaginary person.[53] The methodology which seeks automatically to derive differing views about government from divergencies in metaphysical systems has come under lively attack; there has been much skepticism about the need or possibility of deducing Ockham's socio-political attitudes at all directly from his philosophical presuppositions.[54] On the other hand it would be silly to suggest that round about the year 1328 Ockham's brain underwent some sort of drastic leucotomy, so that the mind henceforward mainly concentrating on polemics was not the mind which in earlier years had been exercised in philosophy and theology. As Stephen McGrade assures us, 'we may still look to specific aspects of Ockham's metaphysics, epistemology ... or logic for at least a partial explanation of various points in his polemical works'; quite recently profitable enquiry along these lines has been made in two theses from Bologna.[55] Moreover, to take a different level of approach, it may well have been the practical fears of a controversial theologian in a hostile world which spurred Ockham to those efforts at autodidacticism in the study of canon law which surface so remarkably in his political works.[56]

It is true that, though Ockham's discourse always claimed to be based on rational argument, there are notably few places in the polemical writings where the school logician is so much to the forefront that the text is not intelligible without an expert understanding of logical technicalities; in the whole of *Dialogus* no more than three passages come readily to mind.[57] Yet it is still proper to emphasise that Ockham the logician was important to the career of the polemicist in at least three ways. First, as McGrade says, because Ockham's 'political works resulted partly from a way of looking at things which came quite naturally to a logician whose preferred response to general propositions was to search for adequate individual equivalents to them'. In the face of possible contingencies, the vastly complicated world of individuals is impatient of absolute and invariable solutions.[58] Secondly, the logician infected the polemicist with that relentless energy in argument which takes every discussion through to the ultimate conceivable position, however unlikely or ridiculous that may appear. No one can have consulted any of Ockham's major political writings without recognising the trait. One well-known example will suffice: the line of argument in book v of part I of *Dialogus*. Christ's promises assure us that the Christian faith shall not fail. Does this mean that the pope cannot fall into heresy? No. Does it mean that the college of cardinals cannot fall into heresy? No. Or a general council or every member of the clerical body? No. Or – by this time after 36 folio pages of print we have reached chapter 36 – all male Christians? No: for the Christian faith can be saved in women, as it was in Mary at the time of Christ's Passion (a proposition, of course, not peculiar to Ockham or his time: he could have found it in Bonaventura or Alexander of Hales or the decretists).[59] But among the whole multitude of rational Christian men and women is someone necessarily immune from error? A final 'No' marks the end of the line: Christ's promise that the Christian faith shall persist can be saved in baptized infants not yet capable of using reason.[60] There is the *jusqu'auboutisme* of the true logician. The third way in which the logician was important to the polemicist has been suggested earlier in this paper: Ockham the writer on politics was carried into public notice mainly on the back of Ockham the philosopher and theologian. The reputation he won by the non-political works, particularly his writings on logic, eventually, in the right conjuncture, ensured him readers for at least some of the polemics.

What was the right conjuncture? When and in what circumstances did Ockham come to be at all widely read as a commentator on government and politics? No doubt, within restricted academic circles, books and ideas could travel fast in the fourteenth century.[61] All the same, there is some danger of exaggerating the speed with which publistic writings became widely known and available. In 1324, we are asked to believe, Marsilio of Padua's *Defensor pacis* 'burst like a bomb'.[62] But it seems quite likely that only extracts from it had as yet become known at Avignon when John XXII condemned it in October 1327.[63] No mention was made of Marsilio or his doctrines during the great debate on Church-State relations at Vincennes in December 1329 and January 1330.[64] From 1330 onwards, whenever Marsilio's path chanced to cross Ockham's in Munich, we may guess, if we like, that they spat blood at each other; but it was not until the very late 1330s or early 1340s that Ockham can be shown to have concerned himself at all deeply with the text of *Defensor pacis*, though probably both Alvarus Pelagius and Pierre Roger had tackled it before then.[65] The doctrine of *Defensor* may have affected the form of Lewis the Bavarian's coronation as emperor in 1328; but Marsilio was present in Rome at the time and could have exerted his influence in person. There was a translation of *Defensor* into French (now lost), earlier than the Italian version of 1363 which was based on it.[66] Yet in the early 1350s Conrad of Megenberg was complaining that he still had been unable to acquire a copy of *Defensor pacis*.[67] If this notorious book can be said to have burst like a bomb, the bomb had a longish time-fuse. The dates of most of the thirty or so surviving manuscripts point to the conclusion that the *Defensor* became well enough known to be influential not far short of a century later than 1324, during the conciliar debates engendered by the outbreak of the Great Schism.[68]

The progress into public notice of Ockham's independent polemical works – as distinct from those cooperative efforts by the group of Michaelist dissidents at Munich to which presumably he contributed[69] – seems no less tardy. Here the contrast with the rapid impression made by some of his philosophical and theological writings is striking. Possibly even they failed to awaken much immediate resonance in Oxford.[70] But certainly it was a different story at Paris. There apprehensions by the regent masters in Arts, especially those belonging to the English-German nation, about the spread of *scientia Okamica* resulted between 1339 and 1341 in statutes against it and the *secta Occanica* formed by its neophytes.[71] The target of the prohibitions, it has been suggested, was Ockham's teaching on physics, which involved a reinterpretation of the Aristotelian categories; neither his theology nor logic came into question.[72] In any case, the prohibitions were short-lived and had little or no appreciable effect on Ockham's popularity at Paris. Scholars possessed and studied the *Summa logicae*. Even if we ought not to assume that Ockham invented Terminist logic or was alone in using its techniques, his intellectual influence was undeniably extensive and powerful at Paris during the 1340s.[73] Early in the next decade the conservatively minded Conrad of Megenberg was raging against the vogue of Ockhamist 'modernism' at his old university.[74] Despite attempts at counterattack, the *via moderna* (perhaps we should more properly say Terminism), imbued to a greater or less extent with Ockham's methods and ideas, continued to prevail at Paris, if not wholly without interruptions, until late in the fifteenth century.[75]

On the other hand there are few early traces of the diffusion of Ockham's polemical writings. By 1343 Abbot John of Viktring in Carinthia knew of Part I of *Dialogus* and quoted its prologue, though significantly he immediately went on to refer to Ockham's prowess as a logician.[76] Soon after 1356 a short summary of *Dialogus* taken from the prologues of Parts I and III was transcribed in a manuscript of German provenance.[77] By 1376 a copy of *Octo Quaestiones* had become available in France to the compiler of the *Somnium viridarii*; the lengthy borrowings he made from it were not acknowledged, and they continue to cause confusion even today.[78] At about the same date Pierre d'Ailly made his abbreviation of as much of *Dialogus* as he could find, while a few years later, perhaps between 1378 and 1381, the English Benedictine and later cardinal Adam Easton composed a rebuttal (now lost) of *Dialogus* and knew of another of Ockham's political treatises, possibly *De imperatorum et pontificum potestate*.[79] But the fact cannot be burked: for the most part the tradition of Ockham's polemical works is thin and late. It was known or suspected that they existed, but they were hard to come by, so that *c.* 1390 the Wycliffite author of the *Opus arduum* could accuse the friars of having deliberately hidden away Ockham's anti-papal writings together with other contentious works.[80] Leaving out of account a couple of treatises whose authenticity is very doubtful, for six out of the eleven acceptable polemical works no more than a single manuscript is known, while three of the eleven are incomplete.

Only for two works are the surviving manuscripts at all numerous, and even then they are mostly late. Perhaps it is too soon to talk with complete confidence about the tradition of *Dialogus*, further investigation of which may be hoped to throw fresh light on the problems how that massive work was designed, reshaped and eventually cobbled together.[81] But it is worth remark that the copy which Peter of Luna acquired between 1375 and 1393, which formed part of his travelling library when he was Pope Benedict XIII, did not contain the most controversial section of the whole work: the first treatise of Part III, *De potestate papae et cleri*.[82] The version used by Pierre d'Ailly in making his *Abbreviatio* was deficient in the same way.[83] While Jean Courtecuisse, when composing *c.* 1375 the *quaestio* later to be called *Tractatus de fide et ecclesia, Romano pontifice et concilio generali*, clearly made considerable resort to Ockham, both to *Dialogus* and the *Commentary on the Sentences*, his borrowings from the former were confined to Part I; it does not appear that he knew Part III at all.[84] Indeed, in as full a form as has been available in print from 1476 onwards *Dialogus* is now known only in a single manuscript, written as late as *c.* 1460.[85] About the manuscripts of *Octo Quaestiones* there is little need for reserve. Of the thirteen I have examined, at most five can be referred to the fourteenth century. No manuscript of *Octo Quaestiones* has come to light which can be securely dated earlier than a generation after Ockham's death. The inference seems inescapable: not until the period of the Great Schism and the subsequent councils – say between 1380 and 1440 – did *Octo Quaestiones* achieve an appreciable measure of diffusion, other than as an unacknowledged source pillaged by the compiler of *Somnium viridarii*.[86]

Scholars turned to earlier authors to seek from them what was useful to themselves. The textual history of Ockham's *An princeps* illustrates the point. He wrote this treatise, probably in 1338 or 1339, to defend Edwards III's right to tax the English churches, even despite papal prohibition, for the needs of his war against Philip of Valois. *An princeps* was long thought to survive only in a single manuscript, datable to 1411, whose scribe used an exemplar which had already been truncated. In 1963, however, another witness for the text of *An princeps* came to light in a manuscript at Balliol College, Oxford; it was a rewriting of the treatise, rather than an accurate transcription. This manuscript too comes from the early fifteenth century; for the most part it comprises a collection of writings concerning the Great Schism, perhaps put together by someone close to the entourage of Benedict XIII.[87] Its version of *An princeps* has some value for establishing the text. But it is even more significant as an illustration of how a later age was prepared to attend to its own preoccupations at the cost of discarding much of the author's original intentions. For this rehandling was done by someone not at all interested in Edward III's financial problems at the beginning of the Hundred Years War, the discussion of which he mostly leaves out. His great concern is to preserve what Ockham had said in general about the question of papal power. In the circumstances of the early 1400s that for him was the relevance of *An princeps*, and he treated the text accordingly.

The extent to which the tradition of Ockham's polemical writings depends on the interest taken in them during the period of the Schism and the councils has its ironies. For that age could not hope to resolve its troubles by taking over from Ockham some perfected theory of conciliar superiority. He had no such theory to offer, as an impressive consensus of scholarly opinion during the last thirty years has stressed.[88] Some care needs to be taken, of course, to distinguish here between Ockham's own views and those expounded in the cooperative works of the whole group of Franciscan dissidents at Munich, in which he figured alongside Michael of Cesena, Henry of Talheim, Francis of Ascoli and Bonagratia of Bergamo. In the late 1320s and early 1330s that group, under the pressure of political events and probably much under the influence of Bonagratia, did perhaps work out something like a coherent theory of conciliar superiority in the government of the Church. But though Ockham's name was sometimes associated with the group's manifestos, and like other members he borrowed freely for his own writings from a common stock of arguments and references, his own flirtations with conciliarism were unimportant. In Lagarde's words: 'among Ockham's preoccupations the general council holds only a passing and secondary place.'[89] Ockham had little to offer by way of prescriptive doctrine for the practical problems which had become acute in 1378.

Mistaken belief that he had such a doctrine was by no means universal. Long before modern times some readers of Ockham had regretted his lack of true conciliar conviction; others had found in him material for anti-conciliar argument. For an illustration of how Ockham's very limited enthusiasm for conciliar authority needed to be supplemented to meet the views of a Gallican traditionalist, we need look no further than the exposition of his *Octo Quaestiones* composed at Paris by Jacques Almain *c.* 1512.[90] Finding in Ockham's discussion of whether it is licit to appeal from the pope's judgement no mention of conciliar power except a glancing reference to the case of an heretical pope,[91] Almain felt obliged to supply the deficiency: 'And this is the conclusion which all the doctors of Paris and other Frenchmen hold, that the power of the pope is subject to the power of the council.' He took his stand on the declaration of the Vth session of Constance, which he quoted; appeal from the pope lies to the council, he may be judged by the council and deposed by the council.[92] Only by such distorting reinforcement could Ockham's ideas be dragged into some approximation to Gallican theory. On the other hand, resort might be made to Ockham in order to counter extreme conciliar claims. An anonymous pamphleteer *c.* 1395 wished to throw doubt on an opinion alleged to be held by the University of Oxford that the right way to end the Schism was by a general council, 'because some say that a general council is God on earth'. To deflate this pretention the pamphleteer simply appropriated, without attribution, some lengthy extracts from book v of *Dialogus* Part I.[93] Ockham's polemical writings were compendious and various enough to serve diverse and sometimes contradictory purposes.

Here is at least some of the reason why learned men turned increasingly to them in the decades after the outbreak of the Schism. If it is true that *c.* 1400 western Europeans became less afraid of disorder than of the pressure exerted on them by official superiors, such a change in climate would favour the growth of Ockham's influence: claim to excessive power by human authority was his bugbear.[94] Above all, men equipped to read him found in his lengthy disquisitions an almost inexhaustible warehouse of material for their contemporary debates: little may have been definitely determined, but scarcely any issue had been left untouched – and that by a master whose philosophical and theological writings had been potent in the formation of many of them. The interminable details of the two major theological debates which burdened so much of his polemical writing soon lost topical interest. Controversy about the retardation of the Beatific Vision and associated problems, heated in the early 1330s, was rapidly tidied up after John XXII's death, not to become urgent again till the time of the Council of Florence in the fifteenth century.[95] Though the dispute about Evangelical Poverty had in it substance of perennial interest, John XXII had handled the practical consequences with such determined skill as to spare his immediate successors much trouble. Only among those poor, harrassed enthusiasts, the Fraticelli of central Italy, can interest in *Opus nonaginta dierum* be discerned lingering on into the third quarter of the fourteenth century.[96] Of course, it would be wholly mistaken to believe that these disputes had not decisively shaped Ockham himself as a polemicist. But later generations could and did read him without paying them much, if any, attention.[97] They found plenty of other matter in the treatises to interest them.

The codicological evidence is persuasive: by 1450 more than a few learned men had been exposed to the influence of Ockham's political treatises. To affirm or deny that this or that particular author was directly influenced by Ockham's ideas is, however, a delicate business. 'Direct influence' is not always easy to define or establish. It can be exercised by attraction, and is then sometimes manifested in more or less crass pillaging and repetition by the later writer of his predecessor's ideas and language. Influence in this sense, for example, affected some of the literary relationship between Jean Courtecuisse and Ockham.[98] On the other hand, one author can arouse in another the sort of revulsion which provokes the latter to an effort of systematic refutation; it is not unreasonable to say that Dante's influence led Guido Vernani of Rimini to write *De reprobatione Monarchie*. Between these extremes innumerable intermediate positions are possible, varying degrees of acceptance or rejection or a combination of both attitudes. What identifies 'direct influence', I suggest, is less often large-scale reproduction or reprobation of the earlier author by his successor than evidence that the latter has taken the former seriously and paid him knowledgeable attention. Even if Pierre d'Ailly's ecclesiastico-political works did not show resort to Ockham's writings (as they do abundantly), the fact that d'Ailly composed for himself an abbreviation of *Dialogus* would sufficiently establish that he was directly influenced by Ockham.[99] In contrast, John Wyclif exhibits so scanty and vague an acquaintance with Ockham's polemical writings that a direct influence of them on him can be discounted.[100] Clearly, we must be careful about imputing 'influence'. But also about denying it. This communication may fitly end by examining an over-confident assertion that a particular fifteenth-century scholar did not come under the 'direct influence' of Ockham's thought.

Werner Krämer's study of conciliar thought at Basle naturally found much to say about John of Segovia, the council's historian and intellectually one of its most powerful members. Krämer was especially eager to refute a charge in the bull *Etsi non dubitemus* (April 1441) in which Pope Eugenius IV claimed that his opponents at the council had formed their impious views under the malign influence of such notoriously heterodox thinkers as Marsilio of Padua, John of Jandun and William of Ockham.[101] In a special excursus Krämer attempted to exculpate the fathers at Basle from this accusation; he devoted much of it to discussing whether John of Segovia was in fact 'directly' influenced by Ockham.[102] His flatly negative answer, I shall argue, is contradicted by the evidence he himself produced.

John is known to have owned a copy of Ockham's *Dialogus*.[103] Scholars can own books without reading them very hard or indeed at all, though perhaps not many in the fifteenth century could afford to keep manuscripts they did not intend to use. On Krämer's own showing, John made at least a couple of references in his writings to Part I of *Dialogus*.[104] He was also acquainted with *Octo Quaestiones*, as Krämer revealed by printing for the first time a series of excerpts from question i of Ockham's work made by John himself and surviving in his own hand at Salamanca.[105] The extent of John's engagement with Ockham's thought shown by these excerpts deserves scrutiny.

The first of the eight questions canvassed by Ockham is whether supreme spiritual power and supreme lay power are so essentially opposed that no one man is capable of exercising both at the same time. About this Ockham offers three opinions, with arguments for each. The first denies the possibility of the two supremacies being united; the two powers are so different in nature that it is formally impossible for them both to fall into the same hands simultaneously.

The second opinion holds that the two powers can and do belong to the same man, i.e. the pope; he is supreme in spirituals, and in temporals has as much power as or even greater power than the emperor or any other layman. The third opinion steers a middle course. While exercise of the two supreme powers does not habitually pertain to the same man, nor ought it to, this results not from their formal incompatibility, but rather from God's ordinance and divine law; on occasion, indeed, the holder of supreme spiritual power can also exercise supreme temporal power, though in the ordinary course of events he does not do so. Though Ockham never determines this question explicitly, his preference for the third opinion can be inferred from the question's structure. He propounds arguments for the first opinion in chapter 1; for the second in chapter 2; for the third in chapters 3 and 4. Chapter 5 presents arguments in favour of the third opinion against those alleged for the first; then follow twelve chapters (6–17) refuting the case for the second opinion in favour of the third. Only in chapters 18 and 19 are earlier arguments militating against the second opinion answered; the final chapter does what it can to defend the first opinion against objections against it made in chapters 2 and 3.

John of Segovia made his excerpts from only the first six chapters of *Octo Quaestiones* i, together with a single sentence from chapter 7. Comparison of the excerpts with Ockham's text does credit to his accurate understanding of his source.[106] He combined literal transcription with a good deal of paraphrase and abbreviation, but ventured to add little that was not in the original;[107] he showed himself very well able to follow Ockham's sometimes complex and subtle argumentation.[108] Beyond doubt he had earnestly studied at least that part of *Octo Quaestiones* i from which his excerpts have survived.

Krämer felt it necessary to belittle this indication of John's interest in Ockham's work. For this purpose he adduced the *Repetitio de superioritate et excellentia supremae potestatis ecclesiasticae et spiritualis ad regiam temporalem*, dated 6 July 1426, in which, he believes, John summarised a lecture course he had delivered at Salamanca during the previous academic year.[109] The *Repetitio* (which, of course, is far from representing John's final position on the subject of papal power) shows him at this stage in his career enunciating high papalist doctrine about Church-State relations.[110] Assuming that John had made his excerpts from *Octo Quaestiones* in preparation for his lectures, and comparing them with the pro-papal tendency of the *Repetitio*, Krämer argued that the latter work proves that John deliberately rejected Ockham's standpoint.

Krämer's evidence, however, falls short of demonstrating the priority of the excerpts to the *Repetitio*.[111] What he printed of the latter's text is insufficient to constitute a convincing case that John composed it after making the excerpts.[112] Moreover, some of his procedures are unsatisfactory; in trying to link John's two productions more plausibly he suggested amendments to the text of the excerpts which are otiose and clearly wrong.[113] Even if his claim that the excerpts were made earlier than the *Repetitio* were as well substantiated as he supposed, that could hardly justify his conclusion that the *Repetitio* amounted to a 'beweisbare Ablehnung Ockhams durch Johannes von Segovia'.[114] As displayed in the *Repetitio* in 1426 John's views came closer to the second opinion set out in question i of *Octo Quaestiones* than to the first or third. It is indeed likely that Ockham's own preference was for the third opinion. But he did not say so openly; his declared method in *Octo Quaestiones* was to eschew dogma and to provoke debate by reciting contrary views with the arguments for and against them.[115] He did not parade a personal doctrine which could be demonstrably rejected by John of Segovia or anyone else. At whatever date John made his excerpts, he seems to have understood Ockham rather better than Krämer has done. The indisputable fact is that he took the trouble to acquaint himself thoroughly and intelligently with at least six chapters of the longest of the *Octo Quaestiones*. That must surely indicate that he thought Ockham worthy of serious attention. Viewed in this light Krämer's attempt to use the excerpts to support the claim that John was uninfluenced by Ockham seems almost perverse.

Later on Krämer unwittingly undermined his case still further. He printed another series of excerpts made by Segovia, this time concerned with faith and heresy and the sort of revocation a heretic is obliged to make.[116] Krämer identified the source of these excerpts as the *Directorium inquisitorum* written in 1376 by Nicholas Eymeric, to whom he attributed a beneficent influence on John;[117] they were used by John, he claimed, in treatises he wrote during the late 1430s.[118] But the supposition that John made these excerpts from Eymeric is wrong.[119] His source was in fact very different; its identification is calamitous for Krämer's argument. Comparison of the texts shows that here John was once again copying Ockham; this time his extracts are taken from chapter 10 of the first treatise *De dogmatibus Johannis papae XXII*, later inserted with a companion treatise into *Dialogus* to form its so-called Part II.[120] Here again John has mingled literal transcription with paraphrase and abbreviation, adding little of his own.[121] These excerpts are either pure or very slightly diluted Ockham throughout, from the accurate reproduction of the chapter's opening lines, through each of Ockham's *notabilia* in turn, down to the contention that the heretic who abandons his heresy, though thus ceasing to be a heretic, does not thereby free himself from the taint of having been a heretic, and the final considerations about the necessary form for a satisfactory revocation of heresy.[122] Nearly at the end of his excerpts John harked back to an Ockhamist sentiment expressed in an earlier chapter of *De dogmatibus*; he finished them with a flourish by quoting a definition of heresy taken explicitly from Part I of *Dialogus*.[123] These excerpts, then, drawn upon by John when writing his later works, were made by him from Ockham. Krämer's flat denial that John experienced Ockham's influence has lost its last shreds of credibility.

Of course this does not turn John of Segovia into 'ein wahrer Ockham redivivus', as has been rashly asserted;[124] undeniably the charge in *Etsi non dubitemus* that the fathers at Basle had been poisoned by Ockham's ideas contained an element of tendentious exaggeration. Ockham may well have seemed a doubtful, even unnatural ally to some of the more extreme conciliarists at Basle, among whom were those of an opposed theological persuasion, followers of *via antiqua* rather than *via moderna*.[125] But whichever way their intellectual loyalties pointed, and however much the practical problems they faced differed from those of the western Church a hundred years earlier, educated churchmen *c.* 1430 must have found Ockham's influence hard to escape completely. Some might suspect or even abhor his ideas and his temperament. But there was no way of erasing him from the learned tradition of the Latin Church. His polemical writings had made available an immense corpus of material for the discussion of ecclesiology and, despite his show of non-committal caution, an example of freedom in approaching its complexities. There was no dearth of independent thinkers in the fifteenth century. They did not necessarily agree with what they understood to be Ockham's views, nor follow them slavishly. But they read him whenever they could get hold of his works, because he was rightly reputed to have interesting things to say about topics important to them. At Rome itself the curial official Lawrence of Arezzo, *sacri palatii causarum auditor*, in the prologue to the second book of his treatise *De ecclesiastica potestate*, dedicated to none other than Pope Eugenius IV, could declare warm appreciation of Ockham's learning as displayed in *Dialogus* and, it would seem, *Opus Nonaginta Dierum* (though his mistaken belief that Ockham was also the author of *Defensor pacis* caused him to review his favourable judgement later).[126] Ockham's better-known polemical writings were in demand, as the number of surviving fifteenth-century manuscripts testifies; so too were works by other authors, often attributed to him in error: *Defensor pacis*, John Quidort's *De potestate regia et papali*, and the anonymous *Disputatio inter clericum et militem*.[127] As early as 1476 competitive commercial enterprise saw *Dialogus* into print at Paris, five years before John of Westphalia could publish at Louvain the epitome of *Dialogus* Part I made in 1460–1461 by Henry of Zoemeren at the behest of Cardinal Bessarion.[128] To deny that churchmen like John of Segovia, Lawrence of Arezzo or Heinrich Kalteisen were in some sense 'influenced' by their study of Ockham is as unprofitable as to brand them as his disciples because they bothered to read him.[129] Many historians today can truthfully reject the imputation of being Marxists; few can honestly claim that Marx's ideas have played no part at all in their intellectual development.

Notes

References to Ockham's philosophical and theological works are to the editions in *Guillelmi de Ockham Opera Philosophca et Theologica*, produced by the Franciscan Institute at St. Bonaventure from 1967 onwards [*OPh* and *OTh*]. So far as they have appeared in *Guillelmi de Ockham Opera Politica* (Manchester: vol. 1^2, 1974; vol. 2, 1963; vol. 3, 1956), his political works are cited in this edition [*OPo*]. For *Breviloquium* references are to Richard Scholz's edition in *Wilhelm von Ockham als politischer Denker und sein Breviloquium de principatu tyrannico*, Schriften des Reichsinstituts für ältere deutsche Geschichtskunde (MGH) 8, Stuttgart 1944, repr. 1952. For *De imperatorum et pontificum potestate* the edition used is Scholz's, in *Unbekannte kirchenpolitische Streitschriften aus der Zeit Ludwigs des Bayern (1327–1354)* ii, Rome 1914, supplemented by my own reconstruction of chapter 27 from the manuscripts. As the pagination of the most accessible edition of *Dialogus*, in M. Goldast, *Monarchia* ii, Frankfurt 1614, is unreliable, in references to it page and line numbers have been given only exceptionally.

Periodicals have been designated by the sigla used in the bibliographies of *Revue d'Histoire Ecclésiastique*.

1. See *The Listener*. London, 1 December 1949, 949–951; *L'Encyclopédie* xiv, 776a, art. 'Scolastiques'.
2. Only some of the immediately relevant can be mentioned here: "Zur Bedeutung der Ekklesiologie für die politische Theorie im späteren Mittelalter". In: *Soziale Ordnungen im Selbstverständnis des Mittelalters*. Albert Zimmermann (ed.), Miscellanea Mediaevalia 12/2, Berlin/New York 1980, 369–388; "Die handschriftliche Überlieferung der Schriften des Juan González, Bischof von Cádiz (†1440)", *QFIAB* 60 (1980) 275–324; "Die Konzilien als Forum der öffentlichen Meinung im 15. Jahrhundert", *DA* 37 (1981) 736–773; "Les genres littéraires dans les sources théologiques et philosophiques médiévales", *Actes du Colloque international de Louvain-la-Neuve 25–27 mai 1981*. Université Catholique de Louvain: Publications de l'Institut d'Études Médiévales, 2ᵉ série, 5, 1982, 193–211; "Marsilius und Ockham. Publikum und Leser ihrer politischen Schriften im späteren Mittelalter", *Medioevo* 6 (1980 ⟨1983⟩) 543–567.
3. "Ockham: Avignon, before and after". In: Michael Wilks and Anne Hudson (eds.), *From Ockham to Wyclif*. Oxford 1987, 18; cf. E.F. Jacob, *Essays in the Conciliar Epoch*, 1st edn. Manchester 1943, 103.
4. J.J. Ryan, *The Nature, Structure and Function of the Church in William of Ockham*. Missoula, Montana 1979, 1.
5. W. and M. Kneale, *The Development of Logic*. Oxford 1962, 243–244.
6. Ockham, *Summa logicae*, eds. P. Boehner, Gedeon Gál and Stephen F. Brown, *OPh* I, 11*–31*.
7. On whom see Katherine H. Tachau, "The influence of Richard Campsall on fourteenth-century Oxford thought". In: *From Ockham to Wyclif*, 109–123.
8. I. Thomas, "Oxford logic and logicians in the seventeenth century". In: *Oxford Studies presented to Daniel Callus*. Oxford Hist. Soc. n.s. 16 (1964) 301–331.
9. Ockham, *Scriptum in Librum Primum Sententiarum (Ordinatio)*, eds. Gedeon Gál and Stephen F. Brown, *OTh* I (1967) 11*–18*.
10. IusIIIae *Dial.* ii.3–8; cf. Mario Grignaschi, "L'interprétation de la Politique d'Aristote dans le *Dialogus* de Guillaume d'Ockham". In: *Liber memorialis Georges de La-*

garde, Studies presented to the International Commission for the History of Representative and Parliamentary Institutions 38, Louvain/Paris 1970, 59–72.

11. R. Creytens, O.P., "Une question disputée de Galvano Fiamma O.P. sur le pouvoir temporel du pape", *AFP* 15 (1945) 107.
12. S.H. Thomson, "Walter Burley's Commentary on the *Politics* of Aristotle". In: *Mélanges Auguste Pelzer.* Louvain 1947, 557–578; Conor Martin, "Some medieval commentaries on Aristotle's *Politics*", *History* 36 (1951) 29–44; Anneliese Maier, *Ausgehendes Mittelalter* i, Rome 1964, 93–99. On Conrad's 'trilogy', of which only the *Monastica* and *Oeconomica* are known, see Konrad von Megenberg, *Werke,* ed. S. Krüger. MGH Staatsschriften d. späteren Mittelalters III.5, 3 vols., 1973–1984, introduction to vol. i, xxi.
13. J.W. Baldwin, *Masters, Princes and Merchants: the social views of Peter the Chanter and his circle* i. Princeton 1970, xi.
14. See L. Schmugge, *Johannes von Jandun, 1285/89–1328.* Stuttgart 1966, 67–75. For the debate on the relation to John's *Questions* of the 'Questiones super Metaphysice libros i–vi' in Florence, Biblioteca Laurenziana, cod. Fesulan. 161 see J. Quillet, "L'aristotélisme de Marsile et l'averroïsme", *Medioevo* 5 (1979) 89, 98, 124–142; M. Grignaschi, "Marsilio e le filosofie del Trecento", *ibid.,* 204–212; R. Lambertini and A. Tabarroni, "Le *Quaestiones super Metaphysicam* attribute a Giovanni di Jandun. Osservazioni e problemi", *Medioevo* 10 (1984) 41–104.
15. According to G.H.M.Posthumus Meyjes, *Jean Gerson, zijn kerkpolitiek en ecclesiologie.* The Hague 1963, 302, n.104.
16. See Raymond de Roover, *La pensée économique des scolastiques: doctrines et méthodes.* Conférence Albert-le-Grand 1970. Montreal/Paris 1971, 26–42, 63–66. Langenstein's *Tractatus* is printed in J. Gerson, *Opera* iv. Cologne 1484, fos. 185–220; discussed by Winfried Trusen, *Spätmittelalterliche Jurisprudenz und Wirtschaftsethik,* Beiheft 43 to *VSWG.* Wiesbaden 1961, 15–20.
17. Georges de Lagarde, *La naissance de l'esprit laïque au déclin du moyen âge.* III. *Secteur social de la scolastique.* Paris 1942, 222–275.
18. Ockham, *Quodlibeta septem,* ed. J.C. Wey, *OTh* IX (1980); cf. Jürgen Miethke, *Ockhams Weg zur Sozialphilosophie.* Berlin 1969, xii, 305, n.583a; *id.,* "Wilhelm von Ockham und die Institutionen des späten Mittelalters". In: *Ockham and Ockhamists,* eds. E.P. Bos and H.A. Krop, *Artistarium* Supplementa IV, 1987, 131.
19. Ockham, *Summula philosophiae naturalis,* pr., ed. Stephen F. Brown, *OPh* VI (1984) 153: quomodo agnus primo sequitur omnem ovem et post discernit – 'just as a lamb begins by running after each and every ewe, and then picks out its dam'. Brown accepts the authenticity of this work and suggests that it was composed between 1319 and 1321. For the context of this passage, see Miethke, *AFH* 60 (1967) 67–73.
20. Ockham, *Epistola ad fratres, OPo* 3, 16–17. Marino Damiata's attempt, *Guglielmo d'Ockham: Povertà e Potere* ii. Florence 1979, 102, to claim for Ockham a 'vero tatto politico' is unconvincing.
21. Ockham, *Contra Benedictum* vii.10, *OPo* 3, 316.
22. *Docendus,* D.62 c.2: cited I *Dial.* vi.94, Goldast, 616.8–15., though here Ockham reserves the superior authority of Scripture and of the sempiternally orthodox Church to that of teachers in matters of faith.
23. For example, I *Dial.* vi.8, Goldast, 514.9–13; *An princeps* 4, 37–39, *OPo* 1^2, 240; *Octo Quaest.* ii.6.56–59, *OPo* 1^2, 78; *Breviloquium* ii.14., ed. Scholz, 136; IIusIIIae

Dial. i.26, Goldast, 899.13–14. Discussed by W. Kölmel, "*A Deo sed per homines.* Zur Begründung der Staatsgewalt in Ordnungsverständnis des Mittelalters", *FS* 48 (1966) 332 seqq.; G. L. Potestà, "Rom. 13,1 in Ockham. Origine et legittimità del potere civile", *Cristianesimo nella storia* 7 (1986) 489–491.

24. See Joseph Canning, *The Political Thought of Baldus de Ubaldis.* Cambridge 1987, 24–28; John of Paris, *De potestate regia et papali* xix, ed. Bleienstein, 173.
25. On Ockham's views about the social utility of property rights, see L. Baudry, "L'Ordre franciscain au temps de Guillaume d'Occam", *FS* 27 (1965) 204, n.9, citing *Op. Nonaginta Dier.* 12.118–119, 65.205–206, *OPo* 2, 426, 578.
26. Even that staunch defender of Ockham's 'democratic' instincts (and, even more strangely, of his 'anticlericalism'), Marino Damiata, has nevertheless to concede that Ockham conclusively rejected the principle of majority decisions: *Guglielmo d'Ockham* ii, 77, 105, 118, 429.
27. A veritate enim non a multitudine vinci nullatenus erubescam ... cum ut communius multitudo erret: ed Scholz, 455.
28. See Sabine Krüger, "Krise der Zeit als Ursache der Pest". In: *Festschrift für Hermann Heimpel* ii. Göttingen 1972, 845.
29. G. de Lagarde, *La naissance de l'esprit laïque au déclin du moyen âge.* IV. *Guillaume d'Ockham: Défense de l'Empire.* Louvain/Paris 1962, 253; cf. 221.
30. Ockham, *Octo Quaest.* iv.6.199–210, *OPo* 1^2, 141–142.
31. Ockham, *Consultatio de causa matrimoniali* 7–31, *OPo* 1^2, 278–279; cf. *Octo Quaest.* ii.6.81–82, *OPo* 1^2, 78; iv.6.154–160, 140; iv.9.39–42, 147–148; I *Dial.* vi.8, vi.91. Tierney, "From Thomas of York to William of Ockham. The Franciscans and the papal *sollicitudo omnium ecclesiarum,* 1250–1350". In: J. D'Ercole and A.M. Stickler (eds.), *Comunione interecclesiale, Collegialità, Primato, Ecumenismo,* ii. Rome 1972, 634.
32. Umberto Eco, *Il nome della rosa,* 8th edn. Milan 1981, 63.
33. L. Baudry, "Les rapports de la raison et de la foi selon Guillaum d'Occam", *AHDLMA* 29 (1963) 33–89; G. de Lagarde, *La naissance de l'esprit laïque au déclin du moyen âge.* V. *Guillaume d'Ockham: Critique des structures ecclésiales.* Louvain/Paris 1963, 35.
34. Ockham, *Contra Benedictum* iv.4, *OPo* 3, 251–252; IIusIIIae *Dial.* ii.8; and still at the end of his life in c.27 of *De imper. et pont. potestate.*
35. By Conor Martin, "Walter Burley". In: *Oxford Studies presented to Daniel Callus,* Oxford Hist. Soc. n.s.16 (1964) 199.
36. *Contra Benedictum* vi.17, *OPo* 3, 299–301; *An princeps* cc.7–13, *OPo* 1^2, 252–267; *De imper. et pont. potestate* c.18, ed. Scholz, 472.
37. *Op. Nonaginta Dier.* 3.279–360, 599–659, *OPo* 1^2, 318–320, 326–328.
38. See Huguccio on Gratian's dictum C.14 q.3 ante c.1, and *Glossa ordinaria* on the same dictum; Laurentius Hispanus to *X* V.19.8 *s. v.* 'de feudo'. The authorities are collected by T.P. McLaughlin, "The Teaching of the Canonists on Usury (xii, xiii, xiv centuries)", *MS* 1 (1939) 101–102, nn.175–178. For earlier scholastic views, see Baldwin, *Masters, Princes and Merchants* [as in n.13] i, 286–287; ii, 200.
39. A.-M. Hamelin, O.F.M., *Un traité de morale économique aux xive siècle: le Tractatus de usuris de maître Alexander d'Alexandrie,* Analecta mediaevalia namurcensia 12. Louvain 1962; the implications are drawn by R. de Roover, "Les doctrines économiques des scolastiques", *RHE* 59 (1964) 854–859.
40. The licence is at Lincoln, Lincolnshire Archives Office, Episcopal Register III (John Dalderby), fo.390v (strictly speaking, a presentation to the bishop for licence), and

another at Trowbridge, Wiltshire County Record Office, Reg. Martival II, fos. 186v, 187 = *The Registers of Roger Martival, bishop of Salisbury 1315–1330* II. ii, ed. C.R. Elrington. Canterbury/York Soc. 58, 1972, 504, 506. I do not share the doubts sometimes expressed whether the fr. William Okam, O.F.M. in the Salisbury Register is our Ockham.

41. Ockham, *Op. Nonaginta Dier.* 93.440–443, *OPo* 2, 681: quia [Christus] neque tenebat parliamenta et curias, neque de rebus temporalibus iudicabat .... The attempt by Cary J. Nederman, "Royal Taxation and the English Church: the origins of William of Ockham's *An princeps*", *JEH* 37 (1986) 377–388, to stress the 'role of English political experience' in *An princeps* calls for some modifications in detail.
42. *Octo Quaest.* iii. 8. 9–10, *OPo* 1^2, 110: [princeps] ad hoc videtur principalissime institutus, ut corrigat et puniat delinquentes; cf. Isidore, *Sent.* iii. 47. Much the same contention appears in IIusIIIae *Dial.* i. 1: Nam illud regnum est maxime universo expediens, per quod mali facilius, iustius et efficacius ac salubrius coercentur et boni vivunt quietius inter malos.
43. See W.D. McCready, "Papal *Plenitudo Potestatis* and the source of temporal authority in late medieval papal hierocratic theory", *Speculum* 48 (1973) 654–674.
44. *Octo Quaest.* i. 7. 30–87, *OPo* 1^2, 34–36; see too IusIIIae *Dial.* i. 16–17; *Breviloquium* ii. 20 (fifth opinion), ed. Scholz, 99–100; *De imper. et pont. potestate* c. 8, ed. Scholz, 465. Ryan's claim, *Nature, Structure and Function* [as n. 4], 9, that Ockham 'qualifies the plenitude out of existence' goes much too far. Damiata's descriptive formula *plenitudo potestatis secundum quid* is attractive: *Guglielmo d'Ockham* ii, 160. Anthony Kenny has recently remarked about Wyclif, *Proc. British Academy* 72 (1986) 111: 'It could not be claimed that his political writings, in this century, have anything to offer to anyone but the historian.'
45. *Epistola ad fratres, OPo* 3, 10, 15–17.
46. B. Tierney, *Origins of Papal Infallibility 1150–1350.* Leiden 1972, 205–237. For controversy with A.M. Stickler about Tierney's general thesis, see *CHR* 60 (1974) 427–441 and 61 (1975) 265–279. Ockham has been defended from Tierney's imputation by Miethke, *Francia* 3 (1975) 765–773, and Ryan, *Nature, Structure and Function,* 24, nn. 48–49. The issue was usefully discussed in a wider perspective by Thomas Turley, "Infallibility in the Curia of Pope John XXII", *JMedH* 1 (1975) 71–101; cf. *AHR* 78 (1973) 666.
47. A.S. McGrade, "Ockham on enjoyment – towards an understanding of fourteenth-century philosophy and psychology", *Rev. of Metaphysics* 34 (1981) 706–728, based on *OTh* I, 371–507.
48. For example, *Op. Nonaginta Dier.* 50. 13–15, *OPo* 2, 539: secundum grammaticos una significatio huius verbi 'abuti' est 'valde uti'. Haec tamen significatio in theologia non est in usu; immo videtur omnino recessisse ab usu.
49. Cited by Lagarde, *Critique* [as n. 33], 295.
50. See H.O. Schwöbel, *Der diplomatische Kampf zwischen Ludwig dem Bayern und der römischen Kurie im Rahmen des kanonischen Absolutionsprozesses 1330–1346.* Weimar 1968; Alois Schütz, *Die Prokuratorien und Instruktionen Ludwigs des Bayern für die Kurie (1331–1345).* Kallmünz 1973; Jürgen Miethke, "Kaiser und Papst im Spätmittelalter. Zu den Ausgleichsbemühungen zwischen Ludwig dem Bayern und der Kurie in Avignon", *ZHF* 10 (1983) 421–446.
51. *Epistola ad fratres, OPo* 3, 11–15; *Contra Ioannem* cc. 22–24, *OPo* 3, 85–103; *Contra Benedictum* i. 2–17, *OPo* 3, 171–213; *Compendium errorum* cc. 1–4, 6–7, ed. Goldast,

Monarchia ii, 958–964, 968–973; *Octo Quaest.* viii.7.49–336, *OPo* 1², 206–214. The list is lacking from the incomplete manuscript of *De imper. et pont. potestate* from which Scholz (1914) and C.K. Brampton (1927) printed their editions, but survives in a muddled form in two other manuscripts; published from Deventer, Athenaeum-Bibliotheek ms. 100 by W. Mulder, S.J., *AFH* 17 (1924) 72–97.

52. The chronology of Ockham's non-political writings is discussed by the editors of *OTh* and *OPh*; cf. Vladimir Richter, "Zu Ockhams Entwicklung in der Universalienfrage", *Phil. Jb.* 82 (1975) 177–187. Miethke, "Wilhelm von Ockham". In: M. Greschat (ed.), *Gestalten der Kirchengeschichte*, iv. Stuttgart 1983, 168, suggests that Ockham may have composed two shortened versions of his logical teaching during the Munich years.

53. C. Eubel (ed.), *Bullarium Franciscanum.* Rome 1898, 274: Facta quidem, quae singulorum sunt, personam veram exigunt et requirunt. Ordo autem vera persona non est, sed repraesentata et imaginaria potius est censenda. Quare quae facti sunt, sibi vere convenire nequeunt, licet ei possint congruere quae sunt iuris; repeated in *Quia vir reprobus, ib.*, 433. Discussed by Baudry, "L'Ordre franciscain" [as n. 25], 188–190. Time and again Ockham gnawed at this bone: *Op. Nonaginta Dier.* 6.413–55, *OPo* 1², 365–366; 62.206–263, 279–289, *OPo* 2, 568–570; *Contra Ioannem* c.24, *OPo* 3, 102–103; *Contra Benedictum* i.8, *OPo* 3, 189–191; *Octo Quaest.* viii.7.112–125, *OPo* 1², 208; *De imper. et pont. potestate* c. 27. But his counter-assertion remained the same for a decade and a half: communitas non est una vera persona, sed est plures verae personae, *Op. Nonaginta Dier.* 6.446–448; quod ecclesia, populus ac multitudo, ac ratione consimili ordo, fratrum scilicet Minorum, potest habere actum realem, et quod non sit persona imaginaria et repraesentata, sed est verae personae, quamvis non sit una persona sola, *De imper. et pont. potestate* c. 27.

54. See Charles Zuckerman, "The relationship of theories of universals to theories of church government in the middle ages: a critique of previous views", *JHI* 35 (1975) 579–594. Among the skeptics are J.B. Morrall, "Some notes on a recent interpretation of William of Ockham's political philosophy", *FSt* 9 (1949) 335–369; Philotheus Boehner, "Ockham's political ideas". In: *Collected Articles on Ockham.* St. Bonaventure, N.Y. 1958, 442–463; Tierney, *Papal Infallibility* [as n. 46], 208, n. 1; *id.*, "From Thomas of York" [as n. 31], 648. A. Gewirth, "Philosophy and Political Thought in the Fourteenth Century". In: F.L. Utley (ed.), *The Forward Movement of the Fourteenth Century.* Columbus, Ohio 1961, 125–164, seems non-committal.

55. Arthur S. McGrade, "Ockham and the birth of individual rights". In: Brian Tierney and Peter Linehan (eds.), *Authority and Power. Studies on Medieval Law and Government presented to Walter Ullmann.* Cambridge 1980, 150. Andrea Tabarroni, *Il tutto e la parte nell'ecclesiologia di Guglielmo di Ockham: ricerca sui fondamenti e le strutture logiche del concetto di Ecclesia Universalis* (typescript thesis, Bologna 1982) has interesting comment on Zuckerman's argument, 266–272; Costantino Marmo, *Guglielmo di Ockham e la controversia De fide catholica: presupposti gnoseologici ed epistemologici* (typescript thesis, Bologna 1982).

56. In what circumstances Ockham turned to serious reading of the canon law is a problem awaiting further investigation. An early example of his concern with the subject is provided by c. 37 of his *Tractatus de Corpore Christi*, C. A. Grassi (ed.), *OTh* X (1986) 206–213, perhaps composed 1323/4. The great importance of canon law as a source for Ockham's polemical writing has rightly been stressed by Brian Tierney: see his essay "Natural Law and Canon Law in Ockham's *Dialogus*". In: J.G. Rowe

(ed.), *Aspects of Late Medieval Government and Society. Essays presented to J. R. Lander.* Toronto 1986, 3–24.

57. Marmo, 244–245, insists that logic remains the theoretic validation of the polemics. The technical passages referred to are examples of *fallacia figure dictionis* in I *Dial.* iv.9 and v.5 and of *amphibolia* in IusIIIae *Dial.* ii.17. I have not seen Roberto Lambertini's thesis (typescript, Bologna 1982) on logical terminology in Ockham's political writings.
58. McGrade, *Birth of individual rights,* 162–164.
59. Y.M.-J. Congar, "Incidence ecclésiologique d'un thème de dévotion mariale", *MSR* 8 (1950) 277–292, repr. in *id., Études d'ecclésiologie médiévale.* London 1983, no. x. See also the gloss *Ecce* to *Decretum* C.24 q.1 c.9, cited by Brian Tierney, *Foundations of the Conciliar Theory.* Cambridge 1955, 44.
60. I *Dial.* v.35: Errante tota multitudine Christianorum usum rationis habentium, possunt salvari promissiones Christi per parvulos baptizatos. Though Peter John Olivi never said quite this, some of his ideas pointed in the same direction, as Congar has remarked, "Les positions ecclésiologiques de Pierre Jean-Olivi d'après les publications récentes", *Cahiers de Fanjeaux* 10 (1975) 160–161, repr. in *Études d'ecclésiologie,* no. xi.
61. Richard of Bury (*potius* Robert Holkot?), *Philobiblon* viii.96–124. Ed. Altamura, Naples 1954, 101–102; cf. Neal W. Gilbert, "Richard de Bury and the 'Quires of Yesterday's Sophisms'". In: E. P. Mahoney (ed.), *Philosophy and Humanism. Renaissance Essays in Honor of Paul Oskar Kristeller.* Leiden 1976, 229–257.
62. Lagarde, *Défense* [as n. 29], 9.
63. This seems safe to infer from the treatises of Sybert of Beek and William of Cremona against *Defensor pacis,* printed by Scholz, *Unbekannte kirchenpolitische Streitschriften* ii, 3–15, 16–28. Danach Mag Fhionnbhairr in his doctoral dissertation *Guillelmi de Villana de Cremona C. S. A. Tractatus cuius titulus Reprobatio errorum* (typescript, University College, Dublin 1975), 271, denied that William had read *Defensor* in full when he set about refuting it.
64. See G. H. M. Posthumus Meyjes, *Jean Gerson et l'Assemblée de Vincennes.* Leiden 1978, 78.
65. Ockham's opposition to Marsilio is specific in IusIIIae *Dial.* iii. cc.1 and 21, and iv. cc.1, 3, 12, 21; see also *Octo Quaest.* i.7.19–89, *OPo* 1^2, 34–36; iii.1.93–120, 98; iii.2.5–13, 99; iii.3.5–28, 101–102; viii.6.147, 204. Of course, Ockham knew about Marsilio's ideas long before he wrote IusIIIae *Dial.* or *Octo Quaest.*; there are indications of this in I *Dial.*, as Léon Baudry pointed out, *Guillaume d'Occam.* Paris 1950, 163, 168–169. I am not convinced by Carlo Dolcini's attempt to link Ockham and Marsilio as collaborators in the authorship of the memorandum *Quoniam scriptura: Marsilio e Ockham.* Bologna 1981, 53–102. It would have surprised Georges de Lagarde, who wrote 'Nul n'oserait prétendre aujourd'hui que les deux hommes sont solidaires': 'Marsile de Padoue et Guillaume d'Ockham', *Études d'histoire du droit canonique dédiées à Gabriel Le Bras* i. Paris 1956, 593. For Alvarus, see his *De planctu ecclesie*, part i, arts. 68–70. In: J. T. Rocaberti, *Biblioteca Maxima Pontificia* iii. Rome 1698, 244. Possibly these articles were not inserted into *De planctu* until 1335 or 1340, but they may have originated as a separate work c.1324–1328; cf. N. Iung, *Alvaro Pelayo.* Paris 1931, 43. Presumably it was between 1335 and 1342 that Pierre Roger extracted 240 heretical propositions from *Defensor pacis* at the behest of Pope Benedict XII; see H. S. Offler, "A political *collatio* of Pope Clement VI, O. S. B.", *RBén* 65 (1955) 135.

66. Jeannine Quillet, *Marsile de Padoue: Le Défenseur de la Paix.* Paris 1968, 23.
67. Conrad of Megenberg, *Yconomica* II.iii.1, ed. Krüger [as n.12], ii (1977), 87.
68. Quillet, *Marsile*, 27; Miethke [as n.2], "Ekklesiologie", 376–380; "Genres littéraires", 207–211; "Konzilien als Forum", 758–766; "Marsilius und Ockham", 549–550.
69. See H.S. Offler, "Zum Verfasser der *Allegaciones de potestate imperiali* (1338)", *DA* 42 (1986) 555–619.
70. As W.J. Courtenay maintains, "The reception of Ockham's thought in fourteenth-century England". In: *From Ockham to Wyclif* [as n.3], 89–107.
71. R. Paqué, *Das Pariser Nominalistenstatut.* Berlin 1970, 253–263; W.J. Courtenay and K.H. Tachau, "Ockham, Ockhamists and the English-German Nation at Paris, 1339–41", *Hist. of Universities* 2 (1982), 53–96.
72. Courtenay and Tachau, 79.
73. Courtenay and Tachau, 71–72; Neal W. Gilbert, "Richard de Bury" [as n.61], 239–240, 245, n.41, 254, 257.
74. Conrad, *Tractatus contra Occam* i., Scholz (ed.), *Unbekannte kirchenpolitische Streitschriften* ii, 347–348; Krüger (ed.), *Yconomica* III.i.1, iii (1984) 7.
75. Sabine Krüger, "Krise der Zeit" [as n.28], 844–851. It is doubtful, of course, whether in his own lifetime Ockham would have been considered more 'modernus' than his contemporaries, or labelled 'terminista'; cf. Neal W. Gilbert, "Ockham, Wyclif and the *via moderna*". In: Albert Zimmermann (ed.), *Antiqui und Moderni.* Miscellanea Mediaevalia 9. Berlin/New York 1974, 85–125. *Via moderna* belongs to the terminology of the fifteenth rather than the fourteenth century.
76. F. Schneider (ed.), *Liber certarum historiarum*, MGH SS. in usum scholarum, 1910, ii.241. John says of Ockham: qui etiam regulis artis loice subtilissima multorum ingenia occupavit.
77. Bremen, Staatliche Bibliothek cod.lat. b.35, fos. 176r-v; described by Colette Jeudy, *Marsile de Padoue: Oeuvres mineures.* Paris 1979, 80–82.
78. See Ockham, *OPo* 1^2, 8. André Leguai, "Fondements et problèmes du pouvoir royal en France (autour du 1400)". In: Reinhard Schneider (ed.), *Das spätmittelalterliche Königtum im europäischen Vergleich.* Vorträge und Forschungen 32 (1987) 53 has quoted a long passage from the *Songe du Verger* i.78 without indicating that it is verbally translated from *Octo Quaest.* v.6.
79. See W.A. Pantin, "The Defensorium of Adam of Easton", *EHR* 51 (1936) 675–680.
80. Printed by R.H. and M.A. Rouse, "The Franciscans and books. Lollard accusations and the Franciscan response". In: *From Ockham to Wyclif*, 372, n.9: per absconsionem librorum Wilhelmi Occam contra papam Romanum.
81. Jürgen Miethke's paper "Ein neues Selbstzeugnis Ockhams zu seinem *Dialogus*". In: *From Ockham to Wyclif*, 19–30, may have revealed a clue.
82. Paris, BN cod.lat.3657, described in *Bibliothèque Nationale. Catalogue général des manuscrits latins* vi, 1975, 468–469; discussed by F. Ehrle, "Zur Geschichte des Schatzes, der Bibliothek und des Archivs der Päpste im vierzehnten Jahrhundert", *ALKG* 1 (1885) 15–17, and *Historia Bibliothecae Romanorum Pontificum* i. Rome 1898, 555, no.1582. Anneliese Maier, *Ausgehendes Mittelalter* iii. Rome 1977, 609 (cf. 15, 26, 60) argued that Benedict XIII possessed a second copy of *Dialogus*, not known to have survived. If, as she tentatively suggested, this second copy was the exemplar for the version of *Dialogus* now in cod.Vat.lat.4115, it too seems to have lacked IusIIIae *Dial.* Even today no more than three versions of this first treatise of Part III are known.

83. See the critical edition of d'Ailly's *Abbreviatio Dyalogi Okam* by Father Ian Murdoch, typescript Ph.D. thesis, Monash University, 1981. As the editor points out, d'Ailly's interest in *Dialogus* seems to have focussed primarily on dogmatic and doctrinal problems (p. xxi).
84. H.-J. Sieben, "Die *Quaestio de infallibilitate concilii generalis* (Ockhamexzerpte) des Pariser Theologen Jean Courtecuisse († 1423)", *AHC* 9 (1977) 178–199; Francis Oakley, "The *Tractatus de fide et ecclesia, Romano pontifice et concilio generali* of Johannes Breviscoxe", *AHC* 10 (1978) 99–130.
85. Frankfurt am Main, Stadtbibliothek, cod. lat. quart. 4, described by Karin Bredehorn and Gerhardt Powitz, *Kataloge der Stadt- und Universitätsbibliothek Frankfurt am Main*, Bd. 4: *Die Handschriften der Stadt- und Universitätsbibliothek Frankfurt am Main*. III. *Die mittelalterlichen Handschriften der Gruppe Manuscripta Latina*, 1979, 7–9. This corrects the dating suggested in Ockham, *OPo* 1^2, 5.
86. See Ockham, *OPo* 1^2, 3–6. A.J. Black's view, "What was conciliarism? Conciliar theory in historical perspective". In: *Authority and Power* [as n. 55], 216, that from 1408 onwards the influence of Ockham and Marsilio on conciliar thinking was 'replaced by orthodox theology and ecclesiastical jurisprudence' needs qualification.
87. Balliol College, ms. 165B, described by R. A. B. Mynors, *Catalogue of the Manuscripts of Balliol College, Oxford*. Oxford 1963, 164–170.
88. See, for example, B. Tierney, "Ockham, the conciliar theory and the canonists", *JHI* 15 (1954) 40–70; *id.*, "From Thomas of York" [as n. 31], 645–646; J. B. Morrall, "Ockham and Ecclesiology". In: J. A. Watt, F.-X. Martin, J. B. Morrall (eds.), *Medieval Studies presented to Aubrey Gwynn, S. J.* Dublin 1961, 481–491; Ryan, *Nature, Structure and Function* [as n. 4], 12; Damiata, *Guglielmo d'Ockham* ii [as n. 20], 61–62, 168, 435. Cf. the conspectus in Miethke, "Konzilien als Forum" [as n. 2], 738–739.
89. Lagarde, *Critique* [as n. 33], 53.
90. Almain's *Expositio circa decisiones questionum Mag. G. Ockham super potestate summi pontificis* was seen into print after his death by his pupil Vincent Doesmier in 1518, and often reprinted; for the date, cf. A. Renaudet, *Préréforme et humanisme à Paris pendant les premières guerres d'Italie (1494–1517)*, 2nd. edn. Paris 1953, 547, n. 4. See the account by Francis Oakley, "Almain and Major. Conciliar theory on the eve of the Reformation", *AHR* 70 (1965) 673–690.
91. *Octo Quaest.* i. 17. 31–2, *OPo* 1^2, 60: a generali concilio – quod etiam super papam haereticum habet iudiciariam potestatem.
92. Almain, "Expositio". In: Gerson, *Opera omnia* ii. The Hague 1728, coll. 1070–1072.
93. Edited from the Munich manuscript clm 7006 by R. N. Swanson, "A survey of views on the Great Schism, *c.* 1395" , *AHP* 21 (1983) 79–103. The extracts from Ockham, I *Dial.* v. 25–6, are at lines 158–229, pp. 99–100.
94. Such a 'climatic change' in the West is suggested by Heinrich Koller, "Der Ausbau königlicher Macht im Reiche des 15. Jahrhunderts". In: R. Schneider (ed.), *Das spätmittelalterliche Königtum* [as n. 78], 426.
95. Anneliese Maier's notable papers on the dispute about the Beatific Vision are reprinted in her *Ausgehendes Mittelalter* iii, Rome 1977, 319–443, 505–590. Father Marc Dykman's numerous contributions down to 1975 are conveniently listed in his *Pour et contre Jean XXII en 1333: Deux traités avignonnais sur la vision béatifique.* Città del Vaticano 1975, 11, n. 1.
96. Ockham, *OPo* 2, xix. Lawrence of Arezzo at the Curia in the 1430s seems to have been aware of *Op. Nonaginta Dier.*; cf. an apparent reference to it in the proem to

book ii of his 'Liber de ecclesiastica potestate': in libro illo responsivo quem edidit [Ockham] ad certum processum Johannis XXII contra magistrum Michaelem de Cesena, A.-H. Chroust and J.A. Corbett (eds.), "The fifteenth-century *Review of Politics* of Laurentius of Arezzo", *MS* 11 (1949) 64–66.

97. Though it should be noticed that when making his *Abbreviatio* of *Dialogus* in the 1370s Pierre d'Ailly paid considerable attention to the so-called Part II, which concentrated on John XXII's 'errors' about the Beatific Vision; see Murdoch, *Abbreviatio* [as n.83], 71–94.
98. See n.84.
99. For d'Ailly's use of Ockham, see n.83 and Francis Oakley, *The Political Thought of Pierre d'Ailly*. New Haven/London 1964, 202–203.
100. W.R. Thomson, *The Latin Writings of John Wyclif.* Pontifical Institute of Mediaeval Studies, Subsidia Mediaevalia 14. Toronto 1983, 299. Wyclif's references to Ockham in his *De concordantia fratrum cum secta simplicis Christi*, R. Buddensieg (ed.), *Wiclif's Polemical Works in Latin* i, Wyclif Society, 1883, 92, 94, 95, seem far too general to warrant Thomson's claim: 'Undoubtedly he implies here Ockham's *Epistola ad fratres minores.*'
101. G. Hofmann (ed.), *Epistolae pontificiae ad Concilium Florentinum spectantes.* Rome 1940–1946, doc. 248: Fuerunt impietatis illius dyabolici fundatores Marsilius de Padua, Iohannes de Ganduno, Guillermus Ocham aliique nonnulli, qui non tantum sui temporis, sed etiam futuri saeculi homines venenarunt. Inde procedit omnis corruptela praesentium ....
102. Werner Krämer, *Konsens und Rezeption: Verfassungsprinzipien der Kirche im Basler Konziliarismus, BGPTM* N.F. 19. Münster 1980, 166–181: 'Exkurs: Gibt es einen direkten Einfluß von Marsilius von Padua und Wilhelm von Ockham auf die Theologen des Basler Konzils?'
103. J. Gonzales, *El maestro Juan Segovia y su biblioteca.* Madrid 1944, no. 50., 166; cf. Miethke, "Marsilius und Ockham" [as n.2], 566, n.73. The manuscript has now disappeared; from what is said below it seems likely that it contained at least Part II in addition to Part I of *Dialogus.*
104. Krämer, 423, 433.
105. Krämer, *Excerptum* I, 416–422, from Salamanca, Cod. bibl. univers. 246, fos. 71r–72v.
106. Ockham, *OPo* 1², 16–34; cited below according to question, chapter and line.
107. Cited according to the marginal numeration in Krämer's edition. John's reference at 2.13–14 to the decretals *Duo* and *Solitae* seems the result of confusion between Popes Innocent III and IV, as also at 2.22–3; his *et dedicavit* at 2.27–8 is not in the original, nor *et successoribus* at 2.32. At 4.7 he omits *Octo Quaest.* i.4.9–55, but supplies a paraphrase of this at 4.13–18.
108. Though at 5.1–4 John does not appear to show convincing grasp of Ockham's difficult argument at *OQ* i.5.5–22. Again, John's *Pro intelligentia, opponit tripliciter* at 6.1 is not perspicuous; the opening of *OQ* i.6 introduces the objections of the third opinion to the reasons for the second.
109. Krämer, 169–170, referring to the version of the *Repetitio* in Valladolid, Biblioteca universitaria de Sta. Cruz, cod. 89, fos. 130r–165v, which is mostly in Segovia's own hand. Krämer printed, 384, only the summary at the end of the *Repetitio*, which gives the conclusions of the eight questions discussed.
110. Thus question 7 concludes: 'Sacred writ in the Old Testament and the New attests that the fullest power both spiritual and temporal was granted to Christ as man for

the governance of all men', and question 8: 'Evangelical authority teaches that Christ's power in its fullness was granted to Peter and his successors for the governance of the whole world', Krämer, 384. Elsewhere Krämer, 171, n. 19, quotes from *Repetitio* fo. 155: in supremo hierarcha ecclesiastico, successore Petri, plenitudo potestatis assistat ad ecclesiam tam in spiritualibus quam in temporalibus gubernandam.

111. B. Hernández-Montes, "Obras de Juan de Segovia", *Repertorio de historia de las ciencias eclesiasticas en España* 6 (1977) 267–347, ranks John's excerpts from *Octo Quaest.* late among his works (no. 77). Krämer, 207, n. 1, does not expatiate on his grounds for disagreeing with this.
112. Krämer, 170–173.
113. Krämer's introduction of *solum* and *spiritualem* into the excerpts at 7.2–3, 422 (cf. 171, n. 19) is quite gratuitous. John's text said what he meant, for he was here faithfully following *OQ* i.7.32–33, 34–35: Petro ... omnem potestatem necessariam ad regimen fidelium.
114. Krämer, 173.
115. *OQ* pr. 16, 15: Personam enim induam recitantis; *OQ* i. 1.6–7, 16: ipsas [quaestiones] breviter conferendo tractare curabo; *OQ* i. 5.1, 27: Quia in isto opusculo censui solummodo recitando et allegando procedere.
116. Krämer, *Excerptum* V, 430–433: Septem notabilia super materia haeresis attendenda; from Salamanca, Cod. bibl. univers. 246, fos. 73v–74r (Segovia's autograph) and Salamanca, Cod. 81, fos. 282v–283v.
117. Krämer, 231, n. 59: 'Dieses kirchliche Handbuch verlieh ihm [Segovia] eine spürbare Sicherheit und Großzügigkeit in allen Fragen des Glaubens und der Häresie.'
118. Krämer, 430, n. 1; see also 173, n. 26; 229, n. 54; 246, n. 92.
119. Part I of the *Directorium*, to which Krämer refers, does indeed discuss twelve questions *de pertinentibus ad fidem*, all of them resolved by resort to Aquinas: Nicolaus Eymericus, *Directorium inquisitorum*. Venice 1607, 58–78. But John's excerpts show no close verbal similarity to Eymeric's discussion; any resemblance is merely generic, deriving from the circumstance that the subject matter of both is the same.
120. The references to II *Dial.* are to pages and lines in Goldast's edn., *Monarchia* ii. John's excerpts are quoted according to the sections and lines in Krämer's edition, 430–433.
121. Peculiar to John: 2.3–4: de quorum ... per circulum anni; 2.17–20: Hinc est ... speculativas; 5.6–7: Unde Christus ... me spernit; 7.3–4 Non enim ... peccavi.
122. John 1.3–5 = Goldast, 753.1; John 2.1 = G, 753.25; John 3.1 = G, 754.8; John 4.1 = G, 754.26; John 5.1 = G, 754.64; John 6.1 = G, 755.11; John 7.1 = G, 755.22; John 8.2–8 = G, 755.63–756.1, 756.37; John 8.9–20 = G, 757.38–42, 757.63–758.3, 758.9, 758.14–16.
123. John 8.21–4: cf. II *Dial.* i.8, G, 751.3–5; John 9.4–5 = *Dial.* ii.6, G, 416.32–3.
124. By P. Ladner, "Johannes von Segovias Stellung zur Präsidentenfrage des Basler Konzils", *ZSKG* 62 (1968) 4.
125. Krämer, 180: 'Theologiegeschichtlich gesehen verteidigten die Basler Konziliaristen (selbst nach dem eigenwilligen Schisma) immer die *via antiqua*.'
126. Lawrence of Arezzo, eds. Chroust and Corbett [as n. 96], 64–66, 73: excellentem ac profunde scientie virum Guiglielmum de Occam de ordine fratrum minorum, inter theologos quasi primum, qui papalem materiam et concilii potestatem inceperit aperire ... ego nomini suo reverebar et virum hunc laudabam, quoniam quod magne scientie vir esset, eius opera, que ad me devenerant, demonstrabant. Until he mistak-

enly took Ockham to be the author of *Defensor pacis* Lawrence's only unfavourable comment on him was: presumptuosum tamen et temerarium in aliquibus suis dictis.

127. See Miethke, "Ekklesiologie" [as n. 2], 388; Offler, "Zum Verfasser" [as n. 69], 557. * John Trevisa's rendering of the *Disputatio* into middle English was the only vernacular version of an 'Ockhamist' work available in fifteenth-century England: ed. A.J. Perry, Early English Text Soc., original series, 167 (1926). They knew better elsewhere. The rubric to the Latin version of the *Disputatio* in Biblioteca Apostolica Vaticana, cod. Borghese 29, fo. 24v notes that while the English attributed it to Ockham, it was really the work of Marsilio of Padua! cited by J.I. Catto, *From Ockham to Wyclif*, 358, n. 15.

128. Cf. *FSt* 37 (1977) 210, n. 12.

129. Evidence of Kalteisen's interest in Ockham is provided by his manuscript, now Koblenz, Staatsarchiv, Abt. 701, no. 230, described by Jeudy, *Marsile de Padoue* [as n. 77], 83–85; cf. Krämer, 315.

XI

A POLITICAL "COLLATIO" OF POPE CLEMENT VI, O. S. B.

That the Benedictine pope Clement VI was a notable preacher has long been recognised. M. G. Mollat has discussed the general characteristics of his pulpit eloquence, while the inventory of the surviving manuscripts of his sermons drawn up by Dom Philibert Schmitz makes clear that they were widely copied and diffused [1]. Of Clement's sermons in the strict sense of the term — delivered during High Mass and devoted to religious matters — some have found modern editors [2]. But Clement was master also, as M. Mollat has pointed out [3], of a related but somewhat different *genre;* the *collatio,* which might be preached at Vespers or later in the day, but was sometimes no more than an allocution made in consistory or elsewhere on an occasion of political or religious importance at the Curia. The *collatio* in this latter sense was in fact a public speech on some matter of topical interest delivered by the head of the Church to a distinguished audience. That here is a potentially valuable source of information for the historian is obvious ; if the vein has not been much worked, that may be because hitherto it has not been readily accessible. A few of Clement's *collationes* were printed in full by Schunck in the late eighteenth century ; fragments of others were published by C. Höfler and Carl Müller or are to be found in M. Mollat's edition of the *Vitae paparum Avenionensium* [4]. But I know of only one complete *collatio* by Clement which is available in a modern edition [5].

---

1. G. Mollat, *L'œuvre oratoire de Clément VI,* in *Archives d'histoire doctrinale et littéraire du moyen âge,* III (1928), pp. 239-74 ; Dom Philibert Schmitz, *Les sermons et discours de Clément VI* in *Revue bénédictine,* XLI (1929), pp. 13-34.

2. Cf. the bibliographical note in G. Mollat, *Les papes d'Avignon* (Paris, 1949), p. 93.

3. *L'œuvre oratoire,* p. 242.

4. J. P. Schunck, *Beyträge zur Mainzer Geschichte* (Frankfurt, 1788 *sqq.*) I, 405 ; II, 332, 341, 353 ; C. Höfler, *Aus Avignon,* in *Abh. d. böhmischen Gesellschaft d. Wiss.,* ser. vi, II (1868), p. 18 *sqq.* ; C. Müller, *Der Kampf Ludwigs d. Baiern mit d. römischen Curie* (Tübingen, 1879-80) II, 361-3 ; S. Baluze, *Vitae paparum Avenionensium,* ed. G. Mollat (Paris, 1916 *sqq.*) II, 303-5, 371, 388-9, 423.

5. Delivered on 6 November 1346 on the text *Salomon sedebit.* The occasion was Clement's formal approval of Charles of Luxemburg as king of the Romans,

That fact alone might serve to justify the present attempt to edit another. For this purpose the *collatio* on the text *Atrium quod est foris* (*Apoc.* 11, 2) delivered by Clement on Maundy Thursday 1343 recommends itself not only as an excellent example of Clement's manner, but also because of the light it throws on a political problem much in men's minds at the time. When Clement became pope in 1342 he inherited a controversy with the German king Lewis the Bavarian which had begun in the early days of John XXII. Since 1324 Lewis had been under the Church's ban ; in 1328 he had aggravated his offences by having himself crowned emperor at Rome in defiance of papal prohibitions, and by setting up an anti-pope ; and though he proved incapable of promoting an effective schism the struggle was obstinately continued. From 1330 onwards Lewis did indeed make repeated attempts to secure absolution from the effects of the long series of papal processes issued against him ; but the papal conditions remained too exigent and Lewis' reserves too obdurate for a satisfactory basis of reconciliation to be found. The pontificate of Benedict XII had seemed at one time to offer brighter hopes, but the serious negotiations between Lewis and the Curia in 1336 were brought to nothing by the political cross-currents set in motion as western Europe prepared for the outbreak of the Hundred Years' War. During the rest of Benedict's lifetime Lewis, his hand strengthened first by an English (1337), then by a French alliance (1341), and his sense of independence sustained by the German movement of national resistance to papal claims which found expression in the great assemblies of 1338 and 1339, was not excessively concerned to pursue the business of his reconciliation ; talks continued, envoys came and went, but in desultory fashion. The sense of urgency is lacking[1].

Clement was not the man to tolerate this drift : particularly in view of the additional affront inflicted on the Church just before his accession by Lewis' behaviour over the Tirolese marriage[2] ; in view also of his well grounded suspicion that Lewis was medit-

---

Edited by K. Zeumer and R. Salomon in *Monumenta Germaniae Historica, Constitutiones* VIII (Hannover, 1926), nr. 100, pp. 143-63.

1. Cf. Müller, *op. cit.; *Mollat, *Les papes d'Avignon*, p. 350 *sqq.;* E. E. Stengel, *Avignon und Rhens* (Weimar, 1930), p. 85 *sqq.;* F. Bock, *Reichsidee und Nationalstaaten* (Munich, 1943), p. 355 *sqq.*

2. Cf. below, lines 100-1 and note. It will hardly have escaped Clement's notice how severely Lewis had damaged his relations with the German princes by his action in Tirol; cf. Johannes Victoriensis, *Lib. certarum historiarum*, ed. Schneider, II (*MGH. SS. in usum scholarum*, 1910), p. 228.

ating another descent into Italy[1]. When the Bavarian's first embassy to Clement in the last months of 1342 refused outright to consider proceeding on the basis of the conditions of 1336[2], the pope inferred that the time had come, if not for a final blow, at any rate for sharper measures to bring his opponent to reason. On Maundy Thursday (10 April) 1343 Clement delivered the *collatio* printed below, by way of introduction to the reading of the *monitionis processus* which was to follow. This process summarizes John XXII's proceedings against Lewis, declares Clement's intention of aggravating the existing sentences and sets a term of three months within which Lewis must lay down the administration of the German kingdom and the empire[3]. Though Lewis wrote in May to announce that he had given the Dauphin Humbert of Vienne power to treat about his reconciliation[4] he had no representative at the Curia when the term expired, and on 11 July he was declared contumacious[5]. That more drastic action was not taken against him at this time may have been due to intervention by the French king on his behalf, as a German chronicler suggests[6]. But Clement maintained the pressure. In August he let fall the hint that he was preparing for the election of an anti-king in opposition to Lewis in Germany[7]. And in time the demonstration achieved the desired result; by the autumn of 1343 Lewis had resumed negotiations with the papacy on terms very similar to those of 1336.

The *collatio* of 10 April 1343 is a noteworthy document in this

---

1. Cf. R. Caggese, *Roberto d'Angio e i suoi tempi*, II (Florence, 1931), p. 276; T. E. Mommsen, *Italienische Analekten zur Reichsgeschichte des 14. Jahrhunderts* (Stuttgart, 1952), nrs. 263-4, pp. 110-11.
2. Below, lines 343-5.
3. Raynaldus, *Annales ecclesiastici*, 1343, §§ xliii-lvii (tom. VI, Lucca, 1750, pp. 323-9).
4. J. P. de Bourchenu, Marquis de Valbonnais, *Histoire de Dauphiné* II (Geneva, 1722), p. 473.
5. S. Riezler, *Vatikanische Akten z. deutschen Geschichte i. d. Zt. Kaiser Ludwigs d. Bayern* (Innsbruck, 1891), nr. 2151, p. 775. An allocution on the text *Impius cum in profundum venerit peccatorum* (Prov. 18, 3), attributed to Clement on this occasion, is preserved in Eichstätt, Staatliche Bibliothek, cod. 698, fos. 494-5. This is the only known copy, and J. Hofer, *Biographische Studien über Wilhelm von Ockham* in *Archivum franciscanum historicum*, VI (1913), p. 664 *sqq.* has produced good reasons for suggesting that as it stands it cannot be authentic. A portion of it is inserted by Conrad of Megenberg in his *Tractatus contra Wilhelmum Occam* of 1354; R. Scholz, *Unbekannte kirchenpolitische Streitschriften aus d. Zt. Ludwigs d. Bayern* II (Berlin, 1914), p. 364.
6. Matthias von Neuenburg, *Chronica*, ed. A. Hofmeister (*MGH. SS. Nova series*, IV, i, 1924), p. 189.
7. Raynaldus, 1343, § lix; Riezler, *Vatikanische Akten*, nr. 2160, n. 1.

successful diplomatic action. Clement displays his wide range of biblical knowledge with a virtuosity which tells us something of his education and his tastes. Of the commentators on Apocalypse he quotes Haymo of Halberstadt (confusing him, as was not uncommon at the time, with Remigius of Auxerre), Ambrosius Autpertus, Richard of St Victor and Rupert of Deutz. St Bernard's *De consideratione* is laid under contribution, as we might expect. But for the rest it is to the Fathers that Clement turns for illustration and authority : to Augustine on half a score of occasions, to Gregory's *Liber moralium* twice, to Origen in the version of Rufinus and to Hilary of Poitiers. Typical perhaps of Clement the Benedictine theologian is the fact that throughout this very political address only once has he recourse to the canon law (for a reference to the *Decretum*). But the *collatio* has something more to offer us than high technical competence in a mode of pulpit eloquence. It interests us most when, from time to time, Clement's passion breaks through the envelope of theological learning and rigidly formal division, and we can catch a glimpse of the strength of his personal feelings and a hint of historical fact for which we have little or no other evidence. Clement's hopes for Lewis' punishment (lines 113-21), his opinion of Marsilio of Padua (lines 177-80), his statement that the extirpation of heretics is a more urgent matter than the recovery of the Holy Land (lines 226-32), his reminiscences of Lewis' dealings with Benedict XII (lines 323-37) : these utterances bring us close to Clement ; they proceed from convictions held with a force which helps to explain why he was probably the most formidable enemy with whom Lewis ever had to contend. In all, the *collatio* was an impressive performance, and it is not surprising that a written version was widely circulated : a few years later Conrad of Megenberg inserted a short passage from it into his tractate against Ockham [1], and Dom Philibert Schmitz has been able to list 7 manuscript versions in addition to the Eichstätt codex from which Höfler published some short extracts in 1868 [2].

I have been unable to consult the Vienna, Cracow and Olmutz manuscripts mentioned by Dom Philibert Schmitz [3], but the following have been collated for this edition :

1. Cf. below, lines 177-80.
2. Höfler, *Aus Avignon*, pp. 18, 20.
3. Schmitz, *Les sermons et discours*, p. 20.

G	Paris	Bibliothèque Ste Geneviève, 240 (saec. xiv), fos. 63-8r.
E	Eichstätt	Staatliche Bibliothek, 698 (saec. xiv), fos. 488-94.
V	Venice	Biblioteca Nazionale di San Marco, cod. lat. IV. 20 (saec. xiv), fos. 95v-98v (incomplete).
C	Cambridge	Corpus Christi College, 534 (saec. xiv), fos. 66v-69v.
M	Munich	Staatsbibliothek, cod. lat. monacen. 21247 (saec. xv), fos. 165-167v.

Both V and M show a family resemblance to G, though neither seems to derive directly from it ; nor does either depend immediately upon the other. E and C belong to another group, with some marked peculiarities. G offers the most consistently satisfactory text, and has been taken as the basis for this edition. But it is by no means impeccable, and on a number of occasions I have preferred readings from the other manuscripts ; when this has been done the reading of G has always been noted in the apparatus. On the other hand only a few of the more important readings from the other manuscripts have been preserved. The spelling of G has been retained, except that consonantal *u* has been written *v* throughout ; punctuation, paragraph divisions and the use of capital letters are my own.

COLLACIO FACTA PER DOMINUM C⟨LEMENTEM⟩ PAPAM VI IN DIE JOVIS SANCTA IN PUBLICACIONE PROSSESUUM CONTRA BAUARUM PONTIFIC⟨II⟩ SUI ANNO PRIMO

Atrium quod est foris, eice foras, Apocalypsis xi°. Remigius super Apocalypsim libro iii° pertractans ista verba dicit sic : *Miranda prorsus locutio, que illud eici foras precipit, quod iam foris existit. Quomodo enim foras eici potest, si intus non est?* Et Ambrosius Anpertus super eodem,

---

Collacio facta in die cene contra Bavarum V ; Collacio Clementis pape VI de Bawaro Ludewico in die cene anno domini mcccxliii E || **3** foris : foras G || **4** Anpertus : expertus E ; *om.* G | eodem : verbo *add. codd.*

---

1 Apoc. 11, 2.

2-4 Haymo Halberstat., *Expositio in Apoc.*, iii, P.L. 117, 1068 ; on the ascription to Remigius of Auxerre cf. M. Manitius, *Gesch. d. latein. Lit. d. Mittelalters*, I, 516-7.

libro suo v° pertractans etiam hoc verbum, dicit sic : *Miranda prorsus locutio, que illud foras eici precipit, quod iam foris ostendit. Quomodo enim atrium hoc foras proici iubetur, quod intus omnino non invenitur? Quod enim non intra sed iam foris est, utique unde foras mittatur non est.* Et licet isti questioni respondeant ipsi dicentes quod talis modus locucionis in scriptura frequenter invenitur (sicut est illud, quod dicitur : *Deleantur de libro viventium, et cum iustis non scribantur* : ' deleantur ', id est ' non scribantur ' ; sicut est illud, quod Deus *induravit cor Pharaonis*, pro eo quod eius duriciam cordis non abstulit, et Ysaias cor populi excecat, quia illi lumen vite non administrat : sic dicitur atrium quod est foris, foras eici, id est ipsum nequaquam infra templi mensuras admitti) : tamen michi videtur quod aliquantulum altius et subtilius contemplanti occurrit, quod aliquid quod est foris, potest foras eici, ymmo foras eicitur de facto, tribus modis.

Videtur enim michi, quod aliquis est foris ecclesiam quandoque per maliciam inique operationis. Peccata enim divident a Deo et ab ecclesia sponsa sua ; unde Ysaie lix° : *Iniquitates vestre diviserunt inter vos et Deum vestrum, et peccata vestra absconderunt faciem eius a vobis ;* et propter hoc dicitur Numerorum v° : *Eiciant de castris omnem leprosum.* Quandoque est aliquis foris per sentenciam iuste excommunicationis. Excommunicatio enim separat a fidelium communione ; et ideo dicit Apostolus II ad Thessalonicenses iii° : *Denunciamus vobis, fratres, in nomine domini nostri Jhesu Christi, subtrahatis vos ab omni fratre ambulante inordinate, et non secundum traditionem, quam acceperunt a nobis ;* et subdit : *Si quis non obedierit verbo nostro, hunc notate, et non commisceamini cum illo, ut confundatur ;* et Amos viii° : *Eicietur, et defluet sicut rivus Egipti.* Quandoque est aliquis foris per adherenciam et pertinaciam dampnate assertionis. Talis enim est hereticus ; hereticus autem divisus est et foris est : et propter hoc Johannes in canonica sua secunda dicit sic : *Si quis venit ad vos, et hanc doctrinam non affert, nolite eum recipere in domum, nec ' Ave ' ei dixeritis. Qui enim dixerit ei ' Ave ', communicat operibus eius malignis ;* et in psalmo : *Vineam de Egipto transtulisti-eiecisti Gentes, et plantasti eam.*

Modo videtur michi, quod qui est foris per maliciam inique operationis, foras eicitur quando publice anathematizatur et eius perversitas propalatur. Unde Richardus de Sancto Victore libro suo iii° super

---

7 foras : foris GV | proici : eici EC || **8** foras : foris GE || **9** isti : huic VEC || **12** est illud : et illud EC || **13** Ysa. vi exceca domine cor populi huius. dicit glosa Deus excecat quia *add.* C || **17** foris, potest foras : foras potest foris G || **18** ymmo foras : ymmo foris GVME | eicitur de facto : de facto est G || **19** aliquis : aliquid G || **24** est : eicitur G || **30** et [1] : *om.* GVE | Eicietur : Eicitur G | sicut : quasi EC || **31** est : eicitur G || **36** et *om.* GVME || **37** Gentes : eos E

5-8 Ambrosius AUTPERTUS, *In Apoc.* v, *Bibl. Max. Patrum* XIII (Lyons, 1677), 521.
10-11 Ps. 68, 29.
12 Exod. 9, 12.
13 cf. Is. 6, 10.
21-22 Is. 59, 2.
23 Num. 5, 2.
26-28 II Thess. 3, 6.
29-30 *ibid.* 3, 14.
30-31 Amos 8, 8.
34-36 II Ioann. 10-11.
36-37 Ps. 79, 9.

Apocalypsim pertractans verba thematis nostri, dicit sic : *Atrium falsi Christiani sunt, qui videntur consecrati, eo quod sunt baptizati, sed pleni sunt cadaveribus, id est viciis et pravis operibus; qui quamvis fidelibus iuncti sint nomine, longe tamen sunt actione. Isti foras eiciuntur, quociens separati a fidelibus predicantur.* De quibus dicitur Thren. iiº : *Jacuerunt in terra foris, et ceciderunt; percussisti, nec misereberis.*

Secundo, ille qui est foris per sentenciam iuste excommunicacionis, foras eicitur quando multipliciter aggravatur et penarum qualitas et quantitas cumulatur vel etiam alio et alio anathemate alligatur : Danielis ivº : *Alligetur vinculo ferreo et ereo in herbis, que foris sunt, et cum feris pars eius in herbis terre;* sicut fuit illa Engeltruda anathematizata, iiiª, q. iv, *Engeltrudam.*

Tercio, qui est foris per adherenciam et pertinaciam dampnate assertionis, foras eicitur quando sentencialiter sicut hereticus condempnatur et curie seculari relinquitur vel, si haberi non potest, contra eum indulgencia conceditur et crux predicatur : prima ad Thimotheum primo : *Quidam circa fidem naufragaverunt, de quibus est Ymeneus et Allexander, quos tradidi Sathane, ut discant non blasphemare.* De talibus dicitur prima ad Corinthios vº : *Eos, qui foris sunt, Deus iudicabit.* Patet ergo quod qui foris est, tripliciter adhuc foras eici potest et eicitur tribus modis.

Modo videtur michi, quod ille sceleratissimus, excommunicatus, scismaticus, hereticorum fautor et verus hereticus, Ludovicus de Bauaria, est istis tribus modis foris extra ecclesiam Dei evidenter. Primo enim est inmanissimis sceleribus, tyranniis et criminibus maculatus. Secundo est gravissimis penis, sentenciis et excommunicacionibus innodatus. Tercio est de perniciosissimis et periculosissimis heresibus, fautoriis et scismatibus condempnatus. Ergo foris est.

Dico primo quod est inmanissimis sceleribus, tyranniis et criminibus maculatus. Ad litteram enim potest dici de illo quod scribitur prima ad Thimotheum primo : *Blasphemus, persecutor et contumeliosus.* Unde potest dici de eo quod dicitur de illo malo Anthiocho rege, II Machabeorum ixº, quod erat *homicida blasphemus* et inde *pessime percussus*

---

42 eo : et GV || **44** sint nomine : *om.* EC | longe... actione : sint longe cum actione E ; sunt longe tamen actione C ; tamen longe sunt actione VM || **45** Tren. G || **48** foras : foris CVE || **51** sicut : sic G || **52** Engeltrudam : Engeldruda uxor Rosoli E || **56** conceditur : concedatur G || **58** tradidi : tradidit GVME || **59** foris : foras G | iudicabit : iudicavit V || **60** foris : foras G | foras eici potest : foris est G || **63** Lodwicus V ; Ludewicus E || **64** foris *om.* VMC || **65** inmanissimis : inhumanissimis V || **65** maculatus : Ergo foris est tripliciter *add.* E || **67** innodatus : Ergo foris est *add.* EC || **67-68** Tercio... foris est *om.* E || **68** est : unde dicitur Atrium quod foris est eice foras *add.* C || **69** inmanissimis : inhumanissimis V || **70** illo : eo ECV || **73** inde : ideo ECV

41-45 Richardus de Sancto Victore, *In Apoc.*, iii, 7, P. L. 196, 792.
45-46 Thren. 2, 21 (much compressed).
50-51 Dan. 4, 20 (a free rendering).
52 *Decretum Gratiani*, c. 12, C. 3, q. 4, ed. Friedberg, c. 514.
57-58 I Tim. 1, 19-20.
59 I Corinth. 5, 13.
71 cf. I Tim. 1, 13.
73 II Machab. 9, 28.
74 *Ibid.* 8, 34.

a Domino. Et ideo potest dici sicut ille Nichanor, qui facinorosissimus dicitur II Machabeorum viii^{o}. Unde iste etiam videtur Pharaonis maliciam superasse. Pharao enim dixisse fertur Exodi ix^{o} Moysi et Aaron : *Peccavi. Dominus iustus : ego et populus meus, impii. Orate Dominum.* Quasi enim in profundum malorum veniens, sic contempnit Deum et ecclesiam, quod iam fere XXVI annis et ultra dimissus Sathane nec ad matrem rediens lapsus est de peccato in peccatum (quia peccatum, quod per penitenciam mox non diluitur, *suo pondere ad aliud trahit*, sicut dicit Gregorius) ; et ideo traditus est *in reprobum sensum, ut* faciat *que non conveniunt*, et que etiam pudet recitare. Unde videtur verificatum de eo cum sibi adherentibus illud II ad Thimotheum iii^{o} : *Instabunt tempora periculosa, et erunt homines seipsos amantes, cupidi, elati, superbi, blasphemi, parentibus inobedientes, ingrati, scelesti, sine affectione, sine pace, criminatores, incontinentes, inmites, sine benignitate, proditores, protervi, immundi, ceci, voluptatum amatores magis quam Dei, habentes quidem speciem pietatis, virtutem autem eius abnegantes. Et hos devita.* Et sequitur : *Quemadmodum Yannes et Mambres restiterunt Moysi, ita et isti resistunt veritati, homines corrupti mente, reprobi circa fidem. Sed ultra non proficient; insipientia enim eorum manifesta erit omnibus, sicut illorum fuit.* Et videte quod iste in tantam prorupit insaniam quod, quemadmodum ille draco absorbere volebat filium, quem paritura erat *mulier amicta sole*, de quo dicitur Apocalypsis xii^{o}, ita iste conatur omnino sanctam ecclesiam et eius potestatem a Deo sibi datam absorbere : et iniquas leges contra ecclesiam condendo ; et episcopos insti-

---

77 iustus : iudex G || **78** enim : *om.* G | et : *om.* G || **79** XXVI : XXVIII VM || **80** matrem : ecclesiam *add.* EC || **84** cum : et EC || **92** proficient *scripsi;* proficiens GM ; proficientes V ; reficient EC | manifesta : est et *add.* EC || **97** ecclesiam : ecclesias V ; eam E

---

77 Exod. 9, 27-28.

78 cf. Prov. 18, 3.

79 XXVI annis : on 31 March 1317 Pope John XXII had issued the constitution *Si fratrum* assuming the empire to be vacant and declaring penalties against those who should meddle with it in despite of the papal claims *vacante imperio : MGH. Const.*, V, nr. 401, pp. 340-1. Lewis' attempts to intervene in imperial matters in Italy up to this time had been few and feeble (cf. *Const.*, V, nrs 195, 239, 333, pp. 179, 207, 282), but that he was thought to have offended against the principles of *Si fratrum* is suggested by the appearance of this constitution as the first item in the *Liber processuum* kept against him at the Curia : cf. Martene et Durand, *Thesaurus Novus Anecdotorum*, II (Paris, 1717), cc. 641-4.

81 Gregorius Magnus, *Moral.*, xxv, 9, P. L. 76, 334.

82 cf. Rom. 1, 28.

84-89 II Tim. 3, 1-5.

90-93 *ibid.*, 3, 8-9.

95 cf. Apoc. 12, 1-4.

97 iniquas leges : presumably the reference is to the great German constitutional declarations of 1338 : the *Kurverein* and *Weisthum* of Rhens, and the imperial law *Licet iuris*. Texts : M. Krammer, *Quellen z. Gesch. d. deutsch. Köningswahl* (Leipzig, 1911), pp. 89, 91 ; K. Zeumer, *Das Königswahlgesetz Licet Iuris, Neues Archiv*, XXX (1904) p. 87.

97-98 episcopos instituendo : cf. for example Lewis' nomination of John of Jandun as bishop of Ferrara in May 1328 : *MGH. Const.*, VI, nr 444, p. 366; A. Hauck, *Kirchengesch. Deutschlands* V, i (Leipzig, 1911), p. 525 ; O. Bornhak, *Staatskirchliche Anschauungen u. Handlungen am Hofe Kaiser Ludwigs d. Bayern* (Weimar, 1933), pp. 67-71.

tuendo ; et interdictum violando et illos qui nolunt violare de beneficiis expellendo, ymmo (ut nobis relatum extitit) etiam aliquos occidendo ; matrimonia solennizata in facie ecclesie separando et in gradibus consanguinitatis et affinitatis prohibitis coniungendo ; ydolum in ecclesia constituendo, illum scilicet antipapam ; claves ecclesie non solum contempnendo, ymmo negando, et non contentus ut hominum maliciam superaret, voluit etiam maliciam demonum superare. Ille enim Lucifer equalitatem Dei appetiit, sed iste se Deo et eius vicario preponere voluit, ipsum papam Dei vicarium etiam de facto deponendo, ymmo quod sibi liceat et omni imperatori papam deponere etiam heretice asserendo : ut merito de eo dici possit illud II Johannis : *Hic est seductor et antichristus.* Sed sicut Michael et angeli eius preliati sunt cum dracone, et *proiectus est ille draco magnus, serpens antiquus, qui vocatur dyabolus et Sathanas, qui seducit universum orbem:* ita et iste, nisi convertatur et redeat, proicietur *in tenebras exteriores: ubi erit fletus, et stridor dentium.* Et certe speramus in Domino, quod nisi peccata nostra obsistant, non solum reservabitur in tartarum eternis ignibus cruciandus, sed etiam hic eius pena inchoabitur et ira Dei deseviet super eum, sicut factum est de Herode rege, Actuum xii°, qui percussus ab angelo Domini *eo quod non dedisset honorem Deo, consumptus a vermibus expiravit:* ut de eo dicatur illud Deuteronomii xxxii° : *Foris vastabit* eum *gladius, et intus pavor ;* ut de eo merito dicamus illud II ad Corinthios iv° : *Qui foris est homo corrumpitur, sed is, qui intus est, renovatur de die in diem.*

---

101 ecclesia : Dei *add.* EC || **102-103** contempnendo : condempnando G || **106** vicarium : deponere *add.* G || **114** servabitur G || **116** est : fuit EC || **118** xxxii° : xxii° G || **120** renovatur : renovabitur E

---

98 interdictum violando etc : cf. *MGH. Const.*, VI, nrs 727, 728, 854, pp. 619, 620, 713 ; Hauck, pp. 525 *sqq.*, 557 ; Bornhak, pp. 45-50.

99 occidendo : that any executions did take place seems wholly improbable. But at least in theory Lewis regarded bishops who opposed him as having incurred the penalties of treason ; cf. *MGH. Const.*, VI, nr 444, p. 366, and the case of Simone Saltarelli, Archbishop of Pisa, quoted by R. Davidsohn, *Gesch. v. Florenz*, III (Berlin, 1912), p. 807.

100-101 matrimonia etc. : presumably Clement VI had in mind the expulsion of John Henry of Luxemburg, husband of Margaret Maultasch, from Tirol in November 1341, followed by the celebration of a form of marriage between Margaret and Lewis' eldest son, Lewis of Brandenburg, at Schloss Tirol in February 1342. Margaret and Lewis of Brandenburg were related in the third degree. Cf. Bornhak, pp. 116-121. But already in 1327 John XXII had complained of the emperor's illegal conduct in a matrimonial case : *MGH. Const.*, VI, nr 274, p. 186.

101-102 ydolum : Peter of Corbara, the anti-pope Nicholas V. He is termed *ydolum* in the letter in which the commune of Florence informed John XXII about his appointment, which took place on 12 May 1328 : *MGH. Const.*, VI, nr 453, p. 372.

107-108 cf. Lewis' constitution *Gloriosus Deus* of 18 April 1328 : *MGH. Const.*, VI, nr 436, p. 344 *sqq.*

108-109 II Ioann. 7.

110-111 Apoc. 12, 9.

112-113 Matth. 8, 12.

115 cf. Iosue 22, 18.

117-118 Act. 12, 23.

118-119 Deut. 32, 25.

120-121 II Corinth. 4, 16 (freely adapted).

Dico secundo, quod ipse est gravissimis penis, sententiis et excommunicacionibus innodatus, sicut apparet in processibus factis per felicis recordationis Johannem XXII predecessorem nostrum, quos statim recollectos in substancia succincte et breviter audietis. Ipse enim fuit ex contumacia excommunicatus ; item, ex inobediencia ; item, ex hereticorum fautoria ; item, ex hereticali perfidia ; item, ex scismate et ecclesie scissura ; item, fere ex omnibus causis, propter quas et in scriptura sacra et in iure aliquis anathematis vinculo innodatur. Quia, sicut dicit Augustimus in libro suo de correptione et gratia, capitulo xxiii° : *Corripiantur a prepositis sui subditi correptionibus de caritate venientibus, pro culparum diversitate diversis, vel minoribus vel amplioribus:* etiam ipsa, que dampnacio nominatur, quam facit episcopale iudicium ; quia pena in ecclesia nulla maior est. Et rationem reddit Augustinus, super Johannem omelia li^a. Dicit enim sic : *Cum excommunicat ecclesia, in celo ligatur excommunicatus ; cum reconciliatur ab ecclesia, in celo solvitur reconciliatus.* Merito ergo ista pena magna est, tamen necessaria. Unde Augustinus ubi supra (scilicet de correptione et gratia) subdit quod *pastoralis necessitas habet, ne per plures serpant dira contagia, separare a sanis ovibus morbidam, ab ipso, cui nichil est impossibile, ipsa forsitan separacione sanandam.* Sic fecit ad litteram Apostolus, prima ad Corinthios v°, qui illum Corinthium tradidit Sathane qui postmodum correctus est, ut apparet II ad Corinthios ii°. Et propterea dicebat Salvator Matthei xviii° : *Qui ecclesiam non audierit, sit tibi sicut ethnicus et publicanus ;* et merito, quia sicut dicit Augustinus in libro suo contra epistolam Fundamenti : *Non crederem ewangelio, nisi ad hoc me ecclesie auctoritas commoveret.* Et ideo de talibus dicitur II Paralip. xxiii° : *Educite extra septa templi foris* et ibi *interficiatur gladio ;* quia Matthei xiii° dicitur de bonis angelis : *Malos autem foras miserunt.*

Tercio dico, quod est de perniciosissimis heresibus, fautoriis et scismatibus condempnatus. Ipse enim est condempnatus de triplici heresi. Primo de paupertate Christi et Apostolorum. Ipse enim asseruit determinationem factam per ecclesiam esse hereticam et iuravit se credere contrarium, sicut apparet in appellacione magna, quam fecit

---

124 quos : quod EV ‖ **125** et : *om.* E ; et etiam V ‖ **127** hereticali : pertinacia et perfidia *add.* E ‖ **130** correptione : corr. G ; correctione ECVM ‖ **131** prepositis sui : proposito cui E | correptionibus : corr. ibus G ; correctionibus VM ; correctione EC ‖ **133** nominatur : nuncupatur V | facit : fecit G ‖ **137** est, tamen : tamen est V ; est cum E ‖ **139** serpant : serpent *ex* serpant G ; serpat *ex* serpentes *manu recentiori* V ; separentur E ‖ **140** contagia : *ex* contagius *corr.* G ; contagio V | ipso : illo VEC ‖ **142** Corinthium : corintheum G

124-125 quos... recollectos : that is, in the *monitionis processus ;* printed RAYNALDUS, *Annales ecclesiastici*, 1343, §§ xliii-lvii.

131-133 Augustinus, *Lib. de correptione et gratia*, c. 15, PL. 44, 944.

135-137 *idem*, *In Ioann. Evangel.*, tr. l, c. 12, P. L. 35, 1763.

142-143 I Corinth. 5, 5 ; II Corinth. 2, 6-8.

144-145 Matth. 18, 17.

146-147 AUGUSTINUS, *Contra epist. Fundamenti*, c. 5, P. L. 42, 176.

148 II Paralip. 23, 14.

149 Matth. 13, 48.

154 appellacione magna : the Sachsenhausen appeal of 22 May 1324, *MGH. Const.*, V, nr 909, p. 722 *sqq.* The *determinatio* of the Church attacked was that of John XXII in his

contra dominum papam Johannem. Secundo de alia heresi, qua asseruit quod ad imperatorem pertinet deponere papam et instituere : que heresis, quam periculosa est et subvertens totum statum ecclesie, quamque contra omne ius naturale, divinum, canonicum et humanum pertransimus, quia etiam dicta heresis nullo colore fulcitur, dicente Apostolo prima ad Corinthios ii° quod *spiritualis* homo *omnia diiudicat, ipse* autem *a nemine iudicatur.* Tercio condempnatus est de heresi, quia citatus super heresi et propter contumaciam excommunicatus, in dicta excommunicatione non solum per annum, sed etiam plus quam per decem pertinaciter stetit. Condempnatus est etiam de scismate, quia tunicam Domini inconsutilem, quam etiam Gentiles horruerunt dividere, ipse scindere et dividere nisus est, antipapam creando, ydolum in ecclesia constituendo. Quam grave autem sit tale scisma incipere, apparet Numerorum xvi° capitulo, ubi legitur quod Datan et Abiron, qui sacerdotium, quod Deus instituerat esse in Aaron, dividere voluerunt, non solum morte solita interierunt, sed etiam infernus absorbuit eos vivos, et etiam eos, qui in eis consenserunt, ignis consumpsit. Unde possumus dicere isti quod dicebat Augustinus in epistola ad Emeritum Donatistam, ubi dicit sic : *Vobis obicimus schismatis crimen, quod etiam heresim male perseverando fecistis.* Fuit etiam condempnatus de fautoria hereticorum. Ipse enim Marsilium de Padua et Johannem de Janduno heresiarchas et de heresi condempnatos sustinuit et secum tenuit usque ad mortem eorum ; et audemus dicere quod vix nunquam legimus peiorem hereticum illo Marsilio. Unde de mandato Benedicti predecessoris nostri de quodam eius libello plus quam ducentos et quadraginta articulos hereticales extraximus. Dicitur etiam multis aliis hereticis favisse. Et ideo merito de eo dicitur, ad Titum iii° capitulo : *Hereticum hominem devita : sciens quia subversus est, qui huiusmodi est.* Et nemirum,

---

159 pertransimus : pertransiens EC ‖ **160** prima : primo G ; Paulo E | iii° G ‖ **167** incipere : *om.* VEC ‖ **169** instituerat : constituerat VEC ‖ **171** in eis consenserunt : consenserant eis EC | consumpsit : combussit EC ‖ **172** isti : istis E ; istud V ‖ **174** heresim : habet *add.* GV ‖ **175** Janduno : Lauduno G ‖ **179** quam : b ne *add.* V ‖ **181** iii° : iv° G ‖ **182** Et nemirum : enim mirum G

---

constitutions *Ad conditorem canonum* and *Cum inter nonnullos ; ibid.*, p. 734 *sqq.* Lewis' oath, *ibid.*, p. 743. Cf. J. Hofer, *Zur Gesch. d. Appellationen König Ludwigs d. Baiern, Hist. Jb.*, XXXVIII (1917), p. 501 *sqq. ;* F. Bock, *Die Appellationenschriften König Ludwigs IV, Deutsches Archiv f. Gesch. d. Mittelalters*, IV (1941), p. 179 *sqq.*

156 deponere papam : cf. note to l. 106 *supra*.

160-161 I Corinth. 2, 15.

164 decem : Lewis was cited for heresy 3 April 1327, declared contumacious 23 October 1327 : *MGH. Const.*, VI, nrs 274, 361, pp. 185, 267.

165-166 cf. Ioann. 19, 23-4.

168-171 Num. 16, 1-36.

173-174 Augustinus, *Epist.* lxxxvii, P. L. 33, 298.

177 mortem eorum : this seems the first evidence for the death of Marsilio. John of Jandun had died at or near Todi in September 1328 : cf. N. Valois, in *Hist. littéraire de France*, XXXIII (1906), pp. 600-2.

177-180 et audemus... extraximus : these lines are inserted *verbatim* by Conrad of Megenberg in his *Tractatis contra Wilhelmum Occam*, printed by R. Scholz, *Unbekannte kirchenpolitische Streitschriften*, II, 364.

181-182 Tit. 3, 10-11.

si de una heresi venerit in aliam, quia, sicut dicit beatus Gregorius IIIº Moralium capitulo xviº : *Habent hoc heretici proprium, quod in eo gradu, quo ab ecclesia exeunt, diu stare non possunt, sed ad deteriora cotidie ruunt, et sentiendo opera peiora in multis se partibus scindunt.* Ideo Amos, vº capitulo, dicit : *In cunctis, qui foris sunt, dicitur Ve, ve.*

Habemus ergo duo. Primo quod ille, qui est foris per maliciam inique operationis, adhuc foras eicitur quando publice anathematizatur et eius perversitas propalatur ; item, quod ille, qui est foris per sententiam iuste excommunicationis, foras eicitur quando aggravatur et penarum qualitas et quantitas cumulatur ; item, quod qui est foris per adherentiam et pertinaciam dampnate assertionis, adhuc foras eicitur quando sententialiter condempnatur et quando contra eum indulgencia conceditur et crux predicatur. Habemus secundo, quod iste sceleratissimus Ludouicus est foris ecclesiam quia inmanissimis sceleribus, tyranniis et criminibus maculatus ; item, quia gravissimis penis, sententiis et excommunicationibus innodatus ; item, quia de perniciosissimis et periculosissimis heresibus, fautoriis et scismatibus condempnatus. Ergo merito ipse, qui foris est, adhuc foras eiciendus est et per sue iniquitatis propalationem, et per sententiarum aggravationem et penarum cumulationem, et etiam per crucis contra eum predicationem : ut merito dicantur verba thematis preassumpti : *Atrium quod est foris, eice foras.*

Ubi tanguntur duo. Primo enim aliquid michi preponitur intuendum : quia *Atrium quod est foris ;* secundo aliquid michi precipitur exequendum: *Eice foras.* Unde primo hic demonstratur flagicium, exaggeratur vicium nefande malignitatis : *Atrium quod est foris.* Secundo imperatur exercitium, imploratur officium iniuncte potestatis et date auctoritatis : *Eice foras.*

Dico primo quod demonstratur flagicium, exaggeratur vicium nefande malignitatis : *Atrium quod est foris.* Istud enim *Atrium* hereticos recte significat. Unde Rupertus super isto verbo dicit sic : *Per illud 'Atrium' hereticos intellige, quia sicut atrium templo quidem vicinum est, sed in templo vel templum non est, ita sunt heretici, ' habentes quidem speciem pietatis, virtutem autem* <*eius*> *abnegantes '.* Cum ergo dicitur : *Atrium quod est foris,* demonstratur flagicium nefande malignitatis. Quantum autem et quale est istud flagicium, deducit Augustinus XXI de civitate Dei, capitulo xxviº, dicens expresse quod peiores sunt quam Iudei

---

183 venerit : venit VEC || **185** quo ab : in quo de EC || **186** opera : se G ; *om.* V || **187** qui : que G | dicitur : duo dicuntur G ; *om.* V || **188** duo : *om.* G || **189** foras eicitur *om.* GV || **192** quantitas et qualitas *trs.* G || **196** Lud. E ; lodwicus V | foris : extra *add.* E | inmanissimis : inhumanissimis V || **200** foras : foris GE || **202** merito : michi *add.* ECVM || **204** Ubi tanguntur duo : tanguntur *om.* V ; ubi duo sunt notanda EC || **209** Eice foras *om.* G || **211** foris : foras G || **212** Rupertus *scripsi ;* B. G, Bernardus *in marg. addens ;* Rabanus ECVM || **215** autem *om.* G | eius *supplevi ; om.* GVM ; anime EC || **217** XXI *ex* XXII *corr.* G || **218** capitulo xxviº *om.* G

184-186 Gregorius MAGNUS, *Moral.*, iii, 25, P. L. 75, 623.
187 Amos 5, 16.
203 Apoc. 11, 2.
212-215 Rupertus TUITIENSIS, *Comment. in Apoc.*, vi, 11, P. L. 169, 1018 ; cf. II Tim. 3, 5.

vel pagani, qui nunquam fidem susceperunt. Unde dicit sic : Heretici non ideo ab eterno supplicio liberentur, *quod in catholica ecclesia baptizati sunt et sacramentum corporis Christi in vero Christi corpore primitus acceperunt, cum peior sit utique desertor fidei et ex desertore oppugnator eius effectus, quam ille qui non deseruit quod nunquam tenuit.* Et ideo dicit Petrus in canonica sua secunda, iiº capitulo : *Melius illis erat non cognoscere viam iusticie, quam post agnitionem retrorsum converti ab eo, quod illis traditum est sancto mandato.* Et ideo mirandum est de aliquibus, qui quando crux predicatur contra hereticum nec ita assumunt nec ita sumendum putant, sicut quando predicatur in subsidium terre sancte. Et tamen sine comparacione utilius et magis necessarium est ecclesie, ut heretici extirpentur ab ea, qui faciunt ipsi ecclesie seditionem et bellum intestinum, quam terra perdita recuperetur vel quam sit quodcunque bellum contra paganos vel Iudeos. Ideo dicebat Apostolus ad Galathas vº : *Utinam abscindantur, qui vos conturbant;* et primo capitulo dicit : *Si quis aliud ewangelizaverit preter id, quod accepistis, anathema sit.* Et ideo boni Christiani statim ad preceptum vicarii Christi debent opus istud assumere, sicut illi de quibus legitur Levitici xº, qui statim ad preceptum Moysi pergentes, licet essent fratres, eos qui imposuerunt ignem alienum coram Domino confestim *eiecerunt foras, ut sibi fuerat imperatum.* Ideo cuilibet bono Christiano dicitur : Eice *et proice abs te,* Matthei ixº. De isto atrio sic existente foris videtur michi dictum in figura Matthei xxviº, ubi dicitur quod Petrus, cum Christum negavit, erat foris in atrio : qui ad litteram fidem negavit. De hoc etiam videtur michi esse dictum Hester viº capitulo : *Aman est in atrio foris;* de quo etiam Aman dicitur statim in viiº capitulo : *Hostis noster et inimicus pessimus est iste Aman.* Aman, id est Bavarus. Ad litteram Aman interpretatur iniquus, vel coanguscans vel comprimens me. Ad litteram enim ipse in se iniquus (ut *quasi ex adipe* prodiret *iniquitas* eius, ita *ut iniquitas eius* inveniretur *ad odium*) et per odium coanguscat et comprimit ecclesiam quantum potest ; quia, ut verum fatear, ipse omni genere persecutionis ecclesiam suo conamine coanguscat et comprimit. Propheta enim in psalmo exprimit quatuor persecutiones datas ecclesie, a quibus tamen, Deo protegente, non habet timere, scilicet : *A timore nocturno, a sagitta volante in die, a negocio perambulante in tenebris : ab incursu, et demonio meridiano. A timore* inquam *nocturno,* propter nequiciam perpetrati sceleris ; *a sagitta volante*

---

223 quod : qui G ‖ **226** sancto : secundo G ‖ **230** ipsi : Christi E ‖ **240** ixº *codd.; potius* vº ‖ **242** qui : quia ECVM ‖ **245** est iste Bavarus *add.* VE ‖ **247-248** prodiret : prodire G ‖ **248-249** et per odium *om.* ECVM ‖ **252** tamen, Deo protegente : tamen eo protegente E ; cum Deo protegente C ; cum eo protegente VM

220-223 Augustinus, *de Civit. Dei,* xxi, 25, P. L. 41, 742.
224-226 II Pet. 2, 21.
233 Gal. 5, 12.
234-235 *ibid.*, 1, 9.
237-239 Levit. 10, 5 ; cf. *ibid.*, 10.
240 Matth. 5, 29.
241-242 *ibid.*, 26, 69.
244 cf. Esther 6, 5.
245 *ibid.*, 7, 6.
247-248 cf. Ps. 72, 7 ; *ibid.*, 35, 3.
253-254 Ps. 90, 5-6.

in die, propter violenciam et evidenciam patrati scismatis ; *a negocio perambulante in tenebris*, propter perfidiam dampnate heresis ; *ab incursu, et demonio meridiano*, propter violentiam et vehementiam dire tyrannidis. Est ergo *hostis et inimicus noster pessimus*, persequens sanctam ecclesiam sicut peccator gravissimus, sicut scismaticus, sicut hereticus, sicut tyrannus crudelissimus, non attendens illud Matthei xvi°: *Porte inferi non prevalebunt adversus eam*, nec illud quod Hilarius dicit VII de Trinitate capitulo iii° : *Hoc ecclesie proprium est, quod tunc vincat cum leditur, tunc intelligat cum arguitur, tunc obtineat cum deseritur;* et subdit : *Hoc habet proprium ecclesia: dum persequitur, floret; dum opprimitur, crescit; dum contempnitur, proficit; dum leditur, vincit; dum arguitur, intelligit; tunc stat, cum superari videtur.* Merito ergo iste dicitur 'Atrium quod est foris', de quo dicitur in figura Ezechielis xlii° : *Non egredietur de sanctis in atrium exterius*, id est foris.

Dico secundo quod imperatur exercitium, imploratur officium iniuncte potestatis et date auctoritatis, quia michi dicitur : *Eice foras.* Michi enim ad litteram competit ex officio. Unde Bernhardus III de Consideratione ad Eugenium capitulo ii° dicit sic : *Curandum summopere tibi et tota vigilantia considerandum est, quomodo et qui non sapiunt, sapiant ; et qui sapiunt, non desipiant ; et qui desipuerint, resipiscant. Proinde oportet tibi dare operam quam potes, ut infideles convertantur ad fidem, conversi non avertantur, aversi quoque revertantur, porro perversi ordinentur ad rectitudinem, subversi quoque ad veritatem revocentur, subversores invictis rationibus convincantur, et emendentur ipsi, si fieri potest, vel si non, perdant auctoritatem facultatemque alios subvertendi. Sunt enim summo studio aut corrigendi, ne pereant, aut cohercendi, ne perimant.* Et II° libro capitulo vi° dicit sic : *Accingere gladio tuo, ' gladio spiritus, quod est verbum Dei ', glorifica manum et brachium dexterum in faciendo ' vindictam in nationibus et increpationes in populis, ad alligandos reges eorum in conpedibus, et nobiles eorum in manicis ferreis '. Si facis hec, honorificas ministerium tuum, et ministerium te. Cura ergo extirpare malas bestias a terminis tuis, ut greges tui securi in pascua deducantur.* Et in libro IV° capitulo ultimo dicit sic : *Oportere te esse, considera, ultorem scelerum, malorum metum, bonorum gloriam, virgam potentium, malleum tyrannorum, regum patrem, legum moderatorem, canonum dispensatorem, sal terre, orbis lumen, sacerdotem Altissimi,*

---

256 patrati : perpetrati V ‖ **267** cum : *in marg. add.* G ‖ **269** id est foris : idem est exterius quod est foris ECVM ‖ **273** Eugenium : papam *add.* E ‖ **275** sapiunt : sapiant GE | desipuerint *ex* desipuerunt *corr.* G ; desipuerunt V ‖ **276** infideles : increduli ECVM ‖ **277** avertantur *ex* advertantur *corr.* G ; advertantur E | aversi *ex* adversi *corr.* G ; adversi E ‖ **284** faciendo : *desinit* V ‖ **285** manicis : manibus G ‖ **286** honorificas : honorifices G | et : in *add.* G

---

259 Esther 7, 6.

262 Matth. 16, 18.

263-264 Hilarius Pictav., *de Trin.*, vii, 4, P. L. 10, 202.

265-267 I have not found this passage in the editions of Hilary.

269 Ezech. 42, 14.

273-282 Bernardus Claraevallensis, *de Consid.*, iii, 1, P. L. 182, 759.

282-288 Bernardus, iii, 6, c. 749.

282 Ephes. 6, 17.

284-285 Ps. 149, 8-9.

288-298 Bernardus, iv, 7, c. 788.

vicarium Christi, christum Domini, postremo deum Pharaonis. Intellige que dico ; dabit enim tibi Dominus intellectum. Ubi malicie iuncta potentia est, aliquid tibi supra homines presumendum. Vultus tuus super facientes mala. Timeat spiritum ire tue, qui hominem non veretur, gladium non formidat. Timeat excommunicationem, *qui ammonicionem contempsit. Cui irasceris tu, Deum sibi iratum, non hominem putet. Qui te non audierit, auditurum Deum contra se paveat,* dicente Ipso : *Qui vos audit, me audit, et qui vos spernit, me spernit;* Cant. ii^{o} : *Capite nobis vulpes parvulas, que demoliuntur vineas.*

Et videte quod istud *Eicere* est exemplo Christi, qui fecit flagellum de funiculis et eiecit de templo vendentes et ementes, Matthei xxi^{o} et Marci xi^{o} et Luce xix^{o}. Ita est infixum ossibus nostris, quod (sicut deducit Augustinus, Omelia xlvi^{a} super Johannem, pertractans illud Johannis x^{o} : *Mercenarius autem, et qui non est pastor, videt lupum venientem, et fugit;* fugit autem, *quia non pertinet ad eum de ovibus*) dicit quod mercenarius est et non pastor, qui ex quacunque causa, sive propter inimicicias subsequentes sive alias, omittit aliquem excommunicare et a communione fidelium separare. Unde dicit sic : *Quis est mercenarius, qui videt lupum venientem et fugit? Ille qui sua querit, non que Jhesu Christi; qui peccantem non libere audet arguere. Ecce nescio quis peccavit, graviter peccavit; increpandus est, excommunicandus est. Sed excommunicatus inimicus erit, insidiabitur, nocebit cum potuerit. Iamque ille, qui sua querit, non que Jhesu Christi, ne perdat quod sectatur, humane amicicie scilicet commoditatem, et inimicitiarum humanarum incurrat molestiam, tacet, non corripit. Ecce lupus ingreditur, apprehendit et rapit. O mercenarie, lupum venientem vidisti, et fugisti. Respondebit forte et dicet: ' Ecce hic sum, et non fugi '. Certe fugisti, quia tacuisti; et tacuisti, quia timuisti: fuga animi timor est. Corpore stetisti, sed spiritu fugisti.* Quod non faciebat Apostolus, qui, etsi corpore absens, spiritu tamen presens Corinthium Sathane tradidit, prima ad Corinthios v^{o}. Et ideo dicebat propheta : *Ve michi, quia tacui,* Ysaie vi^{o}.

Sed diceres michi : ' Tu videris arguere predecessorem tuum immediatum, qui toto tempore pontificii sui tacuit, nec processit. ' Respondeo et dico quod dictus predecessor, ad convincendum magis istius maliciam, ipsum longo tempore expectavit, credens quod expectatio prodesse posset ad salutem ipsius, quam summe desideravit. Sed ad litteram

---

293 malicie : malicia EC || **296** excommunicationem : orationem P.L. || **298** dicente Ipso : dicit enim ipse EC || **299** ii^{o} : ix^{o} G ; *om.* E | nobis : vobis GE | parvulas, que : parvulas qui G ; parvulos qui E || **301** est : *del.* G || **303** nostris : meis ECM || **304** xlvi^{a} : xvi^{a} G || **305** x^{o} : ix^{o} G || **307** qui *ex* quia *corr.* G ; quia E || **310** venientem : *om.* G || **313** qui : que EC || **314** sua : sunt *add. codd.* | amicicie : amicitiarum G || **323** diceres : dicitur EC || **325** dictus : *om.* G || **327** desideravit : desiderabat EC

298-299 Luc. 10, 16.
299-300 Cant. 2, 15.
302-303 Matth. 21, 12 ; Marc. 11, 15 ; Luc. 19, 45.
305-306 Ioann. 10, 12-13.
309-319 Augustinus, *In Ioann. Evangel.*, tr. xlvi, P. L. 35, 1732.
311 cf. I Tim. 5, 20.
321 I Corinth. 5, 3-5.
322 Is. 6, 5.

verificatum est illud Ysaie v° : Expectavi *ut faceret uvas, et fecit labruscas* (vel spinas, sicut habet ad litteram Augustinus). Unde *dedit ei locum penitentie et ipse abusus est eo in superbiam*, Job xxiiii°. Nota quomodo, cum misisset ad eum episcopum Magalonensem, ipsum quadam die vocavit et quasi vellet aliquid se facturum pro ecclesia in eius presentia vestibus imperialibus se induit et multa enormia contra ecclesiam fecit. Unde ipsemet predecessor sicut bonus pastor non solum expectavit ut ipse veniret, ymmo ipsum volebat super humeros suos imponere et reducere ad ovile. Sed ipse econtra ficte sibi multa promittebat, de quibus etiam litteras suas dedit, sed tamen nichil opere adimplevit.

Et certe nos etiam ipsum fere per unum annum expectavimus, et Deus scit quantum reconciliacionem suam desiderabamus et quam favorabiles et misericordes nos exhibuissemus eidem, et propter salutem suam et multorum aliorum, et etiam propter favorem aliquorum, qui toto corde pro eius reconciliatione instabant. Sed certe ipse illusit eis et nobis. Nam nuncii sui qui venerunt, illa que promiserat et sigillaverat tempore predecessoris dixerunt quod nullo modo faceret, ymmo quasi quidquid ibi erat ad honorem ecclesie resecarunt, et cetera. Ut dicatur

---

329 habet : etiam M | ad litteram Augustinus : littera Augustini EC || **330** superbia G || **338** ipsum *om.* G | unum *om.* EM || **344** quasi : quod EC || **345** resecarunt : reserabit C

328-329 *ibid.* 5, 2.

329 Augustinus, *Enarr. in Ps. xxxv*, P. L. 36, 346 ; cf. Hieronymus, *Comment. in Is.*, ii, P. L. 24, 78.

329-330 cf. Iob 24, 23.

330-333 On the mission of the papal chaplain Master Arnaud de Verdale (bishop of Maguelonne in April 1339) to Lewis in September 1338, cf. Riezler, *Vatikanische Akten*, nr 1974, p. 714. The incident of which Clement complains perhaps occurred at the Frankfort *Reichstag* in March 1339, when the electoral princes published a radical declaration of imperial independence against the pope : cf. E. E. Stengel, *Avignon und Rhens*, p. 174, n. 5 ; *idem*, *Nova Alamanniae* II (Berlin, 1930), nr 613.

335-336 cf. Luc. 15, 5.

337 litteras : presumably Clement refers to the instruments taken by Lewis' envoys to the Curia in March and October 1336 : cf. H. S. Offler, *Ueber die Prokuratorien Ludwigs des Bayern für die römische Kurie*, *Deutsches Archiv f. Gesch. d. Mittelalters*, VIII (1951), pp. 483-487.

337 nichil opere adimplevit : Benedict XII complained to Lewis on 13 September 1338 that a recent envoy from Lewis had stated : quod tue intentionis non erat servare ea, que per te et pro parte tua iam dudum nobis fuerant oblata ; Riezler, *Vatikanische Akten*, nr 1974, p. 714.

338 per unum annum : Clement was elected pope on 7 May 1342.

341 aliquorum : among these Clement would no doubt have included the French king, Philip VI of Valois, who by the terms of his alliance with Lewis dated 15 March 1341 had engaged himself to act as mediator between Lewis and the papacy. According to the chronicler Johannes Victoriensis Philip sent his chancellor and Ulrich of Savoy to support Lewis' envoys at the Curia in late November 1342 : *Lib. certarum historiarum*, ed. F. Schneider, II (*M.GH. SS. in usum scholarum*, 1910), p. 229.

343-345 On this embassy in November-December 1342 cf. Johannes Victoriensis, *loc. cit.* ; Heinrich von Diessenhoven, *Chronicon*, in *Fontes rerum Germanicarum*, ed. J. F. Bohmer IV (Stuttgart, 1868), p. 38. Its members were Albert count of Hohenberg, Wolfram van Nellenburg, Markward von Randeck and Ulrich von Augsburg.

de eo illud ad Romanos iiº : *Secundum duriciam tuam et cor inpenitens thesaurizas tibi iram.* Unde noster predecessor et nos voluimus sibi facere sicut facit bonus medicus, ut primo revocaremus eum lenibus, scilicet exhortationibus et monitionibus ; sed quia infirmitas non curatur sed gravatur, oportet membrum illud eicere et resecare. Quod pulchre pertractat Origenes, Omelia viiª super Joshue loquens de illo anathemate, dicens sic : *Non dicimus ut pro levi culpa aliquis abscidatur, sed si forte commonitus quis et correctus pro delicto suo semel, iterum ac tercio nichil emendationis ostenderit, utamur medici disciplina. Si oleo perunximus, si emplastris mitigavimus, si malagmate mollivimus, nec tamen medicamentis cedit tumoris duricia, solum superest remedium resecandi.* Et ita docet Salvator in illa parabola, cum docet ad suum convivium primo vocari, sed postmodum compelli, Luce xiiiiº, sicut pulchre deducit Augustinus in quadam epistola ad Donatum presbiterum : *Ecclesia enim utitur potestate, ut non solum invitet, sed etiam cogat.* Et idem prosequitur Augustinus in libello suo ad Bonifacium de correctione Donatistarum. Dicit enim sic: *Potestate, quam accepit ecclesia, hii, qui inveniuntur in viis et sepibus, id est in heresibus et scismatibus, coguntur intrare.* Patet ergo quomodo ad officium nostrum pertinet tales eicere de ecclesia. In cuius signum Deus post peccatum eiecit Adam de paradiso, Genesis iiiº ; et ita eiecit, quod *collocavit ante paradisum voluptatis Cherubim, et flammeum gladium atque versatilem, ad custodiendam viam ligni vite.* Iste gladius est potestas ecclesie tradita, per quam mali ab ecclesia arcentur et eiciuntur. Unde de talibus dicitur in psalmo ad litteram : *Cum iudicatur, exeat condempnatus;* et sequitur : *Eiciantur de habitacionibus suis.* Unde Proverbiorum xxiiº dicitur· *Eice derisorem, et exibit cum eo iurgium.* Ut merito possimus sibi dicere illud Ezechielis xxviiiº, et fuit verbum dictum illi Cherub qui elevabat se in superbiam contra Deum ; unde dicitur sic : *Repleta sunt interiora tua iniquitate, et peccasti, et eieci te de monte sancto Dei, et perdidi te;* et multe alie malediciones ibi secuntur. Ut de eo accipiamus illud Johannis xiiº : *Nunc princeps huius mundi eicietur foras,* et verbum dictum est ad litteram a Salvatore de dyabolo, qui non est princeps mundi huius per

---

347 noster : idem EC ‖ **348** eum : *ex* cum *in marg. corr.* E ; cum (?) G ‖ **350** gravatur : aggravatur EC ‖ **353** commonitus : excommunicatus G | pro delicto suo *om.* G ‖ **355** si[1] *om.* G | malagmate *scripsi secundum auctorem laudatum;* malignate G ; malagranate EC ‖ **365** de ecclesia : ab ecclesia ECM ‖ **367** Cherubim, et : Cherubin tenentem G ‖ **367** custodiendum G ‖ **368** gladius... per quam : est gladius potestatis ecclesie traditus per quem E ‖ **369** eicientur G ‖ **372** possim G | illud : quod scribitur E ‖ **376** illud : quod scribitur E ‖ **378** a Salvatore : ad Salvatorem G

346-347 Rom. 2, 5.
351 anathemate : cf. Iosue 6, 17.
352-356 Origenes-Rufinus, *In lib. Jesu Nave*, homilia vii, P. G. 12, 862.
357-358 Luc. 14, 23.
359-360 Augustinus, *Epist.* clxxiii, P. L. 33, 757.
362-364 Augustinus, *Epist.* clxxxv c. 6, P. L. 33, 804.
366-368 Gen 3, 24.
370-371 Ps. 108, 7 ; 10.
371-372 Proverb. 22, 10.
374-375 Ezech. 28, 16.
377 Ioann. 12, 31.

iusticiam, sed solum per tyrannicam violentiam. Et certe, licet iste dicat se imperatorem et regem, tamen nullum in hiis ius habet ; ymmo nec etiam in terris quibuscunque ; ymmo omnibus iusto iudicio est privatus.

Eicietur ergo foras, quia Matthei v° dicitur quod *ad nichilum valet ultra, nisi ut mittatur foras, et conculcetur ab hominibus.* Non quod ei communicetur ab hominibus, quia : *Qui tetigerit picem, inquinabitur ab ea, et qui communicat superbo, induet superbiam,* Ecclesiastici xiii°. Et ideo dicebat Ysaias, lii° : *Recedite, recedite, exite inde, pollutum nolite tangere;* quia, sicut dicit Apostolus II ad Corinthios vi° : *Nolite iugum educere cum infidelibus. Que enim participacio iusticie cum iniquitate? Aut que societas lucis ad tenebras? Que autem convencio Christi ad Belial? Aut que pars fidelis cum infideli? Quis autem consensus templo Dei cum ydolis? Vos enim templum estis Dei vivi. Propter quod exite de medio eorum et separamini, dicit Dominus, et immundum ne tetigeritis, et ego recipiam vos et ero vobis in patrem, et vos eritis michi in filios.* Et prima ad Corinthios v° dicit quod prius debet bonus Christianus de hoc mundo exire, quam talibus commisceri. Unde Deus, II Paralip. xix°, per prophetam dicit Josaphat regi : *Impio prebes auxilium, et hiis qui oderunt Dominum amicicia iungeris, et idcirco iram Domini merebaris.* Et idciro contra fautores et adherentes dicto Bauaro sunt late sententie excommunicationis in personas et interdicti in terris eorum, et omnia iuramenta, pacta, lige et pactiones cum eo habita cassata sunt, et cassa et irrita nunciata.

Ergo cum eo non est communicandum ab hominibus. Unde de eo videtur dictum illud Danielis iv° : *Ab hominibus eicient te, et cum feris erit habitatio tua:* cum feris, id est cum infernalibus demonibus erit habitatio tua. Et causam huius dicti reddit ille Salvator, Johannis xv° dicens : *Si quis in me non manserit, mittetur foras sicut palmes, et arescet, et colligent eum, et in ignem mittent, et ardebit.* Colligent quidem ipsi angeli, qui separabunt malos de medio iustorum, et *mittent eos in caminum ignis. Ibi erit fletus, et stridor dentium.* Et ideo Luce

---

384 ei *om.* E | *post* hominibus : et dixit bene conculcetur ab hominibus non quod communicetur ab hominibus *add.* E || **387** et lii° Ideo dicebat G | ideo *om.* ECM | lii° *om.* G || **388** sicut dicit Apostolus : sicut dicitur G || **395** prima : primo G | v° : *om.* G || **398** amiciciam G || **399** mereberis G || **402** et[1] *om.* G | cassa *altera manu add.* G || **403** Ergo... ab hominibus : Ergo non est communicandum de eo cum hominibus G || **404** eicient : deiciant E || **406** ille : ipse E || **407** dicens *om.* G | foras : foris G || **408** ardebit : ardet EC

379-382 John XXII had declared Lewis deprived of any right to the kingship he might have acquired by his election, 11 July 1324 : *MGH. Const.*, V, nr 944, p. 785. On 3 April 1327 Lewis was declared deprived of the duchy of Bavaria and all his other lands : *ibid.*, VI, nr 273, p. 183.

383-384 Matth. 5, 13.

385-386 Eccli. 13, 1.

387-388 Is. 52, 11.

389-395 II Corinth. 6, 14-18.

396-397 I Corinth. 5, 10.

397-399 II Paralip. 19, 2.

400 late sententie : cf. *MGH. Const.*, V, nr 944, p. 786 ; *ibid.*, VI, nr 273, p. 184.

404-405 Dan. 4, 22.

407-408 Ioann. 15, 6.

410 Matth. 13, 42.

xiiii° dicitur : *Neque in terra, neque in sterquilinio utilis est, sed foras mittetur;* quia Apocalypsis xxii° dicitur : *Foris canes, et venefici et impudici et homicide et ydolis servientes et omnis, qui amat et facit mendacium.* Istum ergo foras eicimus, sentencias et processus contra eum habitos propalando et publicando ; sed, ut iusticiam misericordia temperemus, adhuc foras eum non eicimus sententias aggravando. Sed decrevimus adhuc per tres menses eum expectare, rogantes Eum, Cuius vices (licet immeriti) in terris gerimus, ut velit aufferre cor lapideum de carne sua et dare sibi cor carneum, ut vere penitens ad gremium sancte matris ecclesie redeat et recipi mereatur, ut eius spiritus salvus fiat in die iudicii. Quam salutem nobis et sibi concedat Qui est benedictus in secula seculorum. Amen.

---

412 foras : foris G || **418** decrevimus : determinavimus EC | eum : ipsum EC.

412-413 Luc. 14, 35 (adapted).
413-415 Apoc. 22, 15.
419-420 cf. Ezech. 11, 19.

XII

AN INTERPOLATED « COLLATIO » OF POPE CLEMENT VI, O.S.B. ?

On 10 April 1343 Pope Clement VI delivered a *collatio* on the text *Atrium quod est foris* (*Apoc.* 11,2) by way of introduction to a *monitionis processus* against the excommunicate emperor Lewis the Bavarian. The process declared Clement's intention of aggravating the existing sentences against Lewis, but he was granted a delay of three months within which he was to abandon the administration of the empire and the German kingdom and make his submission in person at the Curia. [1] The only action which Lewis took to avert the threatened aggravation was to write to the pope on 17 May, still using the imperial title, but informing Clement that he had empowered Humbert, Dauphin of Vienne, to treat at the Curia for his reconciliation and promising to follow Humbert's guidance in this business 'salvo honore et iure nostro et imperii'. [2] There is no evidence that Humbert took action on his mandate, though the text of it may have become known at Avignon. [3] When the prescribed term of three months expired on 10 July, neither Lewis nor any representative of his had made an appearance at the Curia. On 11 July he was formally cited, thrice publicly and once again in consistory, but with no result. Thereupon the pope, in public consistory

---

1. RAYNALDUS, *Annales ecclesiastici* 1343, § lvii (tom. VI, Lucca, 1750), p. 328 : 'monemus eundem Ludovicum, ut infra trium mensium spatium, quod ei pro termino peremptorio assignamus, ab omni administratione regni et imperii Romani omnino desistat......nostris et ecclesiae praedictae beneplacitis et mandatis personaliter veniat humiliter pariturus, ac facturus et recepturus quod suadebit iustitia et nobis videbitur expedire'. Cfr H.S. OFFLER, *A political « collatio » of Pope Clement VI, O.S.B.*, in *Revue bénédictine* 65 (1955), p. 126-144 ; H.O. SCHWÖBEL, *Die diplomatische Kampf zwischen Ludwig dem Bayern und der römischen Kurie im Rahmen des kanonischen Absolutionsprozesses, 1330-1346* (Weimar, 1968), p. 312-316.

2. J.P. DE BOURCHENU, marquis de Valbonnais, *Histoire du Dauphiné*, 2 (Geneva, 1722), p. 473.

3. Cfr SCHWÖBEL, p. 317, n. 74. Possibly there is an echo of Lewis's proviso in his mandate to Humbert saving the honour and rights of himself and the empire to be detected in the *collatio* of 11 July (below, lines 58-59) : 'Et si vmquam dixit [Ludovicus] quod vellet redire ad gremium sancte matris ecclesie, semper dixit saluo statu suo'. But this was a reservation which Lewis had made consistently for many years ; cfr his instruction to his proctors at the Curia in October 1336, printed from Munich, Geheimes Haus Archiv 1/5, 259, fol. 12 by S. RIEZLER, *Die literarischen Widersacher der Päpste zur Zeit Ludwigs des Baierns* (Leipzig, 1874), p. 329.

and after consultation with the cardinals, declared Lewis to be contumacious and that he would be proceeded against as such. [1] The legal consequences of contumacy were, of course, severe, and the gravity of Clement's declaration on 11 July ought not to be underestimated. [2]

Thus far the official record. But in addition there survives in the Eichstätt ms. 698, p. 494a - 495b, a 'Collacio et modus procedendi quem tenuit Clemens papa VI contra dominum Ludewicum xi die mensis Iulii anno domini m°ccc°xliii'. In fact the piece is almost entirely a *collatio* or papal allocution ; [3] only at the very end does it refer to the sentences already passed against Lewis and their aggravation *tanquam contra contumacem*, and to further processes to be drawn up against him later *cum consilio et deliberatione matura*. Considerable extracts from it were printed by C. Höfler in 1869 ; [4] the whole is published below from what remains its only known source, the Eichstätt ms.

In its choice of theme from *Prov.* 18,3 : *Impius cum in profundum venerit peccatorum, contempnit : sed sequitur eum ignominia et opprobrium*, the *collatio* of 11 July takes up a text on which Clement had already touched on 10 April and which is echoed in the *monitionis processus* of that date and in the proceedings on 11 July. [5] It is a short piece, almost perfunctory when compared with many of the discourses of that master of formal eloquence whom we know Clement VI to have been considered by his contemporaries ; [6] unlike most of them it was not included in the great collected edition of Clement's sermons now at Paris in

---

1. Only an extract from a late copy of this process in the Vatican Archives is printed by S. RIEZLER, *Vatikanische Akten zur deutschen Geschichte in der Zeit Kaiser Ludwigs des Bayern* (Innsbruck, 1891), nr. 2151, p. 775.

2. As SCHWÖBEL, p. 316-319, may be inclined to do, with his reference to Clement's 'Glimpflichkeit' ; cfr the review of his important book in *Erasmus* 21 (1969), p. 566-571.

3. Cfr the useful distinction quoted from the Vatican ms. Ottoboni lat. 747, fol. 42, by P. HERDE, *Audientia litterarum contradictarum*, 1 (Tübingen, 1970), p. 117 : 'Sermo est ad animarum edificationem et collatio ad scientie acquisitionem'.

4. Constantin HÖFLER, *Aus Avignon*, in *Abhandlungen der königl. böhmischen Gesellschaft der Wissensschaften*, Jhrg. 1868, sechste Folge, zweite Band (Prague, 1869), p. 20-21.

5. Clement's *collatio* of 10 April 1343, *ed. cit.*, p. 133, line 78 ; RAYNALDUS, 1343, § lvii, p. 328 : 'idem Ludovicus in profundum malorum descendens' ; RIEZLER, *Vatikanische Akten*, nr. 2151, p. 775 : 'Ludovicus de Bavaria, qui se gerit pro imperatore Romano et qui descendit in profundum malorum per multas inobedientias'.

6. '... l'homme le plus éloquent de son temps', as P. FOURNIER wrote, *art.* : *Pierre Roger (Clément VI)*, in *Hist. litt. de la France*, 37 (Paris, 1938), p. 224.

Bibliothèque Ste. Geneviève ms. 240.[1] Yet there would be no hesitation about accepting it as a wholly authentic utterance of Clement VI were it not for a single brief but very odd passage referring to two heterodox schoolmen of considerable standing : Nicholas of Autrecourt and William of Ockham (below, lines 27-41). In the first division of the *collatio* Clement maintains that Lewis has been 'brought down to hell, to the sides of the pit' and is to be compared to Oholibah, who in her whoredoms — Clement's audience was assumed to remember — was even more corrupt than her sister Oholah (cfr *Is.* 14, 15 ; *Ezech.* 23, 11 *sqq.*). Lewis fears neither God nor man — the *collatio* continues — for he harbours and favours all heretics who resort to him. By way of example are quoted Nicholas who, the *collatio* claims, after uttering many errors and heresies against the Holy See fled to Lewis and was immediately received by him. As to Ockham, it is from him that Marsilius of Padua and many others learned their errors. After the death of Michael of Cesena (formerly minister-general of the Franciscans and leader of their dissident group at Lewis's court) Ockham, according to the *collatio*, had acquired Michael's seal, with which he had sealed a letter creating himself vicar of the Order ; he continues to call himself vicar although his vicariate has expired.

Extreme difficulties emerge when one attempts to reconcile this passage with the declared date of the *collatio* and with what is known from other sources about the careers of Nicholas and Ockham. Nicholas had been cited to the Curia in November 1340, together with others *contra quos apostolatui nostro aliqua catholicam fidem tangentia sunt relata.*[2] The enquiry into his doctrines appears to have proceeded slowly ; not before May 1346 did the curial commission presided over by Cardinal Guillaume Curti condemn Nicholas's errors, though it seems that the cardinal had already been concerned with the case at the beginning of Clement's pontificate in 1342.[3] But there was nothing very unusual about such deliberation ; for instance, the enquiry into Ockham's teachings, which began at the Curia in 1324, had not

---

1. Ch. Kohler, *Catalogue des manuscrits de la Bibliothèque Sainte-Geneviève*, I (Paris, 1893), p. 146. Of the 87 sermons and discourses attributed to Clement by Dom Philibert Schmitz, *Les sermons et discours de Clément VI*, in *Revue bénédictine* 41 (1929), p. 13-34, no more than 8 are missing from this collection.

2. *Chartularium Universitatis Parisiensis*, ed. H. Denifle and E. Chatelain, II, 1 (Paris, 1891), nr. 1041, p. 505.

3. *Chartularium*, nr. 1124, p. 576-587 ; also printed by J. Lappe, *Nicolaus von Autrecourt*, in Baeumker's *Beiträge zur Geschichte der Philosophie des Mittelalters* 6. 2, (Münster, 1908), p. 31*-45*.

been brought to the point of a formal condemnation when he fled from Avignon to Italy in May 1328. [1] Nor does Nicholas seem to have made difficulties about carrying out the sentence of Guillaume Curti ; as had been prescribed, he publicly recanted the condemned errors and burned his writings containing them at Paris on 25 November 1347. [2] Less than three years later he had achieved the respectable position of dean in the cathedral church of Metz. If the account in the *collatio* is to be believed, it would be necessary to infer that during the course of the enquiry into his orthodoxy, at some date before July 1343 and so long before his condemnation in 1346, Nicholas had fled to Lewis. It is very hard to accept that inference. No other source has been found to support it, and, significantly enough, the condemnation of May 1346 is concerned solely with Nicholas's philosophical errors and their theological implications. If, at some time between Novembre 1340 and July 1343 he had left Avignon and adhered to the excommunicate emperor, could that fact have escaped being noticed when he was condemned in 1346 ? Doubt about what the *collatio* has to say concerning Nicholas has been felt to reflect on its authenticity as a whole. So Denifle could write in 1891 : 'Collationi Clementis VI......vix absoluta fides exhibenda est', and further : 'Merito dubitare debemus an ista collatio sit Clementis VI'. [3] Though the view has been expressed that these doubts are insufficiently grounded, [4] it is not easy to dismiss them. The suggestion that Nicholas's flight to Germany took place at some time between the condemnation at Avignon in May 1346 and his recantation at Paris in November 1347, [5] though it may help his biographer, does nothing to rescue the credit of the *collatio*. For how could flight in 1346 or 1347 possibly be mentioned in a discourse which claims to have been delivered on 11 July 1343 ?

There are similar difficulties about what the *collatio* has to say concerning Ockham. In no sense can he be reputed to have been the master of Marsilius of Padua, who was the product of a

---

1. Cfr Jürgen MIETHKE, *Ockhams Weg zur Sozialphilosophie* (Berlin, 1969), p. 58-74.

2. *Archiv für Literatur- und Kirchengeschichte des Mittelalters* (ed. H. Denifle and F. Ehrle), 5 (Berlin, 1889), p. 324.

3. *Chartularium Universitatis Parisiensis* II, 1, *addenda et corrigenda*, p. 720.

4. LAPPE, *op. cit.*, p. 3, n. 1 ; P. VIGNAUX, *art.* : *Nicolas d'Autrecourt*, in *Dict. de Théologie catholique*, 11 (Paris 1931), col. 562, does not pronounce on this problem.

5. J.R. O'DONNELL, *art.* : *Nicholas of Autrecourt*, in *New Catholic Encyclopedia* 10 (New York, 1967), p. 448.

very different intellectual tradition and whose major work, *Defensor pacis*, was being produced at a time when Ockham was still striving to remain on the path of an orthodox academic career. Since J. Hofer doubted the evidence of the *collatio* in this respect on grounds such as these in 1913, the work of two generations of scholars has served to emphasise the differing standpoints — even the mutual antagonism — of Marsilius and Ockham. [1] Could Clement VI have gone astray over this ? Let us grant that men of eminent position, called upon to make a public pronouncement with perhaps insuffıcent time to prepare their words carefully, can say inaccurate or ill-considered things. But it does seem vastly improbable that Clement VI, whose university career at Paris presumably overlapped that of Marsilius, and who at the command of Pope Benedict XII had made a careful study of Marsilius's works, [2] would have fallen into such an error. Even admitting as a remote possibility that he did, there remains the muddle about Ockham's vicariate. When Michael of Cesena, then minister-general of the Franciscans, went into schism in 1328 over the question of Evangelical Poverty and exiled himself at the court of Lewis the Bavarian, he took with him the seal of his Order. Possibly it was under that seal that Ockham and Heinrich von Talheim had been created Michael's vicars before 12 June 1330. [3] After Michael's death at Munich on 29 November 1342, still in schism with the papacy, [4] the seal passed to Ockham, who sent it back to the Franciscan General Chapter which met at Verona at Whitsun 1348. [5] The statement in the *collatio* of 11 July that after Michael's death Ockham used the seal to make himself vicar of the now tiny

---

1. J. HOFER, *Biographische Studien über Wilhelm von Ockham, O.F.M.*, in *Archivum franciscanum historicum* 6 (1913), p. 664-669. He thinks of a 'Verwechslung' (p. 669), not, it would seem, of deliberate falsification.

2. Cfr Clement's *collatio* of 10 April 1343, *ed. cit.*, p. 136, lines 177-180 : 'et audemus dicere quod vix nunquam legimus peiorem hereticum illo Marsilio. Unde de mandato Benedicti predecessoris nostri de quodam eius libello plus quam ducentos et quadraginta articulos hereticales extraximus'.

3. *MGH Constitutiones* VI, 1, nr. 788, p. 668.

4. Clément SCHMITT, *Un pape réformateur et un défenseur de l'unité de l'Église. Benoît XII et l'Ordre des Frères Mineurs, 1334-1342* (Quaracchi-Florence, 1959), p. 246.

5. The evidence for this is Clement VI's letter of 8 June 1349 to the Franciscan minister-general, William Farinier : *Bullarium Franciscanum*, ed. C. EUBEL, VI (Rome, 1902), nr. 508a, p. 230b-231a. It seems safe to suppose that the *Wilhelmus de Anglia* of Clement's letter refers to Ockham, and that *sigillum antiquum dicti ordinis, quod diu habuit* came to him from Michael. The problem has been fully discussed by Jürgen MIETHKE, *Zu Wilhelm Ockhams Tod*, in *Archivum franciscanum historicum* 61 (1968), p. 79-98.

dissident branch of the Franciscans at Munich is perhaps not in itself completely incredible, even though we know that he had been named as one of Michael's vicars a dozen years before. But the complaint that Ockham was continuing to call himself vicar although his vicariate had expired (because, it must be understood, of the death of his principal, Michael), is a quite extraordinary one to find raised by Pope Clement, implying as it did the admission that at some time or other Ockham's vicariate had been legitimate. This would have been absurdity in the eyes of the canonists, who were bound to take the view that once Michael had been deposed from the office of minister-general by the Franciscan General Chapter at Paris in June 1329 he had no power at all to appoint a vicar. [1] It seems inconceivable that Clement VI, whose taste and capacity for law is well known, [2] could casually have fallen into the trap of recognising even by implication the legitimacy of any of Michael's actions after he had broken with the papacy.

This accumulation of gross improbabilities makes an irresistible case for rejecting the section of the *collatio* which speaks of Nicholas of Autrecourt and Ockham. It does not necessarily follow, however, that the authenticity of the rest of the *collatio* must be impugned. Can the nonsense about Nicholas and Ockham be attributed to incomprehension on the part of whoever was responsible for making the *reportatio* of Clement's words ? His tolerably adequate performance throughout the rest of the *collatio* makes this an unlikely explanation. Deliberate interpolation of an otherwise authentic *collatio* seems a much more attractive alternative. A cogent reason for supposing that the offending section (lines 27-41 : *Quia ipse est......vicarium ordinis*) has been interpolated is the ease with which it can be excised without damaging or disturbing the formal disposition of the discourse as a whole. If this is done, there are good grounds for believing that what remains represents a genuine utterance on the part of Clement VI. The occasion on 11 July was one on which the pope might naturally be expected to deliver some kind of address, though since the business was predetermined and no representatives of Lewis were present to be impressed, any very elaborate speech wes unnecessary. The protocol of the proceedings indicates that Clement spoke on a theme which approximates to the

---

1. Nicholas GLASSBERGER, *Chronica*, in *Analecta Franciscana* 2 (Quaracchi, 1887), p. 146. My view coincides with that of MIETHKE, *Ockhams Tod*, p. 91.
2. Cfr Anneliese MAIER, *Ausgehendes Mittelalter* II (Rome, 1967), p. 313.

text taken in the *collatio*. [1] At line 10 of the *collatio* appears a quotation from Gregory the Great's *Moralia* which Clement had already used three months before. [2] The *collatio* refere in a well-informed fashion to a biblical authority which Clement claims to have used when replying to Lewis's envoys at the end of 1342 (lines 49 - 50). It plays (lines 59 - 62) on the consonance between the pope's own name and the quality of *clementia* in a fashion which Clement affected elsewhere. [3] At lines 11 - 16 it has recourse, quite typical of Clement, to an example from the physical science of his time, and throughout it uses copious and apt quotations from the Vulgate in his habitual manner. If lines 27 - 41 can be regarded as a later addition and the *collatio* thus be freed from this highly suspect passage, there would be little or no reason to doubt its authenticity. There is much to be said for Dr Miethke's opinion that we are faced by 'Verfälschung' rather than 'Erdichtung' of the *collatio*. [4]

If we suppose that a genuine papal *collatio* has suffered interpolation, it is clear that this had occurred by 28 September 1354, for the interpolated version is quoted by Conrad of Megenberg in his *Tractatus contra Wilhelmum Ockham* which he had finished by that date. [5] There remains the difficulty of finding a plausible explanation why anyone should want to interpolate a papal *collatio* of the fourteenth century. What possible purpose could the author of the interpolation have sought to serve ; what advantage or satisfaction did he promise himself from such apparently useless activity ? That problem — which of course becomes still more puzzling if the whole *collatio* is rejected as a falsification

---

1. See above, p. 112, n. 5.
2. Clement VI, *collatio* of 10 April 1343, *ed. cit.*, p. 133, line 81.
3. Clement's *collatio* in the presence of Lewis the Bavarian's envoys on 16 January 1344 on the text *Nolite errare*: *Deus non irridetur* (*Gal.* 6, 7), Eichstätt ms. 698, p. 497b : 'posset esse concepta dulcedo indiscrete remissionis et indulgencie, videlicet quod nos receptas iniurias totaliter laxaremus, et maxime amore cuiusdam quem summe diligimus, qui satis pro isto facto rogauit, ut sibi [Ludovico] clemens essemus quia sic vocamur'. And later in the same *collatio* in a portion printed by S. Baluze, *Vitae paparum Avenionensium*, ed. G. Mollat, II (Paris, 1928), p. 423 : 'Et ideo, licet ab infantia creverit mecum miseratio et de utero matris mee egressa sit mecum, et licet clementiam desponsaverim, tamen clementia non est sine justitia nec misericordia sine veritate'. This was clearly in reply to a phrase in the speech made by Lewis's envoy, Marquart von Randegg, on this occasion, Eichstätt ms. 698, p. 496a : 'Et Seneca in de clementia ad Neronem dicit quod nichil est tam decens in principe sicut clementia et misericordia' [cfr Sen., *De Clem.* I.iii.3 ; I.xvi.1 ; I.xix.1].
4. Miethke, *Ockhams Tod*, p. 92.
5. Ed. R. Scholz, *Unbekannte kirchenpolitische Streitschriften aus der Zeit Ludwigs des Bayern, 1327-1354*, II (Rome, 1914), p. 346-391.

— has hardly been faced squarely by critics of its authenticity in part or as a whole. The falsifier cannot be absolved — as Professor Bosl would absolve most medieval forgers [1] — from conscious purpose to deceive. Nor can his deception be understood as belonging to that class of attempts to use present untruth in order to restore things to an earlier, more just situation, on which Dr Fuhrmann, among others, has laid so much weight. [2] Motives springing from lower but perhaps more readily comprehensible levels of human nature, of the kind used by H. Silvestre to explain the hagiographical forgeries of medieval times, [3] offer a more likely clue. Tentatively I would suggest that in the case of the interpolation of Clement's *collatio* we have to reckon less with the result of rational calculation or literary conceit than with an expression of private malice.

Let us suppose that someone acquires a *reportatio* of the authentic *collatio* delivered by Clement VI on 11 July 1343 and decides to vent a personal spleen against Nicholas of Autrecourt and Ockham by adding a section which relieves his feelings about them : what survives in the Eichstätt manuscript could be a copy of such an effort. On this hypothesis the linking of Nicholas and Ockham (both highly individual thinkers, between whom exist no readily identifiable bonds of personal connexion, while their intellectual relationship remains obscure) [4] would suggest that the author of the interpolation was bitterly opposed to what may in general terms be called the 'modernist' movement in philosophy and theology which was making itself felt strongly at the University of Paris by 1340. Moreover what may be a slip by the interpolator in line 31 is suggestive. Nicholas of Autrecourt, we are told, fled from the Curia and was taken up by Lewis the Bavarian : 'et predicat *ibi* multos et magnos errores cum quibusdam religiosis'. The *ibi* can hardly refer to Avignon, whence Nicholas is supposed to have fled, and where

---

1. K. BOSL, *Zu einer Soziologie der mittelalterlichen Fälschung*, in *Historische Zeitschrift* 197 (1963), p. 567 = *Frühformen der Gesellschaft im mittelalterlichen Europa* (Munich-Vienna, 1964), p. 424.

2. Horst FUHRMANN, *Die Fälschungen im Mittelalter*, in *Historische Zeitschrift* 197 (1963), p. 543.

3. H. SILVESTRE, *Le problème des faux au Moyen Age*, in *Le Moyen Age* 66 (1960), p. 363, where he speaks of 'un esprit......d'égoïsme et de vanité' ; cfr FUHRMANN, p. 551, who there allows for envy and greed.

4. Cfr E.A. MOODY, *Ockham, Buridan, and Nicholas of Autrecourt*, in *Franciscan Studies* 7 (1947), p. 113-146 = *Inquiries into Medieval Philosophy. A collection in honor of Francis P. Clarke*, ed. J.F. Ross (Westport, Conn., 1971), p. 275-313 ; J.R. WEINBERG, *Nicolaus of Autrecourt* (Princeton, 1948), p. 119, 151, 205.

he would scarcely have been allowed opportunity to preach errors. Rather, it reflects the standpoint of an author living and writing in Lewis's realm. That is to say, the interpolation is of German provenance.

If our reconstruction of the author of the interpolation suggests a German inimical to 'modernist' tendencies, at work before 1354, can conjecture about his identity usefully be pushed further ? Two factors may be relevant here. The first is the use made of the interpolated *collatio* by Conrad of Megenberg, who had left the University of Paris in 1342 and, after some time directing the school at St Stephen's in Vienna, had settled down, so it seems, in his canonry at Regensburg in 1348. [1] In chapter 6 of his treatise against Ockham Conrad quotes literally the text of the *collatio* of 11 July from line 34 to line 65, [2] interrupting his citation only in order to insert an explanatory passage about Marsilius of Padua and John of Jandun borrowed from Clement's authentic *collatio* of 10 April 1343. [3] For the most part Conrad follows faithfully enough the text of the July *collatio* as it appears in the Eichstätt ms.. But there are two discrepancies. First, Conrad applies lines 43 - 65 of the *collatio* to Ockham, whereas this is a part of what we take to be the authentic text in which Clement was clearly referring to Lewis the Bavarian. Second, at lines 58 - 59 Conrad shows a slight but significant alteration in the text of the *collatio* when compared with the Eichstätt ms. Whereas the latter has Clement saying this of Lewis : 'Et si vmquam dixit quod vellet redire ad gremium sancte matris ecclesie, semper dixit saluo statu suo'. Conrad's adaptation of the passage to Ockham reads : 'Et *numquam* dixit quod vellet redire ad gremium sancte matris ecclesie, *sed* semper dixit saluo statu suo' (my italics). If the first aberration might just possibly (though not probably) be explained as the result of a misreading by Conrad of the already interpolated *collatio*, no such excuse will serve for the second ; here Conrad would seem quite deliberately to have altered the text, presumably in order to make it more damaging to Ockham.

The second relevant factor in our search for the author of the

1. Cfr H. Ibach, *Leben und Schriften des Konrad von Megenberg* (Berlin, 1938), p. 7 ; R. Scholz, introduction to his edn. of Conrad's *Planctus ecclesiae in Germaniam* (*MGH Staatsschriften des späteren Mittelalters* II, 1, Leipzig, 1941), p. 3 ; A. Pelzer, *art.* : *Conrad de Megenberg*, in *Dict. d'hist. et de géographie ecclésiastiques*, 12 (Paris, 1956), col. 491-495.
2. Scholz, *Unbekannte kirchenpolitische Streitschriften*, II, p. 364-365.
3. *Ed. cit.*, p. 136, lines 175-180.

interpolation is the context in which the *collatio* survives. It has been found only in the Eichstätt ms., where it is followed immediately by Brother Bernard's account of the submission made by Lewis the Bavarian's proctors to the pope on 16 January 1344 — an account which includes a *reportatio* of Clement VI's discourse delivered on this occasion on the text *Nolite errare : Deus non irridetur. Que seminaverit homo, hec et metet* (*Gal.* 6,7). [1] It is preceded by Clement VI's *collatio* of 10 April 1343 (p. 488a-494a). Except for a copy of Lewis's manifesto *Fidem catholicam* dated 6 August 1338 (p. 484a-488a) the rest of this section of the Eichstätt codex (from p. 406 onwards) is taken up by two works, the *Tractatus de translatione imperii* and the *Tractatus contra Wilhelmum Ockham*. Of both these works the author is Conrad of Megenberg. [2]

Guilt needs to be proved by evidence far stronger than that of mere association, which may be wholly accidental. But if one were asked to identify a German academic churchman of such conservative intellectual tendencies that in 1354 he could still be found echoing the declaration against nominalist views put out by the Arts Faculty at Paris in December 1340 ; [3] who pursued Ockham with venom for his pernicious doctrines which had diverted so many of his contemporaries from the virtues of 'solida philosophia' ; [4] who had to hand and quoted *reportationes*

---

1. P. 495b-500b ; cfr C. Höfler, *Aus Avignon*, p. 22-23 ; Schwöbel, *Diplomatische Kampf*, p. 356, n. 218.

2. Cfr the descriptions of Eichstätt ms. 698 (formely 269) by L. Bethmann, *Reise durch Deutschland und Italien in den Jahren 1844-1846*, in *Archiv der Gesellschaft für ältere deutsche Geschichtskunde* 9 (1847), p. 54-55 ; Scholz, *Unbekannte kirchenpolitische Streitschriften*, II, 574. Cfr Add. Note, p. 125.

3. Conrad, *Tractatus contra Wilhelmum Ockham*, ed. Scholz, p. 365 : 'tunc dixi et adhuc dico quod sermones referendi sunt secundum materiam subiectam' ; cfr *Chartularium Univ. Paris.* II, 1, nr. 1042, p. 506. For a suggestion that Conrad may have had something to do with instigating the Paris declaration, see Miethke, *Ockhams Weg zur Sozialphilosophie*, p. 232, n. 349. Moody, *art. cit.*, p. 289, argues that this passage in the Paris declaration can hardly have been directed against Ockham. Cfr Add. Note, p. 125.

4. Conrad, *Tractatus contra Wilhelmum Ockham*, p. 347 : 'fratri Wilhelmo de Occam anglico, qui......virus maximum diffudit in ecclesiam Dei tantamque multitudinem scholasticorum virorum secum traxisse videtur, ut tercia pars uel ultra speculatorum a solida philosophya modernis temporibus apostatasse decernatur'. Conrad again attacks Ockham in his *Œconomica*, pars III. tr.i, c. 1, Vatican, cod. Palat. lat. 1252, fol. 99r : 'quemadmodum frater Wilhelmus de Octhan anglicus atque sui sequaces, qui tam relationes quam situs, habitus, ubi, quando, asserunt preter animam res indistinctas a rebus absolutis atque quantitatem eandem cum substantia rem affirmant ; motus etiam, in quibus actiones rerum et passiones firmantur, dicunt res indistinctas a permanentibus rebus' ; cfr A. Pelzer and Th. Käppeli, *L'Œconomica de Conrad de Megenberg retrouvée*, in *Revue d'histoire ecclésiastique* 45 (1950), p. 559-568. With his

of a least two of Clement VI's discourses :[1] then the answer would be Conrad of Megenberg. If we postulate an interpolator for Clement's *collatio* of 11 July, Conrad, whom we know to have been capable of tampering with texts,[2] has the appropriate characteristics. To say that is not to claim that his culpability has been demonstrated. But if it was Conrad who, perhaps for no other reason than to relieve the burden of spite which he felt for two eminent innovators, added the suspect passage to Clement's *collatio*, he probably did so after the death of Lewis the Bavarian in October 1347,[3] and possibly after the death of Clement VI in December 1352. At any rate, by the summer of 1354 it was ready for him to use when he was quietly rehandling the *collatio* in his *Tractatus contra Wilhelmum Ockham.*

For the most part, then, the *collatio* of 11 July can be accepted as a genuine discourse of Clement VI. But there are very strong indications that it contains an interpolated passage. Though Conrad of Megenberg's responsibility for this appears likely, it cannot be treated as certain. However, the suspicion that he was guilty of this minor literary fraud ought to be borne in mind when we come to consider the authenticity of the treatise *Quia saepe iuris ignari* against Charles IV of Luxemburg, which is ascribed to Ockham on the sole witness of Conrad of Megenberg.[4]

***

---

conservative and moderate instincts (*Œconomica*, fol. 99^v : 'Nam in medio subsistere sanior est usus') and warm feeling for the established system of the University of Paris, Conrad can have had equally little sympathy for Nicholas of Autrecourt, of whom P. VIGNAUX, *art. cit.*, p. 587, has said : 'Son œuvre paraît uniquement signifier : incertitude de la doctrine aristotélicienne ; vanité de la culture d'école'. Cfr Add. Note, p. 125.

1. See above, p. 119, n. 2 and 3.
2. See above, p. 119.
3. A likely, but not absolutely necessary interpretation of line 27 : 'Quia ipse [Ludovicus] est *et fuit* fautor......' (my italics).
4. Cfr CONRAD, *Tractatus contra Wilhelmum Ockham, ed. cit.*, p. 347 : 'ascribitur ille nequiciarum libellus, ut sic dicam, fratri Wilhelmo de Occam' ; *ib.*, p. 348 : 'iste tractatus predicti fratris Wilhelmi, quem nunc pre manibus habeo, si tamen suus est, ut asseritur'. On the question of the authorship of the treatise *Quia saepe iuris ignari*, cfr C.K. BRAMPTON, *Ockham and his alleged Authorship of the Tract* Quia saepe iuris, in *Archivum franciscanum historicum* 53 (1960), p. 30-38 ; H.-J. BECKER, *Zwei unbekannte kanonistische Schriften des Bonagratia von Bergamo in cod.vat.lat. 4009*, in *Quellen und Forschungen aus italienischen Archiven und Bibliotheken* 46 (1966), p. 253-254 ; Anneliese MAIER, *Zwei unbekannte Streitschriften gegen Johann XXII. aus dem Kreis der Münchener Minoriten*, in *Archivum Historiae Pontificiae* 5 (1967), p. 43-57 ; MIETHKE, *Ockhams Weg zur Sozialphilosophie*, p. 133-136.

Ms. Eichstätt *Staatliche Bibliothek* 698, p. 494a-495b

Collacio et modus procedendi quem tenuit Clemens papa VI contra dominum Ludewicum xi die mensis Iulii Anno domini m° ccc° xliii

Impius cum in profundum venerit peccatorum, contempnit, sed sequitur eum ignominia et oprobrium, Prouerbiorum xviii°. In quibus verbis tria considera quantum ad istum hominem. Quia primo considero eius excessum viciosum et abhominabilem ; secundo considero eius progressum iniuriosum et intollerabilem ; tercio considero eius egressum ignominosum et vituperabilem.

Patet primo eius excessus viciosus et abhominabilis, cum dicitur : *Impius cum in profundum venerit peccatorum.* Tunc impius venire dicitur in profundum peccatorum cum addit peccata peccatis, quia secundum Gregorium peccatum cum perpetratum fuerit, *mox suo pondere ad aliud trahit.* Et sic accidit impio in peccatis sicut est in motu lapidis. Dicunt isti naturales quod motus rei grauis in fine forcior et velocior est quam in principio, et quanto magis mouetur supernaturali motu tanto magis descendit et vadit in profundum, sicut ignis quanto magis induitur naturali motu magis ascendit sursum. Et ideo de peccatoribus dicitur Exodi xv° : *Descenderunt in profundum quasi lapis.* Descenderunt impii in profundum peccatorum cum inebriantur viciis et peccatis. Et ideo dicitur impio venienti in profundum peccatorum Ezechielis xxiii° : *Calicem sororis tue bibes profundum et latum:* et *eris in derisum et subsannationem, que est capacissima. Ebrietate et dolore repleberis: calicem meroris et tristicie, calicem sororis tue Samarie. Et bibes illum et potabis usque ad feces.* Et quia impius venit in profundum peccatorum, sibi dicitur Ysaiae xiiii° : *Ad infernum detraheris in profundum laci*, sicut iste de quo loquitur venit in profundum laci et comparatur alteri sorori, videlicet Oolibe, ut iste sit homo qui nec deum timeat nec hominem vereatur, sicut patet.

Quia ipse est et fuit fautor et receptator omnium hereticorum volencium ad ipsum habere recursum. Erat quidam licenciatus in theologia et vocatur Nycolaus de Utricuria uel Aurituria, qui posuit multos errores et multas hereses contra istam sanctam sedem. [494b] Fugit de Romana curia et statim ab ipso receptus fuit et predicat ibi multos

---

14 induetur *cod.* 25 Oolibe : Colibe *cod.*

1-2. *Prov.* 18, 3.

10. Gregorius Magnus, *Moral.* xxv, 9, *PL* 76, 334 ; cfr Clement VI, *collatio* of 10 April 1343, *ed. cit.*, p. 133, line 81.

12-16. isti naturales : presumably the commentators on Aristotle, *De caelo* I, 8, 277a27-277b8. Cfr Jordanus, *Lib. de ratione ponderis*, cited by E.A. Moody and M. Clagett, *The Medieval Science of Weights* (Madison, 1954), p. 216-217 ; M. Clagett, *The Science of Mechanics in the Middle Ages* (Madison, 1959), p. 541-582.

16. *Exod.* 15,6 .

19-22. *Ezech.* 23, 32-34.

23. *Is.* 14, 15.

25. Cfr *Ezech.* 23, 11 *sqq.*

27-41. Printed by C. Höfler, *Aus Avignon*, p. 20 ; this is the passage (Quia......ordinis) which I suggest has been interpolated.

et magnos errores cum quibusdam religiosis. Sed ut scitis inter apostolos fuit aliquis malus, et ideo impossibile est quod in una tanta congregatione non sit aliquis malus. Hoc dicimus propter illum Wilhelmum Ockham <Oquam>, qui diuersos errores contra potestatem et auctoritatem huius sancte sedis docuit et docet. Et ab illo Gwillelmo didicit et recepit errores ille Marsilius et multi alii. Et quid fecit predictus Gwillelmus post mortem illius Michahelis, qui fuerat minister generalis Minorum ? Ipse scripsit literam et sigillauit eam sigillo illius Michahelis et fecit se vicarium ordinis, et quamuis vicariatus ille exspirauerit, vocat se tamen vicarium ordinis. Venit ergo iste impius in profundum peccatorum.

Et deum inuoco testem quod nunquam aliquid tantum desideraui post salutem anime mee quantum desideraui salutem istius hominis et quod ipse reuerteretur ad gremium sancte matris ecclesie. Quia ut Ezechielis xviii^{o} : *Si impius egerit penitentiam ab omnibus peccatis suis que operatus est, et custodierit omnia precepta mea, et fecerit iudicium et iusticiam, vita viuet et non morietur. Omnium iniquitatum* suarum, *quas operatus est, non recordabor.* Et istam auctoritatem nos proposuimus nunciis suis in responsione nostra. Sed semper fuit magis superbus et magis impius, ut de ipso dicatur quod legitur Iob xv^{o} : *Cunctis diebus impius superbit ;* quia ut dicitur in psalmis : *Superbia eorum, qui te oderunt, ascendit semper.* Iste semper superbiuit et stare voluit in profundo peccatorum ut in suis heresibus, sicut patet per literam suo sigillo sigillatam, quam misit pape Johanni predecessori nostro super illa materia, videlicet quod Christus et apostoli nichil habuerant nec in proprio nec in communi, quam positionem non tenet sancta mater ecclesia. Et si vmquam dixit quod vellet redire ad gremium sancte matris ecclesie, semper dixit saluo statu suo. Et deum inuoco testem quod in ista sede non sedit adhuc aliquis qui cicius fuisset sibi misertus quam nos, ymmo aliquando dubitauimus ne nostra clementia posset reputari ad vicium, quia secundum Gregorium libro Moralium aliquando vicia mentiuntur se esse virtutes. Sed *non sic, impii, non sic : sed tam-*

---

33 in una : inv^{a} *cod,* ; in virorum *Höfler* 35 Ockham Oquam *cod.* 36 huius *ex* hoc *in marg.corr.man.alt.* 40 exspirauerit *e* spirauerit *corr.man.alt.* ; exspiraverat *Höfler* 54 profundo *ex corr.cod.*

43-45. Höfler, p. 20.

46-49. *Ezech.* 18, 21-22.

50. nunciis suis : presumably Lewis's envoys to the Curia in December 1342 are meant ; cfr Schwöbel, *Diplomatische Kampf,* p. 305-311 ; Clement's *collatio* of 10 April 1343, *ed. cit.*, p. 141, lines 343-345.

50. responsione nostra : possibly Clement delivered a *collatio* on the text *Ezech.* 18, 21-22 on this occasion. But no such discourse is listed by Ph. Schmitz, *Les sermons et discours de Clément VI*, in *Revue bénédictine* 41 (1929), p. 13-34.

51-52. *Job* 15, 20.

52-53. *Ps.* 73, 23.

53-62. Höfler, p. 20.

54-55. per literam suo sigillo sigillatam : the Sachsenhausen appeal of 22 May 1324, *MGH Constitutiones* V, nr. 909, p. 722 *sqq.* ; cfr Clement's *collatio* of 10 April 1343, *ed. cit.*, p. 135, line 154 and note.

59. saluo statu suo : cfr *supra*, p. 111, n. 3 .

63. Cfr Gregorius Magnus, *Moral.* i, 35, *PL* 75, 549-550.

63-64. *Ps.* 1, 4.

quam puluis, quem proicit ventus a facie terre. Impius ergo, *cum in profundum peccatorum venerit,* quid facit ? *Contempnit.*

Sequitur eius progressus iniuriosus et intollerabilis, quia dicitur : *contempnit.* Sed dices : 'Quare contempnit ?' Dico quia contempnit ecclesiam dei. Et de talibus hereticis dicit apostolus prima ad Corinthios xiº : *Ecclesiam dei contempnitis.* [495ª] Sed non durant tales et ecclesia dei in eternum manet. Unde dicit Crisostomus in sermone de spiritu sancto : Ubi Decius, ubi Iulianus, ubi Nero, ubi Herodes ? quasi dicat : 'Omnes perierunt, omnes in profundum iuerunt'. Sed ecclesia dei semper stat, quia est *tamquam lignum, quod plantatum est* iuxta *aquas, quod fructum suum dabit in tempore suo.* Unde stat ecclesia, quia propter ecclesiam Christus est incarnatus, natus, crucifixus et mortuus, propter ecclesiam resurrectus, ascendit in celum et spiritum sanctum in discipulos misit, et ideo *porte inferi non preualebunt aduersus eam.* Unde dixit Christus Luce xxiiº : *Ego pro te rogaui,* Petre, *ut non deficiat fides tua; et super hanc petram edificabo ecclesiam meam, et porte inferi non preualebunt aduersus eam;* quia ut dicitur Matthei v⟨i⟩º : *Iota unum aut unus apex non preteribit a lege.* Ergo istud verum est quod tales heretici, tales persecutores ecclesie dei, tales impii, qui veniunt in profundum peccatorum, non durant, quia ut dicitur in Deuteronomio, qui contempserit sacerdotem morte moriatur. Et quomodo moriatur ? Tradendo ipsum Sathane, ut dicit apostolus prima ad Thymotheum primo. Iste contempsit summum sacerdotem, quia summum pontificem. Semper persecutus est ecclesiam dei, et habemus figuram primo Regum iiº c. de Azael persequente Abner, cui Abner dicebat quod recederet ad dexteram uel ad sinistram et dum ille a sua via praua nollet recedere, vertit se Abner et hasta ipsum in i[n]gwine percuciens interfecit. Sic iste fuit monitus quod recederet a suis erroribus, et nunquam recedere voluit. Et quare ? Quia contempnit. Ergo dignum est quod feriatur.

Sequitur eius [e]gressus ignominosus et vituperabilis, quia dicitur : [*s*]*et sequitur ignominia et obprobrium.* Loquitur dominus primo Regum iiº capitulo : *Qui autem contempnunt me, erunt ignobiles,* et hoc est quia formalis ratio peccati est contemptus. Unde dicit Augustinus primo de civitate Dei quod *amor sui usque ad contemptum dei* facit ciuitatem dyaboli, sed *amor dei usque ad contemptum sui* facit ciuitatem dei. Iste ergo, qui descendit et venit in profundum peccatorum, contemp-

---

78 Luce ***scripsi*** ; Matth. *cod.* 89 sinistrum *cod.* 90 igwine *cod.* 94 gressus *cod.* 95 set : et *cod.*

64-65. *Prov.* 18, 3.
66. Höfler, p. 20.
69. *I Cor.* 11, 22.
71. I have not found this passage in any of the genuine sermons of Chrysostomus, but similar passages can be found in [*Ps.*-Chrysostomus], *Sermo i in sanct. Pentecost.*, *PG* 52, 807, and *Sermo de pseudo prophetis et falsis doctoribus*, *PG* 59, 560.
73-74. *Ps.* 1, 3.
77-78. *Matth.* 16, 18.
78-79. *Luc.* 22, 32.
79-80. *Matth.* 16, 18.
81. *Matth.* 5, 18.
84. Cfr *Deut.* 17, 12.
85-86. Cfr *I Tim.* 1, 20.
88-91. Cfr *II Sam.* 2, 19-23.
94. Höfler, p. 21.
95. *Prov.* 18, 3.
96. *I Sam.* 2, 30.
98-99. Augustinus, *De civ. Dei* xiv, 28, *PL* 41, 436.

nit, et ideo *sequitur eum ignominia et oprobrium.* Unde dicitur Prouerbiorum vi° : *Turpitudinem et ignominiam congregat sibi, et obprobrium illius non delebitur.* Ita iste, qui nunquam voluit redire ad gremium sancte matris ecclesie, recipiet ignominiam et obprobrium, ut ipse sit *oprobrium habundantibus, et despectio superbis,* ut merito ipse dicat : *Obprobrium insipienti dedisti me.* Et ideo nos de fratrum nostrorum consilio approbamus et confirmamus [495b] omnes sententias latas contra ipsum per predecessores nostros et tamquam contra contumacem aggrauamus, et alias sententias inferemus ut apparebit in processibus qui fient de dicta materia cum consilio et deliberatione matura.

---

106 fratrum *e* fectum *in marg.corr.man.alt.* 107 et *supra lineam add. cod.*

---

101. *Prov.* 18, 3.
102-103. *Prov.* 6, 33.
103-104. HÖFLER, p. 21.
105. *Ps.* 122, 4.
106. *Ps.* 38, 9.

ADDITIONAL NOTE

Since the paper was submitted, a small number of bibliographical additions have come to hand.

To p. 120, n. 2 : For a recent description of EICHSTÄTT ms. 698, which was written c. 1410, perhaps in Regensburg, cfr D. GIRGENSOHN, in *Festschrift für Hermann Heimpel* II (Göttingen, 1972), p. 1069-1072.

To p. 120, n. 3 : For a contrary view to Moody's, cfr R. PAQUÉ, *Das Pariser Nominalistenstatut* (Berlin, 1970), p. 253-260.

To p. 120-121, n. 4 : Conrad's attitude towards the 'modernist' currents of his time have been excellently discussed by Dr S. KRÜGER, *Krise der Zeit als Ursache der Pest*, in *Festschrift für Hermann Heimpel* II, p. 845-851.

XIII

Thomas Bradwardine's 'Victory Sermon' in 1346

1346 was a year of amazing successes for English arms, unbroken except for a minor setback in Flanders. In June Thomas Dagworth had defeated Charles of Blois at St Pol de Léon in Brittany against the odds. A few days before Edward III's great victory at Crécy on 26 August Aiguillon in Gascony had been relieved from its long siege; less than two months later the invading Scots had been routed at Neville's Cross. It may be doubted whether fourteenth-century Englishmen were squeamish about possible imputations of 'triumphalism'. By late October or early November the main English army, concentrated under the king's command at the siege of Calais, was in the mood for celebration and thanksgiving. Edward gave orders for a service to be held, with an appropriate sermon to congratulate and edify his forces. Nearly all the sermon has survived: not however in the vernacular version originally delivered, but as a later elaboration in Latin. This *sermo epinicius* has been in print since 1959.[1] If it has hardly attracted as much attention as its interest warrants, that may be because the text as it stands presents quite numerous difficulties of interpretation. It may be useful to proceed from a revision of the Latin text to a fresh examination of the sermon in its historical circumstances.

If the occasion of the sermon was important, no less significant was the king's choice of preacher. Naturally enough, that fell on one of the royal chaplains accompanying the army. Neither rubric nor text gives his name. But in combination the comparatively slight external evidence and the more weighty internal indications discussed below have allowed the preacher to be identified beyond any reasonable doubt. He was Thomas Bradwardine, who

1 The adjective, which appears only in the rubric and in the form *ephinichius*, is constructed from the Vulgate noun *epinicion / epinicia* at I Par.15.21 and II Machab.8.33. The text, Merton College, Oxford, ms.180 ff.183-188v, is incomplete. It was printed by H.A. Oberman and the late J.A. Weisheipl, 'The *Sermo Epinicius* ascribed to Thomas Bradwardine (1346)', *Archives d'histoire doctrinale et littéraire du Moyen Age* xxv (1959), pp.307-29; introduction, pp.295-306. They were able to consult a transcript made by J.F. Laun, who in this as other ways was a pioneer in the modern study of Bradwardine. My thanks are due to Dr J.R.L. Highfield, librarian of Merton College, for helping me acquire a microfilm of the text.

had been chancellor of St. Paul's since 1337 and had crossed over to Normandy with the king in July 1346.[2] By that date Bradwardine's mathematical studies and his *De causa Dei* had given notice of a formidable scholastic intelligence, not readily equalled on the English scene as long as the ageing Ockham continued to lurk in his German exile.[3] It must be remembered too that Bradwardine was not just a very eminent scholar. As a former protégé of Richard of Bury and as a member of the politically-minded chapter of St Paul's he had not lacked opportunities to become aware of a world outside the schools. With what eyes he regarded that world, as far as I know, has not yet been investigated systematically. Here and there his great theological work *De causa Dei* suggests that his political views were those of a pretty authoritarian high monarchist. He cites with approval the well-worn tag from Aristotle's *Metaphysics* XII.10 1076a 3-4: 'Things do not wish to be ill-ordered, and a plurality of commanders is no good thing. So there should be only one ruler.' Moral reinforces natural philosophy. Those who discuss politics say that monarchy is the best form of government, especially if a properly qualified candidate can be found. So Aristotle taught in his *Politics* and *Ethics*; so teach the civil law of nations and the lawful enactments of all cities, communities and realms.[4] The powers of earthly princes are not small. 'Can they not and do they not in fact decree as just many things not

2 As Oberman and Weisheipl pointed out, p.302, the sermon is attributed to Bradwardine in the medieval table of contents to the Merton ms., on f.189r: *Sermo Epitnicius thome brad' deficiens*. F.M. Powicke's caution about the attribution, *The Medieval Books of Merton College*, Oxford, 1931, p.134, seems excessive. Shortly before his death Dr Weisheipl repeated without hesitation his conviction that Bradwardine was the author; see his essay 'Ockham and the Mertonians' in *The History of the University of Oxford* i, ed. J.I. Catto, Oxford, 1984, p.644. In his account of Bradwardine the fourteenth-century author of *Vitae archiepiscoporum cantuariensium* surely had this sermon in mind. In France Bradwardine taught the king and his army *quod solius Dei potentiâ, et non in multitudine armatorum Rex Angliae tandem suorum habuit victoriam aemulorum;* see Henry Wharton, *Anglia Sacra* i, London, 1691, p.42. A convenient summary of Bradwardine's career is in A.B. Emden, *Biographical Register of the University of Oxford* i, Oxford, 1957, pp.244-6; for his letter from Normandy to his friends in London, dated 17 July 1346 at La Hogue, see Adam Murimuth, *Cont. chron.*, ed. E.W. Thompson, pp. 201-2.

3 *De causa Dei* was edited by Henry Savile, London, 1618. For a general estimate of Bradwardine's significance as a scholar, see Weisheipl 'Ockham and the Mertonians', pp.634-58. His contributions to the science of motion and such problems as insolubles and future contingents, together with his activity as a leader among the 'Oxford Calculators', are discussed in *The Cambridge History of Later Medieval Philosophy*, ed. N. Kretzmann, A. Kenny, J. Pinborg, Cambridge, 1982, pp.247-9, 252-3, 374-7, 533-6, 540-2, 553-5. He bulks large in W.J. Courtenay, *Schools and Scholars in Fourteenth-century England*, Princeton, 1987, esp. pp.234-331.

4 *De causa Dei* i.1. corr.14, p.11; *cf. ib.*i.27, p.262.

sanctioned by the prior demonstration of natural reason, but which are entrusted to the lawgiver's judgement – things of which lawyers say: "What has pleased the prince, has the force of law"? For instance, might not the ruler justly and very reasonably enact that whoever has served strenuously and consistently in the ruler's interests and those of the state over which he presides should be rewarded in perpetuity, while anyone who has behaved in contrary fashion should be punished for all time? For the latter kind, that just personal penalty might last for ever, if they could live for ever. But since they cannot, the punishment is laid upon their descendants as if upon themselves in a certain fashion for ever, when the descendants are excluded from their rights of inheritance and perhaps declared incapable of receiving certain marks of distinction.'[5] The problem envisaged – the possibility that perpetual disinheritance might strike a family because one of its members had been disloyal to the crown – was, of course, a real issue in England during the first half of the fourteenth century. Here Bradwardine can be seen grasping it in a fashion attuned to the harsh doctrine of Bracton and *Fleta* about the treatment of a traitor's heirs. He carried his esteem for kingship very high. It would be difficult to adduce from his English contemporaries so forthright a declaration in favour of the king's thaumaturgical powers as Bradwardine gave in *De causa Dei* when challenging disbelief in Christian miracles: 'Come to England to the present king of the English, and bring with you any Christian suffering from the King's Evil, in however chronic, deep-seated and foul a form. After prayer, the laying on of hands and a blessing given under the sign of the Cross, the king will cure him in Christ's name. This he is doing continually, and he has done it time and time again to badly diseased men and women flocking to him on every side in England, Germany and France. Of this, everyday experiences give most certain warranty, as do those who have been cured, those who were present as witnesses, the peoples of the

[5] *De causa Dei* i.1. corr.29, p.113: Nonne et terreni principes possunt multa iusta statuere statuuntque de facto, ad que ratio naturalis demonstratiua precedens omnino non cogit, sed legislatoris arbitrio committuntur, de qualibus dicunt iuriste: 'Quod principi placuit, legis habet vigorem'? Nonne ergo posset princeps iuste statuere et multum consone rationi, quod quicumque pro principe aut republica, cui preest, perseueranter [et] strenue fecerit, perpetuo premietur, et quicumque contrarium fecerit, perpetuo puniatur? Quod et iuste eternaliter fierit in personis eorum, si possent viuere in eternum. Quod quia non possunt, in eorum posteris, quasi in ipsis quodammodo in perpetuum exercetur, dum a successione hereditaria repelluntur et ad multos forsan honores inhabiles decernuntur. *Cf. Fleta* i.21, ed. H.G. Richardson and G.O. Sayles, Selden Soc. Publ. lxxii, 1955, p.56, on the treatment of the convicted traitor. He is to be punished not only by death but also: omniumque bonorum amissione et heredum suorum exheredacione perpetua, et vix est permissibile quod heredes viuere permittantur.

nations and the often repeated talk of the multitude.'[6] Such unbridled enthusiasm contrasts notably with the caution, verging almost on scepticism, of Ockham's approach a couple of years earlier to this matter of curing the scrofulous by the king's touch.[7]

Both as a convinced royalist and as a scholar of high achievement Bradwardine was thus well fitted to give the victory sermon, preached in English before the king and his magnates in the host besieging Calais, on an unspecified day which the sermon's first editors reasonably supposed to have lain in late October or early November 1346.[8] No record exists of this English sermon, nor of the schema and notes presumably made in Latin by the preacher in preparation for it. What is the relation between the lost vernacular sermon and the surviving Latin version? According to its rubric the latter was made at the bidding (*ad praeceptum*) of a great ecclesiastic,

6 *De causa Dei* i.1. corr.32, p.39: Quicumque etiam negas miracula Christiana, veni et vide ad oculum adhuc istis temporibus in locis sanctorum per vices miracula gloriosa. Veni in Angliam ad regem Anglorum presentem, duc tecum Christianum quemcumque habentem morbum regium quantumcumque inueteratum, profundatum et turpem, et oratione fusa, manu imposita ac benedictione sub signo crucis data, ipsum curabit in nomine Iesu Christi. Hoc enim facit continue et fecit saepissime viris et mulieribus immundissimis et cateruatim ad eum ruentibus in Anglia, in Alemannia et in Francia circumquaque, sicut facta quotidiana, sicut qui curati sunt, sicut qui interfuerunt et viderunt, sicut populi nationum et fama quam celebris certissime contestantur.

7 See Ockham, *Octo Quaestiones*, in *Opp.polit.* i, ed. altera, Manchester, 1974, v.7.34-6; v.9.29-33. Record evidence attests how assiduously Edward touched for scrofula. In the period 12 July 1338 - 27 May 1340, for most of which he was overseas, royal alms were paid at 1d. for each person to 885 infirmis benedictis a rege et per gratiam dei curatis ... a morbo regali: *The Wardrobe Book of William de Norwell*, ed. Mary and Bryce Lyon and H.S. Lucas, Brussels, 1983, p.211. Touching the scrofulous was probably developed as a regular custom at the French court under Louis IX and imitated in England by Henry III towards the end of his reign. Though Edward I does not seem to have touched when in Wales, Scotland or overseas, he did so on a large scale in England, giving alms for 627 cases in 1275-7 and 1219 cases in 1303-4: Marc Bloch, *Les rois thaumaturges*, Strasbourg, 1924, pp. 97 ff., 438 ff.; Frank Barlow, 'The King's Evil', *EHR* xcv (1980), 3-27; cf. G. Vinay, 'Egidio Romano e la "Questio in Utramque Partem"', *Bolletino dell' Istituto storico italiano per il Medio Evo e Archivio Muratori* xliii (1939), pp. 118-119.

8 Oberman and Weisheipl, p.302; according to the sermon (§ 2) Neville's Cross, fought on 17 October, had been won *nouissime*. If the dating of *Rot.Scot.* i.675 can be trusted, news of the victory had reached the regency council at London by 20 October, when thanks were sent to a dozen named captains for their services. Since the battlefield is about 270 miles from London and the issue cannot have been clear until nightfall on 17 October, this seems almost unbelievably quick work. The messenger first to London with the news, Thomas of Byncheste, was rewarded with an annuity on 29 October: *CPR 1345-8*, p.198. Possibly the council's congratulatory letter was backdated. How rapidly the news reached the king from London will have depended on conditions in the Channel.

Annibaldo of Ceccano, cardinal bishop of Frascati, one of the two papal nuncios active from August 1346 in attempting to mediate between Edward III and Philip of Valois.[9] The rubric says that in translation the sermon proceeded *parumper ex causa diffusius* than in English. That, it may be suspected, much underestimates the case. The Latin sermon is an impressively learned composition. Scholarly references, quotations and allusions abound: to 'Hermes Trismegistus', to Plato, to Aristotle's *Physics, Metaphysics* and *Nicomachaean Ethics* and that composite made up from parts of the *Eudemean Ethics* and *Magna Moralia* known to the Latin fourteenth century as *De bona fortuna*,[10] as well as to the pseudo-Aristotelian *De mundo* and *Secretum secretorum*, to Augustine, Boethius and Gregory the Great. Scraps of the poets are quoted, from Ovid and the pseudo-Ovid of *De vetula*, from a garbled Claudian and the author of medieval leonine verses which had found their way into the *Latin Anthology*. Above all, there is a wealth of Biblical (especially Old Testament) reference, incorporated both by direct quotation and by resonance in a fashion which can surely have been appreciated only by those well accustomed to the Vulgate text. Of course, at times learned preachers have not hesitated about pitching their sermons far above the heads of their congregations. But the learning of the Latin victory sermon is omnipresent, unrelenting and ostentatious. It is difficult to conceive of Edward III and his fighting men bearing patiently with the preacher while he regaled them in English with chunks of literal quotation from *Secretum secretorum* and Josephus's *Jewish Antiquities* (§§ 33, 36), with a continuous nine lines from Jeremiah (§ 36), or a catena of almost twice that length put together from four assorted books of the Old Testament (§ 24). The suggestion does not seem rash that when the sermon was delivered in English in October or November 1346 it lacked much of this heavy top-hamper of scholastic display. Despite the rubric's minimising declaration, in all probability the Latin sermon represents not a slightly expanded translation but a thorough rehandling of the English original.

9 See Marc Dykmans, 'Le Cardinal Annibal de Ceccano (vers 1282-1350): étude biographique et testament du juin 1348', *Bulletin de l'Institut historique belge de Rome* xliii (1973), 145-344. Annibaldo had left Avignon on his peace-making nunciature together with cardinal Étienne Aubert in November 1345 and had certainly met Edward III by the beginning of January 1347: Dykmans, pp.219-27. Edward had retained this great lordly prelate (who was also a master of theology at Paris) as a counsellor in 1334, with a yearly pension of 50 marks: Rymer, *Foedera* II.ii.894. For his benefices and dignities in England, see Dykmans, pp.179, 193, 304-5.

10 A. Pelzer, 'Les versions latines des ouvrages de morale conservés sous le nom d'Aristotle, en usage au xiiie siècle', *Revue Néoscolastique* xxiii (1921), 316-41, 378-412.

That is not to say that the line of argument or articulation of the English sermon is likely to have differed radically from what appears in the Latin version. The preacher's choice of text from II Corinthians 2.14 dictated the direction taken: 'Now thanks be unto God, which always causeth us to triumph in Christ.' It is to God that thanks are due for England's victories; He alone has been responsible for them, and those who attribute them to secondary causes are utterly mistaken. Discussion and dismissal of seven errors against this truth provide the sermon's structure. The English had not triumphed, as some claim, because of the power of the stars. Nor because the time was favourable to them. Nor because of the working of Fortune on their behalf. Nor as an outcome of fate and predestined luck in battle (*omen armorum*).[11] Nor because of superior numbers. Nor because of their own military skill and prudence. Nor was any credit due to the pagan god or goddess of love, on the basis of the false argument that victory is the reward of bold and daring spirits and that only those are such who are lustful lovers. The sole author of the English successes is the one and only true Christian God, limitless in His power and energy, to solicit whose grace the preacher at the beginning of his sermon had led his congregation in saying the Lord's Prayer and Hail Mary. There is no reason to suppose that the English version departed from this scheme, or that it omitted any of the few *exempla* exhibited in the Latin sermon. They, it must be admitted, are not particularly striking. The most elaborate (§ 33) tells how two lovers had arranged a nefarious assignation at the Devil's prompting. The man arrived first and the devil, disguised as his beloved, played succubus, then strangled him and hid the body. Disguised as the man, the Devil proceeded to play incubus to the woman before strangling her too. This is rather commonplace stuff, it may be thought, not really in Bradwardine's higher vein; many a preaching friar could have made a livelier use of the material.

Both the theology and the learning of the Latin sermon point unmistakably to Bradwardine as the preacher. The English version, as has been claimed, will have been a 'popular presentation' of Bradwardine's main theological concern, worked out a few years earlier in his *De causa Dei:* 'all goodness, power and victory manifest in human activity' is to be attributed exclusively to God.[12] The close relationship between the Latin sermon and *De causa Dei* becomes quite obvious when the two texts are compared. What the sermon finds to say about Fortune and Fate (§§ 8-16) is clearly based on

11 The sermon pays much attention to what it calls *omen armorum* (§§ 3, 17-18). Exact verbal parallels seem hard to find in fourteenth-century Latin. A modern analogy might be some phrase as 'the luck of the Irish'.

12 Oberman and Weisheipl, p.304.

what Bradwardine had written earlier on these topics in *De causa Dei* i.28-31 and iii.27; indeed the sermon's account of the astrologers' view of Fortune (§ 8) is hardly intelligible without the help of Bradwardine's reference in *De causa Dei* to Albumazar's *Introductorius maior*.[13] Authorities, quotations, instances and turns of speech already used in *De causa Dei* frequently recur in the sermon.[14] Once we accept, as surely we must, that the sermon is Bradwardine's, its theology is wholly predictable in the light of *De causa Dei*. It can be found summarised in § 5: 'Whatever God wills to be or to happen, will occur; whomever God wills to win, will win; whomever God wishes to reign, will reign. For all things are disposed by His irresistible will. And so it is no small sin to attribute to any creature thanks for victory due to the Creator.' As Bradwardine had said in *De causa Dei*, whoever fails to attribute credit and thanks to God for a victory gained, even if he is at least nominally a Christian, shows himself less grateful to the true God than are pagans to their false deities.[15]

It is difficult to suggest how soon after preaching in English Bradwardine produced the elaborated Latin version of the sermon. Contact between him and its instigator, Cardinal Annibaldo, can be assumed at the latest shortly after 22 October 1346, when he was appointed among eight English commissioners to treat with the papal legates.[16] Just possibly a clue for a *terminus ante quem* can be found in § 22, when Bradwardine is enumerating the foreign allies who fought for Philip of Valois at Crécy. He refers to two kings, John of Bohemia and James of Majorca, and 'another

13 1.19, p.268.

14 Thus the sermon's use (§ 24) of the catena of references from Deut.8.17-18, Ps.32.16-19. II Paralip.25.8 and I Machab.3.19 repeats that in *De causa Dei* i.31, pp.276-7; its recourse (§ 16) to the Latin *Asclepius* in the *Corpus Hermeticum* reflects that already made in *De causa Dei* i.1. corr.39, pp.98-9; the verses it quotes (§§ 15, 18) from the pseudo and genuine Ovid had already been used in *De causa Dei* i.28, p. 265 and i.29, p. 267; the unusual noun *eufortunium* (§ 28) had occurred at least twice in *De causa Dei*, at i.9, p. 192 and i.29, p. 271. Further examples appear in the notes to the sources.

15 *De causa Dei* i.31, p. 277: nec dubito si fuerit saltem nomine Christianus, quin erit ingratior Deo vero quam aliquis infidelis Deo falso seu diis falsis cuius vel quorum gratiae et virtuti suam ascribit victoriam et honorem, eique vel eis secundum ritum suum gratias referens caedit victimas et pingues hostias immolat ac solennes.

16 Rymer, *Foedera* III.i.92: Mestre Thomas Bradewardyn, maistre en divinite, chanceller de l'eglise de Loundres. Cardinal Annibaldo will have been in contact with the English negotiators, at least intermittently, until the conclusion of the truce of Calais in late September 1347. He was back at the Curia in November: Dykmans, pp. 225-6.

quasi-king, that is to say the Roman emperor elect.'[17] By 'another quasi-king' Bradwardine meant John of Bohemia's son, Charles of Moravia, whom Luxemburg partisans among the electoral princes had set up on 11 July 1346 as anti-king in Germany in opposition to the Wittelsbach ruler, Lewis of Bavaria; Charles' election as *rex Romanorum* implied for him a presumptive claim to the title *imperator* when he had been crowned by the pope. Charles was consecrated and crowned as king by his supporters at Bonn on 26 November 1346, and news of this must have reached the English camp near Calais by early December. May we not perhaps infer that the Latin sermon had been written before Charles's transformation from 'quasi-king' to a king consecrated and crowned at Bonn was known to Bradwardine, and consequently that it had been completed only a few weeks after the vernacular sermon was preached? Unfortunately any such argument is far from conclusive. There can have been little inclination on the English side to recognise Charles as the legitimate *rex Romanorum* until much later than November or December 1346. Lewis, Edward III's former ally, had no great difficulty in maintaining his position in Germany against the Luxemburger anti-king; after Lewis's death in October 1347 the Wittelsbach party tried hard to persuade Edward himself to become king of Germany. Not until the spring of 1348 did Edward finally reject that prospect and make peace with Charles.[18] As long as Lewis was alive and Charles remained Edward's enemy it seems highly unlikely that Bradwardine would have accepted Charles as a proper king. So the reference to Charles as *quasi rex* does not prove that the Latin version had been completed by early December 1346. The problem when it was produced remains open.

It may be easier to suggest why it was undertaken. Abundant display of learning and calculated rhetorical effects lend the Latin version the air of a sort of prize song or *Paradestückchen*. If that was indeed its character, whom was it intended to impress? Bradwardine was not just an outstanding scholastic; he was also active in practical life, with reasonable expectation of high office in the Church. A member of the king's entourage on the Crécy-Calais campaign, he was quite near the centre of affairs; he continued to enjoy the king's trust after the battles were over. On 28 September 1347 Edward dispatched him from Calais on a confidential mission to London; he was to make known by word of mouth to the chancellor, John Offord, the

17 § 22: et alius quasi rex, el<l>ectus videlicet inperator Rom[anus]. The reading proposed by the previous editors, p. 317, cannot be accepted: et alius quasi rex excellentissimus, videlicet Imperator Romanus.

18 See F. Trautz, *Die Könige von England und das Reich 1272-1377*, Heidelberg, 1961, pp.344-52.

king's intentions about the provincial council of Canterbury called by Archbishop John Stratford for the first week in October.[19] This interesting collocation of names comprised the three highest-flying ecclesiastics in the English church at the time: two lawyers, the primate and Offord, together with the theologian Bradwardine. Next year, after falling ill in June, Archbishop Stratford died on 23 August. Even before he was buried on 9 September, the monks of Canterbury with indecent and perhaps uncanonical haste elected Bradwardine as his successor on 30 August.[20] This precipitate action, it may be suspected, can hardly have been taken without Bradwardine's concurrence. Clearly the chancellor of St. Paul's was not unduly modest in his ambitions. Had the Latin elaboration of the victory sermon – so orthodox in its Christian sentiment, so learned, so adept in its handling of homiletic technique – been produced with the possibility of a vacancy at Canterbury in mind (by now Stratford had possibly reached, if not exceeded, the age of seventy)? More specifically, was it, with the knowledgeable encouragement of Cardinal Annibaldo, intended to impress that great virtuoso of pulpit eloquence, Pope Clement VI, whose influence together with the king's would decide how the vacancy should be filled?[21] We cannot be sure that positive answers to these questions are right. If they are, the reckoning was not immediately successful. On 24 September, at the request, we are told, of Edward III, the pope provided John Offord, chancellor of England and dean of Lincoln, to the vacant archsee. But the Black Death swept Offord away on 20 May 1349, before he could be consecrated. Bradwardine, for whom the deanery of Lincoln had been reserved by the pope, found the next place in the queue for Canterbury. Speedily the monks of Christ Church elected him again, but perhaps even before the news of this election on 4 June could have reached Avignon

19 PRO SC/1/39/198, printed by B. Wilkinson, *The Chancery under Edward III*, Manchester, 1929, p.118 n.1; the document speaks of: nostre cher clerc Maistre Thomas Bradewardyn plus pleinement enforme de nostre intencion. For the date, see R.M. Haines, *Archbishop John Stratford: Political Revolutionary and Champion of the Liberties of the English Church ca. 1275/80-1348*, Toronto, 1986, p.358.

20 Haines, *Stratford*, pp.507-8.

21 See Paul Fournier's description of Clement VI as 'l'homme le plus éloquent de son temps', in *Histoire littéraire de la France* xxxvii (1938), 224. Dr Diana Wood takes account of earlier work on Clement's sermons in her essay 'The sermon literature of Pope Clement VI', in *Studies in Church History* xi, Oxford, 1975, pp.163-72; see also her *Clement VI: the pontificate and ideas of an Avignon pope*, Cambridge, 1989, pp.14-17. As Pierre Roger he had declared in 1326/7: Videtur mihi ut illum decet esse pontificem et non alium qui est praedicationis clamore mellifluus (Paris, Bibliothèque Sainte-Geneviève, cod.230, f.284v). Cardinal Annibaldo was eulogised by Clement in *collationes* in 1343 and 1347: Dykmans, p. 226 n.1; Wood, *Clement VI*, app. 3, nos. 25, 28, pp. 213-4.

Clement VI had provided him to Canterbury on 19 June. He was consecrated in the church of the Friars Minor at Avignon on 19 July, and had to stomach at the subsequent festivity a gross insult put upon him by the pope's brother, Cardinal Hugues Roger. Bradwardine survived his return to England as archbishop by only a few days. He landed at Dover on 19 August and died on the 25th or 26th of the same month.

The fourteenth-century author of the *Vitae* of the Canterbury archbishops, the main source of these details, had obviously read the 'Victory Sermon', presumably in its Latin form.[22] Even if we accept the conjecture – it can be no more – that Bradwardine had prepared this elaboration as a calculated shot in a campaign for ecclesiastical advancement, he cannot fairly be blamed for making the most of the chances to which his abilities entitled him. There is no trace of timeserving or sycophancy in the sermon's message; it did not hesitate to convey truths which its original audience cannot have found wholly flattering or even palatable. But when we read the Latin version today its steady progress to a predetermined theological conclusion is not its most attractive aspect. Precisely because its theology reflects so accurately what Bradwardine had already propounded in *De causa Dei* much of the sermon's appeal lies elsewhere, in the light it throws upon the personality of the preacher and on a particular historical situation. The churchman called upon to give a command performance before the English host in the late autumn of 1346 was highly intelligent, not lacking in ambition, and occupying in the royal household a position which gave him advantages in learning what was going on at the headquarters of England's military organisation. Bradwardine was no actively belligerent clerk in the fashion of a Thomas Hatfield or a William de la Zouche. But even as an intellectual rather than a fighting man in the king's entourage, he cannot have been impervious to the mood and prejudices there prevailing or have failed to reflect them at least in part. Historians concerned with English military affairs in 1346 will find some useful material in his sermon.

From it we get no impression that Bradwardine was at all close in person to the action at Crécy; his appropriate station in battle would have been with the rear elements of the army. When his discussion of the battle (§ 23) declares that on the English side no notable was killed, taken prisoner or gravely wounded *de quo sciam*, this looks like an admission that his standpoint was somewhat remote. Nevertheless, the little he has to say about the course of the battle – for example, how the weight of the repeated French attacks was for the most part borne by the English first division on the right –

[22] See note 2 above.

seem acceptable enough, and he correctly insists that the foreign troops with Edward's army were few.[23] Elsewhere (§ 21) he rightly stresses how widely the military resources of England were extended in 1346, though his compass tour to demonstrate that no less than nine separate areas needed to be manned simultaneously may have owed more to the schematism of a mathematically inclined theologian (*nouemque fuisse porciones seu ordines Anglicorum secundum numerum ordinum angelorum*) than to genuine insight into strategy and logistics, despite the fact that Edward's government was by no means incapable of planning military operations in detail.[24] Bradwardine himself seems aware how anachronistic was his claim that in 1346 the eastern coasts of England needed defence against the Danes; he tried to cover himself by resort to a lame gloss.[25]

Himself a southerner by birth[26] and in 1346 a royal chaplain by occupation, Bradwardine's accounts of English successes other than those gained under the king's direct command are not particularly well-informed. Their interest lies in the light they cast on the sort of things which could be believed at court: not, perhaps, in the innermost circle there, but at any rate not far from it. Thus his statement (§ 2) that recently (*nouiter*) in Ireland four so-called kings had been defeated, had given hostages and had submitted to Edward's rule, though apparently so definite and confident, is in fact difficult to relate closely to specific events. What reality had those four Irish kings, beyond Bradwardine's feeling that Ulster, Connacht, Leinster and Munster each ought to provide one? English arms had indeed prospered in Ireland under the justiciar Ralph Ufford; during 1344 and 1345 he had exacted submissions from *reguli* in Leinster, Ulster and elsewhere. But after Ufford's death in April 1346 his successor Walter Bermingham does not appear to have mounted a major campaign until c. November 1346, too late, it must be supposed, to find mention in Bradwardine's sermon, at any rate in its original

23 See, for example, John of Tynemouth, *Historia Aurea*, in Lambeth Palace Library, ms.12, f.245vb: per primam aciem anglorum gallici deuicti sunt. Geoffrey le Baker, *Chron.*, ed. E.M. Thompson, p.85 agrees that there were three formal French attacks on 26 August. Trautz, *Die Könige von England*, p.333 estimates the German element in Edward's army at no more than one per cent.

24 M.C. Prestwich, 'English Armies in the early stages of the Hundred Years War: a scheme in 1341', *Bulletin of the Institute of Historical Research* lvi (1983), 102-13.

25 § 21: in latere orientis ad custodiendas partes maritimas orientis propter insultum Dacorum, id est hostium alicorum.

26 Though presumably his forebears came from Herefordshire, Bradwardine was ordained priest by letters dimissory from Chichester; see R.M. Haines, *The Church and Politics in Fourteenth-Century England. The Career of Adam Orleton c.1275-1345*, Cambridge, 1978, p.57, n.30.

form. Our fullest narrative source, Friar John Clyn's annals, recount Ufford's success in taking hostages *de pace tenenda* and deposing 'the king of Ulster'. Yet it seems impossible to identify what particular incidents Bradwardine may have had in mind. Probably he had no more accurate understanding of what had been going on in Ireland than most of his contemporaries, and based his statement on scraps of news and rumours which had reached the court over a period of time.[27] Bradwardine's exaggerated figures for the number of combatants at Neville's Cross (§ 20), where he has 60,000 Scots opposed by about 20,000 Englishmen, are in line with those given by sources with less excuse to err.[28] But his rather condescending contrast of the quality of the two armies, when he sees the flower of Scotland, her *nobilissimi bellatores*, defeated by a very ordinary lot of Englishmen,[29] would hardly have been relished by such skilled and experienced northern English warriors as William de la Zouche, Henry Percy, John Mowbray and Ralf Neville. Bradwardine's attitude here reminds us that some military snobberies are perennial; the 'fashionable' English army in 1346 was that led by the king in person on the Continent.[30]

If to Bradwardine the Irish ranked as *ferocissimi hostes nostri* (§ 2), he reserved the full force of his hatred for the Scots. Them he singles out as chopping-blocks to serve an independent and courageous turn in his sermon. He was preaching to a court and army which was not only habituated to the licence of service abroad but which also held in high esteem the cult and trappings of chivalry: to men accustomed to all chivalry's erotic overtones made popular in literature and formal in the ceremonies of the tournament. He must have been brushing shoulders almost daily with some who were to become foundation members of the Order of the Garter. Against the tide,

27 See Friar John Clyn, *The Annals of Ireland*, ed. R. Butler, Dublin, 1849, pp. 30, 32-3; R.F. Frame, *English Lordship in Ireland 1318-61*, Oxford, 1982, pp. 262-86. I am much indebted to Dr Frame for his advice about this.

28 Dr Thomas Sampson in his newsletter written on the spot estimates about 62,000 Scots and 32,000 English: Oxford, Bodleian Library, ms. Bodley 302, ff.142vb, 143ra. *Chron.Lanercost*, ed. Joseph Stevenson, p. 345, numbers the Scots at more than 32,000; *Anonimalle Chron.*, ed. V.H. Galbraith, at more than 41,500. No doubt all these figures are inflated.

29 § 20: cerciter 20 milia Anglicorum talium qualium in partibus illis tunc temporis communiter repertorum.

30 Bradwardine's anecdote (§ 25) that *iam ultimo* an English leader against the Scots refused to await the arrival of considerable reinforcements before giving battle may refer to Neville's Cross, fought before the arrival of Thomas Lucy with his Cumbrian troops. Thus Thomas Sampson, in ms. Bodley 302, f.143rb: Lui sire de Lucie, qe vient hastant uers la bataile tant com il poait ou grant nombre des gentz darmes e ne fust mi a la iournee, ad encountree les enemys fuantz e les pursuit egrement.

Bradwardine spoke out strongly on behalf of conventional Christian morality in sexual matters. Victory was not the due of devotees of heathen Venus, striving to win renown in battle in order to be more amorously cherished by foolish women.[31] He mocks as profane madness the reasoning that victory is to the audacious and audacity is the prerogative of those who make love without restraint.[32] Those who think thus, he declares in language designed to strike home to soldiers mindful of the organisation of their own calling, fight for the Devil, are of his retinue and follow his banner.[33] Here is the explanation of the current military failures of the French and Scots, peoples once of high repute as fierce, courageous and great of heart (§ 35). From of old the Scottish people, and especially their nobles, have been regarded as addicted to the unrestrained pursuit of sexual pleasure, even in its most unlawful forms.[34] Worst of them all is their king, David. Him Bradwardine blackguards mercilessly. David has deserted his lovely wife and, defying God's law, has violated almost all the wives and daughters, the ladies and damsels in Scotland who have caught his fancy; he glories in the repute of being, as it were, the stud bull of the herd or the communal village boar, serving whomever comes up next in turn.[35] This diatribe will have been well received by the English court and host. For David's spurned wife was Edward III's younger sister, Joan, whose child-marriage to David when she was aged seven and he only four had failed to produce the political advantages hoped for. What credence should be given to these allegations about David's sexual excesses remains uncertain. As far as I know, this is the earliest example in the sources of charges for this kind against David; when they wished to abuse him the English chroniclers generally fastened on to his misfortune as an infant at the font when he was being baptised.[36]

31 § 32: ut a mulieribus fatuis amorosius diligantur.

32 § 32: Set dicunt quod nullus esse poterit animosus nisi fuerit amorosus vel diligat amorose, [ita] quod nullus esse poterit milic[i]osus nisi fuerit amorosus vel diligat amorose, quia nullus se potest gerere strenue excessiue nisi diligat excessiue.

33 § 32: Hii igitur milites amorosi militantes dee amoris diabolo militant, de retinencia ipsius existunt, vexillo eius intendunt...

34 § 36: Gens vero Scotorum, et precipue nobiles, eciam ab antiquo maxime venerei reputantur. Ibi nanque, sicud communiter diffamant, consanguinitati non parcitur nec affinitati defertur neque ab adulterio temperatur.

35 § 36: omnes quasi vxores et filias, dominas et ancillas de Scocia in oculis suis placentes violauit, factus, quia est, quasi emissarius taurus seu aper communis seruiens quamquam versuram; et ... talem se puplice iactare gaudebat et gloriabatur se talem ab omnibus predicari.

36 Ranald Nicholson, 'David II, the historians and the chroniclers', *Scottish Hist. Rev.* xlv (1966), 59-78, has little to say about David's sexual behaviour, beyond pointing out that Bower mentioned his adultery among the explanations of his disaster at Neville's Cross.

It is lust, Bradwardine proclaims, which has caused the Scots to lose their martial prowess. But his attack on the vice is not limited to castigating Edward's unsatisfactory brother-in-law and the Scottish people. To Edward and his assembled fighting men he struck the high moral note which his duty as a Christian churchman called for: the one true God, He who alone gives victory, is the God of unsmirched love, modesty and chastity. How the sermon proceeded to ram home this teaching is unknown, for the text breaks off at this point. It may be useful to remember that Bradwardine, for all his stress on God's omnipotence and omniscience, was far from denying the freedom of man's will. 'A reasonable creature has free will and is naturally free'; 'temptation is wholly incapable of vanquishing right will', even though the will cannot overcome temptation by its own strength without God's help and grace.[37] Did the sermon close by repeating the contention in *De causa Dei* that chastity can be striven for, and there is no need for humans to yield to lust? There are human means of suppressing sexual appetite; if camphor, *agnus castus* or mouse's dung fail to do the trick, there is always castration.[38] Whether the sermon's lost conclusion was as forthright as that we do not know. But it is certain that in the climax up to which Bradwardine was building emphasis had shifted from scholastic learning and deterministic theology to pastoral concern. The end of the sermon as it survives – and probably little is missing – is an exhortation to Christian morality, none the less resounding for being conventional. If that was not welcome to all who heard it, at any rate Bradwardine had done his duty as a priest. He had read II Corinthians 2 beyond his text verse through to the end of the chapter: 'For we are not as many, which corrupt the word of God: but as of sincerity, but as of God, in the sight of God speak we in Christ.' That his career as primate lasted only a few days was a heavy loss.

But the only reference Bower, writing c. 1440, makes to David's adultery seems to be in *Scotichronicon* xiv.5, ed. Goodall, ii.345, when he quotes the verses:

Nitens per guerras Anglorum perdere terras.
Testes erit culter, David capietur adulter *etc.*

He had taken these from the *vaticinium* about Neville's Cross in 'Robert of Bridlington's' prophecies, ed. Thomas Wright, *Political Poems* i (1859), 156. On the 'Bridlington' problem, see Paul Meyvaert, 'John Erghome and the *Vaticinium Roberti Bridlington*', *Speculum* xli (1966), 656-64 and A.G. Rigg, ibid. lxiii (1988), 596-613..

37 *De causa Dei* ii.3, p. 449; ii.3, p. 451; *cf.* ii.5, p. 480; *cf.* H.A. Oberman, *Archbishop Thomas Bradwardine: a fourteenth-century Augustinian*, Utrecht, 1957, pp.65-70.

38 *De causa Dei* i.1. corr. 39, p. 119: Nonne pueri, decrepiti et infirmi, maleficiati et frigidi concupiscentiam venereorum non habent? Nonne castratio, camphora, agnus castus, stercus muris et similia extingunt veneris appetitum?

PREFACE TO TEXT

The text of the sermon as it appears in Merton College ms. 180 [*cod.*] is written by an indisputably English cursive hand, a rather coarse and ugly Anglicana. This script, as Dr A.I. Doyle has kindly advised me, points to a date c. 1375 or perhaps somewhat later. The text has a few errors and omissions of the sort characteristic of a copy rather than an original composition. Throughout it shows traces of intervention (not invariably apposite) by what I take to be a different hand of about the same date [*corr.* or *suppl.*]. On this occasion this second hand has made it impossible to recover what *cod.* wrote. As it survives, the sermon is incomplete; presumably something on another folio, now lost, following the word *Aduerte* with which the text breaks off at the foot of f.188vb. But by this stage the main argument has been pretty fully developed; probably little of the text has been lost. The surviving six folios have been bound very tightly, so that parts of the columns adjoining the gutter are sometimes difficult to read on film; cropping of the upper margin has caused the loss of a few words at f. 183rb.

In editing the sermon I have supplied the division into numbered sections; punctuation and the use of capitals have been modernised. On the other hand, the somewhat inconsistent and idiosyncratic orthography of *cod.* has been retained, so far as it can be recovered. At times the scribe writes *i* where *e* would be more usual, and vice versa; quite often he has *c* (or intrusively *sc*) for *s* and a few times for *qu*; unnecessary doubling of consonants is not uncommon, nor the dropping of the second letter in what are normally double consonant forms. Such scribal peculiarities seem unlikely to puzzle readers seriously and for the most part have been allowed to stand. The manuscript gives little indication on how the scribe would have extended abbreviations of the kind *nāque, nūquid, nūquam, eorūdem*; if on the whole I have preferred to supply *n* rather than *m*, this is partly guesswork.

Editorial additions are enclosed within square brackets, [ ]; suggested supressions within pointed brackets, < >. Textual notes are numbered consecutively within the section to which they apply; references to sources (other than to the Vulgate) are designated alphabetically in the same way. The siglum *ed.*[1] refers to the edition by Weisheipl and Oberman.

TEXT

Merton College, Oxford ms. 180, f.183ra

Sermo ephinichius ad mandatum Christianissimi et propterea victoriosissimi principis domini E. Dei gracia regis Anglie et Francie in presencia sua et optimatum suorum in Anglico primo dictus, et postea ad preceptum patris domini Anibaldi sancte Romane ecclesie cardinalis episcopi Tusculani et apostolice sedis legati translatus de Anglico in Latinum, set in Latino parumper ex causa diffusius prosecutus quam in Anglico dicebatur.

[1] *Deo gracias, qui semper trimphat nos:* 2 ad Corinthios 2.[14] Karissimi, licet dominus noster rex habeat multos clericos excellentes, secundum quod decet regiam magestatem, placuit tamen regali prouidencie quod ego pusillus facerem collacionem hac vice ad vestram nostramque omnem gratuitatem excitandam. Quatinus gracias agamus Domino Deo nostro, dignum est enim veraciter atque iustum; Ipse nanque prius multas et magnas gracias gratuito fecit nobis. Set ad ista facienda graciose seu grate adhuc vlterius indigemus communiter ipsius gracia speciali, que sola actus nostros efficit graciosos et opera nostra grata. Igitur in principio collacionis presentis, pro gracia inpetranda dicamus supliciter auctori gracie et auctrici *Pater noster* et *Aue Maria.*

[2] *Deo gracias, qui semper triumphat nos.* Karissimi, mos est in factis armorum dare grates seu gracias melius se gerenti. Vos autem habuistis recenter in locis diuersis diuersa et magna facta armorum: in Francia, in Vasconia, in Flandria et in Britannia, set recentissime in Hibernia et in Anglia, sicud scitis. In Hibernia nanque iam nouiter ferocissimi hostes nostri, ymmo quatuor reges vt fertur – quales ibi habentur – deuicti, datis obsidibus, dicioni se domini regis Anglie subdiderunt. In Anglia vero nouissime, scilicet 17 die Octobris, rex Scocie cum 60 milibus ingressus partes Anglie boriales ab hominibus parcium earundem quasi 20 milibus, prope Dunolmum commisso bello accerimo, est deuictus et captus / [f.183rb] ac caute custodie mancipatus … et …[1] *cecidit flos* [*cf.* Is.40.7] Scocie vniuersus. Omnes enim pene nobiles Scocie perimuntur, ignobiles prosternuntur et omnes fere residui capiuntur et ergastulis contraduntur. Oportet igitur reddere gracias siue grates secundum consuetudinem approbatam in armis superius memoratam.

§2 (1) *Margine sup. conciso, aliqua verba illegibilia*

[3] Set cui? Hic est opinionum varietas, ymo et contrarietas inter multos. Aliqui nanque dicunt quod stellarum potestati, alii quod temporis oportunitati, alii quod fortune seu casus collacioni, alii quod fati seu ominis[1] disposicioni, alii proprie [potencie seu][2] prudencie, alii deo amoris, scilicet falso deo, alii Deo virtutis innumere et vigoris, videlicet vero Deo.

[4] Primi sunt quidam vani astrologi, quia omnia que fiunt sub sole attribunt generi hominum et virtuti stellarum. Vnde et quidam ipsorum curiosius delirantes accipiunt significatores pugnaturorum et inter alias partes multas, quas so[m]pniant, partem victorie, et cum quo significatore illa ceciderit, ibi dicunt victoriam futuram. Set hii sunt similes antiquis gentilibus, qui solem et lunam et stellas ceteras tanquam deos ex causis huiusmodi coluerunt. Tales si quidem sint huius temporis Christiani, vid[eb]untur[1] antichristiani pocius nuncupandi seu Christiani apostate, sicud et olim illi Iudei, qui *adora*uerunt *ad ortum solis* surgentis [*cf.* Ezech.8.16], coluerunt reginam *celi*, puta Dyanam seu *lunam*, et *vniuersam* eius *miliciam* [*cf.* IV Reg.17.16; Jer.8.2], puta stellas ymaginesque stellarum, sicud nostri sanctissimi apices recordantur. Hii igitur horribiliter deuiant et aberrant. Constat enim, litteris nostris sacris tradentibus, quod totum celum, sol et luna et stelle in principio facta sunt per Deum, nec quicquam nisi a Deo [*cf.* Ioann.1.3], et ipsius in omnibus seruiunt voluntati. Quod Baruc attestans veraciter dicit ita: *Stelle dederunt lumen in custodiis suis, et letate sunt: vocate sunt, et dixerunt: Adsumus: et luxerunt ei cum iocunditate, qui fecit illas* [Bar.3.34-5]. Illud et euidenter apparuit quando, Moyse extendente *manum in celum, facte sunt tenebre palpa*biles et *horr*ende *in* tota *terra Egypti tribus diebus*, ita vt nullus Egipcius posset aspicere *fratrem suum: ubicunque* vero *filii Israel habitabant, lux erat* [Exod.10.21-3]. Illud eciam euidenter apparuit in stacione solis et lune spacio vnius diei ad preces magnifici Josue, Deo sic victoriam de hostibus concedente [*cf.* Jos.10.12-14]. Illud / [f.183va] et euidenter apparuit in reuersione solis per 10 linias – spacium 10 horarum – *in orologio Achaz* ad votum mirifici Isaye [*cf.* Is.38.8].[a] Quis astrologus pro[g]nosticasset huiusmodi? Quis astrologus preiudicasset hec fieri? Quis astrologous talia preuidisset? Quis astrologus talia predixisset?

[5] Verum karissimi, ecce pro[g]nosticacio vna certa, nunquam potest fallere, nunquam falli: Quicquid Deus wlt fore seu fieri, illud fiet; quemcunque Deus uult vincere, ille vincet; et quemcunque Deus uult regnare,

§ 3 (1) hominis *corr.*

§ 3 (2) potencie seu *suppl.*

§ 4 (1) vīdūtur *cod.*

ille regnabit. In voluntate nanque sua *cun[c]ta sunt posita*, nec *est qui* eius *possit resistere voluntati* [*cf.* Esth.13.9]; vnde propheta, ymmo Dominus per prophetam: *Consilium meum stabit, et omnis voluntas mea fiet* [Is.46.10]. Licet igitur *celum et terra et quicquid celi ambitu continetur* [Esth.13.10] fueri[n]t vobis contraria, si Deus sit vobis propicius, quid potest vobis nocere? Et licet *celum et terra et quicquid celi ambitu continetur* fueri[n]t vobis propicia, si Deus sit vobis contrarius, quid potest vobis valere? Vnde claret perspicue illos non parum peccare et diuinam iracundiam prouocare, qui gracias siue grates victorie debitas creatori auferentes ab eo tribuunt creature. Quare et propheta, ymmo Dominus ipse locutus est per prophetam aduersus Babilonem, vbi sciencie huiusmodi plurimu[m] viguerunt. *Sapiencia*, inquit, *tua et sciencia tua decepit te. Sta cum incantoribus tuis, et cum multitudine maleficiorum tuorum, in quibus laborasti ab adolescencia tua, si forte quid prosit tibi, aut si possis fieri forcior. Defecisti in multitudine consiliorum tuorum: stent, et <p>saluent te augur<i>es celi, qui contemplabantur sidera et supputabant menses, vt ex eis annunciarent ventura tibi. Facti sunt quasi stipula, ignis combuscit* illos [Is.47.10, 12-15]. Istam quoque artem iudicialem per astra vnacum suis artificibus atque iudicibus beati Augustinus, Gregorius et ceteri sancti patres, iura canonica atque ciuilia[1] concorditer reprobant et condempnant.[a] Sic igitur reicitur primus error; quo diffusiori parumper certamine iam deuicto, alii breuius conuincentur.

[6] Secundum errorem tenentes sunt priorum filii et sequaces. Tales autem fuerunt Egipcii veteres, qui dies in quibus erant deuicti nonantes vocauerunt dies malos, sicud vsque ad presens legitima kalendaria manifestant, quare et *dies Egipciaci* nuncupantur.[a] Qui et dies, in quibus de hostibus triumphabant, dicebant econtrario / [f.183vb] dies[1] bonos, vinci suum et vincere malicie et bonitati diei et temporis deputantes. Verum [h]aut dubie totum tempus quantum est de se est vniformis concimilisque nature, nec vnum melius aut deterius alio neque dans vincere neque vinci, nisi fortassis racione constellacionis bone vel male occurentis[2] in tali, concedentis victoriam vel negantis. Hic igitur error secundus inplicat precedentem; quare et confutabitur sicud ille.

[7] Set de sapientibus Egipciis specialiter[1] admirandum est. *Dicentes enim se esse sapientes*, et *stulti facti sunt* [Rom.1.22], et secundum nomen suum

§ 5 (1) ciuilia; similiter *cod.*
§ 6 (1) dies *rep. cod.*; *del. corr.*
§ 6 (2) occurentes *cod.*
§ 7 (1) spiritualiter *cod.*; supernaturaliter *ed.*[1]

obscuratum est insipiens cor eorum [Rom.1.21]. Nam si hec dies huius anni dicatur mala vtcumque propter malam constellacionem existentem in ea, non ideo sequitur quod semper omni anno, ymmo nec anno proximo, erit mala; non enim semper, ymmo nec anno proximo, suberit illa eadem constellacio, scilicet illa mala, set forcitan alia constellacio bona valde, sicud eciam[2] parum scientes de astrorum sciencia bene norunt. Adhuc autem, si dies, in qua ipsi erant deuicti, fuerit[3] ideo dies mala, consimili racione fuit eadem dies suis hostibus ipsos vincentibus dies bona, et dies, que Egipciis vincentibus fuit bona, fuit hostibus suis mala, sic quod[4] eadem dies fuit mala simul et bona secundum Egipciorum sentenciam insensatam. Set audiant isti et timiant malediccionem propheticam latam in tales: *Ve qui dicitis bonum malum, et malum bonum: ponentes tenebras lucem, et lucem tenebras* [*cf.* Is.5.20]. Horum vero[5] sentencia longe sit a me et a quolibet Christiano. Per hec igitur et huiusmodi potest <ergo> erro[r] secundus corrigi aut corripi.

[8] Errorem 3m profitentes secundum sectam duplicem variantur. Quidam nanque, puta antiqui gentiles, fortunam confixerant vnam deam nutibus[1] suis incertis temporalia dispensante[m];[a] qui error eciam alicos Judeorum antiquitus inuoluebat, de quibus ait propheta: *Qui ponitis Fortune mensam, et libatis super eam* [Is.65.11].[b] Alii vero, puta astrologi, ponunt fortunam quandam virtutem celestem secundum vim stellarum et partes celestis circuli ordinatam. Vnde et inter duodecim / [f.184ra] domos quas fabricant, decimam[2] sibi assignant et inter omnes partes celestes partem principalissimam ei donant, quam et vocant partem fortune. Que secundum doctrinam ipsorum accipitur in die [a] sole in lunam, quia sol est *luminare maius* et *pre*est *diei*; in nocte autem a luna in solem, quia luna est *luminare minus* et *pre*est *nocti* [*cf.* Gen.1.16]. Et proicitur ab ascendente, et vbi computacio terminatur, ibi dicunt pars fortune, que, si[3] cum quocunque aduersariorum in quacunque causa cediderit, ille fortunabitur et bene prosperabitur in agendo.[c]

[9] Set prima harum sectarum est irracionabilis multum valde. Illa nanque dea fortune ceca apud hos veteres dicebatur et inter picturas eorum depingebatur vt mulier quedam ceca, eo quod sine discrescione aut meritis personarum distribuit prospera vel aduersa. Set quam ceca insania colere

§ 7 (2) vere *cod.*; universaliter *ed.*[1]
§ 7 (3) fuerit mala *s.l.add.corr.*
§ 7 (4) set que *cod.*
§ 7 (5) ergo *ed.*[1]
§ 8 (1) deam nutibus: de annutibus *cod.*
§ 8 (2) naturam *cod. ed.*[1]
§ 8 (3) se *cod.*

talem deam, que cultores suos videre non potest nec inter cultores et contemptores discernere! Neque enim magis prodesset colere quam contempnere talem deam. Adhuc autem, hec secta nedum est irracionalis et insana, verumeciam heretica et prophana. *Omnes* enim *dii gencium* atque dee, litteris sacris tradentibus, *demonia* perhibentur [*cf.* Ps.95.5]. Quam igitur prophana vesania[1] et falsa infamia! Grates et gracias debitas soli Deo debemus ex[h]ibere. Secunda secta huius euisdem erroris profitetur primum errorem premissum; quare retunditur sicud ille.

[10] Verumtamen aduertendum quod fortuna non est penitus reprobanda. Solent nanque catholici et perfectissimi Christiani sepius dicere 'forte hoc erit' seu 'forte non erit', nec hoc aliqua religio pro[h]ibet neque culpat. In litteris quoque sacris, eciam in ipso ewangelio veritatis, verba habitus 'forte', 'forcitan', 'fortassis' aliquociens sunt reperta. Hec autem verba videntur fortunam patule importare. Quis igitur presu[m]pserit fortunam penitus reprobare?[a]

[11] Hic igitur est sciendum quod secundum Philosophum, ymmo secundum philosophos, fortuna est causa latens circa ea, que proueniunt preter intencionem agentis, et eius effectus 'fortuitus' nuncupatur. Que, si esset patens et effectum illum intendens, nequaquam fortuna, / [f.184rb] set causa determinata et certa, et eius effectus nequaquam fortuitus, set determinatus respectu sue cause et certus racionabiliter diceretur.[a] Hinc igitur licenter permittitur vt homines, ignorantes causas multorum effectuum contingencium circa eos, ipsos quodammodo fortune atribuant vtentes verbis superius memoratis.

[12] Verum, pro pleniore cognicione fortune parum alcius ordiendum.[1] Est enim fortuna, sicud premititur, causa latens, et hoc [est] secundum philosophos causa agens siue actiua,[2] videlicet voluntas diuina, vel ad illam reducitur sicud causa inferior ad superiorem et summam, sicud causa secunda siue posterior ad priorem seu primam, sicud tam philosophice quam theologice littere contestantur. Quare et fides vniuersalis Deum ipsum esse *factorem celi et terre, visibilium omnium et inuisibilium* fideliter confitetur.[a] Et quomodo facta sunt hec omnia? Procul dubio sapienter. Homo nanque sapiens facit sua opera sapienter ex intencione discreta et deliberacione prouida precedente. Quomodo igitur putandus est Deus, *cuius sapiencie non est numerus* [Ps.146.5], facere aliquod vt contingat[3] temerarie [siue]

§ 9 (1) phesania *cod.*
§ 12 (1) alcius ordiendum; alicuis ordinandum *cod.*; alicuius ordinandum *ed.*[1]
§ 12 (2) acciō *cod*; accio *ed.*[1]
§ 12 (3) contingit *cod.*

negligenter? Quare et teste propheta Ipse *in sapiencia omnia fecit* [*cf.* Ps.103.24]. Hec autem sapiencia Dei magna, sicud Sapiencia testatur, *attingit a fine vsque ad finem* non remisse, set *fortiter, et disponit omnia suauiter* [Sap.8.1]. Vniuersa *ordinacione* quoque *sua perseuerat dies*, non vna, set omnis dies temporis diffluencis [et] dies eternitatis manencis, et omnia tempora et eterna, *quoniam sibi omnia diseruiunt* [*cf.* Ps.118.91] et ordinacionibus suis obediunt et statutis. *Statuit ea in eternum*, atque *in seculum preceptum posuit, et* nullatenus *preteribit* [Ps.148.6]. Nil igitur operum diuinorum inordinatum, remissum, indispositum aut nne[g]lectum. Quare et clariores philosophi atque teologici concorditer attestantur omnia et singula, que in mundo proueniunt, ex diuina prouidencia et solicitudine prouenire. Quapropter et omnes effectus, qui videntur fortuiti, ad voluntatem diuinam latentem originaliter reducuntur. Vnde et Philosophus in libris suis *De mundo* et *De bona fortuna* discu<s>ciens de fortuna, reducit illam principaliter in Deum et operacionem diuinam,[b] cui et consonans Augustinus eandem sentenciam plene docet.[c] Nil igitur a fortuna, videlicet preter intencionem agentis, nisi respectu inferiorum causarum et eciam secundum opinionem hominum ignorancium causas rerum. De casu vero et effectibus casualibus similiter est senciendum. Omnia igitur fortuita atque casualia ad voluntatem diuinam ascendunt et ex ipsa secundum sua iudicia / [f.184va] sibi certa, nobis autem abscondita, defluunt et emanant. Quilibet igitur grates seu gracias fortune seu casui dare voluerit, det illas voluntati diuine, vnico vero Deo. In voluntate nanque sua cun[c]ta posita perhibentur. *Ex Ipso* nempe, sicud testatur Apostolus, *et per Ipsum, et in Ipso sunt omnia. Ipsi* igitur *gloria*, gracia et laus omnis *in secula* seculorum [Rom.11.36]. Hec igitur circa errorem 3m sufficient ista vice.

[13] 4m errorem[1] fingentes in duas sectas erroneas diuiduntur specialiter circa fatum. Aliqui nanque putant per fatum dictum a fando [quod] famen vere deorum gentilium seu dearum circa temporalia specialiter autem humana coerciat et disponat. Vnde poete fingunt 3es sorores fatales facta hominum disponentes. Que istis nominibus, Cloto, Lachesis, A<s>tropos nuncupantur; de quibus poetice scribitur: *Cloto colum baiulat, Lachesis trahit, Atropos occat.*[a] Alii estimant quod fatum sit quedam vis sideria moderans res humanas.[b]

[14] Prima autem harum sectarum est heretica manifeste.[1] Omnes nanque deos gentilium siue deas demones esse constat, sicud dicebatur. Vnde et vere

§ 13 (1) 4m errorem *ex corr.*

§ 14 (1) manifesta *cod.*

dicit Philosophus: *Multa menciuntur poete.*[a] Quis autem[2] Christianus pro triumpho de hostibus demonibus referat gracias et non Deo? Adhuc autem, etsi demones dicantur sicud Platoni placuit *dii secundi,*[b] nichilominus tamen patet [quod][3] ex hoc ipso sunt primo et summo Deo subiecti. Quicquid igitur ipsi dixerint siue concesserint.[4], si summus Deus contradixerit siue negauerit, nil prodest; et quicquid dedixerint siue negauerint, si[5] summus hoc dixerit siue concesserit, nil obest. Est enim plene omnipotens, quare nec aliquis demon potest nec omnes isti possunt resistere preualendo. Nonne igitur pro triumpho nobis concesso pocius referende sunt gracie summo Deo quam talibus *diis secundis*?

[15] Secunda secta erronea circa fatum concordat cum primo errore, quare et redarguitur sicud ille. Illud quoque fatum siderium reprobant Augustinus, Gregorius et alii patres catholici multis locis.[a] Quod Ouidius[1] in libello suo *De vetula* reprobans dicit ita: *Est fatum fatuum: fatui, qui fata secuntur.*[b]

[16] Verum, vt parum magis affatim essemus de fato,[1] sciendum quod adhuc vlterius sumitur 3° modo fatum, videlicet a fando seu famine sum / [f.184vb] mi Dei.[a] Et sic secundum Hermetem patrem philosophorum in *De mundo et celo* et in *De verbo eterno* series tota fati procedit a Deo.[b] Quem et filii eius digni Plato et Aristoteles pens<s>antes, sicud libellus Aristotelis *De mundo* plenius recitat, 3es sorores fatales predictas, 3ia statuta fatalia pro 3bus temporibus preterito, presenti et futuro, et omnia prorsus fatalia reducunt in Deum hec omnia temporibus omnibus moderantem;[c] quos et illa sentencia sociatur Boetius[d] et similiter Augustinus.[e] Nec mirum. In rerum nanque exordio legitur: *Dixit Deus: Fiat* hoc et illud, et factum est hoc et illud [*cf.* Gen.1.3 *sqq.*]; quare dicit propheta: Quoniam *Ipse dixit, et facta sunt* [Ps.148.5]. Qui igitur dixerit omnia fieri fato, famine seu verbo Dei, quamquam verbum fati soleat communius accipi in mala significacione quam bona, videtur bene sentire, set male proferre propter simplices et indoctos, qui ad intelligenciam fati prophanam, falsam et vanam faciliter delabuntur. Mutato igitur periculoso nomine isto fati, dicat catholice et[2] secure cum euuangel[io] Dei dignissimo: *Omnia per ipsum*, scilicet verbo Dei, *facta sunt, et sine ipso factum est ni[chi]l* [Ioann.1.5]. Quicunque igitur pro triumpho

§ 14 (2) eciam *cod.*
§ 14 (3) patet quod; primo *cod. ed.*[1]
§ 14 (4) consesserint *cod.*
§ 14 (5) sine *cod.*
§ 15 (1) Ouidius: quidius *cod.*
§ 16 (1) de fato *ex corr.*
§ 16 (2) et *s.l.add.corr.*

gracias referre voluerit tali fato, referat illas plane et catholice verbo Dei, filio Dei, Deo.

[17] Expedito igitur sic de fato, de omine[1] breuiter est tangendum. Set quid est omen armorum, quod tam crebro nominabunt viri armorum? Vel est aliquid vel ni[chi]l. Si ni[chi]l, ni[chi]l inde uenit. Si aliquid, vel creator vel creatura. Quod sit creator, non recolo me audisse; si creatura, ni[chi]l potest iuvare nec facere sine virtute et efficiencia creatoris. Quandocunque insuper creatura quecunque iuvare voluerit, si creator voluerit, ni[chi]l obest. Set si creator iuvare voluerit vel nocere, procul dubio ita fiat, quicquid voluerit creatura, sicud in superioribus est ostensum. Nullus igitur cultor Dei triumphum suum imputet creature, set pocius creatori.

[18] Verum,[1] vt illud parum exquisiti[u]s patefiat, si omen sit aliqua creatura, vel est aliquis fauor siue auxilium alicuius dei gentilium siue dee, videlicet demonis alicuius, aut aliqua virtus stellarum, aut aliqua gracia Dei alicui gratis data. Si primum dixerit aut secundum, redarguitur patenter sicud prima secta et secunda de fato / [f.185ra] erant superius redargute. Quare et videtur quod omen sit aliqua gracia diuinitus gratis data et ad Deum actorem originaliter referatur; quod videtur poetam sensisse cum dixit:

Omnia sunt hominum tenui pendencia filo.
Ludit in humanis diuina potencia rebus.[a]

Et si isti viri armorum, qui tantum laudant omen armorum, isto modo intelligant, mutent nomen, teneant rem notatam. Mutent nomen nec amplius dicant 'omen', ne forte mentes aliquorum infirme ad malam intelligenciam 'ominis' inclinentur. Teneant rem notatam per nomen et faciant nomen concors, plane et catholice proferentes: 'Gracia Dei hoc fecit', vel illud: 'Gracia Dei fecit nos vincere et de aduersariis triumphare'. Dicantque singuli cum strenuissimo milite Christi Paulo: *Habundancius illis omnibus laboraui: non autem ego, set gracia Dei mecum* [I Cor.15.10]. Non stelle, non tempus, non fortuna, non casus, non fatum, non omen, ymmo nec *ego, set gracia Dei mecum.* Sicque tanquam filii Dei grati[2] agnoscant graciam Dei clare et referant gracias soli Deo tocius gracie gratuito largitori. Sic igitur corrigitur 4us error.

[19] 5um errorem tenentes[1] videntur isti elati, ymmo elaciores quam potenciores, pomposiores quam forciores, iactanciores quam robustiores, similes Moabitis;[a] horum *spiritus quasi turbo inpellens parietem* [Is.25.4],

§ 17 (1) omen *cod. ed.*[1]
§ 18 (1) Verum *ex* Quare verum *corr.*
§ 18 (2) grates *cod. ed.*[1]
§ 19 (1) 5um errorem tenentes *ex corr.*

spiritus grandis et fortis subuertens montes et conterens petras duras [III Reg.19.11]. Talis videtur fuisse Nemphorat *robustus venator* [Gen.10.9], hominum et oppressor, historia Josephi referente.[b] Talis videtur fuisse rex Roboam, qui *minimum digitorum* suorum *dorso* et *lumbis patris* sui asseruit *grossiorem* [*cf.* III Reg.12.10; II Paralip.10.10]. Talis videtur fuisse Sennacherib rex Assur, qui dixit: *[In fortitudine] manus mee* ego *feci, et abstuli terminos populorum, et principes eorum depredatus sum, et detraxi quasi potens in sublimi presidentes. Et inu[en]it quasi nidum manus mea fortitudinem populorum*, sicud littere sacre tradunt [Is.10.13-14].

[20] Set absit quod rex Anglie vel aliquis Anglicus ita sapiat, ymmo ita desipiat[1], / [f.185rb] quin pocius ita insaniat, vt sic dicat. Experiencia nanque doctrice certissima et magistra docente, constat perspicue non sic esse. In vltimo nanque bello apud Dunolmum fuerunt cerciter 60 milia Scotorum, et hii inter omnes naciones istis temporibus corpore fortes, animo fero<s>ces, bene armati, ad prelium docti et, vt in breuibus multa dicam, nobilissimi bellatores. Contra quos venerunt cerciter 20 milia Anglicorum talium qualium in partibus illis tunc temporis communiter repertorum, et commisso bello grauissimo, cessit Anglis victoria gloriosa, sicud superius recitatur. In bello quoque de Cresy[2] erant aduersari[i] nostri incomparabiliter plures nobis et multipliciter forciores.

[21] Quod vt clarius elucescat, aduertatis karissimi et diligencius attendatis, qualis porcio Anglicorum aptorum ad prelium fuit ibi. Constat enim certissime Anglicos aptos ad bellum in nouem partes, seu particulas pocius, iam diu fuisse partitos nouemque fuisse porciones seu ordines Anglicorum secundum numerum angelorum. In[ter] 4oe nanque porciones huiusmodi Anglicorum in Anglia constat esse vnam – vt secundum ordinem et processum celi et celestium rerum incipiam et procedam – in latere orientis ad custodiendas partes maritimas orientis,[1] propter insultum Dacorum, id est hostium alicorum; alteram in latere meridiei, propter incursum hostilem, id est demon[i]um meridianum [*cf.* Ps.90.6] et multa pericula ex latere illo maris probabiliter formidanda iugiter[2], sicud et rei exitus declarauit (aliqui nanque hostes ad portus illarum parcium applicantes statim ab incolis manu valida sunt repulsi); 3iam in latere occidentis[3] propter Wallicorum audaciam, Hibernicorum versuciam, Scotorum proteruiam et quorunlibet aliorum in partibus illis degencium aut illuc venire valencium maliciam reprimendam;

§ 20 (1) dissapiat *cod.*

§ 20 (2) Cresy *ex corr.*

§ 21 (1) orientes *cod.*

§ 21 (2) igitur *cod. ed.*[1]

§ 21 (3) *ex* latere maris occidentis *corr.*

quartam in latere aquilonis propter incursum Scotorum, qui ingerant illas partes: ipsi enim quasi *olla succensa a facie aquilonis* ad partes finitimas Anglie comburendas [*cf.* Jer.1.13]; *ab* illo siquidem *aquilone* verisimiliter timebatur *malum pandendum super omnes habitatores* parcium Anglie vicinarum [*cf.* Jer.1.14]. Quinta porcio Anglicorum fuit in Hibernia ad illorum contubernia / [f.185va] refrenanda. 6a in Vasconia, et preclara septima in Britannia, non ignaua 8a in Flandris, 9a in Francia apud Cresy cum domino nostro rege.

[22] Set quid fuit hec porciuncula Anglicorum ad congregatam potenciam Gallicorum? Illa enim *quasi arena maris* [cf. Os.1.10; Ps.138.18] incomparabiliter multiplicior esse constat in viris, armis, in equis, in curribus et in omni bellico apparatu. Et si quis dicerit quod vna porcio Gallicorum fuit in Vasconia tempore huius belli, fuit re vera. Set ad supplendum illorum absenciam habundanter, ymmo superhabundanter et superhabundancius excessiue, fuit ibi cum rege Francie nominato strenuissimus militum rex Bohemus, rex Maioricarum et alius quasi rex, ell<l>ectus videlicet inperator Rom[anus], et duces, comites et barones ac alii quam multi bellatores de Lotharingia, Bohemia, Hanonia, Sabadia, Alamania,[1] Prouincia, Janua et alienigene plurimi de aliis partibus ampli mundi. Sicud enim olim, sic et tunc: *Astiterunt reges terre, et principes conuenerunt aduersus Dominum et aduersus* dominum *christum* [*cf.* Ps.2.2], dominum nostrum regem *oleo leticie pre* participibus *vn*ctum [*cf.* Ps.44.8]. Aduersus Anglicos suos paucos condixerant enim hostes: *Venite et disperdamus* eum de terra, *eos de gente, et nomen* eorum nequaquam *vl*terius *memor*abi*tur. Quoniam simul aduersus* nos *vnanimiter cogitauerunt* et *testimonium disposuerunt, tabernacula Idumeorum et Hismahelite: Moab et Agareni, Gebal et Am[m]on et Amalec: alienigene cum habitantibus Tyrum. Etenim Assur venit cum illis*, vt *in adiutorium* eis fierent[2] [Ps.82.5-9]. Cum Anglicis vero armis non erant alienigene nisi numero pauci valde: circa 20 aut sicud 30 ipsos audiebam[3] estimari. Set quid inter tantos? Quid hec porcio Anglicorum [ad] tantam multitudinem Gallicorum venditatorum ac talium populorum?

[23] Quinymo, si precisius [loquar],[1] nec tota hec porcio Anglicorum confluxit cum illa tanta multitudine Gallicorum, set quasi 3a pars ipsius. Totus enim exercitus Anglicanus diuidebatur in 3es acies illa vice, quarum prime primogenitus regis Anglie princeps Wallie preficiebat[ur] gubernator.

§ 22 (1) Alamania *cod.*; Alemania *corr.*

§ 22 (2) ferrent *cod.*

§ 22 (3) audebant *cod.*

§ 23 (1) loquar *suppl.*; *om. cod. ed.*[1]

Cum hac acie primo tantum congressa est vero tanta aduersariorum potencia, et deuicta; / [f.185vb] congressa est iterum, et reuicta; congressa est 3°, et euicta. Vbi cecidit ille strenuissimus rex Bohemie, dux Loth[a]ringie, comes Alasonie frater regis Francie nuncupati, cum aliis comitibus, baronibus, militibus et nobilibus in numero copioso; vbi et nonnulli fuerant capti viui. Quod videntes residui tandem finaliter fugiebant, sicud per Jonathan filium regis Saul et eius armigerum de stacione Filistinorum et eorum multitudine nimia contingebat [*cf.* I Reg.14.1-10]. De nostris vero nullus dominus, miles aut armiger in illo conflictu ceciderat aut graue uulnus reciperat aut captus fuerat, de quo sciam, et alii pauci valde. Nunquid illa fiebant per potestatem regis Anglie aut suorum? Non. Plene absit quod quisquam sic dixerit aut cogitauerit. Absit.

[24] Ecce etenim, quando olim *unus persequebatur mille et duo x milia*[1] *fug*auerunt, quam causam Moyses assignauit. *Quia*, inquit, *Deus illas vendidit et concludit* [*cf.* Deut.32.30]. Quare et monuit populum ne *dicere*nt vel *in corde suo: Fortitudo mea et robur manus*[2] *mee, hec michi omnia prestiterunt. Set recorderis*, inquit, *Domini Dei tui, quod Ipse prebuérit tibi vires* [Deut.8.17-18].[a] Quapropter et Dauid rex clarissimus et propheta, huiusmodi miras victorias sufficienter expertus quando interfecit leonem et vrsum robustissimumque Goliam, sic ait: *Non saluatur rex per multam virtutem, et gigas non saluabitur in multitudine virtutis sue. Fallax equus ad salutem: in habundancia virtutis sue non saluabitur.* Set inquit: *Ecce oculi Domini super metuentes eum: et in eis, qui sperant super misericordia eius. Vt eruat a morte animas eorum* [Ps.32.16-19]. Ipse quippe adiutor talium et protector, adiutor fortissimus inuadendo, protector tutissimus in deffendendo, a vulnere, morte et capcione tuendo. Quare et homo Dei ad Amaciam regem: *Si*, inquit, *putas [in] robore exercitus bella consistere*, Dominus *te faciet ab hostibus superari:* Dei quippe est *adiuuare vertere*que *in fugam* [II Paralip.25.8]. Quibus et concorditer strenuissimus ille[3] miles, Judas videlicet Machabeus: *Non*, inquit, *in multitudine ex<c>ercitus belli victoria, set de celo* [I Machab.3.19].

[25] Neque illa[1] tam vetera reputanda, vt modernis temporibus abolita reputentur. Audiui nanque quod dux et capitaneus[2] / [f.186ra] Anglicorum pugnacium iam vltimo contra Scotos cuidam consulenti[3] vt quendam

§ 24 (1) xii milia *cod.*
§ 24 (2) manus *rep. cod.*; *del. corr.*
§ 24 (3) ille *rep. cod.*
§ 25 (1) ita *cod.*
§ 25 (2) capitaneus *rep. cod.*
§ 25 (3) consolante *cod.*; consolanti *ed.*[1]

dominum cum 10 milibus venturum in proximo paululum expectaret, respondit: 'Ad quid tante more dispendium, et iustissima causa nostra, preentibus inimicis? Scio quod victoria nunquam est in numero hominum, set in manu Dei solius [*cf.* I Machab.3.19]. Si Deus propter peccata nostra fortassis voluerit nos punire et perdere, ita faceret etsi essemus in duplo aut quantumlibet plures ipsis, et si voluerit nos iuuare, satis sumus numero[4] copiose.' Et in hac spe statim congredientes cum hostibus, *propin*co *re*ge *glorie fort*i *et potent*i *in prelio* [*cf.* Ps.23.8; Prov.23.11], feliciter triumphabant. Audiui quoque auribus meis quosdam seniores et experciores de nostris militibus hic presentes constanter asserere raro aut nunquam pocius se vidisse, specialiter autem in bellis et conflictibus bellicis concernentibus Anglicos, nimis multis iam annis quasi circiter 60, quin pars pauciorum et debiliorum victoriam optineret et pars meliorum et forciorum subiaceret. Quapropter nullus in tantum dissipiat vt ascribat sue potencie victoriam aliquam seu triumphum.

[26] Set[1] hic fortassis aliquis presumens de viribus propriis cogitabit:[2] 'Quid igitur facit humana potencia et hominis fortitudo?' Cui breuiter respondendum: Certe hoc facit, quod Deus per illum facere disponebat. Deus enim [est] quasi vir pugnator, homo autem sicud gladius aut baculus seu quodlibet instrumentum huiusmodi in manu ipsius, sicud Dominus ipse per Ysaiam de rege Senacherib clare docet [*cf.* Is.37.38]. Quemadmodum igitur gladius, baculus et huiusmodi instrumenta in manu percussientis dant ictus et wlnera, non tamen virtute propria set utentis, sic et homo respectu potentissime manus Dei. Verum, vt istud exemplum propheticum, ymmo dominicum propter reuerenciam exemplantis, parum elucidacius patefiat, ymaginemur vnum militem talis potencie et virtutis quod gladio, quem manu teneret, daret totum penitus suum esse, ita quod, si de manu ex[c]ideret, statim in nichilum verteretur, quodque per illum possit percutere quantum vellet. Tali / [f.186rb] modo re vera se habet manus omnipotens creatoris ad hominem et ad quamlibet creaturam, sicud philosophice et theologice littere contestantur. Set philosophicis pretermissis [h]ac vice, ecce theologicas profit<i>entes quia Ipse *porta*t *omnia verbo sue virtutis* [Hebr.1.3], quodque *in Ipso viuimus, et mouemur, et sumus* [Act.17.28]. Nec dubium quin *omnia quecunque voluit* facere quouismodo per se vel per quamlibet creaturam, Ipse sic *facit in celo* et *in terra* et *in mari et in omnibus*<que> *abissis* [Ps.134.6]. Sicud igitur, milite et gladio ymaginatis superius realiter positis et milite per

§ 25 (4) numero *cod.*: numerus *corr.*
§ 26 (1) Sic *cod.*
§ 26 (2) cogitabat *cod.*

gladium de hostibus triumphante, quicun[que] triumphum ascriberet gladio, potencie probitatiue gladii, et non pocius militi, potencie probitatiue militis, turpiter deliraret et grauem iniuriam militi irrogaret, simili modo[3] de homine et de Deo. Sic igitur retunditur 5us error.

[27] 6m errorem[1] erronie profitentes sunt similes Pharaoni olim regi Egipti iactanti: *Filius sapiencium ego, filius regum antiquorum* [Is.19.11], et Senacherib regi Assur superbienti in auctoritate et dicenti: *In sapiencia mea intellexi: et abstuli terminos populorum, et principes eorum depredatus sum* [Is.10.13] et multa similia. Set absit quod rex Anglie aut aliquis Anglicus ita dicat. Que nanque [fuit prudencia][2] illorum pauculorum Anglorum acephalorum, inprouisorum et preocupatorum per hostes priusquam potuerunt plenari<m>e congregari ad prudenciam, seu pocius secundum philosophicas litteras astuciam,[a] Scotorum tot et tantorum ex tanta et tam prouida deliberacione regis et optimatum suorum ingrediencium Angliam illa vice? Aut que proporcio prudencie Anglicorum ad prudenciam Gallicorum? Certe, sicud Pisonis[b] et Mercurii siue Apollinis. Ipsi nanque sunt Argus, Anglici Polliphemus. Habent enim mille consiliarios contra vnum de nostris; ipsi sunt *pleni oculis ante et retro* [*cf.* Apoc.4.6.], nos autem iuxta [et] retro, sicud Gallici ipsi dicunt. Ipsi more veterum Romanorum *curiam sibi fecerunt*, adinuicem *consulentes cotidie* quasi *3es centos* seu plures *consili*arios[3] sapientes, *vt que digna sunt, gerant* [*cf.* I Machab.8.15]. Set nunquid solet sic esse de Anglicis? Non reuera. Nunquid igitur Anglia per suam prudenciam / [f.186va] de tam prudentibus hostibus triumphabat? Non plane. Nunquid per suum consilium de tam consultis hostibus trumphaba<n>t? Non sane.

[28] Quomodo igitur? Per quid igitur? Sapiens nempe dic[it]: *Vir sapiens fortis est: et vir doctus, robustus et validus. Quia cum disposicione initur bellum, et vbi multa consilia, erit salus* [Prov.24.5-6]. Certe, per eius sapienciam, prudenciam atque consilium a quo omnis vera sapiencia, omnis vera prudencia et omne verum consilium diriuatur. Testatur nempe Philosophus in *De*[1] *bona fortuna* quod ipse est principium boni consilii et origo, quodque sapientes et docti non habent diuinos instinctus, quibus ad eufortun[i]a et prospera dirigantur, set simplices et indocti.[a] Cui et concorditer summus philosophus loquens Patri: *Abscondisti*, inquit, *hec a sapientibus, et prudentibus, et reuelasti ea paruulis* [Matth.11.25]. *Quoniam sapiencia Dei* magna [*cf.* Eccli.15.19]. *Si quis est paruulus*, ipsum vocat. *Et*

§ 26 (3) solummodo *cod.*

§ 27 (1) 6m errorem *ex corr.*

§ 27 (2) fuit prudencia *suppl.*; fuit sapiencia *supplevit ed.*[1]; *om.cod.*

§ 27 (3) consiliarii *cod.*

§ 28 (1) in De: inde *cod.*

insipientibus[2] *est locuta*[3]: *Venite, com<m>edite panem meum, et bibite vinum quod miscui vobis* [Prov.9.4-5]. *Com<m>edite*, inquit, *panem meum, [et bibite vinum]*,[4] de difficilioribus et clarioribus scienciam hauriendo,[5] *quod miscui vobis*, prout melius conuenit temperando. Porro et *cum simplicibus sermocinacio* Domini [Prov.3.32]. Perhibetur[6] hic igitur consilium simplicium Anglicorum, hic sapienncia simplicium Anglicorum, hic prudencia simplicium Anglic<an>orum. Hic autem consiliarius est tam iustus, vt solummodo diligat et foueat causas iustas. Suum *est* enim *consilium et equitas* [Prov.8.14]. Suum est, inquit, consilium. Sed quid seu quale? Certe, cui equitas sociatur, cui iusticia suffragatur. *Iustus* siquidem *Dominus, et iusticias dilexit: equitatem vidit* propius *vultus eius* [Ps.10.8]. Ipse[7] autem *et omnem iniusticiam a*<d>*uersatur* [Deut.25.16].

[29] Consiliarius igitur iste summus, sicud ex euidencia ipsa rerum clare videtur, propter iniusticias aduersariorum nostrorum ipsorum consilium dereliquit et causam eorum[1] despexit, et propter iusticias Anglicorum factus est consiliarius Anglicorum, patronus et aduocatus cause ipsorum. Omnes igitur cogitatus vestri iaciantur in Ipsum et *omnia consilia* vestra *in Ipso permaniant* in eternum [*cf.* Tob.4.20]. Quamdiu nimirum Ipse de consilio vestro esse dignabitur, *consilium* vestrum erit sanum et *stabile* [*cf.* Eccli.37.20] et utilem exitum sorcietur, consilium vero aduersancium erit vanum et labile et inutilem exitum pacietur. Ab Ipso quippe procedit *spiritus sapiencie, et intellectus, spiritus consilii*, et *fortitudinis* [Is.11.2]: spiritus consilii veraciter discernendi et spiritus fortitudinis efficaciter exequendi. Ipse spiritus [f.186vb] paraclitus constat esse suorum continuus aduocatus pro suis non desinens postulare, nisi forcitan desinant esse sui. Nonne et sapiencia Dei patris, filius Dei, Deus magni consilii, angelus perhibetur[2] [*cf.* I Cor.1.20; Ier.32.19; II Reg.14.20]. Ipse *admirabilis, consiliarius, Deus, fortis* [Is.9.6] et aduocatus magnus suorum, et procul dubio *consilium*, scilicet *Domini, in eternum manet: cogitaciones cordis eius in generacione et generacionem* [Ps.32.11], consilium scilicet et cogitaciones Ipsius destinatum effectum, nunquam deffectum, eternaliter sorciuntur. Quare et[3] per

§ 28 (2) insipientibus *sec. Vulg.*; sapientibus *cod.*
§ 28 (3) locata *cod.*
§ 28 (4) et bibite vinum *suppl.*; *om. cod. ed.*[1]
§ 28 (5) haurienndo *ex corr.*
§ 28 (6) prohibetur *cod.*
§ 28 (7) ipsum *cod.*
§ 29 (1) earum *cod.*
§ 29 (2) prohibetur *cod.*
§ 29 (3) et *s. l. add. corr.*

prophetam sic ait: *Consilium meum stabit, et omnis voluntas mea fiet* [Is.46.10]. Consiliarium igitur talem habentibus cuius sapiencia timescenda, cuius prudencia metuenda, cuius hastucia tremiscenda?

[30] Porro, *non est sapiencia*, et *non est*[1] *prudencia*, et *non est consilium contra Dominum. Equus paratur*[2] *ad diem belli:* Deus *audtem salutem tribuet* hiis, quos fouet [Prov.21.30-1]. *Scriptum est enim* de Domino: *Perdam sapienciam sapiencium, et prudenciam prudencium reprobabo. Vbi sapiens? Vbi scriba? Vbi* in*quisitor huius seculi? Nonne stultam fecit Deus sapienciam huius mundi?* [I Cor.1.19-20]. Quoniam *que stulta sunt mundi elegit Deus, vt confundat sapientes: et infirma mundi elegit Deus, vt confundat forcia: et ignobilia et contemptibilia, et ea, que non sunt, vt ea que sunt destrueret: vt non glorietur omnis caro in conspectu eius* [I Cor.1.27-9] de sapiencia, prudencia aut alio quouis bono tanquam iugiter[3] a se proprio, set Dei intuitu[4] sibi dato. Ipse *prudencia* sua *percussit superbum* [Job 26.12]. Ipse *ponit humiles in sublimi, et merentes*[5] *erigit sospitate.* Ipse *dissipat cogitaciones malignorum, ne possint inplere manus eorum quod ceperant.* Ipse *comprehendit sapientes in astucia eorum, et consili*a *prauorum* dissipat*: per diem incurrent tenebras, et quasi in nocte, sic in meridie palp*it*abunt* [Job 5.11-14], in manifestissimis scilicet ignorabunt et in clarissimis aberrabunt. Ipse est qui *miscuit in medio* sapiencium Egipti *spiritum vertiginis: et errare fecerunt Egiptum in omne opere suo, sicud er[r]at ebrius* insensatus [Is.19.14], vnde sciendum est quod *sapientes consiliarii Pharaonis dederunt consilium insipiens* / [f.187ra], scriptura et propheta recitante [Is.19.11]. Ipse est qui infatuauit et *nutu* suo *discipa*uit *consilium Achitofel* versipellis, vt destrueret regem iniustum et saluum faceret regem iustum [*cf.* II Reg.17.14]. Ipse est qui misit *spiritum menda*cem *in* os *omnium prophetarum*, quasi quadringentorum virorum consulencium concorditer regi Achab vt ascenderet ad pugnandum, quia prospera cederent[6] ei cuncta [*cf.* III Reg.22.6, 22-3). Hoc autem ideo factum esse scriptura commemorat, vt deciperetur, preliaretur et occideretur rex ille, quin magis tyrannus, propter vineam Naboth, quam iniuste ei abstulit et possedit [*cf.* III Reg.21.1-16]. Cur igitur non similiter faceret hiis diebus regibus Scocie et Francie nuncupatis, qui nedum[7] vnam

§ 30 (1) est *s. l. add. corr.*
§ 30 (2) paratus *cod.*
§ 30 (3) igitur *cod.*
§ 30 (4) intus *cod. ed.*[1]
§ 30 (5) marentes *cod.*
§ 30 (6) cederunt *cod.*
§ 30 (7) nedum *ex corr.*

vineam paruulam auferunt[8] regi Anglie minus iuste et detinent violenter, verumeciam multas amplas prouiincias ac insuper duo[9] regna, quanta et qualia bene nostis? Verisimiliter igitur, ymmo veraciter est credendum quod Deus istis temporibus excecat et fatuat et discipat consilium Gallicorum similiterque Scotorum, quodque illuminat, adiuuat atque effectuat consilium Anglicorum. Quapropter et quamdiu aduersarii nostri, ymmo iusticie atque Dei, similes Pharaoni in sua iniusticia permanent obdurati, nos autem cum Melchisedec rege iusticie iusti iuste prosequimur causam iustam, confidens in Deo iusticie dicam eis fiducialiter cum propheta: *Congregamini et confortamini, et vincemini: inite consilium,* et *dissipabitur*[10]: *loquimini verbum, et non fiet: quia nobiscum Deus* [*cf.* Is.8.9-10]. Sic enim factum est hucusque [a] temporibus retroactis.

[31] Set nunquid tot et tantas victorias fecit sapiencia regis aut populi simplicis Anglicani? Non, veraciter. Non, constanter. Set sapiencia Dei secum. *Hec*, vt utar verbis sapientibus Sapientis, *iustum deduxit* <dominus> *per vias rectas;* et *in fraude circumueniencium illi affuit, et honestum fecit illum. Custodiuit illum ab inimicis, et [a] seductoribus tutauit illum, [et] certamen forte dedit illi vt vinceret, et sciret quoniam omni[um] potencior est sapiencia. Hec venditum*[1] *iustum non dereliquit, set a peccatoribus liberauit eum: descenditque*[2] *cum illo in foueam, et non dereliquit illum, donec afferret illi sceptrum regni, et potenciam aduersus eos,* / [f.187rb] *qui* illum *deprimebant. Hec populum iustum, et semen sine querela liberauit a nacionibus, que illum* comprimebant. Hec *intrauit*[3] *in animam serui Dei, et stetit contra reges horrendos in portentis et signis. Et reddidit iustis mercedem laborum suorum, et deduxit illos in via mirabili;* et *transtulit illos per mare rubrum* – in bello nauali in finibus Flandrie nuper gesto hostium sanguine rubricatum – *et transuexit illos per aquam nimiam. Inimicos autem illorum demersit in mari, et ab altitudine inferorum eduxit illos. Ideo iusti tulerunt spolia impiorum, et decantauerunt Domine nomen sanctum tuum, et victricem manum tuam* – non suam – *pariter laudauerunt: quoniam sapiencia aperuit os [mutorum], et linguas infancium fecit disertas*, ipsorumque opera dirigebat [Sap.10.10-21; 11.1]. Per hanc sapienciam Dei, non suam, *iustos* simplicitas *dispon*et *populos; et naciones erunt* sibi *sub*iecte. *Timebunt* eam[4]

§ 30 (8) auferunt *ex corr.*
§ 30 (9) duo *corr.*: dua *cod.*
§ 30 (10) dissepabitur *cod.*
§ 31 (1) vendidum *cod.*
§ 31 (2) descenditque *ex corr.*
§ 31 (3) intrans *corr.*
§ 31 (4) eum *cod.*

audientes reges horrendi; et per hanc *videb*itur *bonus* in pace *et fortis in bello* [*cf.* Sap.8.14-15]. Hec nempe *sapienncia* Dei, non hominis, *vincit maliciam* rebellantem [*cf.* Sap.7.30]. Sapiencie igitur, prudencie et prouidencie Dei, non vestre, gracie triumpho omnibusque triumphis.

[32] Errorem 7m amplexantes simulari videntur antiquis gentilibus colentibus Hymeneum siue Cupidinem deum carnalis amoris. Hii dee Veneri militantes, hii Affrodisiis famulantes, hii milites Epicuri, hii animositati seu audacie imputant probitatem, victoriam seu triumphum. Set dicunt quod nullus esse poterit animosus nisi fuerit amorosus vel diligat amorose, [ita][1] quod nullus esse poterit milic[i]osus nisi fuerit amorosus vel[2] diligat amorose, quia[3] nullus se potest gere strenue excessiue nisi diligat excessiue. Set quam prophana hec vanitas quam falsa et insan<i>a et vesana! Quid enim est iste deus huius amoris nisi, sicud ceteri dii gencium, demonium: demon luxurie, incentor luxurie et nutritor? Constat enim certissime quod verus Deus, cuius *oculi sunt* tam *mundi* vt *nec videa*t quid *malum, et respicere ad iniquitatem non poterit* approbando (*cf.* Hab.1.13], qui concipi de virgine dignabatur eternaliter permanens Ipse[4] virgo, feditatem luxurie detestatur et sanctitatem castimonie amplexatur. / [f.187va] Hii igitur milites amorosi militantes dee amoris diabolo militant, de retinencia ipsius existunt, vexillo eius intendunt et ipsi deseruiunt specialiter in duobus. In superbia laborant enim vehementer in armis, vt faciant sibi *nomen iuxta nomen magnorum, qui sunt in terris* [*cf.* II Reg.7.9], ymmo vt faciant sibi *nomen quod* sit *super omne nomen* [cf. Philip.2.9], vt sic ipsi in nomine et in fama alios transcendere videantur et soli digni nomine militari. Ecce superbia exsecrabilis[5] coram Deo. Et quare finaliter appetunt tale nomen? Vt a mulieribus fatuis amorosius[6] diligantur. Ecce luxuria abhominabilis coram Deo. Et quis reddet horum stipendia et mercedem laborum suorum? Quis, nisi deus cui militant, cui deseruiunt et quem colunt? Et que stipendia, quem mercedem? Pro superbia confusionem puplicam et immensam, et pro luxuria combuscionem fetidam et intensam.

[33] Adhuc autem et hii turpes amatores turpitudinis turpi deo turpe seruicium ex[h]ibentes turpiter deluduntur. Constat racione et auctoritate docente quod huiusmodi turpis amor nequaquam, vt dicunt, audaciam generat, sed magis vecordiam[1] administrat. Qui enim sic amat, querit ea, per

§ 32 (1) ita *suppl.*; *om. cod.*
§ 32 (2) nisi *cod.*
§ 32 (3) quod *cod.*
§ 32 (4) ipse *corr.*: ipsa *cod.*
§ 32 (5) excecrabilis *cod.*
§ 32 (6) amorosius *ex corr.*
§ 33 (1) vecordiam *ex corr.*

que suam valeat persequi voluptatem, et prohibita et contraria horum fugit. Hec autem sunt persecuta in agone vulnera, carceres, et mors summe. Et qui ista immoderate timuerit, quomodo animosus, quomodo strenuus aut quomodo probus erit? Constat enim militibus et militaribus viris certissime, nullum posse esse milisiosum aut probum veraciter, nisi libenter et prom[p]te, prout res postulat, talibus periculis se exponat. Quare et Philosophus ad nobilem Alexandrum sic scribit: *Declina conatus bestialium voluptatum. Carnales enim appetitus inclinant animam ad corruptibiles voluntates anime bestialis*[2]*, nulla discrecione prehabita, et* ideo *corpus corruptibile letabitur, et contristabitur incorruptibilis intellectus.*[a] Et iterum: *Noli te inclinare ad co<n>itum mulierum, quia co<n>itus est quedam [proprietas] porc[orum]. Que gloria est tibi, si excerceas vicium irracionabilium bestiarum et actus brutorum? Crede michi indubitanter quod co<n>itus est destruccio corporis et abbreuiacio vite et corrupcio virtutum, legis transgressio et mores generat feminicios.*[b] Vnde et propheta: *Fornicacio, et vinum, et ebrietas aufer[un]t cor* [Osee 4.11]. Quapropter et precipiebatur in lege quod congregatis ituris ad bellum duces publice proclamarent: *Quis est homo, qui despondit vxorem, et non accepit eam? Vadat et reuertatur in dom/*[f.187vb]*mum suam, ne forte moriatur in bello, et alius homo accipiat eam* [Deut.20.7]. Cuius causa statim videtur annexa: *Quis est homo formidolosus* in *corde pauido? Vadat et reuertatur in domum suam, ne pauere faciat corda fratrum suorum* [Deut.20.8]. Nonne et olim in Anglia contigit mirabilis casus iste? Quidam condixit cum quadam affectu venereo, vt destinatis loco et tempore conuenirent. Quod audiens mediator eorum diabolus precucurrit ad locum accedenteque viro, in speciem sue amasie se transformat, et dum vir ipsam amplectitur, in ipso actu nephario ab ipso demone succubo strangulator reponiturque ad partem. Deinde femina veniente, se in specie[m] sui amasii transfigurat, et dum ab ipso complectitur et ipso actu venereo ab ipso demone incubo suffocatur. Nec mirum: *ipse* nempe quandoque *se in lucis angelum transfigurat* [II Cor.11.14]. Legimus quoque quod demonium Asmodeus septem viros Sare occidit *mox vt ingressi fuissent ad eam* [Tob.3.8]. Illis nanque, Raphaele testante, *perualere potest demonium, qui coniugium ita suscipiunt vt sue libidini ita uace[n]t [sic]vt equus et mulus, quibus non est intellectus: super* tales *habet demonium potestatem* [Tob.6.16-17]. Verum karissimi, si demonium habet potestatem super suscipientes coniugium vt tantum in coniugio libidini sue vacent, quanto magis super fornicarios, adulteros, incestuosos et ceteros huiusmodi potestatem creditur habiturus, licet misericordia Dei quandoque eius

§ 33 (2) bestiales *cod.*

maliciam temperat et refrenat? Set de misericordia Dei tanta non est rebellibus, miseris et indignis regulariter construendum. Et quis tam horrenda pericula non timebit?

[34] Adhuc autem, quis vel modice fidei [nesciat][1] peccatoribus et specialiter, luxuriosis *stagnum ignis* ardentis *et sulphuris* preparatum [*cf.* Apoc.20.9]? Quis nesciat mulieris stulte stultis conuiui<i>s in *profundo inferni* hospicium, seu carcerem pocius, preparatum [*cf.* Prov.9.13-18]? Et quis non timeat carcerem infernalem, preserti[m] cum a carceribus aliis captiui per redempcionem sepius liberentur, in inferno autem nulla redempcio, nulla liberacio est speranda? Alii enim carceres dantur ad custodiam, non ad penam; carcer autem inferni ad custodiam perditoriam et ad penam non momentaneam, set eternam, ymmo et ad penas multiplices incomparabiliter transcendentes omnes penas in seculo consuetas, quinymmo et ad mortem non vnam semel transcursam, set quasi continue reuocatam, ad mortem perpetuam / [f.188ra] sine morte, vbi mori finaliter dulcissimum miseris videretur, set hec mors optantibus denegatur. Cum igitur secundum Philosophum mors consueta momentanee transcurrenda vltimum terribilium iudicetur,[a] quam terribilis mors predicta! Quare et Veritas ipsa monet: *Ne terrea[mini] ab eis, qui occidunt corpus, et post hec non habent amplius quid faciant: timete eum, qui postquam occiderit, habet potestatem mittere in gehennam. Ita dico vobis, hunc timete* [Luc.12.4-5]. Quomodo igitur luxuriosi erunt ad mortis pericula animosi, et non pocius timorosi? Aut quomodo erunt tales cordati et probi, et non pocius vecordes[2], reprobi et ignaui? Quinymmo audiant isti Veneri[s] insensati graciam Dei in luxuriam transferentes, addiscant humiliter veraciterque cognoscant quod timorositas et animositas, vecordia et audacia, ignobilitas et nobilitas siue strenuetas inmittuntur a Deo prout sibi placuerit et congruere videret cause, tempori et personis. Nonne et contemptoribus legis sue Dominus per Moysen comminatur: *Ponam faciem meam contra vos, et coram hostibus corruetis, subiciemini* inimicis, *fugietis nemin*i *persequente. Dabo pauorem in cordibus eorum, terrebit eos sonitus folii volantis, et* ideo *fugient quasi gladium: cadent, nullo persequente, et corruent singuli super fratres suos quasi bella fugientes, nemo vestrum audebit resistere inimicis* [Lev.26.17, 36-7]? Qui et iterum per prophetam: *Erunt*, inquit, *in montibus quasi columbe conuallium omnes trepidi, vnusquisque in iniquitate sua. Omnes manus dissoluentur, et omnia genua fluent aquis. Operiet eos formido, et in facie* eorum *confusio* requiescet [Ezech.7.16-18]. Quare et Sapiens: Frequenter, inquit, preoccupant

§ 34 (1) nesciat *suppl.*; *om. cod. ed.*[1]

§ 34 (2) vecordi *cod.*

pessima, redarguente consciencia, et *cum sit nequicia timida*, data est in condempnacionem omnium peccatorum; *semper enim presu*p[p]on*it seua, consciencia* con*turbata* [*cf.* Sap.17.10]. Nonne et Domino deduc<c>ente filios in terram Chanaam, quam ipsis promiserat, Chananei[3] senserunt veraciter et dixerunt: *Irruit in nos terror vester, et [e]languerunt omnes habitatores terre. Pertimuimus, et elanguit cor nostrum, nec remans<c>it in nobis spiritus ad introitum vestrum. Dominus enum Deus vester, ipse est Deus in celo sursum, et in* / [f.188rb] *terra deorsum* [Jos.2.9,11]. Quelibet et multa similia in sacris litteris continentur, neque magna necessitas multum de longe querere horum exempla.

[35] Constat nanque, experiencia et fama testantibus, Francos et Scotos feroces animo, cordatos et audaces quamplurimum retroactis temporibus extitisse. Set nunquid modernis temporibus videantur in aliquo declinasse? Quid a me queritur? Queratur a facto, queratur a mundo, a crebra experiencia perquiratur et a fama celebri requiratur. Set cur sic modo *elanguit cor* eorum [*cf.* Jos.2.11]? Cur sic modo *emarcuit arcus*[1] ipsorum [*cf.* Jer.51.56]? Cur sic modo *cecidit flos* illorum? Nescio, nisi *quia spiritus Domini sufflauit in eo* [*cf.* Is.40.7]. Exsufflauit audaciam, et ignauiam insufflauit propter peccata sua forsitan[2] publica vel priuata, Domino disponente illos corripere atque corrigere aut, quod absit, corrumpere, illo modo scilicet superius prelibato.[3] *Pauor hiis, qui operantur malum* [Prov.10.29]. *Formido* enim *et pauor in magnitudine brachii* Domini *irruit super eos* [*cf.* Exod.15.16]. Quo contra bonis et obseruatoribus legis sue Dominus remittit: *Absque pauore habitabit[is] in terra vestra. Dabo pacem in finibus vestris: dormietis, et non erit qui exterreat. Persequemini inimicos vestros, et corruent coram vobis. Persequentur 5. de vestris .C. alienos, et centum de vobis decem milia* [Lev.26.5-8]. Et hinc est quod iustus *non timebi*t *milia populi circumdantis* [*cf.* Ps.3.7]; Dominus enim *saluator* suus, inquit, *fiducialiter* aget, *et non timebi*t [*cf.* Is.12.2]. Vnde et propheta: *Dominus illuminacio mea et salus mea, quem timebo? Dominus protector vite mee, a quo trepidabo* [Ps.26.1]*? Si consistant aduersum me castra, non timebit cor meum. Si exsurgat aduersum me prelium, in hoc ego sperabo* [Ps.26.3]. Qui et virum iustum confortans: *Scuto*, inquit, *circumdabit te*[4] *veritas eius: non timebis a timore nocturno, a sagitta volante in die, a negocio perambulante in tenebris: ab incursu, et demonio meridiano. Cadent a latere tuo mille, et decem milia a*

§ 34 (3) Chananei *ex corr.*
§ 35 (1) ausus *cod.*
§ 35 (2) forsitan *ex corr.*
§ 35 (3) prelibata *cod.*
§ 35 (4) me *cod.*

dextris tuis: ad te autem non appropinquabit [Ps.90.5-7]. *Super aspidem et basiliscum ambulabis, et conculcabis leonem et draconem* [Ps.90.13]. Horum autem exempla de Josue, Dauid, Juda /[f.188va], Machabeo et aliis multis iustis se offerunt gloriosa. Set ad quid transibimus maria ad querendum exampla? A vobis ipsis vos ipsi,[5] rex et populus paruulus Anglicanus, exempla patula sumite predictorum, propter iusticiam cause vestre. Sapiente nanque testante, *iustus* vt *leo confidens absque terrore* faciet facienda: iniustus vero et *impius fugiet, nemine persequente* [*cf.* Prov.28.1]. Iusticia gentem exaltat; [in]iusticia autem et peccatum miseros efficit populos et pessumdat. Quapropter karissimi colite Dominum, iusticiam et virtutem; cauete offensam Domini, iniusticiam et peccata, vt Ipso nobis propicio offenso, ignauiam incurratis.

[36] Verum karissimi, vt ad materiam redeam principalem, si deus fedi amoris vel de[a] aliquos animaret et sic ipsos de hostibus triumpharet, hoc in cultoribus suis precipuis precipue demonstraret. Tales autem esse feruntur rex et gens Scotorum. Fama nanque communi seu pocius infamia lacius deuulgante, rex ille Scotorum, vxore propria licet pulcher[r]ima derelicta et lege Dei contempta, omnes quasi vxores et filias, dominas et ancillas de Scocia in *oculis* suis *plac*entes [*cf.* Esth.2.5] nepharie violauit, factus, quia est, quasi emissarius taurus seu aper communis seruiens quamquam versuram;[1] et sic *in profundum* malorum per*uen*iens [*cf.* Prov.18.3], tamen, verecundia propulsata, talem se puplice iactare gaudebat et gloriabatur se talem ab omnibus predicari, sicque, *cum esset in honore* regio positus, nullatenus *intellexit*, set *comparatus est iumentis insipientibus, et similis factus est illis* [*cf.* Ps.48.13]. Gens vero Scotorum, et precipue nobiles, eciam ab antiquo maxime venerei reputantur. Ibi nanque, sicud communiter diffamant, consanguinitati non parcitur nec affinitati defertur neque ab adulterio temperatur. Et licet pessima pestis illa retroactis[2] scilicet temporibus ibi viguerit excessiue, exuberancius tamen temporibus huius regis. Quod enim a principe geritur, de facili trahitur a subditis in exemplum, et *qualis rector* in *ciuitat*e, *et hab* /[f.188vb] *itantes in ea* [*cf.* Eccli.10.2]. Quare et dicit poeta:

*Regis ad exempl*ar totus *componitur orbis*.
Mutatur varium *cum principe vulgus*.[a]

Vnde et Josephus de antiquitate Judaica disserens: *Cum moribus*, inquit, *principum corrumpitur conuersacio sub*d*itorum. Et cum viderint illorum*

§ 35 (5) nobis ipsis nos ipsi *cod.*
§ 36 (1) versuram *ed.*[1]; *lectio dubia*: vs̄r *cod.*
§ 36 (2) retroacta *cod.*

luxurias, sue castitatis merita respuentes, quasi virtutem eorum imitari nituntur illecebras. Cum igitur *Roboa[m] filius Salamonis*[3] *ageret impie et inique, studebant et illi non esse iusti, ne rex videretur offendi.*[b] Quod et testantur concorditer historie veteres et recentes. Set quomodo ille deus eorum ipsos iuuerit[4] et ipsos animauerit et ipsos triumphauerit in bellis iuxta Dunellum, Berewyc cum Duppilino[5] et aliis multis bellis gestis cum eis iam multis temporibus, licet vbique essent plures Anglicis excessiue, experiencia manifestat et vos ipsi[6] nos[ci]tis plenarie veritatem. *Non sic* igitur *impii*, nec *sic* vere [*cf.* Ps.1.4]. Set audite sentenciam verbi Dei: *Ibo*, inquit, *ad optimates: et ecce magis hii simul confregerunt iugum, ruperunt vincula. Iccirco percussit eos leo de sil<l>ua, lupus ad vesperam vastauit eos, pardus vigilans super ciuitates eorum: omnis, qui egressus fuerit ex eis, capietur, quia multi[plicate] sunt preuaricaciones eorum, confortate sunt auersiones*[7] *eorum. Saturaui*[8] *eos, et mechati sunt, et in domo meretricis luxuriaba[n]tur. Equi amatores* in feminas, *et emissarii facti sunt. Vnusquisque ad vxorem proximi sui hinniebat.*[9] *Nunquid super hiis non visitabo, et in gente tali non vlci[sc]etur anima mea?* [Jer.5.5-9]

[37] Ipse nempe est Deus inpolluti amoris, castimonie, pudoris. Ipse luxurie aduersatur et castimonian amplexatur. Castos inanimat, roborat et triumphat. *Qui* enim *diligit cordis mundiciam, propter graciam labiorum suorum habebit amicum regem* [Prov.22.11], meum Regem, veraciter *Re*gem *glorie, fort*em *in prelio et poten*tem [*cf.* Ps.23.8-10], Regem inquam glorie. Aduerte...

SOURCES

Biblical quotations and echoes have been identified in the text.

§ 4 (a) *Cf.* Bradwardine, *De causa Dei* i.1 corr.32, ed. Savile, p.37.

§ 5 (a) *Cf.* Augustinus, *De Civ. Dei* v.1-7, CC 47, 128-35; Gregorius Magnus, *In Evang.* hom.x.3-5, PL 74, 1111-2; *Decretum Gratiani* C.26, q.5 *per totum*, ed. Friedberg i, 1027-36; *X* V.21.1-3, ed. Friedberg ii, 822-3 *Cod.Iust.* 9.18.1-9.

§ 36 (3) Roboa filia Salamonis *cod.*
§ 36 (4) iuuare *cod.*
§ 36 (5) Dupplinum *cod.*
§ 36 (6) ipsi *cod.*; ea *corr.*
§ 36 (7) aduersiones *cod.*
§ 36 (8) saturaz *cod.*
§ 36 (9) hunliebat *cod.*

§ 6 (a) The *dies Egipciaci* were accepted into Christian calendars; see Lynn Thorndike, *A History of Magic and Experimental Science* i, New York, 1923, pp.685-8, 695-6.

§8 (a) *Cf.* Isidorus, *Etymol.* viii.11.94.

(b) Cited *De causa Dei* i.29, p.267.

(c) Based on *De causa Dei* i.29, p.268, which refers to Albumazar's *Introductorius maior*, differentia 3a. Erhard Radolt published Hermann of Dalmatia's Latin version of this work at Augsburg in 1489.

§ 10 (a) Verbal echoes of Augustinus, *Retractat.*I.i.2, CC 57, 7, quoted in *De causa Dei* i.29, p.270.

§ 11 (a) *Cf.* Aristoteles, *Phys.*II.5 196b 17sqq.; *De causa Dei* i.29, p.268.

§ 12 (a) *Symbolum Nicaenum*, clauses 2-3 in Denzinger-Schönmetzer, *Enchiridion Symbolorum*, ed. 34a, no. 125.

(b) Aristoteles, *De bona fortuna* = *Eth.Eudem.*VII.14 1248a 23-33; pseudo-Aristoteles, *De mundo (ex vers. Nicholai Siculi)* 7, ed. W.L. Lorimer, 1924, p.93; *Arist.Lat.* (1965) XI.1-2; cited by *De causa Dei* i.29, p.268.

(c) *Cf.* Augustinus, *Retractat.*I.i.2, CC 57, 7.

§ 13 (a) Medieval leonine verses preserved in *Anthologia latina*, ed. Alexander Riese, i.2, Leipzig, 1906, no. 792, p.270:

> Tres sunt fatales quae ducunt fila sorores:
> Clotho colum baiulat, Lachesis trahit, Atropos occat.

Hans Walther, *Proverbia Sententiaeque Latinitatis Medii Aevi* (*Carmina Medii Aevi Posterioris Latina* II.1) i (1963) no. 2879b gives a variant form. *Cf.* Ovidius, *Epp.ex Ponto* i.8.64: nerunt fatales fortia fila deae: pseudo-Aristoteles, *De mundo* 7, p. 95; *Arist.Lat.* XI (1965) 1-2; cited *De causa Dei* i.1. corr.39, p.109 and 1.28, p.266.

(b) *Cf. De causa Dei* i.28, p.265.

§ 14 (a) Aristoteles, *Metaphys.*I.2 983a 4 = *Auctoritates Aristotelis*, ed. Hamesse, p.117, no. 26; cited *De causa Dei* i.1. corr.19 p.14.

(b) *Cf.* Calcidius, *Commentarius in Timaeum Platonis*, comm.cxxix-cxxxvi, ed. J.H. Waszink, *Plato Latinus* IV, 1962, pp.171-7; *ib.*, comm. cxlvi, p.184 for *dii secundi*.

§ 15 (a) *Cf.* Augustinus, *De Civ. Dei* v.1, CC 47, 128; Gregorius Magnus, *In Evang.* hom.x.4, PL 76, 1112.

(b) Pseudo-Ovidius, *De vetula* 490: nichil ergo / est fatum fatuum; fatui qui fata sequuntur (ed. Paul Klopsch, Leiden, 1967). Cited *De causa Dei* i.28, p.265.

§ 16 (a) See Isidorus, *Etymol.*VIII.11.90-1; *De causa Dei* i.28, p.266.

(b) By *De verbo eterno* of 'Hermes' Bradwardine clearly meant the Latin *Asclepius; cf. De causa Dei* i.1.corr.39, pp.98-9 and p.114, where Hermes is called 'pater philosophorum'; see also W. Scott and A.S. Ferguson, *Hermetica* IV, Oxford, 1936, p.xlviii. Just possibly he termed the opening section of the same work *De mundo et celo*, though Ferguson, *Hermetica* IV, p.xlvi says he has failed to identify this piece, which Bradwardine refers to in *De causa Dei* iii.27, p.711. See *Asclepius* §§ 2, 39-40, in *Corpus Hermeticum*, ed. A.D. Nock and A.-J. Festugière, ii, Paris, 1945, pp.297-9, 349-51; D.N. Wigtil, 'Incorrect apocalyptic: the Hermetic *Asclepius* as an improvement on the Greek original', in *Aufstieg und Niedergang der römischen Welt* II.xvii.4 (1984), 2282-97; Garth Powden, *The Egyptian Hermes*, Cambridge, 1986, pp.5-11, 38, 142-6, 198.

(c) *Cf.* Pseudo-Aristoteles, *De mundo* 7, pp. 93-5.

(d) Boethius, *Phil.Consol.*iv. prosa 6.11, 14, CC 94, 79-80. Cited *De causa Dei* i.28, p.266.

(e) *Cf.* Augustinus, *de Civ. Dei* v.9, CC 47, 138; Isidorus, *Etymol.*VIII.11.90-1.

§ 18 (a) Ovidius, *Epp.ex Ponto* iv.3.35, 49; cited *De causa Dei* i.29, p.267.

§ 19 (a) Jer.48.30: Ego scio, ait Dominus, iactantiam eius [i.e. Moab]: et quod non sit iuxta eam virtus eius.

(b) Flavius Josephus, *De Antiq.Jud.*i.4.2, ed. B. Niese, i, Berlin, 1887, p. 26; on f.7rb of the Latin version in Durham, Dean & Chapter Library ms. B.II.1.

§ 24 (a) This and the three following O.T. passages are cited together in *De causa Dei* i.31, pp.276-7.

§ 27 (a) *Cf.* Cicero, *Epp.ad Familiares* iii.10.9; non astutia quadum sed aliqua sapientia secutus sum.

(b) On Piso's defect, see Hieronymus, *Ep.*lxix.2, CSEL 54, 681: cum loqui nesciret, tacere non potuit.

§ 28 (a) *Cf.* Aristoteles, *De bona fortuna* = *Eth.Eudem.*VII.14 1248a 23-33; cited *De causa Dei* i.9, p.192 and i.29, p.269. *Eufortunia:* the form *enfortunium* in *De causa* i.9, p.192 and i.29, p.271 is perhaps corrupt.

§ 33 (a) Pseudo-Aristoteles, *Secretum secretorum* i.8, ed. R. Steele in *Opera hactenus inedita Rogeri Baconi* v, Oxford, 1920, p.46.

(b) *ib.*i.13, p.51.

§ 34 (a) Aristoteles, *Eth.Nic.*III.6 1115a 26 = *Auctoritates Aristotelis*, p. 236, no. 56.

§ 36 (a) Claudianus, viii *(Panegyricus de quarto consulatu Honorii Augusti)*, 299-300, 302, ed. Theodor Birt, MGH *Auct.Antiquiss.* X, 161. See Walther, *Proverbia Sententiaeque* ii (1964), no. 14986 and iv (1966) 26481 for examples closer to Bradwardine's quotation.

(b) Flavius Josephus, *De Antiq.Jud.*viii.10.2, ed. Niese, ii, 231; for the Latin version, *cf.* Durham, Dean & Chapter Library, ms.B.II.1, fo.79vb.

ADDENDA AND AUTHOR'S CORRIGENDA

I Aspects of government in the late medieval Empire

Angermeier, *Königtum und Landfriede im deutschen Spätmittelalter* (Munich, 1966).

F.R.H. Du Boulay, *Germany in the Later Middle Ages* (London, 1983).

K. Jeserich, H. Pohl, G.C. von Unruh, eds., *Deutsche Verwaltungsgeschichte*,vol. 1, 'Vom Spätmittelalter bis zum Ende des Reiches (Stuttgart, 1983).

K.F. Krieger, *Die Lehnshoheit der deutschen Könige im Spätmittelalter* (Aalen, 1979).

K.F. Krieger, 'König, Reich und Reichsreform', *Oldenbourg Enzyklopädie deutscher Geschichte*, vol. 14 (Munich, 1992).

P. Moraw, 'Von offener Verfassung zu gestalteter Verdichtung. Das Reich im späten Mittelalter', *Propyläen-Geschichte Deutschlands*, vol. 3 (Berlin,1985).

E. Schubert, *König und Reich. Studien zur spätmittelalterlichen deutschen Verfassungsgeschichte* (Göttingen, 1979).

E. Schubert, *Einführung in die Grundprobleme der deutschen Geschichte im spätmittelalter* (Darmstadt, 1992).

E. Schubert, 'Fürstliche Herrschaft und Territorium im späten Mittalalter', *Oldenbourg Enzyklopädie deutscher Geschichte*, vol. 35 (Munich, 1996).

H. Thomas, *Deutsche Geschichte des Spätmittelalters, 1250–1500* (Stuttgart, 1983).

II Empire and papacy: the last struggle

F. Trautz, 'Die Reichsgewalt in Italien im Spätmittelalter', *Heidelberger Jahrbücher*, 7 (1963), 45–81.

M. Berg, 'Der Italienzug Ludwigs des Bayern. Das Itinerar der Jahre 1327–1330', *Quellen und Forschungen aus italienischen Archiven und Bibliotheken*, 67 (1987), 147–97.

R. Pauler, *Die deutschen Könige und Italien im 14. Jahrhundert: von Heinrich VII. bis Karl IV.* (Darmstadt, 1997).

See also the biographies by Benker and Thomas detailed below for chapter III.

III England and Germany at the beginning of the Hundred Years' War

There are a couple of substantial recent biographies of Ludwig the Bavarian which might be worthwhile consulting for more general interest, as they synthesize post-Offler work on the diplomatic history of the reign: G. Benker, *Ludwig der Bayer* (Munich, 1980); H. Thomas, *Ludwig der Bayer: Kaiser und Ketzer* (Graz, Vienna, Cologne, 1993).

p. 608, note 3: Cf. F. Bock, *Reichsidee und Nationalstraten* (Munich, 1943), 355–479; ibid., *Das Deutsche-Englische Bündnis von 1335–1342: I.Quellen* (Quellen und Eröterungen zur bayerischen Geschichte. N.F. XII, 1956); F. Trautz, *Die Könige von England und das Reich, 1272 1377* (Heidelberg, 1961).

p. 610, note 2: Printed by Trautz, *Beilage*, ii, 423–9.

p. 611, note 3: Printed by Bock, *Quellen*, no. 530–31, pp. 120–22.

p. 611, note 4: H. Fricke, *Reichsvikare, Reichsregenten und Reichsstatthalterdes deutschen Mittelalters* (Phil. Diss., Göttingen, 1949).

p. 615, note 4: R. Gandilhorn, 'La frontière de la Meuse', *Bibliothèque de l'Ecole des Chartes*, 106 (1946), 80–105.

p. 615, note 7: Cf. L. Hüttebräuker, 'Cambrai, Deutschland und Frankreich, 1308–78', *ZSRG*, 59 (1959), *Germ. Abt.*, 103 *et seq.*

p. 617, note 3: Cf. G. Barraclough, 'Edward I and Adolf of Nassau', *Cambridge Historical Journal*, 6 (1940), 225–62; F. Bock, 'Musciatio dei Francesi', *Deutsches Archiv*, 6 (1943), 521–44. Trautz, pp. 151–71, contests Kern's interpretation and doubts whether Adolf was 'bribed'.

p. 618, note 3: Printed by Bock, *Quellen*, no. 533–4, 537–41, pp. 122–4, 127–32.

p. 620, note 3: Another 7000 fl. (=£1050) was given before May 1340: E36/203, p. 368. The total of Wardrobe prests to Lewis recorded in MBE 203 comes to £8277. 1s.; cf. the figure of £8237 given by BL Harley MS. 782, f. 71. Trautz, p. 284, n. 235, makes the total 55, 292 florins of Florence – but they were worth only two-thirds of the florins de Scuto.

p. 624: See end of section II. For a detailed criticism of this view cf. H.O. Schwöbel, *Der diplomatische Kampf zwischen Ludwig dem Bayern und der römische Kurie im Rahmen des kanonischen Absolutionsprozesses, 1330–1346* (Weimar 1968), 291–4.

p. 626, note 3: Cf. Bock, *Quellen*, p. 87, no. 489.

p. 626, note 5: Otto of Cuyk and Philip de Weston, Canon of York, had been empowered to treat with Lewis King of the Romans on 23 February 1345 (Rymer III. i. 32) – probably on Lewis's initiative: cf. Trautz, p. 323, n. 483.

p. 627, note 4: Trautz, pp. 322–30.

p. 629, note 4: But Trautz, p. 352, maintains it was a proper election.

p. 630, note 2: Printed by Trautz, p. 348, n. 23.

IV Meinungsverscheidenheiten am Hof Ludwigs des Bayern für die römische Kurie

H.-J. Becker, 'Das Mandate "Fidem catholicam" Ludwigs des Bayern von 1338', *DA*, 26 (1970), 454–512.

C. Dolcini, 'Marsilio e Ockham', *Medioevo*, 6 (1980).

C. Pfaff, 'Die Münchner Minoriten - Ratgeber Ludwigs des Bayern', in *Zur geistige Welt der Franzikaner im 14. und 15. Jahrhundert*, ed. R. Imbach, E. Tremp (Fribourg, 1995), 45–57.

p. 193, note 9: A date after the abjuration of Peter of Corvara (25 July 1330, renewed 25 August) is indicated by a phrase in the proem: 'pontificalis auctoritas ad presens divino iudicio videtur expirasse de medio' (p. 1344). So it seems likely that the assembly for which the letters were prepared was that summoned for Frankfurt in January 1331.

V Über die Prokuratorien Ludwigs des Bayern für die römische Kurie

C.A. Lückenrath, 'Zu den Rekonziliationsverhandlungen Ludwigs des Bayern', *DA*, 26 (1979), 549–55.

A. Schütz, *Die Prokuratorien und Instruktionen Ludwigs des Bayern für die Kurie* (Kallmünz, 1973).

C. Dolcini, 'Marsilio e Okham', *Medioevo*, 6 (1980).

C. Pfaff, 'Die Münchner Minoriten - Ratgeber Ludwigs des Bayern', in *Zur geistige Welt der Franiskaner im 14. und 15. Jahrhundert*, ed. R. Imbach, E. Tremp (Fribourg, 1995), 45–57.

VII The origin of Ockham's *Octo Quaestiones*

A.G. Weiler, 'The foundations of the superior secular and spiritual powers according to William of Ockham's *Octo Quaestiones de Potestate Papae*', in *Ockham and Ockhamists. Acts of the symposium organized by the Dutch Society for Medieval Philosophy Medium Aevum on the occasion of its 10th anniversary* (Leiden, 10–20 September 1986), ed. E.P. Bos, H.A. Krop (Nijmegen, 1987), 145–152.

D.E.H. De Boer, 'Ludwig the Bavarian and the scholars', in *Centres of Learning: Learning and Location in Pre-Modern Europe and the*

Near East, ed. J.W. Drijvers, A.A. MacDonald (Leiden, 1995), 229–44.

IX Notes on the text of Marsilius of Padua's 'Defensor minor'

Cf. Cary J. Nederman's translations, *Marsiglio of Padua, Writings on the Empire: Defensor Minor and De Translatione Imperii* (Cambridge, 1993).

X The 'influence' of Ockham's political thinking: the first century

p. 365, n. 127: Cf. N.E. Erikson, 'A Dispute between a Priest and a Knight', *Proceedings of the American Philosophical Society*, 111.5 (1967), 288–309.

XI A Political *collatio* of Pope Clement VI, O.S.B.

Cf. Diana Wood, 'The Sermon Literature of Pope Clement VI', *Studies in Church History*, 11 (Oxford, 1975), 163–72, and *Clement VI: The Pontificate and Ideas of an Avignon Pope* (Cambridge, 1989).

XII An interpolated *collatio* of Pope Clement VI, O.S.B.?

Cf. Diana Wood, 'The Sermon Literature of Pope Clement VI', *Studies in Church History*, 11 (Oxford, 1975), 163–72, and *Clement VI: The Pontificate and Ideas of an Avignon Pope* (Cambridge, 1989).

GENERAL INDEX